PMP Certification

A BEGINNER'S GUIDE

THIRD EDITION

PMP Certification

A BEGINNER'S GUIDE

THIRD EDITION

George G. Angel, PMP, SAPM

UNIVERSITY PRESS OF COLORADO
Boulder

Second edition 2014
Third edition 2017

Published by University Press of Colorado
5589 Arapahoe Avenue, Suite 206C
Boulder, Colorado 80303

Printed in the United States of America

The University Press of Colorado is a proud member of
the Association of American University Presses.

The University Press of Colorado is a cooperative publishing enterprise supported, in part, by Adams State University, Colorado State University, Fort Lewis College, Metropolitan State University of Denver, Regis University, University of Colorado, University of Northern Colorado, Utah State University, and Western State Colorado University.

∞ This paper meets the requirements of the ANSI/NISO Z39.48-1992 (Permanence of Paper).

ISBN: 9781607325987 (third edition)

The Library of Congress has cataloged the second edition as follows:

Library of Congress Cataloging-in-Publication Data

Angel, George G.
PMP certification : a beginner's guide / George G. Angel. — Second Edition. pages cm
Summary: "This accessible guide bridges the gap between being a project manager and becoming a globally recognized Project Management Professional (PMP). Aligned with A Guide to the Project Management Body of Knowledge (PMBOK)" ISBN 978-1-60732-306-8 (paperback)
1. Project management. 2. Project management—Case studies. I. Title. HD69.P75A54 2014
658.4'04—dc23
2014009471

Design by Daniel Pratt

This book is dedicated to the Angels in my life.

Pam, my wife, who is also my best friend; she is not only supportive but thinks this book is a way to climb to a new level in my life, and because of her love of books, she is very excited about this opportunity.

Candy, our oldest daughter, is also my good friend and has a sense of clarity in her life that is truly inspiring. She has the ability to see things that no one else sees, even in the things we take for granted. A leaf with small insect bites appears to her as an image of a butterfly, and she can see a smile in the clouds on a gray or sunny day. Her laugh warms my heart and makes me glad she is our daughter.

And Dawn, our youngest daughter, who is amazing; she loves to read, she is an editor by trade, and she is a published writer herself. She is truly a friend and is so supportive that she makes me feel like I am on top of the world when I am with her. She has been understanding and thoughtful even when I was traveling on business and was not able to be with her. She truly lights up a room and our lives when we are with her.

And to our four grandchildren, who are full of energy and smiles. They bring so much joy to our lives. Thanks to all the Angels in my life; I am truly blessed and so very fortunate to be surrounded by all their love, laughter, and caring.

Contents

PART II THE TEN KNOWLEDGE AREAS

Acknowledgments

This book, like any other, is the end product of a lot of hard work by many people. I'd like to thank some of the people who were involved with its creation.

I would like to thank Julie Clark, former student, co-instructor, and the technical editor for this book. Thanks for all your hard work and dedication to make this revision possible.

Many thanks go out to the students for their interest in project management and the great questions and input they provided through the years to give me the ideas for this book. And to the production and editorial staff at University Press of Colorado, including Darrin Pratt, director and acquiring editor, and indexer Linda Gregonis.

Also a big thanks to my fellow instructors (Joe Keim, Lee Varra-Nelson, Julie Clark, and Pat McDonald) who provided input and reviews to help make this book a useful resource for our project management classes.

Introduction

This book's focus is on bridging the gap between being a project manager (PM) and being a globally recognized Project Management Professional (PMP®). It takes you through the everyday challenges of managing projects and provides tips on how to prepare for and pass the Project Management Institute, Inc. (PMI®) exam.

The differentiators in this book are the straightforward approach to project management details, the proven examples, and the collection of checklists and references that serve as guides for newcomers to project management as well as for even the most experienced project managers. This book takes you through the fundamentals of project management using real-world examples of what works and what doesn't work in this dynamic profession. To demonstrate how sound PM principles can improve the efficiency and effectiveness of you and your project team, sample documents and a real-project case study build on the topics discussed throughout the book.

Project management is recognized as one of the fastest-growing professions in many of today's industries—software and hardware product development, government, military, construction, and information services (just to name a few). It is rapidly becoming a required skill for career advancement and improved project and program management success.

This book helps PMs better understand the importance of balancing project constraints (barriers) and communicating timely and accurate project status to all key stakeholders.

It is also important to note that this book is just a starting point in this large and growing profession. I hope it whets your appetite for more on the topic of project management.

Assumptions

This book assumes the readers have varying degrees of knowledge and experience—from little or no formal project management (PM) experience to more advanced experience.

Because of this range of experience, this book is designed to be a primer and to confirm the further steps needed to become a more successful project manager.

Organization

Because this book is designed to meet the needs of a wide range of project managers, it is broken into two major sections. The first section, which consists of Chapters 1–3, discusses the value and benefits of PM certification and serves as an introduction to PMI credentials and exams. The first section bridges the gap between being a PM and becoming a certified PMP.

The second section contains Chapters 4–13, which detail the ten knowledge areas, and Chapter 14, which explains how to bring a project to successful closure.

If you are not familiar with project management (PM) credentials or are not sure you want to pursue PMI certification right away, you definitely want to start this book from the beginning. If you have a few years of project experience and already know about PMI and the benefits of their credentials, you may want to jump right into the knowledge areas, starting at Chapter 4.

Now here's a brief summary of the book's organization and contents.

Part I: Essentials of Project Management and PMP Certification

This part of the book looks at project management from a real-world perspective and then offers insight into the benefits of PM credentials:

- **Chapter 1:** Changes to This Book and Bridging the Gap between Project Manager and Project Management Professional
- **Chapter 2:** The Emerging (Evolving) World of Project Management
- **Chapter 3:** Project Management Process Groups and Processes

Part II: The Ten Knowledge Areas

Part II contains ten chapters, starting with Chapters 4–13, which cover PMI's ten knowledge areas, and ending with Chapter 14, which discusses how to successfully close a project. Here's a list of the knowledge area chapters:

- **Chapter 4:** Project Integration Management
- **Chapter 5:** Project Scope Management

- **Chapter 6:** Project Schedule Management
- **Chapter 7:** Project Cost Management
- **Chapter 8:** Project Quality Management
- **Chapter 9:** Project Resource Management
- **Chapter 10:** Project Communications Management
- **Chapter 11:** Project Risk Management
- **Chapter 12:** Project Procurement Management
- **Chapter 13:** Project Stakeholder Management
- **Chapter 14:** Closing the Project (Are We There Yet?) explains the importance of properly closing the project and offers a checklist for effectively bringing the project to successful completion.

Tips, Notes, Try This, and Ask the Expert Elements

This book also includes Tips, Notes, Try This, and Ask the Expert series elements. These elements are based on collaborative input from a number of reviewers and instructors and are intended to share a specific experience, address a common problem, or highlight key information that will help you understand the topic better and provide helpful information toward your PMI exam application, preparation, and successful completion of these highly sought-after credentials.

Project Management Institute (PMI), Inc.

This book ties directly to the sixth edition of the *PMBOK Guide** and can be read in tandem with it chapter for chapter, or you can jump into any of the chapters to focus on specific areas of interest.

This book not only will help you improve your project knowledge, but will help explain the PMBOK by offering real-world project examples and tips to help increase your success on your projects and help prepare you for the PMI exam.

* Project Management Institute *A Guide to the Project Management Body of Knowledge (PMBOK® Guide)—Sixth Edition*, Project Management Institute, Inc., 2017. Copyright and all rights reserved. Material from this publication has been reproduced with the permission of PMI.

PMP Certification

A BEGINNER'S GUIDE

THIRD EDITION

PART I

Essentials of Project Management and Introduction to PMP Certification

Changes to This Book and Bridging the Gap between Project Manager and Project Management Professional

Key Skills & Concepts

- Welcome to the third edition—what changed and why?
- A brief history of project management
- Project Management Institute (PMI) and the *PMBOK® Guide* (A Guide to the Project Management Body of Knowledge)
- Reasons for getting certified
- Benefits of certification/credentials
- Introduction to PMI credentials

Welcome to the third edition of this book. The reason for this revision is that project management is constantly changing with new processes, new tools and techniques, and new focus areas. This edition maps processes to the 2017 *PMBOK Guide* and updated PMI exams.

What Changed and Why?

To answer the question of what changed in this edition of the Beginner's Guide, the biggest changes in this third edition are as follows:

1. The role of the project manager has changed based on a Delineation Study conducted by PMI. The new role of the PM increases their level of involvement and accountability on not only the projects we manage but how those projects fit into the overall business objectives. Without going into a lot of detail, the project manager's role is viewed as being (or needing to be) more business oriented and more strategic in nature rather than tactical. More details are provided below and in Chapter 2.

2. Another reason for this revision is to map this book to the sixth edition of the *PMBOK Guide* (see information below and Chapter 3 for more details).
3. PMI updates their Project Management Body of Knowledge (*PMBOK Guide*) every four years or so to keep up with the changing world of project management.

The good news is the changes to the *PMBOK* from the fifth to sixth edition are fairly minor and include two Knowledge Area title changes, moving a process (Plan Human Resource Management) between Knowledge Areas, and the addition of three new processes as outlined below:

TITLE CHANGES

- Manage Project Knowledge is part of the Executing Process Group and Project Integration Management Knowledge Area.
- Implement Risk Responses is part of the Executing Process Group and Project Risk Management Knowledge Area.
- Control Resources is part of the Monitoring and Controlling Process Group and the Project Resources Management Knowledge Area.

Next, PMI changed the names of six processes in the *PMBOK Sixth Edition* as shown in Table 1.1 below:

TABLE 1.1 Changes to the *PMBOK Guide* Processes

PMBOK Fifth Edition	PMBOK Sixth Edition
Perform Quality Assurance	Manage Quality
Plan Human Resource Management	Plan Resource Management
Control Communications	Monitor Communications
Control Risks	Monitor Risks
Plan Stakeholder Management	Plan Stakeholder Engagement
Control Stakeholder Engagement	Monitor Stakeholder Engagement

As you might know, project management is very dynamic, using globally recognized tools, techniques, methods, and processes that often evolve and change to keep up with the demands of projects such as software, use of virtual teams, many new applications for digital communications, tablets, cell phone apps, and so forth.

Even though the fundamentals remain constant, the project manager's role is emerging, with the level of involvement and responsibilities of the PM growing. Companies, agencies, and organizations in both public and private sectors are realizing the importance of good solid project management discipline, not only embracing it but striving to build these practices into the foundation of their organization. Large corporations and medium and small companies are all built by fulfilling objectives and completing a series of projects; no matter what type of business they are in, everything comes down to project management.

While project management goes back to nearly the beginning of time, the way we manage projects is ever changing. The tools and techniques are getting more advanced every day. The team dynamics and sponsor expectations are continually in flux. The role of the PM has been elevated to that of a strong member of decision makers who have a huge influence in the success of the business, organization, or agency. PMs "have arrived" in many cases and are viewed as a major player in growing the business, for example, increasing revenue, increasing profit margin, or improving efficiency.

Project management is by definition the "application" of knowledge, skills, tools, and techniques to project activities to meet approved requirements. As with any application, there are tasks that must be performed in order to complete the work. One of the major changes in the Project Management Professional (PMP) exam is the increased focus on the tasks of the project manager. The tasks we (as PMs) perform are broader and often cut across many Knowledge Areas of the project; PMI refers to these as "Cross-cutting Knowledge and Skills"; some examples:

- Active listening
- Applicable laws and regulations
- Benefits realization
- Brainstorming techniques
- Business acumen

As project managers we must be able to interact with and effectively manage across a much broader audience and on a higher scale than ever before. For more details on the new role of the PM, see "The Expanded Role of the PM" in Chapter 2.

To help educate and certify PMs, there are several PM credentials available internationally. These include PMI-issued credentials totaling over 750,000 Project Management Professionals (PMPs) and 35,000 Certified Associates in Project Management (CAPMs) in 2017 and another 300,000 people certified in one or more of the International PM credentials such as Certified International PM (CIPM) and Certified PM (CPM) under the umbrella of the International Project Management Association (IPMA), just to name a few. These credentials are noteworthy, as the demand for certified project management competence spreads globally. All of these international certifications combined don't add up to the PMI Project Management Professional (PMP) credential, which has been around the longest and continues to prevail as the most globally recognized and highly sought after certificate.

There is a huge difference between being a project manager and managing projects as a globally recognized certified PMP and holder of other International PM credentials. The difference can often be seen in the reduced number of failed projects. As project managers develop the skills needed to manage projects effectively and then go on to get certified, their success rate typically increases, as does their salary.

According to the *PMI Salary Survey, Ninth Edition,* IT professionals who hold the PMP credential report median earnings worldwide of $81,000 USD annually; however, the upper 25 percent of survey respondents earn at least $110,000 USD. Depending on factors such as the complexity and size of the project, location, field of expertise (IT, construction, or healthcare, for example), or experience, salaries for PMP credential holders may be much higher.

To get a better understanding of these changes, let's look first at project management in general. It is in practically everything we do—creating a new technology, designing an office building or a new home, managing a major event (such as the Olympics), or running a fund-raiser for a church or school. Project management principles can also be used in our personal lives—remodeling a basement or kitchen, designing a landscape, and planning a wedding or a family vacation. A large number of these projects are done with little or no formal training. Because projects (by definition) are unique in nature, we tend to manage them in various ways and with different degrees of success. Most of the time when the project reaches the end, everyone is fairly happy with the results.

Project management goes back thousands of years. Look at the pyramids of Egypt (some date back to 2550 BC), the Roman aqueduct was believed to be the first one built (in 312 BC), and the Great Wall of China (sections began to emerge as early as 700 BC). Many of these engineering marvels are still standing today (with some renovation).

How do you suppose these marvels were designed and built? Project management. Project management existed in one form or another early on, and our ancestors somehow mastered it without written scope statements, communications plans, or activity schedules.

Even though many early project managers were successful, their processes were independent (ad hoc), inconsistent, and mostly not repeatable; thus the need for structure—documented, proven, and repeatable processes; standard tools, techniques and methods—and solid project management discipline.

Even some "successful" projects were anything but successes by today's standards (i.e., on time and on budget). For example, the Sydney Opera House—one of the most recognizable images of the modern world—was designed by Jørn Utzon of Denmark in 1957 and deemed, at the time, a spectacular failure. Even though it is now revered as an icon of Sydney, it was originally labeled a "white elephant" and an "acoustic nightmare." When construction started on the opera house in 1959, it was estimated to cost AU$7 million and take five years to build. However, it was finally completed in 1973 (nine years behind schedule) at a cost of over AU$100 million (AU$93 million over budget). Even though this project failed to meet the traditional project management success metrics, it is considered a huge success.[1]

Note

If you are already familiar with PMI's credentials or if you are not planning to pursue certification just yet, that's okay. Please feel free to jump to Chapter 2. You can always come back to Chapter 1 as a reference when you are ready for more information regarding exam eligibility, PMI credentials, or exam information.

Introduction to the Project Management Institute

A lot of us have been managing projects longer than we care to admit, and for the most part we have been doing pretty well, mainly going on basic instincts and "gut feelings." However, the growing need to modernize has caused the world of project management to really take off. The 1950s marked the beginning of the modern era of project management as we know it today. This new era ushered in the need for a framework of globally recognized standard processes, tools, and methods. A small group of project management professionals recognized this need and in 1969 founded a nonprofit organization called the Project Management Institute. PMI began documenting a proposed set of project management standards it called a "white paper" (an authoritative guide) in 1987. Its intent was to standardize project management information and practices. The white paper later became the original *A Guide to the Project Management Body of Knowledge* (*PMBOK Guide*), published for the first time in 1996. This guide became recognized as a worldwide standard and provided common processes, principles, Knowledge Areas, tools and techniques, and a global project management discipline. PMI saw the need to take this new discipline into the twenty-first century and make it official by creating an examination for project managers to validate their ability to understand the new standards. To do this, PMI launched the Project Management Professional certification exam in 1994. Since that time, the PMP credential has skyrocketed in popularity.

To demonstrate the emerging demand for certified PMPs, you need only look at the job postings for project managers. Only a few years ago, advertisements for project manager jobs stated, "PMP certification a plus." Now they read, "PMP certification required." This is true for public and private sector companies as well as government agencies that require their PMs to be certified. To meet this increased demand, PMs are getting serious about acquiring those important initials after their names. The number of PMPs has grown exponentially since 1998, when there were only 11,000 PMPs worldwide. In 2017 the number of PMPs exceeded 750,000—and this number continues to grow each month.

For those who don't have the three years of PM experience leading project teams that are required to apply for the PMP certification, there is the Certified Associate in Project Management (CAPM) credential available from PMI.

Why Get Certified? What's in It for Me?

Anything worthwhile, such as getting certified, requires commitment. A lot of people wonder, "Why should I subject myself and my family to the extra time it takes to prepare for the PMI exam, especially in today's demanding work environment?" Most of us are already working long hours on several different projects at the same time and with less time for family and friends.

Current studies indicate a huge shortage of project managers worldwide. Many qualified workers with a ton of experience are working multiple projects and may not have the time to put in the extra effort to get certified.

Getting certified can be demanding and competitive—so why put yourself through the extra work? The biggest reason, I believe, starts with the feeling you get when you walk out of the test center with a "Congratulations, you passed" printout in your hand, knowing you reached a goal that millions of project managers are thinking about pursuing. A chill runs down your spine, and the smile on your face can be spotted a mile away. You want to tell the world, "I have arrived. I passed the PMI exam!"

Then come the real benefits. You will be able to "talk the talk" (know a common language to be able to communicate with PMs on a global basis) and "walk the walk" by being able to apply standard, proven processes on global projects.

Your family and friends will be proud of you because they know the time and energy you put into studying for the PMI exam. Your boss and coworkers will admire your commitment and achievement. Some companies even reward employees who rise to the level of certification with recognition bonuses, salary increases, and promotions for their dedication.

Benefits of Achieving PMI Credentials

The benefits go far beyond the initial congratulations. Once you are certified, you have a newfound sense of awareness and understanding, knowing there is a standard, recognized worldwide, that provides a roadmap to guide you toward improved project results.

You can be content in knowing there are thousands of PMs across the globe facing the same challenges you are—and in some cases stumbling over similar barriers and "potholes." Your job is made a little easier with the realization that you are not alone on your project. There is a global network of professionals working together to help make the job easier.

Here's a summary list of the benefits of certification:

- Demonstrated commitment and proof of professional achievement
- Increased credibility with customer and team
- Increased marketability of your skills
- Potential for higher compensation
- A better understanding of how to manage resources
- Improved communications skills

Introduction to PMI Credentials

PMI offers a comprehensive certification program for project managers with different levels of experience. The program supports a career framework in the project management profession. PMI's credentials and professional development can help business professionals start, build, or advance their careers in project management, program management, scheduling, and risk management. For current information on PMI and their credentials, go to www.pmi.org.

PMI credentials establish your dedication and proficiency in project management. To attain one of PMI's credentials, you must first satisfy the education and professional experience requirements. To better understand PMI credentials and the requirements needed to obtain certification, review the following definitions and then refer to Table 14.2 or the PMI.org website for the necessary requirements, project roles, and details. There are a number of different PMI credentials, and new ones are being added to the PMI portfolio along the way. Several of the credentials are specialized and all are not included in this chapter. For more information and to see any changes or additions to the PMI credentials, go to the PMI website (www.pmi.org).

Types of PMI Credentials

The 2014 PMI Pulse of the Profession study found that organizations with more than 35 percent PMP certified project managers had better project performance. And according to an earlier PricewaterhouseCoopers survey, 80 percent of high-performing projects use a credentialed project manager. A summary list of PMI credentials appears below:

- Certified Associate in Project Management (CAPM)
- Project Management Professional (PMP)
- Program Management Professional (PgMP)
- PMI Portfolio Management Professional (PfMP)

Other credentials are specialized and shown here:

- PMI Agile Certified Practitioner (PMI-ACP)
- PMI Risk Management Professional (PMI-RMP)
- PMI Scheduling Professional (PMI-SP)
- PMI Professional in Business Analysis (PMI-PBA)

Certified Associate in Project Management (CAPM)

The CAPM credential is geared toward people who contribute to a project team but who are not leading or directing the team. (See the PMP credential, explained next, for those who are leading and directing project teams.) The CAPM credential recognizes a person's ability to demonstrate their capabilities by

- Having a fundamental knowledge of the *PMBOK Guide*
- Understanding the standard *PMBOK* processes and terminology
- Demonstrating knowledge of basic project management practices
- Being responsible for individual project tasks in their area of expertise (e.g., finance, marketing, legal, customer care, market research, fulfillment, and processing)
- Contributing to the project team as a subject matter expert (SME)

Project Management Professional (PMP)

The PMP credential is for people who are leading and directing a project team. PMPs are

- Responsible for all aspects of the project through its entire life cycle
- Capable of leading and directing cross-functional teams in delivering project results
- Able to demonstrate sufficient knowledge and experience to apply a methodology to projects within the constraints of schedule, budget, and resources
- Responsible for managing risk, communications, and stakeholder expectations and for effectively performing their duties in a professional manner

Program Management Professional (PgMP)

PMI's Program Management Professional credential is specifically developed to acknowledge the qualification of the professional who leads the coordinated management of multiple projects toward a strategic goal and ensures the ultimate success of the overall program. PgMP responsibilities include the following:

- Achieving an organizational objective by overseeing a program that consists of multiple projects

- Defining and initiating projects and assigning project managers to manage costs, schedules, and performances
- Maintaining alignment of program scope with strategic business objectives
- Effectively monitoring and responding to the needs of the PMs in their program

Note

Unlike other PMI credentials, you must pass a sequence of three evaluations to obtain the PgMP credential. This process takes approximately four weeks to complete.

- **Evaluation 1.** Panel Review
  + The initial evaluation occurs through an extensive application review during which a panel of credentialed program managers will assess your professional experience based on your responses to the Program Management Experience Summaries provided on the application.
- **Evaluation 2.** Multiple-Choice Examination
  + The next step occurs with the multiple-choice examination, in which you will be called upon to demonstrate your competence in both situational and scenario-based questions.
- **Evaluation 3.** Multi-Rater Assessment (MRA)
  + Once you pass the examination, you will be moved to the third and final evaluation, which is the MRA. Similar to a 360-degree review process, a team of raters that you select will assess your history of demonstrated performance of tasks that are pertinent to program management.

PMI Agile Certified Practitioner (PMI-ACP)

In January 2013 PMI added the PMI-ACP (Agile Project Management) Certification. Agile is a topic of growing importance in project management. The PMI-ACP certification recognizes an individual's expertise in using Agile practices in their projects, while demonstrating their increased professional versatility through Agile tools and techniques. In addition, the PMI-ACP certification carries a higher level of professional credibility as it requires a combination of Agile training, experience working on Agile projects, and examination on Agile principles, practices, tools, and techniques. Sample PMI-ACP capabilities include the following:

- Demonstrating to employers their level of professionalism in Agile practices, tools, and techniques
- Increasing the practitioner's professional versatility in Agile techniques

- Holding a certification that is more credible than existing offerings based in entry-level experience, training, or exams only

PMI Risk Management Professional (PMI-RMP)

The PMI Risk Management Professional credential recognizes knowledge, skills, and experience in the area of project risk management. An RMP provides expertise in the specialized area of assessing and identifying project risks, along with plans to mitigate threats and to capitalize on opportunities. RMPs are typically

- Responsible for identifying project risks, assigning owners, and reviewing mitigation plans
- In direct support of PMs and the project team as a contributing member
- Able to document a minimum of three years of project risk management experience

PMI Scheduling Professional (PMI-SP)

The Scheduling Professional credential recognizes the specialized skills needed for developing and maintaining the project schedule. SPs are

- Responsible for creating and maintaining the project schedule
- In direct support of the PM and project team as a contributing member in managing the overall schedule
- Able to document a minimum of three years of project-scheduling experience

PMI Professional in Business Analysis (PMI-PBA)

Another certification PMI offers is the Professional in Business Analysis (PMI-PBA) credential (announced in 2014). This role is the PM's "business office manager" for the project or projects. Think of a business analyst (BA) as the person who helps set the budget and tracks progress and performance. The BA is essential to large and even medium-sized projects. The BA role varies depending on the type and complexity of the project or projects. As a PM, life gets a whole lot easier if you have a BA to help you run your project(s).

The BA helps the PM and project teams identify business needs, set goals, and recommend solutions. According to PMI's Pulse of the Profession report on requirements management, 53 percent of organizations believe there will be an increase in demand for the BAs in the next few years.[2] The BA skill is not easily found and is great to have.

For more information on the role of the BA, go to the www.pmi.org website and print out the latest PMI-PBA Handbook.

Additional details on the PMI credentials, what to expect on the exams, and next steps can be found at the end of this book after "Next Steps: Where to Go from Here" (Chapter 14).

References

1. "Jørn Utzon Pritzker Prize," *Architecture Week*, April 23, 2003, http://www.architectureweek.com/2003/0423/news_2-3.html, accessed March 12, 2017.

2. PMI's *PULSE OF THE PROFESSION, 2015*, http://www.pmi.org/-/media/pmi/landing-pages/business-analysis-tools-silverpop/pdf/business-analysis-communities-thriving.pdf.

2 The Emerging (Evolving) World of Project Management

Key Skills & Concepts

- How the world of project management is evolving
- Project framework
- What is a project?
- What is project management?
- Different views of project management
- The expanded role of the project manager
- Importance of communications
- Difference between projects, programs, and operations
- What is a portfolio, a project management office (PMO), and organizational project management (OPM)?
- Three takeaway points for this chapter
- The project life cycle
- Organizational structures
- How to measure success on a project
- The "Ready, Fire, Aim" dilemma
- The AIM (analyze, implement, manage) strategy

The best way to describe how the world of project management is evolving is to start by defining the project management framework, defining a project and project management, and, most important, the role of the project manager (PM).

Project Framework

A framework implies structure, a solid foundation, processes, and governance (guidelines, tools, techniques, and methods). Even though there are many organizations that like to think they set the standard for project management, the Project Management Institute (PMI) has emerged as the globally recognized standard to help guide us in how we manage projects; when used properly, it works.

As part of this standard, PMI continues to provide and update its Project Management Body of Knowledge (*PMBOK Guide*). The *PMBOK Sixth Edition* is divided into two parts. Part I is the "Standard for Project Management," and Part II is the main body of the *PMBOK*, with breakouts by Knowledge Area, processes with their associated inputs, tools and techniques, and outputs. This standard is viewed as the project framework, and it defines key project management concepts including the relationship of project management to business/organizational strategy, program management, and portfolio management, how projects are governed, the project environment, and how to measure results of a project.

This standard also outlines the project life cycle, defines stakeholders, and describes the processes necessary to manage most projects. PMI processes will be covered in depth in chapters 3–14.

What Is a Project?

Even though project management has been around a long time, there still tends to be a fair amount of confusion, even among experienced project managers, concerning the definition of a project. People often use the term *project* to describe everything from designing software to building a new house, planning a major event, installing a computer or new computer equipment, finding a way to fix a problem, or setting up a lemonade stand.

So, what is the correct definition of *project*? I suggest we first look to the experts in the PM profession. According to PMI, a *project* is "a temporary endeavor undertaken to create a unique product, service or result."[1] Projects are put in place to create a unique product, service, or result. Most everyone has a pretty good idea about what products and services are, but what about "results"? This was added to the 2004 version of the *PMBOK*, and it means that the results of the project may far outlive the project itself—for example, increasing productivity by installing new energy-efficient equipment saves a company money for years to come after the project is complete. Mount Rushmore was a massive sculpture project brought to a close in 1941, yet it has over 2 million visitors a year even long after the project has ended. Reduced pollution from hybrid cars will benefit the planet far beyond the design project. Automated systems often lead to increased savings over time. These are all long-term results from temporary projects.

To be a little more specific, let's look at some of the characteristics of typical projects. All projects should have the following characteristics:

- They are temporary in nature—that is, they have a definite start and a definite end. (If it is long term—perhaps even never ending—it is likely a program or an ongoing operation instead of a project.)
- They create a unique product, service, or result. Even if the project has been done before, there is usually something unique about repeating it, such as its location, size, team members, or type of materials.
- They have (or should have) clearly defined goals and objectives with measurable results. (If a project is open ended, part of a larger group of projects, or changes significantly over time, it is most likely a program instead of a project.)
- They should reach an end when their approved requirements have been achieved.

What Is Project Management?

Now that you know what a project is and have seen some examples of projects, programs, and operations, let's discuss project management. What is project management, and what does the PM need to do to perform this dynamic, often challenging role?

In practice, *project management* is all about being able to look across the entire project—from the requirements (i.e., what the customer or project sponsor wants) to what is being accomplished (i.e., what needs to be done to meet the requirements). In Chapter 8 this is referred to as *meeting specifications* and *fitness for use*—for example, does the product, service, or result do what we said it will do (provide the functions and features as specified) and work the way we designed it to work in order to meet the approved requirements of the project (fitness of use)?

Project management may involve staffing the project team (who will do the work) and planning, estimating, and managing the schedule (when each phase of the project will be completed), as well as the cost of the project. Note that hiring or assigning the team members may be managed by the human resources (HR) department (or the contracts and procurement department in some companies), and the PM may not get to pick the team members to work on the project. Team members may be preassigned or provided by a functional manager as part of a "pool" of skilled resources.

According to PMI, project management is the *application* of knowledge, skills, tools, and techniques to project activities to meet project requirements. This is accomplished through the appropriate application and integration of the logically grouped project management processes in the *PMBOK Guide*.

Tip

The PMP exam focuses on the ability of PMs to apply knowledge and skills to solve various problems and to be able to think on their feet (that is, to be able to manage in many different situations).

Two Project Management Perspectives

In this chapter and throughout this book, we will look at project management from two different perspectives. These views differ and are based on the extent of formal training and experience you may have. Yet, when the views are combined, they provide synergy and benefits to you as a PM.

Here are the two project management perspectives:

- **The real-world view.** Managing projects using common sense (instincts, gut feelings) and informal practices
- **The Project Management Institute (PMI) view.** Project management as a distinct profession, using globally accepted standards and common processes that fall into five Process Groups (note that experience across all five Process Groups is required to sit for the PMP exam):
  - Initiating
  - Planning
  - Executing
  - Monitoring and Controlling
  - Closing

The Real-World View: Managing Projects by Instinct

Many of us apply project management skills in our daily jobs and in everyday activities by using sheer gut instincts (often referred to as managing by the "seat of our pants"). Many project managers are put into projects with little or no formal training and must trust their instincts.

A large number of project managers perform well using nothing but common sense. Others perform poorly and don't even know it. They tend to make the same mistakes over and over, developing bad habits that may never be realized or corrected.

The good news is that common sense goes a long way, and chances are you have been managing projects with good to reasonable success much longer than you might realize. Think about putting on those puppet shows as a kid, working on school projects (there's that word again, *projects*), and planning a surprise birthday, anniversary, or wedding party for a friend or family member—all of these are examples of projects.

Common sense and basic instincts are at the core of being a good, solid project manager. However, having good instincts is great up to the point at which you have to lead others and present the project status to the key stakeholders (i.e., anyone affected by the project). For that you need more than common sense—you need a common language.

Once you learn the language of project management, the standard processes, and the tools and techniques, then the "aha" moments come (when you see the link between what you do instinctively and what these components are called in the professional world of project management).

As a project manager, you need to see the bigger picture (across the entire project, as previously mentioned). This includes the identification of risks; using effective communications; and addressing the various needs, concerns, and expectations of the stakeholders. One of the most important skills is balancing the competing project demands and constraints (limitations or barriers).

The Project Management Institute (PMI) View

PMI's view of project management is to have a globally recognized discipline with a standard, accepted framework and processes to assist in the pursuit of improved project success. PMI's vision is to provide a network of highly skilled professionals to share experiences and knowledge and to help promote the project management profession.

Strong PM skills are not easy to acquire and in many cases need to be developed over time by working on real projects; this is one field that can't be totally learned from books. PM skills must be developed and practiced to ensure success. That is why PMI calls us "practitioners" and requires recertification every three years at the PMP level.

Project and program managers face many variables and challenges, and, at the end of the day, it all comes down to being able to apply sound project management judgment, leadership, and organizational skills to balance competing project demands. This constant balancing act, if done well, can help you reach a higher level of success on your projects. PMI's goal is to provide the broader perspective and assist the PM community in striving for continuous improvement.

The Expanded Role of the Project Manager

The project manager is the "glue" that holds the project together. The PM is responsible and accountable for the project and must take charge as the project leader.

To be a good leader, the project manager must be a good communicator, be organized, play well with others (i.e., be team oriented), be a team builder, and motivate the team to reach the project objectives. The PM must be willing and able to take calculated risks, be an advocate for the team, solve problems, and understand stakeholders' needs and expectations. As the person responsible for project success, the PM is in charge of all aspects of the project, including but not limited to the following:

- Developing the project management plan and updating it as needed to ensure that it remains current, accurate, and applicable
- Keeping the project on track in terms of budget, schedule, scope, and deliverables
- Managing risk and providing timely and accurate reports on project status and metrics
- Managing stakeholder needs and expectations

Ideally, the PM should be assigned to the project early in the project life cycle to assist in developing the project charter, creating the planning documents, and establishing the project team. Depending on the type of organizational structure, the team may already be assigned or may be assigned by the functional (line) manager based on location, skills, and availability.

The role of the project manager is distinct and should be focused on the project. If, for example, this person is a functional (line) manager in addition to being assigned the PM role, there will likely be conflicting demands on the individual's time and priorities.

Being a good project manager requires employing a specific set of competencies (skills). According to PMI, there are three dimensions (layers) of project management competency often referred to as the PMI Talent Triangle:

- **Technical Project Management.** This refers to what the PM knows about project management and the technical aspects of performing the role of a PM.
- **Leadership.** This refers to the PM's ability to apply their project management leadership to guide and motivate project team members and stakeholders.
- **Strategic and Business Management.** This refers to the project manager's industry and organizational knowledge and experience and how they apply this knowledge when managing the project to meet approved objectives and balancing project constraints.

Even though the role of the PM varies based on the size, type, and complexity of the project, the fundamental skills required are universal (the primary PM skills and disciplines can be plugged into practically any industry). This is not to say "one size fits all," because projects by definition are unique. However, project management, as a skill, is extremely versatile and can be used in a broad spectrum of applications.

Finally, a good PM must be a strong leader to control the project effectively. Being a leader means taking control of the project.

PMI's view of project managers is as follows:

Who Are Project Managers?

- PMs are skilled communicators, leaders who are passionate and goal-oriented and who are focused on project and product deliverables. They are strategic in nature and able to use their organizational skills, negotiation, and other skills to ensure success on their project.
- PMs are flexible, adaptable, and willing to take control and responsibility to meet project goals. They use their skills and expertise to inspire a sense of confidence and shared purpose within the project team. They thrive on new challenges, managing risks and taking their responsibility seriously to drive business results.
- They work well under pressure and are good presenters. They are good at leading and directing the work of a project and understand the diversity and complexity of the project environment. They understand and effectively manage change on their project(s).
- PMs are good team builders and know how to motivate team members. They have excellent interpersonal skills and know how to develop trust among all project stakeholders, sponsors, and team members.
- They know how to use a broad range of tools and techniques to get results. They know how to resolve complex problems and how to break work into tasks and subtasks for ease of assignment. They know projects are unique and that no "one size" can fit all the needs of the business or organization.
- They are always looking for ways to improve their own and their teams' skills through lessons learned, training, and sharing knowledge and experience with others to develop a solid skill set and a global network of highly trained professionals.
- They are in demand as senior executives, and HR managers recognize project management as a strategic and indispensable role to project and business success.

Tip

The true measure of success for you as a project manager is when team members say they want to work with you on future projects. The only way you gain this kind of trust and dedication is by being an advocate for the team, being able to admit when you have made a mistake, and being honest and respectful. This will go a long way toward establishing your credibility and integrity.

Having the skills and knowledge of a good PM are great; however, remember project management is about application. So when you are assigned to a new or existing project, you will be expected to apply those skills and knowledge to perform in a prompt and effective manner. So, what do you need to do when asked to step in and take control of a project? I recommend the following steps for taking control of either a new or existing project:

1. Get (and stay) informed. Be like a sponge and absorb as much about the project as possible by reviewing project objectives and requirements, the project management plan, output documents, the contract, work orders, change requests, and the status reports of the project. This means listening more than talking. One of my previous managers has a saying that goes like this: "My daddy always said I have two ears and one mouth, so I should listen twice as much as I talk."
2. Document key issues and concerns. Early on, review actions and options with key individuals to understand as much as possible about pervasive (chronic) issues, staff issues, customer contacts, organizational structure, environmental factors, and organizational assets (standard tools, templates, forms and so on) as appropriate and available.
3. Meet with the customer to begin establishing a relationship. Seek to understand the customer's concerns, likes, and dislikes when it comes to the project, the team, and the deliverables.
4. Bring these steps together by holding a project kickoff meeting. Use all the information you have collected to establish yourself as the leader of the project. This is where steps 1–3 pay off, because you need to demonstrate your awareness of the project, the stakeholders, the project objectives, customer expectations (hot buttons, constraints), and the project's overall status. You need to provide clear direction (a plan) and reiterate the roles, responsibilities, and assignments, all while using proven project management tools, techniques, and processes to demonstrate your competency as the project manager.

Ask the Expert

Q: Once you are assigned as a PM, what is the best way to take control of a project?

A: The best way to take control of a project is to establish yourself as the leader (not by being bold or dictatorial, but by showing interest, knowledge, and professionalism). When you, as the PM, take responsibility and accountability for the project, you show the team you are in control. Being in control also means you need to support your team in their effort to deliver the approved scope of the project. Being firm but fair helps lead to positive results.

As mentioned in Chapter 1, the role of the project manager is constantly changing. With the size and breadth of projects in today's dynamic workplace, the PM has to be able to step up to the additional challenges that companies and organizations face, such as virtual teams working in different time zones and speaking different languages, and very diverse work environments.

According to PMI (and in the real world), we know that the PMs' knowledge and skills are essential to the success of any project. Often these skills cross over into different Knowledge

Areas and, again, are referred to as cross-cutting knowledge and skills. PMI even identifies tasks that apply to each of the five Process Groups (also known as domains) and which of the knowledge and skills might apply to a given Process Group/domain. These tasks, their alignment to the five performance domains, and specific cross-cutting knowledge and skills that cross multiple domains were incorporated into the 2016 PMP exam; changes were introduced in PMI's PMP Exam Content Outline dated June 2015.[2] For introduction purposes, a short sample of these tasks and the applicable cross-cutting knowledge and skills are shown below.

Project Manager Tasks

Each of the five performance domains (Process Groups) contain tasks, specific knowledge and skills, and cross-cutting knowledge and skills that are measured through the PMP certification progress.

Performance Domains

1. Initiating
2. Planning
3. Executing
4. Monitoring and Controlling
5. Closing

A sample list of tasks for the first three of five domains are shown below:

Domain 1: Initiating

Task 1: Perform project assessment based on available information, lessons learned from previous projects, and meetings with relevant stakeholders in order to support the evaluation of the feasibility of new products or services within the given assumptions and /or constraints.

Task 2: Identify key deliverables based on the business requirements in order to manage customer expectations and direct the achievement of project goals.

Task 3: Perform stakeholder analysis using appropriate tools and techniques in order to align expectations and gain support for the project.

Task 4: Identify high-level risks, assumptions, and constraints based on the current environment, organizational factors, historical data, and expert judgment in order to propose an implementation strategy.

Domain-specific Knowledge and Skills:

- Analytical skills
- Benefit analysis techniques
- Elements of a project charter
- Estimate tools and techniques
- Strategic management

Domain 2: Planning

Task 1: Review and assess detailed project requirements, constraints, and assumptions with stakeholders based on the project charter and lessons learned and by using requirement-gathering techniques in order to establish detailed project deliverables.

Task 2: Develop a scope management plan, based on the approved project scope and using scope management techniques in order to define, maintain, and manage the scope of the project.

Task 3: Develop the cost management plan using estimating techniques based on the project scope, schedule, resources, approved project charter, and other information in order to manage project costs.

Domain-Specific Knowledge and Skills:

- Estimating skills
- Change management planning
- Communications planning
- Contract types and selection criteria
- Resource planning
- Risk management planning

Domain 3: Executing

Task 1: Acquire and manage project resources by following the resource and procurement management plans in order to meet project requirements.

Task 2: Manage task execution based on the project management plan by leading and developing the project team in order to achieve project deliverables.

Task 3: Implement the quality management plan using the appropriate tools and techniques in order to ensure that work is performed in accordance with required quality standards.

Task 4: Implement approved changes and corrective actions by following the change management plan in order to meet project requirements.

It takes a lot of "know-how," knowledge, and skills to successfully execute these tasks. For an overview of knowledge and skills that should be used across all domains, see the partial list below:

All-Domains Cross-Cutting Knowledge and Skills

- Active listing
- Applicable laws and regulations
- Benefits realization
- Brainstorming techniques
- Business acumen (able to see the bigger picture at the business and organization levels)
- Coaching, mentoring, training, and motivational techniques
- Change management techniques and configuration management
- Decision-making, team-building and delegation techniques
- Effective communications and presentation tools and techniques
- Brainstorming and analytical tools and techniques
- Conflict resolution (use peer review processes)
- Data-gathering tools and techniques
- Facilitate discussions and meetings
- Expert judgment and risk assessment techniques
- Meeting management and organizational skills
- Quality assurance and control techniques
- Stakeholder management and virtual/remote team management

As you can see from this partial list, the new role of the project manager is much more involved at the strategic level of the organization. According to PMI, the institute's view of the required knowledge and skills is much higher level than in years past because many projects are run remotely and/or with virtual team members or virtual sponsors, and often with subcontractors, vendors, and suppliers from many different countries. This brings a whole different set of risks and challenges.

What are business goals and objectives? This question comes up a lot from students and people who are new to project management as they may not have business experience or business acumen. Business goals represent a clear statement of intention on the part of the business to reach high-level achievements such as increasing revenue or profit to grow the business or increase its market share.

A few examples of business goals: to release two new products every quarter, to produce increased income (or revenue) by 10 percent year over year, to ensure that 90 percent of a marketing team meet or exceed sales quotas by a minimum of 5 percent.

Business goals should be measurable and have specific attainable targets. We often call the measurements measures of performance (MOPs) or key performance indicators (KPIs). Companies may have goals or objectives to reduce cost by *x* percent, increase customer satisfaction by *y* percent, improve performance (e.g., such as on-time arrivals in the airline industry) by *z* percent, or reduce defects by ± 1 sigma (68.26%), and so on.

One way to look at the new role of a PM is to break the focus areas into three categories, as shown in Table 2.1.

TABLE 2.1 Three Focus Areas for Project Managers

I. Project Manager	II. Resource/People Manager	III. Task/Technical Manager
1. **Visionary—able to see the bigger picture.** Seeks information from a number of sources using a variety of tools and techniques to facilitate effective planning, decision making, and problem solving.	1. **Interpersonal skills.** Motivates and inspires team members. Sets clear roles and responsibilities and is a good negotiator to ensure the team has the tools needed to get the job done.	1. **Analytical thinking.** Problem solver. Able to identify the root cause of a given problem, quickly assess the impact to the project, and look at options (alternatives) before making informed decisions.
2. **Communications (two-way).** Able to effectively communicate at multiple levels in a timely manner. Confident in presentation skills. Overcommunicates when necessary to ensure results.	2. **Fosters teamwork.** Able to get groups to work together by establishing trust and confidence. Has good presentation and facilitation techniques.	2. **Results orientation.** Looks for effective solutions to get the job done in an efficient manner. Dedicated to meeting approved requirements based on approved objectives.
3. **Organizational skills.** Has an eye for detail and a tendency to maintain order. Plans well and knows where to go next and how to get things done.	3. **Performance management.** Able to provide direction, sets clear goals and expectations, makes clear assignments, provides clear feedback, serves as a coach and mentor to team members.	3. **Attention to detail.** Focuses on ensuring information is clear, complete, and accurate by preparing effective meetings and presentations. Follows up with stakeholders to ensure agreements and commitments have been met to validate scope and requirements.
4. **Interpersonal skills.** Motivates team members. Assigns clear roles and responsibilities and is a good negotiator to ensure the team has the tools needed to get the job done.	4. **Negotiation skills.** Able to negotiate for the right resources at the right time and for the right amount of hours or cost to ensure proper funding to successfully fulfill the resource needs of the project.	4. **Resource management.** Able to look at both functional and nonfunctional (technical) requirements and is capable of getting the right skills needed to ensure proper results.

How is this new role different from the old project manager role? As noted in the table above, the focus areas for project managers includes a lot of general management skills in addition to those traditionally associated with project managers. As a project manager, you should constantly watch for and manage the various aspects of a project such as time (schedule), cost (budget), and scope. At its end, a project's success is measured by product and project quality, timeliness, budget compliance, the degree it meets approved requirements, and of course overall customer satisfaction. It is important to note that not all companies support the changing role of the project manager and have stuck with the old view of project managers, which is that they are expected to only focus on their piece of the project and let the program manager or portfolio manager manage across multiple projects and deal with the larger business perspective.

Importance of Clear Communications: Learn the Language

Being able to speak and understand the language of project management is essential to the combined success of the project stakeholders and the project itself.

On average, PMs spend about 90 percent of their time communicating. Communications occur in many different ways: formal, informal, written, verbal, and nonverbal (through body language). The types of communications are varied and should be tailored to meet the needs of the project. The common forms of communications on most projects include the project management plan document, various process documents (for example, the work breakdown structure [WBS]), communications plan, various written reports, status meeting minutes, emails, phone messages, and general discussions with project stakeholders. The project manager is either communicating or planning communications during the majority of the time on a given project. Multiply this several times over if the PM is managing multiple projects or programs at the same time. This can become quite a juggling act for the PM.

The primary purpose of project communication is to ensure that everyone associated with the project is rowing in the same direction (on the same page) and making sure everyone on the project understands the deliverables, roles, responsibilities, schedule, and expected results.

The best way to keep everyone focused is through clear two-way communications. To communicate effectively, you need to learn the language of project management. Using this book, you will learn how to keep the team focused on the project. Given the importance of communication management, you can bet it is a key PMI Knowledge Area (to be discussed in more detail in Chapter 10 of this book).

Competing Project Constraints (Demands)

Regardless of which project management book you read (and there are many), you will hear about the need for the PM to balance competing demands and constraints. A constraint is any limiting factor or restriction that affects the execution of a project or process. What used to be called the *triple constraints* was often illustrated as a triangle with time, cost, and scope (or quality) constituting the respective sides of the triangle (see Figure 2.1).

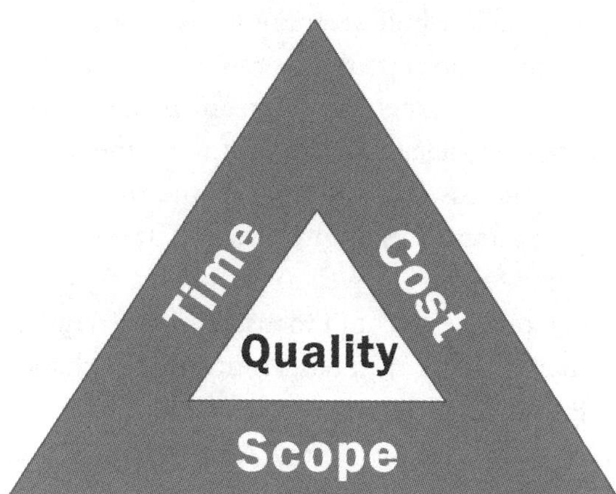

FIGURE 2.1 Triple Constraints

FIGURE 2.2 Good, Fast, or Cheap Concept

To put this in perspective, a friend of mine, when faced with the challenge of balancing project demands, often says, "Good, fast or cheap—pick any two," meaning that if you want something good and fast, it will likely cost more; if you want it good and cheap, it may take more time (see Figure 2.2). Any change to the triple constraints throws the triangle out of balance.

Because of the dynamics of managing projects in today's complex world, we need a broader view beyond just the three primary constraints. Most authors agree on time (often shown as schedule) and cost (often shown as budget), but the third key component varies between scope, quality, resources, and risk. PMI recognizes that multiple components must be managed (balanced) and therefore has pulled away from using the term *triple constraints* in favor of recognizing that a number of factors can constrain projects (see Figure 2.3).

The basic concept is still the same in that the project manager and team must balance the key constraints to keep them in line with the project sponsor's requirements. If time (the schedule) is compressed (e.g., the customer needs the solution sooner), then the other components of the constraints shift, thus increasing cost or decreasing quality and potentially affecting the scope of the project. If scope changes, then time and cost are surely affected. The key is to clearly understand the driver (or main component) of the project constraints. For example, the primary constraint on the Olympics project is time—making sure the torch is lit at a specific time on a specific date, even if the paint is not dry on the bleachers.

Project stakeholders will have different priorities and sometimes changing demands, which can make the balancing act extremely difficult. Also, as a project progresses the constraints and their interactions will also change. This is why I often refer to project managers as "jugglers." We constantly have to keep the plates spinning and all the balls in the air (so to speak) at the same time.

FIGURE 2.3 The Bigger Picture of Project Constraints

Finally, I believe there is another side to these constraints that is rarely mentioned—and that is keeping the team happy. If the PM is focused on the team as the number-one asset to the project, the rest of the pieces tend to fall into place. If the team is happy, working well together (using interpersonal skills), and focused on the requirements, the project has a much higher chance for success.

Now that we know what projects are, what project management is all about, and the expanded role of the project manager, let's look at the next level: programs, operations, and portfolios.

What Is a Program?

Programs are different from projects in that they usually are a collection (or group) of projects, they tend to be longer in duration, and they have no defined end date. An example would be a company's education program, which might include several development projects to create new courses, combined with ongoing projects for the continued operation, maintenance, and updating of the courses.

Program management is a way for us to bundle (or group) similar projects and support operations into a logical manner. Grouping projects into a program makes them easier to assign and manage. A project management education program, a government healthcare program, a specific software application program—they all tend to be ongoing and usually include multiple projects and often include ongoing operational support.

What Is an Operation?

Usually an *operation* is the activity of operating something (such as a machine or a business). On a larger scale, a company may have multinational operations. In the world of project management, the key words to look for to help distinguish operations from projects or programs are *enhancement* (e.g., improving existing software application code or adding a process to enhance [or improve] the operation of computer installations), *daily activities*, or *ongoing*.

Operations are usually repeatable activities performed to establish a product (e.g., an assembly line operation to manufacture cars).

A good way to clarify the differences between projects, programs, and operations is to think about the characteristics of each, as detailed in the preceding definitions, and then look at the examples presented in Table 2.2.

Ask the Expert

Q: What happens when a person is called a project manager yet is responsible for various aspects of a program and even daily operations (systems availability, staffing, and so on)?

A: There are times when the staff is limited and the person in charge of leading the project is expected to be all things (one-stop shopping) across the entire program. When the PM is handling daily operational issues and problems or a long-term program (multiple projects or subprojects), then the specific project tends to get neglected. The end result, at best, is controlled chaos, and the most likely result is uncontrolled chaos. When subjected to this cross-section of responsibilities, the PM can rarely focus on the specific project and may fail at the project management level. If you find yourself in this situation, the solution, in my opinion, is to work with the sponsor(s) to verify the priorities of the project (or program) and reason with them to allow you to have the staff needed or time required to focus on the project at hand.

Tip

There is no hard-and-fast rule on what is called a *project*. Therefore, don't correct your boss or project sponsor when they tell you to go manage a "project" that may not be one by strict definition. Simply smile and take comfort in knowing the difference for yourself, and do your best to help train the rest of the world a little along the way.

TABLE 2.2 Examples of Projects, Programs, and Operations

Event/Activity	Project	Program	Ongoing Operation
Design software	X		
Testing software	X (if new)		X (if repetitive)
Maintain the software support once promoted to production		X	
Manage a group of software application products		X	
Design a hybrid fuel-efficient car	X		
Set up an assembly line to build hybrid cars	X		
Assemble/build hybrid cars		X	
Plan a major event (like a wedding)	X		
Develop a new PM risk management class	X		
Manage new class development as part of a series of PM courses including delivery and support		X	

What Is a Portfolio? What Is Portfolio Management?

In the world of project management, a *portfolio* refers to a collection of projects or programs and other work operations that are grouped together at a company level to achieve strategic business objectives. When they hear the word *portfolio*, most people think of a financial portfolio, which refers to any collection of financial assets such as stocks, bonds, and cash that are either held or managed by an individual or a financial institution. A portfolio of any kind is designed according to the investor's business objectives and risk tolerance.

The event management industry is a prime example of a company that offers a portfolio of products and services, such as the events center facility itself and its support staff (including promotions and contract management, as well as the changeover project managers who convert the building within hours from one venue to another, as from a hockey rink to a concert arena to a motocross race track and back to an ice rink). As part of the company's portfolio, the event managers might also provide ticketing, parking, concessions, and security, to name a just few operations.

Portfolio management refers to the centralized management of one or more portfolios, which includes identifying, prioritizing, authorizing, managing, and controlling projects and programs, as well as the governance of the collective work to achieve specific strategic objectives. The programs and projects that make up the portfolio may not be related, other than by their helping to achieve a common strategic goal for the organization.

Table 2.3 provides an overview of project, program, and portfolio management. It compares how projects, programs, and portfolios differ in key areas, such as how they are

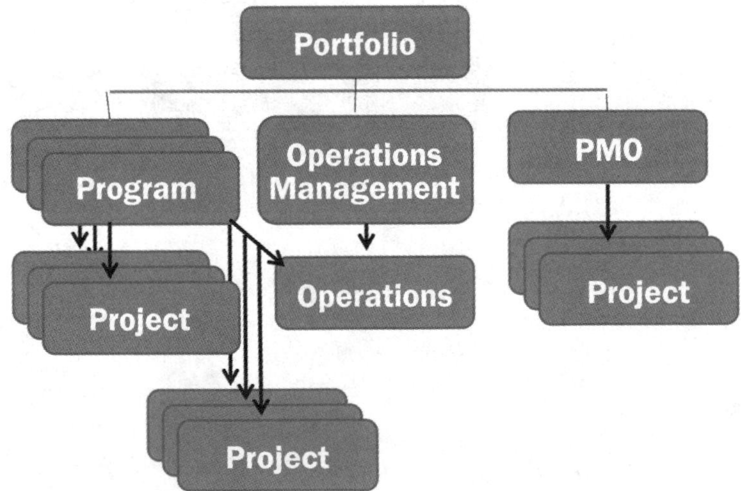

FIGURE 2.4 Portfolio Management

planned, managed, and measured, and how scope is defined. Figure 2.4 shows a pictorial view of how such a portfolio management organization may look, with its components for projects, programs, operations, and project management offices (PMOs).

TABLE 2.3 Comparative Overview of Project, Program, and Portfolio Management

	Projects	Programs	Portfolios
Scope	Projects have defined objectives. Scope is progressively elaborated upon (i.e., it builds) throughout the project life cycle.	Programs have a larger scope than projects and provide more significant benefits.	Portfolios have a business scope that changes with the strategic goals of the organization.
Change	Project managers expect change and implement processes to keep change managed and controlled.	The program manager must expect change from both inside and outside the program and be prepared to manage it.	Portfolio managers continually monitor changes in the broad environment.
Planning	Project managers progressively integrate high-level information into detailed plans throughout the project life cycle.	Program managers develop the overall program plan and create high-level plans to guide detailed planning at the component level.	Portfolio managers create and maintain necessary processes and communication relative to the aggregate portfolio.
Management	Project managers manage the project team to meet the project objectives.	Program managers manage the program staff and the project managers; they provide vision and overall leadership.	Portfolio managers may manage or coordinate portfolio management staff.
Success	Success is measured by product and project quality, timeliness, budget compliance, and the degree of customer satisfaction.	Success is measured by the degree to which the program satisfies the needs and benefits for which it was undertaken.	Success is measured in terms of aggregate performance of the portfolio components.
Monitoring	Project managers monitor and control the work of producing the products, services, or results that the project was undertaken to produce.	Program managers monitor the progress of program components to ensure the overall goals, schedule, budget, and benefits of the program will be met.	Portfolio managers monitor aggregate performance and value indicators.

Project Management Office (PMO)

Project management offices (PMOs) are emerging mostly in larger companies to set up a common approach to providing standards across many projects. When projects are managed inconsistently, the overhead cost of setting up, running, and reporting using different types of procedures, tools, and reports can be prohibitive.

PMOs also provide "governance" (controlled direction) to projects and programs. The word *governance* originates from the Greek verb *kubernáo*, meaning "to steer"; Plato was the first to use it in the metaphorical sense of directing or managing people rather than, say, boats. The term *governance* as used in the industry—especially in the information technology (IT) sector—describes the processes that need to exist for a successful project.[3]

Governance works best when standards are selected and enforced across projects and programs within a portfolio or organization.

Ask the Expert

Q: Are there standard templates and real-world examples of scope statements and other project documents to help me manage my project in a more consistent manner?

A: Yes. I recommend an internet search on "PM Templates" for a wealth of project management freeware and great examples used in real-world projects. For great examples, see the template library designed by Dr. Gary Evans at http://cvr-it.com/PM_Templates/. You can also talk to fellow project managers inside and outside your team or organization for examples as well.

Note

The message here is to use the tools available (never reinvent the wheel if you don't have to) to manage projects in a shared learning environment (working together to learn from one another and gain synergy). Most project managers are happy to offer templates they have designed or used on successful projects to share their knowledge and experience.

Organizational Project Management (OPM)

A term you may not be familiar with but that is emerging in popularity is *organizational project management* (OPM). OPM is the systematic management of projects, programs, portfolios, and other organizational practices (see Figure 2.5). It serves as a framework for keeping an organization, as a whole, focused on overall strategy and goals. It provides direction on how work should be prioritized, managed, executed, and measured to best achieve strategic goals. Think of OPM as the overall umbrella covering the strategic direction and oversight of an organization.

Being Audit Ready

The best way to be "audit ready" is to have a project control book (PCB), preferably in an electronic database, team room, content management application (such as Microsoft SharePoint), or other form of a central repository to ensure easy access by the project stakeholders. The PCB should also be included in the overall project management information system (PMIS). The PMIS is where you should keep all your project plans and output documents (status reports, risk and communication plans, schedule updates, approved changes, and so on).

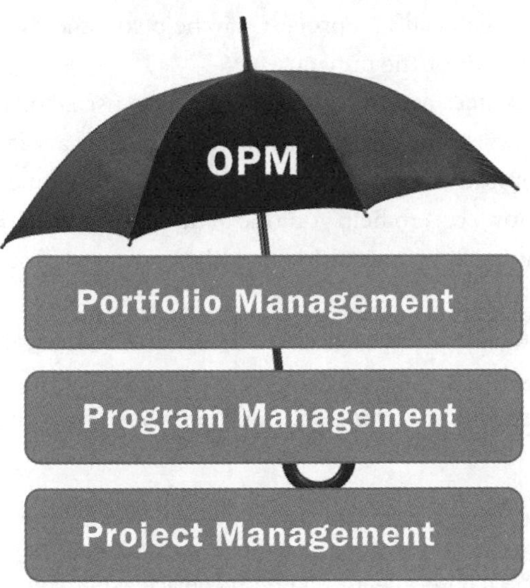

FIGURE 2.5 Organizational Project Management (OPM)

With a PMIS comes the responsibility to keep it current, which means version control (making sure you have the latest version of all project documents). Being "audit ready" means being able to demonstrate that you are effectively managing all aspects of the project. It is a great feeling to walk out of a project audit with no negative findings and no action items because you were able to show that your project is well organized, that you are current with all documents, and that you are in control of the project.

Three Takeaway Points from This Chapter

Understanding the importance of applying clear communications, common processes, tools, techniques, and practices in a consistent manner is essential for quality delivery and measured results on your projects. Many of my students, associates, and clients often ask for the "magic bullet" to successful project management—that is, "what are the key focus items that will help me manage my project more effectively?"

In my opinion, three primary points (focus items) will assist you in achieving your goals of managing your projects effectively:

- **Stay focused on the end goals and objectives.** It is very easy in the real world to get distracted by the many requests from sponsors, the potential risks identified by the team, changes in scope, and the natural tendency to want to add value (do more) to the project. Change management, as a process, can help you and the team stay focused on the approved scope and goals of the project.

- **Use the tools and resources available.** It is important to use standard tools and templates from the *PMBOK*, from your project management office (if available), from other projects in your group or company, and from other resources. Also, you can acquire shareware tools at no cost (or low cost) to help you track and manage the cost, schedule, and scope of your project. This includes consulting or collaborating with subject matter experts (SMEs).
- **Work as a team.** Remember, the number-one asset on a project is the team. As a PM, you cannot do it all. The best way to ensure that the team is working together is through clear communications and with rewards or recognition when things are done right.

Note

There is a saying in the PM world that goes like this: "If you have more than one person on a project, you have a team, and if you have a team, you have conflict." Therefore, be aware of the ongoing need to keep the team informed, engaged, and focused. As a project manager, you must provide clear direction to the team for success.

Roles of the Stakeholders: Who Are They and Why Do We Care?

I have mentioned the term *stakeholders* several times in this chapter and want to take a minute to define who they are and their importance to the project.

- Who are project stakeholders?

  Answer: Anyone or any organization that is positively or negatively affected by the project.

- Why should we care who the project stakeholders are?

  Answer: The project cannot exist without stakeholders. They are the sponsors (i.e., they provide the budget), the customer, the team, and the end users of the product produced by the project. The project team (led by the PM) is responsible for bringing the project to a successful close to meet the needs of the other key stakeholders. The stakeholders are so important to the project that PMI added Project Stakeholder Management as a new Knowledge Area in the *PMBOK Fifth Edition in 2013*. It is extremely difficult to meet stakeholder needs if we don't know who they are.

Try This

WHO ARE THE PROJECT STAKEHOLDERS?

Say you are the overall project manager working on a major event (such as a concert). It is your job as PM to identify all the stakeholders (including whom to call boss) on the project.

Take a few minutes and write a list of who you think the stakeholders are for an events center and then compare your list to the following:

- Corporate sales representative
- Marketing representative
- Contract manager
- The client/customer or entertainer
- Business-office manager
- Event manager
- Ticket sales (box office)
- Operations manager and team
- Changeover project manager and team (setting up the venue for concert seating)
- Hundreds of part-time employees, including security; ushers; lighting, sound, and dressing-room setup technicians (to meet artist requirements); food and merchandising workers; audio/video (AV) technicians; post event cleanup personnel; parking and traffic control employees; and, of course, the people attending the event
- The artist and performing band, riggers, wardrobe personnel, makeup artist, and managing agent
- The boss. This is the person to whom you report and to whom you are accountable on the project. The person you call "boss" varies depending on where you are in the pecking order (chain of command). At the end of the day, the project manager is the "boss" of the project, and of course the sponsor (the person or persons paying for the project) is the "boss" of the project manager. Remember, everyone has a boss (usually several).

The Project Life Cycle

The life cycle of a project can differ in type and terms used. Software development is a good example, in which there are concept, development, test, implementation, and closing phases (remember, projects should have a beginning and an end). Because of the high potential for change, the project and associated project management plan are iterative in nature, meaning they go through what PMI calls "progressive elaboration" throughout the project's life cycle. Progressive elaboration involves continuously looking for ways to improve on the work and

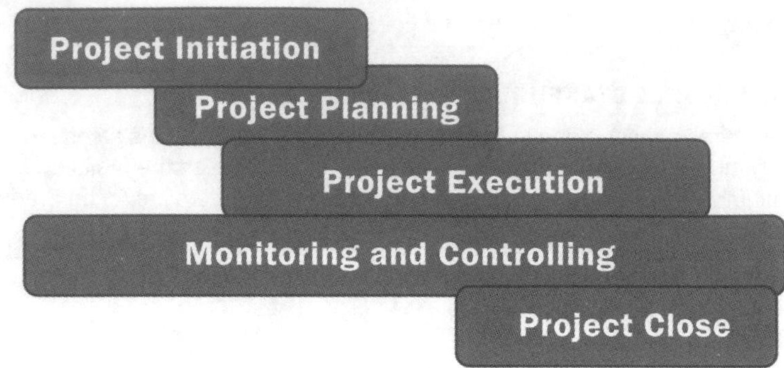

FIGURE 2.6 Project Life Cycle

results of the project. As the project evolves, you learn more and you have more information (more "knowns" and less risk), and with information comes knowledge. This increase in knowledge allows the project team to manage a higher level of detail as the project evolves.

No matter how large, small, simple, or complex the project, in general all projects have a basic structure:

- Initiating the project (getting it started)
- Organizing and preparing the project through planning (planning the work)
- Carrying out the work of the project (working the approved plan)
- Monitoring and controlling results
- Closing the project (transitioning the product or result of the project to its intended use)

In summary, a project life cycle is a collection of sequential (but sometimes overlapping) project phases (see Figure 2.6).

Project Phases

Project management is all about organizing the work of the project in manageable, logical chunks (groups or categories of work). With the many dependencies that exist on a project to get from one phase to the next, it is almost like managing many subprojects or subsets of the project. Take the case of setting up an ice rink for a hockey game or any other show on ice event. Clearly the event will not occur unless the ice is properly frozen, and even if the ice rink is ready for play, unless marketing, advertising, and the box office do their jobs, no tickets will be sold or delivered. These are often considered project phases, especially when setting them up for the first time. Once these steps become repeated, documented, and approved, the steps may ultimately become ongoing operations.

Also consider a project that is coming to a close. Even though you are in the final phase of the original project, the closing phase becomes, and should be managed like, a project. Closing a project (as you will see in Chapter 14) has a project life cycle of its own and should be managed accordingly.

Organizational Structures

There are many different organizational structures as well as multiple methods of managing projects. However, it is best to focus on the basic structures (especially if you are planning to take the PMI exam).

Basic Organizational Structures According to PMI

Organizational structure is an enterprise environmental factor that can affect the availability of resources and influence how projects are managed. *Organizational structure* refers to the way a company or group is formed or aligned. The basic structures (according to PMI) are as follows:

- **Functional.** This structure is usually hierarchical (with line managers) or by skill (e.g., plumbers, event planners, programmers, security administration, and so on). With this type of organizational structure, the power tends to be retained by the functional manager, not the PM.
- **Matrix (weak, balanced, and strong).** This structure is usually a pool (group) of people aligned similarly to the functional structure; however, the people are used across multiple projects and organizations and have much more flexibility in cross-coverage between projects. *Weak*, *balanced*, and *strong* relate to the level of power or authority the PM has in the matrix organizational structure. As you would expect, the PM has more authority in a strong matrix than in a weak matrix organizational structure.

> **Tip**
>
> Don't get these organizational structure terms confused with the term *tight matrix*, which means to have the project team co-located (working) in the same room or building.

- **Projectized (aligned and managed by project).** This structure provides the project manager with the highest level of authority of all the structure types because the team usually reports directly to the PM. However, there are disadvantages. For example, when a project ends, the PM and team will have to find a new project; otherwise, they close with the project.

Note

Remember organizational structures are part of the enterprise environmental factors (EEFs) that need to be considered on your project. These EEFs can affect a number of areas of your project, such as how you obtain resources (people and equipment), how you execute your project, how payments are made, and so on. Some companies may have a combination of these structures, or spin-offs, they use to manage their business and projects. Because of the importance of enterprise environmental factors, more information is provided in Chapter 3 of this book.

Organizing the Project: Using Different Breakdown Structures

Several tools are available to assist the PM in organizing a project. The most common are the work breakdown structure (WBS), the risk breakdown structure (RBS), resource breakdown structure (also RBS), and the organizational breakdown structure (OBS).

The WBS is extremely beneficial in helping to identify the work of the project and to break the work into manageable chunks (groups or categories.) The WBS provides a systematic way to carve out (identify) what needs be done to meet the deliverables of the project. The WBS also provides a way to capture key categories of work and put them into logical groups (work packages) that can be assigned to different work groups or departments.

Tip

A deliverable is a product of work completed on a project. Deliverables are sometimes described as inputs or outputs. One person's output is the next person's input, until the project is complete. You often have both product and project deliverables. An example of a product deliverable is a set of blueprints for a construction project, a training manual, or survey results that are needed as an input to the type of classes being developed to meet a particular program curriculum. On the other hand, you have project deliverables, which are the project documents, such as the Project Charter document, the PM Plan, the risk plan, communications plan document, and so on. Think of project deliverables as more related to the work of the project to get us to the finished product.

It is important to note that PMI is really big on the work breakdown structure (WBS)—it is mentioned many times in the *PMBOK Guide*. When you take a PMI exam, you will likely see many questions concerning the WBS. Creating the WBS is a process in the Project Scope Management Knowledge Area and will be covered in detail in Chapter 5 of this book.

The OBS typically shows the organization's departments, units, or teams aligned to the project activities or work packages that they are responsible for delivering. The OBS shows "who" is doing the work of the project.

The risk breakdown structure (RBS) shows how the risk should be managed. The RBS should show the risk events that have been identified, provide analysis of impact and probability, and identify the risk event owner, should the risk occur. Risk response strategy and how to manage risk on the project are covered in detail in Chapter 11 of this book.

The resource breakdown structure (RBS) breaks the work down by type of resource, such as programmers, plumbers, electricians, testers, trainers, and so on.

Now that you are up to speed on the primary breakdown structures and their use, let's look at how project success is achieved.

Success Is in the Eyes of the Customer

The customer is always right, right? It is important to know that in the real world, the customer is not always right; however, the customer is always the customer, right? So we have to be sensitive to the customer's needs and expectations.

According to PMI, customer satisfaction is a measure of success on a project. It is important to keep the customer in the loop and involved in many aspects of the project planning and tracking, areas of risk, communications, and so on.

Customer needs and expectations can be a dichotomy. Needs are usually fairly precise and measurable, whereas expectations vary early and often, depending on "selective amnesia." For example, the customer often remembers the extra features you presented in the sales pitch but may conveniently forget that for reasons of affordability, those features were not subsequently purchased—yet still expects the extras. The customer may change focus on what they want at the end of the project for various reasons (this is especially true when requirements or scope are unclear going into the project). These and a host of other reasons can cause "scope creep" or even "scope leap" (that is, when project requirements change significantly from the start of the project to the end).

In general, the measure of success on any project should be quality delivery (on time and on budget) based on customer approved scope and deliverables.

Note

PMI states that, in general, all conflicts on the project should be resolved in favor of the customer. Therefore, make sure you are in close communication with the project sponsor (customer) to help ensure you meet the customer's needs and expectations (which at the end of the project is the true measure of success). In the real world, however, this could be viewed as a "yes-man" approach and could be costly. So, what is the answer? The answer is to be very aware of the customer's needs and expectations, and to add value to the project without giving away the store (i.e., without giving extras at no additional cost).

Try This

WHAT DOES THE CUSTOMER WANT?

Suppose you are the project manager on a kitchen remodeling project in a home. You hire a plumber (subcontractor) to do the plumbing and sink installation. You obtain the bid from the plumber, and when you roll this into your overall bid with the other work, the total estimate is three months to complete the project at a cost of $30,000. You present the bid to the customer, who signs a contract, and the work begins. You are two months into the project and the plumber tells you that the special fixtures (brushed-nickel sink and faucet) are backordered and will delay the project by six weeks. As a competent PM, you discover that the fixtures are available at a higher cost from an alternate supplier in another state. The purchase of the fixtures from the alternate supplier will cost an additional $3,000.

Now that you have the analysis (expected impact), you take it to the customer, who has a decision to make. Here are the key questions that need to be answered from the customer:

1. How important are the special fixtures? Is the customer willing to allow the project to be delayed? If time is not as important as having the brushed-nickel fixtures, the customer may decide to accept the delay.
2. If both time and cost are important (say, for example, that the customer has planned a special event at their home, and the delay will spoil the plans), is the customer willing to go with alternative (standard) fixture selections, saving the extra time and cost? Or are the special fixtures so important that the customer is willing to pay extra for the additional cost and shipping?

As the project manager, you need to learn from this lesson and establish a strategy to prevent this from happening in the future. The best strategy for the PM is to check project status frequently with the team to minimize the risks that this type of problem will occur again. You must be prepared and have action (backup) plans to help mitigate the risks should they occur. In summary, the strategy as a PM should be to plan well to help ensure there are no (or minimal) surprises!

Adding Value to the Project

There are ways to add value to a project without "giving away the store." How is this possible, especially given that value is often very difficult to measure? You can add value by consistently showing integrity in how you manage the project. Provide on-time and accurate status reports even if the story is not good—being behind schedule or over budget are real situations, and you do not want to hide, ignore, or delay bad news in your status reports.

Always present the impact to the project in clear terms. More important: present a plan of action or alternative options so the sponsor can make an informed decision about where the project needs to go next. Try to anticipate the questions. If you were the customer, what would you want to know about a risk event and its possible impact? Is it a threat or possible opportunity? Is it going to cost more or delay the project in any way?

Try This

BUILDING A CORRAL FOR RODEO ANIMALS

Suppose you are the PM on a project to build a corral fence. As your team is digging the post holes, they encounter an unforeseen event—they hit solid rock. The equipment is damaged, and the impact to the project is a two-week delay and a $1,000 repair to the equipment.

Because you are an experienced PM, you know the first step is to assess the situation. You gather the team together and discuss the situation. One of the team members mentions she has probed the ground around the rock and found that the soil is more favorable if the fence line were to be moved ten feet in from the original boundary. This would allow the team to continue building the corral around the remaining property. If you remain on the original fence line, you will need to bring in special equipment at great expense, and you will have not only a delay but also a big impact to the cost of the project.

What do you do?

Your answer should be to balance the competing demands of time, cost, and scope. It is best to determine the priorities from the customer to determine which factor is the more important. Once the priority is clear and you realize that time is of the essence, it appears that moving the fence line in ten feet is the best approach. It will save time and money. You present this as the recommended option to the customer in the form of a change request. Once this is approved (signed) by the customer, you direct the team to move the fence line and proceed with the project.

It is important to remember to report the status (finding) to your sponsor and other stakeholders honestly in a professional and timely manner. Provide a best estimate of impact to the project. You always want to provide the all important recommended action plan as to how best to solve the problem and to keep it from happening again in the future. This is how you add value and gain the much needed trust and confidence from the customer, other key stakeholders, and sponsors.

Many different approaches can be used to manage projects. As mentioned previously, we tend to manage using our personal experiences and instincts. These methods work in some cases, but in many cases they don't. We fall into certain habits (some of them bad), and as everyone knows, habits are often hard to break. The most common bad habit is often referred to as the "Ready, Fire, Aim" dilemma.

The "Ready, Fire, Aim" Dilemma

Too often we get ahead of ourselves on projects. We live in a world in which most people are used to, and expect, instant gratification. We want an all-in-one, state-of-the-art gadget that is a phone, camera, and personal planner that plays music and can shine our shoes, all at the same time. The end result is distractions—and lots of them. This can lead to a "jump the gun" mentality, in which we frequently start doing the work without having a clear scope and then wonder why we continue to miss the target. It is the PM's responsibility to bring the team back to the beginning and talk about the problem rather than start planning the work.

This tendency comes to light in the book *The Toyota Way Fieldbook*, by Dr. Jeffrey Liker and David Meier, who caution against the tendency in most Western companies to shortchange the problem solving process:

One of the signs of a "Ready, Fire, Aim" culture is the tendency to "jump" immediately from the "problem" to the "solution." In many cases the problem may be mentioned casually, and much time is spent proposing various "solutions" before the "problem" has been clearly defined. At this stage in the process it is likely that a symptom has been observed rather than the true problem.[4]

The Toyota problem-solving approach is implemented in four steps:

1. Develop a thorough understanding of the situation and define the problem.
2. Complete a thorough root-cause analysis.
3. Consider alternative solutions while building consensus.
4. Use Plan-Do-Check-Act (*f*)—the Shewhart-Deming cycle:
   - **Plan.** Develop an action plan.
   - **Do.** Implement solutions rapidly.
   - **Check.** Verify results.
   - **Act.** Make necessary adjustments to the solutions and action plan and determine future steps.
   - Finally, reflect and learn from the process.[5]

The "Ready, Fire, Aim" dilemma was painfully realized when a project manager began working on a nine-month software application project without clearly defined requirements. There was no project charter to authorize the project. Because this was a new and exciting product and had never been done before, the PM decided the requirements and features were to be "open-ended" code. The work needed to start immediately, and the customer was excited about the potential of this new product. At every meeting the customer brought many great ideas to the team for additional features they wanted added to the code. Because of the added features, the PM kept adding more and more people to the project. As you can imagine, at the end of nine months they had some good code, but a very unclear product that tried to do everything—from paying bills online to automatically balancing checkbooks. However, the team couldn't get it to work reliably. They needed more time. Unfortunately, the customer ran out of patience, time, and money and decided to take the development work back in-house. "Thanks for the hard work." the customer said, "We will take it from here." The customer and service provider were not happy with the results, and the project was deemed a failure.

In looking at our "Ready, Fire, Aim" dilemma, let's go back to the first word: *ready*. If everything is done properly—we have a project charter, we know what the project deliverables are, and we can begin the planning cycle (the "aim" part)—then we are ready to begin. Many projects begin without anyone knowing who the real customer is or what the requirements are, and yet we continue to jump right into that "new opportunity." We gather a team of people and schedule the kickoff meeting (PMI is big on kickoff meetings). We may not even have all the details of the project yet, but we *fire* it off. We introduce the project (or what we think the project should be), we set target dates (based on when the sponsor wants the project completed, which is often a date drawn out of thin air), and we start building the project—only to find we are building the wrong solution, in the wrong place, with down-level specifications lifted from earlier projects. Oh my!

Project management is all about communication, and yet we rarely ask questions or make sure we understand what the sponsor wants or expects from the PM and team.

In this discussion the word *fire* ahead of the word *aim* alludes to pulling the trigger of a gun before actually aiming it. You will never hit the target if you don't aim. This comes from years of being pushed to deliver results without knowing exactly what the customer wants. The customer always knows what they want, right? This is like a kid watching commercials on TV at Christmastime, and his wish list changes and grows with every series of commercials.

To close on the "Ready, Fire, Aim" dilemma, let's talk about aim. We always seem to be in such a hurry to do the work even if the scope is not clear, that we don't take the time to plan (aim). And then we wonder why we continue to miss the target.

You would think a concept as basic as planning (aiming) before executing the project (firing) would be something we would do instinctively, and yet we do it so rarely that it causes a high percentage of failed projects—we keep making the same mistake over and over again!

I often wonder why we don't take the time to aim (i.e., plan our projects). The only excuse I can come up with is that we are so distracted, we fool ourselves into thinking that we don't need to take aim before we fire (or we don't think at all and simply react to the pressure). The cost to industry and to ourselves in lost time and energy is enormous.

So, what are the lessons learned? If we properly prepare (get ready with adequate planning) and take the time to aim before we fire off a project (i.e., ensure that the proper processes, procedures, and expectations are in place), many headaches can be avoided.

How do you know if you have the right order? What is the proper sequence of planning a project to avoid stepping in front of the proverbial bullet? For an answer, let's look at the AIM strategy.

Ask the Expert

Q: What is the solution to the "Ready, Fire, Aim" dilemma?

A: The solution is what I call the *AIM strategy*. Many of my clients agree that sponsors are quick to throw a project at them without any thought for the time it takes to complete the project, the planning needed, or even how much it will cost. Many sponsors just want a problem to go away fast or to be first to market with a new product or service. The AIM strategy breaks the solution down into a manageable flow and allows the PM and team to analyze the problem systematically, implement a solution, and manage the project effectively.

AIM Strategy

To better understand the AIM strategy, let's look at why we need a strategy in the first place. A strategy requires planning. In the *PMBOK Guide Sixth Edition* and Table 3.1 in Chapter 3 of this book, the majority of processes are planning processes. This should be your first clue to take a deep breath and think about what it takes to manage a project. We need to prepare not only the project itself, but how we are going to manage the project.

Far too often when projects are priced, we fail to consider adequately the cost of project management, the time it takes to build the team, and how to manage the flow of information. Rarely do we take time to actually build communication and risk plans, document and verify the scope of the project, look at the Process Groups to see where we are in the life cycle of the project, or determine which processes are necessary to help us effectively manage the project. Instead, we just jump right into "fire"!

The AIM strategy is all about staying focused on the task at hand and understanding what the goals are before pulling the trigger to start the project. This requires planning and coordination, and this is where we need to look at the whole project, to ensure we have a solid project management strategy.

What Does AIM Stand For?

- First, *analyze* the situation and get involved with the key stakeholders, develop the plan as a team, and obtain formal acceptance (approval) for the project plan.
- Second, *implement* the approved plan.
- Last but not least, *manage* the whole project and nothing but the project. If you stray, which is far too easy to do with the many distractions mentioned earlier, your project is likely to fall into the category of a failed or troubled project.

Why Projects Fail: What Can You Do about It?

First, let's review what constitutes a failed or troubled project. The definition varies based on the size, type, and complexity of the project.

According to the Standish Group, which specializes in independent research and analysis of IT project performance, project results can be divided into three categories:

- **Project that succeeds.** The project is completed on time and on budget, with all features and functions as initially specified.
- **Project that is challenged.** The project is completed and operational but over budget, or over the time estimate, or it offers fewer features or functions than originally specified.
- **Project that is impaired.** The project is canceled at some point during the development cycle.

Reports from The Standish Group and other sources show that approximately 30 percent of projects succeed, over 50 percent are challenged in some way, and fewer than 20 percent fail, which is an improvement from several years ago when over 30 percent of projects failed for one reason or another.

A project can fail for several reasons. As discussed earlier in the chapter, under "Success Is in the Eyes of the Customer," success is meeting the customer's needs and expectations. So, failure is *not* meeting those needs. Failure can occur when project objectives are not met, such as delivering the project late, going over budget, not meeting quality standards, or not completing all of the agreed-upon scope of the project.

Business requirements change so quickly these days that unless the PM is fully aware of the issues at a business level, even a project that delivers the planned scope within time and cost may be deemed unsuccessful because its deliverables are no longer relevant to the business.[6] 

Statistics from the Gartner Group state that 30 percent of IT projects never come to a fruitful conclusion. On average, 51 percent exceed budget by 189 percent while only delivering 74 percent of the originally stated functionality.[7]

Factors that drive poor performance range from lack of disciplined project management to lack of communication between the IT organization and the business unit directors. It is essential that the project managers have a solid understanding of the enterprise's business objectives so they can continually measure the project in terms of delivering these business objectives.

Here are several factors that may cause failed projects:

- Project sponsors are often not committed to the project objective. They have a lack of understanding of the project and are not involved in the project strategy and direction.

They may have their own agenda, biases, pet projects, or pet peeves concerning other projects.

- Some projects do not meet the strategic vision of the company, or the direction has changed. When business needs are not clearly defined, the result is a project that does not add value to the bottom line or enhance business processes.
- Projects are started for the wrong reasons. Some are initiated purely to implement new technology without regard for whether the technology is right for the business needs.
- Staffing is often a reason for failure. For example, not enough dedicated staff (project managers and project team members) is allocated to projects. Project team members may lack experience and do not have the required qualifications.
- Incomplete project scope. There's no clear definition of the project's benefits and how they will be delivered.
- The project plan is nonexistent, out of date, incomplete, or poorly constructed. Not enough time and effort are spent on project planning.
- Project value management is not put into practice to evaluate the baseline cost agreed upon during baseline transfer against actual costs spent at any given time.
- Insufficient funds and incorrect budgeting are a major reason that projects do not deliver their goals and objectives within the quality framework required.
- Formal project management methodologies and best practices aligned to the company's specific needs aren't used to assist project performance.
- Projects don't go through a normal signoff using a proper postmortem (Lessons Learned) process to build a reference model for future use.

Here are some things you can do to help keep your projects from failing:

- Use proven project management disciplines.
- Ensure clear two-way communication.
- Work with the stakeholders to focus on the end results (including end users).
- Manage change, risk, scope, time, and cost diligently.
- Review and report status frequently and honestly.
- Be an advocate (cheerleader) for the project team (catch them doing something right).
- Use project management standards (tools and resources available) for planning, executing, and controlling the project.
- Verify the overall health of the project by asking yourself and the team the following questions:
  - Were deliverables produced on time, within the approved scope, and within the approved budget?

+ Did the project satisfy the business requirements of the stakeholders? (e.g., was the problem solved, or the solution accomplished?)
+ Has the project met the business value goals (such as cost savings, increased market share, or streamlined processes that are needed to improve quality)?
+ Most important, do the business owners (sponsors) believe the project was successful? Did you deliver a quality product and meet stakeholder expectations?

Projects Fail for Many Reasons

Keep in mind that projects may be deemed a failure for reasons outside of your control as a PM. Even when everything is executed properly, there may be changes in direction, strategy, funding, or limited availability of key skilled-staff members to complete the project effectively. As a PM, you need to keep these influencing factors in mind and realize there are times when projects are considered failures through no fault of your own. It is difficult not to take this personally. Still, you must perform a lessons learned session, document the issues as well as what worked and what didn't work (including input from the customer), and then move on. We discuss this in more detail in Chapter 14.

At the end of the day, the success or failure of a project depends entirely on measured results and perception—a project may be on time and on budget but may not meet the customer's expectations.

Pop Quiz

By now you should have a better understanding of what a project is, what a program is, and what project management is, this chapter's three takeaway points, the AIM strategy, what constitutes failed projects, and things you can do to help prevent projects from failing. To test yourself on these important topics, take the following simple pop quiz:

1. What is a project?
2. What is a program?
3. What are the three takeaway points from this chapter?
4. What does AIM stand for?
5. Name three reasons why projects fail.

Take a few minutes and write down your answers. Then refer back to the appropriate sections in this chapter for confirmation or check out the answers that follow.

Answers:

1. A project is a temporary endeavor to create a unique product, service, or result. It has a definite start and end, is usually short-term in duration, and has clearly defined goals and objectives.

2. A program is a collection of projects, usually has no end date, and tends to be longer term in duration.
3. The three takeaway points are
   - Stay focused on the end goal and objectives of the project.
   - Use the tools and resources available to help effectively manage the project.
   - Work as a team (remember, the number-one asset on the project is the team).
4. AIM stands for
   - *Analyze* the situation and get involved with the key stakeholders, develop the plan as a team, and obtain formal acceptance for the project plan.
   - *Implement* the approved plan.
   - *Manage* the whole project and nothing but the project.
5. Here's a sample summary list of reasons of why projects fail:
   - Lack of project management discipline
   - Lack of user (key stakeholder) involvement
   - Lack of project sponsors committed to or involved in the project strategy and direction
   - Projects do not meet the strategic vision or business needs of the company
   - Projects started for the wrong reasons
   - Lack of properly trained or skilled people to work the project
   - Lack of cultural skills and ability to manage in a multicultural environment

Why Projects Succeed

Rather than end the chapter on a negative note, let's look at what constitutes a successful project and ways to help ensure success on your projects.

Project success is all in the measurements. If you don't set goals and measurements, how will you know when you have completed the project? We noted earlier that one of the key characteristics of a project is that it must have measureable results. If you don't measure the progress and results, how do you know when you're done, and how will you even know what "done" is supposed to look like?

According to PMI, project success should be measured in terms of completing the project within the constraints of scope, time, cost, quality, resources, and risk as approved between the project managers and senior management. The PM is responsible and accountable for setting realistic and achievable boundaries for the project and for accomplishing the project within the approved baselines.

Dimensions of Project Success

Another perspective on project success is provided by William R. Duncan in an article titled, "Defining and Measuring Project Success."[8] Project success requires a combination of product success and project management success:

- Was the product (service, result, or outcome) of the project a success?
- Was the project well managed?

Simple yes-or-no answers will not suffice. We should not be asking, "Was your project a success?" We should be asking, "How successful was your project?"

Different stakeholders will use different measures. The health and safety officer wants no injuries. The manufacturing manager wants a product that is easy to build. The ISO 9000 compliance team cries, "Success" if the documentation is complete. The VP of marketing will be delighted if you get to market before your competition.

The bottom line is this: Your project will be measured. Your stakeholders will decide whether it was well managed. Someone will decide whether or not the product of your project was a success. Do yourself, your team, and your organization a service and get these measures documented and agreed to right from the start.[9]

It is also important to be able to handle changes, because they are inevitable. However, even though project specifications might become altered, the project can still be successful—as long as the changes go through a well-defined change control system.

References

1. *A Guide to the Project Management Body of Knowledge (PMBOK® Guide), Sixth Edition* (Newtown Square, PA: PMI Project Management Institute Global Standard, 2017), page 6.

2. PMI, "PMP Exam Content Outline" (Newtown Square, PA: Project Management Institute, June 2015), pages 5–11, https://www.pmi.org/-/media/pmi/documents/public/pdf/certifications/project-management-professional-exam-outline.pdf, accessed February 17, 2017.

3. "Governance," *Wikipedia*, http://en.wikipedia.org/wiki/Governance, accessed February 17, 2017.

4. Jeffrey K. Liker and David Meier, *The Toyota Way Fieldbook: A Practical Guide for Implementing Toyota's 4Ps* (New York: McGraw-Hill, 2004), page 325.

5. Ibid., page 313.

6. AST Group, "The Top 10 Reasons Why Projects Fail," *TechForum* (July 12, 2001), http://www.itweb.co.za/office/ast/0107120730.htm, accessed June 14, 2008.

7. Ibid.

8. William R. Duncan, "Defining and Measuring Project Success," *LinkedIn* (April 19, 2015 [2004]), https://www.linkedin.com/pulse/defining-measuring-project-success-bill-duncan, accessed May 29, 2017. See also William R. Duncan, "Project Success," *PM Theory into Practice* (February 15, 2010), https://pmtip.wordpress.com/2010/02/15/project-success/, accessed February 17, 2017.

9. Ibid.

3 Project Management Process Groups and Processes

Key Skills & Concepts

- Definition of a process
- Importance of the five PMI Process Groups
- Mapping processes to Process Groups and Knowledge Areas
- Process inputs, tools and techniques, and outputs
- Initiating Process Group
- Planning Process Group
- Executing Process Group
- Monitoring and Controlling Process Group
- Closing Process Group
- Introduction to the ten *PMBOK* Knowledge Areas
- Importance of global standards
- Code of Ethics and Professional Conduct

This chapter identifies and defines project processes and describes how they align within PMI's five Process Groups (also referred to as domains). It explains the importance of the five Process Groups as covered in the new standards outlined in the *PMBOK Guide Sixth Edition*. This chapter also briefly introduces the ten *PMBOK* Knowledge Areas and their associated processes required for most projects. The Knowledge Areas will be covered in more detail in Chapters 4 through 13.

Lastly, this chapter introduces PMI's Code of Ethics and Professional Conduct and its importance for project managers (PMs) and project teams.

What Is a Process?

"A process is a set of interrelated actions and activities performed to create a pre-specified product, service, or result. Each process is characterized by its inputs, the tools and techniques that can be applied, and the resulting outputs."[1] In other words, a *process* is a series of actions that bring about a result. It serves as a guide of what needs to be done to convert inputs (information) into outputs (often referred to as a deliverable, e.g., a PM plan document or training manual, or a set of blueprints). A process is often considered synonymous with a procedure; however, a process is usually viewed at a higher level that can include multiple procedures. A *procedure* usually defines a series of steps, which when completed achieve a consistent and repeatable product or result. Many companies and organizations follow standard operating procedures (SOP), which may be referred to as "best practices" to help ensure quality.

Processes also tend to overlap and interact in a variety of ways. Some processes run in series in which one process can build on the next. However, many processes are repeated within the different Process Groups, or phases of the project. The good news is that the PM and key project stakeholders usually get to decide which processes are appropriate for their specific project.

In order for a project to be successful, the project team must

- Select the appropriate processes required to meet the project objectives.
- Use a defined approach to meet the requirements of the project.
- Establish and maintain appropriate communication and engagement with stakeholders.
- Comply with requirements to meet stakeholder needs and expectations.
- Balance competing constraints of scope, schedule, budget, quality, resources, and risk to produce the specified product, service, or result of the project.

Project processes should be performed by the project team with input from stakeholder interactions. Project processes usually fall into one of two categories:

- **Project management processes.** These processes focus on the overall management of the project and the activities needed to create project documents. Process-oriented activities focus on the process to help ensure the effective flow of the project throughout its life cycle. Process-oriented activities focus on the processes of project management and not the outcome of the project. This book focuses on project management processes, and it is important to note that PMI is really big on processes (there are 49 project management-related processes in the *PMBOK Guide Sixth Edition*).

- **Product-oriented processes.** These processes specify the products (outcome) of the project (what the project will deliver) when it is complete, for example, the donation check to be presented at the end of a fundraising project; that is, the big check is the "product" of the project, or the house (or building) is the finished product of a construction project.

Each process has inputs, tools and techniques, and outputs that should serve as a high-level guide for the project management team. The project management team should "tailor" each process to the individual needs of the project. Project management processes tie directly into the five Process Groups. All processes interact throughout the project via their inputs and outputs. According to PMI, successful project management includes actively managing these interactions to successfully meet project requirements. More detail will be provided later in this chapter.

Now that you have a better understanding of the concept of project processes, the next step is to group them into Process Groups.

What Are Process Groups and Why Are They Important?

PMI recognizes and endorses five basic Process Groups (sometimes referred to as *domains*). These five Process Groups have clear dependencies and are typically performed in each project and are highly interactive with one another. These five Process Groups are independent of application areas or industry focus.

Process Groups serve as independent groups of processes that are linked by the respective inputs and outputs they produce. The output of one process often becomes the input to the next process. A Process Group can also be performed independently—for example, planning a project that ultimately doesn't get funded, or closing a project at the end of its life cycle, where closing the project is a project in itself.

Process Groups and processes are iterative in nature, meaning that they are repetitive and build on one another. *Iterative* can also be defined as a method for getting to a decision or desired result by initiating a series of repetitive cycles of analysis. Note that Process Groups are NOT synonymous with project phases. There are many different types of projects, and the phases are often very different.

The five Process Groups are briefly described as follows:

- **Initiating Process Group.** Defines and authorizes the start of a project or a phase.
- **Planning Process Group.** Establishes the overall project management plan, defines the scope and objectives of the project, and helps identify how the project, scope, schedule, budget, risk, and so on are to be managed throughout the project life cycle.

- **Executing Process Group.** Integrates people and other resources to complete the work of the project according to the defined and approved project management plan.
- **Monitoring and Controlling Process Group.** Includes those processes required to track, review, and regulate the progress and performance of the project and identifies areas where changes or corrective action needs to be taken to meet project objectives.
- **Closing Process Group.** Includes those processes performed to finalize all activities across all Process Groups to formally close the project or phase.

Tip

Why are the five Process Groups important? If you are planning to take the PMP exam, it is important to note that the questions on this exam align with the five Process Groups and not with the Knowledge Areas (as in the past or in the CAPM exam). The reason for this is that it is more important to know when a process should occur relative to the five Process Groups rather than which Knowledge Area it happens to fall into. The important thing to remember is that project dynamics change according to where you are in the project life cycle. For example, the types of risk will vary from phase to phase during the project life cycle. Risks are typically higher at the beginning of the project life cycle and change during the project, depending on the phase or the project life cycle. Another example is if a team member leaves the project, the PM may have to go back to the Planning Process Group to review and adjust the estimate of the activity resources, cost, and project schedule.

If you plan to take the PMP exam, you must look at the processes vertically from top to bottom (by Process Group), moving down the Initiating Process Group, then to the Planning Process Group, and so on in a "rolling wave" approach much like a "waterfall" as opposed to a horizontal or "swim-lane" view for the CAPM exam, which follows more of a left to right by Knowledge Area pattern.

Process Groups provide a logical sequence of events rather than simply grouping processes into their area of knowledge. For example, Identify Stakeholders is one of the Project Stakeholder Management Knowledge Area processes. It is extremely important to initiate this process early in the project management life cycle, which is why it is grouped in the Initiating Process Group. This can be a bit confusing because all the PMI recognized processes are associated with their respective Knowledge Areas *and* the processes are grouped in one of the five Process Groups (see "Mapping Processes to Knowledge Areas and Process Groups" in Table 3.1 later in this chapter for more details).

Ask the Expert

Q: Do most project managers use Process Groups to manage real-world projects?

A: PMs frequently make use of these Process Groups and Knowledge Areas instinctively and may not even realize they are doing so. Even experienced PMs without formal training use these Process Groups and often could not tell you what the Process Groups are called.

For example, this was evident when my daughter started planning her wedding. Even though she has no formal project management training, she instinctively sat down and wrote out her idea (scope) of the perfect wedding, thus initiating the project (in project management terms we call this *developing the project charter*, which is the first process in the Initiating Process Group). Her documented view of the wedding set up the criteria, requirements, and expected results to be met for this project to be successful. These requirements were the input to the project charter and to the scope statement.

Next, my daughter and her fiancé put together a list of guests and participants, including the attendants and the person who would preside over the ceremony. In doing so they identified the stakeholders, which is the second process under the Initiating Process Group. Not even realizing it, my daughter had just completed the first Process Group of any project (initiating).

Next, she approached my wife and me to negotiate the size of the wedding and a preliminary budget. She estimated the number of attendees, and based on her expectations and research, she was able to provide a best-guess estimate of the cost. This is known as a rough order of magnitude (ROM) cost estimate, which is used in one of the processes in the Project Cost Management Knowledge Area under the Planning Process Group.

Once my wife and I reviewed the estimate and were convinced my daughter and her future husband were serious about keeping the budget reasonable without our having to take out a second mortgage on our home, we all agreed. This became our formally accepted project charter and budget. With the charter (including the preliminary scope) and the budget estimate in hand, we officially "authorized" the project to begin.

Establishing a budget and funding the wedding up front turned out to be a great idea because it kept my wife and me from being involved in every detail and from having to negotiate for each item along the way. This approach also kept my daughter from feeling guilty about the cost of a particular item (such as the wedding dress or the cake) because she had the decision to make and the budget to manage. Talk about a lesson learned (a key project management principle)! I highly recommend this approach for all parents of a bride because it really instills a sense of ownership in the wedding project and encourages the bride and groom to manage their budget well.

I must admit the credit for this great idea goes to one of my project management students at Colorado State University (CSU) who was planning her own wedding during the time she was taking a project management class. We used her wedding as a team project during this eight-week class. It was great to see even the older men in the class take such an active role in helping plan her wedding, using all the project management processes and Knowledge Areas as we discussed them in class. The bride was able to use the work of the team to make her wedding project a complete success, and the class had fun as a team working on the project.

The Process Group interactions diagram in Figure 3.1 shows how each of the Process Groups interact with one another. Note the multiple interdependencies between Process Groups, linked especially through the project documents at the center. Also note that even

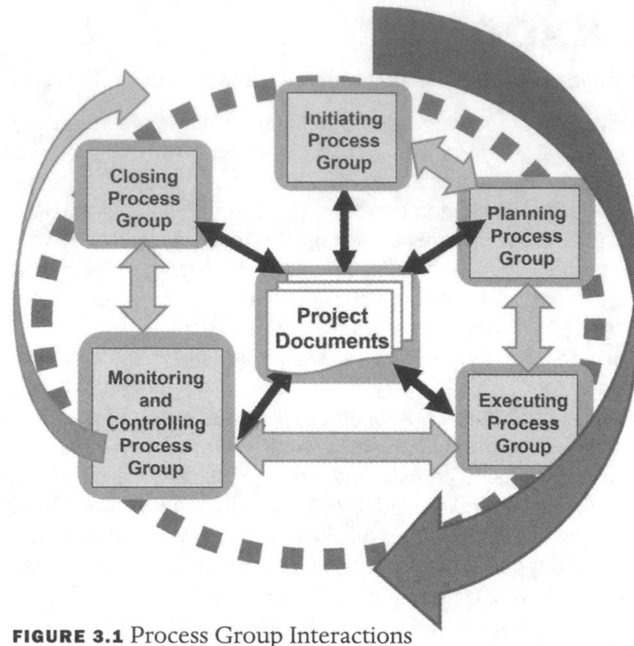

FIGURE 3.1 Process Group Interactions

though it is not shown in this diagram, the Monitoring and Controlling Process Group overlaps the other Process Groups and should be followed throughout the project life cycle.

Mapping Processes to Process Groups and Knowledge Areas

A Guide to the Project Management Body of Knowledge (*PMBOK Guide*) is a collection of processes and Knowledge Areas generally accepted as best practices within the project management discipline. It is also an internationally recognized standard (IEEE Standard 1490–2011) that provides the fundamentals of project management, regardless of the type of project being managed—construction, hardware or product development, software development, engineering, aviation, automotive, and so on.

Table 3.1 maps the *PMBOK* processes to both the ten Knowledge Areas (in the first column) and the five Process Groups (across the top of the table, in columns 2 through 6).

Note

Each process is identified by its *PMBOK* chapter and section number. For example, 4.1 is the Develop Project Charter process, which is discussed in Chapter 4 of the *PMBOK Guide*, and is the first process in the Project Integration Management Knowledge Area.

TABLE 3.1 Mapping Processes to Knowledge Areas and Process Groups[2][Comp: Remove vertical lines from this and all other tables in this chapter.]

Knowledge Areas	Initiating	Planning	Executing	Monitoring and Controlling	Closing
Project Integration Management	4.1 Develop Project Charter	4.2 Develop Project Management Plan	4.3 Direct and Manage Project Work 4.4 Manage Project Knowledge	4.5 Monitor and Control Project Work 4.6 Perform Integrated Change Control	4.7 Close Project or Phase
Project Scope Management		5.1 Plan Scope Management 5.2 Collect Requirements 5.3 Define Scope 5.4 Create WBS		5.5 Validate Scope 5.6 Control Scope	
Project Schedule Management		6.1 Plan Schedule Management 6.2 Define Activities 6.3 Sequence Activities 6.4 Estimate Activity Durations 6.5 Develop Schedule		6.6 Control Schedule	
Project Cost Management		7.1 Plan Cost Management 7.2 Estimate Costs 7.3 Determine Budget		7.4 Control Costs	
Project Quality Management		8.1 Plan Quality Management	8.2 Manage Quality	8.3 Control Quality	
Project Resource Management		9.1 Plan Resource Management 9.2 Estimate Activity Resources	9.3 Acquire Resources 9.4 Develop Team 9.5 Manage Team	9.6 Control Resources	
Project Communications Management		10.1 Plan Communications Management	10.2 Manage Communications	10.3 Monitor Communications	
Project Risk Management		11.1 Plan Risk Management 11.2 Identify Risks 11.3 Perform Qualitative Risk Analysis 11.4 Perform Quantitative Risk Analysis 11.5 Plan Risk Responses	11.6 Implement Risk Responses	11.7 Monitor Risks	
Project Procurement Management		12.1 Plan Procurement Management	12.2 Conduct Procurements	12.3 Control Procurements	
Project Stakeholder Management	13.1 Identify Stakeholders	13.2 Plan Stakeholder Engagement	13.3 Manage Stakeholder Engagement	13.4 Monitor Stakeholder Engagement	

Inputs, Tools and Techniques, and Outputs

All processes have inputs, tools and techniques, and outputs. These components provide links (or common threads) from one process to the next. Many of the processes have the same inputs. For example, project documents, enterprise environmental factors, and organizational process assets are the inputs to almost all the processes and should be considered as an input even if not specifically identified in each process.

Tip

Any time you see a particular topic mentioned frequently in this book or the *PMBOK*, you should take note because this means the topic is viewed as highly important by PMI, and you can bet it will be on the PMI exam. This is especially true with process inputs, tools and techniques, and outputs (watch for the ones repeated often between processes and focus on them if you plan to take a PMI exam). There are many questions on PMI exams around process inputs, tools and techniques, and outputs to the various project management processes.

Further, an *input* is something that needs to be considered as part of the influencing factors to complete a process. Inputs to a particular process are often the outputs from the previous process. In some cases there tends to be a logical sequence, and in other cases the processes may be totally independent.

Tools and techniques are the methods in which the information (input) is applied to get the process to the intended output. For example, you may use "expert judgment" as a tool or technique to help ensure you have the right skilled resources to review the input and provide expert recommendations on how the input information or conditions may affect the output. *Meetings* are an effective tool or technique for transferring information or presenting project status, for example, a kickoff meeting or weekly project status meetings.

An *output* of any process is the finished product or result of the process—for example, the project charter is the output of the Develop Project Charter process.

Two of the more common inputs are enterprise environmental factors and organization process assets, which show up frequently in the *PMBOK* as inputs to most all processes.

Enterprise environmental factors (EEFs) refer to both internal and external environmental factors that surround or influence a project's success. An enterprise is nothing more than an organization (including corporations, small and large businesses, nonprofit institutions, and government bodies). In practice, the term *enterprise* is used more often to describe larger organizations than smaller ones.

Environmental factors may come from any or all of the enterprises involved in the project. These factors may enhance or constrain the project management options and may have a positive or negative influence on the outcome. The various environmental factors are to be considered as inputs to most planning processes and include, but are not limited to, the following:

- Organizational culture, structure, and processes
- Government or industry standards (regulatory agency regulations, codes of conduct, product standards, quality standards, and workmanship standards)
- Infrastructure (existing facilities and capital equipment)
- Existing human resources (skills, disciplines, and knowledge)
- Personnel administration (staffing and retention guidelines, performance reviews, training, overtime policies, and time tracking)
- Company work-authorization systems
- Marketplace conditions, stakeholder risk tolerances, political climate
- Organization's established communication channels

Ask the Expert

Q: Can you provide an example of how enterprise environmental factors may affect a real project?

A: Yes. A Fortune 500 company initiated a service agreement (contract) to have a project team come into its offices to conduct a physical (wall-to-wall) inventory of its computers. The cost estimates were developed based on a certain set of assumptions. As the project plan was developed and verified, the customer informed the PM that its organization's culture and structure (an EEF) is "management by consensus." This meant that the organization had a committee of managers that set certain policies. In this case the company policy first required all the people conducting the inventory to go through four hours of training on sensitivity in the workplace (for example, how to be respectful of the employees' time when conducting the data-collection process). Also, the entire inventory team had to provide very detailed background information and to sign nondisclosure statements, because some of the buildings where they would be conducting inventories were highly confidential research and development centers. As you can imagine, with all the additional requirements and constraints, the cost and the time to conduct the inventory more than doubled.

The moral to this story is that you need to fully understand the environmental factors prior to the final agreement for the time, cost, and scope of the project.

To begin a project of any kind, you must first initiate the project. That is, to ensure the project is approved to begin and formally recognized to allow the project manager the authority to assign resources and start the work of the project. There are usually two primary steps needed to get a project rolling. First is the authorization through some form of a project charter and next is to identify who the key (primary) stakeholders are so the PM can begin the dialog with them to understand what the project is all about, its purpose, and expected results. The first Process Group to accomplish this is Initiating.

Initiating Process Group

As you might imagine, the Initiating Process Group should be the first in the series of Process Group activities and consists of those processes performed to define a new project or a new phase of an existing project. This Process Group is focused on obtaining authorization to start the project or phase (see Figure 3.2).

The Initiating Process Group includes only two processes:

- Develop Project Charter.
- Identify Stakeholders.

Project Integration Management

Develop Project Charter

Stakeholder Management

Identify Stakeholders

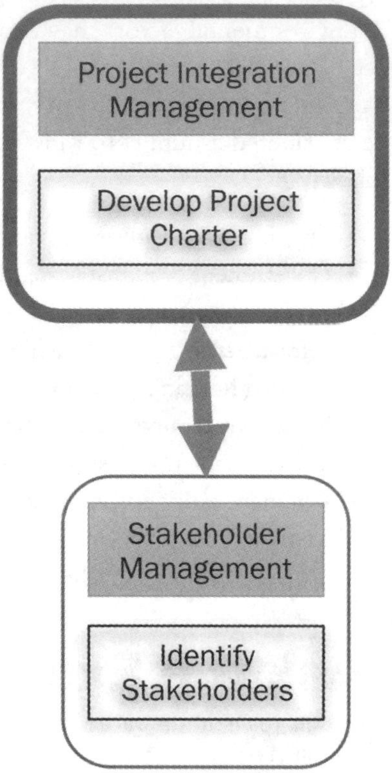

FIGURE 3.2 Initiating Process Group

Tip

On real projects there are many more processes (beyond the two listed in the *PMBOK*) associated with initiating a project. Activities or processes such as selecting a project manager, collecting historical information, determining high-level requirements, understanding the business needs and objectives, and so on are essential to jump-starting (initiating) a project. The CAPM exam will focus more on the *PMBOK* view of processes where the PMP exam will focus more on the real-world view of the expanded list of processes and actions needed to initiate a project.

Develop Project Charter Process

The project manager should be assigned as early in the project life cycle as possible, either during or shortly after the project charter is written, because this is when things can go well if the PM is represented or can go wrong if a PM is not assigned.

Note that some projects are only authorized or funded (budgeted) for one phase, such as a "feasibility study" or a concept phase, to determine whether the project is appropriate and if it will provide the correct solution to meet the need or solve the problem it is intended to resolve. You have probably seen a project charter in one form or another—and may not have realized it. The charter can come in many different forms. It can be formal (such as a contract), informal (such as a phone call from your boss or customer), or in writing (such as an email or memo). If at all possible it is best if you can get it in writing, even if only in an email. Some examples are provided in the following list (additional details can be found in chapter 4):

- **Informal.** A work order or service order/request to upgrade a computer system, thus changing the scope of the project; an email from your boss telling you to get a team together and fix a design problem on a software application
- **Formal.** A written contract for any product, service, or result (an example of a result would be a project to consolidate work to decrease production costs by 10 percent), statement of work (SOW), service agreement (SA), project change request (PCR), service request (SR), or request for service (RFS) to modify or change a project

The inputs and outputs of this process are shown in Table 3.2.

TABLE 3.2 Develop Project Charter Inputs and Outputs

Inputs	Outputs
Business documents	Project charter
Agreements	Assumption log
Enterprise environmental factors	
Organizational process assets	

Note

The inputs and outputs shown in this chapter are high-level (summary) to give an example of the flow of information (inputs) into a process and outputs for each process. A more detailed list of inputs, tools and techniques, and outputs will be covered in the Knowledge Area chapters, 4–13. As a reminder, rather than replicate many of the standard inputs or outputs, one can group them under the title of "Standard Inputs" or "Standard Outputs." For an even more detailed view of the ITTOs for each process, you will need to refer to the *PMBOK Guide*.

When the project charter is approved (signed off on and accepted), the next step is to identify the stakeholders on the project. These are the people, departments, or organizations that are involved with or associated with the project.

Identify Stakeholders Process

The Identify Stakeholders process is the first in the Project Stakeholder Management Knowledge Area and is extremely important within the Initiating Process Group. A stakeholder can be anyone who is positively or negatively impacted by the project. It is the PM's responsibility to identify the stakeholders of the project. Additional details on this process and other Stakeholder Management Knowledge Area processes are provided in Chapter 13. The inputs and outputs of this process are shown in Table 3.3.

TABLE 3.3 Identify Stakeholders Inputs and Outputs

Inputs	Outputs
Project charter	Stakeholder register
Business documents	Change requests
Project management plan	Project management plan updates
Project documents	Project document updates
Agreements	
Enterprise environmental factors	
Organizational process assets	

The best way to identify stakeholders is to ask questions to anyone that has been involved with this or a previous similar project. A stakeholder register is a good way to keep track of who the stakeholders are and their level of authority or expectations from the project. Microsoft Excel spreadsheets or other tools may be used to create the stakeholder register. When working with stakeholders, you should get an idea of their timeline and priorities. The best way to manage a timeline is breaking the project into manageable phases.

Manageable Phases

It is common (or should be) to divide projects into separate, manageable phases. Identifying stakeholders and knowing their expectations for the different phases of the project make the phases more manageable. Repeating the initiating processes at the start of each phase helps keep the project team focused on the key deliverables for each project phase. This doesn't mean creating or obtaining a new project charter at the beginning of each phase, but it does mean ensuring you have authorization to proceed to the next phase of the project. The best way to know when a phase is complete is by setting key measurements and identifying phase deliverables and making sure the measurements (metrics) have been met and the deliverables completed.

Tip

Setting and verifying key measurements and jointly determining project success criteria with key stakeholders will help ensure project success. The success criteria–once documented, approved, and communicated–provide key indicators of the health and progress of the project and will help you manage the primary project constraints more effectively. An example of success criteria is having an events center facility fully set up, tested, and ready to host a concert prior to curtain up time.

It is also important to involve the customers and other key stakeholders identified in the Initiating Process Group, because it generally improves the probability of shared ownership, deliverable acceptance, and customer / stakeholder satisfaction.

After the project is officially sanctioned or approved (chartered) and we have identified the key stakeholders who will be involved in or affected by the project, it is time to start the planning processes.

Planning Process Group (Planning the Work)

The Planning Process Group consists of processes performed to establish the overall project management plan, to define the total scope of the project, to define and refine objectives, and to develop the course of action required to attain the approved objectives (see Figure 3.3).

The Importance of Planning

The importance of planning a project is evident as the majority (24 of 49) of processes in the sixth edition of *PMBOK Guide* are included in the Planning Process Group.

In the real world, projects are far too often managed with little, if any, planning. We are lucky if we get three hours (much less three days or three weeks) of actual planning before we begin the work of a project. This, in my opinion, is due to the current culture (especially in the United States) where we have grown to expect instant gratification. Between watching the problems of the universe being solved in a 30-minute television show and the wonders of modern technology (phones that play music; take pictures; receive up-to-the-minute sports scores, traffic, and weather updates; and use global navigation systems), it is no wonder we have little or no patience. We are multiplexing our way into sleep deprivation, frustration, accidents, and potentially death. Our cultural changes and distractions are often hazardous to our health.

How Distractions at Work Take up More Time Than You Think

Multiple studies confirm distractions don't just eat up time during the distraction but also derail your mental progress for up to a half hour afterward (that's assuming another distraction

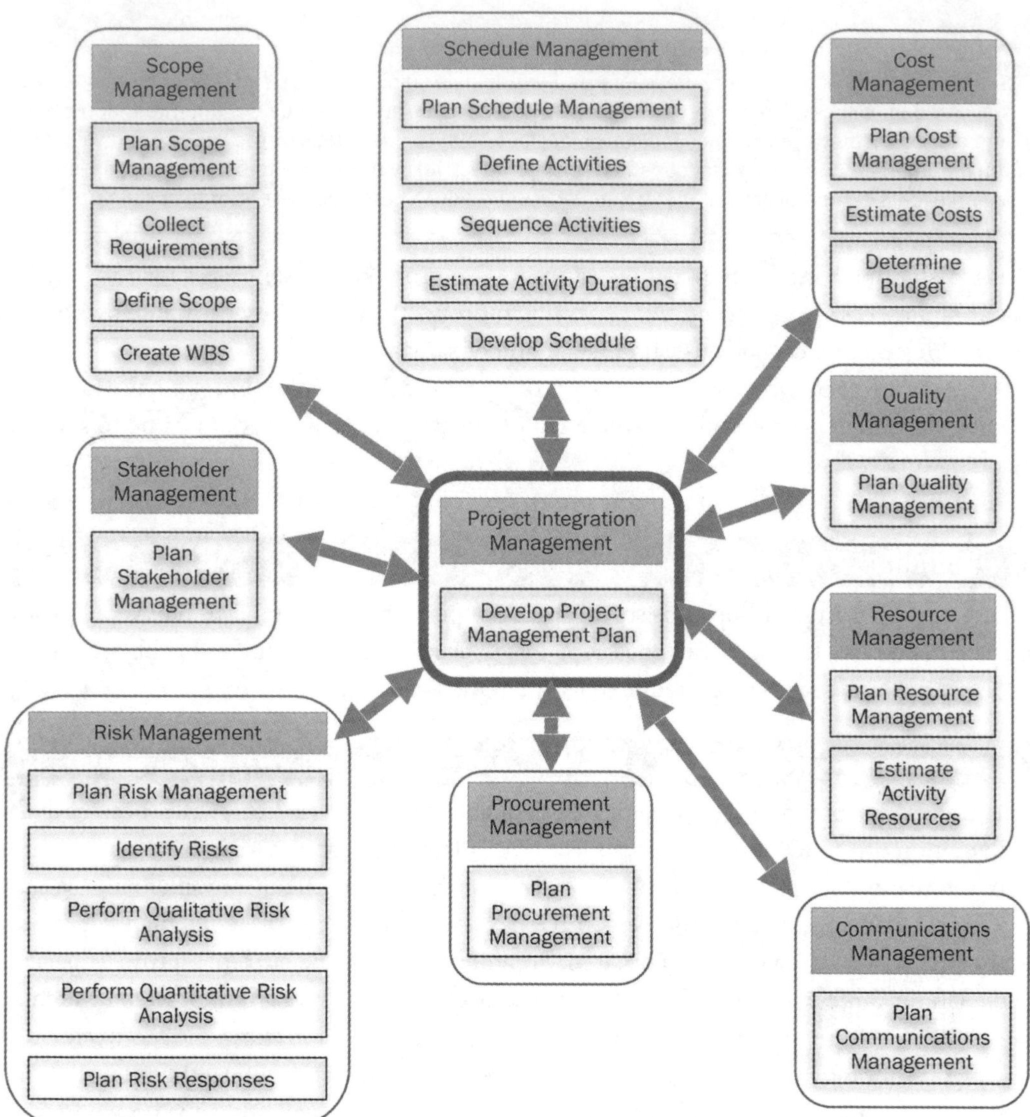

FIGURE 3.3 Planning Process Group

doesn't show up in that half hour). In other words, that "30 seconds to check Twitter" isn't just 30 seconds down the drain. It's 25 minutes and 30 seconds. And all these distractions not only hurt productivity but also have negative emotional effects. "Our research has shown that attention distraction can lead to higher stress, a bad mood and lower productivity."[3]

The following facts are from the DistractedDriversAccidents.com website:

- Over 2.5 million people in the United States are involved in road accidents each year. The population of the United States is just 318.9 million. At this rate, the American people could be extinct in two human lifespans. This is an astounding number of traffic accidents.
- Of these, 1.6 million have a cell phone involved in them. That's 64 percent of all the road accidents in the United States. Over half the road accidents in the States have cell phones involved, and if this doesn't make you realize how potent it is, what will?
- 37,000+ people die in automobile crashes in the United States every year.
- Every year about 421,000 people are injured in crashes that have involved a driver who was distracted in some way.[4]

Distractions often account for limited, delayed, or lack of planning. As you would imagine, the processes grouped into the Planning Process Group should occur early in the project life cycle, when there are many unknowns. The risk for failure is increased if the planning processes are not performed, are unclear, or are not communicated properly. Too many distractions during the planning process and during the development of the project plan endanger the success of the project.

An example of this occurred when I was asked to manage a new global project, and in the first meeting with the project sponsor he boldly stated, "We don't have time to plan; we are already three weeks behind before we even started."

The same is true with project activities—the project team and manager are constantly being distracted. Because over 90 percent of the PM's time is spent communicating, the unscheduled interruptions of phone calls, new concerns and issues, and project changes are like a juggling act. With the urgent demands from the project stakeholders and almost immediate response expected from everyone, it is no wonder we don't take the time to plan properly how to manage a project.

Poor planning and lack of project management discipline are two common reasons for project failure. Therefore, it is essential to develop a solid project plan and to work the plan. (Don't just let it collect dust in a desk drawer or in your briefcase.)

The iterative, multidimensional nature of project management creates an atmosphere for repeated input and feedback loops for further consideration and analysis. Remember, everyone likes to make informed decisions, and the more information you can provide, the better the chances of hitting the target.

Tip

Success is not possible unless you plan first and then validate, validate, and validate again the scope and deliverables throughout the project life cycle.

Ask the Expert

Q: How long, on average, should one spend planning on a 12-month project?

A: It all depends on the uniqueness of the project (has it been performed before? or is it a unique, first-time project?), the experience of the team and PM, and the level of commitment from the sponsors and other stakeholders. Also to be taken into account for the estimate is whether the scope is clearly defined and if there is an approved project charter.

The answer also will vary depending on the country in which the project is being performed. For example, in Asia planning is a way of life, and project teams often will spend several months on this phase. One of my students from Korea stated that in his country, planning would take approximately 8 to 9 months on a 12-month project. Granted, the planning process is viewed differently in different countries. In the United States we often want to dive right in to the work and begin the project prior to having a clear scope, a charter, or, in many cases, approved funding.

So what is the right amount of planning? On average, I would suggest 100 hours for every 1,000 hours of work on the project. The key thing to remember is that the real answer to the amount of planning needed depends entirely on the variables previously mentioned and the experience of the PM and the project team. We must first aim at the target before we fire (start the project) to maximize our chances of hitting the target.

The Planning Process Group is all about revisiting one or more of the planning processes and possibly some of the initiating processes in a progressive fashion to ensure that the requirements are clear and communicated properly, and that the work of the project is in line with the scope and deliverables to be provided by the project. This iterative, progressive detailing of the project management plan is often called "rolling wave planning," which means you keep coming back and checking for the ripple effect—in other words, when you identify a risk or make a change to the project, you are likely to affect something else and will need to update the scope, budget, or schedule along the way.

The planning processes, along with a brief description of these processes, are listed below. It is important to note that planning processes are spread across all ten Knowledge Areas; for more details and the distribution across the project management Process Groups, refer to Table 3.1.

Develop Project Management Plan (Integration Management Knowledge Area)

Developing the project management (PM) plan is the process of defining, preparing, and coordinating all plan components (or elements) and consolidating them into a single project management plan. The purpose of this process is the development of a comprehensive document that defines how the project will be managed throughout the project life cycle.

Ask the Expert

Q: Does the project manager really need a project management plan if the project has been done before?

A: Yes, the PM should have a documented and approved project plan to serve as a guide to how the project is to be managed, to help ensure the accountability and audit-readiness of the project, and to help ensure success. The plan can later be refined into an operations guide for repeat projects. In either case you need a documented plan to guide the work of the project.

For example, let's say you are working on the event-changeover project for a large convention center, and the requirements for the next event are to set up a rodeo. Because this project has been done before, you begin the process by setting up the usual corrals, gates for bull and bronco riders, and so on. Then you hear over lunch that this is a 4-H Special Olympics rodeo, and the main events are goat roping and mutton busting—there will be no bulls and broncos. You've just lost several hours, if not days, of setup time and money because you didn't fully understand the requirements.

For more information regarding this process, go to Chapter 4. The inputs and output of the Develop Project Management plan process are shown in Table 3.4.

Tip

One of the latest changes to the *PMBOK Guide Sixth Edition* is an increased focus on project management documents, which are also referred to as "components" of the project management plan. This increased focus means that all project documents created for the project, including the project management plan, should be considered as inputs to most all processes. To minimize confusion and repetition, these common inputs will be grouped under the common title of "Standard inputs" in the process charts throughout this chapter. When you see the input in the process tables as Standard inputs, one, several, or all of the common inputs shown below should be considered inputs to that particular process.

Inputs that are grouped as "Standard inputs" are listed below:

- Project management plan
- Project documents
- Enterprise environment factors
- Organizational process assets

Similarly, there are some common outputs that appear frequently in many of the process outputs, such as "Project management plan updates and Project document updates" and "Organizational process assets updates," and these will be grouped under the common title of "Standard outputs" in the process tables.

The results of this grouping will allow us to focus more on the unique inputs and outputs to each process and allow for increased focus to help with the learning process.

TABLE 3.4 Develop Project Management Plan Inputs and Outputs

Inputs	Outputs
Project charter	Project management plan
Outputs from other processes	
Enterprise environmental factors	
Organizational process assets	

Plan by Using Progressive Elaboration

If the project management plan is developed properly, it serves as a guide to how we manage the project. Typically, this process is done early in the project life cycle and may not be very detailed at first. The project management plan should be a working document that we build on as we learn more about the project. Because we learn more after each process is performed (PMI calls this *progressive elaboration*), it is important to be very aware of those things that may affect or change the project, product, or results.

Progressive elaboration is a concept or technique that uses repeated feedback loops to help guide us to improved work habits and results. Usually this approach brings about the need for additional analysis and often allows, or requires, us to modify the work activities, response, and so forth as more detailed information becomes available. When using progressive elaboration properly, it helps us modify and improve our work or approach to the project based on lessons learned from that new detailed information, providing a higher level of quality.

The output of the Develop the Project Management Plan process is the project management plan document itself, which becomes the input to many follow-on (downstream) processes.

The next process in the Planning Process Group is the Plan Scope Management process.

Plan Scope Management (Scope Management Knowledge Area)

This is the process of creating a scope statement or document that is used to identify all the work of the project and the product (service or result) of the project. This process should include information about how the scope of the project will be managed and controlled. Additional information about this process can be seen in Chapter 5. An example of the inputs and outputs of this process are shown in Table 3.5.

TABLE 3.5 Plan Scope Management Inputs and Outputs

Inputs	Outputs
Project charter	Scope management plan
Standard inputs	Requirements management plan

The needs (size, type, and complexity) of the project will determine which components of the project management plan and which project documents are needed to effectively manage the overall project. One example of a component needed for the project management plan is the project life cycle. The life cycle often will provide a clearer picture to the phases needed, constraints, assumptions, and so on.

Once the project management plan (at least the preliminary draft) is complete, it is time to collect the project and product requirements to allow us to manage the scope (breadth) of the project.

Collect Requirements (Scope Management Knowledge Area)

The Collect Requirements process is the act of determining how to collect the project and product requirements, which tools and techniques should be used, and how to effectively identify, validate, and track requirements. The inputs and output of this process are shown in Table 3.6.

TABLE 3.6 Collect Requirements Inputs and Outputs

Inputs	Outputs
Project charter and standard inputs	Requirements documentation
Business documents	Requirements traceability matrix

There are many ways to collect requirements, which are described in detail in Chapter 5 in Scope Management.

Other inputs for the collecting requirements process as components of the project management plan include, but are not limited to, the scope management plan, requirements management plan, and stakeholder engagement plan documents.

Define Scope (Scope Management Knowledge Area)

Define Scope is the process of developing a detailed description of the project and product of the project (what will be produced at the end). Defining the scope of the project helps everyone understand the purpose, the boundaries, and constraints to allow us to focus on the actual approved scope and avoid being distracted by things that are exclusions. The inputs and outputs of this process are shown in Table 3.7.

TABLE 3.7 Define Scope Inputs and Outputs

Inputs	Outputs
Project charter	Project scope statement
Standard inputs	Project documents updates

Project documents updates might include updates to the project scope statement and requirements documentations as an output to the Define Scope process.

Tip

When you see the word *updates* in regards to processes, this is likely an "output" of many of the project management processes. As a reminder, since "Project management plan updates" and/ or "Project documents updates" are outputs to most all processes, we will only show the unique outputs to minimize repetition.

Once the scope has been defined, it is time to identify the work (activities) needed to move the project forward. The next step in this process is to create the Work Breakdown Structure (WBS).

Create Work Breakdown Structure (Plan Scope Management Knowledge Area)

Create the Work Breakdown Structure is the process of subdividing the work of the project into more manageable components such as categories or phases.

The WBS should be created by the project team and allows the PM and the team to clearly identify the work of the project. The benefit of this process is that it creates a clear vision of the activities of the project. It provides a way to package the work for ease of assignment, duration, cost estimating, and progress reporting. For more details on the WBS and *Work Packages*, go to Chapter 5, "Scope Management."

The inputs and output of this process are shown in Table 3.8.

TABLE 3.8 Create WBS process Inputs and Outputs

Inputs	Outputs
Standard inputs	Scope baseline

Note

The scope baseline is the approved version of a collection of components such as the scope statement, WBS, and associated WBS dictionary. Most projects have a scope baseline, a schedule baseline, and a budget baseline. Remember a baseline is the approved version of any of the key project documents.

Plan Schedule Management (Schedule Management Knowledge Area)

Plan Schedule Management is the process of developing a project schedule and documenting the plan for how to manage the schedule, including the policies, procedures, and documentation for planning, managing, executing and controlling the project timeline (schedule). The plan should include which tools should be used and who should be involved in the schedule development process. The inputs and output of this process are shown in Table 3.9. For more details on this and all schedule related processes, go to Chapter 6.

TABLE 3.9 Plan Schedule Management Inputs and Outputs

Inputs	Outputs
Project charter	Schedule management plan
Standard inputs	

The output of the plan schedule management process is the schedule plan document itself, which should include any updates deemed necessary to the scope statement and scope baseline or other components of the project management plan.

Define Activities (Schedule Management Knowledge Area)

Define Activities is the process of identifying specific actions to be performed to produce the project deliverables identified during the define scope process. For more details, see Chapter 6. The inputs and outputs of this process are shown in Table 3.10.

TABLE 3.10 Define Activities Inputs and Outputs

Inputs	Outputs
Standard inputs	Activity list
	Activity attributes
	Milestone list
	Change requests
	Standard outputs

Another output includes updates to the project management plan documents such as the schedule baseline and cost baseline.

Sequence Activities (Schedule Management Knowledge Area)

Sequence Activities is the process of identifying and documenting the relationships between activities. These relationships help the PM and team determine when activities need to be performed relative to their predecessor and successor activities. The result is a logical sequence or timeline (flow) of when activities need to be completed. The inputs and output of this process are shown in Table 3.11.

TABLE 3.11 Sequence Activities Inputs and Outputs

Inputs	Outputs
Standard inputs	Schedule network changes
Project documents	Project documents updates

Outputs may include updates to project documents that pertain to project schedules, the activity list, the attributes, activity attributes, or the assumptions log and milestone list.

Estimate Activities Durations (Schedule Management Knowledge Area)

Now that the Schedule Activities process is complete, the next step is the process of estimating the amount of time or number of work periods needed to complete the different individual activities. This process typically begins with the WBS activities already identified, and with input and knowledge from the team or subject matter experts (SMEs), it provides an estimate of the duration of each WBS activity. The inputs and outputs of this process are shown in Table 3.12.

TABLE 3.12 Estimate Activities Duration Inputs and Outputs

Inputs	Outputs
Agreements	Duration estimates
Standard inputs	Basis of estimates
	Standard outputs

There are a number of project documents (inputs) that should also be considered for this process, such as activity list, assumptions, milestone list with target dates, project team member assignments, resource calendars, and risk register, just to name a few.

When the Estimate Activities Duration process is complete with updates to appropriate project documents—for example, the assumption log—and the duration estimates and the basis of estimates are documented (as outputs), the next step is to develop a project schedule, which is to lay the activities out in a logical order.

Develop Schedule (Schedule Management Knowledge Area)

Develop Schedule is the process of analyzing activities to see where they fit into the overall schedule, the sequence, the duration, and any constraints to allow the PM and team to create the schedule (often referred to as a network diagram). The project schedule provides guidance into how the project is executed, managed, monitored, and controlled, and when it should be closed. The inputs and outputs of this process are shown in Table 3.13.

TABLE 3.13 Develop Schedule Inputs and Outputs

Inputs	Outputs
Standard inputs	Schedule baseline
	Project schedule
	Schedule data
	Project calendars
	Change requests
	Standard outputs

There are a number of project documents (inputs) that should also be considered for this process: activity list, activity attributes, activity duration estimates, and project schedule network diagrams, just to name a few.

Plan Cost Management (Cost Management Knowledge Area)

Plan Cost Management is the process of establishing policies and procedures, including assumptions needed for planning, managing, executing, and controlling project cost.

For more details on this and other cost management processes, go to Chapter 7.

The inputs and outputs of this process are shown in Table 3.14.

TABLE 3.14 Plan Cost Management Process Inputs and Outputs

Inputs	Outputs
Project charter	Cost management plan
Standard inputs	

Project management plan components that should also be considered as inputs include the schedule management plan, the risk management plan, and other plan documents.

Estimate Costs (Cost Management Knowledge Area)

Estimating Cost is the process determining the amount of money it will take to complete the work, including all resources such as labor, materials, equipment, and contractor services. The inputs and output of this process are shown in Table 3.15.

TABLE 3.15 Estimate Cost Management Process Inputs and Outputs

Inputs	Outputs
Standard inputs	Cost estimates
	Basis of estimates
	Standard outputs

Once the estimate is complete, it is time to determine the budget needed to adequately fund (support) the cost of the project.

Determine Budget (Cost Management Knowledge Area)

During this process we take all the information collected, such as the cost estimate and other assumptions (e.g., type of estimate), to determine what the overall budget should be for the entire project. It is also important to look at the risk register for potential cost of risks in the event you need to include contingency funds in the budget (see Chapter 11, "Risk Management," for more details).

The inputs and outputs of this process are shown in Table 3.16.

TABLE 3.16 Determine Budget Process Inputs and Outputs

Inputs	Outputs
Agreements	Cost baseline
Standard inputs	Project funding requirements
	Project documents updates

Additional planning processes include the quality management plan, the resource plan, how we plan to communicate to the stakeholders, the risk management plan (and other risk planning processes), the procurement management plan, and the stakeholder engagement plan, just to name a few. These planning processes are listed below.

Plan Quality Management (Quality Management Knowledge Area)

This process involves reviewing quality policies and procedures to help develop a plan to manage quality on the project. It is important to ensure your plan includes what needs to be measured and tracked. This process should also provide guidance and direction on how quality will be managed and verified throughout the project life cycle. The inputs and outputs of this process are shown in Table 3.17.

TABLE 3.17 Plan Quality Management Process Inputs and Outputs

Inputs	Outputs
Project charter	Quality management plan
Standard inputs	Quality metrics
	Standard outputs

The next step is to plan resources and how they will be managed on your project.

Plan Resource Management (Resource Management Knowledge Area)

Planning resource management includes determining the experience, timing, and length of commitment and costs of the resources needed to meet the project objectives. Keep in mind that inputs come from many sources on real projects and that the *PMBOK Guide* looks at the more general view of project processes, meaning there is often relevant information, contracts, work directives, and so on that are not specifically included in the *PMBOK Guide* inputs. With this in mind, some other project documents that should be considered as inputs to this and other processes include the schedule, requirements documents, risk register, and the stakeholder register, to name a few. The *PMBOK Guide* inputs and outputs of this process are shown in Table 3.18.

TABLE 3.18 Plan Resource Management Process Inputs and Outputs

Inputs	Outputs
Project charter	Resource management plan
Standard inputs	Team charter

Estimate Activity Resources (Resource Management Knowledge Area)

This process is all about determining the resources needed for the project, including number of team members and contractors and quantities of materials, equipment, and supplies necessary to perform the work of the project. Inputs and outputs of this process are shown in Table 3.19.

TABLE 3.19 Estimate Activity Resources Process Inputs and Outputs

Inputs	Outputs
Standard inputs	Resource requirements
	Basis of estimates
	Resource breakdown structure

Plan Communications Management (Communications Management Knowledge Area)

Plan Communications Management process consists of developing the plan for how to effectively communicate with the various stakeholders, including the format, frequency, and type of communications. Stakeholder analysis (Chapter 13) will help you determine stakeholders' level of interest and level of authority to provide direction to help guide decisions about what to communicate, to whom, and how often. The inputs and outputs of this process are shown in Table 3.20.

TABLE 3.20 Plan Communications Management Process Inputs and Outputs

Inputs	Outputs
Project charter	Communications management plan
Standard inputs	Standard outputs

Plan Risk Management (Risk Management Knowledge Area)

Developing a plan for how to manage risk on your project is essential as risks happen. A risk is an event that has not yet happened; planning for how to manage risk is the best way to stay ahead of risks on a project. The last thing you want to happen is for a risk event to occur and not have a plan to address the risk if it becomes a reality. Inputs and outputs of this process are shown in Table 3.21.

TABLE 3.21 Plan Risk Management Process Inputs and Outputs

Inputs	Outputs
Project charter	Risk management plan
Standard inputs	

Identify Risks (Risk Management Knowledge Area)

The best way to identify risks is to first look at historical information from previous similar projects, then conduct brainstorming techniques as a team to identify all potential risks. For more details on identifying risks, go to Chapter 11. Inputs and outputs of this process are shown in Table 3.22.

TABLE 3.22 Identify Risks Process Inputs and Outputs

Inputs	Outputs
Procurement documentation	Risk register
Standard inputs	Risk report and Standard outputs

Perform Qualitative Risk Analysis (Risk Management Knowledge Area)

Qualitative risk analysis evaluates identified risks to determine the probability and impact of the risks should they occur. This process helps determine the level of priority of the risks identified based on the impact to the project. Inputs and outputs of this process are shown in Table 3.23.

TABLE 3.23 Perform Qualitative Risk Analysis Process Inputs and Outputs

Inputs	Outputs
Standard inputs	Project documents updates

The risk report document should be updated with any new information gained from the Qualitative Risk Analysis process, including a list of risks based on priority.

Perform Quantitative Risk Analysis (Risk Management Knowledge Area)

This process involves determining the potential probability and impact of each risk in quantitative (numerical) terms. There are various tools and techniques available, such as decision tree analysis and expected monetary value calculations that help put a dollar amount on risks. The inputs and outputs of this process are shown in Table 3.24.

TABLE 3.24 Identify Risks Process Inputs and Outputs

Inputs	Outputs
Standard inputs	Project documents updates

Plan Risk Responses (Risk Management Knowledge Area)

During the Plan Risk Responses process, it is time to apply expert judgment to those risks that are most likely to occur (high probability) and will have the highest impact on the project. The best way to do this is by developing a response strategy to those risks. In other words, what needs to be done, and whom are you going to call should the risk occur?

Because risks can impact the project in so many ways, some of the inputs that need to be considered are the project schedule, budget, resource breakdown structure, risk register, risk management plan, and risk report. Inputs and outputs of this process are shown in Table 3.25.

TABLE 3.25 Plan Risk Response Process Inputs and Outputs

Inputs	Outputs
Standard inputs	Change requests
	Standard outputs

Because risks can occur at any time and across all aspects of a project, it is important to manage change requests promptly and update the appropriate project documents. Some of the project management plan components that may require updates are the scope plan, schedule management plan, cost management plan, quality plan, resource plan, and procurement plan, just to name a few.

Some risks that often impact a project are in the area of contracts and procurements, which brings us to the next process.

Plan Procurement Management (Procurement Management Knowledge Area)

Plan Procurement Management is the process of documenting the approach to procurements, identifying potential sellers (vendors or suppliers), and establishing a plan on how to manage procurements. Inputs and outputs of this process are shown in Table 3.26.

TABLE 3.26 Plan Procurement Management Process Inputs and Outputs

Inputs	Outputs
Project charter	Procurement management plan
Business documents	Procurement strategy
Standard inputs	Bid documents
	Procurement statement of work (SOW)
	Source selection criteria
	Make or buy decisions
	Independent cost estimates
	Change requests
	Standard outputs

For more details on procurement management, see Chapter 12.

Plan Stakeholder Engagement (Stakeholder Management Knowledge Area)

This is the process of creating a plan for how to identify and effectively engage project stakeholders based on their needs and expectations for the project. Inputs and outputs of this process are shown in Table 3.27.

TABLE 3.27 Plan Stakeholder Engagement Process Inputs and Outputs

Inputs	Outputs
Standard inputs	Stakeholder engagement plan

As you can see from the high number of planning processes, PMI and the project management industry realizes the importance of planning projects. Once the planning is complete, it is time to start figuring out how to effectively execute the work of the project.

Executing Process Group (Work the Plan)

The Executing Process Group is where the real work begins, and as you would expect, the largest portion of the project budget is usually spent during the executing processes. This

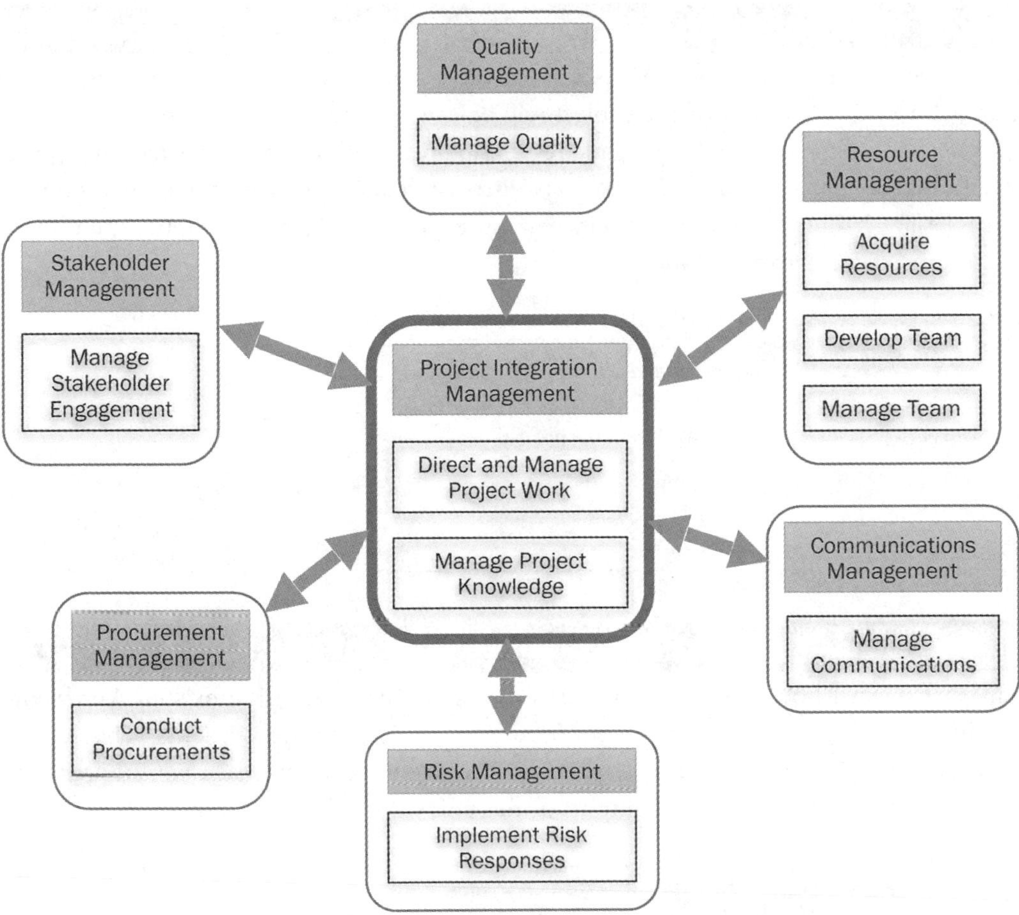

FIGURE 3.4 Executing Process Group

is where the majority of the team is engaged in performing the work of the project. This group consists of ten processes that are performed to complete the work defined in the project management plan (see the list below and refer to Table 3.1 for mapping to the Process Groups).

The goal of the PM in the Executing Process Group is to coordinate the people and other resources, as well as integrate and perform the activities of the project to meet the requirements by satisfying the approved specifications. For the processes associated with the Executing Process Group, see Figure 3.4.

The following processes fall under the Executing Process Group:

Direct and Manage Project Work (Integration Management Knowledge Area)

During the Direct and Manage the Work of the Project process, you need to establish a clear approach to how the work of the project will be executed (performed). This is where the work begins and the direction, roles, and responsibilities need to be crystal clear. Any confusion during this process can cause delays and increase cost to the project. For details on this process, see Chapter 4, Integration Management Knowledge Area. The inputs and outputs of this process are shown in Table 3.28.

TABLE 3.28 Direct and Manage Project Work Process Inputs and Outputs

Inputs	Outputs
Approved change requests	Deliverables
Standard project inputs	Work performance data
	Issue log
	Change requests
	Standard outputs

Manage Project Knowledge (Integration Management Knowledge Area)

Manage Project Knowledge is the newest process and involves using existing knowledge to achieve project objectives and to contribute to consistent improvements. This process includes identifying subject matter experts on and off the team who can contribute to the success of the project. Inputs and outputs of this process are shown in Table 3.29.

TABLE 3.29 Manage Project Knowledge Process Inputs and Outputs

Inputs	Outputs
Deliverables	Standard outputs
Standard inputs	

Other examples of project documents that may be considered as inputs to this process include project team assignments, the resource breakdown structure, the contractor source selection, and the stakeholder register.

Keep in mind that true knowledge comes from the project manager and the project stakeholders' experience, decision-making skills, capabilities, and willingness to take pride, ownership, and accountability in the project. The true measure of success on any project is when the team members respect the project manager, perform the work of the current project per the guidelines to meet the approved schedule and budget, and are willing to work on the next project with the same PM.

Manage Quality (Quality Management Knowledge Area)

The Manage Quality process involves understanding the quality management plan and translating that plan into executable actions. These actions include making sure quality measurements are clear and manageable and that quality is being tracked and communicated accurately and in a timely manner. The inputs and outputs of this process are shown in Table 3.30.

TABLE 3.30 Manage Quality Process Inputs and Outputs

Inputs	Outputs
Standard inputs	Quality reports
	Test and evaluations documents
	Change requests
	Standard outputs

Remember, the PM is responsible for having a quality plan and managing it effectively; however, quality is a team sport and should be every team member's goal.

Acquire Resources (Resource Management Knowledge Area)

Acquire Resources is the process of obtaining team members, facilities, equipment, materials, supplies, and other resources necessary to complete the work of the project. For more information about this process, go to Chapter 9. The inputs and outputs of this process are shown in Table 3.31.

TABLE 3.31 Acquire Resources Process Inputs and Outputs

Inputs	Outputs
Standard inputs	Physical resource assignments
	Project team assignments
	Change requests
	Standard outputs

Develop Team (Resource Management Knowledge Area)

The Develop Team process is focused on improving team member capabilities, competencies, and interactions to ensure a high-performing team. This includes training, mentoring, and other means of developing team members and team performance. The inputs and outputs of this process are shown in Table 3.32.

TABLE 3.32 Develop Team Process Inputs and Outputs

Inputs	Outputs
Standard inputs	Team performance assessments
	Change requests
	Standard outputs

Manage Team (Resource Management Knowledge Area)

Manage Team is the process of keeping track of team member and team performance, managing conflict, and resolving issues. Remember, the team is your number-1 asset; it is important to manage the team effectively. Providing feedback in a timely manner, gaining the trust and confidence of team members, and ensuring they have the tools and training necessary to get the job done properly is the focus of this process. The inputs and outputs of this process are shown in Table 3.33.

TABLE 3.33 Manage Team Process Inputs and Outputs

Inputs	Outputs
Work performance reports	Change requests
Team performance assessments	Standard outputs
Standard inputs	

Manage Communications (Communications Management Knowledge Area)

Manage Communications is the process of conducting project communication activities according to the communications management plan. This includes proper and timely collection, distribution, and storage of project communications. For more details on this process, see Chapter 10. Inputs and outputs of this process are shown in Table 3.34.

TABLE 3.34 Manage Communications Process Inputs and Outputs

Inputs	Outputs
Standard inputs	Project communications
	Standard outputs

Implement Risk Responses (Risk Management Knowledge Area)

The Implement Risk Responses process involves ensuring you have a response strategy to activate when risks occur. It is best to assign owners who are responsible to implement the agreed-upon response as appropriate. For more information on this and other risk management processes, see Chapter 11. Inputs and outputs of this process are shown in Table 3.35.

TABLE 3.35 Implement Risk Responses Process Inputs and Outputs

Inputs	Outputs
Standard inputs	Change requests
	Project document updates

Conduct Procurements (Procurement Management Knowledge Area)

This is the process of initiating seller selection activities such as holding a bidder's conference, obtaining responses from bidders, and selecting sellers from outside the project team. The inputs and outputs of this process are shown in Table 3.36.

TABLE 3.36 Conduct Procurements Process Inputs and Outputs

Inputs	Outputs
Procurement documents	Selected sellers
Seller proposals	Agreements
Standard inputs	Change requests
	Standard outputs

Manage Stakeholder Engagement (Stakeholder Management Knowledge Area)

This process includes communicating and working with project stakeholders to meet their needs and expectations. The goal is to establish a good working relationship with all key stakeholders. Inputs and outputs of this process are shown in Table 3.37.

TABLE 3.37 Manage Stakeholder Engagements Process Inputs and Outputs

Inputs	Outputs
Standard inputs	Change requests
	Standard outputs

Clearly the Executing Process Group is where the work is performed (work the plan), and the processes in this group are vitally important to the success of the project. There are many risks that surface during this Process Group, and that is why it is important to keep a close eye on the work being performed and the progress being accomplished. The way you do this is by performing the Monitoring and Controlling processes.

Monitoring and Controlling Process Group

The Monitoring and Controlling Process Group is the "eye in the sky," so to speak, making sure that the project is following the management plan for reviewing and tracking the overall performance and attainment of the deliverables per the approved scope and budget.

This step is where many projects fail—the PM is either too distracted with the daily work or is in too much of a hurry to monitor the overall progress of the project effectively. In many cases the PM simply does not have enough resources (people) to measure progress in a timely manner or is just not familiar with the tools and techniques to monitor and control the project effectively. In any event, things slip when the project manager's eyes are taken off of this Process Group. Monitoring and controlling the project must start early in the project life cycle and be performed diligently throughout the life of the project.

There are currently twelve processes in the *PMBOK Sixth Edition* Monitoring and Controlling Process Group. Some of the key processes include determining how you and the team will track progress, deciding what tools and techniques you will use to measure the progress, and choosing how you will report that progress (using which types of reports, and how frequently) to the key stakeholders of the project.

The Monitoring and Controlling Process Group consists of processes needed to track performance and review and manage progress, as well as reporting the status of the project. When focusing on this Process Group, think about measurements and ask yourself questions such as "Are we on schedule, on budget, etc.? If the project is not on track, why not, and what needs to be done to get it back on schedule, on budget, etc.?" For the processes associated with the Monitoring and Controlling Process Group, see Figure 3.5.

The following list of processes fall under the Monitoring and Controlling Process Group:

Monitor and Control Project Work (Integration Management Knowledge Area)

Monitor and Control Project Work is the process of tracking, reviewing, and reporting the project's progress. The intention of this process is to allow the PM to accurately report project status to key stakeholders. Inputs and outputs of this process are shown in Table 3.38.

TABLE 3.38 Monitor and Control Project Work Process Inputs and Outputs

Inputs	Outputs
Work performance information	Work performance reports
Agreements	Change requests
Standard inputs	Standard outputs

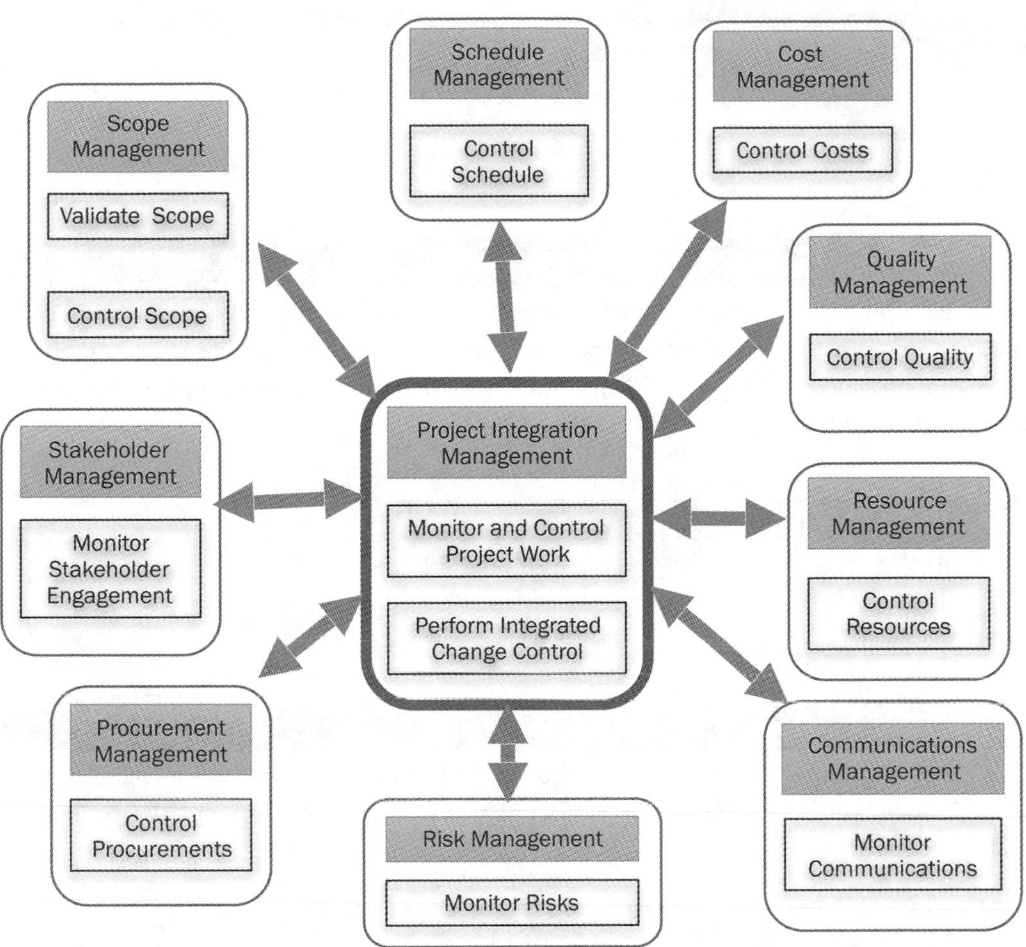

FIGURE 3.5 Monitoring and Controlling Process Group

Perform Integrated Change Control (Integration Management Knowledge Area)

The Perform Integrated Change Control process involves reviewing all change requests as well as approving and managing changes to the project deliverables, organizational process assets, scope, project documents, and the project management plan. The change process (like the risk management process) should be conducted early and often throughout the project life cycle.

For details on this and other Integration Management processes, go to Chapter 4.

Inputs and outputs of this process are shown in Table 3.39.

TABLE 3.39 Perform Integrated Change Control Process Inputs and Outputs

Inputs	Outputs
Work performance reports	Approved change requests
Change requests	Standard outputs
Standard inputs	

Validate Scope (Scope Management Knowledge Area)

Validate Scope is the process of obtaining formal acceptance of the completed project deliverables. This process should be carried out throughout the project life cycle. Additional details are provided in Chapter 5 ("Scope Management"). Inputs and outputs of this process are shown in Table 3.40.

TABLE 3.40 Validate Scope Process Inputs and Outputs

Inputs	Outputs
Verified deliverables	Approved deliverables
Work performance data	Work performance information
Standard inputs	Change requests

Control Scope (Scope Management Knowledge Area)

This process monitors the status of the project, and this includes managing changes to the scope baseline and ensuring that baseline integrity is upheld throughout the project life cycle. The inputs and outputs of this process are shown in Table 3.41.

TABLE 3.41 Control Scope Process Inputs and Outputs

Inputs	Outputs
Work performance data	Work performance information
Standard inputs	Change requests
	Standard outputs

Control Schedule (Schedule Management Knowledge Area)

The process of monitoring and controlling the status of the project schedule ensures that deliverables and progress are being met. Inputs and outputs of this process are shown in Table 3.42. Other inputs that might be considered for this process are project calendars, project schedule, and schedule data. Project management plan document updates might include the schedule baseline and cost baseline.

TABLE 3.42 Control Schedule Process Inputs and Outputs

Inputs	Outputs
Standard inputs	Work performance information
	Schedule forecasts
	Change requests
	Standard outputs

Control Costs (Cost Management Knowledge Area)

This is the process of monitoring the cost of the project and managing changes to help minimize and control costs. Inputs and outputs of this process are shown in Table 3.43.

TABLE 3.43 Control Cost Process Inputs and Outputs

Inputs	Outputs
Standard inputs	Work performance information
	Cost forecasts
	Change requests
	Standard outputs

Control Quality (Quality Management Knowledge Area)

This process consists of monitoring and recording results of executing the quality management activities to assess performance and ensure outputs meet customer expectations. Additional details are provided in Chapter 8. The inputs and outputs of this process are shown in Table 3.44.

TABLE 3.44 Control Quality Process Inputs and Outputs

Inputs	Outputs
Approved change requests	Quality control measurements
Deliverables	Verified deliverables
Work performance data	Work performance information
Standard inputs	Change requests and Standard outputs

Control Resources (Resource Management Knowledge Area)

Control Resources is the process of ensuring the physical resources (people, equipment, etc.) are assigned and properly allocated to the project. A resource calendar is a great tool to help ensure resources are available when needed to perform the work of the project. Inputs and outputs of this process are shown in Table 3.45.

TABLE 3.45 Control Resources Process Inputs and Outputs

Inputs	Outputs
Work performance data	Work performance information
Resource allocation	Resource allocations updates
Agreements	Change requests
Standard inputs	Standard outputs

Monitor Communications (Communications Knowledge Area)

The Monitor Communications process helps ensure the information needed by the stakeholders is provided in an accurate and timely manner. This process provides the guidelines for ensuring effective and efficient flow of information to the right people at the right time. The inputs and outputs of this process are shown in Table 3.46.

TABLE 3.46 Monitor Communications Process Inputs and Outputs

Inputs	Outputs
Work performance data	Work performance information
Standard inputs	Change requests
	Standard outputs

Monitor Risks (Risk Management Knowledge Area)

The Monitor Risks process tracks identified risks and includes risk analysis of new risks to ensure there are as few surprises as possible. As with all monitoring and controlling processes, this process should be conducted early and throughout the project life cycle. Inputs and outputs of this process are shown in Table 3.47.

TABLE 3.47 Monitor Risks Process Inputs and Outputs

Inputs	Outputs
Standard inputs	Work performance information
	Change requests
	Standard outputs

Control Procurements (Procurement Management Knowledge Area)

Control Procurements is the process of establishing and maintaining procurement relationships. This process also involves monitoring contract performance and change control to ensure proper procurement deliverables are being met. Inputs and outputs of this process are shown in Table 3.48.

TABLE 3.48 Control Procurements Process Inputs and Outputs

Inputs	Outputs
Agreements	Closed procurements
Selected sellers	Work performance information
Procurement documentation	Procurement documentation updates
Approved change requests	Change requests
Quality reports	Standard outputs
Standard inputs	

Monitor Stakeholder Engagement (Stakeholder Management Knowledge Area)

Monitor Stakeholder Engagement is the process of building and maintaining relationships with stakeholders and making sure their needs and expectations are clear and being met. It also involves engaging stakeholders to work on ways to enhance the relationship throughout the project life cycle. The inputs and outputs of this process are shown in Table 3.49.

TABLE 3.49 Monitor Stakeholder Engagements Process Inputs and Outputs

Inputs	Outputs
Work performance data	Work performance information
Standard inputs	Change requests
	Standard outputs

Closing Process Group

Last but not least is the Closing Process Group. In the sixth edition of *PMBOK Guide*, PMI has combined closing procurements into closing the project or phase process to make up a single process in the Closing Process Group; see Figure 3.6.

The only process that falls under the Closing Process Group is the Close Project or Phase process, which is the last of the Integration Management Knowledge Area processes.

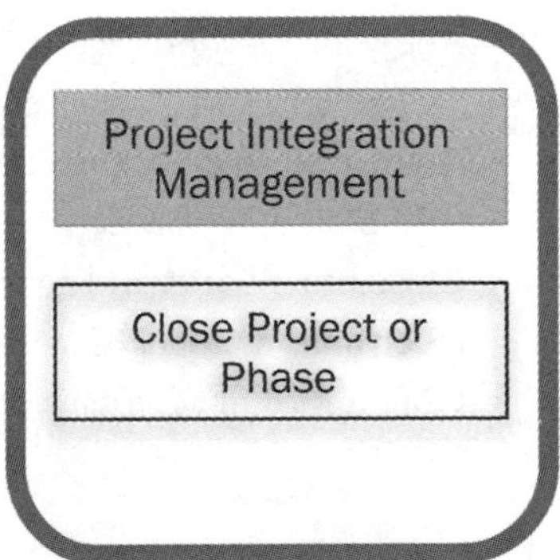

FIGURE 3.6 Closing Process Group

Close Project or Phase (Integration Management Knowledge Area)

Close Project or Phase is the process of bringing the project to a successful end. It involves completing all activities and deliverables, making sure the project or phase meets approved scope, schedule, and cost. The inputs and outputs of this process are shown in Table 3.50.

TABLE 3.50 Close Project or Phase Process Inputs and Outputs

Inputs	Outputs
Project charter	Final product, service, or result
Quality reports	Organizational process assets updates
Standard inputs	
Accepted deliverables	
Business documents	
Agreements	
Procurement documents	

The Closing Process Group is all about bringing the project (or phase) to an orderly and hopefully successful completion. The Closing Process Group now includes closing procurements to ensure all contract deliverables have been met and formally accepted.

The steps involved with the Closing Process Group are essential for the formal completion of the project or phase or to meet contractual obligations. Once the process is completed, a number of signoffs (*formal acceptance*) should occur. For example:

- Conduct post-project or phase-end review.
- Document open issues relating to changes or the tailoring of the project or its processes (sometimes referred to as "After Action Report").
- Document lessons learned from the team and customer. It is a good idea to complete this step throughout the project and not just at the end.
- Apply all appropriate updates to organizational process assets.
- Obtain formal acceptance of all project and product deliverables.
- Archive all relevant project documents in the Project Management Information System (PMIS) as appropriate.
- Close out all outstanding procurements (purchase orders, accounts payable, accounts receivable, supplier agreements, equipment rentals or leases, software licenses, and so on).
- Obtain formal acceptance from the customer and other key sponsors.

Ask the Expert

Q: What happens when the project manager receives an invoice from a subcontractor (supplier) for services rendered, but three months after the project is officially closed?

A: If the invoice is for legitimate services provided for approved work from an approved supplier, then the invoice must be paid.

The key questions that need to be reviewed and addressed are: How was this invoice overlooked? What steps should have been taken to ensure that it was accounted for as part of the Closing Process Group? The main thing is to do what you can to ensure this doesn't happen on other projects in the future.

Tip

Missing or late invoices are far too common. The best approach is to set up a project closeout checklist using the project management plan documents, information system, and all the startup-phase deliverables to help ensure a clean closeout of the project. Even though billing may be the responsibility of the finance department, the PM is still responsible for closure of all aspects of the project.

Introduction to PMI Knowledge Areas

Knowledge areas are fields of specialization. The ten globally recognized *PMI Knowledge Areas* are as follows:

1. Integration Management
2. Scope Management
3. Schedule Management
4. Cost Management
5. Quality Management
6. Resource Management
7. Communications Management
8. Risk Management
9. Procurement Management
10. Stakeholder Management

This section provides only a brief introduction to Knowledge Areas; more details are provided in Chapters 4 through 13.

Knowledge areas apply to all projects or phases to some degree and can, in some cases, be used to organize project startup. That is, each of the ten Knowledge Areas contain project management processes that cross over some or all of the five Process Groups. Keep in mind, the *PMBOK* Knowledge Areas should be used as a guide for managing projects using globally recognized processes, terms, and methods. And at the end of the day, the PM is responsible for the application of knowledge, skills, tools, and techniques for project activities to meet project requirements.

Tip

Focusing on the ten Knowledge Areas and the processes in each is essential if you are planning to take PMI's CAPM exam. The CAPM exam questions are grouped by Knowledge Area as opposed to grouped by Process Group like in the PMP exam. The best way to study for the CAPM exam is by using the "*Swim lane*" (left to right) approach to learn the processes in each of the Knowledge Areas. It will also be helpful if you take as many sample questions as possible (available from several sources) that tie to the sixth edition of *PMBOK*.

The ten Knowledge Areas, according to PMI, with a brief introduction and a list of associated processes are shown below:

Project Integration Management

The Project Integration Management Knowledge Area includes the processes and activities needed to identify, define, combine, unify, and coordinate the various processes and project management activities within the project management Process Groups. Project integration is the capstone (it brings the project together), it is crucial to project completion, and it provides the key components of project management. Another key ingredient to success is managing stakeholder expectations and meeting the approved requirements and objectives of the project in accordance with the approved charter.

Here's a list of the Project Integration Management processes and associated Process Groups in parentheses. Note: the numbers at the beginning map to the chapters and sections in the *PMBOK (and in this book)*. For example, 4.1 refers to Chapter 4 and the .1 indicates the first process for that Knowledge Area.

- **4.1.** Develop Project Charter (Initiating Process Group).
- **4.2.** Develop Project Management Plan (Planning Process Group).
- **4.3.** Direct and Manage Project Work (Executing Process Group).
- **4.4.** Manage Project Knowledge (Executing Process Group).
- **4.5.** Monitor and Control Project Work (Monitoring and Controlling Process Group).
- **4.6.** Perform Integrated Change Control (Monitoring and Controlling Process Group).
- **4.7.** Close Project or Phase (Closing Process Group).

Project Scope Management

The Project Scope Management Knowledge Area includes the processes required to ensure that all the work required (and only the work required) to complete the project successfully is identified. Managing project scope is primarily concerned with defining and controlling what is and is not included in the project. Here's a list of the Project Scope Management processes:

- **5.1.** Plan Scope Management (Planning Process Group).
- **5.2.** Collect Requirements (Planning Process Group).
- **5.3.** Define Scope (Planning Process Group).
- **5.4.** Create WBS (Planning Process Group).
- **5.5.** Validate Scope (Monitoring and Controlling Process Group).
- **5.6.** Control Scope (Monitoring and Controlling Process Group).

Project Schedule Management

The Project Schedule Management Knowledge Area includes the processes required to manage timely completion of the project. Here's a list of the Schedule Management processes:

- **6.1.** Plan Schedule Management (Planning Process Group).
- **6.2.** Define Activities (Planning Process Group).
- **6.3.** Sequence Activities (Planning Process Group).
- **6.4.** Estimate Activity Durations (Planning Process Group).
- **6.5.** Develop Schedule (Planning Process Group).
- **6.6.** Control Schedule (Monitoring and Controlling Process Group).

Project Cost Management

The Project Cost Management Knowledge Area includes the processes involved in estimating, budgeting, and controlling costs so the project can be completed within the approved budget.

Here's a list of the Project Cost Management processes:

- **7.1.** Plan Cost Management (Planning Process Group).
- **7.2.** Estimate Costs (Planning Process Group).
- **7.3.** Determine Budget (Planning Process Group).
- **7.4.** Control Costs (Monitoring and Controlling Process Group).

Project Quality Management

The Project Quality Management Knowledge Area includes the processes and activities of the performing organization that determines quality policies, objectives, and responsibilities so that the project will satisfy the needs for which it was undertaken. Here is a list of the Project Quality Management processes:

- **8.1.** Plan Quality Management (Planning Process Group).
- **8.2.** Manage Quality (Executing Process Group).
- **8.3.** Control Quality (Monitoring and Controlling Process Group).

Project Resource Management

The Project Resource Management Knowledge Area includes the processes that organize, manage, and lead the project team. The project team is composed of people with assigned roles and responsibilities for completing the project. Project Resource Management processes:

- **9.1.** Plan Resource Management (Planning Process Group).
- **9.2.** Estimate Activity Resources (Planning Process Group).
- **9.3.** Acquire Resources (Executing Process Group).
- **9.4.** Develop Team (Executing Process Group).
- **9.5.** Manage Team (Executing Process Group).
- **9.6.** Control Resources (Monitoring and Controlling Process Group).

Project Communications Management

The Project Communications Management Knowledge Area includes the processes required to ensure the timely and appropriate generation, collection, distribution, storage, retrieval, and ultimate disposition of project information. It is important to note that PMs spend the majority of their time communicating. Project Communications Management processes:

- **10.1.** Plan Communications Management (Planning Process Group).
- **10.2.** Manage Communications (Executing Process Group).
- **10.3.** Monitor Communications (Monitoring and Controlling Process Group).

Communications management processes are interrelated and overlap with processes in the other Knowledge Areas. Good clear communications are essential to the overall success of the project.

Project Risk Management

The Project Risk Management Knowledge Area includes the processes of conducting risk management planning, identification, analysis, response planning, monitoring, and control on a project. The objectives of risk management seek to increase the probability and impact of positive events and decrease the probability and impact of negative events in the project.

The Project Risk Management processes are as follows:

- **11.1.** Plan Risk Management (Planning Process Group).
- **11.2.** Identify Risks (Planning Process Group).
- **11.3.** Perform Qualitative Risk Analysis (Planning Process Group).
- **11.4.** Perform Quantitative Risk Analysis (Planning Process Group).
- **11.5.** Plan Risk Responses (Planning Process Group).
- **11.6.** Implement Risk Responses (Executing Process Group).
- **11.7.** Monitor Risks (Monitoring and Controlling Process Group).

Project Procurement Management

The Project Procurement Management Knowledge Area includes the contract management and change control processes required to develop and administer contracts and purchase orders issued by the authorized project team members. It also includes administering contracts issued by an outside organization (the buyer), acquiring the project from the performing organization (the seller), and administering contractual obligations placed on the project team by the contract. Here's a list of the Project Procurement Management processes:

- **12.1.** Plan Procurement Management (Planning Process Group).
- **12.2.** Conduct Procurements (Executing Process Group).
- **12.3.** Control Procurements (Monitoring and Controlling Process Group).

Project Stakeholder Management

The Project Stakeholder Management Knowledge Area includes the stakeholder management processes needed to identify stakeholders, plan for stakeholder management, manage stakeholders, and control stakeholder engagement. The list of the Project Stakeholder Management processes is show below:

- **13.1.** Identify Stakeholders (Initiating Process Group).
- **13.2.** Plan Stakeholder Engagement (Planning Process Group).
- **13.3.** Manage Stakeholder Engagement (Executing Process Group).
- **13.4.** Monitor Stakeholder Engagement (Monitoring and Controlling Process Group).

Importance of Global Standards

Global standards are crucial to the project management profession because they ensure that a basic project management framework is applied consistently worldwide. The American National Standards Institute (ANSI) has recognized PMI as a standards-development organization.

With the increased focus on project management across the globe, it has become more and more important to operate in a common, consistent manner wherever possible. PMI provides generally recognized "good practices" for processes, applications, skills, tools, and techniques to enhance the chances of success over a wide range of projects. This, however, does not mean the knowledge should always be applied uniformly across all projects.

PMI offers a standard vocabulary for discussing, writing, and applying project management concepts. Having a globally recognized standard in terms, methods, and processes is an essential element of a professional discipline such as project management.

Several recommended standards can be found in the *PMBOK* and in some of the inputs of many of the processes. Earlier, we discussed enterprise environmental factors and how they must be considered as inputs to most processes (especially the planning processes). Another input that needs to be considered as key to most processes is organizational process assets. This is where standard processes reside. The organization's processes and procedures for conducting work include the following standards:

- Organizational standard processes such as company policies (e.g., safety and health, ethics, project management policy, standard project audits, and quality policies)
- Standard guidelines, work instructions, proposal evaluation criteria, and performance-measurement criteria
- Standard templates (risk breakdown structure, work breakdown structure, project schedule network diagrams, and contract templates)
- Communication requirements and guidelines
- Change control procedures and approvers (including how project documents will be modified)
- Risk control procedures (including risk categories, probability definition, and impact analysis)

PMI Code of Ethics and Professional Conduct

PMI formed the Ethics, Standards, and Accreditation Group in 1981. This group has evolved through the years. However, the topic of ethics, standards, and accreditation is so dynamic and has gone through so many changes that it is published as a separate document rather than as part of the *PMBOK*.

Tip

> You should not be fooled by the minimal appearance of the Project Management Institute Code of Ethics and Professional Conduct in the *PMBOK*, as there are several questions in the PMP exam around the topic of ethics. I like to think of these questions (which cross over multiple Process Groups and Knowledge Areas) as similar to those in the game of *Scruples* (by Milton Bradley), in which a situation is described and you are asked what you would do in the scenario mentioned. The best answer is always to follow the "do good and avoid evil" mantra, and you should do fine on these types of questions on the PMP exam.

PMI's Code of Ethics and Professional Conduct is specific about the basic obligation of responsibility, respect, fairness, and honesty. It requires PM practitioners to demonstrate a commitment to ethical and professional conduct, including complying with laws, regulations, and organizational and professional policies. Acceptance of the code is required for PMP certification by PMI. "Ethics is about making the best possible decisions concerning people, resources and the environment. Ethics diminish risk, advance positive results, increase trust, determine long term success and build reputations. Leadership is absolutely dependent on ethical choices."[5]

With all the changes to this section and only a small amount of coverage in the *PMBOK*, it is best to view the latest details on the PMI.org website. The document can be downloaded from https://www.pmi.org/about/ethics/code.

To better understand the reason for the code of ethics and its purpose, let's look at PMI's Vision and Applicability statement.

Vision and Applicability Statement

As practitioners of project management, we are committed to doing what is right and honorable. We set high standards for ourselves, and we aspire to meet these standards in all aspects of our lives: at work, at home, and in service to our profession.

The PMI Code of Ethics and Professional Conduct describes the expectations we have of ourselves and our fellow practitioners in the global project management community. It articulates the ideals to which we aspire as well as the behaviors that are mandatory in our professional and volunteer roles.

The purpose of this code is to instill confidence in the project management profession and to help an individual become a better practitioner. We do this by establishing a profession-wide understanding of appropriate behavior. We believe that the credibility and reputation of the project management profession are shaped by the collective conduct of individual practitioners.[6]

Persons to Whom the Code Applies

The Code of Ethics and Professional Conduct applies to all PMI members and individuals who are not members of PMI but who meet one or more of the following criteria:

- Nonmembers who hold a PMI certification
- Nonmembers who apply to commence a PMI certification process
- Nonmembers who serve PMI in a volunteer capacity

Structure of the Code

The Code of Ethics and Professional Conduct is divided into sections that contain standards of conduct aligned with the four values of responsibility, respect, fairness, and honesty, which are identified as most important to the project management community.

Each section of the Code of Ethics and Professional Conduct includes both aspirational standards and mandatory standards.

ASPIRATIONAL STANDARDS

The aspirational standards describe the conduct we strive to uphold as project management practitioners. Although adherence to the aspirational standards is not easily measured, conducting ourselves in accordance with these standards is an expectation that we have of ourselves as professionals, and it should not be viewed as optional.

Note

The conduct covered under the aspirational standards and the conduct covered under the mandatory standards are not mutually exclusive; that is, one specific act or omission could violate both aspirational and mandatory standards. Also, both aspirational and mandatory codes are further divided into values of responsibility, respect, fairness, and honesty.

Here are examples of "respect" under the aspirational standards:

- As practitioners in the global project management community, we inform ourselves about the norms and customs of others and avoid engaging in behaviors they might consider disrespectful.
- We listen to others' points of view, seeking to understand them, and we approach directly those persons with whom we have a conflict or disagreement.

MANDATORY STANDARDS/REQUIREMENTS

The mandatory standards establish firm requirements and in some cases limit or prohibit practitioner behavior. Practitioners who do not conduct themselves in accordance with these standards will be subject to disciplinary procedures before PMI's Ethics Review Committee.

As practitioners in the global project management community, we require the following of ourselves and our fellow practitioners:

- Regulations and Legal Requirements
  - We inform ourselves about, and uphold, the policies, rules, regulations, and laws that govern our work, professional, and volunteer activities.
  - We report unethical or illegal conduct to appropriate management and, if necessary, to those affected by the conduct.
- Mandatory Standards
  - We negotiate in good faith.
  - We do not exercise the power of our expertise or position to influence the decisions or actions of others in order to benefit personally at their expense.
  - We respect the property rights of others.

Ask the Expert

Q: I have a trusting relationship with my team and project sponsor and don't feel I should enforce rigid change control on my project. Why should I take extra time for "bookkeeping" when it is not needed?

A: Clearly, you have to manage the sponsor and team in a trusting and effective manner; however, there are times when a simple "do me a favor" request from the sponsor, a team member, or other stakeholder is a request to look the other way or to perform "extras" on the project without proper change management. These "favors" often pose a conflict of interest and should not be performed because there will likely be negative consequences. As a project management professional, you should be prepared for these requests and respond in a straightforward, professional manner.

The term in the world of project management for providing extras (giving away something that is not in the scope of the project) is *gold plating*. Gold plating is often viewed as a bad thing, though many people feel it is a good thing, and they want to provide the extras to show commitment to the project. However, there is a big difference between gold plating and providing added value on your project. If you understand the difference, you can always provide high-quality, value-added management to the project without giving away things that are not in the scope agreement.

Value-added service can come in the way of streamlining a process (making it more effective or efficient) and offering suggestions to the stakeholders to save time or money. Showing integrity and operating in an honest manner is what the PMI Code of Ethics and Professional Conduct is all about.

What to Expect on the PMP Exam for Code of Ethic Questions

To give you an idea of what to expect on the PMP exam crossover questions when it comes to the PMI Code of Ethics and Professional Conduct section, here are a couple sample questions:

1. A project you are managing is at the end of the Closing phase. During the lessons learned meeting, the customer informs you of a number of activities and deliverables that have not been completed. What do you do first?
   A. Tell the customer you will check on the incomplete deliverables and get back to them within a few days, even though you know these deliverables are not in the project scope.
   B. Review the project deliverables in question during the meeting to understand the status and the customer's expectations to ensure you reach formal acceptance for all approved deliverables.
   C. Ask for the customer's schedule and compare it to your own schedule.
   D. Tell the project team to work overtime to complete the deliverables.

Answer: B. Openly reviewing and discussing the project activities and deliverables with all the stakeholders (including the customer) shows respect and helps ensure you are clear on the expectations, the status, and what it will take to obtain formal acceptance from the customer prior to closing the project.

Note

PMI is big on (in favor of) "formal acceptance." Getting signoff in writing or even in the form of an email helps you stay audit ready on your project.

2. You have just been assigned as the project manager for a new global project and have been told by one of the four sponsors to work only with him (Bob) because the other three sponsors live in different countries with different time zones. Bob asks you to conduct a project kickoff meeting (face-to-face for local team members and via conference call for the international team and sponsors) and tells you not to invite the other sponsors because "they are too busy." What should you do?
   A. Work only with Bob because this will make communications much easier.
   B. Insist on inviting the other sponsors.
   C. Notify the other sponsors that Bob doesn't want them invited to the meeting.
   D. Talk to Bob to better understand the reasons for not inviting the other sponsors and strongly encourage him (politely insist) to allow you to include the other sponsors.

Answer: D. It is important to ensure that all sponsors of the projects have the opportunity to participate in the kickoff meeting so they can provide their input, expectations, and support. The sponsors are making an investment in their share of the project and have specific expectations for the end results. Thus, they need to be included in the kickoff meeting.

What Else is Missing from the PMBOK?

Remember, the *PMBOK* is only a "guide." It cannot possibly cover all the aspects and variations documented in the many textbooks, journals, and articles across the globe. Therefore, don't expect to use only the *PMBOK* when preparing for a PMI exam. To pass the PMP exam, for example, you will need a good cross-section of knowledge, experience, and problem-solving capability, and to be able to apply all your knowledge and skills to real-world situations. If this tip makes you nervous and you are thinking you might not have enough PM experience to pass the PMP exam, you should consider taking the CAPM exam, which is based mostly on the *PMBOK Guide* (for more details on exam eligibility go to Chapter 14 under "Next Steps").

References

1. *A Guide to the Project Management Body of Knowledge* (*PMBOK® Guide*), *Sixth Edition* (Newtown Square, PA: PMI Project Management Institute Global Standard, 2017), page 49.

2. Ibid., page 31 (Process Map).

3. Blake Thorne, "How Distractions at Work Take Up More Time Than You Think," *I Done This Blog*, July 23, 2015, http://blog.idonethis.com/distractions-at-work/, accessed May 29, 2017.

4. Kiernan Hopkins, "Distracted Driver Accidents," *DistractedDriverAccidents.com*, January 23, 2015, http://distracteddriveraccidents.com/25-shocking-distracted-driving-statistics/, accessed May 29, 2017.

5. PMI, "Code of Ethics and Professional Conduct," *Project Management Institute*, https://www.pmi.org/about/ethics/code, accessed February 17, 2017.

6. Ibid.

PART II

The Ten Knowledge Areas

4 Project Integration Management

Key Skills & Concepts

- Overall project integration management
- Project selection process (how projects are chosen)
- The project charter and who owns it
- Jumpstarting a project (Checklist)
- Project management plan (planning the work)
- Execution of the project (working the plan)
- How to know whether the project is on track
- Importance of the closing phase of the project

Think of project integration management as what the project manager sees while flying over the project on a daily basis, 1,000 feet in the air, to see how everything is going. Are all the boats rowing in the right direction? Are the barriers (levies, dikes, and dams) all holding properly, or is there a flood coming that could break down the barriers and ruin the project?

As the project manager, it is up to you to be the pilot in command, the "eye in the sky," the one who keeps the project moving forward as planned. It is up to you to provide clear direction and support to all the stakeholders while keeping everyone focused on the end results (project objectives). The Project Integration Management Knowledge Area also involves reporting the progress and overall status of the project accurately and in a timely manner to ensure that adjustments can be made if needed.

Integration management is also about the team. Is the project team fully staffed? Do they have the right skills? Are they at the right place at the right time? Do they have all the information, tools, and support they need to manage their portion of the project? Are the team members clear on the goals and objectives of the project? Are they playing well together? Are they productive? These are only a few of the questions you need to ask yourself and address to manage project integration effectively across the entire project.

The PM must effectively manage the interdependencies between groups and individuals to ensure a smooth flight while traveling through the project life cycle and different Knowledge Areas. Integration management not only entails making choices about resource allocation but is also about making trade-offs among competing objectives and alternatives to solve problems and address concerns and issues before they become problems.

A PM who is too close to the details of the project might not be able to see the bigger picture beyond the project itself. The PM needs to think strategically (from beginning to end) and look at the whole project, not just the pieces and parts. This is where project integration management is essential; if done properly, it will help ensure success on your project.

Project Integration Management According to PMI

Project Integration Management (which was introduced in the 2000 version of the *PMBOK Guide*) is the first Knowledge Area in the *PMBOK* (Chapter 4) and probably the most important in that it crosses all five Process Groups. It sets the overall framework for how the project will be managed. According to PMI, project integration management includes the processes and activities needed to identify, define, combine, unify, and coordinate the various processes and activities across the project management Process Groups.

In the context of project management, integration management includes a variety of characteristics, such as being able to articulate project deliverables (what are the products of the project?) and taking integrative actions to make sure all the work products and packages (activities) fit together properly. This also includes successfully managing stakeholder expectations and meeting all approved project requirements (which is easier said than done).

Ask the Expert

Q: Is it easier to manage integration of the project without including the team?

A: Many project managers feel they can conduct integration management faster on their own without the involvement of, and questions from, their teams. This may work for a little while early in the project life cycle; however, without the team's input or involvement, the PM misses a wealth of knowledge, experience, and, most important, "buy-in" (acceptance) from the team. Even though the PM must be the "pilot in command" of the project, integration management revolves around the team and works best if the team is involved.

Tip

Integration management is a "team sport," and the PM is ultimately responsible (as the overall integrator) for the project and integration management. However, the PM cannot do it all; therefore, it is very important to include the team in the integration management process activities.

Overview of Project Integration Management Processes

The Project Integration Management Knowledge Area, according to Chapter 4 of the *PMBOK*, includes the following processes:

- **4.1. Develop Project Charter (Initiating Process Group).** The process of developing a document that formally authorizes the existence of a project and provides the project manager with the authority to apply organizational resources to project activities.
- **4.2. Develop Project Management Plan (Planning Process Group).** The process of defining, preparing, and coordinating all subsidiary plans and integrating them into a comprehensive project management plan. The project's integrated baselines and subsidiary plans may be included within the project management plan.
- **4.3. Direct and Manage Project Work (Executing Process Group).** The process of leading and performing the work defined in the project management plan and implementing approved changes to achieve the project's objectives.
- **4.4. Manage Project Knowledge (Executing Process Group).** The process of using existing knowledge and creating new knowledge to achieve project goals and objectives. Project knowledge should be developed and shared with others for best results for current and future projects.
- **4.5. Monitor and Control Project Work (Monitoring and Controlling Process Group).** The process of tracking, reviewing, and reporting project progress against the performance objectives defined in the project management plan.
- **4.6. Perform Integrated Change Control (Monitoring and Controlling Process Group).** The process of reviewing all change requests; approving changes (as appropriate), and managing changes to the deliverables, organizational process assets, project documents, and the project management plan; and communicating their disposition.
- **4.7. Close Project or Phase (Closing Process Group).** The process of finalizing all activities across all the project management Process Groups to formally complete the phase or project. This process now includes closing procurements as well.

Note

Project phases can actually be projects or subprojects within themselves. For example, closing the project involves the same Process Groups and Knowledge Areas that should be used for managing the whole project. The same can be true with any of the project phases. I have seen many cases in which the project plan and schedule were aligned with and grouped by the project phases or Process Groups, in essence breaking the project down into more manageable subprojects.

Project integration management is complex, and often the time and cost to perform this Knowledge Area are overlooked during estimating processes. We usually do a pretty good job of estimating the cost of the work necessary to complete the finished product or to solve the problem the project is created to address; however, we tend to underestimate the cost to manage the time and effort it takes to oversee and integrate the overall project.

Integration management includes setting up meetings, building the team, and setting up a tracking mechanism, collecting information, addressing issues, and reporting project status. A project manager needs to be assigned early in the project life cycle to focus on the project for these reasons. Far too often the existing operations manager or program manager who will inherit the product or result of the project is also expected to oversee the project, in their spare time and at no extra charge. A host of activities are involved with integration management, and these activities are rarely considered as part of the project. Because the work of the project will benefit the ongoing operations, it is often assumed the project work will be done by the daily operations manager and operations support team without cost or schedule impact. This is a great idea if it works; however, it rarely does.

For example, suppose a business need is identified in our case study: to reduce call center operations costs by 10 percent. A PM is brought in to identify a solution. The PM and solutions team agree that an automated VRU (voice response unit) would expedite call handling with fewer handoffs, thus reducing both time and cost. The estimated time to complete the project is two months. The project proposal is reviewed and approved for immediate implementation. However, instead of assigning a PM to initiate and manage the project, the company executives feel they can save costs by having the call center's operations manager oversee the project (in addition to his full-time operations job) because he will own the solution once it is installed. Do you think this will work? No, because the operations manager already has a full-time day job (and coincidentally has very little project management experience in most cases). Therefore, both roles will be done poorly. Between lack of PM experience and the distractions of the day-to-day operations, the operations manager will be too distracted to perform well in either function. This usually leads to a failed project.

The Selection Process: How Projects Are Chosen

Projects are usually chosen (initiated) for one of two primary reasons:

- Business needs (e.g., to increase revenue, reduce cost, or increase market share [profit])
- Problem that needs to be solved (e.g., equipment failure causing lost productivity, or a construction project needed to stimulate the economy)

Think about it: All the projects you have ever worked on probably fall into one of the two categories mentioned.

Because business needs may often be a matter of perception as much as they are a direct result of a real problem, we tend to use both the primary reasons mentioned as drivers in the project selection process. For example, take an IT (information technology) project to consolidate the number of servers. The justification for this project is to reduce cost and to increase reliability of the servers. Reducing cost meets a business need (to be more competitive), just as increasing reliability reduces outage and service problems while also saving money and improving customer satisfaction. All are great benefits that can justify the project—thus, a project is created (born).

Usually the company's executive committee, together with its subcommittees, identifies the need for projects and approves project funding (budgetary) commitments. This committee or delegate is responsible for establishing the strategic direction and plans for ensuring that projects are consistent with the organization's overall strategy. It is also responsible for ensuring that approved policies or practices are, in fact, followed.

Define the Business Need/Opportunity or Requirement

The best way to get a project approved is to identify the opportunity, benefit, or business need for the project. If the benefits (results of the project) outweigh the cost and time to create the product or service, then the project proposal should be an easy sell. If the project is to satisfy a safety or regulatory compliance requirement, it may be mandated.

Tip

Many companies or organizations have a project review board or project management office (PMO) that serves as a governing body to determine which projects are worthy to be funded and chartered/approved.

The project statement, justification, or proposal should explain, in clear business terms, how the project will address specific needs or opportunities. Why should the company spend time and money on this project? Here are some examples of how to help satisfy business needs, opportunities, or a regulatory requirement:

- Streamline/improve quality, reliability, or effectiveness of a product, or efficiency of a service, procedure, or operation.
- Meet mandated or regulatory compliance requirements of an internal or external authority (Sarbanes-Oxley, OCC, OSHA, FDA, ISO, ITIL, and so on). For more details on these regulations/organizations, simply perform an Internet search.
- Reduce operating or overhead costs or increase revenue.
- Gain market share or provide a strategic business advantage.
- Improve the skills of the team (through education, on-the-job training, or mentoring) to enhance their ability to perform more effectively.

Here are some additional details that can (or should) be provided in the discussion of the business need/opportunity to help provide a better understanding of the project:

- How the need/opportunity was recognized, and who benefits.
- A best estimate of the size or impact of the need/opportunity in specific terms.
- Results or contributing factors, such as increased workload, reduction in staff, budget or time constraints, increased risk, and the need to introduce new technology.
- Alternatives, risk analysis, advantages, and disadvantages.
- The potential cost of the project if approved and the potential cost if no action is taken (e.g., a continued failure rate of 15 percent if no action is taken). You should be as specific as possible about failure or improvement rates.

Remember, the information you provide in the project proposal will help the project sponsors make informed decisions and will help promote support for the project. The business need or opportunity can be better justified if it is based on sound information and facts. Unfortunately, there are many variables and you may not always have the answers.

Two Famous Words in Project Management: "It Depends"

A fellow PM instructor (and friend of mine) frequently says that the two magic words in project management are "it depends." This is true because every project tends to be unique in one way or another. No matter how many times a project is performed, many variables make each occasion different, and the way the project is managed depends entirely on these variables.

PMs have to be able to solve problems, handle different situations, and be able to think on their feet to come up with the best answers based on the information available at that time. If it were easy, anyone could do it, right?

Project Methodology and Sample Checklist

In the PM classes I teach at businesses and universities, two questions are frequently asked by my students:

- What is a project methodology?
- Are sample checklists and templates available for the different aspects of a project?

I'll answer the second question first: Yes, hundreds of sample checklists and templates are available from the Internet and from fellow PMs, who are usually more than willing to share their tools and techniques, such as checklists, sample documents, and so on. To get an idea of what is available, simply perform an Internet search for "PM Templates." Some are available at a fee, of course, but many are free "shareware." One such website (discovered by a student in my class) is a website showing a fantastic list of templates. They are explained clearly, organized well, and cover a host of topics on project management. The website is owned by Dr. Gary Evans, PMP, and the URL is http://www.cvr-it.com/PM_Templates/. The templates from CVR/IT Consulting LLC are free for educational use or for governmental and nonprofit agencies. However, there is a nominal licensing fee for commercial use, which is well worth the cost.

Now let's tackle the first question: What is a project methodology?

Methodology is the theoretical analysis of the methods applied to a particular field of study (such as project management) and/or of the principles associated with a branch of knowledge, set of procedures, or group of processes. A methodology does not set out to provide solutions but offers the theoretical view to help us understand which method, set of methods, or "best practices" can or should be applied to a specific set of activities or a situation.

Methodology has also been defined as "the analysis of the principles of methods, rules, and postulates employed by a discipline" and as "the systematic study of methods that are, can be, or have been applied within a discipline."[1]

The term "methodology," then, refers to more than a simple set of methods; it refers to the rationale and the assumptions that underlie a particular study or approach relative to the method.

Many companies are realizing the importance of a standard approach, or methodology, to help ensure consistency and a greater degree of success across the projects and programs they manage. To do this in an organized manner, more companies are creating project management offices (PMOs). As part of its charter, a PMO is responsible for ensuring and maintaining a documented project management methodology for use across all projects. This methodology is designed to meet the needs of all segments of the organization. It serves as a guide to the organization concerning the projects it selects, to project teams as they plan their work and report the status of their projects, and to management as it supplies the required oversight.

Often the chosen project management methodology is designed around the *PMBOK*; in other cases companies develop their own project management methodologies. Either way, it is important to remember that the *PMBOK* is only a guide (not a methodology). A project management methodology should work equally well on large and small projects. Standard templates are typically part of the methodology, and hundreds of great templates are available on the Internet or within your company's project management methodology (if one exists). If your company doesn't have an approved, standard, project management methodology, now is a good time to create one. You will realize time savings from using the same methodology on your projects. Your boss will see the benefits and shower you with bonuses, keys to the VIP washroom, and executive parking . . . or at least a pat on the back.

The best way to set up a clearly defined project methodology is to use a set of tried-and-true checklists. One constant with PMs around the world is that we love checkmarks, and checkmarks work best on a checklist. To this end, I have included several bulleted and numbered checklists in this chapter for your review.

A standard project management methodology is extremely beneficial and the goals are quite simple. Per CVR/IT Consulting LLC, the following goals or objectives should apply when defining a project management methodology:

- Provide a common point of reference and a common vocabulary for talking and writing about the practice of project management.
- Increase awareness and use of good project management practice by those charged with the responsibilities defined in the methodology.
- Define the roles of the executive committee, sponsor, project manager, stakeholders, and other team members, and obtain consensus within the organization about critical success factors (CSF).
- Create the basis for a collaborative environment in which those engaged in technical project work understands what is required of them and why those requirements are key factors for improving project results.[2]

Project Integration Management Processes: Charter to Close

To better understand project integration management, we need to look at the individual processes. The details of the processes in the Project Integration Management Knowledge Area are defined and explained throughout the remainder of this chapter.

Develop Project Charter Process (Initiating Process Group)

What is a project charter? In simple terms it is the authorization for a project or phase of a project to begin. It also authorizes the PM to be assigned and allows the PM to begin assigning resources (people and equipment) to the project. In other words, it is the official green light for the project to begin.

When Does a Project Officially Become a Project?

In reality, many projects are born (created) long before they receive the official charter. PMI views the project charter as the first official authorization and recognition of a project or phase of a project. There are many ways for a project or phase to begin, and many organizations don't even use or recognize the term "project charter."

Tip

The term "project charter" is not commonly used in many government agencies, nor in many public and private sector companies. It is more often referred to as one of the following: work order, service request, statement of work (SOW), request for service (RFS), contract, work initiative, work action, grant, legislative bill, or any of a number of other different names (especially on government contracts).

The Develop Project Charter process is the first in the series of processes in the *PMBOK*, and it occurs during the Initiating Process Group. It is the process of developing a document that formally authorizes the project or phase to begin. It is also the process for documenting the initial requirements that satisfy the stakeholders' needs and expectations; defining the product, service, or result of the project; and outlining acceptance criteria.

Here's a list of some of the key activities that should occur during this process:

- Identify project sponsor(s).
- Identify and document project deliverables (i.e., what is expected from the project).
- Identify and document project constraints (limitations).
- Determine project success criteria.
- Document project assumptions.
- Develop and analyze cost benefits.

Where Does a Project Charter Come From?

The project charter can come in many forms and in different names. It may be formal, such as a contract or letter of agreement (LOA), or informal, such as a call or email from your boss or the customer telling you to proceed with the project or phase. It is best if the charter is in writing to minimize confusion and to meet audit requirements.

To clarify the term project phase, let's use as an example a specific project to estimate the cost of designing a new fuel-efficient car. The approval may be to conduct a preliminary review or feasibility study (concept phase analysis) to determine whether there is sufficient business justification to proceed. The prudent approach to any project is to determine first whether it is doable or can be cost justified before the company commits to the project in its entirety.

In today's economy many companies are not able to afford long-term investments and need to realize benefits and ROI (return on investment) sooner than later, thus the need to take projects in smaller steps using fewer investment dollars.

Sample Components of a Project Charter Template

As mentioned, many great templates and forms are available that provide a good starting place for documents such as the project charter (see Figure 4.9 toward the end of this chapter for an example). Here is a summary list of the key components of a sample project charter template:

1.0. General project information

- **1.1.** Project name
- **1.2.** Sponsors (who is funding or will be the primary benefactor of the project)
- **1.3.** Document history (for tracking changes and version control)

2.0. Identify stakeholders and key contacts

- **2.1.** Project manager
- **2.2.** Team leads (responsible for certain areas of the project)
- **2.3.** Project sponsor(s)
- **2.4.** Customer or client
- **2.5.** Other key stakeholders as appropriate for the project

3.0. Project description

- **3.1.** Project purpose, business need, opportunity, or justification (problem to be solved)
- **3.2.** Project objectives (measurable outcomes, such as reducing cost, increasing performance, increasing sales, etc.)
- **3.3.** Deliverables or major milestones (products of the project, such as working software code, training manual, completed call center, user test document, etc.)
- **3.4.** What the project is intended to do and not do
- **3.5.** Risks or constraints (barriers/limitations)

4.0. Financial or resource information

- **4.1.** Budget assumptions

- **4.2.** Reporting strategy (frequency and format)
- **4.3.** Type of estimate
- **4.4.** Funding source(s)

5.0. Acceptance criteria

- **5.1.** Approvers
- **5.2.** Change control process

6.0. Final signoff (formal acceptance signatures) of the project charter[3]

Note

When filling out a template, remember that all projects are unique in some way, so the template might not fit the project exactly. Therefore, consider all the inputs, tools and techniques, and outputs of the processes to ensure that you haven't missed anything.

Case Study Introduction

Now that we have discussed the project charter, I would like to introduce a case study that we will use throughout this book to help apply the concepts discussed in this section and other chapters covered in this book.

The hard part is finding a case study that most people can relate to and one that can demonstrate what works and what generally doesn't work on a given project to serve as a learning experience.

The best way to learn about project management is to see one in action (being a part of it), and if that is not possible, the next best thing is to read about the project and the events that occurred—and if we can discuss events that are of an interesting nature, we may learn more about projects and hopefully have some fun along the way.

I have chosen an Information Technology (IT) project that had a diverse set of requirements and deliverables. I think you will find this project and various events that occurred over the life of the project informative, interesting, beneficial, and even entertaining. The objective is to learn from the experiences in this case study and to apply this knowledge to your own projects. Other project examples and sample project documents will also be provided to show a broader perspective than just IT-related projects.

This case study is real, and the events are based on real-world examples that occurred on a large project that I managed several years ago. It was a project with a series of services that should fit pretty well in the topics that we will cover in this book.

Let's start with a little background on the customer, service provider, and contract for this case study.

Case Study Background

This project is for a Fortune 500 company, and we all use its products. The company is Procter & Gamble, also known as P&G, which is an American-based multi-national consumer goods company with headquarters in Cincinnati, Ohio (USA). The company was founded in 1837 by candlemaker William Procter and soap maker James Gamble. In 2015 P&G reported over $76.2 billion dollars in annual sales. Most of these brands—including Bounty, Crest, and Tide—are global products available on several continents. Its products include everything from cleaning agents, to snacks, to personal care products. In 1995 P&G decided to focus on their core competencies (consumer products) and contracted (outsourced) with IBM to consolidate their help desk services, office equipment order processing, distribution of office systems, and training, in addition to providing on-site desktop support in the greater Cincinnati, Ohio, area.

Contract scope of services included:

1. Help desk consolidation of five P&G support centers into a single professional call center in Boulder, Colorado.
2. Physical (wall-to-wall) inventory of all office equipment in 30 facilities of approximately 12,000 employees in Cincinnati to establish a baseline of equipment to be supported.
3. Setting up an order processing center (OPC) complete with leasing a local warehouse for receiving new laptops and printers. Setting up the equipment, testing (burn-in), delivery, and training the receiving end users to use their new office equipment on the operating system and applications as part of what they called the Standard Equipment Workstation Platform (SEWP).
4. Creating a central on-site desktop and client/server support network to service all P&G employees.
5. Vendor/supplier contract management of key support services with over 40 different companies that provided extended services and support to P&G.

Project Goal

The goal of this group of projects, including five years of ongoing support after the transition, was to change everything about P&G's desk support services from the inside out without disrupting day-to-day operations. This would allow the customer to focus on their core competency (consumer products) instead of worrying about their information technology needs.

In order to reach this goal, IBM assembled an initial project management team of 11 subject matter experts and a PM for a total of 12 team members to work on-site at P&G headquarters in Cincinnati. The project team grew to a peak of over 38 people during transition with an ongoing operations (day-to-day) support team of around 20–25 people, including managers, after the transition was complete.

First Challenge

The first challenge occurred when the project management team (core team) arrived in Cincinnati ready to work, only to find their laptops had not been shipped. On the first day the team was without the tools of their trade. Note: in 1995 laptops were hard to come by on short notice and cost around $6,000 to $7,000 per unit. The wait time was expected to be three to four weeks. As the project manager, what would you do?

If you are reading the book alone, write down your answer to the following four questions and then compare to the results shown below. If you are in the classroom and can work in a team, pick an acting PM for this discussion and answer the following four questions:

1. What is the primary problem?
2. What is the potential impact to the project?
3. What are the alternatives (options) to address the problem?
4. What are your findings and recommendations (next steps) to resolve this situation?

After you have written down your answers, compare to the solution below:

Case Study Results

1. The primary problem was the project team was not equipped to begin work on the project without their laptops. Everything discussed had to be captured using pen and paper, which would have to be entered into the laptops when they arrived, very old fashioned and a redundant use of resources.
2. The impact to the project was (a) delay in the start of work, and (b) the team looked unprepared and unprofessional.
3. Options discussed by the PM and team were the following:
   a. Escalate the equipment delay to the capital assets manager to expedite shipment.
   b. Try to rent laptops locally. Note that there was limited availability and this solution was cost prohibitive.
   c. Ask the customer if they had spare laptops the team could use temporarily to allow the team to get up to speed more quickly.

4. Steps taken to solve this problem: the PM reviewed all options above and chose option c: the customer was asked if spare laptops were available so the project team could get familiar with the SEWP applications and see the configuration they would need to support. The customer agreed and provided 12 preloaded laptops, and the team was able to begin work immediately, which resulted in a win-win situation for all parties. The team's laptops arrived three weeks later, and the team members were allowed to continue using customer laptops to learn more about the customers' standard SEWP applications. By using the customer's laptops, the team was also able to communicate easier with the customer employees through their email system (in the mid-1990s, mail did not port easily across different email systems).

Next Challenge

The next challenge was the logistics of transitioning the customers' support environment from the current or "as-is state" to the new "to-be state." This challenge, without a doubt, was the biggest as "time was of the essence" on this contract; all transition projects were to be completed and ready for operation within 60 days. This objective was unattainable as there were too many constraints and "moving parts" from the beginning of the project. This was a clear case of a lack of communications between middle- and upper-management in the customer's organization. The executives made the decision to move forward very quickly on the contract without input from middle management as to the feasibility. This is an example of what happens far too often when company executives make big decisions without including their own managers. Only guessing here, but maybe the executives felt that including the middle managers would slow down the decision to outsource the IT services. At the end of the day, however, because the customer's organizational structure was "management by consensus," it slowed the implementation down by over two months. This delay surfaced about halfway through the first project kickoff meeting after the contract was signed, when the Project Executive at P&G boldly stated that they "needed more time to understand the contract between P&G and IBM and that IBM team members were not to interact with P&G team members until they sorted out the contract." When the customer was asked how much time they would need to figure out their needs and expectations, their response was "three months." Remember the contract was to provide full service transition of the six subprojects within 60 days. This news was a "showstopper" and what can happen (and did) on a contract when executive-level management makes very high-level decisions about when a project will be complete without actually talking to middle managers or the first line of managers and people who are expected to do the work of the project. The results were that unrealistic expectations were set and contracted without a reality check on what it would take to complete the project in a more realistic time frame.

As the Project Manager, What Would You Do?

If you are reading the book alone, write down your answers to the following four questions and then compare to the results shown below. If you are in the classroom and can work in a team, pick an acting PM for this discussion and answer the following questions: 1. What is the primary problem? 2. What is the potential impact to the project? 3. What are the alternatives (options) to address the problem? 4. What are your findings and recommendations (next steps) to resolve this situation to yourself or to the group?

After you have written down your answers, compare to the solution below:

Case Study Results

1. Primary problem identified was that the project momentum was lost, the contract was potentially in breach, and the project team members were now idle with nothing to do on this project.
2. The impact to the project was (a) delayed start to the work of the project by approximately three months, (b) the contract issues had to be addressed by legal teams, and (c) the project team would need to be reassigned as its members couldn't sit around waiting for P&G to open up the engagement.
3. Options and outcomes discussed by the team were:
   a. Negotiate for PM and top two to three team leaders to continue working the project startup plan and to gather as much information as possible without disrupting the P&G staff/managers.
   b. Ask P&G to begin paying the monthly service fees for the project.
   c. Reassign the project team to other projects.
   d. Call the contract management team to try and renegotiate the long-term contract based on this new information.
4. Steps taken to solve this problem: the PM exercised all of the options suggested by the team as outlined above.
   a. PM successfully negotiated for access to three primary P&G focal point contacts, and the IBM PM and two team leads were allowed to stay on site to jumpstart the project planning and data collection.
   b. Legal teams reviewed the contract and required the customer to pay monthly service fees.
   c. PM had to regroup the full project team after 60 days to prepare for project activities when P&G staff were finally approved to engage at the three-month mark.
   d. The contract was renegotiated for an open-ended startup date (with many changes along the way; the project took 18 months instead of the original contract of full

startup within 60 days). The updated contract was deemed a success because everything was managed through a formal change control.

Additional Discussion Points

As project managers we need to be proactive (think ahead) so we can avoid potential risks prior to the start of the project.

What should the Project Manager have done before showing up at P&G?

1. Called ahead and introduced him/herself to the P&G Project Executive several weeks before the engagement was scheduled to begin to make sure that the expectations and timing were still on track
2. Started speaking with and getting to know the key stakeholders at P&G before the team was brought on-site
3. Identified the key stakeholders at P&G and made arrangements to meet them early before kick-off with the entire team

Now that the case has been introduced, let's look at an example of a project charter for this project case study to set the stage (so to speak) regarding the many variables and challenges often faced on real projects. An example of a project charter can be seen in Figure 4.9 toward the end of this chapter. Some of the components that are often included in a project charter are shown below:

PURPOSE OF THE PROJECT (BACKGROUND OR PROJECT SUMMARY)

You need to answer the question: "Why are we doing this project?" That is, what problem does the project solve or business need does it fulfill?

- **Goals**
  What are the goals you hope to achieve and when? The goals need to be specific and measurable using the "SMART" acronym, which stands for Specific, Measurable, Attainable, Relevant, and Time Bound. For example, "Increase revenue by 10 percent year over year" or "Reduce cost by 12 percent by the end of the current year." Simply saying, "Improve customer satisfaction" is a bad goal because it does not meet the SMART objectives; for example, it is not measurable. If you say "Improve customer satisfaction by 10% year over year," the goal is now measurable.

- **Scope**
  What is the product, service, or result you expect to create from this project? And what actions will your team take to successfully complete the project? It is important to

clearly document what will be included in the scope of the project and what is not included (out-of-scope / exclusions) to eliminate any confusion as you go forward.

- **Key Stakeholders**
  Make a list of the primary people involved or affected by this project. It is also good to list the title of the required position, department name, and contact information. This is often referred to as a Stakeholder Register.

- **Project Milestones**
  Identify significant dates of your project: start date, end date, invoicing dates. It's important to understand that these dates are merely estimates at this stage. When writing the project charter, you may not have firm dates as yet because it is early in the project life cycle.

- **Project Budget**
  List the expected project expenses; if the level of confidence in the estimate is not firm, identify them as rough estimations. It is best to focus on those costs that are direct to the project; however, don't overlook the overhead (indirect) costs that will charged or allocated to your project.

- **Constraints, Assumptions, Risks, and Dependencies**
  + **Constraints:**
    These are the limiting factors that impact your project, such as schedule, budget, or resources. For example, when developing a new website, the number of people such as programmers or testers often have limited availability as they often are working on multiple projects at the same time. This needs to be taken into consideration.

  + **Assumptions:**
    Assumptions are factors that may not be clear and are important to the success of your project. For example, contractors will be used for 30 percent of the project work, and their invoices are to be paid within 30 days of receipt of approved invoices for all work completed (deliverables) within the accepted time frame.

  + **Risks:**
    Document all identified risks that might get in the way of project goals, the team, the schedule, or budget. A few examples:
    - Aggressive schedule; for example, the deadline doesn't allow for force majeure (acts of God)
    - High number of changes expected from the customer

- 30 of the team are volunteers with limited motivation and training
- Technical risks; for example, equipment compatibility or availability

+ **Dependencies:**

  Cases when work depends on inputs or completion by others that can delay the project. The customer will provide the requirements prior to the start of the design, testing needs to be completed prior to final coding, or the building permit must be obtained prior to start of construction.

- **Reviewers/Approvers:**

  It is also important to list the people who need to review and sign off (approve) the project charter by name, position, and date so there is no confusion over the acceptance of the charter.

Who Owns the Project Charter?

Because the project charter is the official authorization document of the project, it should be initiated by the primary champion or executive owner (sponsor). Because most high-level managers are not usually document creators, it is up to the PM to draft the charter, review it with the sponsor, and obtain formal acceptance or approval of the document. This can even be in email format, as long as it is in writing.

Ask the Expert

Q: Who owns the project charter?

A: The project sponsor is responsible for the financial resources of the project owns the project charter. The sponsor is usually the person who promotes or supports the benefits of the project to higher levels of management. In the real world, however, the PM (or project leader) usually documents the details of the charter and obtains approval for the project to begin. At the end of the day, the PM is responsible for ensuring there is a project charter and to obtain acceptance of the charter from the appropriate project sponsor(s).

Definition of a Project Sponsor

According to Dr. Gary Evans, the sponsor is the individual (or individuals), generally an executive, who is responsible for the strategic direction and financial support of a project. A sponsor should have the authority to define project goals, secure resources, and resolve organizational and priority conflicts.

It has been shown, but may not be generally recognized, that lack of project sponsorship can be a major contributor to project failure. Conversely, an appropriately placed and fully engaged sponsor can bring a difficult project to a successful conclusion. Assumptions that a formal sponsor is not needed (or for political reasons can be avoided) are misplaced. Steering committees are no substitute. A powerful but uninvolved sponsor is no help. Even big-budget and highly visible projects require a formal sponsor.

Here's a sample list of sponsor responsibilities:

- Champion the project from initiation to completion.
- Participate in the development and selling of the project business case.
- Present the overall vision and business objectives for the project.
- Assist in determining and approving the final funding and project direction.
- Serve as executive liaison to key stakeholders (e.g., senior management, department directors, and support managers).
- Support the project team.[3]

For best results it is also important for the PM to be assigned early in the initiation phase so that the charter can be reviewed and developed by the person responsible for the execution of the project.

The project sponsor provides the direction, executive sponsorship, and expectations that need to be met to consider the project a success. These components must be considered as key inputs to the project.

Develop Project Charter Inputs, Tools and Techniques, and Outputs

As a reminder, every process has inputs, tools and techniques, and outputs. An input often comes from the output of the previous process, so there is a logical progression in many cases. Figure 4.1 shows the inputs, tools and techniques, and the outputs for the Develop Project Charter process.

INPUTS

As mentioned previously, inputs are items that need to be considered for the process to be administered. Further, "input" is a term denoting either an entrance or changes inserted into a system or process. The quality of the input can be crucial to the value of the output of the process, which brings us to the famous saying "garbage in, garbage out" (GIGO). There are several inputs to the Develop Project Charter process, as listed here:

- **Business documents.** Based on demands in the marketplace, organizational needs, customer needs, advances in technology, legal requirements, ecological impacts, and social needs. This ties the project to the strategic business objectives of the organization.
- **Agreements.** This could be any form of contract, memorandum of understanding, letter of agreement, statement of work (SOW), and so on.

- **Enterprise environmental factors.** Influenced by laws, regulations, and industry standards. This includes the culture and structures of the organizations involved. Marketplace conditions can be a strong motivator for new projects to take advantage of emerging trends.
- **Organizational process assets.** These are your company's processes, policies, and templates. This is also where your lessons learned and historical information maintained by your company come into play.

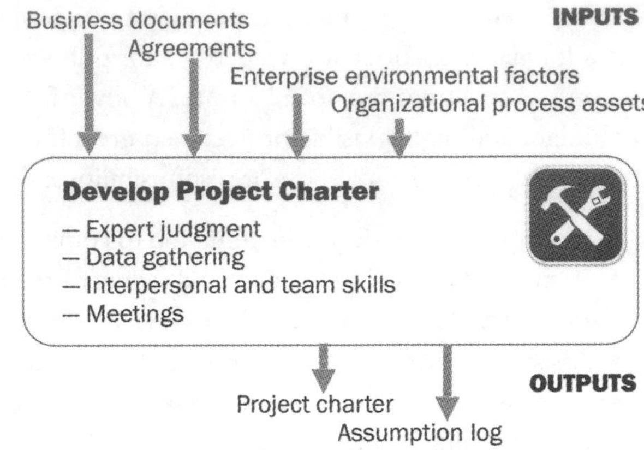

FIGURE 4.1 Develop Project Charter Process ITTOs

TOOLS AND TECHNIQUES

Tools and techniques are used to analyze the inputs received for a particular process. Subject matter experts (SMEs), focus groups, and specialists are often used as consultants; they can be considered to be the tool or technique used to assess the inputs for a process. These experts apply their knowledge and experience to help determine the best approach to accomplish specific outputs of the process. In the Develop Project Charter process, the primary tool and technique is simply expert judgment. Note that the SMEs may have (and certainly can use) a variety of tools and techniques to help them develop the project charter. Facilitation techniques will also be employed during this process as the project manager solicits and coordinates the inputs of key stakeholders in defining the project.

FACILITATION TECHNIQUES

As a PM, you will lead and manage individual and group interactions of your project team and other stakeholders. This is a critical skill area, requiring leadership and patience. Consider the most efficient format for a meeting. You will need to schedule meetings at convenient times, provide an early snapshot of the proposed agenda with a focused purpose for the meeting, and solicit inputs. The meeting should start on time and maintain the schedule, being respectful of other team members' time. Critical issues should be discussed and the status of action items reviewed.

Other facilitation techniques include brainstorming, conflict resolution, and problem solving. The greatest value of the team sport of brainstorming is learning from the perspectives of others and building a more holistic picture of the problem environment and potential solutions. During these team activities, the need for conflict resolution may arise. These topics are covered in more detail in Chapter 10, Project Communications Management.

OUTPUTS

The outputs of a process are the documents or results being developed as part of the process. For example, the outputs of the Develop Project Charter process include the project charter document and an assumptions log.

When the project charter (or alternative authorization document) is received, the PM needs to dive right in and jump-start the project.

How to Jump-Start a Project

Projects usually come at you with little warning. You get a tap on the shoulder from your boss (usually via email or a phone call) with the all-too-familiar line, "Have I got an opportunity for you!" And as always, the project is high priority and needs to begin immediately. So what do you do?

Ask the Expert

Q: How do I "hit the ground running" to jump-start a project?

A: I suggest you use a standard checklist and templates from previous, similar projects, or you can use the sample checklist I provide in this section. The key is to have a checklist ready before you receive "the call."

Once a checklist is chosen, the next step is to select the templates that can be used. Templates can be your friend or your enemy. They are great for getting your thoughts flowing and to apply synergy based on other people's experiences. However, if the templates you select are then used simply as "fill-in-the-blanks" forms, you and your team could waste countless hours collecting information or answering questions that really don't apply to your project. A template is just a shell until you fit it into your project. I have seen many PMs and project teams lose focus and creativity on their project when using a template whose blanks they filled in with little thought about how (or whether) the template fits their project.

The best way to collect and organize the templates is to put them in a binder or electronic folder—often referred to as a project control book (PCB). The PCB provides a great way to organize documents or templates so you can dive right in when starting a new project or updating an existing project.

To help you begin, I've provided a sample PM jump-start checklist. Although your actual checklist will likely be different from this one, the good news about project management is that the fundamentals tend to apply to most all projects. With that in mind, here is a sample project jump-start checklist:

- Review project objectives from the project selection process. What is the problem to be solved? What is the business need or opportunity to be addressed?
- Identify / verify the project sponsor (or sponsors) who needs (need) to be satisfied that the project does what is expected of it. The PM's job is to identify the sponsors and other stakeholders on the project (in other words, know your audience).
- Obtain the project charter and other inputs (contract, work order, service request) to review what is authorized (in scope) in the project. In the world as the PM, you might need to write the first draft of the project charter and obtain signoff approval from the project sponsor instead of the sponsor providing a project charter document to you. The current view indicates it is the PM's responsibility to create the charter and obtain approval signatures from the project sponsor(s).
- Review and verify logistics such as building location, maps, access (e.g., badges and or escorts), on-site work space (offices), equipment (e.g., printers and computers), parking, phones, special training, disclosure requirements, and so on.
- Acquire the project team and other resources needed to perform the work. In some cases a letter of commitment from management for key resources (especially "mission critical" or highly skilled people) is recommended to ensure their availability.
- Assess and maintain staff technical proficiency and provide training where needed.
- Gather the team to begin introductions and conduct skill and capability reviews.
- Review constraints (financial, resource, and time) to help establish the scope.
- Document and review the scope statement with key stakeholders and obtain scope verification from the project sponsor(s).
- Create a resource assignment matrix (RAM) and organizational breakdown structure (OBS), and review these with the team.* (This should include backup resources.)
- Schedule a kickoff meeting to officially announce the project, get everyone on the same page, set the ground rules, show the project structure "chain of command," and so on.
- Develop the project management plan, including the tools and techniques needed to manage the project.*
- Develop the work breakdown structure (WBS).*
- Begin development of the project schedule (time management).*
- Begin cost estimating (cost management) with input from the stakeholders.*
- Conduct risk management assessment and assign owners to the high-priority risks.*

---

* **With team involvement**—Keep in mind that the team development "forming stage" may have certain constraints, such as personality conflicts, lack of skilled resources for the assignment, lack of commitment, and lack

- Develop the project communications plan, including format and frequency. Review this with the stakeholders for approval and determination of how issues will be tracked and managed.
- Once the project is underway, begin the *PMBOK* execution and controlling processes.
- Review the project status on a regular basis and report the status to key stakeholders weekly (or as needed, based on the size, type, and complexity of the project).
- Set up a project management information system (PMIS). This is often called an electronic "team room" or "central database repository." Its purpose is to allow the project manager and team to store the project plan and output documents for easy access and audit readiness. Note: There are many tools available such as Dropbox, Google, or SharePoint that will help with this process.

Dr. Bruce Wayne Tuckman is an American psychologist who has carried out research on the theory of group dynamics. In 1965 he published one of his theories, called "Tuckman's Stages," where he states that "groups initially concern themselves with orientation accomplished primarily through testing. Such testing serves to identify the boundaries of both interpersonal and task behaviors. Coincident with testing in the interpersonal realm is the establishment of dependency relationships with leaders, other group members, or existing standards. It may be said that orientation, testing, and dependence constitute the group process of forming."[4]

The best approach to help form a project team is to make time for the team members to get to know one another and for you to get to know the team members—they are your number-one asset on the project.

Once the project initiation (startup) has begun and the preliminary team is formed, it is time to lock in (verify) the project deliverables.

What Are Project Deliverables?

In project management a deliverable can be a product or service that is given to the customer/client. A deliverable usually is tangible, unique, verifiable, and has a due date; it should be measurable and specific whenever possible. Deliverables can be either project or product related.

Project deliverables typically are project management related work documents needed to perform the PM tasks such as the Project Management Plan, the Project Charter, or Risk Plan. Usually there are several deliverables that lead to a milestone. Project deliverables can

of trust from a team member or from a manager. Therefore, it is important to allow time for the team to get to know one another on a new project.

often include both the outputs that comprise the product or service of the project as well as ancillary results, such as project reports and other documents.

Product deliverables, on the other hand, are usually tied to the "product" of the project and can be a software application product, a design document (i.e., blueprints or specifications), a training manual, or another asset that is required by the customer to be produced as part of the product of the project.

Deliverables can also be described at a summary level or in great detail, depending on the needs of the project.

Note

The only way to be completely clear on the project deliverables is to collect and verify the requirements of the project with the sponsor(s). The requirements usually dictate the deliverables. As important as it is to clearly identify project deliverables, it is equally important to identify and document what is excluded (out of scope) from the project. Project exclusions should be precise enough to leave little room for confusion and to prevent challenges about what is and is not included in the project scope. An example of project exclusion is, "The training manual will only be provided in English." Or, "Special sound effects and laser light show equipment for the concert must be provided by the artist, not the events center."

Try This

WHO PROVIDES THE REQUIREMENTS?

A famous rock star's booking agent contacts the events center manager to book it for a concert. The requirements for the stage placement, seating, and special effects (for example, pyrotechnics/fireworks) pose a safety hazard. The booking agent is contacted, and he insists on the requirements as stated. What do you do?

Answer: Even though the customer (booking agent) provides the requirements, if these requirements pose a hazard or are in conflict with a city or fire ordinance, they will need to be changed. Otherwise, the event cannot go on as requested.

The requirements must be clear, documented, and approved and must pose no conflicts in the safe delivery of the project. Once the requirements are approved, the PM should schedule a kickoff meeting and begin developing the project management plan.

Kickoff Meetings

The *kickoff meeting* helps set the stage (framework) for the project and demonstrates the team's importance in the planning and execution process.

Note

There can be more than one kickoff meeting; however, there should be at least one such meeting conducted fairly early in the project life cycle to get everyone up to speed quickly and to formally announce the project scope, schedule, deliverables, team members, sponsors, and so on. Be careful not to over invite (large audience) to the initial (preliminary) kickoff meeting as you may want to have a project team meeting first, then you can hold other kickoff meetings as you see fit that might include the customer, subcontractors, vendors, extended project team, and so on.

So who should attend? A sample list is shown below:

- Project sponsor(s)
- Project manager
- Project leads (coordinators)
- Project team members and support personnel
- Key subject matter experts (SMEs)
- Others as appropriate:
    + Administrator or scribe (to take minutes of the meeting)
    + Financial representative (person tracking budget and expenses)
    + Vendors, suppliers, subcontractors, or volunteer leaders
    + Customer, end user management, or lead representatives

What topics are covered in the kickoff meeting? It depends (you knew that was coming, right?) on the size, type, and complexity of the project. If the project is an extension of an existing project, this step should be pretty easy. However, a totally new project with a totally new team and new technology can be labor intensive. At the end of the meeting, the attendees should leave with a clear understanding of the following:

- Project organization, key stakeholders, and team members assigned. Where the plan and output documents, meeting minutes, and assignments will be posted and stored (preferably in an electronic team room). How to access and update the product documents in the PMIS.
- The project charter, including goals and objectives of the project.
- The scope of the project and how the scope will be managed (e.g., through formal change control).
- Success factors (measured deliverables and results expected).
- General schedule, budget, and preliminary next steps (action items).

- Benefits or business results expected upon completion of the project.
- Known issues, constraints, or risks that need to be considered going into the project.
- Key assumptions and milestones, if identified.
- Activities planned for the next several days/weeks.

With the kickoff meeting complete, you are now ready to develop the more detailed overall project management plan with input from the team (remember, this should be a team sport).

Develop Project Management Plan Process (Planning Process Group)

The Develop Project Management Plan process involves documenting the actions necessary to define, prepare, integrate, and coordinate all the other work plans of the project. It defines how the project will be executed, monitored and controlled, and then closed.

The project management plan, once developed, serves as a guide to how the project will be managed. This guide should be used as a working document. It should be used for various purposes and is the first step in demonstrating that the PM is effectively managing the project based on an approved methodology and formal plan.

At the end of the day (or the end of an audit), the true measure of control over a project is whether the PM has a plan and is working (managing) the plan.

The primary owner of the project management plan is the PM. The PM has total responsibility and accountability for the overall project and its successful completion. To succeed, the PM must work closely with the sponsor, the team, and other key stakeholders to ensure that adequate plans are put in place for all aspects of the project, including (but not limited to) resources, funding, risk management, communications, schedule, and change control.

On some real-world projects the PM may not be assigned to the project until the planning or even execution phase (after the project has started), in which case there may be a handoff or orientation meeting to bring the PM up to date on the agreements made during the initiation phase. In these cases the PM must thoroughly review all the materials previously collected or created, as well as ensure that they are reasonable in scope and delivery capabilities and are approved. Once approved, and all project history and current status have been reviewed, the PM must then finalize the project management plan development.

Try This

PLAN THE WORK

In Chapter 2 the "Ready, Fire, Aim" dilemma was introduced. This is the stage at which you can avoid this dilemma. Planning the work of the project will help ensure the proper order of project planning and a smooth project. There are far too many variables—thus the importance of planning.

Consider the following: Your boss comes to you on Monday and says, "You are the new PM of a software-development project to create a tracking system for downloads from the EZtrack.com website, and you need to deliver the project plan to the sponsor on Friday." What is the first step to get you started?

This is a great time to begin the first step of the AIM strategy:

1. Analyze the situation, including what needs to be done, target dates, limitations, and possible roadblocks and barriers.
2. Lock in a preliminary plan first at the team level. A good approach is to use a checklist (such as the "Sample Checklist for PM Management Plan Development," shown next).
3. Then take the plan forward for review and validation by the key sponsors/stakeholders. Once approved, you now have a plan to work from for your new project.

Sample Checklist for Project Management Plan Development

The following sample checklist can be used to assist in the Develop Project Management Plan process (note that many of these steps are also included in the project jump-start check list):

- Develop a detailed project management plan with the assistance of the project team, including how changes will be managed; how risks will be identified, tracked and reported; and so on.
- Create a work breakdown structure (WBS), organizational breakdown structure (OBS), and risk breakdown structure (RBS) with assistance from the project team.
- Develop or assist in the development of a scope statement, project schedule, and communications plan.
- Create a preliminary risk management plan (including owners and contingency plans) and cost-benefit analysis (or other tools and techniques as appropriate).
- Create a procurement plan. This plan will vary depending on organizational structure (i.e., a centralized procurement department vs. a decentralized procurement department, where the PM has more involvement and control).
- Develop the project budget, assumptions and exclusions, and the tracking and reporting plan. Note that it is important to identify and document the type of estimate used (e.g., order of magnitude or definitive).

- Obtain management commitment (agreement), such as a document of understanding (DOU), statement of work (SOW), or contractor (vendor/supplier) agreement for key resources to clearly state the work they are expected to perform.
- Assign resources to the project and assign work packages from the WBS to specific team members (resource plan or resource assignment matrix [RAM]).
- Approve project quality management processes and procedures, measurements and tracking format, and reporting frequency.
- Develop a baseline and obtain approval (*baselining* the plan means to establish a starting point or a point of reference for comparing against for changes).

Once these items are complete, as the PM you must provide clear direction and ongoing management of the project management plan. It is all about planning the work and working the plan. The plan also serves as a guide to how you are planning to manage the different aspects of the project, including risks, communications, schedule, cost, and changes.

Example of a Project Management Plan

The events center project management plan is the event data sheet (EDS), which is created by the event manager, using a standard process and template that clearly defines how the project is to be managed down to the following items. Another example of a project management plan is shown in Figure 4.10 toward the end of this chapter:

- The schedule (including event date, setup date, sound check, and doors-open times)
- Contacts (including promoter, tour manager, production contacts, operations manager, media/PR manager, box office, finance/HR, concessions, and catering)
- Box office information (including attendance/seating and ticket handling)
- Staff (number of supervisors, number of staff needed for each category—sound/lights, runners, receptionists, cleaning, video, pyro shooter, and so on)
- First responders (local law enforcement, emergency medical, fire department)
- Security (including parking lot, entrances, loading dock, and dressing rooms)
- Parking lot management
- Concessions/catering
- Setup (stadium seating, stage, tables, dressing rooms)
- Show production (trucks, buses, food/beverages, stagehand labor)
- Miscellaneous

The standard format and flow of the EDS offers consistency in how events will be managed, regardless of the type of event. From the customer's point of view, the measure of success will be whether the project is completed on time, within budget, and at an acceptable level of quality.

Develop Project Management Plan Inputs, Tools and Techniques, and Outputs

Figure 4.2 shows the inputs, tools and techniques, and the outputs for the Develop Project Management Plan process.

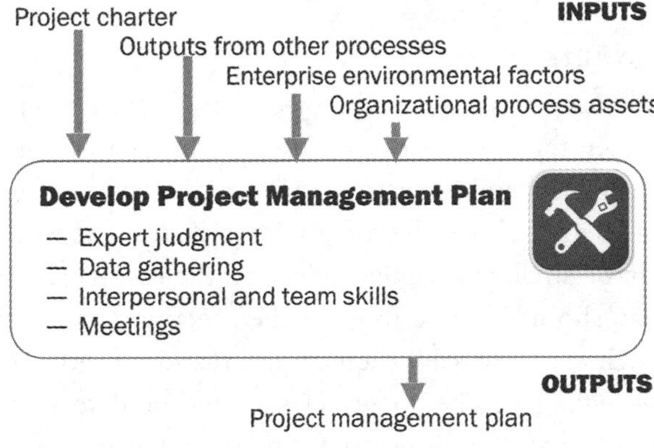

FIGURE 4.2 Develop Project Management Plan

INPUTS

Some key inputs to the Develop Project Management Plan process are as follows:

- **Project charter.** Describes the stakeholder's high-level needs (requirements) for the project, as well as early time and cost estimates. The project charter should provide a good picture of the expected outcome of the project.
- **Outputs from other processes.** As planning progresses, plans should be folded into the master project management plan and updated throughout with each iteration.
- **Enterprise environmental factors.** Always consider external factors that may influence your project. These may include such factors as government and industry standards, the project management body of knowledge, and the project management methodologies appropriate to your project, as well as your organization's structure and infrastructure.
- **Organizational process assets.** Also, always consider the internal factors that influence your project. Determine which organizational processes, standards, and policies will affect your project. In addition, take advantage of the history your organization has collected in lessons learned and re-using (and tailoring) appropriate templates.

TOOLS AND TECHNIQUES

The tools and techniques for this process are expert judgment and facilitation techniques.

EXPERT JUDGMENT

Be sure to take advantage of the knowledge and experience of others. In crafting the project management plan you will probably have to rely on support from finance, human resources, and engineering departments. Even if a subject matter expert (SME) is not assigned to your team, if you ask for information or help, people will almost always give it.

FACILITATION TECHNIQUES

Facilitation techniques will be covered in more detail in Chapter 10, "Project Communications Management."

OUTPUTS

The output is the actual project management plan document. Don't be fooled by the single output for this process, because the project management plan is essential to the success of the project and is a compilation of all the key components of the project. The project management plan can be a fairly large document with many volumes (subsidiary plans), or it can be small in size, depending on the complexity of the project. The project management plan should be used to guide the execution of the project. It will be the first place someone (such as a new team member or an auditor) goes to understand the project and how it is to be managed. The copies/files should be date stamped and clearly marked with a version number so there is no confusion over which is the latest version to be used for reference by the PM and the team.

Tip

The project management plan should be used early and often throughout the project life cycle. It should be a "working document" kept readily available in a centrally located file cabinet or an electronic team room (such as a Wiki or SharePoint location). It is extremely important to keep the document up to date and accurate without multiple versions. The rule of thumb is to keep the current version, and the previous two versions, for reference. To see sample project charter and management plan documents, go to Figure 4.9 and Figure 4.10.

Direct and Manage Project Work Process (Executing Process Group)

This is where the actual work execution begins. The bulk of the project budget is spent during this phase of the project. As Project Manager, you need to exercise your leadership skills and put them into action. Be proactively involved, constantly looking for ways to keep the team focused on the deliverables of the project. Provide clear direction. Be available to the team and ensure they have the tools necessary to do their job. Ensure that schedules are being met, and work the details of the project plan to anticipate breakdown or risks, such as missed handoffs. For example, you should be aware of dependencies where someone needs to provide information or work products to allow the project "assembly line" to continue operating.

Figure 4.3 shows the inputs, tools and techniques, and the outputs for the Direct and Manage Project Work process. Notice that one of the primary inputs on top of the standard inputs of project documents is approved change requests. Remember that as we move though the processes each step of the way on any project, we learn more about the project, which often requires us to make changes.

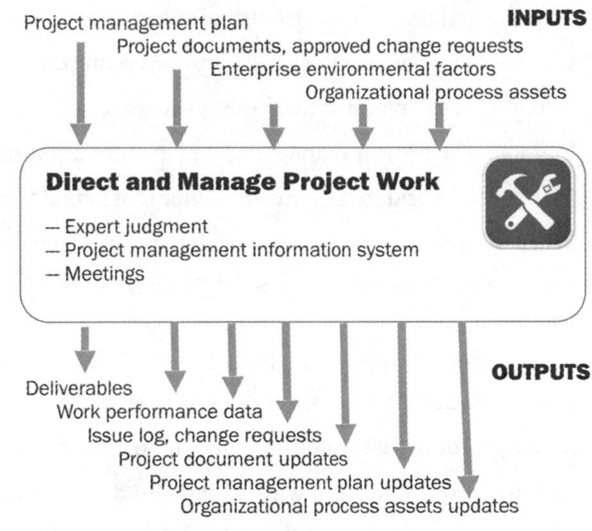

FIGURE 4.3 Direct and Manage Project Work Process ITTOs

Key outputs of the Direct and Manage Project Work process include deliverables, work performance data, an issue-tracking log, and any new change requests. As always, we may need to update project documents as an output of this and most all other processes.

The PM, along with the team, directs the performance of the planned project activities as well as manages the various technical, operational, and organizational interfaces that exist within the project to achieve project objectives.

Project Execution Activities Checklist

During the project execution phase, it is helpful for the PM and project team to perform their work in an organized fashion. As always, a good way to begin is with a checklist of key activities.

> **Tip**
>
> Notice that the action words (verbs) change during the execution phase (perform, maintain, manage, and review) when compared to the earlier initiation phase (develop, create, and assign). In most cases the verbs will change during each phase of the project life cycle.

The following checklist includes some key activities that should be considered when executing the work of your project (note that the order of activities may change depending on the needs of your project):

- Perform activities to accomplish project requirements and deliverables.
- Create project deliverables per approved requirements.
- Implement the planned methods, processes, and standards.
- Maintain the project management plan and output documents from other processes.
- Manage risks and make sure an owner is assigned to each of the highest-priority risks.
- Work with risk owners to ensure that mitigation plans as well as response action plans and procedures are in place and are being monitored as well as managed, should the risks occur.
- Maintain staff levels and technical proficiency, providing training and mentoring where needed (including sellers, vendors, and suppliers, as appropriate).
- Manage productivity and the schedule to ensure that the work is being done on time.
- Manage communication with all stakeholders, including timely and accurate reporting.
- Manage day-to-day activities and provide clear direction to team members.
- Review project status, comparing budgeted costs to actual costs and the value of the work performed (earned value analysis) on a regular basis (weekly is recommended).
- Manage the scope, budget, and schedule, and update them based on approved changes.
- Make recommendations and adjustments as needed to improve the project.
- Manage quality results to ensure compliance.
- Manage the change process and participate in the Change Control Board (CCB) to approve product/project changes.
- Document lessons learned, and implement approved process improvements.

Clearly defined processes and a firm understanding of inputs, tools and techniques, and outputs are great; however, in the real world of project management, something invariably gets in the way—time or cost constraints, resource turnover, skills or experience limitations, misguided (or distracted) project sponsors with unrealistic expectations, risk events, and so on. Therefore, managing projects in the real world is sometimes easier said than done.

There are many methods used to help PMs organize the work to help them direct and manage the project: things like checklists or standard guidelines and processes. As mentioned earlier, a process is a series of actions to bring about results. When it comes to directing and managing the work of the project, it is important to focus on all aspects of this process.

Try This

SKY'S THE LIMIT: PET PROJECTS ARE OUT OF SCOPE

You are a seasoned project manager for an international project, and the primary sponsor (director) is a good person who knows a lot about the project. However, he has his own "pet" subproject that is not funded and is outside the scope of the project you are managing. The director has asked you to write a proposal to get funding for his pet project, and he wants it completed as soon as possible. You are fully committed right now for your in-scope deliverables, and you politely explain to him that his request is outside the scope of your project. The director gets very upset and says you are not a team player. How do you handle the situation?

A. Write up the proposal to prove you are a team player and to get him off your back.

B. Hold your ground (be firm) in your position and remind him that his request is not part of the funded project, and you will not have time to work on his pet project.

C. Negotiate with the director and tell him you will write the proposal; however, you need more time on the original project from him in return.

D. Tell the director that his plan to get additional funding is a good idea and you will be happy to assist in the proposal when time allows; however, his request needs to go through the approved change control process to assess the impact to the funded project.

Answer: D is the best answer in this case. However, this is easier said than done because the director can impact your career and your future by telling others you are not a "team player" or even firing you. Unfortunately, this sort of thing happens occasionally when one plays by the rules.

If all project sponsors were easy to work with and stuck to the approved scope statement, anyone could be a PM. At the end of the day, you have to stand firm on managing scope and feel that you are doing the right thing—which may require you to update your résumé and be prepared for a change.

Manage Project Knowledge Process (Executing Process Group)

This process was added in the sixth edition *PMBOK* in 2017 and involves using existing project knowledge from the PM, team members, and other SMEs, along with any new knowledge that can be gained from previous similar projects, consultants, or specialists to achieve the project's objectives. As the PM, it is important for you to be available to the team and ensure they have the tools and information necessary to perform their work in a timely and accurate manner.

Figure 4.4 shows the inputs, tools and techniques, and the outputs for the Manage Project Knowledge process.

The PM, together with the team needs to share knowledge and experience to ensure project performance and achieve project objectives. Typically there are many years of combined experience on any given team, no matter how small. It is up to the PM to know the

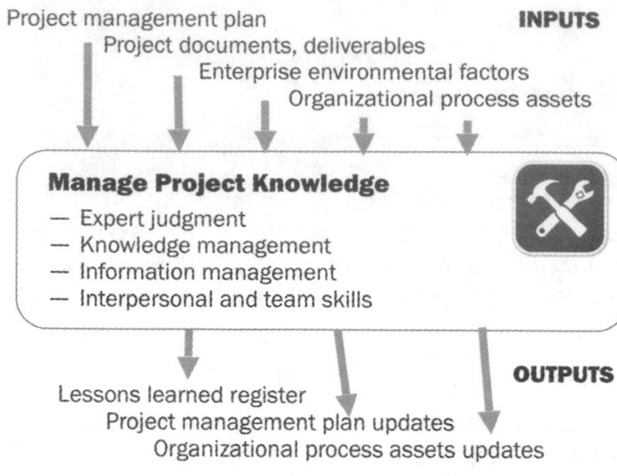

FIGURE 4.4 Manage Project Knowledge Process ITTOs

strengths and weaknesses of his/her team members and to engage them to gain synergy across the entire team. Managing the project should be a shared learning experience. A good thing to help with managing project knowledge is the use of a Project Management Information System (PMIS). A PMIS is an information system (often a software application or central electronic storage capability such as a team room, Dropbox folder, SharePoint server, or storage partition) that consists of standard planning documents, tools, and templates, along with processes and procedures laid out for easy access to the project team to organize and maintain control over the project. The PMIS is generally used to support all aspects of the project, which often includes planning documents and output documents; for example, meeting minutes, inventory reports, issue- and risks-tracking log, change request log, and other project knowledge that is generated throughout the project life cycle.

Monitor and Control Project Work Process (Monitoring and Controlling Process Group)

The Monitor and Control Project Work process involves tracking, reviewing, regulating, and reporting the progress of project activities necessary to meet performance objectives as defined in the project management plan. This process needs to be implemented early during plan execution to ensure that the project is on track. Many tools and procedures are available to assist the PM and team with this process.

The PM must constantly keep an eye on the project, team performance, change requests, the issues and concerns that surface, and the risk events that occur to ensure that the project is under control. The following is a simple list of some of the things the PM needs to watch for during the Monitor and Control Project Work process:

- Monitoring and controlling the quality of the deliverables of the project
- Comparing the actual project performance against the approved project management plan
- Assessing performance to determine if corrective or preventive actions are needed

- Monitoring risks and identifying, analyzing, and tracking new ones
- Maintaining timely and accurate status reports and updates to the information system (including up-to-date documents, version control, and audit readiness)
- Providing accurate forecasts to update the current cost and schedule
- Monitoring the implementation of approved changes as they occur

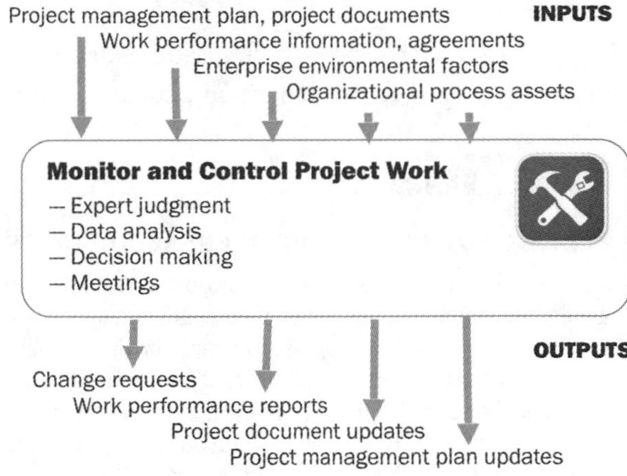

FIGURE 4.5 Monitor and Control Project Work Process ITTOs

Figure 4.5 shows the inputs, tools and techniques, and the outputs for the Monitor and Control Project Work process.

Monitor and Control Project Work Inputs, Tools and Techniques, and Outputs

As for the inputs, tools and techniques, and outputs of this process, there are only a few differences from the previous processes.

INPUTS

Some of the key inputs of the Monitoring and Controlling of project work are the work performance information (such as status reports, schedule activities and issue tracking reports, milestone report, etc.), project agreements, and standard project management documentation. Also important to this process are the schedule and the cost forecasts used to measure project performance and the standard inputs of enterprise environmental factors (such as building codes or regulatory requirements) and organizational process assets (such as standard forms or templates) to be used for consistency within your department or organization.

TOOLS AND TECHNIQUES

Some tools or techniques that can be used in this process are *expert judgment*, which is used to interpret the information provided by the Monitoring and Controlling processes so the PM (in collaboration with the team) can determine any actions required to ensure that the project performance matches approved requirements and sponsor expectations.

OUTPUTS

The outputs for this process focus on work performance reports, change requests, and updates to the project management plan and other project-related documents, as needed.

Try This

KEEPING YOUR EYES WIDE OPEN: ACCURATE PROGRESS REPORTING

A project team lead (Joey) has reported for the last three weeks that he is 85 percent complete on a "test script" work package that he has been working on for the application test group. It appears that there is either no progress on this activity or Joey has failed to accurately update his report. However, when asked about it he replies with a definite, "Yes, progress is being made and I am on schedule," which should mean about 98 percent completion. The test group lead (Mary) says she has not seen any progress on the test script and that this activity is on the critical path of the project and will impact the end date if not provided. What do you do?

A. Request that Joey show you the test script and hand-carry it with Joey to the test group to verify it is usable for the upcoming test sequence.

B. Ask Joey to update the status report to accurately reflect the 98 percent completion.

C. Work out the details with Joey one-on-one and then schedule a checkpoint meeting with all appropriate team members to verify the current status of the script and its readiness for handoff to ensure there are no surprises.

D. Let it go because Joey knows people in high places and you don't want to rock the boat.

Answer: C. It is best to work out the details with Joey first and then meet with the appropriate team members (especially for activities on the critical path) to help ensure proper progress of activities, accurate reporting, and a smooth handoff of dependencies to meet the project schedule.

One of the key outputs mentioned during the Monitor and Control Project Work process is "change requests." Change requests may include the following:

- Taking corrective action to resolve a problem
- Taking preventive action to avoid a problem
- Repairing a defect in a project component (the action taken may be to repair or replace the component)

Perform Integrated Change Control Process (Monitoring and Controlling Process Group)

The key inputs to this process are the project management plan, other project documents, work performance reports, and, of course, change requests, along with the other standard inputs.

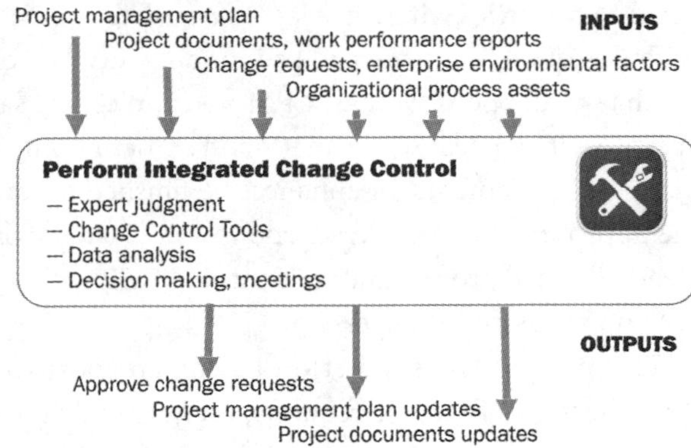

FIGURE 4.6 Perform Integrated Change Control Process ITTOs

The tools and techniques are the people who have the experience (expert judgment), the change control tools, and meetings. Outputs are the approved change requests (usually kept in a change log for tracking purposes) as well as updates to the project management plan and other project documents as appropriate.

The Perform Integrated Change Control process involves reviewing all change requests as well as approving and managing changes to the project deliverables, organizational process assets, scope, project documents, and the project management plan. The change process (like the risk management process) should be conducted early and often through the project life cycle.

Figure 4.6 shows the inputs, tools and techniques, and outputs for the Perform Integrated Change Control process.

Change Management Activities

This process includes, but is not limited to, the following change management activities:

- Ensuring that a change management system is in place to review, analyze, and approve change requests in a timely manner (including a request form, log, and work order)
- Identifying the people authorized to request and approve project changes
- Ensuring that only approved changes are implemented
- Managing and enforcing the change control process
- Coordinating changes across the entire project (e.g., a proposed schedule change will often affect cost, risk, quality, and staffing)
- Documenting and communicating the complete impact of change request
- Updating appropriate documents, deliverables, and activities based on approved changes

Importance of Change Control (Be Stubborn on Change)

I love to use the quote, "change is inevitable, except from a vending machine" (unknown source) when teaching my project management classes—it is always good for a laugh (except in some countries where it is lost in translation). One of my students even gave me a placard with this quote on it, which I prominently display for all to see (in my home office).

Change happens, and as a PM you can't "just say no." Instead, you must be willing to accept change because it is real—and sometimes it can even benefit the project, resolve regulatory requirements, or enhance the finished product (as long as the change is approved by the appropriate stakeholders/sponsors). Change control is best managed when you have a clearly defined process and an identified CCB with authorized decision makers to review and vote on requested changes.

This process focuses first on having an approved change process. The process involves the collection of change requests, logging and reviewing all change requests, analyzing the potential impact to the project, obtaining proper acceptance (or deferral/rejection) of the change, and last, making sure you document and communicate changes. Remember, change tends to have a ripple effect to the project deliverables, organizational process assets, project documents, and the project management plan itself.

Typically, there are two different types of changes:

- Changes that impact the project's constraints (and may increase cost, time, or scope)
- Daily operational changes, such as shift coverage, material adjustments, and so on, that may not impact the overall project's cost, schedule, or scope

Tip

All changes should go through a change control system—especially anything that potentially impacts the project's scope, cost, or schedule. All changes must be reviewed and approved prior to implementation. In the real world many PMs have a certain amount of authority in making daily change decisions without going through the full-blown change process. This can be risky, though—depending on the size, type, and complexity of the project; and the criticality of the project; as well as the trust and confidence in the project team.

Change Control System

The best way to manage change is to establish a change control system (an electronic tool or database is recommended) to more easily document, log, and track the change requests, and document the response action to the requests. This system doesn't have to be elaborate or expensive; it can be simple and should include at least these three components:

- A request form (keep it simple—a one-page request form in the project team room)
- Tracking log with response (can be an ordinary spreadsheet)
- Work order (requirements, direction, response strategy, guidance, and back-out plan)

Response actions in the tracking log are typically one of the following:

- Accept
- Reject
- Defer (postpone)

Tip

The most important action for all changes is to document and communicate the response. The response action/status should go first to the requester and then to the team, so that everyone is crystal clear on the request and the response.

Also, in the change management process it is good to have categories or priorities of changes with an approved response time. Here's an example:

Urgency:

- **1 = Emergency change.** For example, one- to four-hour fix required if something is broken and impacts a high number of users. This could be a system outage, down network, out-of-service train, and so on.
- **2 = Normal change.** For example, three- to five-day response time, with accepted solution or work-around (temporary fix).

It is also important to track the results of a change to determine whether or not it was successful. If it failed, how will the results be tracked and reported? Usually, results are recorded in a standard template and reported weekly or at least monthly with action plans and future planned change activity.

The only way to manage change effectively is to have a regularly scheduled change control meeting (usually weekly; the meeting can be canceled if no change requests are submitted for the change review period). You should identify key representatives (authorized decision makers and SMEs) in the meeting to vote on the change requests and to identify potential risks or conflicts if changes are approved for implementation.

Tip

A single change may not pose a serious risk to the project; however, when coupled with or installed out of sequence with other changes, it could fail or cause other things to fail. Also, when unauthorized changes are forced into the system, they can catch you by surprise. If they are installed without going through the proper review and approval channels, this is a recipe for failure.

Try This

CRYSTAL BALL: FIX IT BEFORE IT BREAKS

You are the PM on a software application development project, and the IT manager (Bob) comes to you with a request for the installation of a new software product he just read about in a trade journal. Bob is so impressed with this product—the "Fix It before It Breaks" (FIBIB) Wizard—that he wants it installed on 500 laptops before the end of next week.

The normal change process takes at least two weeks, but Bob, who has been a good friend and customer, is asking you to expedite the change because it will make him a hero with his end users (customers). What do you do? Take a few minutes to formulate your response and then look at the following answer.

Answer: Politely sit down and say, "To ensure I get the request accurate, let's fill out the request form together. It will just take a few minutes, and it will give me the specifics to ensure we get this right. We will also need to discuss the level of urgency because the change will need to go through the emergency-change process."

After reviewing the priority with Bob and questioning him on management approval, Bob decided not to submit the request. This was a good thing because it turned out he did not have approval from his manager to request the change, and the software product requested was "beta" (still being tested and not yet available to the general public).

The moral of the story:

- Follow the change process; and
- Ask questions to fully understand the importance, level of sponsorship from management, and level of priority of all changes.

Close Project or Phase Process (Closing Process Group)

Closing down a project or a phase of a project is as important as the startup/initiation phase. A project may have a predetermined "kill point," at which a decision is made either to stop the project or to continue into the next phase. An initial phase may be a feasibility study that would investigate the feasibility of the proposed product, service, or result. For example, it may be determined that the proposed product is not fundable (no budget) or is not marketable (limited demand). The closing phase would then document the reasons why the project was terminated.

Close Project or Phase Inputs, Tools and Techniques, and Outputs

The closing process involves finalizing all the activities across all of the Process Groups to allow you to formally close the project or phase.

INPUTS

There are many inputs to this process with the key inputs as always the project management plan (you must have a plan and stick to it unless an approved change causes a re-direct), the project charter, project and business documents, agreements, and accepted deliverables.

The project management plan is key because it is like a contract or service agreement between the PM and the project sponsor to ensure that the project meets its approved requirements and provides its deliverables. Part of the approved plan is any accepted deliverables, such as approved product specifications, and any work performance documents or reports, such as a project status report or an audit report.

TOOLS AND TECHNIQUES

One difference in the tools and techniques for this process compared to others is to use any analytical techniques needed to develop the process. Of course, the primary output in this case is the final product, service, or result of the project and updates to the organizational process assets as appropriate.

This process is the act of engaging expert judgment from SMEs to assist with the steps needed to successfully close the project or phase and using analytical tools (such as trend analysis or progression analysis) to determine the level of achievement or performance results needed to ensure a graceful shutdown of the systems and utilities, the release of equipment, and finding a home for the team. It also involves managing the communications, such as lessons learned meetings and celebration meetings, to reward and recognize the team members who helped bring the project or phase to completion.

OUTPUTS

Outputs for this process include the final product, service, or results, such as the transition of the finished product to production (e.g., a new software application product that has been tested and approved for launch can now be released or "promoted" to production, which means it is transitioned from a prototype to a customer deliverable product). Also included is the proper archiving of the project documents as intellectual capital for use on future, similar projects. Figure 4.7 shows the inputs, tools and techniques, and the outputs for the Close Project or Phase process.

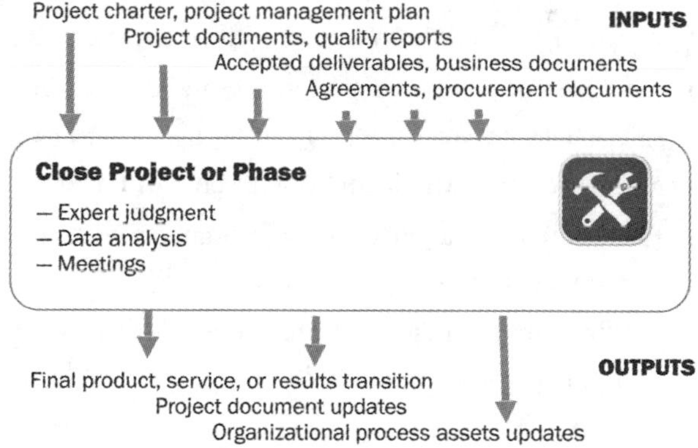

FIGURE 4.7 Close Project or Phase Process ITTOs

The closing phase should be handled as a project in itself. It oftentimes is difficult because the team members are aware the project is ending, and they want to focus on their next project. Most project teams start abandoning the ship toward the end of the project because no one wants to be the last person out the door. This attitude makes it more difficult to manage a project during the closing phase.

Ask the Expert

Q: Who is responsible for turning out the lights and closing the door on a project?

A: The janitor, right? Actually, it would be the PM. And, like a warranty period on a new product, a project should have a set time period for closing down, even after the lights are turned out and you think the doors are closed and locked. This period of time allows for any residual charges or delayed billings (invoices) that can come in after the project is complete. Time is needed to compile and report final performance and accomplishments to ensure assets and people have been officially transferred (to pay final utility bills, vendor services, and such).

The best way to effectively turn out the lights on a project and make sure you don't miss anything is to use a "project closeout" checklist. A good input to this checklist is the "startup" checklist you used when you initiated the project (assuming you have one). Closing a project is like opening it in reverse—but the closing phase should be more complete because you will have identified things along the way that have been added or that were missed during the startup phase.

You'll have numerous important considerations to make during the closing phase of a project, and the following list represents only a sampling of those things. The actual list you use will depend on the specifics of your project.

- Determine the targeted project close date, and develop a right-to-left plan schedule (back into the schedule by working from the must-finish-on "close" date).
- Close out all open action items, and develop action plans for any product deficiencies, open issues, and follow-up activities needed to satisfy the approved deliverables.
- Create a project closure document, and review it with the customer and team.
- Conduct a final customer acceptance meeting, and take meeting minutes (distribute and retain a copy of the minutes).
- Obtain customer and management formal acceptance of the completed project (in writing, if possible), and retain the acceptance document for audit purposes.
- Find homes (new assignments) for the project team members and project assets.
- Conduct a lessons learned assessment meeting (include the customer). Note that you should be collecting lessons learned throughout the project, not just during the project close phase.

- Close out any financial accounts or accounting charge codes.
- Assist as needed with any project delivery activities.
- Assist purchasing and contract administrators in contract closeout.
- Archive all project documents (ensure that record retention complies with company and outside audit or regulatory agency requirements).
- Celebrate success with the key stakeholders and project team.

A big dilemma during the closing phase is that there may be a mountain of documentation (paperwork) to go through, much of it old and outdated. So how do you handle this dilemma?

The answer is, get the team together for a casual-dress day, get a large shredder and file boxes, and then carefully go through and organize the documents, files, and such (you don't want to throw away important papers, but you also don't want to keep old documents that have been replaced or updated with newer versions). This is where electronic storage media comes in handy because it is small and easy to store.

Try This

PASS THE SHREDDER: CLOSING THE PROJECT IS SO THERAPEUTIC

Doug is one of your lead project coordinators on a ten-month project. There were a number of problems on this project, and the team was pushed hard to complete on time and on budget—which they did. After the celebration lunch, you go back to your office feeling pretty good about the successful completion—and there is Doug shredding all the project documents. You stop him and ask, "What are you doing?" Doug smiles and replies that he is closing down the project by shredding the project documents, and that it feels very therapeutic. What do you do?

Take a minute to formulate your response and then look at the following answer.

Answer: You stop him immediately, collect all the documents from Doug, determine which were shredded, and try to recapture them from soft copy (or other sources) to ensure that all key documents are retained for audit purposes. You inform Doug that the latest project documents must be stored in a safe place to ensure that you meet record retention and other business control and audit requirements.

In my experience, closing the project is one phase that is often neglected. You should plan for closing the project from the very beginning of the project. That is what project integration is all about—looking across the entire project (charter to close) and planning adequate time and resources for the all-important closing phase.

The biggest factor that may negatively impact the closing process is when the project was not clearly defined in the first place or may have experienced significant or uncontrolled changes. In many cases the project was not truly a project to begin with (i.e., it might actually have been ongoing operations or programs). If your project seems to be never ending, you might want to go back to the basic definition of a project (definite end date) and see if it still meets the criteria.

The closing phase of projects is generally where the gap between noncertified PMs and certified PMPs is the widest. Our natural instincts tend to be to wrap up the project as it ends. Often we forget about the length of the runway needed to gracefully shut down the systems, close the financial accounting, conduct lessons learned meetings, make arrangements for record retention storage, and, most important, obtain the "formal acceptance" (signoff from the sponsor or customer) of the closing phase of the project. Chapter 14 provides more details on effective project closure.

Summary of Project Integration Management

To summarize, project integration management should be viewed as the starting and the ending point of the project (charter to close). It is the PM's job to look across the entire project at a high level even before beginning to determine how to plan, manage, control, and effectively close the project or phase.

Remember, the processes associated with integration management are distributed across all five Process Groups.

Integration management is one of the tougher Knowledge Areas in real life and on the PMI exam, as it covers all aspects of the project throughout the project life cycle; it is not a sequential series of steps that you can address once and then move on. The steps are highly interactive with other processes and across all the Knowledge Areas. To be a successful PM you must be able to look forward, be proactive, be flexible, and adapt to the needs of the project stakeholders; you must be a professional problem solver who can think on your feet to respond quickly to risks, issues, and changes to the project environment.

It is important to remember that the PM is expected to be the overall project integrator (i.e., conductor of the orchestra, air-traffic controller, coach, and cheerleader) for the project. The PM should be diligent and be constantly looking at the bigger picture to reach successful completion of the project.

Also, remember that PMI expects the PM to be able to look at project management from a large project perspective that includes financials, contracts and procurements, risks, and scheduling, and to be able to forecast project and stakeholder needs for the best results.

Figure 4.8 shows how integration management maps (overlaps) the Knowledge Areas and Process Groups (also see the process map in Chapter 3 of the *PMBOK* and this book for process relationship details).

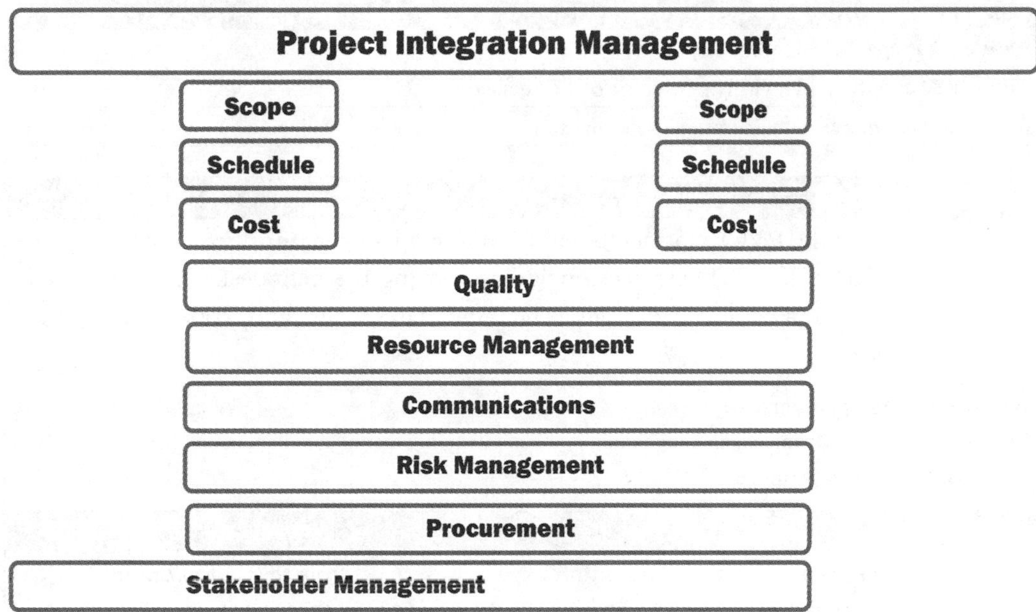

FIGURE 4.8 Integration Mapping to Process Groups and Knowledge Areas

Also, to aid you in further understanding the products of these processes, see Figure 4.9 (Sample Case Study Project Charter) and Figure 4.10 (Sample Project Management Plan for a fundraising event), which are provided as examples for these two project documents.

FIGURE 4.9 Sample Project Charter

P&G IT Transition Project Charter	
Project Manager:	George A.
Primary Sponsor:	David W., Director of IT Services, P&G
Document last edited: Date: March 1995, Version 3.1	

Project Overview

Proctor and Gamble (P&G) contracted with IBM to manage the transition of its employee Information Technology (IT) services, including moving the help desks (5) into a single Call Center to IBM in Boulder, Colorado. The target dates, goals, and scope of the project are detailed below.

Target Start Date: January 1995
Target Completion Date: March 1995
Address: P&G Plaza, Cincinnati, OH

Project Goals

The goals of this project are to fully transition IT support services from P&G locations in Cincinnati, OH, to IBM in Boulder, CO, within the approved contract period to ensure seamless employee support with minimal disruption in their day-to-day operations. The overall intent of this project is to "Outsource" P&G's IT services from Cincinnati to Boulder to allow P&G to focus on their core competencies (consumer product sales and research and development).

Project Description

IBM will develop a project management plan, schedule, and budget to accommodate this transition to include the following services:

Project Scope

1. Help desk consolidation of five P&G support centers into a single professional call center in Boulder, CO
2. Physical (wall-to-wall) inventory of all office equipment in 30 facilities of approximately 12,000 employees
4. Creating a central on-site desktop support network to service all P&G employees and client/servers
5. Vendor/supplier contract management of key support services with over 40 different companies

P&G is to provide detailed requirements and information as needed to allow IBM to meet all approved deliverables, milestones, schedule, and budget.

FIGURE 4.9—*continued*

P&G IT Transition Project Charter	
Project Manager:	George A.
Primary Sponsor:	David W., Director of IT Services, P&G
Document last edited: Date: March 1995, Version 3.1	

Stakeholders

- Project sponsor (P&G) including project executive (Lynn G.), transition PM (David W.) and other key contact manager and team leads and end users
    - On-site project team (including PM and IBM project executive)
    - Boulder support services departments (receivers of the support services)
    - Vendors and suppliers

Project Deliverables

Deliverables list for this project will be refined as the planning progresses and the needs of the clients and project team continue to evolve. Deliverables for the overall project may include, but are not limited to, the following:

- Overall project management plan
- Time and cost estimates with schedule of activities
- Associated permits: FCC requirements, move permits
- Logistics plan to stage and facilitate the physical move
- Staff attainment, training, and management
- Vendor and subcontractor selection process
- Both internal and external communications plans
- Deliverables relating to the subproject include those items mentioned above
- Contracting with all moving companies needed to relocate equipment and services
- Summary of the completed project, including lessons learned for proper closeout

FIGURE 4.9—*continued*

P&G IT Transition Project Charter	
Project Manager:	George A.
Primary Sponsor:	David W., Director of IT Services, P&G
Document last edited: Date: March 1995, Version 3.1	

Project Milestones

Project milestones and target dates will be determined through the planning process. They may include but are not limited to the following:

- Contract signed (3/1/1995)
- Project charter approved (5/1/1995)
- Project management plan approved (5/15/1995)
- Project kickoff meeting conducted (6/1/1995)
- Logistic plan and schedule accepted by client (6/15/1995)
- Vendor/subcontractor selection plan complete (7/1/1995)
- Communications and risk plans complete (7/12/1995)
- Staffing, training, and management plan complete (7/15/1995)
- Setup of the new help desk in Boulder (8/1/1995)
- Execution of the move (8/15/1995)
- Final training, testing, and start-up services verification (9/1/1995)
- Final cleanup and closeout, including project status and financial reports (9/15/995)
- Transition Project complete (closing); for example, all invoices paid, hand-off meeting with steady-state team for ongoing support and operations
- Staff recognized and transition complete party (ribbon-cutting ceremony)!

Sample List of Risks

- Lack of proper skilled staff and limited availability or training
- Customer dependencies not met in a timely manner
- Limited access to the customer employees during transition
- Unclear or changing scope and schedule
- Uncooperative or limited availability of supplier/vendor support
- Limited access to, or attainment of, needed equipment
- Staff turnover during key installation, testing, or training
- Adverse weather conditions during the move
- Other unknown events such as lost equipment

FIGURE 4.9—*continued*

P&G IT Transition Project Charter	
Project Manager:	George A.
Primary Sponsor:	David W., Director of IT Services, P&G
Document last edited: Date: March 1995, Version 3.1	

Project Budget

- Rough order of magnitude (ROM) estimate will be created for initial transition budget with more definitive budget at the halfway mark when more information is available; for example, all bids received, staffing complete.
- Monthly payments will be made by P&G starting with the first month period after the contract is signed.
- Penalties will be paid by IBM for missed SLAs per table provided in the contract.
- All approved vendor and contractor services will go through IBM with direct "pass-through" billing for all approved invoices, which are to be paid within 60 days of services rendered.

Closing the Project

The project will be considered complete when the approved scope of services is complete and formally accepted by P&G representatives. The IBM project team will take the time to properly close the project to include the following actions:

- Provide a closing management plan including schedule, cost, risks, and communications plan for review and approval prior to the work beginning to close the project(s).
- Obtain scope and deliverables validation and acceptance at approved checkpoints.
- Conduct final testing to ensure all systems are working properly prior to transition handoff to the ongoing operations team.
- Conduct a lessons learned meeting to capture what worked and what needs to be improved for future similar projects and delivery of a final project status report.
- Obtain final acceptance (formal signoff) of the project.
- Celebrate the project, project team, and vendors.

Project Charter Acceptance

P&G Project Executive Approval	Date
IBM Project Executive Approval	**Date**
Project Manager Approval:	**Date**

FIGURE 4.10 Sample Project Management Plan

	Cat Wranglers	**PROJECT SCOPE STATEMENT** *Rev. 2.1, 1/27/2017*

Note: Any work not explicitly included in the *Project Plan Statement* is implicitly excluded from the project.

Project Name:	Boulder Pedal 4 a Paws
Prepared by:	Carolyn K.
Date (MM/DD/YYYY):	01/27/2017

Version History (*insert rows as needed*)		
Version	Date (MM/DD/YYYY)	Comments
1.0	1/27/2017	Develop initial PM Plan draft—Carolyn K.
1.1	1/29/2017	Suggested edits from Simone G.
1.2	1/30/2017	Reviewed changes with team members
1.3	2/1/2017	Plan submitted for review and approval

1. Executive/Project Summary
Provide below a brief overview of this project (e.g., project purpose and justification):
The Boulder Pedal 4 a Paws is a bicycle race benefiting the Humane Society of Boulder County. It raises funds for homeless pets through private donations, corporate donations, rider sponsorship, and rider/team fundraising efforts. The donations will be used to add an expanded wing to the current facility as well as to fund future outreach programs for spaying/neutering pets.
1.1 Business or Project Objectives, Product Description, Planned Solution (e.g., problem to be solved or product to be delivered)
Raise $300,000 for the Humane Society of Boulder County.
1.2 Business Objectives (goals and benefits of the project to the organization)
With the money raised, the Humane Society of Boulder County will be able to execute plans to expand their current facility and to fund future outreach programs for spaying/neutering pets.

FIGURE 4.10—*continued*

	**Cat Wranglers**	**PROJECT SCOPE STATEMENT** *Rev. 2.1, 1/27/2017*

2. Project Scope
Brief overview of this project scope:
The scope of Boulder's Pedal 4 a Paws bicycle race includes planning, design, communication plans for and about the event, implementation, and closing of the event. This event will meet or exceed the fundraising goals as established in the project charter. Project completion will occur once the Humane Society receives the final donation check and all financial reports are completed and submitted for approval.
2.1 Project Scope Details
Includes (List Primary Deliverables) • Overall project management plan • Time and cost estimates to cover logistics • Route map and associated permit applications • Both internal and external communications plan • Vendor and subcontractor selection process • Logistics plan including schedule, locations of rest stops, Emergency Medical Team (EMT) support plan, vendor location layout, entertainment, etc. • Volunteer recruitment, training, and management plan • Execution of event schedule by assignments • Summary report, including financials
Does not include (out-of-scope exclusions) • Actual construction of the Humane Society's addition and expansion of spay/neuter program • Any additional communications/publications for sponsors/vendors not related directly to the race • Tents and vendor-related supplies • Rider and volunteer transportation to and from the event
2.2 Project Completion Criteria (what has to be provided to meet project successful completion)
• Completed bike race including teardown and cleanup • All donations received and accounted for • All invoices paid and reconciliation of all financials • Present final check to the Humane Society of Boulder County • Conduct lessons-learned project meeting (what worked and what needs work?) • Present final project status (including any after-action items for follow up) • Recognize and reward the team (celebration meeting or event) • Finalize all project documents and post them in the project control book (archive)

FIGURE 4.10—*continued*

	**Cat Wranglers**	**PROJECT SCOPE STATEMENT** *Rev. 2.1, 1/27/2017*

2.3 External Dependencies (such as client requirements, vendor/supplier deliverables)
• Permit approvals • Sponsorship agreements • Vendor and supplier contracts • Volunteers
2.4 Assumptions (customer to provide ongoing support when the project is complete, materials will be provided in English only, subcontractor provides their own tools, etc.)
• Sponsors will provide their own product booths, workforce, signage (banners), and cleanup. • Vendors and subcontractors are responsible for their own setup and cleanup of areas; they will have their own tools and materials. • Riders will provide their own riding gear and bicycles (minus assigned numbers). • Appropriate number of volunteers will be available and properly trained prior to race day. • The majority of riders will pre-register for the event prior to race day. • Boulder County Fairgrounds has enough parking/overflow to accommodate riders, spectators, staff/volunteers, vendors, etc. • Materials including route map will be provided in English only (with the exception of ADA-required accommodations).
2.5 Constraints (limitations such as schedule, budget, resources, or quality measures, etc.)
• The race will only be able to handle a maximum of 8,000 riders. • The project cost should not exceed $100,000. • Volunteer resources will be limited. • Training resources for volunteers will be limited. • There are many worthy organizations to which people can donate. We will be competing with other charities for support as well as competing with other bike races for participants.

FIGURE 4.10—*continued*

	**Cat Wranglers**	**PROJECT SCOPE STATEMENT** *Rev. 2.1, 1/27/2017*

3. Project Milestones	
Estimated Schedules—List key project milestones relative to project start (Insert rows as needed)	
Project Milestone	Target Date (MM/DD/YYYY)
Project plan accepted by client	02/05/2017
Route planning and mapping	02/13/2017
Permits received	03/01/2017
Implement the communications plan	03/15/2017
Vendor/subcontractor selection	03/18/2017
Logistics plan accepted by client	03/22/2017
Finalization of additional project sponsors	04/01/2017
Completion of volunteer recruitment and training	05/01/2017
Execution of the event and donation of proceeds check	06/22/2017
Cleanup including financial accounting	06/22/2017
Project closing – present check to Humane Society	07/01/2017
Lessons-learned meeting complete	07/12/2017
Final project status presented and approved	07/14/2017
Final project documents updated and archived	07/15/2017

4. Project Approach (how the project will be managed)
4.1 Primary Plans—Will the project have formal written plans—formal change control, shared project schedule, budget, quality measures, risk plan and issues tracking, etc.? Describe briefly in the space below.
We will have a SharePoint site folder set up that holds all documents related to the project.
• Documents section: project charter, project management plan, minutes, etc. • Changes workflow request: People will be able to submit their change requests at this location. They will be able to add details and priority levels. It will then be reviewed and approved/denied by the project manager, given an appropriate due date, and assigned to the appropriate project team member. • A dashboard will highlight the pending tasks, current budget, and issues. • Schedule section: A Gantt chart will be created that will help monitor current tasks and associated subtasks.

FIGURE 4.10—*continued*

	**Cat Wranglers**	**PROJECT SCOPE STATEMENT** *Rev. 2.1, 1/27/2017*

Briefly describe how each of the following will be handled. Provide links to relevant documents as appropriate. Modify example text provided or enter your own text to explain how you plan to manage your project.
Review the sample list of focus areas below and update the information for your project
4.2 Risk/Issue Management
• Project-related issues and risks will be identified, tracked, prioritized, assigned, resolved, and communicated in accordance with the project management methodology. Issues will be tracked on the SharePoint server site.
4.3 Change Management. The change control procedures as documented in the change management plan will be consistent with the project management methodology and consist of the following processes:
• A change request log will be established by the project manager to track all changes associated with the project effort. • All change requests submitted via change request form on the SharePoint site will be assessed to determine possible alternatives and costs. • Change results will be tracked and reported on a weekly basis.
4.4 Communication Management. The following strategies have been established to promote effective communication within and about this project. Specific communication policies will be documented in the communication plan.

• Project manager will provide a written status report to the project sponsors on a monthly basis and distribute the project team meeting minutes. Or the documents will be placed in the project team room folder.
  ◦ All urgent issues will be brought to the sponsor's immediate attention via email or a phone call.
  ◦ Minor issues will be reviewed by the PM, and they will assess whether or not they need to be brought to the sponsor's attention.
• Project team will have weekly status meetings to review completed tasks and determine current priorities. Minutes will be kept on meetings.

4.5 Resource Management. The project management team will produce a resource management plan that will document the following:
• Indicate which goods and services will be obtained from sources outside the organization and who is assigned to the project and when.

FIGURE 4.10—*continued*

	**Cat Wranglers**	**PROJECT SCOPE STATEMENT** *Rev. 2.1, 1/27/2017*

5. Authorizations (Modify lists as needed)
This section identifies the approvers/decision makers on the project that should review key documents such as the scope statement, WBS, project schedule, risk management plan, staffing plan, communications plan, and project budget for buy-in/signoff: • Project sponsor • Project manager Project deliverables will be approved/accepted by the • Project sponsor • Key stakeholder(s)
Specific task responsibilities of project resources will be defined in the Responsibility Assignment Matrix (RAM) or RACI table.

6. Project Management Plan Approval/Signatures/Date			
I have reviewed the information contained in this Project Scope Statement and agree:			
Name	Role	Signature	Date (MM/DD/YYYY)
Pets 'R' Us	Project Sponsor		
Cat Wranglers (Pedal 4 a Paws)	Project Manager		
Humane Society of Boulder County	Key Stakeholder / Benefactor		

References

1. "Methodology," usage notes, *Merriam Webster*, https://www.merriam-webster.com/dictionary/methodology, accessed February 2017.

2. CVR/IT Consulting LLC, by Dr. Gary Evans, http://www.cvr-it.com/PM_Templates/, accessed February 2017.

3. Ibid., Project Charter Lite template.

4. See Bruce Tuckman's model on team development, described in an article by M. K. Smith, "Bruce W. Tuckman: Forming, Storming, Norming, and Performing in Groups," *InfEd: The Encyclopedia of Informal Education* (2005), http://infed.org/mobi/bruce-w-tuckman-forming-storming-norming-and-performing-in-groups/, accessed February 2017.

5 Project Scope Management

Key Skills & Concepts

- Importance of scope management
- Definition of scope management
- What are deliverables and milestones?
- The importance of clear completion criteria
- Scope management processes
- Difference between project and product scope
- How to manage scope on your project
- Who owns and should provide project requirements
- Ways to collect requirements
- Creating a work breakdown structure (WBS)
- Avoiding scope creep and scope leap
- Summary of project scope management

As the project manager (PM) on a large project many years ago, I was conducting a kickoff meeting and presenting the scope statement to the team when the project executive sponsor spoke up and said, "Hold on! Scope is a mouthwash, and we don't talk about it to the customer!" He went on to say, "Whatever the customer wants, they get it, as long as they are willing to pay." Knowing the importance of scope management, I cringed and had the feeling of being on a ship that was rolling on very high waves with no sign of land in sight.

My response to the executive was a bit abrupt when I stated, "Scope is not a mouthwash, and yes, we do need to talk about it." The executive said, "If the customer is willing to pay, we will do whatever they ask." Because I didn't want to make a scene in front of the team,

I chose to ease up and approach him later (one-on-one). When I spoke to him about the importance of scope management, he wouldn't budge. It was his customer and his project after all, and he had the final word. He was the boss, and the boss may not always be right, but the boss is always the boss, right? The executive's decision made it painfully clear that the scope of the project was going to be wide open. The next step was to take a deep breath and look at the potential impact to the project, the team, and the customer. For a brief moment my gut was saying, "Update your résumé and move on!" However, PMs are not quitters. As a team we pulled together and performed an impact analysis based on the number of requests already received from the customer. Based on these results, I made the decision to seek out and obtain a temporary change management tool (database) and called a meeting to implement a control process to track the change requests.

In the change meeting we introduced a very simple (three-step) change process to the executive, the customer management, and the project team. Everyone agreed the process was needed, and weekly meetings would be implemented to review and approve changes to help manage the process. We captured the minutes of the meeting, which included a list of attendees, details of the process, and formal approval to implement the change process. We also included an explicit disclaimer that stated that if any information had been misstated or omitted in the document, corrections or suggestions needed to be submitted within five business days, and the lack of response within that time would imply acceptance of the document as written.

The minutes were communicated, distributed, and posted in an electronic team room folder, and the approved process was implemented immediately.

At first the change process was a little difficult for everyone to get used to, but all agreed that it was the right thing to do. Before long it became a habit.

As expected, the changes did flow, and at the end of the first three months of the project, we had 40 pages of requests in the tracking log. I called another meeting and raised the red flag as to the impact on the team, the delays caused by the high number of changes, and the additional cost in terms of person hours to keep track of all the change requests. The executive acknowledged the need for additional resources and allowed us to bring in a full-time change control coordinator to manage the many requests. That helped; however, the PM and project team were distracted with all the changes that continued to come in, and soon the project schedule slipped and costs soared.

At the end of six months, the customer's chief financial officer (CFO) raised a big red flag to the chief executive officer (CEO) on the additional cost, which turned out to be 30 percent higher (several million dollars) than the original approved budget. The CEO called for an independent (external) audit of the project. The project team was interviewed extensively by the auditors, and the change process and minutes of meetings were reviewed as well. The saving grace was the fact that we had a documented and approved change control process that was being managed and enforced. Because of this finding, the auditors ruled in favor of the project team. As a result of the finding, the customer CEO made significant changes (he fired the top three change requesters) and set tighter controls over who could request and approve changes. The number of changes went down by over 60 percent, allowing the project support teams to focus on the planned activities of the project, and almost everyone (except the managers creating all the changes) lived happily ever after.

We not only realized the importance of change and scope management but also the importance of keeping meeting minutes. The minutes from the meeting introducing the change process saved the day! They demonstrated that we had a plan and were working the plan to manage changes to the project. More details on effective meetings will be provided in the Communications Management Knowledge Area (Chapter 10).

Tip

To help ensure proper focus on and response to important documents such as minutes to meetings, I highly recommend using the following statement for meeting minutes and other important communications: "If any information is misstated or omitted in this document, please reply with corrections or suggestions within five business days. No response implies acceptance of this document as written."

Definition of Scope Management

Scope management involves the processes of defining and documenting all the work (and only the work) required to complete the project successfully. Scope is the essence of the project—it defines what the project is all about, the deliverables to be provided, and the foundation on which the team builds. Once the scope is defined for your project, it should be documented in a *project scope statement*, which is a narrative description of the purpose and objectives for the project as well as the specific business need or problem to be solved. The document should clearly state key contacts, key milestones (major events), the project target completion date, and so on. The next step is managing what is included and not included (exclusions) in the project scope statement. The last and most intensive part of scope management is the act of constantly checking to ensure that all the work is being completed and managed effectively to ensure the integrity of the approved scope of the project.

Project Deliverables for Scope Management

Deliverables are tangible products (usually stated at a high level) that the project will produce. They describe what the customer or project sponsor will get at key intervals and when the project is complete. They also state *exclusions*, or what will *not* be included in the project.[1]

Table 5.1 provides some examples of project deliverables.

Ask the Expert

Q: What is the best way to manage scope and deliverables on a project?

A: Once scope is validated, the best way to manage scope and the related deliverables is through an agreed-upon, documented, communicated, and enforced change control process.

TABLE 5.1 Examples of Project Deliverables

Includes	Design document for a new product or service
	Specifications for a new automation system
	A feasibility study for a product or project
	A customer-level procedures manual
	A user's guide or training manual
	A new voice response system for a call center
	Installation of standard lighting and sound equipment for a concert event
Excludes	Implementation of a new service
	Implementation of feasibility-study recommendations
	A user's guide available in other languages (English only)
	Training material provided in printed form (electronic form only)
	Maintenance or ongoing support of a new system
	No "backline" equipment for the concert will be provided without advance reservations

The project requirements should provide, or help identify, the key deliverables for the project. Several deliverables often lead to a milestone. A *milestone* is a major event on the project that (when completed) allows the project to move to the next phase. For example, a set of deliverables on a construction project might be (1) a set of blueprints from an architect, (2) a bill of materials (BOM) list of features, fixtures, and built-in appliances, and (3) the application for a building permit. All are deliverables that may be required to provide to city planning to obtain a building permit. Once the building permit is received, this is considered a major milestone that allows you to begin building the structure.

Note

Regular change control meetings (I recommend weekly) are essential to allow the PM and team to stay focused on scope, risk, and other key aspects of the project.

Project Completion Criteria

Project completion criteria may be listed by project phase, by functional department, or as a milestone. The criteria should describe what will be created in terms of deliverables and their characteristics. The completion criteria (sometimes referred to as "exit criteria") should also describe what will constitute a successful phase completion.

The scope statement should contain clearly expressed criteria for success, describing quantitatively what must be accomplished at the completion of the project (i.e., measurable results). A good rule of thumb is to have five to seven (maybe more on a large project) concisely documented criteria presented in a "priority" list or table that shows the expected results of the project.

Case Study: Sample Completion Criteria

Looking at our case study for the P&G IT services contract as an example of what project completion criteria might look like, you should get a better idea of how this works and the importance of clear completion criteria.

We first looked at the contracted scope of products and services for the project and then listed the high-level deliverables that, if done properly, would constitute a successful project completion.

The completion criteria are key to the overall success of the project because if unclear, the PM and team won't know what "done" looks like. In other words, how do you know when the project is complete, when the project should be complete, and by whom (subproject owners are assigned to ensure accountability)? As you can see in this case, a simple table or spreadsheet can serve us well in identifying the completion criteria, the measure of success, and who the primary owner is for that specific criteria item (see Table 5.2 for the case study example).

TABLE 5.2 Sample Case Study Project Completion Criteria

Priority	Criteria	Measure of Success	Owner
1	Complete physical inventory of all office equipment located at P&G facilities in Cincinnati, OH.	Final inventory report delivered to the customer (project exec.) by the due date and accurate to within ± 1%.	Project manager
2	Meet or exceed approved budget/ financials.	Meeting of approved budget within ± 1% and reporting monthly to the customer in the approved financial report format.	Project manager and business analyst
3	Obtain and set up a central warehouse to facilitate receipt of all new office equipment, setup, testing, and delivery of equipment to the end user.	Location and system in place to allow effective management of all equipment orders and prompt delivery of new office equipment to end users within 3 days of receipt.	Joe T. warehouse manager

continued on next page

TABLE 5.2—*continued*

Priority	Criteria	Measure of Success	Owner
4	Meet or exceed facility and equipment objectives.	No daily operational performance interruptions due to equipment or facility failures.	Operations manager
5	Have fully operational Call Center (Help Desk) ready to receive customer calls by approved "go-live" date.	Call Center set up, tested, and staffed to receive customer calls according to contracted services and able to meet service-level agreements (SLA).	PM and call center manager
6	Put all procedures in place to fully support client/server systems throughout customer network	Fully staffed support team on-site in customer locations to respond to and effectively maintain client/service equipment, including access and availability SLA agreements.	Client/servicer support manager
7	Develop and approve end-user training curriculum and material prior to start of training target date.	All training materials complete (in English only), instructors in place 4 weeks prior to pilot class. Classroom scheduled and pilot class ready for delivery by the approved state of training date.	Education program manager.

Note: a service-level agreement is a measurable goal or contract requirement to meet agreed-upon requirements such as the average hold time of 90 percent of customer calls to be answered within 90 seconds when received at the help desk (call center), or system/server availability of 95 percent during peak periods of usage, and so on.

In summary, the best way to document completion criteria is to look at the work to be done and then pick the top deliverables as measures of performance (MOPs). Review these with the customer and project sponsor; once approved, they become your approved completion criteria.

The processes for the Scope Management Knowledge Area are shown below:

Project Scope Management Processes

Six processes are included in the Project Scope Management Knowledge Area, and four of the six are in the Planning Process Group as listed below.

- **5.1. Plan Scope Management (Planning Process Group).** The process of creating a scope management plan documenting how the project scope requirements, WBS, and validation will be defined and controlled
- **5.2. Collect Requirements (Planning Process Group).** The process of determining, documenting, and managing stakeholder needs to meet project objectives
- **5.3. Define Scope (Planning Process Group).** The process of developing a detailed description of the project and product
- **5.4. Create WBS (Planning Process Group).** Involves subdividing the project into smaller, more manageable components

- **5.5. Validate Scope (Monitoring and Controlling Process Group).** The process of formalizing acceptance of the completed project deliverables
- **5.6. Control Scope (Monitoring and Controlling Process Group).** Involves monitoring and reporting project status and product scope as well as managing changes to the approved scope baseline

These processes and the processes in other Knowledge Areas interact with each other and are interdependent.

It is also important to recognize the difference between project scope and product scope:

- *Project scope* is the work that needs to be accomplished to deliver a product, service, or result with approved specified features and functions.
- *Product scope* is the feature or function identified, designed, and approved for the product that the project is to produce.

Tip

The processes used to manage project scope vary based on the project's size, type, and complexity and by the applications, tools, and techniques needed to produce the project's product, service, or result.

1. Plan Scope Management Process

The best way to ensure project success is to plan for it in the very beginning. Continue this process by creating a formal document (the scope management plan) to guide you and your team within your organization's expectations to meet your customer's requirements. This can be challenging because external factors will always exert a change influence on your project. However, if you have an agreed-to starting point (a contract with set requirements), you can manage these changes in a measured and controlled fashion. Consider this document your "how-to guide" for creating your requirements management plan and for managing the scope of your project.

Inputs to this process should start with an approved project charter. This will set the boundaries for your project and help you understand what is desired and what is not. As you progress through the planning phase, subsidiary plans should be used to update your understanding and control of project's scope. Always be sure to research your organization's process assets and lessons learned. This research could save you lots of headaches later on.

Tools and techniques for this process should include planning meetings and the use of subject matter experts (SMEs). These experts can help guide you and your team by helping you understand internal processes and learn how to leverage available resources. Take advantage of their knowledge and experience and never hold back from asking questions.

The outputs, as shown in Figure 5.1, are a requirements management plan and a scope management plan. Once approved, these documents should go under configuration control with changes managed by a change control board (CCB), covered later in this chapter.

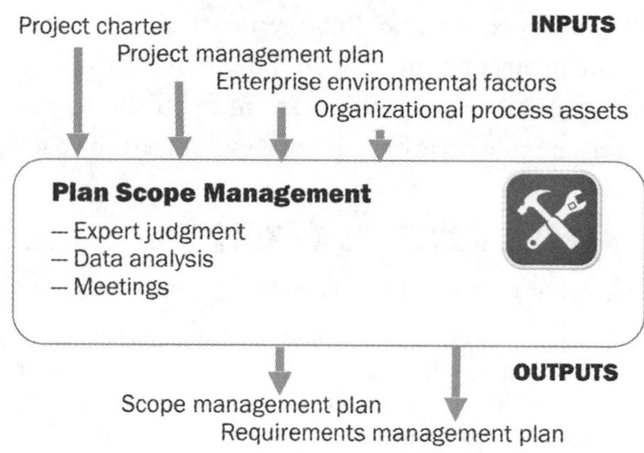

FIGURE 5.1 Plan Scope Management Process ITTOs

Scope is all about understanding what the project is and what the product or service is that your team is creating. Begin managing for success by controlling scope. Control scope by planning for it. Figure 5.1 shows the inputs, tools and techniques, and the outputs for the Plan Scope Management process.

2. Collect Requirements Process (Planning Process Group)

In my opinion the Collect Requirements process is one of the most important processes due to its negative impact on the project if not done properly.

One of the biggest reasons for project failure is incomplete or inaccurate requirements. The Collect Requirements process is one of 24 processes grouped with the Planning Process Group in the *PMBOK Sixth Edition*. This means it should be performed during the planning phase.

Gathering requirements can be an art form in itself. Because of this, and the importance of requirements to the success of the project, I will spend a fair amount of time on this process. Gathering and agreeing on requirements together is a fundamental step. Although their importance does not necessarily imply that all requirements need be fixed before any architecture and design are done, the project team should understand what needs to be built.

The best place to start with the Collect Requirements process is to look first at the project's goals. These goals represent planned outputs or results of what should be accomplished as a result of the project.

Collecting requirements should involve review and analysis of information and business/organizational objectives. What is it that the company or group needs done, and what does it expect at the end of the project? The answers to these questions should be the cornerstone of the project's scope. Requirements should match the scope, and the scope must map back to the project charter. (See a trend here?) By now you should be getting a better feel for how one process links to the next, and you should more fully understand the importance and interdependency of the inputs and outputs of each process.

Ask the Expert

Q: What is the best way to collect requirements?

A: The best way to collect meaningful requirements is through interviews. The trick is to interview the right people. If you talk to the wrong people, you may get skewed, bogus, or varied information and expectations, which will waste time and money. Also, interviews help to establish relationships and show that you are willing to listen and learn and that you care about the people involved in the project.

Q: How do you know you are interviewing the right people to gather requirements?

A: First, make sure you are talking to the key sponsors, end users, or other stakeholders who have a vested interest in the project results. Next, make sure the people you interview are knowledgeable about the project and expected results. Once you have the input from key sponsors and stakeholders, you need to document, communicate, and, most important, validate the requirements.

Remember, there are many techniques for conducting interviews. One technique may work well on a given day with a specific person but might not work for someone else in another circumstance.

Interview Techniques for Gathering Requirements

Good interview techniques for gathering requirements are "all in the approach," and because projects and project managers are unique, the approaches taken to collect requirements vary. To demonstrate this, I offer three distinctly different approaches, and you can pick which works best for you:

- **Open approach**, in which the PM and team have a high degree of trust and open communications. The PM frequently allows time for checking and rechecking requirements to ensure that they are clear and aligned with the deliverables of the project.
- **By the book**, in which the PM may be a bit rigid in the ways of collecting requirements. The PM sticks to the rule book (so to speak) and is somewhat resistant to change once the requirements are collected.
- **The "one-sided" interview**, in which the interviewer maintains eye contact and will ask only a few open-ended questions, allowing for pauses in the conversation that (it is hoped) the interviewee will fill in with additional information. This is an unusual but effective technique, and it does take some practice (unless you are the silent type already). This tech-

nique is rare and not recommended, but since I have seen it used a few times, I wanted to make you aware of its existence.

Too often time is of the essence, and we don't seem to do a good job interviewing people to learn about the details and expectations prior to initiating the project. It seems our interview tactic is more like this:

- **The impatient interviewer**, in which the attitude of the impatient interviewer is, "Who has time for interviews anyway? We know what this project is about and what to deliver, so why waste the time interviewing key stakeholders? Let's move forward; we can adjust later if we have to."

When not taking the time for properly interviewing the people most knowledgeable about the project, the PM and team are most likely get into trouble. It is best to take an open-minded approach and to learn about the project details for the best results.

Tip

Interview techniques tend to vary depending on the situation, how well you know the people involved, the location, and cultural considerations. For example, in Australia it is said that people don't care how much you know until they know how much you care, meaning Australians are wary of authority and of those who consider themselves "better" than others. According to the authors of *Kiss, Bow, or Shake Hands*, in conducting an interview, you should "be modest in interactions, and downplay your knowledge and expertise. Let your accomplishments speak for themselves."[2]

Another good approach (technique) to collecting requirements is to form focus groups or facilitated workshops to obtain valuable opinions and input (more details on these methods are covered later in this chapter).

Who Owns and Provides Requirements?

The project sponsor who is providing the funding or authorization to begin the project owns the requirements. This person is responsible for providing the requirements and expectations for the project. In some companies the project sponsor is also called the "champion" or "requester." No matter what name they go by, that person should clearly identify the desired product, service, or result (for example, a 10 percent increase in revenue, an 8 percent reduction in cost, or a 12 percent improved call center response time).

Requirements Should Map to the Project Goals and Objectives

The business or organization's goals and objectives will dictate which requirements are important. Also, requirements are best divided into project requirements and product or service requirements. The primary purpose for collecting requirements is to allow the project team to focus on what the project will deliver. The deliverables and the product, service, or result of the project must map back to the customer's business or organization's needs and expectations.

Business objectives can be described in two different ways:

- **Hard objectives**, which relate to the time, cost, and operational objectives (scope) of the product or process. Here are some examples:
  + Reduce event staffing expenses by 15 percent.
  + Reduce utility cost by 10 percent.
  + Reduce maintenance and operational expenses by $25,000 per year.
- **Soft Objectives**, which relate more how the objectives are achieved and which may include attitude, behavior, expectations, and communications. Here are some examples:
  + Improve customer service by developing a unique way for all staff to address guests when they arrive.
  + Improve the timeliness and accuracy of the building changeover process through improved communications and active participation by the team.
  + Improve intercompany communication by discussing event requirements one month in advance with all departments.

Try This

DEALING WITH UNUSUAL DEMANDS: THE CUSTOMER WANTS WHAT?

Entertainers are known for their unusual demands. For example, in the early 1980s Van Halen had a demand in his concert rider (contract) that said promoters had to provide M&Ms in the band's dressing rooms, and they had to remove all the brown M&Ms.

Lead singer David Lee Roth explains that at the time when the demand was made to concert promoters, Van Halen was one of the biggest acts in the United States and had one of the most sophisticated stage setups to work with. The "no brown M&Ms" clause was worked into their contract for safety reasons. The band and their management wanted to make sure that those in charge at each venue and the crews brought in to build their sets actually read through the tour rider—which gave all the specifications on what was needed to ensure everyone's safety. If they saw brown M&Ms in the dressing room, they knew the riders had not been properly read or complied with. (For Roth's video explanation of the no-brown M&Ms clause in the Van Halen rider, see www.npr.org/blogs/therecord/2012/02/14/146880432/the-truth-about-van-halen-and-those-brown-m-ms.)

There are many types of requirements, and most tie back to the needs of the business, opportunities to be capitalized on, or problems to be solved, or they help focus on improved quality. Most requirements are straightforward and easy to understand; however, two of the requirement types are worth more discussion: functional and nonfunctional requirements.

Functional vs. Nonfunctional Requirements

Identifying requirements can be like trying to nail JELL-O to a tree—it gets a little wiggly and the consistency tends to change with the weather. Let's look at functional and nonfunctional requirements.

Functional Requirements

Functional requirements are used to describe the capability of a product. They often describe characteristics that the product must have (or functions the product must perform) if it is to provide useful functionality for its operator. Functional requirements are typically stated in general, nonspecific terms. Here are some examples:

- The system will produce an updated easy-to-read report.
- The conference will educate suppliers on the product development process.
- The new data retrieval unit will deliver data faster than the old one.
- The vacation will be at the seashore to provide warmth and relaxation.
- The new doghouse will accommodate a full-grown St. Bernard.

Nonfunctional (Technical) Requirements

Nonfunctional requirements tend to revolve around areas such as service levels, performance, safety, security, regulatory compliance, and supportability. Nonfunctional requirements are often referred to as "technical requirements" or "performance requirements" that focus on the properties or features the project's product must have. They describe what the product needs to do so that it meets the functional requirements. Here are some examples:

- **Usability requirements (based on the intended user).** A newly trained call center service representative will be able to use the problem ticket-tracking system, with nominal errors or assistance. The audiovisual equipment directions in the classroom will be easy to follow.
- **Performance requirements (how fast, big, accurate, safe, reliable, and so on).** The new doghouse must be four feet high and have a 24-inch-wide door. The garment must be 100 percent waterproof during one hour of exposure to three inches of rainfall per hour.

Collect Requirements Inputs, Tools and Techniques, and Outputs

The inputs, tools and techniques, and outputs for the Collect Requirements process are shown in Figure 5.2.

Note

As a reminder, because all process inputs, tools and techniques, and outputs are shown in the *PMBOK*, I discuss only those that are new or have significant pertinence to the topics of this book's discussion. For a complete list of all processes and associated inputs, tools and techniques, and outputs, refer to the *PMBOK Guide, Sixth Edition.*

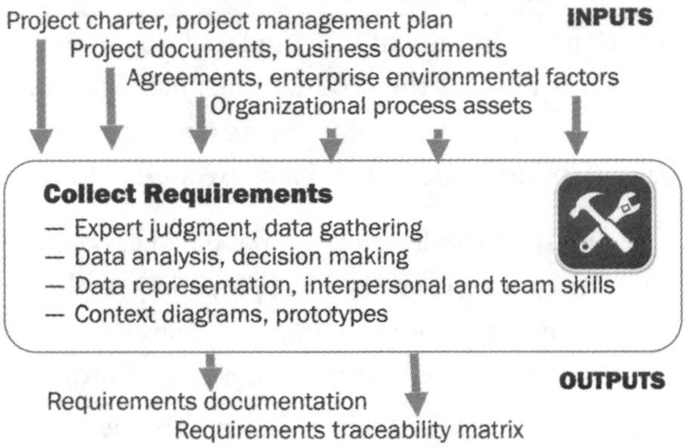

Inputs

According to PMI, along with the standard inputs, there are two primary inputs for the Collect Requirements process:

- **Project charter.** Used to provide high-level project and product requirement descriptions so that greater-detailed requirements can be developed
- **Business documents (including standard project documents).** Various documents are used as inputs to the collect requirements process to ensure alignment of the project objectives to the needs of the business or organization/agency.

FIGURE 5.2 Collect Requirements Process ITTOs

In the real world of project management, collecting requirements can occur at different times and may surface in different ways (casual conversations over coffee or lunch, in the hallway, during meetings, while reviewing processes, or as part of procedural documents). Therefore, it is important to listen more than talk during the requirements-gathering phase of the project. The information provided often becomes a valuable input and can be the difference between success and failure for the project.

Going back to the "Ready, Fire, Aim" dilemma discussed earlier in this book, we need to make sure we know what and where the target is before we can ever hope to hit it. We must take the extra time to collect and validate project requirements (i.e., we must aim before we fire).

Tools and Techniques

A number of tools and techniques are available to assist the PM and project team in collecting requirements:

- **Interviews.** As mentioned earlier in this chapter, there are many interviewing styles or techniques. Interviews provide a formal or informal way to collect information from stakeholders and are a great way to discover the "real" situation and the areas of concern, as well as what is working if the project is already underway.
- **Focus groups.** One form of interview is a focus group. It involves bringing together pre-qualified stakeholders or SMEs (people with similar and perhaps vested interests) in the project to learn their interests, preferences, concerns, and expectations. For example, a company is planning to build a new fitness center in a particular location and wants to get input from the residents of the local community to see what they would like in the way of facilities, child care, pool (or no pool), tennis courts (indoor or outdoor), hours of operation, available classes, and so on.
- **Facilitated workshops.** These are sessions that bring a variety of people together to discuss options, help define product requirements, build trust, and create or strengthen relationships on the project team, and, most important, improve communications. These workshops are sometimes called quality function deployment (QFD) workshops, joint application development (JAD) design workshops, or joint application requirements (JAR) definition workshops.
- **Group creativity techniques.** One or more of the following group creativity techniques can be used to help collect requirements:
  + **Brainstorming.** A good way for a group to generate and collect many ideas (uses synergy, where one idea helps generate another).
  + **Nominal group technique.** Same as brainstorming, only a voting process is added to help rank the most useful ideas for further brainstorming.
  + **Delphi technique.** Used to build a consensus of experts who participate anonymously. A request for information is sent to a select group of experts, their responses are compiled, and the results are sent back to the expert group for further review until consensus is reached.
  + **Idea or mind mapping.** Ideas created through individual brainstorming are consolidated into a single map to reflect the commonalities and differences in understanding to help generate new ideas.
  + **Affinity diagram.** Allows large numbers of ideas to be sorted into groups for review and analysis.
- **Group decision-making techniques.** An assessment process with many alternatives to help prioritize requirements. Here are some of the methods in this process:
  + **Majority.** Support is received from more than 50 percent of the group.
  + **Plurality.** The largest block of the group decides, even if it's not a majority.
  + **Unanimity.** Everyone agrees on requirements or the course of action.
  + **Dictatorship.** One person makes the decision for the group.

- **Questionnaires and surveys.** A written set of questions designed to quickly collect information from a wider audience.
- **Observations.** Involves usability labs, job shadowing, or other types of viewing to collect needed information or requirements from end users.
- **Prototyping.** Involves putting the early release (prototype) product in the hands of the user to see how it works.
- **Benchmarking.** Comparing your project or product to other similar projects. This helps you to understand industry and customer expectations better.
- **Context diagrams.** These drawings help illustrate the project scope by showing the relationships between the business need, how people interact with it, and the desired outputs.
- **Document analysis.** Never underestimate the value of research. By exploring what has already been done and written, you can save yourself time and money and avoid the pitfalls others may have already experienced. Document analysis can be performed just on project documents (business plans and marketing brochures), but it is best to explore other industry and academic sources to create a more rounded perspective.

Outputs

According to PMI, there are two outputs from the Collect Requirements process. The details of each are as follows:

- **Requirements documentation.** This details how requirements will meet the business need/opportunity or the solution to the problem the project is intended to address. The components of the requirements documentation include:
  + Acceptance criteria
  + Business need
  + Quality measurements and tracking
  + Organizational impacts (e.g., training and support)
  + Assumptions and constraints
- **Requirements traceability matrix.** This is typically a spreadsheet or table that shows requirements and the links to their source and traces them throughout the project life cycle.

Creating a traceability matrix helps ensure that each requirement adds business value by linking it to the business and project objectives. Because requirements are so important to the Project Scope Management Knowledge Area, properly using a requirements traceability matrix can provide a structure for managing change to the product scope. The matrix can include the following:

- Requirements to business needs, opportunities, goals, and objectives
- Requirements to project objectives, project scope, and WBS deliverables
- Requirements to product design, development, and test strategy

Some of the attributes (components) captured in the traceability matrix include a unique identifier, a description of the requirement, and the relationship to other requirements, as well as the owner, source, priority, version, and current status (e.g., active, canceled, deferred, added, approved, and date completed).

Managing Requirements

Once the requirements are validated and approved, the job of managing the requirements should be focused—unless, of course, there is turnover in the project sponsors, team, project funding (budget), or overall expectations. There are times when a project has a long duration, resulting in changes to the requirements or expected results. This is where the change control process is extremely important to combat scope creep or scope leap.

3. Define Scope Process (Planning Process Group)

The Define Scope process involves the development of a detailed description of the project and the expected product, service, or result. This process is grouped with the Planning Process Group.

The scope definition may be an iterative (evolutionary) process, starting with a preliminary scope statement and growing in detail as the project progresses and more information is known. In fact, the approved scope definition is the baseline (point of reference) for the project and should not be taken lightly. Some PMs are a bit reluctant or shy about setting the project baseline for schedule, cost, or scope. If you are using Microsoft Project as a scheduling tool, one option is to save a file as a *baseline*. This enables us to save this file as an approved point of reference to use for change management.

Tip

The quicker you establish an approved baseline, the easier it is to manage to that baseline. I have seen case after case in which a customer complains that the project is behind schedule, only to find that there were many approved changes that moved out the target completion date, but that the PM didn't establish or update the baseline. The customer often only remembers the original target date and does not fully appreciate how even approved changes are likely to move the project end-date. Because the PM didn't reset the baseline, the customer viewed the original completion date as being missed.

Define Scope Inputs, Tools and Techniques, and Outputs

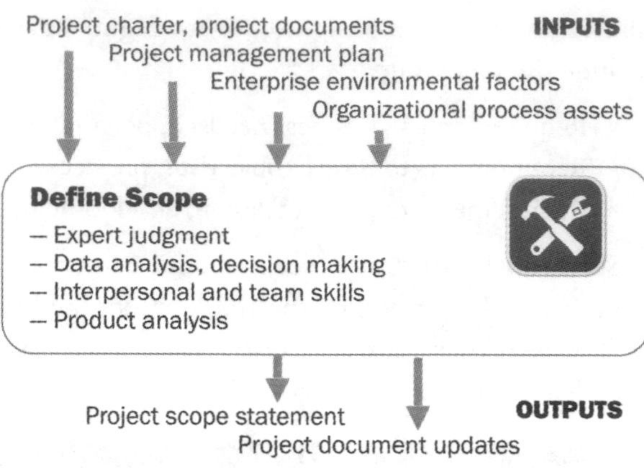

FIGURE 5.3 Define Scope Process ITTOs

Note that some of the inputs to the Define Scope process, such as the project charter (shown in Figure 5.3) and standard project documents, are the same for several other processes, which demonstrates their importance.

The tools and techniques for the Define Scope process often include expert judgment to help analyze the inputs. In this case we should also take a closer look at the product analysis and any alternatives or workshop findings that should be considered prior to finalizing the scope statement.

The outputs for this process are straightforward. The primary output of the Define Scope process is the project scope statement. However, project management is all about realizing that as we go further into the project life cycle, we learn more. After almost every process comes more knowledge and a clearer view of what needs to be done on the project. With the clearer vision, it is important to review and update project documents as appropriate. This approach ties back to the PMI term *progressive elaboration*, which is a technique for increasing the accuracy of plan documents and estimates as more and more information becomes available.

Note

PMI is big on the concept of *progressive elaboration* as a way to effectively manage a project; it is the iterative process of increasing the level of detail in a project management plan or other project documents as greater amounts of information and more accurate estimates become available. If you are planning to take a PMI exam, take note of this concept.

Project Scope Statement

According to PMI, The project scope statement is the description of the project scope, major deliverables, assumptions, and constraints. The intent is to provide a common understanding of the project scope so there is no confusion between project stakeholders.

The scope statement serves as a guide to the PM and team during the execution of the project. It should be used as a "working document," not locked up in a drawer or cabinet. It can be used for team member orientation to the project, to help answer questions, and for audits when they occur. The project scope statement is also an agreement among the project team, the project sponsor, and key stakeholders. It represents a common understanding of the project for the purpose of facilitating communication among the stakeholders. The scope statement includes relating the project to business objectives and defining the boundaries of the project in multiple dimensions, including approach, deliverables, milestones, and budget.

The best way to develop a scope statement is to use a template from a previous, similar project or from an experienced PM source. A number of great templates are available on the Internet (e.g., CVR/IT Consulting LLC at http://cvr-it.com/PM_Templates/) to assist you in defining the scope of the project and ensuring that you have the important components identified to render the scope statement useful in the scope management process.

Here are examples of some key components of a scope statement:

- **Executive/Project summary.** A brief summary of the project using the project charter or work authorization as its basis
- **Business or project objectives (business need/opportunity).** The purpose of the project and how it will benefit the company or organization
- **Project description.** What is in (and not in) the scope of the project
  + Proposed solution, deliverables, and completion criteria
  + Risks, constraints, dependencies, assumptions, and success factors
  + Roles and responsibilities (critical skills, high-level staffing plan)
  + Target date for completion
  + Exclusions (e.g., project documentation will not be provided in languages other than English)
- **Project planned approach.** Methodology to be used and implementation strategy
- **Project estimates.** Duration, cost, resources, hours, and so on
- **Project controls.** How the project will be measured, tracked, and managed (change control, risk management, issue management, and communications)
- **Authorizations.** Project sponsor/owner, approvers, version control, and reviewers
- **Scope statement approval signatures**

Tip

In many cases the contract, work order, or statement of work (SOW) will have all the pertinent information needed to identify the project and its major deliverables, key contacts, and constraints, to the point where these documents may serve as (or replace the need for) a separate scope statement.

Case Study: Scope Statement

Let's take another look at our case study and how the scope of the project was defined and managed by the service provider (IBM). The scope statement for P&G IT was based on the needs of the business, that is, outsource IT support services to IBM to allow P&G to focus on their core competency: consumer products sales and development.

The original scope statement was developed by the transition project manager using the signed contract as the basis of IT services to be provided. The preliminary scope statement detailed the requirements, deliverables, milestone dates, roles, and responsibilities for both the customer and service providers as well as the completion criteria outlining what needed to be done to get to successful completion of the overall project. Additional subprojects that were listed in the scope statement included unique deliverables and products of the project such as locating and leasing a warehouse for receiving new equipment, order-processing procedure for setup, burn-in testing of the new equipment and the end-user training when the equipment was delivered to the employee. The scope also included a physical (wall-to-wall) inventory of existing personal computer equipment at P&G locations, consolidating the five call centers at the customer locations to a central help desk in Boulder, Colorado, and managing a number of vendor/supplier contracts on behalf of P&G. The scope statement, once completed, was submitted for review and approved.

To provide a broader example, a sample scope statement for a fundraising project is shown in Figure 5.10, toward the end of this chapter.

Importance of Clear Language in a Scope Statement (Did You Hear What I Meant to Say?)

To demonstrate the importance of clear language in the scope statement, let's look at one of the many challenges that surfaced on the P&G case study.

The contract called for "End-user orientation" when all new office equipment was installed for an employee. The contract and project team interpretation of end-user orientation was the installer was to spend 15–20 minutes with the end user when the installation of new office equipment was complete to walk them through a brief introduction to their new computer. The orientation was to cover the startup procedures, system login, and other basic functions. The customer's interpretation of the word *orientation* was significantly different. They expected a full blown three- to four-day training for each employee prior to (or within a few days) of receiving their new equipment. P&G's viewed orientation as including very interactive hands-on training for every application on the laptop, including the Microsoft Office suite, call- and problem-tracking system access, and how to call the help desk for assistance, printer setup and testing, and so on. And all this training had be performed on-site in one of the formal classrooms at P&G's main offices in downtown Cincinnati, at which P&G charged $1,000 per day for classroom rental.

The good news is the customer provided great snacks in their classroom break area, but the bad news was the scheduling of classrooms was difficult as there was always a high demand and limited availability. On top of the $1,000 per day rental for the classrooms, we had to provide our own instructors, course material, and so forth.

So, between the misinterpretation of the scope, the added cost and time to develop the course curriculum and material, and testing and implementing a full-blown training program, the change in scope was significant. We ended up having to assign an education project manager to manage this new subproject because of a lack of clear understanding (interpretation) of the project's contract scope. Fortunately, P&G was very understanding and allowed us the extra time to develop the training and paid for a fair portion of the extra cost. The lessons learned from this case study proved that you must first clearly understand the scope (all aspects) of the project and then validate not only the initial scope statement but also the deliverables along the way. A good way to do this is by creating a clear work breakdown structure (WBS).

Create WBS Process (Planning Process Group)

In the world of project management, we often use breakdown structures (BSs), and the work breakdown structure (WBS) is one of the most-used BSs to manage projects.

So, what is a work WBS? The PMI answer is, it is a decomposition of the work to be performed on the project. In plain English, the WBS is a planning tool that helps the project team document the work (activities) needed to build or develop the identified and approved deliverables of the project.

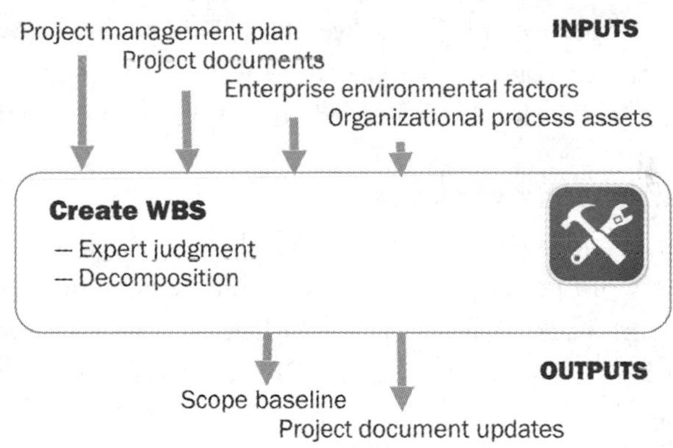

FIGURE 5.4 Create WBS Process ITTOs

The Create WBS process is located in the Planning Process Group and can be created at any time during the project life cycle. However, it works best at the beginning of the project. Figure 5.4 shows the inputs, tools and techniques, and the outputs for the Create WBS process.

Tip

> The WBS is a useful tool, and PMI views it as an important part of project planning and management. Therefore, you can expect a number of questions on the PMP exam regarding the WBS.

Here are some key points to remember about the WBS:

- It should be used on every project (and can be reused on similar projects).
- It identifies all the work of the project. (PMI feels that if the work is not in the WBS, it is not part of the project; therefore, you should view the WBS as the foundation of the project.)
- It shows the hierarchy of the project (groupings or categories) and work packages.
- It should be deliverables oriented. (It should be aligned and focused on project deliverables.)
- It forces you and the team to look at all aspects of the project.
- It should not show dependencies. (That comes later, in the Project Schedule Management Knowledge Area processes.)

Creating the WBS

Creating a WBS is the act of sub-dividing (decomposing, breaking down) the project into manageable chunks (or categories) of work, often called *work packages*, to accomplish the defined and approved project deliverables. This is why the WBS is often referred to as a "deliverables oriented" hierarchical decomposition of the total scope of the work to be performed on the project. It should be focused on and created around the project objectives and deliverables.

WBS WORK PACKAGE

The work package is considered to be the lowest level managed by the PM in the WBS. A work package may contain multiple activities. The benefit for the PM to manage at the work package level as distinct from the activity level is that the PM can better manage the summary work as packages. It requires less of the PM's time to manage at the work package level, because many projects end up with hundreds if not thousands of activities. If you manage at the activity level, you are too deeply involved in the details to manage the overall project effectively. You also need to give the team members some credit and allow them to manage at the activity level and to report statuses at the work package level.

At the work package level, it is also easier to schedule the work, assign owners, perform cost estimates, make duration estimates, and control the deliverables and phases throughout the life cycle of the project. Because the WBS is developed around project objectives, deliverables, milestones, and progress, reporting is much simpler as well.

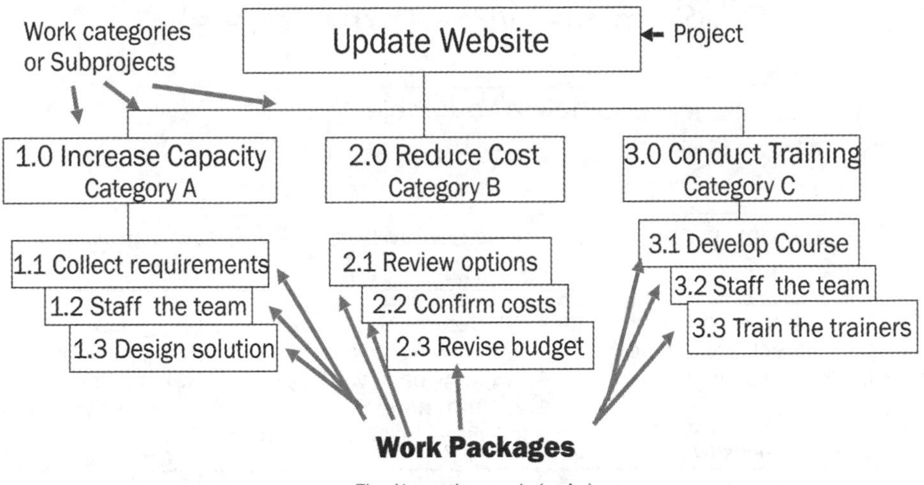

FIGURE 5.5 Sample WBS with Work Packages

The WBS can be created and shown in a number of different ways:

- Using major deliverables of the project as the first level of decomposition
- Using project phases as the first level of decomposition, with product and project deliverables shown in subsequent (second and third) levels of the WBS
- As a listed WBS using a numbering system, called a "code of accounts," to show the relationship and hierarchy, as distinguished from using a diagram view (which looks much like an organization chart)
- As a fishbone diagram, in the five Process Groups, as an outline, or in other form

Example of a WBS and Work Packages

Figure 5.5 shows a high level WBS with several work packages. Each work package can then be expanded later on by adding one or more activities.

Activities should be managed by the project team member assigned to a particular work package, and the PM should focus on the status at the work package level (see Figure 5.6).

Many project management authors talk about the 8-to-80-hour rule (or simply the 80-hour rule), which states that work should be broken into activities or groups of activities that can be performed within 8 to 80 hours (which translates into a one-day minimum and not more than two weeks). This range helps ensure that work is grouped in a way that is easier to track, report, and manage. This heuristic method (rule of thumb) is simply a guide or recommendation to think about the work of the project in a way that allows you to group the work so that it is easy to assign and easier to estimate duration and cost.

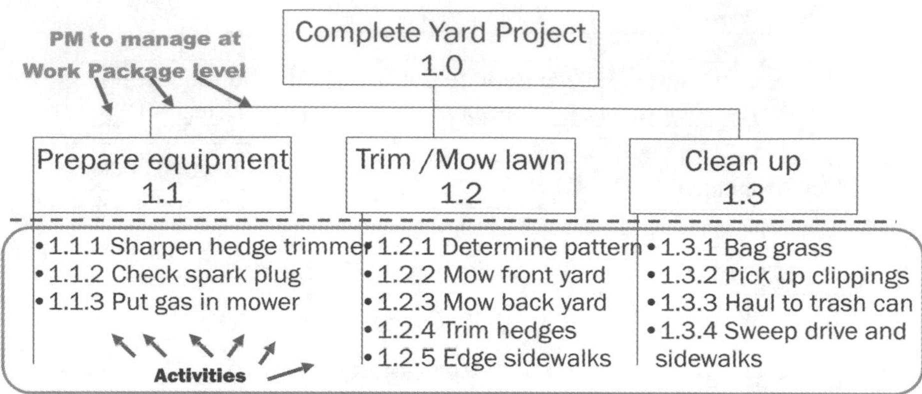

FIGURE 5.6 Sample WBS with Activities

If an activity takes less than eight hours, it is being tracked to a level far too granular (detailed) for the PM and perhaps even for the team member responsible for the work. If it takes more than 80 hours, it will span a longer duration, possibly not be tracked closely enough, potentially slip through the cracks, and therefore not be monitored and managed in a responsive time frame.

Note

Keep in mind that the 80-hour rule is just a "rule of thumb" recommendation; if the activities take more than 80 hours or less than 8 hours, then use logic and assign the realistic estimated time needed and disregard this rule. Other authors suggest up to 300 hours for a large activity or work package. The bottom line is the size of the work package or activity needs to be manageable in time and duration.

Sometimes the 8-to-80-hour rule is not practical, and it can be difficult to determine how much the project should be decomposed. There are no hard-and-fast rules. Generally the WBS should be decomposed until you have met these criteria:

- It has a deliverable.
- It can have time limits (i.e., a duration with start and end times).
- It can have costs assigned to it.
- It can have resources assigned to it.
- It can be used to track performance against cost, schedule, and resource allocations.

Creating the WBS Should Be a Team Sport

The best way to create the WBS is to get the team together and brainstorm using sticky notes, preferably placed on flip chart paper (you can tape several pages together if you need a larger space). This also makes the work portable, as you can roll up the charts and take them with you. Start with the deliverables from the scope statement, project charter, or contract. After the deliverables are listed, continue the brainstorming session to identify the work (activities) of the project for each of the deliverables. Group them in a logical order that will help you and the team better manage the work of the project. You can group by product, by project phase, or by function (e.g., design, develop, test, implement, and close project). If you are working on a construction project, you could create the WBS by stage, such as pour the foundation, frame the structure, install the plumbing, install the electrical, finish the trim, and so on.

The good news is, there is no set rule on how you create a WBS. The only recommendation is that you create it in a way that makes sense and works best for you and the project team.

Have Some Fun Creating the WBS

The process of creating the WBS can be fun and a great way to get to know the team in a relaxed environment.

One time on a project for a Fortune 500 company in Cincinnati, Ohio, we initiated the Create WBS process in a customer's home on his dining room wall. The day the contract was signed, several of the project team leads met for dinner and afterward went back to the host's home and created a WBS by filling his dining room wall with sticky notes. We even used different colors for the different key areas of the project. We had a good time and were able to get a great start on the project. We then captured the work from the dining room wall into a well-known scheduling tool (application software) for portability and for future updates.

Next, we showed the preliminary WBS to the team and entered the work packages into the scheduling tool. We then worked the project from the scheduling tool. As a last step, we assigned the work packages and deliverables to the appropriate team leads and key SMEs. They agreed to add the activities to the work packages, track to the detailed activity level, and report to the PM weekly at the work package level.

Another WBS Story: "Butterflies on the Floor"

Several years ago, I was called in to help jumpstart a project in southern California. The lead PM and I agreed that the best way to start this project was by creating the WBS. We used sticky notes to identify the activities (work packages) needed on a new strategic outsourcing contract. We filled his office wall with the sticky notes and used a numbering system to identify the activities and deliverables. After about nine hours the first day, when we were at a good stopping place, we called it a day.

The next morning, we found all the sticky notes lying on the floor. The paint on the office wall was old, and the sticky notes were unable to hold. There was our work from the day before, resting like butterflies on the floor. I could envision the notes slowly releasing in the night one by one and drifting to the floor. The only thing that saved us was the numbers on the notes, which allowed us to reconstruct the WBS in about an hour (this time, however, we used taped-together sheets of flip-chart paper, so we could roll everything up and take it with us at the end of each day).

Tip

It is best to put the results of the Create WBS process into a scheduling tool or some other digital media prior to going home to ensure that you don't lose the work. I have seen cases in which the WBS was created on a whiteboard or on a conference room wall and the cleaning people erased it that night. (In one case, they cleared the wall of sticky notes. Ouch!) A friend of mine is always quick to use the camera on his cell phone. He takes a snapshot of the WBS whiteboard in stages of development and then immediately distributes it via email.

WBS Dictionary

The WBS dictionary, when combined with the WBS and the scope statement, is part of the scope baseline, which is an output of the Create WBS process. Just as you would think, a WBS dictionary is a document generated by this process that supports the WBS. The dictionary provides a more detailed description of the activities in the WBS. It provides a clear description of the work to be done for each WBS work package and helps make sure the resulting work better matches what is needed. Therefore, the PM uses this tool to prevent scope creep. Here are some of the components that can be built into the WBS dictionary:

- Number identifier and related control account (for tracking and cost)
- Work package description
- Resources assigned (who is responsible for doing the work)
- Deliverables for the work in the work package
- Assumptions, interdependencies, and expected duration
- Schedule milestones (major events)
- Due date and approved by signature field

The WBS dictionary includes work packages and control accounts. It can include account codes (numbering system or a chart of accounts) that identify work packages and a detailed

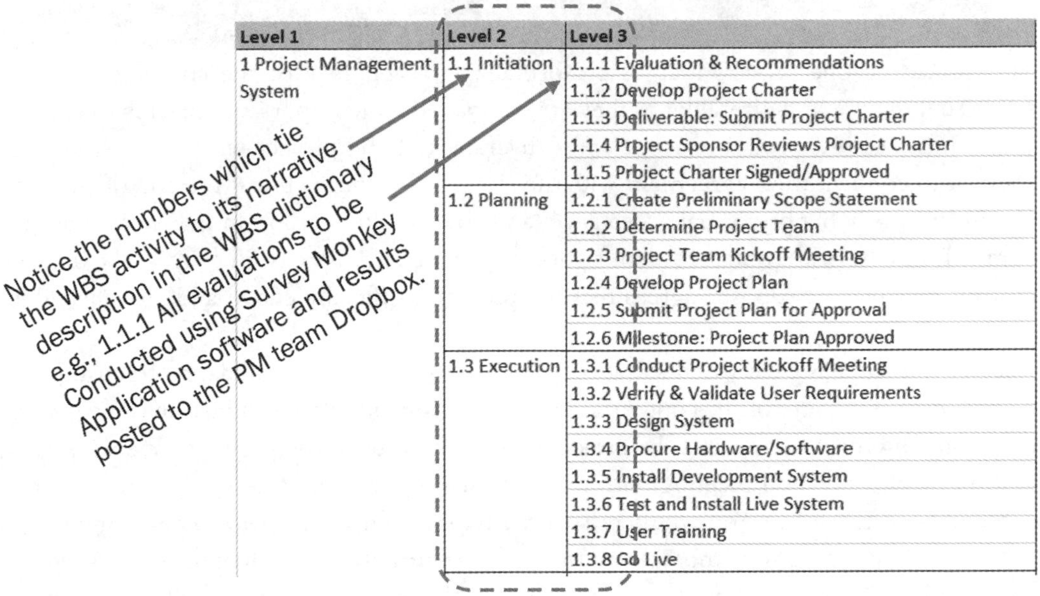

Level 1	Level 2	Level 3
1 Project Management System	1.1 Initiation	1.1.1 Evaluation & Recommendations
		1.1.2 Develop Project Charter
		1.1.3 Deliverable: Submit Project Charter
		1.1.4 Project Sponsor Reviews Project Charter
		1.1.5 Project Charter Signed/Approved
	1.2 Planning	1.2.1 Create Preliminary Scope Statement
		1.2.2 Determine Project Team
		1.2.3 Project Team Kickoff Meeting
		1.2.4 Develop Project Plan
		1.2.5 Submit Project Plan for Approval
		1.2.6 Milestone: Project Plan Approved
	1.3 Execution	1.3.1 Conduct Project Kickoff Meeting
		1.3.2 Verify & Validate User Requirements
		1.3.3 Design System
		1.3.4 Procure Hardware/Software
		1.3.5 Install Development System
		1.3.6 Test and Install Live System
		1.3.7 User Training
		1.3.8 Go Live

Notice the numbers which tie the WBS activity to its narrative description in the WBS dictionary e.g., 1.1.1 All evaluations to be Conducted using Survey Monkey Application software and results posted to the PM team Dropbox.

FIGURE 5.7 WBS Dictionary Relationship to the WB

description of the work; in some cases it even identifies the responsible organization, though that component usually falls into the organization breakdown structure (OBS). It may also have a list of schedule milestones, quality requirements, and technical references, along with key contact information as it relates to the WBS. Figure 5.7 shows the WBS dictionary relationship to the WBS.

It has been my experience that the real-world applicability of the WBS dictionary is that it is used more often on larger, more complex projects with many different applications and the need for more detail at the work package level. However, the WBS dictionary can be used on projects of all sizes. According to Rita Mulcahy's PMP Exam Prep, the WBS dictionary can be used as part of a work authorization system to inform team members of when their work package is going to start. The WBS Dictionary describes the schedule milestones, acceptance criteria, durations, interdependencies, and other information about the work package. You can also use it to control what work is done when, prevent scope creep, and increase stakeholders' understanding of the effort required for each work package. The WBS dictionary essentially puts boundaries on what is included in the work package (similar to the way the project scope statement puts boundaries on what is included in the project).[3]

5. Validate Scope Process (Monitoring and Controlling Process Group)

The Validate Scope process focuses on formalizing acceptance of the completed project scope statement and deliverables as they are completed. One important aspect is validation, which includes reviewing the scope and deliverables of the project with the customer or sponsor to confirm their agreement with the needs to be completed at the end of the project. PMI is really big on formal acceptance (and you should be, too). In many cases project completion letters are obtained with signed acceptance by the customer to show that the customer or project sponsor agrees that the project is officially ended and all deliverables have been met.

Once the scope is clearly defined, it is up to the PM and team to validate it to ensure that everyone is fully aware of the content and that it is attainable. Scope validation is the process of comparing the work against the project management plan, the project scope statement, and the WBS, and then meeting with the customer and project sponsor to obtain formal acceptance of the scope. You would be surprised how often this step is not performed.

Often we are either too embarrassed to ask for confirmation (it will make us look like we were not listening) or too busy to stop and confirm the scope of the project. Then if you add in changing or unrealistic customer expectations, it makes for a moving target. The result is a failed project due to unclear or un-validated scope. We end up building the wrong product or the right product with the wrong features.

Ask the Expert

Q: Everyone on our project team knows the scope of the project, so why do I need to bother with scope validation and formal signoff from the customer or sponsor?

A: If the scope is clearly understood, then getting validation and signoff from the customer or sponsor should be easy. However, with the dynamics of most projects, there frequently are deliverables that were not clearly understood or communicated to the PM. There may also be subprojects or activities that the customer is expecting from you that were not part of the original scope. These sometimes surface only when you ask for formal signoff or validation from the customer or project sponsor.

The best way to approach the customer/sponsor to obtain scope validation is to set up a meeting for a time when no one is rushed and in a comfortable place with minimal distractions. Be sure to have a concise project scope statement and report showing the status of the deliverables. It is also best to provide a signature and date line on the scope document. If you have done your homework, the customer should not raise any concerns and will be more than happy to sign off on the scope of the project. Note that you should retain this validation document to meet your company record retention or audit-readiness requirements.

Validate Scope Inputs, Tools and Techniques, and Outputs

Figure 5.8 shows the inputs, tools and techniques, and outputs for the Validate Scope process. Also note that this process falls under the Monitoring and Controlling Process Group. An important input is verified deliverables and work performance data. One way to validate scope and deliverables is through inspection. This is a simple word that can require significant time and resources, depending on the number of documents that need to be reviewed and validated prior to finalizing the list of accepted deliverables.

The outputs are clear and extremely important, because if there is confusion, incomplete results, or poor documentation, you are wide open for scrutiny. The primary outputs are accepted deliverables, work performance information, and change requests based on any new information gained during this process. The best approach for this process is to be organized and keep copious records on the status and acceptance of each of the deliverables and phase signoffs along the way. This is something you should do throughout the project life cycle, not just at the end of the project.

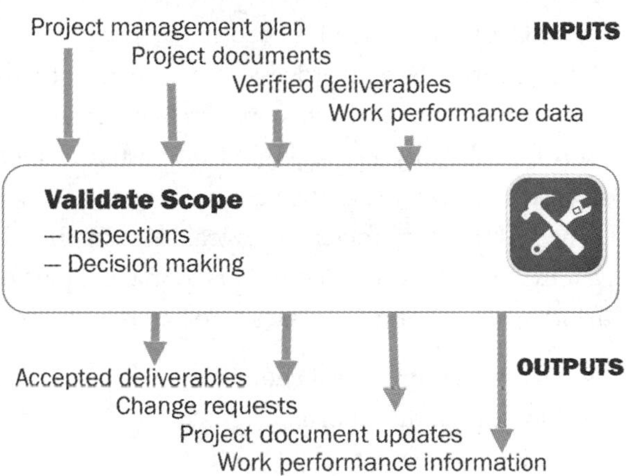

FIGURE 5.8 Validate Scope Process ITTOs

Tip

The PMP exam focuses more on situations than on definitions and may describe a situation that relates to scope validation without actually using the term. With this in mind, it is a good idea to be familiar with alternative phrases that potentially describe scope validation—for example, conducting inspections, reviews, and audits; determining whether results or work products are completed according to (or conforming to) approved requirements; and gaining formal signoff. Keep in mind the exam questions tend to be very subjective.

It is also important to note that scope validation is a close cousin to quality control. The only real difference is that quality control tends to be more product specific, whereas scope validation is at the overall project scope level. There is a huge risk in not being able to close the project successfully if the Validate Scope process is not formally accepted—not to mention that you will likely miss the target unless you are clear on the scope and deliverables of the project. (Don't wait until near the end of the project and find out that you missed the target.)

6. Control Scope Process (Monitoring and Controlling Process Group)

Figure 5.9 shows the inputs, tools and techniques, and the outputs for the Control Scope process. The only way to control a project effectively is to control the scope of the project; these go hand-in-glove (you can't have one without the other). The Control Scope process is accomplished by monitoring the status of the project and the product scope and then setting a baseline to measure against and manage to throughout the project phases. It involves constantly looking at the impact of changes on the scope of the project. As a PM you need to be very proactive in controlling project scope.

The Control Scope process is grouped with the Monitoring and Controlling Process Group. If done properly, this process helps ensure effective control of the project scope. This is accomplished by managing all requested changes and taking or making recommended corrective or even preventive action as needed to keep the project scope aligned.

The PM needs to focus on several key activities during this process. The best way to manage and control scope effectively is to make it part of the discussion and put it on the agenda during meetings and processes associated with the following focus areas:

- Steering committee meetings
- Monthly status reports
- Risk management
- Issue management
- Change management
- Communication management

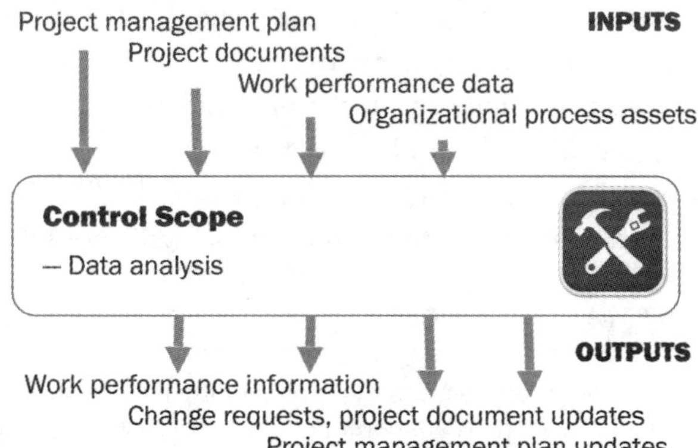

FIGURE 5.9 Control Scope Process ITTOs

Here's a sample communication plan for presenting scope management status:

- The PM presents the project scope status to the project owner on a weekly basis.
- Ad hoc (as needed) meetings are conducted at the PM's discretion as issues or change control items arise.
- The PM provides a written status report to the project owner on a monthly basis and distributes the project team-meeting minutes.
- The project owner will be notified via email on all urgent issues. Issue notification will include time constraints and impacts, which will identify the urgency of the request.
- The project team will have weekly update/status meetings to review completed tasks and determine current work priorities. Minutes will be produced from all meetings.

- The PM will provide the project sponsors with project team-meeting minutes and steering committee status reports.

Another consideration is to establish a project website (Dropbox, Google.doc or "team room") to provide access to the project documentation to anyone, including geographically dispersed project team members. Additional details on communications are covered in Chapter 10 of this book.

What Is Scope Creep?

If you have been around project management for even a short time, you have surely heard the term *scope creep*, a seemingly silly yet frightening phrase that can turn the PM's world upside down. Scope creep occurs when the scope of the project takes on a different size, shape, or complexity over time and requires changes in scope, schedule, or cost on the project.

Scope creep is often a result of uncontrolled change. In today's world scope creep tends to grow quickly into *scope leap*, which is the big brother of change on a project. Scope leap occurs when the final product, service, or result is significantly different from how it started out in the original scope. This is why clear project definition and effective change management are needed to manage scope on the project.

Wikipedia.com offers the following definition of *scope creep*:

> Scope creep (also called focus creep, requirement creep, feature creep, and sometimes kitchen sink syndrome) in project management refers to uncontrolled changes in a project's scope. This phenomenon can occur when the scope of a project is not properly defined, documented, or controlled. It is generally considered a negative occurrence that is to be avoided. Typically, the scope increase consists of either new products or new features to already approved product designs, without corresponding increases in resources, schedule, or budget. As a result, the project team risks drifting away from its original purpose and scope into unplanned additions . . . Thus, scope creep can result in a project team overrunning its original budget and schedule.[4]

If, through change control, the budget and/or schedule are adjusted (up or down) along with the scope, the change is usually considered an acceptable change to the project, and the term *scope creep* is not used. Scope creep can be a result of the following:

- Poor change management or scope control (or both)
- Lack of proper identification of what is required to meet project objectives
- Weak project management discipline or weak executive sponsorship
- Poor communication between the project's PM, sponsor, and other stakeholders

Scope creep is a very common risk in most projects, is difficult to overcome, and remains a difficult challenge for even the most experienced PMs.

Case Study Example of Scope Creep

To give you an example or scope creep in the real world, let's look at our case study:

The original contract with P&G for their call center ticketing system chose to use a software product called Remedy, which is a great call- and problem-tracking tool for entering and documenting status of help desk tickets. The ticketing system requires a server with a fair amount of data storage. The configuration for this server system was determined, and a cost estimate was factored into the contract. When the customer reviewed the system configuration, they saw a single server was to be set up for tracking all tickets and they flagged this as a risk, that is, single point of failure should the server go down (offline). The risk was documented, and during the risk review the customer felt that the probability and impact were low in the event the server dropped out of service for short periods. The mitigation for the risk was simply to have the call center agent take the ticket information on a tablet of paper and enter the ticket when the server was back up and running.

Later, P&G brought this risk up again and determined they wanted a backup server to mitigate the risk. Then the customer went into full scope creep mode by saying that they not only wanted a backup server but that they wanted a development server to be able to update the system to improve the ticketing system if needed. Then they also felt with any new development or changes, the program would need to be tested, so the customer asked for a test server as well. So, what just happened?

Answer: The configuration went from a single production server to multiple servers, including a backup, a development, and test servers for a total—along with the ticketing server—of four new servers. With this change in scope came the need for increased power, installation time, and ongoing support as well as an increase in space for the additional equipment. This is a clear case of *scope leap* and increased cost, time, and resource requirements significantly over the original approved scope.

How to Prevent Scope Creep (or Scope Leap)

The best way to prevent scope creep is to start with a clearly defined scope statement and have formal change control, as mentioned earlier. However, controlling scope creep is easier said than done. Change happens; projects are dynamic in nature and don't just stand still over the project's course. Many PMs equate the attempt to manage scope much like trying to herd cats in an open field.

Managing scope creep is one of the more difficult parts of a project manager's job, but solid documentation, clear communication, and detailed information will minimize any risk to the project and the client relationship. When in doubt, draw on the expertise of your team to determine a few options your client can choose from. In the end, this will help ensure your projects are delivered on budget and on time.[5]

How Do You Identify Scope Creep?

In order to identify scope creep, a PM must be able to prove that a given item falls outside the original agreement. The best way to do this is to reference the project plan, project charter, statement of work, or similar documentation. This means project documentation needs to define the work effort of an initiative or deliverable in a very precise manner. More important, exclusions and assumptions will also support the identification of scope creep by clearly spelling out any items that are considered additional work (and thus are out of scope).[6]

By communicating early and often within the project team and with the key stakeholders regarding the scope status and the approved change control process, you can help lead the team toward controlled success. The change control process, when used correctly, isn't an excuse to just say "no"; rather, it is a tool to help you say, "maybe, but . . ." and then describe the potential impact to the project.

What Do You Do When Scope Creep Occurs?

When you are confident that the client or project team has requested a change that is out of scope, it's important to document the change immediately and initiate the change process. This sends a message and sets expectations that the change must be handled as an out-of-scope change request.

As part of the documentation, you should clearly state the reason the request is out of scope and what the impact might be to the project if you move forward with the change. Note that the specific impact may require further evaluation, and it could be costly to perform this analysis; therefore, as part of the change process, the client must agree to the additional time and cost to review and respond to the change request, even if the change is not approved at the end of the review.

Ideally, you want to be able to go back to the requester and clearly articulate the impact of the requested change. You may also want to look at alternative solutions that might yield the same benefits with lower cost or schedule impact to the project. Another approach is to recommend a postponement of the requested change to a later date or phase of the project to allow you to stay focused on the deliverables and schedule at hand. Regardless of the solution, be very clear, and work with your team and customer to come to agreement on the solution. Then document the outcome in the change log and communicate the results to the team.

Seven Steps for Avoiding Scope Creep

Scope creep can originate from several sources and is a leading cause of project failure when handled poorly. You must take measures to control project embellishment and to ensure that you and your team don't fall victim to its undesired results—deadline delay and budget shortage. Controlling the scope of your project begins before the first line of code is written (or the first design document begins). Each development effort should have a corresponding project plan or project agreement, regardless of the situation. Even if you're just one developer trying to make the boss happy, you'll benefit greatly from documenting your efforts before you begin them. Use the following guidelines (from "Seven Steps for Avoiding Scope Creep" by Shelley Doll) to set yourself up for successful control of the scope of your project:

1. Thoroughly understand the project vision, objectives, and stakeholder expectations. Meet with the project sponsor and provide an overview of the project as a whole for the sponsor's review and approval.
2. Understand project priorities. Make an ordered list for review throughout the project life cycle. Items should include budget, deliverables, target milestone dates, and completion date. Quality metrics (e.g., features, functions, customer satisfaction measurement, and employee / team satisfaction) should also be used to determine priorities.
3. Define the deliverables with the project team. Deliverables should be descriptions of functionality and specific features of the product(s) to be completed during the project.
4. Break the approved deliverables into actual work requirements. The requirements should be as detailed as necessary and can be completed using a simple spreadsheet.
5. Break the project down into major and minor milestones. Whatever your method for determining activity duration, leave room for contingency, especially when working with an unfamiliar staff. If your schedule is tight, re-evaluate your deliverables.
6. Once a schedule has been created, assign resources and determine your critical path. Your critical path may change over the course of your project, so it's important to evaluate and re-evaluate it fairly often. Manage the critical path to determine which deliverables must be completed on time (more details are provided in Chapter 6).
7. Expect that there will be scope creep. Implement change-order request forms early, and educate the project stakeholders on the change process. A change order form will allow you to perform a cost-benefit analysis before scheduling changes.

"If you can perform all of these steps immediately, great, however, even if you start with just a few, any that you're able to implement will bring you that much closer to avoiding and controlling scope creep. That way, you are in a better position to control your project, instead of your project controlling you."[7]

Tip

There is a strong connection between scope control and integrated change control, covered in Chapter 4. Also, keep in mind there are many types of changes, and they tend to come from many different (and seemingly innocent) sources. The best bet is to run all changes through the change control process using the steps shown in the next section on change management. The change procedures, if used properly, will take out a lot of the emotion and personal decision making, putting final decisions in the hands of the change review board.

Additional Information on Change Management

The change management procedures (listed here) should be followed and should be consistent with your project management methodology and overall project integrated change control process:

1. A change request log should be established early to track all changes associated with the project effort.
2. All change requests should be assessed to determine possible alternatives and costs.
3. Change requests will be reviewed and approved by the project owner.
4. The effects of approved change requests on the scope and schedule of the project will be reflected in updates to the project plan.
5. The change request log will be updated to reflect the current status of change requests.

The best way to ensure that formal change control procedures are enforced is to establish a change control board (CCB).

Change Control Board

The CCB should be a mixed panel of organizational and project representatives. It works best if it is made up of a small group of decision makers with appropriate authorization to approve change requests that can impact the overall project. It is also best if you have an odd number of CCB members, because occasionally you will need a tie breaker to move forward on certain changes.

PMI defines a CCB as a group formally chartered who are usually responsible for reviewing, evaluating, approving, delaying, or rejecting changes to the project, and for recording and communicating such decisions.

The Importance of Solid Project Scope Management

Like the saying goes, "When it's right, you know it," and when you have a clearly defined and approved scope for your project, you know it and are more likely to hit the target. Managing scope effectively on your project is like getting a strike in the game of bowling—the points add up a lot quicker. I can't emphasize enough the importance of having a clearly defined, documented, and approved scope statement; clear completion criteria; and solid management of your project's scope to increase your chances of success.

Summary of Project Scope Management

Sadly, many projects fail because scope is poorly understood or controlled. It's hard to hit a fuzzy target or one that keeps moving. However, change is inevitable and will happen. By using the Scope Management processes coupled together with the Integrated Change Control process (described in Chapter 4), you can ensure a greater probability of success by knowing what you build and building what you know. To aid you in this process, I have included a sample scope management plan in Figure 5.10 on the following pages.

FIGURE 5.10 Sample Scope Statement for Cat Wranglers

	Cat Wranglers	**PROJECT SCOPE STATEMENT** *Ver. 1.2 5/01/2017*

PROJECT SCOPE Lite (for Tier 1 "Small" projects)

Note: Any work not explicitly included in the *Project Scope Statement* is implicitly excluded from the project.

Project Name	Boulder Pedal 4 a Paws' Site Construction and Setup
Project Manager	Beverly B.

Version History (*insert rows as needed*)		
Version	Date (MM/DD/YYYY)	Comments
1.0	05/01/2017	First draft completed and sent for review
1.1	05/04/2017	Suggestions by Carolyn K. and team
1.2	05/06/2017	Final Draft Ready for Review (PM)

1. Project Executive Summary
Brief overview of this project (e.g., project purpose and justification):
To construct and set up the main stage (located near the start/end tour area), team sites, and seven rest stops in support of the "Boulder Pedal 4 a Paws" fundraising event. These areas are critical to the staging of the event and in providing rider support throughout the 100-mile bike course.

FIGURE 5.10—*continued*

	**Cat Wranglers**	**PROJECT SCOPE STATEMENT** *Ver. 1.2 5/01/2017*

2. Business Objectives	
2.1 Product Description (Solution)	*Describe what this project will produce and how it will tie to the overall program or company's business objectives, e.g., increase sales, reduce cost, increase customer satisfaction or market share.*
To provide site facilities to support the fund raising event "Boulder Pedal 4 a Paws."	
2.2 Business Objectives	*What specific business impact will this project have? Business Objectives should be objectively measurable.*

2. Business / Project Objectives

In order to provide a safe, clean, supportive environment, the following facility areas will either be constructed or set up:

- A main stage built to provide a central location platform for event announcements and entertainment
- Team sites where cyclists and their crews can set up and provide maintenance and support for their team members
- Seven rest stops at 12–14-mile intervals for riders participating in the event.

The construction and setting up of these facilities will

- Provide refreshments and waste management (Porta Potty, trash, recycling) facilities at each rest stop and main stage area.
- Set aside designated areas to accommodate vendors providing bike mechanical services, for sponsor booths, and for medical volunteers and emergency medical staffing (EMS) first responders to provide medical care (mile markers 37 and 75).
- Ensure the safety of all volunteers and tour participants by establishing safety protocols and providing EMS to administer medical services and address any injuries in a timely fashion.
- Help to ensure overall participant satisfaction during the event.
- Increase the number of early sign-ups by cyclists knowing that proper facilities are being provided throughout the tour course.

FIGURE 5.10—*continued*

	**Cat Wranglers**	**PROJECT SCOPE STATEMENT** *Ver. 1.2 5/01/2017*

3. Project Description
For each area below, provide sufficient detail to define this project adequately or link to the scope section of the overall Project Management Plan document.
3.1 Project Scope Summary
Construct/set up facility sites for the bicycle tour "Boulder Pedal 4 a Paws."
Includes: *(List primary Project Deliverables—can be narrative or bullet list)* • Project management plan including scope statement, work breakdown structure, and schedule network diagram • Project budget including earned value, statements of work, vendor evaluation, vendor contracts • Risk management plan and communication plan • Determination of site locations for main stage, team sites, and rest stops • Creation of architectural design and specifications for main stage • Work with city/county officials to ensure that event sites are in compliance with all building, health, and event legal codes and requirements • Contract for construction of main stage • Installation of electrical outlets and hookups (20, 30, 50 amps) to the main stage • Contract for rental materials to set up and equip tent sites used for team and rest stops sites • Contract for waste-management facilities • Recruitment of volunteers for setup/breakdown of event sites • Set up of tent sites for pre-event opening • Breakdown of all sites post-event • Formal presentation of the proceeds (check) to the Humane Society • Summary of completed project, including lessons learned

3. Project Description
Does not include *(for clarification, list what is not included in this project, i.e., out of scope/exclusions):* • Providing staff to operate/man sites during event • Providing, constructing, or cleanup of facilities for sponsors/vendors • Providing equipment, such as PA systems, lighting, electrical power service, heating, air conditioning, refrigeration, and generators to the main stage, rest areas, or any other tour site(s)

FIGURE 5.10—*continued*

	**Cat Wranglers**	**PROJECT SCOPE STATEMENT** *Ver. 1.2 5/01/2017*

3.2 External Dependencies
Whom outside the project team will you depend on for successful completion of this project? • Tour route to be mapped and approved, and permits obtained • Architectural design and specifications for main stage to be created • Outside vendors to deliver supplies and conduct setup in timely manner • Consult with city and county regarding building and health codes, and other applicable regulations
3.3 Assumptions / Constraints
For example, mandated completion date, staffing limitations, funding assumptions • Contractors and subcontractors will supply their own tools and equipment to construct and/or set up facilities. • County fairgrounds will supply electrical power services to main stage. • Sponsors will provide their own product booths, workforce, signage (banners), and cleanup. • Vendors and subcontractors are responsible for their own setup and cleanup of areas. In addition, they will have their own tools and materials. • Each rest stop will be able to accommodate/handle an average of 100 riders at any given time. • Construction of sites and rental materials to set up sites shall not exceed $40,000. • Event will take place regardless of weather.

FIGURE 5.10—*continued*

	**Cat Wranglers**	**PROJECT SCOPE STATEMENT** *Ver. 1.2 5/01/2017*

4. Project Milestones	
4.1 Estimated Schedule	Key project milestones relative to project start are as follows. (Insert rows as needed):

Project Milestone	Target Date (MM/DD/YYYY)
• Project management plan including scope statement, work breakdown structure, and schedule network diagram reviewed and approved	05/01/2017
• Project Budget including earned value, statements of work, vendor evaluation, vendor contracts, as well as change control process approved	05/07/2017
• Risk management plan, communication plan, and issues-tracking log complete	05/15/2017
• Determination and finalization of site locations	05/24/2017
• Architectural design and specifications of main stage complete	06/01/2017
• Construction of main stage complete	06/20/2017
• Setup of tent sites and waste-management facilities complete	06/20/2017
• Breakdown of sites complete	06/22/2017
• Rental materials/equipment returned	06/23/2017
• Check donated, review and lessons learned meeting conducted, and record retention planned	06/25/2017

FIGURE 5.10—*continued*

	**Cat Wranglers**	**PROJECT SCOPE STATEMENT** *Ver. 1.2 5/01/2017*

5. Project Approach
Describe primary plans briefly in the space below or link to the overall project management plan document. A phased approach is used to break the project into manageable steps for completion. The route maps and architectural design documents will be the primary sources used to determine the site location setups and construction of the main stage. This document provides the project scope and deliverables to be completed.
How will project issues/risks be dealt with?
Issues/risks will be addressed as follows: • Urgent issues will be addressed with the project sponsors and project manager in a timely fashion to ensure quick resolution. • All project-related issues and risks will be identified, tracked, prioritized, assigned, resolved, and communicated in accordance with the project management methodology. Issues will be tracked on the SharePoint site.
How will change requests be dealt with?
The change control procedures to be followed will be consistent with the project management methodology and consist of the following processes: • A SharePoint change request ticketing system, which includes a log of all change requests, will be used by the event sponsor(s), stakeholders, vendors, and support staff to track and manage changes. • All change requests submitted via the change request form on the SharePoint site will be assessed to determine possible alternatives and costs. • Change results will be tracked and reported on a weekly basis.
List any regularly scheduled project team meetings, planned status reports, and so on
• The project manager will have daily communications with the construction contractor during the construction of the main stage. • The event project team will have weekly updates/status meetings to review upcoming and completed tasks. Minutes will be produced from all meetings. • The project manager will provide a status report to the sponsor(s) on a weekly basis.

FIGURE 5.10—*continued*

	**Cat Wranglers**	**PROJECT SCOPE STATEMENT** *Ver. 1.2 5/01/2017*

6. Project Scope Statement Approval/Signatures	
Project Name	Boulder Pedal 4 a Paws' Site Construction and Setup
Project Manager	Beverly B.

The purpose of this document is to provide a detailed scope statement for the project. It is used to reach a satisfactory level of mutual agreement between the project manager and the project sponsors with respect to the objectives and scope of the project before significant resources are committed and expenses incurred.

I have reviewed the information contained in this Project Scope Statement and agree:

Name	Role	Signature	Date (MM/DD/YYYY)
Pets 'R' Us	Project Sponsor		
Cat Wranglers	Project/Program Manager		

The signatures above indicate an understanding of the purpose and content of this document by those signing it. By signing this document, signees agree to this as the formal project scope statement document.

References

1. Gary Evans, "Project Description—Scope Statement Template Instructions," CVR/IT Consulting, sections 3.1–3.3, page 4, http://www.cvr-it.com/PM_Templates/, accessed February 2017.

2. Terri Morrison, Wayne A. Conaway, and George A. Borden, *Kiss, Bow, or Shake Hands* (Avon, MA: Adams Media Corporation, 1994).

3. Rita Mulcahy, *PMP Exam Prep*, Eighth Edition (Minneapolis, MN: RMC Publications, Inc., April 2013), page 180.

4. "Scope Creep," *Wikipedia*, http://en.wikipedia.org/wiki/Scope_creep, accessed February 2017.

5. Gina Lijoi, "How to Manage Scope Creep," *The Project Management Hut* (July 14, 2007), http://www.pmhut.com/how-to-manage-scope-creep, accessed February 2017.

6. Shelley Doll, "Seven Steps for Avoiding Scope Creep," *TechRepublic* (March 13, 2001), http://www.techrepublic.com/article/seven-steps-for-avoiding-scope-creep/, accessed February 2017.

7. Ibid.

6 Project Schedule Management

Key Skills & Concepts

- The true measure of success on a project
- The importance of schedule management
- Precedence diagramming method (PDM)
- Schedule management processes
- Managing the schedule (setting a baseline)
- Forward pass, backward pass, and float
- How to find the critical path (CP)
- Types of dependencies and relationships
- The impact of constraints on a project
- Types of reports and charts (PERT and Gantt)

When you read project management trade journals, magazines, and books, one true measure of success that's often discussed is bringing the project in "on time." The other measure of project success, as you may have guessed, is being "on budget" (a topic that's covered in Chapter 7). These two areas (time and cost) are tightly linked and are the primary constraints (or challenges) project managers (PMs) encounter on a day-to-day basis.

It has also been said that the highest source of conflict on a project is the schedule. More projects miss their target schedule dates than anyone would like to admit. The misses are often due to changes to scope or deliverables that affect a project's scheduled completion date.

Schedule management, in a broad sense, involves both planning and execution. Time, unlike money, once spent, is gone and cannot be earned back. That is what makes schedule management an important Knowledge Area. The bad news is there is no universally agreed-upon way to manage time. How time is managed and how activities are prioritized depend on the individual PM. The good news is that there are some standard processes (discussed in this chapter) that, if followed, can help in this area.

To manage the schedule on a project effectively, it is recommended that you use a schedule management system (SMS). An SMS is a designed combination of processes, tools, and techniques that allow the PM and team to identify, analyze, sequence, and estimate the duration for all project activities. One of the important components is a network diagram. A network diagram can be created in a number of ways, as we discuss later in this chapter. The important thing to remember is that the tool, type, and format you choose should make sense to you and the team and must help you with managing the schedule. Too often we try to fit the process to the tool. The tool you use must work for you, not against you. An SMS usually includes a resource calendar, resource assignment matrix (RAM), and a network diagram to help identify the overall duration and critical path activities of the project (all of these components are discussed in detail throughout this chapter).

Schedule management as a project management Knowledge Area involves a significant number of concepts, tools and techniques, and methods that challenge even the more experienced PMs. This chapter is designed with both the beginner and the experienced PM in mind and addresses real-world project management and tips to help if you are planning to pursue PMP certification.

Tip

If you are not planning to pursue PMI's CAPM, PMP, or PMI-SP (Scheduling Professional) exam in the near future, I recommend that you scan this chapter as a high-level overview and not for detailed comprehension. You can always come back to this chapter later when you are ready to prepare for PM certification. The good news is many of the calculations for schedule management are performed by today's high-tech PM software tools; however, it is still important to learn the concepts.

Managing the Schedule

To give you an idea of the potential size and breadth of schedule management, consider that PMI has a separate independent credential (with its own exam) called Scheduling Professional (PMI-SP) that focuses on developing and maintaining project schedules.

Even though there is a separate PMI credential for schedule management, don't be confused between time management and schedule management. The two go hand in hand—you can't have one without the other.

This chapter is all about how to manage the project schedule to bring your project in on time. Most people think of time management as how to get better organized so they have more time in their day to do other things—how to focus on the "A-list" of to-do's and not get distracted by the small stuff that tends to eat up every spare moment. I submit to you that schedule management is about learning how to better manage the schedule of events and activities on your project to allow you to come in on time according to the approved schedule.

Managing the schedule involves getting focused on the importance of supply-and-demand concepts. It is about making sure we have everything we need—resources, including people, tools, equipment, software, and materials—to get the job rolling and keep the project rolling.

Schedule management in the real world is about knowing when to bring the right people in on the project and making sure that the materials and equipment are available when the workers arrive so they can perform the work needed to complete the activities on time.

An example of this concept is as follows:

Try This

Say you and your team have done a great job identifying and defining the work of a construction project to begin framing a new home. As the PM, you ensured that the appropriate building materials were ordered and scheduled for delivery from the lumberyard, and you also confirmed the arrival time for the framing crew to be on site at 7 a.m. sharp on a Monday morning. As you have a great relationship with the framing crew that you wish to maintain, you arrive at the building site promptly at 7 a.m. to greet them—only to find that the materials were delivered early (Friday afternoon) and were stolen over the weekend. Now what do you do? As the PM, you have a big problem because the crew (if other project jobs are in their queue) may not be willing to wait a day or more for you to reorder the materials. If the crew is in demand, they may have to go on to the next project and you will have just lost three to four weeks of work from your schedule. Risk happens . . . fortunately in this case, because of your relationship with the crew, they are willing to work with you and take a day off or take on a short, one-day project to give you time to obtain the materials so that they can begin the work right away on your project. Of course, to protect your project and keep you on schedule thereafter, you would next need to come up with a plan to help ensure against future thefts of materials, such as by securing them in a lockable storage shed.

Project Schedule Management Processes

You have probably heard the saying, "time is money." This saying is especially true when you are managing a project. Project schedule management is the area that is least understood by many PMs and most often missed (underestimated) when it comes time to manage the amount of work needed to get the job done properly and on or before the deadline.

Schedule management is the organization of tasks, activities, or events by first estimating how much time is required to complete them successfully and by adjusting activities or events that would interfere with their completion, so the tasks are done in the appropriate amount of time.

As a key Knowledge Area, schedule management includes six processes that center around effectively managing the project's work packages and activities (the actual work of the project). The ultimate goal is to bring the project to successful completion on time, according to the approved delivery date. One thing that makes schedule management difficult is that time is constantly moving, and like the many dynamics we face on our projects, the milestones and target dates can be moving targets.

Here are the processes of the Project Schedule Management Knowledge Area:

- **6.1. Plan Schedule Management (Planning Process Group).** This involves identifying and documenting the policies for planning and managing the project schedule.
- **6.2. Define Activities (Planning Process Group).** This involves identifying and documenting specific actions to be performed to produce the approved project deliverables.
- **6.3. Sequence Activities (Planning Process Group).** This involves identifying and documenting relationships between the project activities (e.g., between predecessor and successor activities).
- **6.4. Estimate Activity Durations (Planning Process Group).** This involves estimating the number of work periods needed to complete individual activities with estimated resources.
- **6.5. Develop Schedule (Planning Process Group).** This involves analyzing the activity sequences, durations, resource requirements, and schedule constraints to create the project schedule.
- **6.6. Control Schedule (Monitoring and Controlling Process Group).** This is the process of monitoring the status of project activities to update project progress and manage changes to the schedule baseline to achieve the plan.

Tip

PMP exam takers find schedule management one of the more difficult Knowledge Areas. The reason is usually lack of experience creating, planning, and executing network diagrams, including understanding the forward and backward pass, calculating float, and identifying activities on the critical path (terms to be defined shortly in this chapter). Also, PMI has changed the method used in calculating the forward and backward pass, which adds to the confusion. This change, combined with the fact that we rely on software tools to do the calculations for us, makes for less awareness of the mechanics involved with schedule management.

No matter the size or type of project, the one constant seems to be "time is of the essence." The feeling seems to be—especially in today's environment—to "get it done fast." After all, the faster we get the project completed, the less it will cost. Between our lack of patience, ever-pressing budget concerns, and the number of changes, PMs and team members alike seem to be running on "fast forward."

A PM friend of mine from Australia flew to the United States to participate in a project-planning session several years ago, and at the end of the week-long planning session I asked her what she thought of the session and of how we conducted planning in the United States. Her response was abrupt but not surprising. She proclaimed, "You Yanks are so impatient, and you never want to take the time to plan the details of the project. You just want to jump in and start the activities, even if you are not sure what needs to be done." Does this sound familiar? It sounds a lot like the "Ready, Fire, Aim" dilemma mentioned in Chapter 2.

To investigate my friend's statement further, I raised the same question to some of my project team members from Japan and some of my Asian students; their responses were the same. Most other countries actually spend time planning their projects (on average they said they spend around 60 percent to 70 percent of the project time planning, compared to less than 10 percent in the United States). To further substantiate this, Dr. Liker in *The Toyota Way Fieldbook* uses the phrase, "Ready, Aim, Aim, Aim, Aim, Fire" to describe Japanese project teams.[1] The Japanese approach tends to be the other extreme from that of the United States, and it really shows the need for a happy medium when it comes time to plan our projects. Planning is essential to effective project management.

Following are discussions of each of the six schedule management processes. Remember two things: first, schedule management is a team sport. Second, five of the six schedule management processes are planning processes. (Remember, PMI is big on planning.)

Plan Schedule Management Process (Planning Process Group)

Before you begin working with your subject matter experts (SMEs) to develop the project schedule, it's helpful to create a high-level plan for how you will manage the events, planned and unplanned, of the project. Generally, each project is unique in its content, resources, expected deliverables, and desired result. Having a plan that is specific to the project you are about to undertake can keep your entire team focused on the unique requirements necessary to complete the project successfully. Planning for schedule management is like creating a roadmap for you to guide the project stakeholders during the planning, developing, managing, executing, and controlling of the project. Figure 6.1 shows an overview of the inputs, tools and techniques, and the outputs for the Plan Schedule Management process.

Define Activities Process (Planning Process Group)

Define Activities is the process of identifying the specific actions (activities) to be performed to produce project deliverables. The Create WBS process performed in Chapter 5

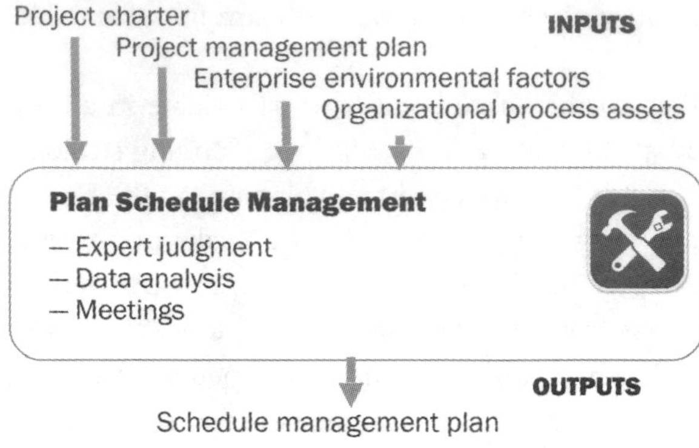

FIGURE 6.1 Plan Schedule Management Process ITTOs

creates work packages, which is the level of detail that you, as the PM, should manage to. However, this is not the level at which you should create a schedule. Work packages must be broken down into smaller-level activities before you begin creating your project schedule. Your SMEs or team leads will manage the project deliverable at the activity level. It is extremely important to break down work packages to this level so you can estimate required project resources, apply the correct time durations, monitor issues during execution, and manage the schedule to complete the project successfully.

The best place to start with the Define Activities process, other than the WBS, is to go back to the scope baseline and other inputs such as organizational process assets and environmental factors. Activities from previous similar projects help provide great insight into the activities needed (why reinvent the wheel, right?). The main outputs of the Define Activities process are the activity list, activity attributes, milestone list, and change requests, as well as updates to the project management plan document based on any new information gathered during this process.

FIGURE 6.2 Define Activities Process ITTOs

Milestone Lists

The best way to organize the work of the Define Activities process is with a milestone list. A milestone, as you may recall from Chapter 5, is a major event on the project. Think of the milestone list as an outline (high-level view) of the deliverables of the project. The milestone list will help the team focus on the deliverables identified in the Create WBS process, and it helps promote discussion and synergy from the team to get you to the next level of detail (activities). It also serves as a very effective input tool for the PM to generate a monthly milestone report. The milestone report can be used to communicate success or concerns of overall progress on the project to upper-level managers. Additional details are provided on the milestone report and other reports in Chapter 10.

The milestone list should also identify whether the milestone is mandatory (such as those required by contract or by outside agencies) or optional (such as those based on similar projects or historical information).

As an example, take a construction project in which the milestone list ties to the major handoffs (changeovers) between the different subcontractors. It is important to be keenly aware of the scheduled completion of a major milestone, such as having the foundation complete and ready for the framer. In our example such handoffs require city inspections and signoffs before the project can go to the next phase. If you don't receive signoff from the inspector for the framework of the building, you cannot move on to the electrical and plumbing phases. You may lose valuable time, not to mention getting a bad reputation, if you are not able to keep the project on schedule. You might want to use a milestone table such as the one shown in Table 6.1.

TABLE 6.1 Sample Milestone List

Milestone	Schedule date	Comments (M = Mandatory, O = Optional)
Approved blueprints	April 15	Dependencies: Client/sponsor and city building permit office review and approval. (M)
Foundation complete	April 30	Dependencies: Land surveyed and marked, forms set, cement poured and cured, and city inspection (signoff). (M)
Framing complete	May 25	Dependencies: Materials available for crew to begin as scheduled. Building framed according to approved blueprints, and rough plumbing installed, and all must meet building code inspection. (M)
Roof decked and frame structure "dried in" against weather	June 15	Dependencies: Roofing crew complete decking according to design, windows and doors installed, and signoff from city inspector. (M)
Electrical and plumbing complete	June 28	Dependencies: Wiring and plumbing installed according to design and building codes and signoff complete. (M)
Project complete	July 15	Dependencies: Customer signed acceptance. (O)

Tip

Milestones are usually shown in the scheduling tool or on a network diagram as a diamond-shaped event that has zero time duration and uses zero project resources. For example, an inspection on your construction project is performed by a city or county employee who is not part of the project team and who doesn't charge time or money (well, not directly, as they are included in the cost of the building permit) to the project.

When reporting milestones, the PM often uses a milestone chart. Figure 6.3 shows the milestone chart for the construction project detailed in Table 6.1.

ID	Milestone	March	April	May	June	July
1	Start Project	◆ 3/30/17				
2	Blueprints approved		◆ 4/15/17			
3	Foundation complete		◆ 4/30/17			
4	Frame complete			◆ 5/25/17		
5	Structure complete "dried in"				◆ 6/15/17	
6	Electrical & Plumbing complete				◆ 6/28/17	
7	Finish work complete					◆ 7/10/17
8	Final Inspection (CO) complete					◆ 7/30/17

CO = Certificate of Occupancy

FIGURE 6.3 Sample Milestone Chart

Activity List and Attributes

The finished activities list and the associated attributes should comprise a comprehensive list that includes all schedule activities required to complete the project successfully.

ACTIVITY LIST

The activity list is an output of the Define Activities process and includes all the schedule activities to be performed on the project. The creation of the activity list relies on the combined knowledge, skills, and experience of you and the team, and on all completed and approved documents generated thus far on the project to use as a guide.

The list should include the activity identifier and a scope of work description for each activity so that the project team members clearly understand the work to be performed and the required outcome. Remember, it is up to you as the PM to keep the team focused on the approved work during this process.

ACTIVITY ATTRIBUTES

Activity attributes extend the description of an activity by identifying the many components associated with the activity. Attributes are the characteristics of schedule activities.

Activity attributes can be (and ideally should be) sorted, organized, and/or summarized according to some specific categories. Some types of activity attributes can include those related to time needed (elapsed time) to complete specific components, costs related to completion of an activity [——], activity codes, [——] specific locations in which the activity may be taking place, and/or other miscellaneous categories into which these attributes can be conveniently and appropriately organized. Activity attributes can also include discussion of specific constraints that may make completion more difficult.[2]

Other types of activity attributes include any measure of capacity, cost drivers, cycle time, and other such cost and performance characteristics, such as installing increased memory in a computer. The activity is installing the new memory chip, and the attribute is the size of the memory being installed (for example, 8GB of memory).

During the initial phase of the project, activity attributes may include the activity identification (ID) number, WBS ID number, activity name, activity codes, and logical relationships. As the project progresses, the attributes tend to evolve into more complex descriptions, resource requirements, locations of the work, and activity types, such as level of effort (LOE), discrete (independent) effort, and apportioned (spread over multiple activities) effort (AE).

The number of attributes varies by application area.

Note

According to the *Wideman Comparative Glossary of Project Management Terms*, level of effort (LOE) is usually "work that does not result in a final product (such as liaison, coordination, follow up, or other support activities) and which cannot be effectively associated with a definable end product process result. Level of effort is measured only in terms of resources actually consumed within a given time period."[3] Once you and the team have defined the project activities, the next step is for the team to begin the "what needs to be done and when" relationship placement on the schedule. This is where the Sequence Activities process comes into the picture.

Sequence Activities Process (Planning Process Group)

Now that you have identified the milestones, activities, and attributes, you need to start thinking about the sequence of the activities (i.e., the order in which the work will be performed). Sequencing is when you start "connecting the dots" between which activities come first, second, third, and so on. Certain terms in this process tend to throw people for a loop—terms such as *predecessor and successor relationships*, *lead and lag time*, not to mention *float*, *total float*, *slack*, *PERT* and *Gantt charts*, and more. All of this should be a lot clearer by the time you get to the end of the chapter.

The good news is, several great project management software applications are available that do a lot of the work for you. However, you still need to have a fundamental understanding of the terms and concepts to be able to effectively use these software products; otherwise, you'll fall back into the "garbage in, garbage out" situation.

Tip

Don't fall into the trap of thinking the scheduling tool takes the place of the overall project management plan. I have been asked by a number of PMs to review and provide suggestions on their "project plan" only to have them send me a project schedule. I will be the first to admit the scheduling tools today do a lot more than help track and manage the schedule, but they should not take the place of having an overall project management plan. The scheduling tool is part of the overall management plan.

Figure 6.4 shows an overview of the inputs, tools and techniques, and the outputs for the Sequence Activities process.

What Is the Critical Path?

Before we get into the details of schedule activity sequencing and network diagrams methods, it is important to mention that the primary purpose for this effort is to be able to determine which activities are on the critical path. In other words, which activities, if not completed, will delay the overall project end date?

Please note that a "path" is a complete sequence of activities that will take you from the beginning of the project to the end of the project. A project will have multiple paths through the project.

The *critical path* (CP) is the longest path through the network that represents the shortest amount of time to complete the project. The most important elements of determining the critical path are accurate activity duration estimates and correct identification of relationships between activities.

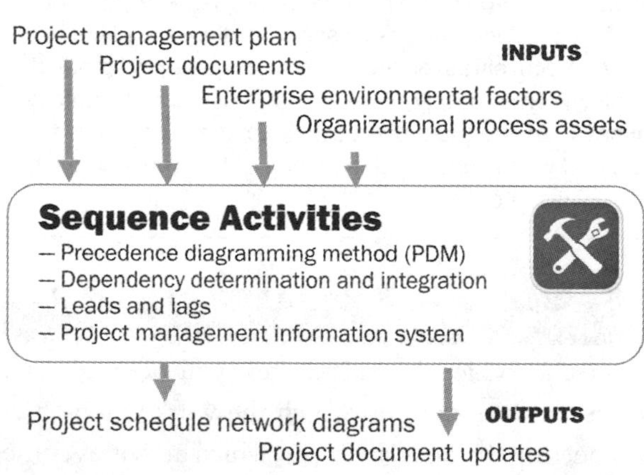

FIGURE 6.4 Sequence Activities Process ITTOs

Why is it important to know which activities are on the CP? Because this is where you get the most "bang for the buck" (return on investment) when it comes time to compress or adjust the schedule. Knowing the specific activities on the CP gives you a direct line to where you need to focus to ensure against slippage (delays) in the schedule.

The best-known method for finding the CP on a project is the critical path method (CPM). CPM is a schedule network-analysis technique to determine the amount of flexibility (called float or slack) for each of the paths in the network diagram. Additional details on the history of CPM, how it is used, and definitions of *float* and *slack* are provided later in this chapter.

Creating Project Network Diagrams

To develop a network diagram, start by getting the team together and then use the diagram from a previous similar project, standard templates, or the scheduling tools available from your organization process assets. The message here is to never reinvent the wheel if you can help it. You will save valuable time if you have tried-and-true work samples and templates from which to begin.

PRECEDENCE DIAGRAMMING METHOD

The precedence diagramming method displays the activities in nodes (boxes) to visually show the relationships between activities. The PDM shows these relationships by using lines or arrows to depict which activity should come first (predecessor activity) and which are dependent activities (successor activities). PDM is also referred to as an activity-on-node (AON) network diagram (see Figure 6.5).

Any project network diagram drawn in such a way that the positioning and length of the activity represents its duration is also known as a time-scaled network diagram.

The precedence diagramming method is also used in what is known as the "critical path method," in which the network diagram and activity-duration estimates can be used to determine the activities on the critical path of the project.

PDM uses four different types of dependencies between activities (see Figure 6.6). These dependencies, listed next, are called *relationships*.

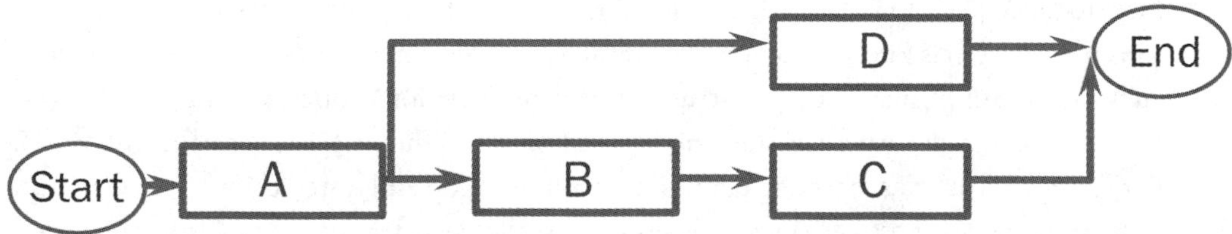

FIGURE 6.5 Sample Precedence Diagram Method (PDM)

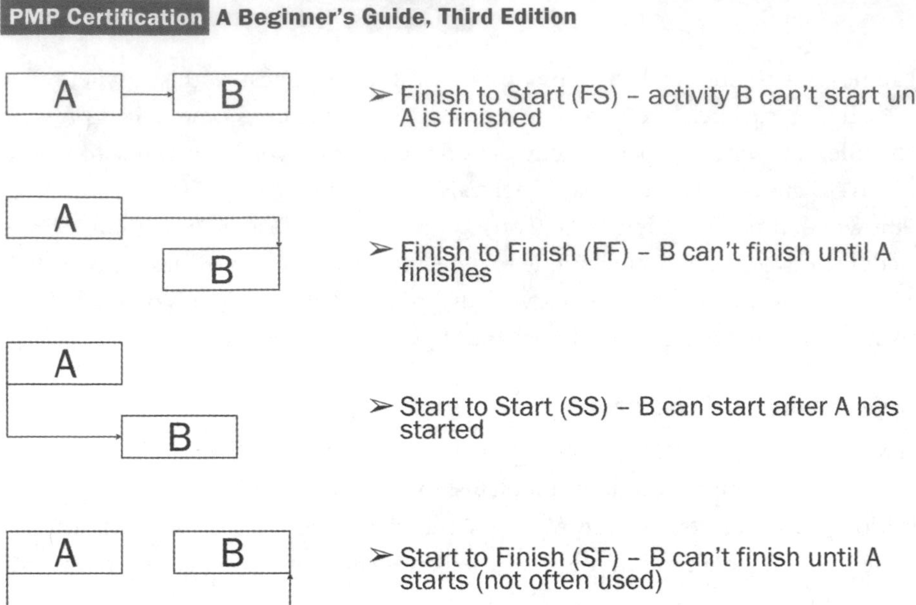
A
B
➢ Finish to Start (FS) – activity B can't start until A is finished
A
B
➢ Finish to Finish (FF) – B can't finish until A finishes
A
B
➢ Start to Start (SS) – B can start after A has started
A
B
➢ Start to Finish (SF) – B can't finish until A starts (not often used)

FIGURE 6.6 Sample Activity Relationships (Dependencies)

- **Finish-to-start (FS).** This is the most common logical relationship and shows that a predecessor activity (or "from" activity) must finish before the successor activity (or "to" activity) can start. This relationship is sequential in nature.
- **Finish-to-finish (FF).** A predecessor activity (A) must finish before the successor (B) can finish. This relationship is often used at dinner time, when you would like all the food to be put on the table at the same time (finish-to-finish). This is tricky because each type of food (activity) takes more or less time to prepare and must be scheduled to complete as near as possible at the same time. Another example is a website for ordering tickets for an event. The website must be up and running at the same time the tickets are printed and ready to sell (finish-to-finish).
- **Start-to-start (SS).** A predecessor activity (A) must start before the successor activity (B) can start. This relationship means the two activities can run in tandem (parallel); however, activity A must start before activity B can start.
- **Start-to-finish (SF).** A predecessor activity (A) must start before the successor (B) can finish. This relationship is rarely used. It is also known as just-in-time (JIT) scheduling in manufacturing, event planning, and construction. For instance, for a concert event project, you would back into the activities' start times based on when the curtain goes up (finish time). For example, you must have the lighting and sound set up and tested prior to concert start time, so you start those activities early enough to allow the team adequate time to complete them prior to the "curtain being raised" time.

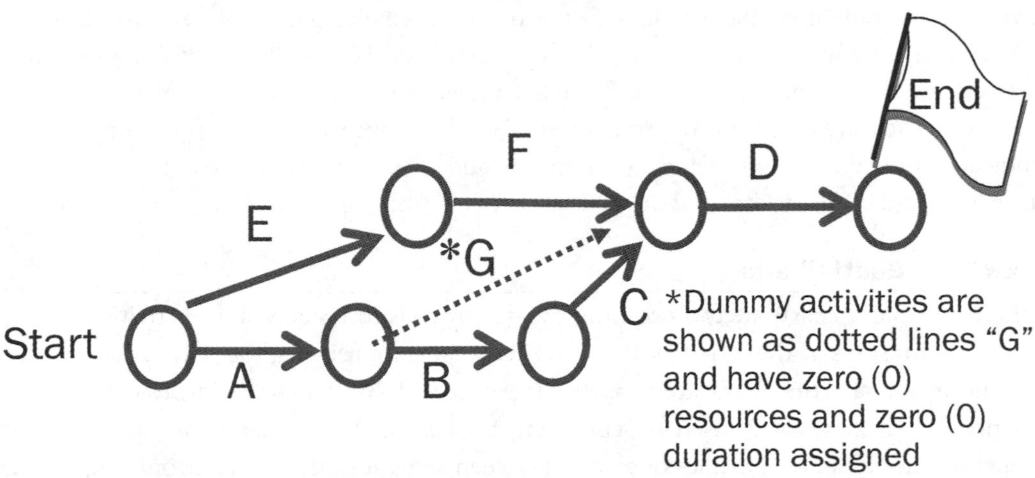

FIGURE 6.7 Sample Arrow Diagram Method (ADM/AOA)

The best way to determine the relationship to use or to find the right link between two activities is to decide which one is driving or positioning the other activity. The driving activity (or task) is the predecessor; the other (driven) activity is the successor.

You also need to be aware of the following types of dependencies:

- **Mandatory (also known as hard logic).** Dependencies that are required by contract or that are inherent in the nature of the work. These often involve physical limitations; for example, the foundation (cement) must be set before the structure can be built.
- **Discretionary dependencies (also known as soft logic or preferred logic).** The project team determines which dependencies are discretionary (those that can wait or those that should proceed) and the preferred logic sequence for best results.
- **External dependencies.** These dependencies include activities that are project related (e.g., the testing of software is dependent on having the hardware received, installed, and running prior to installation of the software application). Or, in some cases, outside the project (e.g., the project can't begin until the building materials are received onsite from the lumberyard). Other external dependencies might be government regulations that must be met, or special reporting, such as with regulatory organizations such as the Occupational Safety and Health Administration (OSHA) or the Sarbanes-Oxley (SOX) Act (for financial reporting).

ARROW DIAGRAMMING METHOD

The first thing to remember about the arrow diagramming method is that the activity is shown on the line (or arrow) itself, and not in a box (see Figure 6.7). AOA (activity-on-arrow) is less common than AON (activity-on-node). Also, AOA has no formal relationships other than the placement of the activities in the diagram. Unlike the AON network diagram, where you can show any relationships between activities (FS, SS, FF, and SF), the AOA network diagram can only show FS (Finish-to-Start) placement of activities.

Another feature of AOA (not found in AON) is the "dummy activity." A dummy activity indicates a dependency between two activities and is shown as a dashed (or dotted) line. *Dummy activities* carry zero time duration.

PERT and Gantt Charts

PERT and Gantt charts are tools commonly used by PMs to visually show activities and the time relationships of the activities for controlling and administering the project schedule.

The PERT and the Gantt are probably the two best known charts in project management. Each of these can be used for scheduling, but because Gantt charts don't illustrate task dependencies (relationship lines or arrows between activities), they can be confusing. Some PMs use both types of charts. The critical path can be found using CPM on either PERT or Gantt charts.

PERT CHARTS

A PERT (Program Evaluation Review Technique) chart is a project management tool used to schedule, organize, and coordinate tasks within a project. PERT is a methodology developed by the US Navy in the 1950s to manage very large, complex projects, such as the Polaris submarine missile program, which had a high degree of intertask dependency. A similar methodology, the critical path method (CPM), was developed for project management in the private sector at about the same time. Classical PERT charting is used to support projects that are often completed using an assembly-line approach. The PERT method extends the CPM by considering the uncertainty in estimating activity duration in order to estimate the probability of finishing a project in a given time.[4]

Tip

Some scheduling software refers to the PERT chart as a "Gantt chart" (see Figure 6.8). This is not completely accurate, because the Gantt chart is more of a bar chart and usually does not have relationship lines between activities. Also, it is important to know that even though PERT is similar to CPM, PERT uses Expected Value, which is calculated using the three-point (weighted value) estimate shown later in this chapter (in Figure 6.15).

GANTT CHARTS (OFTEN SHOWN AS BAR CHARTS)

The Gantt chart was developed by Henry Gantt in the years between 1910 and 1915. He focused on the sequence of activities necessary to complete a project. Gantt charts were

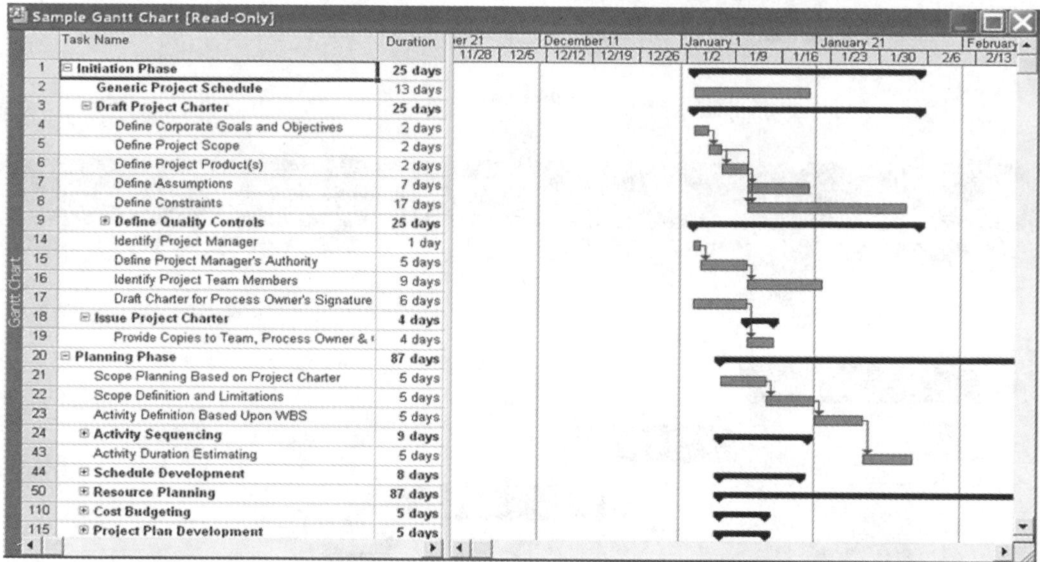

FIGURE 6.8 Sample PERT Chart (referred to as a "Gantt chart" in this scheduling program)

employed on major infrastructure projects, including the Hoover Dam and the Interstate Highway System, and continue to be an important tool in project schedule management. Each activity on a Gantt chart is represented as a single horizontal bar on a graph. The horizontal axis (X-axis) of the graph is the timeline of the project and the length of each activity (or task) bar corresponds to the duration of the activity. The vertical axis (Y-axis) shows the list of WBS activities (see Figure 6.9). A Gantt chart is also a useful tool for planning and scheduling projects and is helpful when monitoring and reporting progress.

Note

Essentially, the Gantt chart is a "time-scaled network diagram" shown as a bar chart with no lines to indicate relationship between activities. As mentioned, some scheduling software tools inappropriately show Gantt charts with relationship lines between activities, much like a PERT chart.

Other Charts Used in Schedule Management

A variety of other charts and methods are available to the PM and project team for presenting schedule progress. In this section I introduce just a few of them.

- **Milestone chart.** As previously mentioned, this type of chart is great for project sponsor/executive-level reporting on schedule status (refer back to Figure 6.3 for an example of a milestone chart).

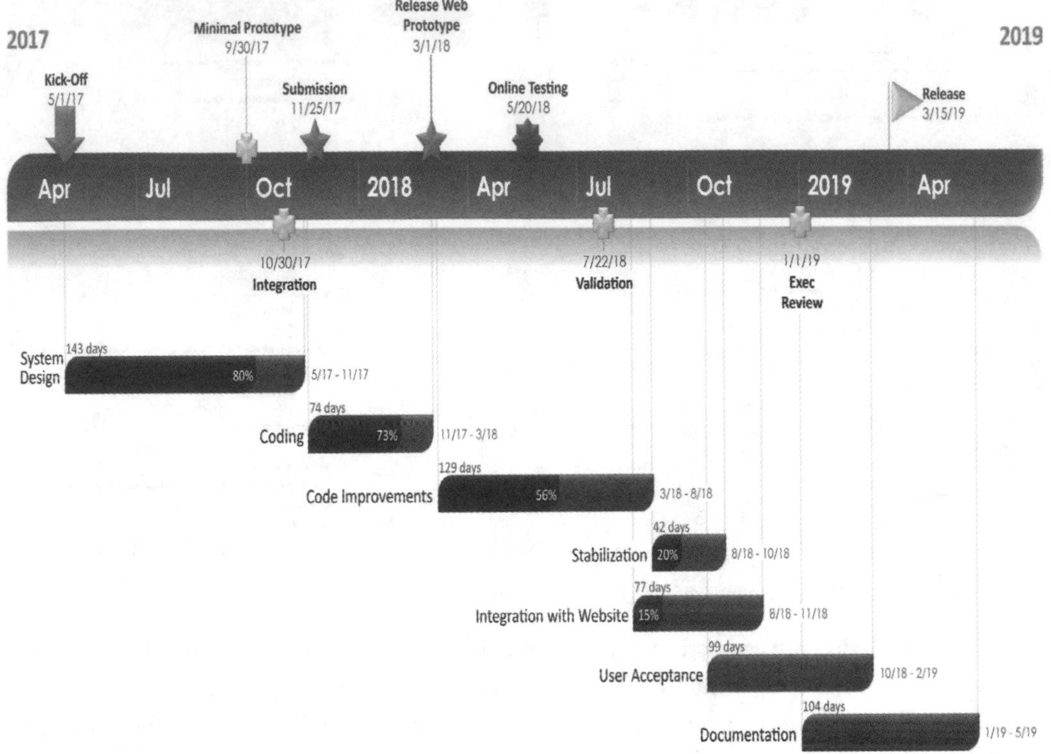

FIGURE 6.9 Sample Gantt Chart

- **Dashboard.** This is typically a single-page, summary-level report of compressed project information, usually displayed with "traffic light" (red, yellow, green) indicators. The indicators show overall status of the project and its key metrics (measurement components). The dashboard serves as a "heads-up display (HUD)" to sponsors on the schedule and other aspects of the project, such as cost, deliverables, and risk (see Figure 6.10). Using the dashboard report also requires a legend to clearly show criteria for each category (red, yellow, green) rating.
- **Burn chart.** Shows the status and progress of the project and is the conceptual equivalent to earned value reports. These types of charts are commonly used in Agile project management methodologies such as Scrum and Extreme Programming (XP). Burn charts can be a useful addition or alternative to more conventional charts. (For more details on burn charts, Agile project management, or other terms mentioned here, I recommend that you perform an Internet search.)

Weekly Status: Project Name

Executives: list sponsors' names

Leads: other PM's or team leads you're working with in the program

Overall Status: (Y)

Last Updated: mm/dd/yyyy

Status Summary: Project objective and progress against that objective

Major Initiatives - Milestones/Deliverables	Due Dates		Dependencies on		Comments
Milestone #1	Target: Actual:	G	Dependency: Due date:	G	Reason for status: Issues
Milestone #2	Target: Actual:	Y	Dependency: Due date:	Y	Reason for status: Issues:
Milestone #3	Target: Actual:	G	Dependency: Due date:	G	Reason for status: Issues:
Milestone #4	Target: Actual:	R	Track: Dependency:	R	Reason for status: Issues:
Milestone #5	Target: Actual:	G	Track: Dependency:	G	Reason for status: Issues:

FIGURE 6.10 Sample Dashboard

Regardless of the process or type of chart you use to report project schedule status, there are some basic terms and techniques you should be familiar with such as lead time, lag time, and hammocks (not the kind you swing in).

Leads and Lags

Lead and *lag* are terms describing techniques (including values) used to control the timing of activities. For example, if the work package is to paint the living room of your house, you must first prepare the surface to be painted by removing pictures, sanding, and so on. Once the walls are painted, you must wait for the paint to dry prior to hanging the pictures back on the wall. This is lag time. An example of lead time is that you must preheat the oven prior to cooking a turkey dinner; thus, the activity to preheat the oven involves lead time (starting the activity sooner than it's associated activity—cooking the turkey).

If you need to alter the relationship between two work packages or activities, you can use lead or lag time. *Lead time* removes time from the start of the activity, allowing an acceleration of the successor activity, whereas *lag time* adds time to the start of the activity (allows

- **Finish-to-Start with lag time**

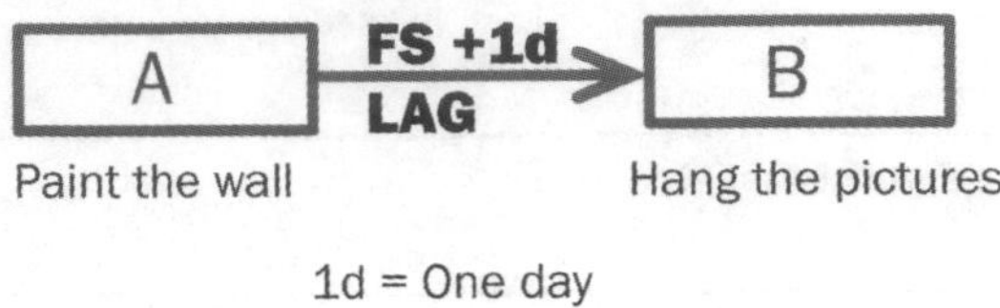

- **Finish-to-Start with lead time**

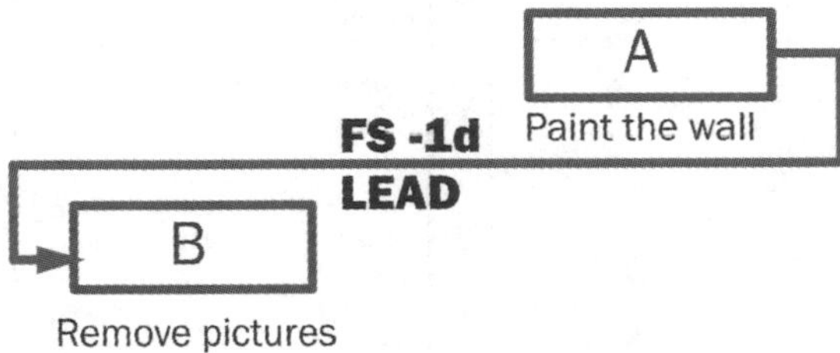

FIGURE 6.11 Sample Lead and Lag Time Relationship

a delay in the successor activity). Lead time is usually shown as a negative number, and lag time is a positive number (see Figure 6.11).

The concepts or techniques to manage time on your project schedule are better understood via examples.

First, let's use the P&G help desk transition case study for an example of lead time. While finalizing the transition project plan and staffing requirements to move the call center support from Cincinnati to Boulder, Colorado, the PM needs the readiness test results of the Boulder call center systems and support capabilities at least two weeks prior to the actual cut over. This could be shown as lead time on the network diagram. This commonly shows as a Finish-to-Start relationship with a two-week lead (FS 2 weeks). Another example of lead-time would be like pre-heating the oven before we can cook the turkey for Thanksgiving dinner.

Second, lag time is best described as a forced or planned delay, such as in a construction project where we can begin restoring each room (hanging pictures, replacing the furniture, etc.) once the paint has dried (in assembly-line fashion). Lag time can be shown as a Finish-to-Start relationship, where the painting ends with one day of lag time for the paint to dry prior to the room being restored. Another example often used is when pouring concrete; you must wait two days (lag time) to remove the forms after the concrete has dried (FS + 2 days).

HAMMOCK ACTIVITY

A hammock activity (also known as a "summary activity") represents a group or collection of related (or unrelated) activities aggregated at a summary level. It often groups subtasks or even subprojects that are not related in a logical sense of a dependency in which one subtask must wait for another. For example,

- Grouping dissimilar activities that lead to an overall capability, such as preparations under a summary label; for example, "project initiation or construction-site preparation"
- Grouping unrelated items for the purpose of a summary such as a calendar-based reporting period; for example, "first-quarter plans"

- Grouping ongoing or overhead activities that run the length of an effort; for example, "project management"

Tip

Remember, change is inevitable. As you and the team are working the details of the Sequence Activities process, you will discover the need to make changes to the project plan, WBS, and perhaps other project documents. Requested changes can surface at any time by any stakeholder. Watch for the changes and manage them as part of the Perform Integrated Change Control process, as mentioned in Chapter 4.

To emphasize the importance of network diagrams and how they can help you as a PM, let's discuss their benefits.

Ask the Expert

Q: How does a network diagram help me as a PM?

A: Network diagrams can help with schedule management in the following ways:

- They provide a visual relationship of the work to be performed on the project.
- They show interdependencies of all activities and the workflow from one to the next.
- They help in the project planning and organizing, and tracking progress of the project.
- They identify activities on the critical path for improved schedule awareness and control.
- They identify activities on the noncritical path (you can temporarily reassign resources to help expedite an activity on the critical path to potentially eliminate a schedule overrun).

Resource Calendars and Resource Leveling

Remember, in project management the team is (or should be) the number-one asset. One way to manage the team, the individuals on the team, and other key resources is with organized scheduling. Without the scheduling tools of resource calendars and resource leveling, you will have conflicts and missed deadlines.

RESOURCE CALENDARS

As a PM, you live and die by the calendar. You need to know who is available on your team at all times. A resource calendar is a great way to do this. More details on this appear in Chapter 9, "Resource Management."

With more team members working across multiple projects at any given time, or working in virtual teams from other countries with different time zones, you have limited availability in this shared resource environment. The problem then becomes a matter of making sure you have people on-board and fully trained to get the work done according to the schedule. The best way to manage this challenge is by using a resource calendar. More details will be provided in Chapter 9 (Resource Management Knowledge Area). Figure 6.12 shows an example of a Resource Calendar.

Try This

WHO'S ON FIRST? (KNOWING THE SCHEDULE)

You are the PM on a global project that requires "all hands on deck" availability during a critical test of a new call center scheduled to go live after the Labor Day weekend (a holiday in the United States on the first Monday of September). The majority of the project preparation work effort is to occur during the month of August. One of your team members in Asia casually mentions that most of the Asian team members will be out honoring religious holidays most of the month of August. What do you do? Take a few minutes to jot down possible solutions before reading the following answer.

Answer: If the schedule is set and the deliverable is firm, use team members from other countries that don't recognize the same holidays, or pay higher rates to the people who are available and willing to work over the holiday period to keep the project on schedule.

To manage resources effectively, you need to do your research ahead of time. You need to know that many countries in both Asia and Europe have major holidays and vacations during the month of August. Therefore, you should plan accordingly. Useful tools include a resource/responsibility assignment matrix (RAM) (see example in Chapter 9) and, of course, a resource calendar for quick reference to see who is assigned to critical activities and whether they are available when needed.

Make-or-Buy Decision

When it comes to managing the project schedule, one of the decisions you will have to make is the *make-or-buy decision*, which means you have to determine if your team has the skills, tools, talent, equipment, and materials necessary to perform the work internal to your project team. Alternatively, you may need to go outside the project team to buy a product or the expertise to perform the work. The make-or-buy analysis is a way to help ensure that you and the team are focused on those things you can do internally and allows you increased flexibility when you are better off going outside for the skills or products needed. This option can work well or may add costs and risk to your schedule. The make-or-buy analysis will be discussed more in the Project Risk Management and Project Procurement Management Knowledge Areas (Chapters 11 and 12, respectively).

Estimate Activity Durations Process (Planning Process Group)

Congratulations! By this time, you and the team have identified the work, what needs to be accomplished, and who is going to do the work. Now it is time to get the team together

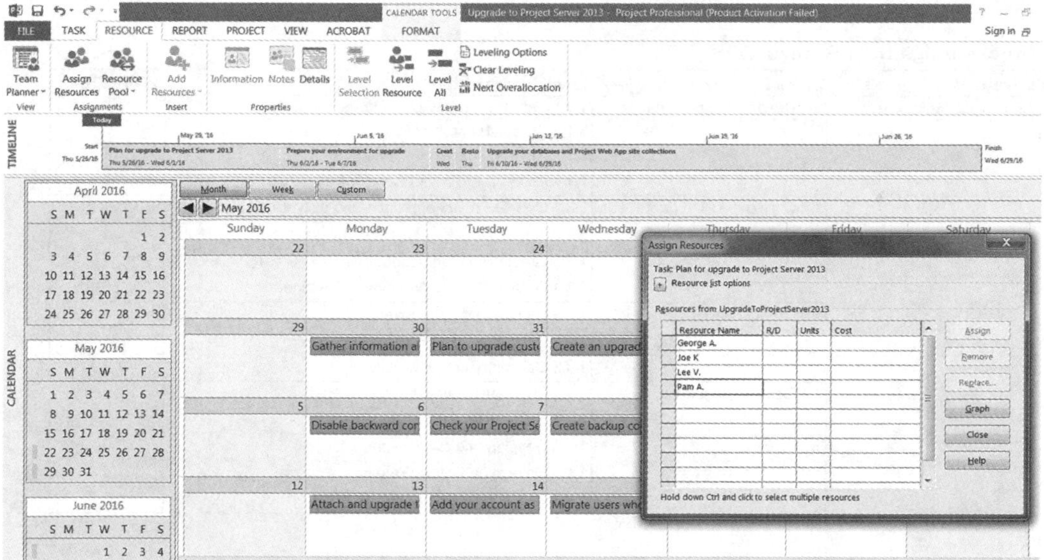

FIGURE 6.12 Sample Resource Calendar

again and perform the Estimate Activity Durations process for all the activities on the project.

I can't emphasize enough the importance of performing this process as a team sport. This is where the team provides their input and expertise in estimating the duration of the work activities. You will have a better chance of getting buy-in if you work this process as a team. Besides, two heads (or many heads) are better than one. The synergy and brainstorming will provide you a more complete package when the process is finished.

I should also mention that duration estimating is usually measured in days, as opposed to "effort," which is usually estimated in hours. Duration estimating is the length of time the activity will take, whereas effort is the labor applied to the activity. Duration estimating should take into account meetings, unscheduled interruptions, and project management activities other than hands-on work, which tends to always take longer than expected. See Figure 6.13 for an example of activity duration estimates as it would appear in a WBS.

Effort (or level of effort) estimating is used more extensively in estimating cost, where you are only charged for the actual time spent on the project. These two types of estimating usually go out the window if the person is assigned to your project full time (dedicated), and you will be paying them for total time worked, regardless of the specific hours spent in direct support of the project.

Breckenridge Beer Festival WBS			Estimated
Level 1: Categories	Level 2: Work Packages	Level 3: Activities	Work Days
1.0 Project Management	1.1 Develop Project Charter	1.1.1 Gather or review project requirements	2
		1.1.2 Create 1st draft of Project Charter	2
		1.1.3 Review Charter and submit for approval	1
		1.1.4 Approval of Project Charter (milestone)	0
	1.2 Create PM Plan document	1.2.1 Outline Project approach and deliverables	5
	(including scope)	1.2.2 Validate requirements and milestones	4
		1.2.3 Create PM Plan document (deliverable)	1
		1.2.4 Obtain PM Plan Approval (milestone)	0
	1.3 Create Budget	1.3.1 Review budget requirements	1
		1.3.2 Determine resources	1
		1.3.3 Calculate budget w/ risks	1
	1.4 Develop Schedule	1.4.1 Estimate activity durations	1
		1.4.2 Incorporate risks	1
		1.4.3 Develop and review schedule	3
		1.4.3 Determine Critical Path	2
		1.4.4 Obtain schedule approval (milestone)	0

FIGURE 6.13 Sample Activity Duration Estimates

Note

Let's say we are working on our painting project. The team has determined it will take 80 hours (level of effort) over a two-week period to complete painting the house. Now, if we have two people painting, we can complete the job in 40 hours (duration). Therefore, the estimate based on resources available is 40 hours (or one business week). If we add two more people to the project, we should be able to complete the job in 20 hours duration; however, we are still expending 80 hours of effort (four people times 20 hours of work each).

Other dynamics need to be considered when estimating activity duration. For example, it has been my experience that sometimes the actual time to complete an activity actually goes *up* with the more people you assign to it. After a certain point, putting more people on the project may lead to more distractions, the workspace may become limiting, and the workers can become counterproductive. Therefore, instead of 80 hours, the activity could very well take 100 hours.

Another common problem occurs when making the team work more overtime. At some stage, you reach the point (or law) of diminishing returns when throwing more overtime hours at an activity. The result of this dilemma is a decrease in quality, more mistakes, and potential injuries due to employee fatigue—all while costing more for overtime pay.

Some common mistakes or shortfalls when defining project activities include underestimating the time involved in managing the overall project. You should try to think outside the box to identify possible risks ("known unknowns" and "unknown unknowns," which are discussed in more detail in Chapter 11).

Estimate Activity-Durations Inputs, Tools and Techniques, and Outputs

There are a large number of inputs, tools and techniques, and outputs associated with the Estimate Activity Durations process. Also notice the many types of tools and techniques (see Figure 6.14) that can assist the PM and team in estimating activity durations. Let's take a closer look at some of them. For more details on inputs, tools and techniques, and outputs see the *PMBOK Guide*.

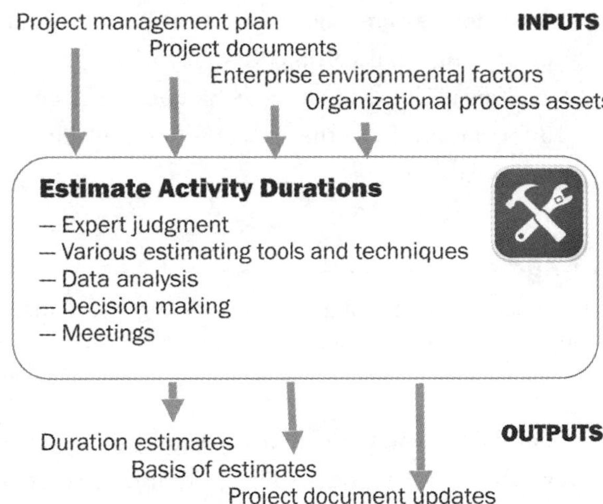

FIGURE 6.14 Estimate Activity Durations Process ITTOs

Types of Duration Estimating

PMI recognizes several tools and techniques for estimating both the duration and cost of the activities identified during the previous processes (more details related to cost estimating will be covered in Chapter 7, Project Cost Management):

- **Expert judgment.** This is the preferred technique, especially if you have worked with the project team before and you know whom to call on for the best answers to certain questions. For example, if you are estimating how long it takes to change over from an ice hockey arena to a rodeo at the event center, you call on Jake or Matt, who have done this activity a hundred times or more, to tell you how long it takes. You might also want to qualify the estimate based on the skill level required (for example, an expert can do things quicker than a novice employee).

Tip

When using expert judgment, the tendency is for the expert to provide a "one-time estimate" (one estimate per activity). There are advantages and disadvantages to a one-time estimate. The advantage is you get the estimate directly from the expert, and usually this is the most accurate. The disadvantage, especially if the activity is new or not frequently performed, is you tend to get "padding" in the time estimate. The best solution is to have the team members participate in creating the WBS and then work from it for the best estimates possible.

Also keep in mind the estimating types discussed in this section apply to either duration estimating or cost estimating.

- **Analogous estimating.** This is a form of expert judgment that's also called "top-down estimating." It involves taking historical estimates from previous, similar projects (an analogy). This estimation technique is used to determine the duration when the detailed information about the project is not available, usually during the early stages of the project.

Tip

PMI seems to prefer analogous estimating due to the use of historical information from previous, similar projects and tends to lean toward this type of estimating on the exam questions.

- **Parametric estimating.** This type of estimating uses a "duration per unit" (quantifiable/mathematical) model, such as duration or cost per square foot (for a construction project), cost per line of code (for a software-development project), and units per hour (for a manufacturing project) to determine how long an activity will take. You simply multiply the duration per unit (or price) by the quantity (*P* [or D] times *Q*) to get the estimated amount of work to determine the overall duration and cost.
- **Three-point estimating.** In the real world, the probability of completing a project on a set date (especially when change is inevitable) is pretty low. Therefore, the best way to determine the range of estimating accuracy is to estimate the probable date (or cost) using a weighted average of a three-point estimate. Here is how it works: A SME who is very familiar with the activity estimates the best (optimistic = *O*), the worst (pessimistic = *P*), and the most likely (*M*) time (*t*) or cost to perform the activity. Then you can use the following formula, known as a *beta distribution*, to calculate the three-point estimate of the expected duration (*tE*):

$$tE = (tO + 4tM + tP)/6$$

Depending on the assumed distribution of values within the range of the three estimates, the expected duration *tE* can also be calculated using the *triangular distribution* formula as follows:

$$tE = (tO + tM + tP)/3$$

Note that PMI refers to the three-point time estimate as a PERT estimate along with two other formulas that may appear on the PMP exam for activity duration and cost estimating (see Figure 6.15). It would be a good idea to memorize them.

Three-point estimate for an activity:	Standard deviation of an activity:	Variance of an activity:
$\frac{(P + 4ML + O)}{6}$	$\frac{P - O}{6}$	$\left(\frac{P - O}{6}\right)^2$

Note: to estimate duration for the project you need to add up the activity estimates on the critical path, and since statistically you can't add standard deviations, you must calculate the variances for the activities.

FIGURE 6.15 PERT Formulas

- **Group Decision-Making Techniques.** These techniques are used to bring the estimating process to closure. It is best to use a combination of estimating methods, but ultimately, the team needs to step back and assess the quality of the data they have created and commit to numbers they believe in. Group decision-making techniques were also discussed in Chapter 5.

Try This

USING THREE-POINT ESTIMATE FOR TRAVEL TIME

You have driven the same route to work for the past three years, so you are the SME on how long the trip takes. You have determined it takes you 45 minutes to get to work on a good (optimistic) day (with good weather and minimum traffic). On a poor-weather or heavy-traffic day, it takes as long as 75 minutes. However, the most likely drive time is one hour (60 minutes). Plugging these numbers into a three-point beta formula results in the following:

$$(45 + (4 \times 60) + 75)/6, \text{ or } (45 + 240 + 75)/6, \text{ or } 360/6 = 60 \text{ minutes}$$

Therefore, knowing the three-point formula, what do you get?

Answer: It will take one hour (60 minutes) on average to drive to work. This type of estimate is used when accuracy is important; however, it does take more time as you need to collect data from a reliable source and to factor in the different elements.

- **Meetings.** No one likes meetings; however, they are an important tool or technique used in many different processes to help communicate status, identify issues, and to review needed changes. Face it, meetings are a way of life but should be used appropriately to help keep everyone focused and on the same page.

Develop Schedule Process (Planning Process Group)

Figure 6.16 shows an overview of the inputs, tools and techniques, and the outputs for the Develop Schedule process.

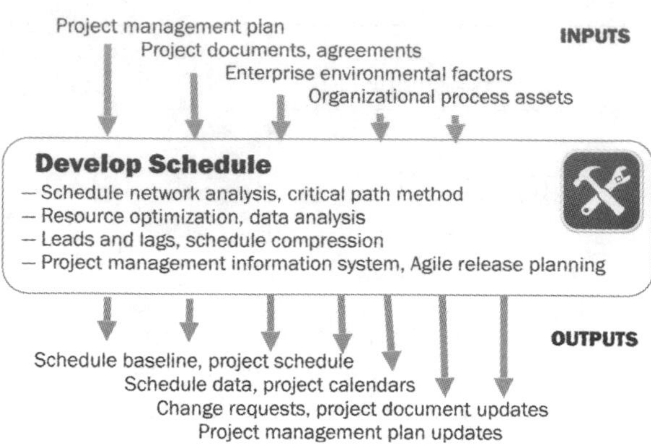

FIGURE 6.16 Develop Schedule Process ITTOs]

Schedule development is where the rubber meets the road, so to speak. It's where the schedule management work really begins, and the results of this process will have a huge impact on your project management capability and credibility.

Once you have a network diagram and activity and resources estimates, it is time to put the information into a schedule. (The difference between a time estimate and a schedule is that the schedule is calendar based.)

Ask the Expert

Q: Is there a checklist that can help me and my team develop a schedule for our project?

A: Yes, there is. This is one I have used that seems to work pretty well.

- Start with a clear understanding of the work required on the project (scope statement, charter, stakeholder priorities, expectations, time frame, deliverables, and so on).
- Clearly define the activities (WBS, WBS dictionary, and activity list) and alternatives.
- Have a clear idea of the order of how the work should be done (activity sequencing).
- Obtain an estimate of the resources needed (activity-resource estimating).
- Obtain an estimate of the duration of each activity (activity-duration estimating).
- Obtain a company calendar identifying working days and nonworking days (this varies by country) as well as key stakeholder (team members and sponsor) vacation days.
- Identify imposed dates (deadlines or major deliverable target dates).
- Identify and verify milestones and dependencies (internal and external agents).
- Identify and document assumptions (in scope and out-of-scope exclusions).
- Identify constraints (time, cost limitations, lead times, lag times, and dependencies).
- Identify other potential impacts to the schedule such as resource availability.
- Obtain formal stakeholder acceptance of the schedule.

The Develop Schedule process involves analyzing activity sequences, activity durations, resource requirements, and schedule constraints to create a project schedule.

So, how do you effectively develop the project schedule? This process starts with the outputs from other previous processes. With your team, focus on activity duration estimates to help ensure that the schedule is both realistic and achievable.

The question that must be answered at the end of this process is, How long will the entire project take to complete? Armed with the activity duration estimates, your team, and the outputs already collected, you work very closely with all the stakeholders to develop the project schedule. As with all project management processes, having a planned approach always helps. Here are some things to consider when developing your project schedule:

- First and foremost, remember to make this a team sport by getting all the information, constraints, and expert judgment you can. At the end of the process you should have buy-in from the team and other key stakeholders.
- Next, you need to fully understand the requirements and stakeholder priorities (don't be afraid to ask and verify these key components).
- Be open minded and look at various options. Also, document the options even if they are not used right away. This will give you a head start on risk management plan development (see Chapter 11).
- Look across the entire project (charter to close), as mentioned in Chapter 4, to see how the project can impact (or be impacted by) other projects—for example, limited resources, changes in priorities, and shift in sponsors (turnover) or budget dollars. To this end, you might want to get managers to provide you with "letters of commitment" for key resources to ensure that the necessary people will be available on your project for the time needed without interruptions from other work or projects.
- Factor in special project requirements, methods, or techniques such as Agile project management. So what project-specific data must be added to create an Agile schedule? An Agile project starts with a backlog, which is a list of features to be implemented, and a number of iterations, or sprints, to implement those features. These are the tasks in the schedule. In addition, each feature will have a priority and a size estimate in story points and will be mapped to an iteration, or sprint. Each feature and sprint will also require a status—e.g., not started, in progress, or done.[5]
- Last, when the schedule is developed, you must manage it continually. Never put the schedule in a desk drawer or on a shelf. It should be a working document that's reviewed, worked, and revised (through change control) early and often, as needed, to be up to date and accurate.

Also, it is important for you to use progressive elaboration (iterative processing) to apply the things you have learned as you progress further into the project life cycle to update the schedule and other documents. As much as we would like to "lock in" on the schedule at the beginning, a phenomenon called "discovery" surfaces as we get deeper into the project. As we learn more about the project, we need to make updates to the schedule. This is often called *hindsight* (which people say is 20/20). This means historical information is a good thing.

Tip

Be very aware of project constraints, limitations, or barriers that can cause you and the team to stumble and fall. It is extremely difficult to see all the constraints at the beginning of the project. This is why you need to be aware of possible constraints and the possible impact to the project throughout the life cycle. Constraints can appear in many forms; some are self-inflicted and in some cases can be turned into real opportunities. A good example of a project with a schedule constraint is the Olympics: it doesn't matter whether or not the paint is dry on the stadium seats; the torch is to be lit at a specific time on a specific date.

Impact of Project Constraints

Constraints are imposed on projects from many sources—even from within (self-inflicted). Suppose you are putting activities into your scheduling software tool and you decide the date for a particular activity is fixed (e.g., "must start on" or "must finish on"). What do you think this does to the scheduling software that works so hard to calculate float, overall duration, and the critical path of your project? It can really mess things up! I have seen this happen many times. When the dates don't make sense in the scheduling tool, chances are that you or someone has set a constraint without fully understanding the impact to the overall project. Don't get me wrong— there are times when fixed-date constraints are needed. Just be aware that when a date is fixed (constrained), it will likely force an override in the software tool and change the overall schedule.

Types of Schedule Constraints

The four common types of schedule constraints are listed and described in Table 6.2. The two used most often are as follows:

- Start No Earlier Than (SNET)
- Finish No Later Than (FNLT)

It is important to remember that constraints can be tied to individual project activities or the entire project. Also, constraints are often tied directly to a milestone, which may be outside the project team. Remember, milestones are major events on the project and require zero resources (from the project team) and carry zero duration.

TABLE 6.2 Schedule Constraints

Constraint	What the Constraint Does	Examples
Start No Earlier Than (SNET)	The constraint sets when an activity can begin, based on a predetermined date or time, often because of a dependency (usually customer imposed).	Setting up the church for a wedding. This activity cannot begin until Monday after the Sunday evening church service has been completed. The electrician on a construction project can start no earlier than when the milestone of the building inspector signing off on the roof decking is complete.
Start No Later Than (SNLT)	The constraint indicates the activity must start prior to a predetermined deadline. This is also known as "right-to-left scheduling."	A changeover project to convert the events center from a rodeo to a concert takes two weeks; therefore, the changeover can start no later than June 1 to be ready for a June 15 concert date.
Finish No Earlier Than (FNET)	This constraint requires the activity to be in progress up until a predetermined date.	The tests for software are required to run continuously until June 15 to obtain adequate results.
Finish No Later Than (FNLT)	This constraint states that an activity or project must finish on a predetermined date.	Federal income taxes must be mailed (postmarked) no later than April 15.

Reporting Schedule Status

Different styles for different stakeholders are an easy way to think about the type of report to use (as well as format and frequency) when reporting the project schedule. This topic will be discussed in more detail in Chapter 10. There are a few things to think about before you set up your status reports.

Some PMs, when asked, "Are we on schedule?" are so detail oriented that they are quick to tell you how to build a watch rather than just tell you the time of day. Too often we feel the need to tell the whole story rather than the only-the-facts version. This is especially true on project status reports—keep them short and to the point. This is where milestone charts are great for reporting status to middle-level or executive-level managers.

Remember there are times when "less is more." Less information—as long as it is the right information—is often more than enough detail to get the message across. The key is to know your audience—know what their interests are and be sure to work on providing the right information, as needed, in a suitable format. For example, a "dashboard" report provides a great way to show high-level status.

It is difficult to stay focused on the overall project schedule if you are trying to manage time only. You must be able to manage both time and the overall project sequence of activities to bring the project in on schedule.

Types of Schedule Reports

As you know, a number of report types and styles are available to present the status of a project schedule. Most PMs send the current copy of their project schedule as a Microsoft Project (.mpp) file. This is easy to do; however, not everyone on the team or your sponsors will have licensed software to view Microsoft Project files. This or any other scheduling software can be expensive. Fortunately, most software products today allow you to save the file in HTML or other viewable formats, such as exports to Microsoft Excel or other software that allows you to view files from other applications.

Ask the Expert

Q: When should I baseline the project schedule?

A: The sooner you baseline, the better (as mentioned in Chapter 5). The longer you wait, the more changes will likely occur, thus making the schedule end date a moving target. When there are many changes, you need to document, verify, and obtain formal acceptance of the target date. Once the target date is approved, you should baseline the schedule and use change control, which will give you an opportunity to renegotiate a new adjusted target date and re-baseline the schedule when changes are likely to move out the project completion date.

Critical Path Method (CPM)

As mentioned earlier, the critical path (CP) is defined as the longest path through the network that represents the shortest amount of time to complete the project. The activities on the CP have the biggest impact on the project end date. The way to calculate CP is by using the critical path method (CPM).

As part of the precedence diagramming method, the CPM helps you determine where the flexibility (or lack of flexibility) resides. The CPM involves calculating the earliest start (ES) date, earliest finish (EF) date, latest start (LS) date, and latest finish (LF) date for each activity in the network diagram. Sounds pretty ominous. However, it is much easier done as a team exercise, and it adds validity (buy-in) to the time it takes to complete the project.

In Chapter 5, Project Scope Management, we discussed creating the WBS and the use of sticky notes to identify activities. For a recommended layout of CPM activities and how to use a sticky note to assist with the calculation of forward and backward pass and float, see Figure 6.17.

It is also important to remember that activities on the critical path always have zero float. Float (or slack) time is determined by performing a forward and backward pass through the network and calculating the amount of time an activity takes in relationship to the other activities. The goal is to identify activities that will potentially impact other activities or the overall project end date if delayed (details and examples will be discussed later in this chapter).

You should also be aware that the critical path can change if delays occur or if milestones or dependencies are missed. Also, an approved scope change or a triggered risk may cause you to have to recalculate the critical path.

Early Start	Id #	Early Finish
	Activity (verb)	
Late Start	Duration (days)	Late Finish

FIGURE 6.17 Sample Sticky Note Layout

Basic Scheduling Terms

Here are several terms you should be familiar with prior to calculating the critical path:

- **Forward pass and backward pass.** These terms are related to ways of determining the early start or early finish (forward pass) and late finish or late start (backward pass) for an activity. Forward pass is a technique to move forward through a diagram to calculate activity duration. Backward pass is its opposite.
- **Predecessor.** An activity (A) that exists on a common logic path that occurs before another activity (B).
- **Successor.** An activity (B) that exists on a common logic path that occurs after another activity (A).
- **Free float.** The amount of time an activity can be delayed without delaying the early start of any immediately following (successor) activities.
- **Float.** Also called *total float* or *slack*. The amount of time an activity can be delayed from its early start without delaying the project finish date.
- **Near critical path.** The path through the network with the lowest total float (if changes occur to the network, the near critical path may then become the critical path).
- **Lag time.** Fixed delay between the start and finish of one activity and the start or finish of another (e.g., letting the paint dry before hanging the pictures).
- **Lead time.** Modification of a fixed relationship to accelerate the start of a successor activity (for example, preheating the oven prior to the "cook the turkey" activity).
- **Dangler.** An unintended break in the network path or an activity in the network diagram that is missing a dependency from its predecessor or successor activity.
- **Loops.** Circular relationships that won't allow an activity to end (e.g., a software test cycle that continuously identifies corrections and enhancements that are never ending).

Calculating the Critical Path

To determine the critical path duration of a project, you must first perform a forward pass and then a backward pass. A forward pass will identify how early each activity in the network diagram can start (ES) and finish (EF), and a backward pass will show you how late each activity in the network diagram can start (LS) and finish (LF). This process will allow you to calculate the float of each activity. The formula to calculate the total float for an activity:

- Late Start (LS) Early Start (ES); or
- Late Finish (LF) Early Finish (EF).

The activities that have zero float are those activities that determine the critical path. You simply add the duration of every activity with zero float across the network, and that will confirm the overall project duration. This means that any activity, if changed, that impacts the project end-date is likely to be on the critical path.

By identifying all paths in the network and adding the activity durations along each path, you can determine which path is the longest duration—and that is the critical path. This process will also help identify if you have more than one critical path. (Yes, you can have more than one CP on a project.) It is also important to know the path that is nearest to the critical path in case the CP changes for some reason.

There are several steps in determining the critical path of the network diagram. The following summary-level checklist can be used as a guide to help you through this process:

1. All network diagrams should have a start milestone (this is different from an activity). Activities have durations and resources assigned; the start of a project has neither. The start milestone will have zero duration. Currently there are two methodologies used to calculate the forward and backward pass: the Zero Method and the One Method. (Most PMs like to start at day 1 and most scheduling software defaults to the one method; however, there is no hard rule on this.) You may see either or both methods used in the PMI exams. Calculating the forward and backward pass will be explained in detail later in this chapter.
2. Identify all activities that can begin immediately. These will be the starting activities of different paths, and they are successors to the start milestone.
3. Identify the next dependent or associated activity to continue the logical relationship of the network path. In essence what you are doing is continuing to identify the next successor activities.
4. Complete the process until all predecessors and successors have been identified (with no danglers).

5. Identify the activities that signify completion of the project (always have an "end" milestone).
6. Calculate the forward pass. Note that when multiple activities converge into a single activity, you should select the activity with the highest early finish (EF) to carry forward to the early start (ES) of the successor activity (see details and Figure 6.20, later in this chapter).
7. Find the latest early finish dates of the project. This will give you an idea of the overall length of the project.
8. Calculate the backward pass. Note that when multiple activities converge into a single activity, you should select the lowest late start (LS) to carry over to the late finish (LF) single-predecessor activity (see details and Figure 6.21, later in this chapter).
9. Calculate the float. Note that the total float is within the activity, and free float is between two activities.
10. Identify the critical path (or critical paths) and the near critical path.
11. Validate the network to ensure that it is correct and complete.
12. Become familiar with the characteristics of the network.
13. Verify that the work can be done with the available resources.
14. Take actions to adjust the schedule as needed.
15. Be sure to include project management activities.

Activity Convergence and Divergence

Other terms you need to be aware of when calculating the forward and backward pass are *activity* or *path convergence* and *activity* or *path divergence*:

- **Path convergence.** This state occurs when deliverables of two or more predecessor activities are required for the start of a single successor activity (see Figure 6.18). On a forward pass, when predecessor activities converge into a single successor activity, you should always use the latest of the EF dates of the predecessor activities as the early start date of the successor activity. On a backward pass, always use the smallest late start date as the late finish date of the successor activity. Convergence calculations will differ based on the Zero Method or One Method, whose calculations will be explained in the next section.
- **Path divergence.** This state occurs when deliverables of one predecessor activity are required for the start of two or more successor activities. On a forward pass, when diverging a single predecessor activity into multiple successor activities, you should use the early finish of the predecessor activity as the early start date of each of the successor activities. On a backward pass, when diverging a single activity into multiple activities, use the late

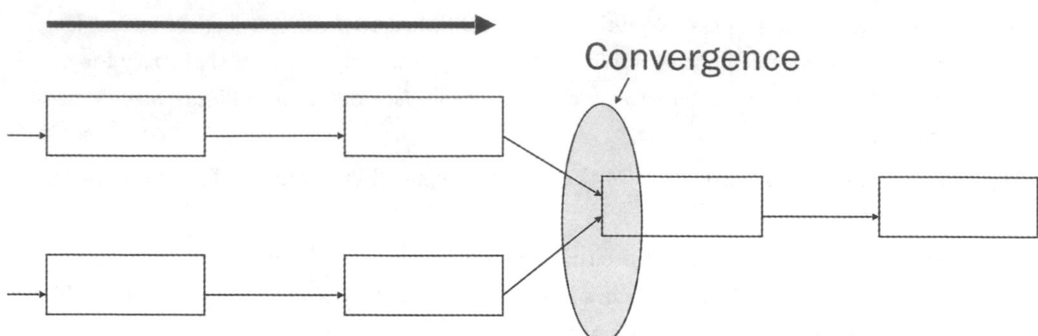

FIGURE 6.18 Sample Converging Paths

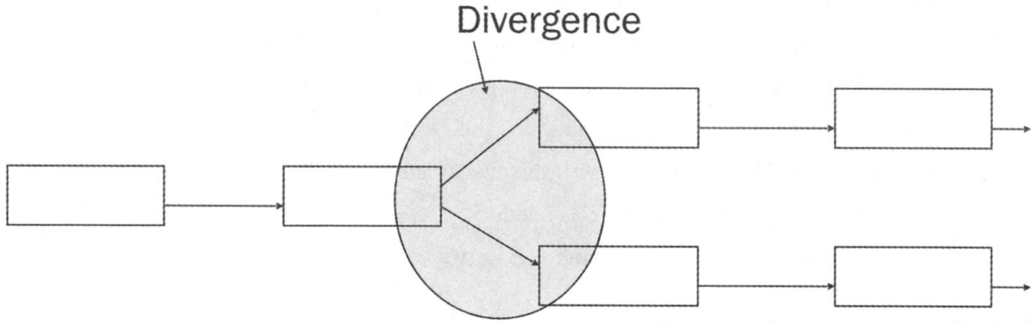

FIGURE 6.19 Sample Diverging Paths

start of the predecessor activity as the late finish date of each of the successor activities (see Figure 6.19). Divergence calculations will differ based on the Zero Method or One Method, whose calculations will be explained in the next section.

Tip

Here are a couple tips to help when you are running the forward and backward pass:

- "Mind the line," which means pay close attention to the relationship lines (convergent paths, finish-to-start, and so on).
- "Mind the sign (+/–)," which means watch for lead and lag times. Lag is a delay (+ time) going forward; however, it's a minus sign (–) coming back on the backward pass. Lead time is "negative" lag—that is, a minus sign (–) on the forward pass and a plus sign (+) on the backward pass.

These tips will make more sense as you work through your own network diagrams.

Two Methods to Calculate Forward and Backward Pass

There are two methods that can be used to determine starts and finishes. One of the methods is easy to use for the exam, while the other method is more often used and seems to work well in real life.

So which method is better to learn? If you are planning to take a PMI exam and plan to be involved with schedule management as a PM, you should be aware of and learn both.

The two ways to calculate early starts and early finishes and late starts and late finishes are sometimes called the One Method and the Zero Method. These titles refer to the early start number you use in the calculations—either a 1 or a 0. Although the starts of the two methods are somewhat different, they both calculate the same finishes. Most project scheduling software programs use the One Method.

Because there are different assumptions associated with each method, you will need to think of the two methods in different ways to grasp the concepts. This differentiation is likely to cause even more confusion if you do not fully understand the basic concept of a forward pass and a backward pass and the purpose of these calculations.

Tip

Feedback indicates there may be questions on the PMI exams using either or both methods for calculating the forward and backward pass. A couple of things to keep in mind will help with determining which method is being used in a particular question.

- Zero Method always starts on day 0 and you do not advance (+ 1 day) from the late start (LS) of an activity to the early start (ES) of the next (successor) activity.
- One Method always starts on day 1 and does advance + 1 day from the last start of an activity to the early start of the next (successor) activity.

The big difference between these two methods is the One Method assumes full workdays (inclusive) with work starting at the beginning (top) of the ES of a given day and finishing work at the end (LS) of the last workday that was estimated in the duration of that activity). The concept is simply giving you full availability of each duration workday. For example, say activity A starts on day 1 and has a duration of four days; with the One Method you would show the ES on day 1, then add +4 workdays duration and then −1 day due the inclusive full use of each day. The formula is therefore ES + duration − 1 for the LS. As mentioned earlier, you then add + 1 day from this activity (activity A) to its successor (next) activity B, giving the successor activity B an ES of 4 + 1 = day 5 and so on. The fact that you have all day of day 1, day 2, day 3, and day 4 using all available duration days, you have to add a day if you are using the One Method to advance through the schedule.

These tips will make more sense as you practice creating network diagrams and calculating the forward and backward passes.

ONE METHOD

Because the One Method is the concept used in most scheduling software on real projects and since it tends to be the more intuitive method, let's take a look at the One Method's basic assumption: all starts are at the beginning of a time period, and all finishes are at the end of a time period.

STEPS TO CALCULATE THE FORWARD PASS USING THE ONE METHOD

The forward pass is where the activity duration estimate comes in, and it is crucial to the accuracy of the critical path calculations. Most PMs will use a software tool to calculate the forward and backward pass of the project network diagram. If you plan to take the PMP exam, you need to master calculating the forward and backward manually. In the Fifth Edition of the *PMBOK*, PMI began using a calculation methodology often referred to as the One Method. This means that the first successor activities from the start milestone begin with 1. And each following successor activity will have an early start that increments by 1 from the predecessor early finish activity. The detailed steps to calculate the forward pass are as follows:

1. Calculating the forward pass will determine the early start (ES) and early finish (EF) days for each activity. The ES and EF numbers go in the upper-left (ES) and upper-right (EF) corners, respectively, of each activity (refer to Figure 6.17).
2. The ES for the first successor activity (A) will be the duration of the predecessor activity early finish, plus 1. Typically you start the forward pass from the start milestone, which has a duration of zero. In this case, because an activity cannot start on day 0, you will place the number 1 in the ES of the first successor activity from start. This formula will hold true through the entire forward pass. The philosophy is that, in general, the successor activity cannot start on the same day the predecessor activity finished. The value of the activity ES should be placed in the upper-left corner of the node representing the activity in the network diagram. Another way to look at this is if we assume that we start an activity at the beginning of the early start day, and if the duration is four days, then we use all of day 1, day 2, and day 3 and end at the end of the day on day 4, then we have four full days of work for that period.
3. The EF of Activity A is calculated by adding the duration of A to its early start (early start + duration 1 = early finish). Place this number in the EF upper-right corner of the sticky note.
4. The early finish of Activity A then becomes the early start for the successor activity plus one day. The formula is EF of the predecessor activity + 1 = ES of the successor activity.

5. Remember, if you have multiple predecessor activities converging on a single successor activity, you must choose the latest EF date of all the predecessor activities and add one; that total will be the ES date for the successor activity. It sounds difficult, but after you create a few network diagrams and apply the forward and backward pass methodology, the process will seem more intuitive. Just keep in mind these few logic keys:
   - The first activity of a project cannot start on day 0.
   - A successor activity cannot start on the same day the predecessor activity ended.
   - When multiple predecessor activities converge on a successor activity, that activity cannot start until all the deliverables of each of the predecessor activities are complete.
6. Complete the forward pass for the entire network diagram using the following formula: EF of the predecessor activity + 1 = ES of the successor activity. To determine the successor activity, use the following formula: ES + the activity duration 1 = EF. Continue to use this formula until you have completed the forward pass. The final activity EF is the network diagram duration and should be moved into the end milestone. Do not add 1 to the final EF of the network diagram. However, if you have multiple activities converging on the finish milestone, you must continue to use the forward pass convergence rule, choosing the latest EF as the final duration of the network diagram.

Table 6.3 is used as input to help demonstrate the forward and backward passes. Using the information in Table 6.3, Figure 6.20 shows how the forward pass might look.

TABLE 6.3 Sample Table Used to Calculate Forward and Backward Pass

Activity	Predecessor	Duration
Start	None	0
A	Start	7
B	D	3
C	A	8
D	A	2
E	C	5
F	B, H	6
G	E	1
H	D	5
I	F, G	9
End	I	0

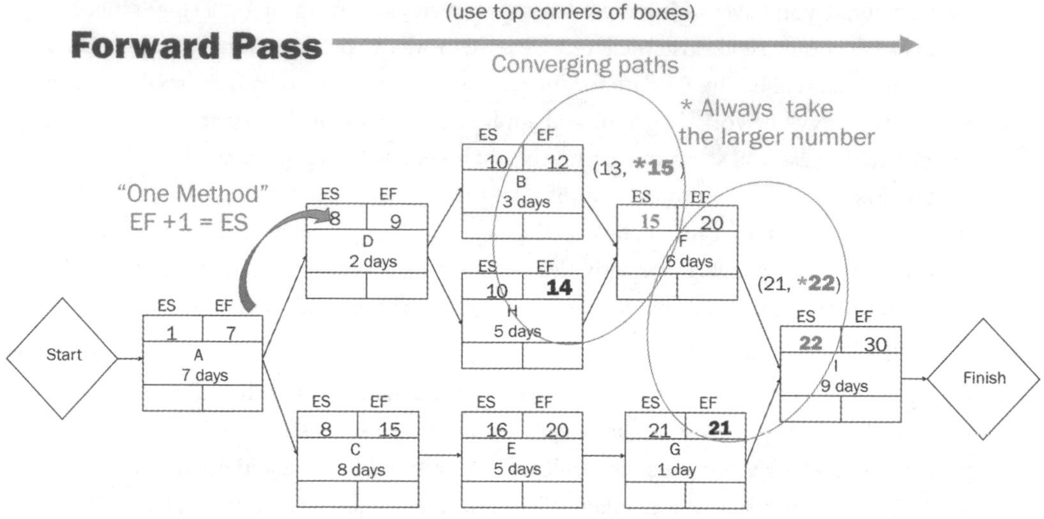

FIGURE 6.20 Forward Pass (One Method)

STEPS TO CALCULATE THE BACKWARD PASS USING THE ONE METHOD

The backward pass, if calculated properly, should get you back to the start milestone with a zero. The backward pass provides the numbers to help you calculate float. To perform the backward pass, use the late start (LS) in the lower-left corner box and the late finish (LF) in the lower-right corner box of the sticky note for each activity (see Figure 6.21).

- **Late start (LS).** The latest date an activity may begin as logically constrained by the network.
- **Late finish (LF).** The latest date an activity may finish as logically constrained by the network.

The detailed steps involved with calculating the backward pass are as follows:

1. Doing the backward pass will determine the late start (LS) and late finish (LF) duration times for each activity in the network diagram.
2. Begin with the end milestone and work backward (right to left). The first predecessor activity of the end milestone will take on the duration of the network diagram as the predecessor LF. To calculate the LS, subtract the activity duration from the LF and add 1.

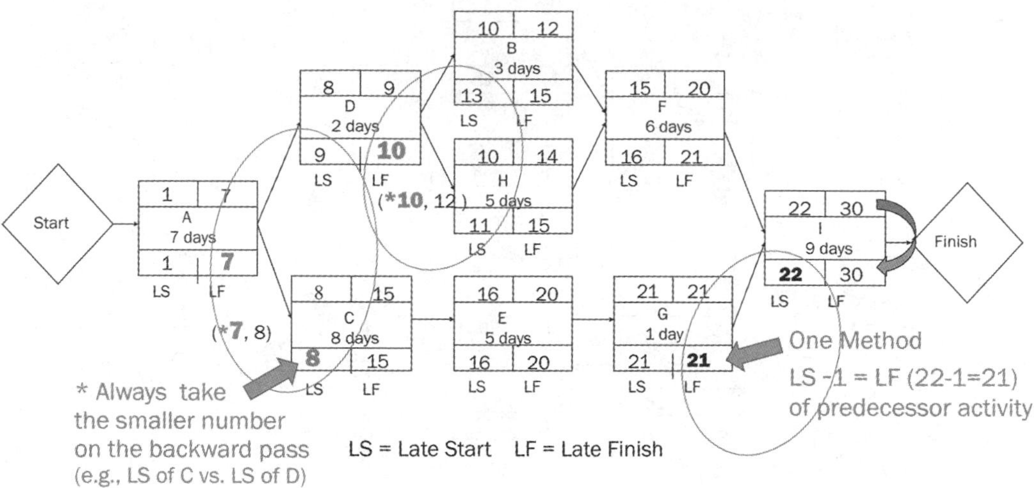

FIGURE 6.21 Backward Pass (One Method)

3. Complete the backward pass for the entire network diagram using the following formula: LS of the successor activity 1 = LF of the predecessor activity. To determine the predecessor activity LS, take the LF - the activity duration + 1 = LS. Continue using this formula until you complete the backward pass. Subtracting 1 from the final LS should give you an end result of 0 into the start milestone. If you have multiple activities converging on the start milestone, you must continue to use the backward pass convergence rule, choosing the smallest LS as the final duration of the network diagram.

Note

Always take the lowest number when multiple paths converge going back through the network diagram in either method.

4. When more than one activity succeeds a given task, the earliest of the LS dates of the successor activities is selected to become the LF date.
5. The LF is the latest that a given activity may finish without delaying the completion of the project.

Calculate Activity Float (Slack)

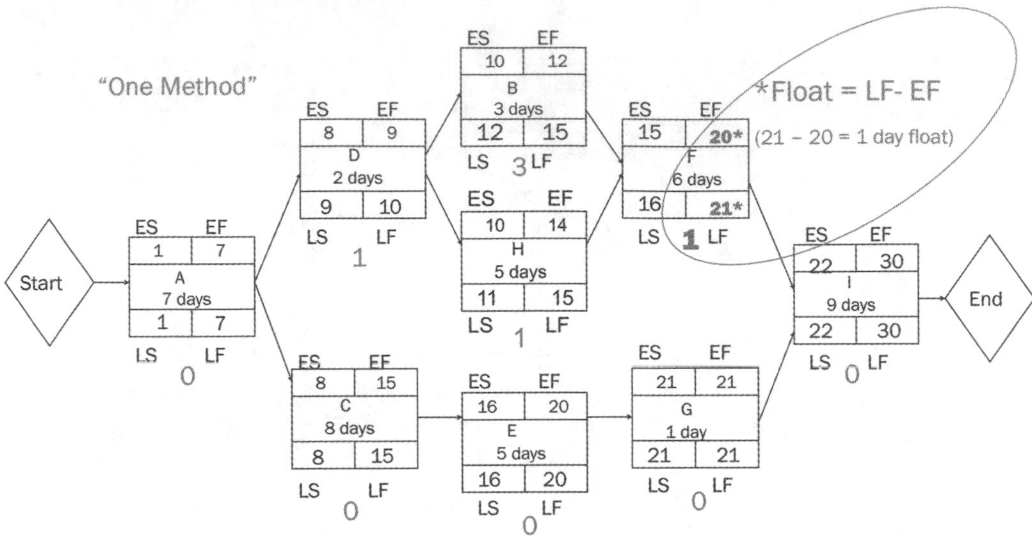

FIGURE 6.22 Float Calculation (One Method)

6. Complete the backward pass for the entire project, and calculate float to determine the critical path.

Float and Slack

The good news is that most project management software will calculate float (synonymous with *slack*). To make sure you have an idea of what is going on (or should be going on) in the software and to be able to check the software results, you should have at least a fundamental understanding of these calculations (see Figure 6.22).

- **Total float (slack).** The amount of time an activity can be delayed without delaying the project end-date or an intermediary milestone. To calculate a task or activity's float, use the following formula: (LS ES) or (LF EF) = Float
- **Free float (slack).** The amount of time an activity can be delayed without delaying the ES date of its successor activities. Here's the formula to use: (ES F EF B) = Free Float of B
- **Project float (slack).** The amount of time a project can be delayed without delaying the externally imposed project completion date required by the customer, or management, or the date committed to by the PM.

Critical Path (One Method)

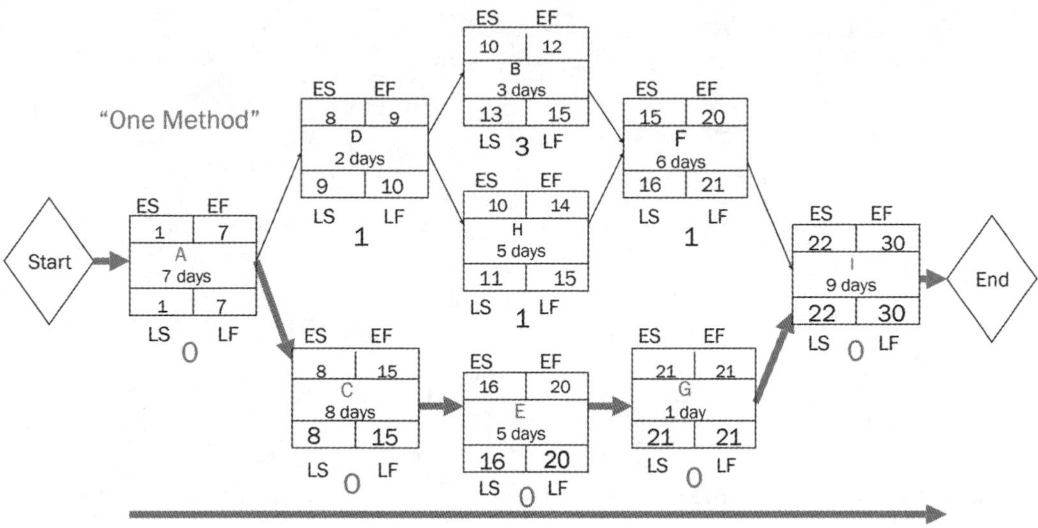

* Critical Path = 30 Days, * CP Float = 0 Days of Float

FIGURE 6.23 Critical Path (One Method)

One thing to keep in mind using the One Method is when you start at day 1 for ES of the first activity, you must end at day 1 when you have completed your calculations for both the forward pass and the backward pass, which indicates your calculations are correct.

Another important reminder is that activities on the critical path have zero float. After float has been calculated, you take the activities with zero float, and those are the activities on the critical path (see Figure 6.23).

ZERO METHOD

Next, let's look at the Zero Method assumption: all starts and ends are at the end of a time period.

STEPS TO CALCULATING THE FORWARD PASS USING THE ZERO METHOD (REFER TO FIGURE 6.24)

These methods are similar in that you should get the same overall duration of the project using either method; that is, the Zero Method or the One Method on the same network diagram will result in the same end duration. The only difference is how the ES, EF, LS, and LF

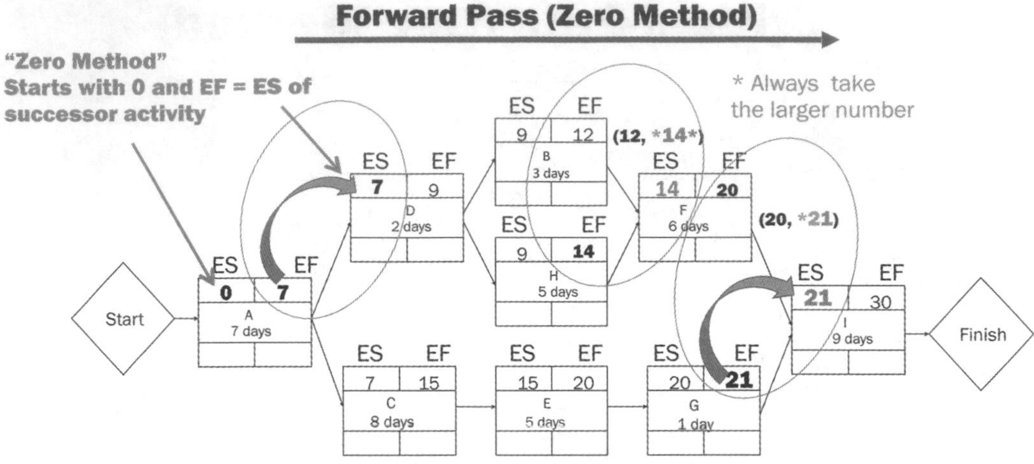

FIGURE 6.24 Forward Pass (Zero Method)

of each activity are calculated. This means that when using the Zero Method, the first successor activities from the start milestone begin with 0. And each following successor activity will have an early start that is equal to the predecessor EF.

1. To begin the forward pass you add 0 to the ES of each successor activity from the start milestone. To calculate the EF, add the duration to the ES. The EF of the predecessor activity is then moved to the ES of the successor activity. In this methodology, predecessor EF and successor ES are the same number. The same principle applies on a convergence: the largest EF of the predecessor is the successor ES.
2. Continue with the calculations from left to right until you complete the forward pass. The last activity EF is the end duration of the network diagram.

STEPS TO CALCULATE THE BACKWARD PASS USING THE ZERO METHOD (REFER TO FIGURE 6.25)

1. The first predecessor activity of the end milestone will take on the duration of the network diagram as the predecessor LF. To calculate the LS, subtract the activity duration from the LF. The LS of the successor activity is used as the LF of the predecessor activity. The same rule applies on a convergence: the smallest LS of the successor is the predecessor LF. In this methodology, successor LS and predecessor LF are the same number.

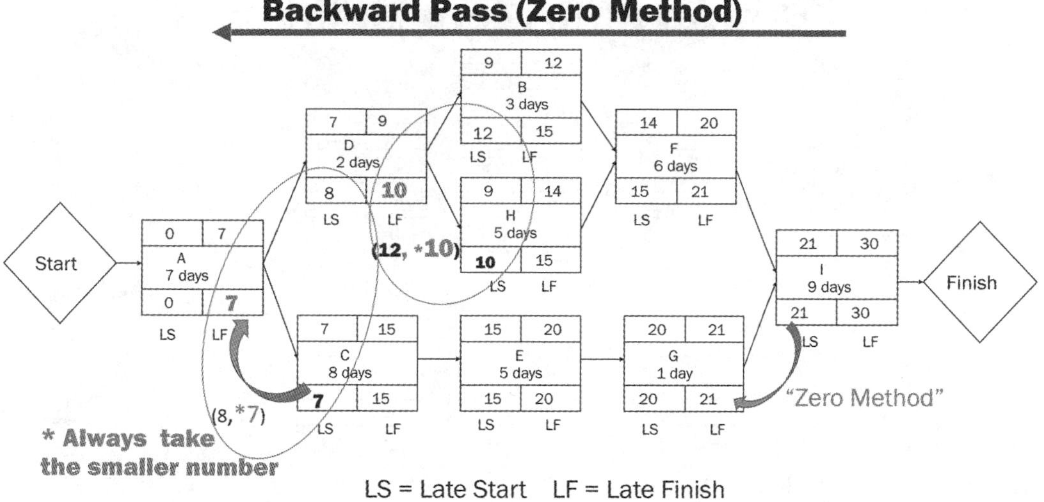

FIGURE 6.25 Backward Pass (Zero Method)

2. Continue calculating the backward pass from right to left using this formula. If your calculations are done properly, the last activity LS back at the activity just after start must be equal to the start milestone of zero (day 0). So, if you start at zero using the Zero Method, you must end at zero when you have completed your calculations for both the forward pass and the backward pass, which indicates your calculations are correct.

Figure 6.26 shows the critical path following the bolded arrows.

Control Schedule Process (Monitoring and Controlling Process Group)

The Control Schedule process involves monitoring the status of the project and reporting progress on the schedule toward project completion. Remember, all projects have an end date (or they should), so controlling the schedule is the only way to get the project to successful completion. Figure 6.27 shows an overview of the inputs, tools and techniques, and the outputs for the Control Schedule process.

Progress Reporting

Many forms and templates are available to report progress. I recommend performing an Internet search on "project progress reports" for a plethora of real-world examples.

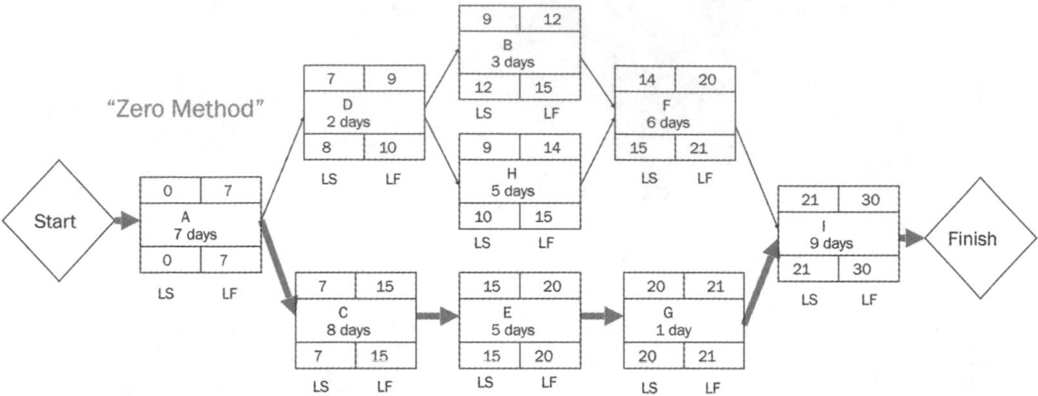

FIGURE 6.26 Critical Path (Zero Method)

Tip

For reporting high-level progress to top and middle managers and executives, you should use a dashboard or milestone charts to show major accomplishments without all the details. Also, there are ways to produce summary-level charts directly from your PM software tools using filters and such. For example, Microsoft Project has reporting options such as Overview, Current Cost, Assignments, Workload (Resource Leveling), Earned Value (EV), and Custom Reports.

A progress report is a useful method to control the schedule and costs. Many PMs determine how much work has been accomplished by asking team members for an estimate of "percent complete" for each work package or activity. On projects where work cannot be measured, this estimate is a simple guess. This is time consuming and almost always a complete waste of time because a guess does not provide a confident estimate of the actual percent complete.

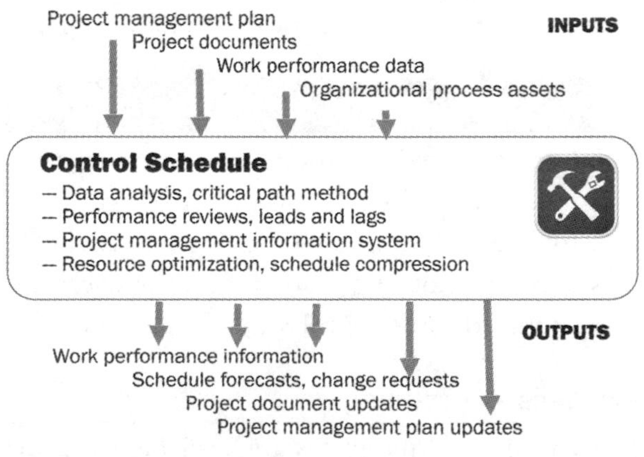

FIGURE 6.27 Control Schedule Process ITTOs

If a project has been planned using a WBS, and work packages require about 80 hours of work, there are alternatives to percent complete. Because work packages will be completed faster and more frequently, we can forget percent complete and use one of the following rules:

- **50/50 rule.** An activity is considered 50 percent complete when it begins and gets credit for the last 50 percent only when it is completed.
- **20/80 rule.** An activity is considered 20 percent complete when it begins and gets credit for the other 80 percent only when it is completed.
- **0/100 rule.** An activity does not get credit for partial completion, only full credit when complete.[6]

Tip

The PM must work with the team to get consensus to ensure that all team members have the same expectation of what, for example, 20 percent or 50 percent complete really means, so that schedule updates are reported consistently throughout the project.

Earned Value Management

Earned value management (EVM) is one tool that can be used to assess the magnitude of variation to the baseline schedule. Schedule performance measurements such as schedule variance (SV) and schedule performance index (SPI) are used. See Chapter 7 for more discussion on earned value management (EVM).

Managing the Schedule (Compression)

A project rarely follows the planned schedule. A PM must continually monitor the progress reporting and determine if the project is ahead or behind schedule. A PM may want to take corrective action to get back on schedule. There are two ways to compress the project schedule. The first is *fast tracking*, which is doing things in parallel that are normally done in sequence. The other is *crashing*, which is bringing in additional resources for the least incremental cost. If there are options for crashing, then the least-expensive option would be used. As with any form of compression, there are increased risks and tradeoffs, such as increased cost (e.g., the cost of rework or training if the added resources are not experts in the activity).

With fast tracking, you add risk by doing multiple things at the same time (a form of multitasking). When you bring more people on the project (crashing), you add cost and additional risk. Therefore, you might want to use a combination of compression techniques, as needed, to minimize cost and risk whenever possible.

One way to remember "crashing" is to think of a party. Someone who arrives uninvited is said to "crash" the party (likely eating more food than the host had planned). Therefore, remember that crashing the schedule involves bringing more people to the party, and it usually costs more than planned.

Try This

OUT-OF-CONTROL SCHEDULE

The customer comes to you (the PM) in the hallway and says, "The date for opening the help desk to begin receiving calls in Boulder, Colorado, has been moved up (sooner) by two weeks. I need to know if there is any way you can move this project schedule ahead to meet the new start date?" What do you say?

A. Sure, we can do that! No problem.

B. I will need to get with the team and see what our options are and the level of risk if we compress the schedule by two weeks. Give me a day or two to work this out.

C. I will be happy to work with you to better understand the changes to the schedule and will help initiate the request as part of our urgent change control process.

D. Sorry, if we move the schedule ahead, the team will have to work overtime. We are coming up on vacation time and will be short on staff.

Answer: C. You should always manage the schedule by using a documented and approved change control process.

Work the Plan (Project Execution)

At the end of the day, it is all about execution. You can have the best plan and the best schedule ever, but if you can't effectively execute (work) the plan, you might as well update your résumé and move on. The primary job of PMs is to be able to put our money where our mouth is to deliver what we said we would, on time and on budget. Effective schedule management enables us to perform our job as the PM with confidence and successful results. With that said, the interesting thing (and you will need to remember this if you are taking a PMI exam) is project schedule management processes mostly (five out of six) fall under the Planning Process Group and one process (control schedule) falls under the Monitoring and Controlling Process Group; there are no schedule management processes in the Executing Process Group. Go figure . . .

References

1. Jeffrey K. Liker and David Meier, *The Toyota Way Fieldbook: A Practical Guide for Implementing Toyota's 4Ps* (New York: McGraw-Hill, 2004), page 325.

2. "Activity Attributes," *Project Management Knowledge*, http://project-management-knowledge.com/definitions/a/activity-attributes/, accessed March 10, 2017.

3. *Wideman Comparative Glossary of Project Management Terms*, http://www.maxwideman.com/pmglossary/PMG_L01.htm, accessed March 10, 2017.

4. "PERT Chart (Program Evaluation Review Technique)," *SearchSoftwareQuality.com*, http://searchsoftwarequality.techtarget.com/sDefinition/0,,sid92_gci331391,00.html, accessed February 2017.

5. Vincent McGevna, "Creating an Agile Schedule with MS Project," *MPUG* (May 2, 2012), http://www.mpug.com/articles/creating-an-agile-schedule-with-ms-project/, accessed May 29, 2017.

6. Rita Mulcahy, *PMP Exam Prep*, 8th edition (Minnetonka, MN: RMC Publications, Inc., 2013), page 235.

7 Project Cost Management

Key Skills & Concepts

- The importance of cost management
- The role of the project sponsor
- How cost management ties into schedule management
- Project cost management processes
- Types of costs
- Types of estimates
- Range of estimating accuracy
- Reserve analysis (contingency)
- Types of reports
- Earned value management (EVM)
- Tips on how to remember EVM formulas
- Life cycle cost

The Importance of Cost Management

Cost management is one of the key project management measurements. Remember the project constraints? Cost is one of the primary focus areas when managing projects.

In any economy, managing cost can mean the difference between whether or not a project can survive. Companies are sometimes forced to cut budgets (or move to other suppliers or markets) to stay competitive. The projects that cost the most or that are not moving as quickly as the company feels they should are the ones that are frequently terminated. The end result is that projects live and die by the almighty dollar (or peso, euro, yen, and so on).

If you have managed projects, even briefly, chances are you have had one terminated due to budget problems. I was caught by surprise five months into a six-month project in New York when my boss called and informed me that the project I was working on had just been canceled due to budget cuts. It is a fact of life, so what can you do? The answer is pretty clear: you manage the budget as closely as you can. You must get (and stay) cost conscious and manage the budget as if it were your own money. If you don't manage cost wisely, the project may go away and your paycheck with it.

If managing a budget were easy, anyone could do it. After all, it is like balancing your checkbook, right? You have a budget, and you have costs and expenses that bleed down the budget. In the world of finance we call this a "two-line chart" (budget versus actual cost). In the world of project management, you need to be familiar with additional tools and techniques to estimate, manage, and report progress against your project budget more effectively.

One of the tools for managing cost as a project manager (PM) is *earned value* (EV), which in PMI terms is the value of the work performed. I like to call it a "three-line chart" because EV looks beyond the budget and actual dollars spent. EV takes a real look at the work that has been completed and allows you to put that accomplishment into dollars and cents so you can show the true financial health and performance of your project. The objective is to give you a better understanding of the benefits of performance tracking as opposed to just looking at the dollars spent.

Many PMs are either unfamiliar with earned value or simply choose not to use it, because it takes some time to incorporate and manage it. Another reason PMs shy away from the financial aspects of a project is a lack of a financial background. For example, how much finance or accounting experience do you have? If not that much, don't worry. This chapter provides some easy tips and tricks to help you manage cost on your project and to help you remember the formulas needed to answer the earned value management (EVM) questions on the PMP exam. More details are provided on EVM later in this chapter.

Tip

There are sometimes several questions on earned value on the PMP and CAPM exams, and the formulas, for the most part, are pretty easy to remember. You will need to remember the formulas and their interpretation (what the results mean) to be able to pass a PMI exam. Another tip is as soon as you sit down to take a PMI exam, do a brain-dump (write down the key formulas) before you push the button to begin taking the test.

An Offer I Couldn't Refuse

In 1984 I was invited to interview for a big promotion in Chicago with IBM, and the regional manager truly made me an offer I couldn't refuse. I accepted the promotion as a technical program manager (TPM). After the move, and with only one month on the job, my boss came into my office and introduced me to my new manager in the finance department.

I was stunned and promptly made what could have been a career-limiting announcement: "I never, ever wanted to be a bean counter," I declared. "Well," my boss said, "you are one." The reason I received this "opportunity" was because I had personal computer (PC) experience. I had, in fact, purchased a PC in 1983, only two years after PCs were introduced in 1981. The one I bought didn't even have a hard drive (only dual floppy 5.25" disks). Because I had taken the time to learn how to set up basic spreadsheets and graphs (with mentoring from my previous branch manager, who had said, "The PC is the wave of the future!"), I was now a "Financial Analyst."

It turns out that getting involved with finance for the company's 26 branch offices and 2 regional offices in the Chicago area was one of the best things that happened to me. It forced me to learn about the world of finance and how to set budgets as well as track and report performance more effectively. I also believe this experience helped me manage my projects and my own finances more effectively. Thanks, boss!

The Role of the Project Sponsor (How Do You Spell "$ponsor"?)

Of all the stakeholders on a project, the most important is the sponsor. I tell my students that when they think of the sponsor, they should visualize a dollar sign as the first letter of the word to help remember who the real customer is and who is funding the project.

In my Chicago days I often said, "Funding is fun." Not that the process is fun, but that without funding the project doesn't exist. Thus, no funding equals no project, and that is no fun!

The Project Selection process was discussed in Chapter 4. Well before the first diaper is purchased for a newborn project, you need a sponsor. Money is what makes the project real. Someone, somewhere is authorizing the project, and that takes funding. Most funding (budgets) are considered internal (at IBM we called these "blue dollars") as opposed to external funding (green dollars) from a customer. In managing internal funding we often keep track of the hours and blended rates, that is, rates including labor costs, general benefits, and occupancy rates for office space, equipment, phones, and so forth. Many companies actually use "project accounting" as opposed to general ledger accounting. For example, at IBM we had a full-blown project financial tracking system and used a tool called CLAIM developed to track hours spent by a person on any given project as part of our project accounting system. When tracking hours, it is best to report actual hours spent on the project compared to an agreed-upon average monthly productivity rate often referred to as "person months." At IBM we usually considered an average productive person month to be 140 hours due to vacations, unproductive time such as training, and so on. And the average person year (usually referred to as a "Full time equivalent [FTE]") as 2,080 hours back in the year 2009.

Tip

PMI considers an average productive number of hours for a given year to be 1,500 hours, which is how they came up with the minimum requirement of 4,500 experience hours (36 nonoverlapping months) over an eight-year period to be eligible to sit for the PMP exam. The experience hours required goes up to 7,500 hours (60 months over an eight-year period) for people who don't have a bachelor's degree or higher education. For the CAPM exam you only need 1,500 experience hours or 23 education contact hours to be eligible to sit for the exam. For more details on eligibility, go to Chapter 14.

How Cost Management Ties into Schedule Management

Assuming at this point that your project is part of the business strategy and has been recognized as essential (and is therefore funded), let's look at how cost management ties into the work you just completed in the previous chapter on schedule management.

We left off in Chapter 6 on the topic of controlling the schedule, which is the last process in the Schedule Management Knowledge Area. The good news is, all the time and work you and the team invested in estimating the duration of each activity (or work package) will be a key input in converting these items into costs.

Cost estimating is a simple process in most cases. You take the activity duration (usually in number of days) and further decompose this into estimated hours of work effort by WBS activity. Once you assign the activities to different people, you can use this simple formula:

$$P \times Q = \textit{estimated cost}$$

where the quantity (Q) of hours is multiplied by the price (P) or hourly rate of the different people working on the project to determine cost of labor.

Notice that I started with labor in the Estimate Costs process because it represents the highest source of cost to your project. There are exceptions (equipment and materials can be high-dollar costs), but almost always the cost of labor is the top of the list (usually around 80 percent of the overall cost to the average project).

The rest of the cost estimating can be pretty easy because the cost of materials, equipment, leases, supplies, and such are what they are. You can shop around and negotiate for the best prices for these things (and even for labor rates, in some cases), but the amount quoted is usually straightforward. Clearly, other factors need to be considered in cost estimating and management, and these other factors can come at you in many ways. For example, changes in project scope as well as unexpected events and delays (such as bad weather on a construction project) may drive up overtime or cause a turnover in personnel (which in turn drives training costs up). Also, natural disasters such as hurricanes can drive up the cost of building materials and supplies. If any of these factors occur, the original cost estimate goes out the window. This is why you also need to plan for risk (see Chapter 11 for more details on risk management). Many dynamics must be considered when planning, estimating, and managing the costs for your project. See Figure 7.8 (at the end of this chapter) for an example of our case study cost estimate and tracking spreadsheet.

Project Cost Management Processes

Project cost management includes the processes needed to plan, estimate, budget, and control costs so that the project can be completed within the approved budget. Cost management is primarily concerned with developing a plan and sticking to it by tracking actual spending and the impact to the budget. Four primary processes are associated with cost management:

- **7.1: Plan Cost Management (Planning Process Group).** The process of establishing the policies, procedures, and documentation needed for planning, managing, spending, and controlling costs on the project
- **7.2: Estimate Costs (Planning Process Group).** The process of developing an estimation of the monetary resources needed to complete project activities
- **7.3: Determine Budget (Planning Process Group).** Aggregating the estimated costs of each activity or work package to establish an approved cost baseline
- **7.4: Control Costs (Monitoring and Controlling Process Group).** Monitoring project status to update the budget and manage changes to the cost baseline.

In the real world of project management (and especially on smaller projects), cost estimating and cost budgeting are tightly linked and may be viewed as, or even combined into, a single process. As you may have noticed, three of the four cost management processes are Planning processes, with the last one falling into the Monitoring and Controlling Process Group. Clearly, the focus is on planning the cost, how to track and manage it, and the tools and methods available to ensure the project is on track to come in at or under the approved budget.

In order to create an accurate cost estimate, you need to consider the inputs (which are often outputs from previous processes). These include the project scope statement, WBS, project constraints, the schedule, company policies, existing systems, standard tools or procedures, and lessons learned from previous or similar projects. Historical information is always a great place to start. You also need an approved, documented plan.

A cost management plan cannot be complete without measurements and rules of engagement, such as procurement; preferred vendors (suppliers or sellers as well as procedures for purchase order processing); and tracking tools, techniques, and methods. The cost management plan should be part of the overall project plan and needs to have a clear set of estimates, measurements to be tracked, and reporting status to show that you:

- Are in control of the project cost and budget
- Can demonstrate your overall capability through accurate forecasting to bring in the project at or below the approved budget

As a PM you may have the authority to negotiate for resources (people, equipment, and materials). However, many of us work in a centralized procurement organization, meaning we have to engage and work closely with purchasing and accounts payable departments. These departments may have strict rules that you need to be aware of prior to spending (or committing) money to obtain goods and services.

As part of the planning process, you and the team should, as early as possible in the project life cycle, determine which processes or tools you will use to manage cost on your project. Once you decide how you are managing the project costs and how you are going to track and report progress, you need to include these components in your project's cost management plan. The cost management plan should address the following areas:

- Type of estimate used (more detail on specific types are shown later in this chapter)
- Level of accuracy needed for estimates (e.g., ±10 % within budget or within delivery schedule)
- Units of measure (e.g., hours, currency, cost per square foot, number of widgets produced in an hour, cost per widget, hours per day worked, cost per hour of labor)
- Type of tracking (e.g., plan versus actual, milestones, trends, and earned value)
- Type of reporting (e.g., format, frequency, and distribution of reports)
- Record retention (where they are stored and for how long) and who has access

These are only a few of the things you might include in a cost management plan. It can be formal or informal and provide lots of detail or just the basics. At the end of the day, however, the plan needs be in place to help you manage the cost of the project with an acceptable level of control based on the needs of the project. The plan needs to meet the needs of the stakeholder requirements for capturing and reporting project costs.

When planning for cost, keep in mind that it is common to see a lot of money (or hours) being charged to a project at the beginning without much to show for it. Unless the PM manages the startup carefully (using entrance criteria, with a good orientation on what is needed vs. what may have been done on similar projects), costs can go over budget very quickly.

Tip

It is important to tie the cost of the project to its expected life cycle. As you can imagine, the lowest costs will be at the ends (starting and closing), with the highest cost occurring during the execution phase, when you are fully staffed and using the most equipment and materials. Also, you want to plan for some residual costs after the project is shut down for "punch list" or warranty corrections.

Plan Cost Management Process (Planning Process Group)

Planning Cost Management is very similar to the work you do as a project manager to Plan Schedule Management. The benefits of having a cost management plan are similar as well, and the key benefit of this process is that it provides guidance and direction on how the project costs will be managed throughout the project. In Planning Cost Management you are establishing policies, procedures, and documentation for planning, managing, expending, and controlling project cost. Keep in mind that you are now creating a project cost roadmap for your team. Figure 7.1 shows an overview of the inputs, tools and techniques, and outputs for this process.

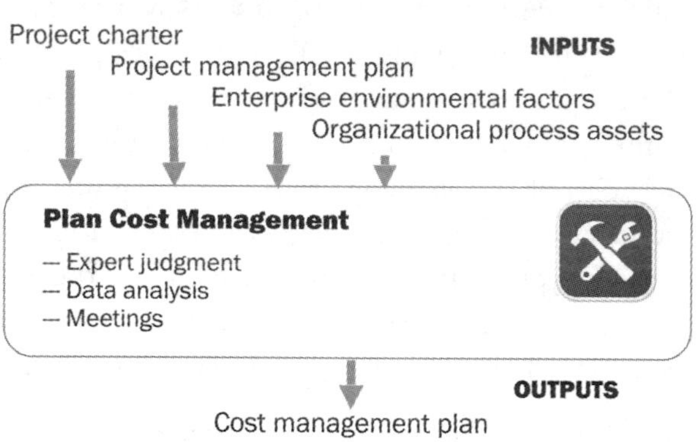

FIGURE 7.1 Plan Cost Management Process ITTOs

Estimate Costs Process (Planning Process Group)

The one question that comes up for every project (especially new projects) is: How much will it cost? The only thing that can make this question easier to answer (unless you have a really clear and accurate crystal ball) is to utilize a similar project that has been completed recently for an actual cost comparison. This is called top-down or analogous estimating.

We talked about it in Chapter 6 and will discuss it further in this chapter—as it is one of several estimating tools and techniques for determining the estimated cost to run your project.

Estimating cost involves developing a best guess (approximation) of the resources needed to complete project activities and their associated costs. The estimates should be refined during the course of the project as more information becomes known through progressive elaboration.

As you progress through the project life cycle, cost estimates should be reviewed and refined as you learn more about the project. The accuracy of your cost estimate will increase accordingly.

Range of Estimating Accuracy

The range of accuracy for estimating cost on any project can vary depending on the level of knowledge, experience, and confidence of the person or people providing the estimates. Early in the project life cycle there is a lot of uncertainty, so it is more appropriate to use a rough order of magnitude (ROM) estimate with a higher range of accuracy. As more information becomes available and confidence grows, especially during the middle to later phases of the project, it is common to use a more definitive estimate (see Table 7.1).

TABLE 7.1 Range of Estimating Accuracy

Type of Estimate	Accuracy Range	When Used
Rough order of magnitude (ROM) estimate (some PMs simply used ±50%)	−25% to +75%	Early in the project life cycle or when confidence is low concerning the information available (e.g., for a new and unique project estimated to cost $100,000, the range of accuracy would calculate to between $75,000 [−25%] and $175,000 [+75%])
Budget estimate (some PMs adjust the cost estimate based on a higher degree of confidence)	−10% to +25% from actual	Usually made after the project is underway (if the project has been done before) and is checked against the actual cost for higher degree of accuracy than ROM
Definitive estimate (some PMs use the range of ±10% from actual)	−5% to +10%	Later in the life cycle or when confidence is high concerning the information available (e.g., for a repeat project)

The decision about when to use each range depends on the degree of confidence in the data available and the timing of the estimate during the project life cycle. For example, during the initiating phase (early in the project life cycle) there are many unknowns and a lot of uncertainty concerning the cost and information. The project team may be new or the project may be unique; this is the time to use a ROM estimate.

Note

Rough order of magnitude (ROM) is sometimes called order of magnitude (OM) and carries a wider range of accuracy to estimate the cost of a project early in the life cycle. This is because of the lack of information (unknowns) at the beginning of a project.

As you get further into the project life cycle, you should have more accurate information and your confidence level will increase to the point where you may choose to use a narrower range (definitive or budget level) of accuracy. In either case the decision is up to you and your team as to the range of accuracy you feel is appropriate for your estimate.

The main thing to remember when determining the type of estimate and range of accuracy is to document the assumptions made, the type of estimating you used, and the percentage of expected accuracy. It is your call. Once the team agrees, you document and communicate the information to the appropriate stakeholders to minimize any confusion as to the degree of confidence in the range chosen.

Tip

There are times when a project sponsor will come to you and say, "I just need a best guess as to the estimated cost before I can agree to start the project." And far too often the number you provide gets "set in concrete," and the sponsor wants to hold you accountable for that guess without giving you time to conduct a proper estimate. This would be a great time to use a ROM estimate and document the type of estimate used and the range of accuracy you predict based on your (and the team's) confidence level.

As always, the best place to start the Estimate Cost process is to look at the work (inputs and outputs) collected and created thus far from previous processes. However, you need to look at the information from a slightly different perspective—for example, dollars and cents as they tie to work (time, resources, deliverables, etc.) as opposed to descriptions. For example, instead of looking at the scope statement as a way to define the deliverables, look at it for signs of the cost of the deliverables to the project. You should also look for language that translates into a direct or indirect cost to your project, such as "Security services will continue to be provided by Watchdog, Inc." This means you are forced to use a security resource and are likely bound by an existing contract for a predetermined cost to the project. While reviewing the contract for Watchdog, Inc., you also see it is a five-year contract with 5 percent cost of living adjustment (COLA) increases every year over the life of the contract. See what I mean? Now you are looking at the dollars and cents of cost management. This makes a big difference.

Tip

More and more companies are requiring that the PM calculate the project costs and factor the ROI (return on investment), ROS (return on sales), and other cost-benefit models into the project as well as the cost of the product of the project. The goal is to see the value of the project once its deliverables are actually in production or operation. Another cost to consider is the Cost of Project Management, as many organizations simply *do* project management "on the side." (E.g., they might have an operations manager running the move of a data center that she manages, or an IT manager in charge of implementing a new system upgrade—either one of the managers with little experience in project management.) This often leads to projects being underfunded from a project management cost perspective and ultimately disbanded halfway during the project.

COST VERSUS PRICING

Keep in mind that cost and pricing are two different things. *Cost* is an expenditure of money, time, and labor to acquire or provide goods and services, whereas *pricing* is the cost plus profit margin.

PROFIT MARGIN

Profit is important to a company's ability to stay in business. Profit margin (or net profit) is a measure of profitability that is calculated by finding the net profit as a percentage of the company's revenue (see Figure 7.2).

$$\text{Net profit margin} = \frac{\text{Net profit (after taxes)}}{\text{Revenue}} \times 100$$

FIGURE 7.2 Net Profit Margin Formula

A low profit margin indicates a low margin of safety: the risk is higher that a decline in sales will erase profits and result in a net loss.

For example, suppose a company produces a product that sells for $10. The cost to produce the product is $6, leaving the company with a $4 gross profit. However, the company also has to pay $2 in taxes. That makes the company's net income $2. Because the revenue is $10, the profit margin would be (2/10) or 20 percent.

> Profit margin is an accounting measure designed to gauge the financial health of a business or industry. In general, it is defined as the ratio of profits earned to total sales receipts (or costs) over some defined period. The profit margin is a measure of the amount of profit accruing to a firm from the sale of a product or service.[1]

Estimate Costs Inputs

Several inputs are often included in the Estimate Costs process:

- **Project management plan.** The PM plan often includes subsidiary plans, and other project documents are shown below: also note that any change to the PM plan should go through the organization's change control process.
  - **Cost management plan.** Costs are estimated for all resources that will be charged to the project. These include labor, equipment, services, supplies, and facilities, and also include inflation costs for lengthy projects or contingency costs.
  - **Scope baseline.** The scope baseline often includes a scope statement, WBS, and WBS dictionary.
  - **Resource plan.** Staffing is key to labor costs, including subcontractors, vendors, suppliers, hourly rates, cost of employee benefits (sometimes called a burden rate), cost of office space (occupancy), and equipment (phones, desks, PCs, and so on).
- **Enterprise environmental factors.** The cost of information, impact of market conditions, and so on.
- **Organizational process assets.** Cost-estimating policies, templates, historical information, and cost to store the project documents.

Figure 7.3 shows an overview of the inputs, tools and techniques, and the outputs for the Estimate Costs process.

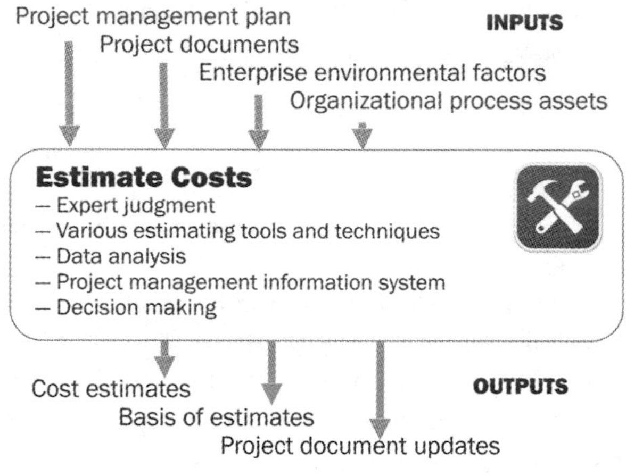

FIGURE 7.3 Estimate Costs Process ITTOs

Types of Estimates

The cost of work (activities) should be estimated using the same tools and techniques introduced in Chapter 6, such as one-cost, analogous, parametric, and three-point estimates, with an additional type called bottom-up estimating.

Things to Know about Estimating Cost

As project managers, we love checklists. Here is a list that I find especially helpful (excerpted from Rita Mulcahy's *PMP Exam Prep, Sixth Edition*):

- The cost estimates should be based on the WBS to improve accuracy.

- The cost estimates should be done by the person (or persons) doing the work (to get accuracy and buy-in).
- Use historical information when available from similar projects.
- A cost baseline should be set and only changed after approved changes.
- The budget should be managed to the cost baseline for the project.
- Estimates are more accurate if tied to work packages rather than at higher work levels.
- Corrective action or preventive action should be recommended when cost problems occur (as with other types of problems around scope, schedule, quality, etc.).
- A PM should always analyze requirements and not just accept them as delivered by management (they should be realistic and achievable).
- Padding is not an acceptable project management practice.
- The project manager must meet any agreed-upon estimates (need to keep estimates realistic).[2]

Types of Cost

A number of different types of cost can be associated with project management. This is also consistent with other real-world applications besides project management. The categories are listed next. It is recommended that you study them and be able to differentiate one from the other for the PMP or CAPM exam:

- **Variable costs.** Costs that change with the amount of work or production (e.g., the cost of salaries, supplies, equipment, and materials).
- **Fixed costs.** Fixed costs don't usually change (e.g., fixed monthly fees for maintenance agreements on computers, monthly lease payments, and rent).
- **Direct costs.** Costs that are directly associated with the project (e.g., materials, project labor, travel, cell phones, or other discretionary costs).
- **Indirect costs.** Costs that are incurred across multiple projects. This can include facilities, Project Management Office (PMO) costs, employee benefits, and other overhead costs.

Things to Consider When Estimating Costs

Value analysis and risk are often not considered when estimating the cost of a project. As mentioned earlier, PMs usually do a good job at estimating direct cost; however, they often underestimate (or miss altogether) some of the key ingredients (components), such as the following:

- Cost of managing the project (the PM's time, meetings, documentation, etc.)
- Cost of quality (cost of nonconformance; rework, scrap cost, etc.)
- Training or company-related meetings not related to the project

- Expenses for office space, phones, computers, raised floor, and network costs
- Estimated profit and ROI (return on investment), ROA (return on assets), or ROS (return on sales), where applicable (usually not a cost component, but it can be in some cases)
- Overhead (indirect costs)

Estimate Costs Tools and Techniques

The list of tools and techniques for cost estimating are similar to the Estimate Activity Durations process from Chapter 6, with just a few differences.

BOTTOM-UP ESTIMATING

Bottom-up estimating is considered very accurate because the estimate is provided by the subject matter expert (SME) or person doing the work. The estimates collected from the team are then rolled up to make the aggregate cost estimate for the project. The accuracy of the cost can be influenced by the size and complexity of the individual activity or work package.

PARAMETRIC ESTIMATING

Parametric estimating uses a statistical relationship between historical data and other variables to calculate an estimate for activity parameters, such as cost, budget, and duration. This technique usually provides a high degree of accuracy because you have historical information to draw from. As always, you can use this estimating method with other methods, as needed, to reach a level of confidence in the accuracy of your cost estimate for the entire project.

Try This

PARAMETRIC ESTIMATING

Your manager is aware of a "Green Data Center" in Boulder, Colorado, and asks you to contact the company (IBM) to obtain a cost estimate to set up five mainframe systems and 300 servers in their center. What do you do?

Answer: You contact IBM and ask the Data Center Manager for a parametric cost estimate (cost per square foot) for hosting your systems and servers. When you receive the cost estimate, you provide this and other pertinent details to your boss.

THREE-POINT ESTIMATING

Introduced in Chapter 6, the three-point estimate adds a degree of accuracy over the one-point estimate (which is the most common). You may recall the three-point estimate is a PERT (Program Evaluation and Review Technique) that takes input from a SME. Based on the SME's understanding of an activity (in this case, the cost), apply their best estimates for optimistic (O), pessimistic (P), and most likely (M) outcomes, and work through the formula to determine expected cost. The formula can be shown in different ways (see Figure 7.4). Refer to Chapter 6 of this book or *PMBOK* for other methods.

$$c^E = \frac{c^O + 4c^M + c^P}{6}$$

Legend

c^E (Cost Estimate)

c^O (Cost Optimistic)

$4c^M$ (4 x Cost Most Likely)

c^P (Cost Pessimistic)

FIGURE 7.4 Three-Point Estimate (Beta Distribution Formula)

RESERVE ANALYSIS (CONTINGENCY)

Contingency: What is it and why do we care? *Contingency* is a reserve accomplished by setting aside money either inside the project cost baseline (called *contingency reserves*) or outside the project cost baseline (called *management reserves*). Contingency reserves are used to cover those risk events that you and the team have identified (known) that are likely to occur on the project. Management reserves are held at the management level (outside the project budget for many companies) for unknown risk events that are not identified or foreseen at the specific project level. Management reserves are not usually project specific and can be used across multiple projects, as needed, and at management's discretion. An example of this would be FEMA (Federal Emergency Management Agency) funds for disaster recovery.

COST OF QUALITY (COQ)

Cost of quality (COQ) is the cost of work needed by the PM and team to ensure that quality management is part of the project. In the real world, COQ is also a measurement used for assessing the waste or losses from some defined process (machine, production line, plant, department, company, etc.).

The COQ measurement can track changes over time for one particular process or it can be used as a benchmark for comparison of two or more different processes (e.g., two machines, production lines, sister plants, and competitor companies).

Most COQ systems are defined using categories of costs. The information in Table 7.2 comes from Process Quality Associates, Inc. COQ systems are sometimes assisted by specially designed COQ software and are helpful in the identification and tracking of COQ.

TABLE 7.2 Categories of Cost of Quality (COQ)

COQ Category	Typical Descriptions (May Vary between Different Organizations)	Examples
Internal	Costs associated with internal losses (e.g., within the process being analyzed).	Off-cuts (waste), equipment breakdowns, spills, scrap, yield, and productivity
External	Costs external to the process being analyzed (i.e., occur outside, not within). These costs are usually discovered by or affect third parties (e.g., vendors or customers). Some external costs may have originated from within or have been caused, created by, or made worse by the process being analyzed. They are defined as "external" because of where they were discovered, or who is primarily or initially affected.	Customer complaints, latent defects found by the customer, warranties
Preventive	Costs associated with the prevention of future losses (e.g., unplanned or undesired problems, lost opportunities, breakdowns, work stoppages, and waste).	Planning, mistake-proofing, scheduled maintenance, and quality assurance
Assessment	Costs associated with measurement and assessment of the process.	Key performance indicators (KPIs), inspections, quality checks, dock audits, third-party audits, measuring devices, reporting systems, data collection systems, and forms

Ask the Expert

Q: How are cost estimating and cost management done in the real world?

A: A PM in the real world first must ask one very important question of the project sponsor: "How accurate do you want me to be?" The answer should be based on the time allotted, the information and resources available, and the degree of accuracy the sponsor needs to sell the project (e.g., getting the funding/budget approved). Then the PM should look at the scope and deliverables to determine which estimating tools and techniques to use based on the type and complexity of the project. It is also important to know if a similar project has been done before. Then the PM takes all this information into consideration and usually rolls the details into a software estimating tool, if one is available.

Tip

If you are planning to take the PMP exam, not only should you know the different types of estimating tools and techniques, but you should also be able to identify the advantages and disadvantages of each. Examples are provided in Tables 7.3 and 7.4.

TABLE 7.3 Analogous Estimating

Analogous Estimating Advantages	Analogous Estimating Disadvantages
Quick and easy	Less accurate than bottom-up estimating
Don't need to estimate at activity level	Less detail based on limited information
Less costly to create	Requires higher experience to do well
Higher level of management expectation	Difficult for projects with a lot of uncertainty
Based on historical information of similar previous projects	Doesn't consider project differences and requires accurate history from previous projects

TABLE 7.4 Bottom-Up Estimating

Bottom-up Estimating Advantages	Bottom-up Estimating Disadvantages
More accurate than most other methods	Takes more time to create and is more expensive
Gains buy-in from the team members because they create the estimates	There is a tendency for team members to "pad" the estimates to provide a comfort zone
Developed based on detailed analysis	Requires the scope and activities to be clearly defined and understood by the team members
Provides a level of detail that should be easier to monitor and control	Requires more time to perform the details as they relate to the WBS activities and work packages

Estimate Costs Outputs

Here are the three key outputs from the Estimate Costs process:

- **Activity cost estimates.** Quantifiable assessments of the probable cost required to complete the work of the project. The cost estimates can be presented in various forms—for example, at the summary level or in a bill of materials (BOM) with cost broken down into details of labor, facilities, equipment, materials, IT, travel, and so on. It can be in a spreadsheet distributed over time by month, by Process Group, or phase of the project life cycle.
- **Basis of estimates (BOEs).** This is where you should show the type of estimating tools and techniques used as well as other supporting details, such as the following:
  + Documented basis of how the cost estimate was developed—bottom-up, top-down (analogous), parametric, and so on—and a clearly documented range of expected accuracy (e.g., ±50 percent or –10 percent to +25 percent)
  + The list of assumptions made by you and the team to come up with the estimate
  + The known constraints (time, cost, resources, permits, compliance, etc.)
  + An indication of the confidence level of the final estimate (for example, high, medium, or low) and the reasons for your conclusion
- **Project document updates.** Updates include changes to the scope statement, WBS, WBS dictionary, schedule, risk register, and communications plan based on findings during this process.

Reporting Formats and Frequency of Delivery

The format and frequency used to report progress should be applicable to the type and complexity of your project. The reports and when they are presented (and in what format) must meet the needs and expectations of the sponsor and other key stakeholders. You should fit the report to the need. For example, for executive-level reporting, keep it simple and concise. I recommend using a milestone report for middle- to high-level managers and customers just to show the status and progress on major events.

Weekly status reports should provide adequate details for the team to understand the specifics needed and potential delays due to dependencies, and so on.

For monthly financial reports, such as earned value measurements and other sponsor-level interests, keep the format focused on dollars and cents and show accurate forecasts if possible (with supporting assumptions and justification data).

Determine Budget Process (Planning Process Group)

In the Determine Budget process you combine all the estimates from the Estimate Costs process into one overall project cost budget. You also add in any cost contingency, usually in conjunction with risk management (e.g., those risk events that have a high probability of impacting the project, if they occur). Remember, contingency reserves should be included as part of the overall project budget. Collectively, the project budget should consist of the approved funds to begin executing the project.

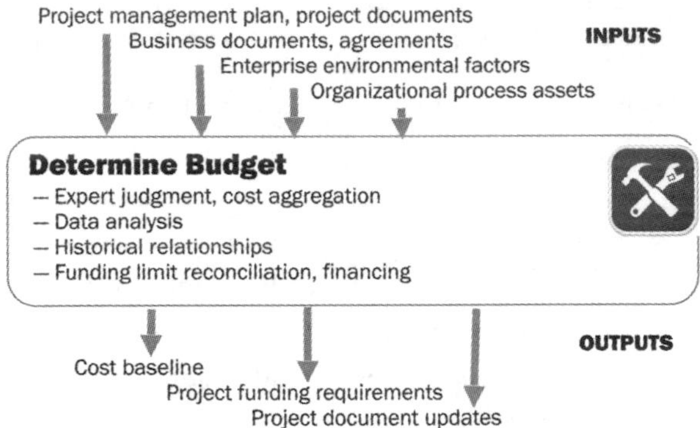

Figure 7.5 shows an overview of the inputs, tools and techniques, and the outputs for the Determine Budget process.

Tip

There will be times when only a portion of the project budget will be authorized for a particular phase; for example, the concept phase may be funded to cover the costs of prototyping the solution so you can demonstrate that the solution will work, before the total project is funded.

Once the budget is authorized, you need to establish and confirm the key measurements. These measurements will need to be tracked and reported on a regular basis (usually monthly) to the project sponsor(s) to demonstrate that you are managing the project budget.

Budget Estimating and Measuring Project Health

The project status (i.e., the health of the project) can be measured in a number of ways. To perform any "health checking," you must first have an agreed-upon cost-performance baseline. You should remember baselines from Chapter 5. Earned value (EV) is a good way to measure progress and the overall health of your project. It is covered in more detail later in this chapter.

Cost Baseline

The cost baseline is an authorized time-phased budget at completion (BAC). BAC is one of the key components in calculating earned value (EV).

In setting the cost baseline, you must first look at the scope baseline to ensure that the cost is aligned with the scope. The cost baseline should also take the scheduled activities and work packages into consideration because this is where the budget will be spent.

Other key considerations should be the project contract, the statement of work (SOW), and specific performance requirements of these documents.

Sample Cost Baseline Overview

Each project should have a formally approved and communicated performance baseline (PB) that describes the integration of the technical objectives and requirements with the schedule and cost objectives.

Here are the main reasons for establishing, approving, controlling, and documenting a performance baseline:

- To ensure achievement of project objectives
- To manage and monitor progress during project execution
- To define the project for approval and authorization by the office of management
- To ensure accurate information on the final configuration (as-built drawings, specifications, expenditures, etc.)
- To establish performance measurement criteria for projects

According to "Performance Baseline Development and Validation," by the US Department of Energy, development of the PB begins with the planning cost, schedule estimate, and the preliminary scope included in the mission need statement, and is further defined in conceptual design documents. The PB development process should be a continuous, iterative, and recursive process. For any PB development effort to be successful, it should be developed by motivated and qualified people, follow well-defined processes, be subject to rigorous quality assurance requirements and processes, and be supported by the careful consideration and application of appropriate project definition tools.[3]

Control Costs Process (Monitoring and Controlling Process Group)

Now that you have an approved budget, which is the main output of the Determine Budget process, you need to be thinking about how to control costs.

The key to effective cost control is the management of the approved performance baseline and the changes to that baseline. It is common to reset the performance baseline, especially on larger projects, and this should only be done through proper change control.

Project cost control includes the following:

- Ensuring that all change requests are responded to in a timely manner
- Reviewing possible impact to the project (cost, time, scope, risk, etc.)
- Managing the actual changes when and as they occur (document and communicate)
- Preventing unapproved changes from impacting the project and budget
- Managing the cost expenditures to not exceed the approved funding by period and in total for the project
- Monitoring cost performance to isolate and understand variances
- Monitoring work performance (value of work performed, or EV) against approved budget and time
- Accurately reporting to appropriate stakeholders all approved changes and costs
- Managing any cost overruns within the acceptable limits (consistent with approved contingency reserves)

The bottom line intent of project cost control is to manage the approved budget effectively and to seek out potential impact variances (both positive and negative) against the budget. The best way to ensure cost control is through effective change management and close monitoring and reporting of earned value.

Tip

For readers not planning to pursue PMI's PMP exam in the near future, I recommend you scan this section on earned value for a high-level overview and not for detailed comprehension. You can always come back to this chapter later when you are ready to prepare for PM certification.

Control Costs Tools and Techniques

PMBOK Sixth Edition shows several tools and techniques for this process, some of which are discussed in this section. Figure 7.6 shows an overview of the inputs, tools and techniques, and the outputs for the Control Costs process.

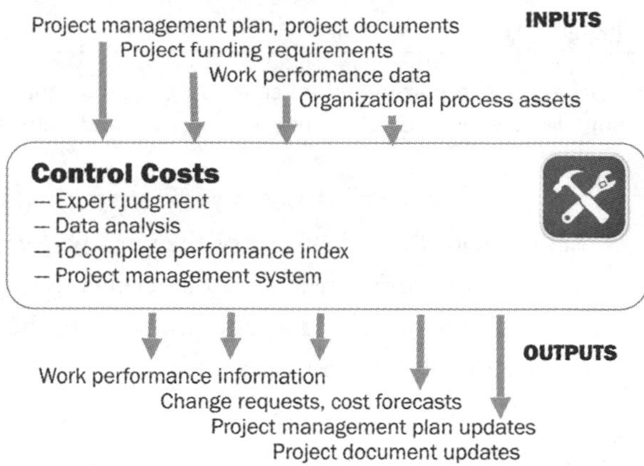

FIGURE 7.6 Control Costs Process ITTOs

The first is earned value management (EVM). EVM is growing in popularity, especially in large companies and on government projects. Some companies even have an earned value analyst (EVA) or business analyst (BA) working with the PMs and teams across multiple projects, tracking and reporting on their EV status while using a consistent format and frequency.

Note

Earned value management involves a number of concepts, calculations, and methods that are performed by today's high-tech project management software tools. Even the more experienced PM is often not completely comfortable with EV tracking because it requires extra time and a degree of judgment on when or how to report the completion and progress of activities.

Earned value management can be used in various ways. It is most often used as a method of measuring project performance in dollars and cents. The principle of EVM is used to develop and monitor three key dimensions (components) for each work package (or at the control account level). To manage EV, you collect key data at regular intervals (e.g., weekly or monthly, depending on the size and duration of the project) to establish a checkpoint (snapshot) in time to measure progress on your project. The key components of EVM are as follows:

- **Planned value (PV).** The authorized budget assigned to the work planned to be accomplished based on historical or expert knowledge for activities or work packages. PV is the amount you planned to spend at a given time on the project. If nothing changes, the original PV adds up to be the budget at completion (BAC) at the end of the project.
- **Actual cost (AC).** The total cost actually incurred and recorded for the work performed.

Note

Tracking and reporting actual cost can be somewhat elusive in the case of delayed invoices from suppliers, allocated costs that are apportioned across multiple projects, and missed or hidden charges.

- **Earned value (EV).** The value of the work performed (e.g., those activities or work packages that are complete and should receive appropriate credit for the expected dollar value they are assigned). EV must be compared to the PV baseline and actual cost (AC) to determine schedule and cost variance.

Tip

Earned value should clearly show not just how much of your budget has been spent (AC) against what you thought you were going to spend (PV), but it should also show the value of work completed (EV). EV is becoming more widely used, especially in large companies and government projects.

When reporting the progress of work performed and EV in dollars and cents for a particular activity or work package, use the progress reporting rules introduced in Chapter 6:

- **50/50 rule.** Fifty percent credit for the value of an activity when it begins and 50 percent when complete
- **20/80 rule.** Twenty percent credit for the value of an activity when it begins and 80 percent when complete
- **0/100 rule.** Zero percent credit when the activity begins and 100 percent credit when it is complete

Note

It is important to discuss and ensure a clear understanding of which rule (or rules) you plan to use when measuring and reporting EVM with the team, to minimize any confusion.

Earned Value Formulas

You should be familiar with several formulas (especially if you are planning to take the PMP or PMI Scheduling exam) to enable yourself and the team to effectively perform and understand EVM. You should also be familiar with the definition or interpretation of each of the key components of EVM, as detailed in Tables 7.5 and 7.6.

TABLE 7.5 EVM Terms and Interpretations

Acronym	Term	Interpretation
PV	Planned value	As of today, what is the estimated value of the work planned to be done?
EV	Earned value	As of today, what is the estimated value of the work actually accomplished?
AC	Actual cost	As of today, what is the actual cost incurred for the work accomplished?
BAC	Budget at completion	How much did we budget for the total project?
EAC	Estimate at completion	What do we currently expect the total project to cost (a forecast)?
ETC	Estimate to complete	From this point on, how much more do we expect it to cost to finish the project (a forecast)?
VAC	Variance at completion	As of today, how much over or under budget do we expect to be at the end of the project?

Tip

Using the work performance information gathered through earned value analysis, a project manager can create reports, including forecasts, and other communications related to the project's performance. EVMs may also result in change requests to the project.[4]

How to Remember the EVM Formulas

A few tips are going around the PM world concerning how to remember the EVM formulas. They are as follows:

- Variances are always "minus." For example, EV minus (−) either cost (AC) or schedule (PV).
- Indexes (CPI, SPI, and TCPI) are always "divide." Think, "I = divide."
- EV is almost always first in the formula (the exceptions are EAC, ETC, and VAC).

TABLE 7.6 EVM Formulas

Name	Formula	Interpretation and Tips
Schedule variance (SV)	SV = EV − PV	Ahead or behind schedule. Minus (negative) is behind schedule (bad), and plus (positive) is ahead of schedule (good).
Cost variance (CV)	CV = EV − AC	Ahead or behind budget. Minus (negative) is over budget (bad), and plus (positive) is under budget (good).
Schedule performance index (SPI)	SPI = EV/PV	The project is currently progressing at ____% of the rate originally planned. (Note: > 1.0 is good.)

continued on next page

TABLE 7.6—*continued*

Name	Formula	Interpretation and Tips
Cost performance index (CPI)	CPI = EV/AC	Currently getting \$____ worth of work out of every dollar spent. Budget is or is not being spent wisely. (Note >1.0 is good). CPI is an index showing the efficiency of the utilization of the resources on the project.
To-complete performance index (TCPI)	TCPI = (BAC – EV) / (BAC – AC)	Efficiency that must be maintained in order to complete on-plan budget based on the current EAC (estimate of completion). (Note: If the resultant number is higher than 1.0, the chances of getting back to the original budget [BAC] are extremely difficult.)
Estimate to complete (ETC)	ETC = EAC – AC	How much more do we expect the project to cost from this point forward?
Estimate at completion (EAC)	There are several ways to calculate EAC, depending on the assumptions made.	At this time, how much do you expect the total project to cost? (See the formulas to the left and below.)
	EAC = AC + Bottom-up ETC (Note: This formula is most often asked for on the exam.)	This formula calculates actual cost plus a new estimate for the remaining work.
	EAC = BAC / Cumulative CPI	Used if no variances from BAC have occurred or if you plan to continue at the same spend (burn) rate.
	EAC = AC + ETC	Actual cost plus the new estimate to complete remaining work. Used when original estimate is not appropriate.
	EAC = AC + (BAC – EV)	Actual to date plus remaining budget. Used when current variances are thought to be atypical (it is essentially AC plus the remaining value of work to be performed).
Variance at completion (VAC)	VAC = BAC – EAC	How much over or under budget do we expect to be at the end of the project?

Ask the Expert

Q: How do we know where we are in the project? Can you show an example?

A: Earned value management is a good way to tell where you are on your project. The important thing to remember if you are planning to use EVM is to set it up early in the project life cycle. You need to determine which progress reporting rule (or rules) mentioned earlier in this chapter you plan to use. Also, you need to be consistent in how you credit the work performed and how you report the progress. This may take some education for both you and your project team. See Figure 7.7 for an example of how the earned value key components would map out in a chart.

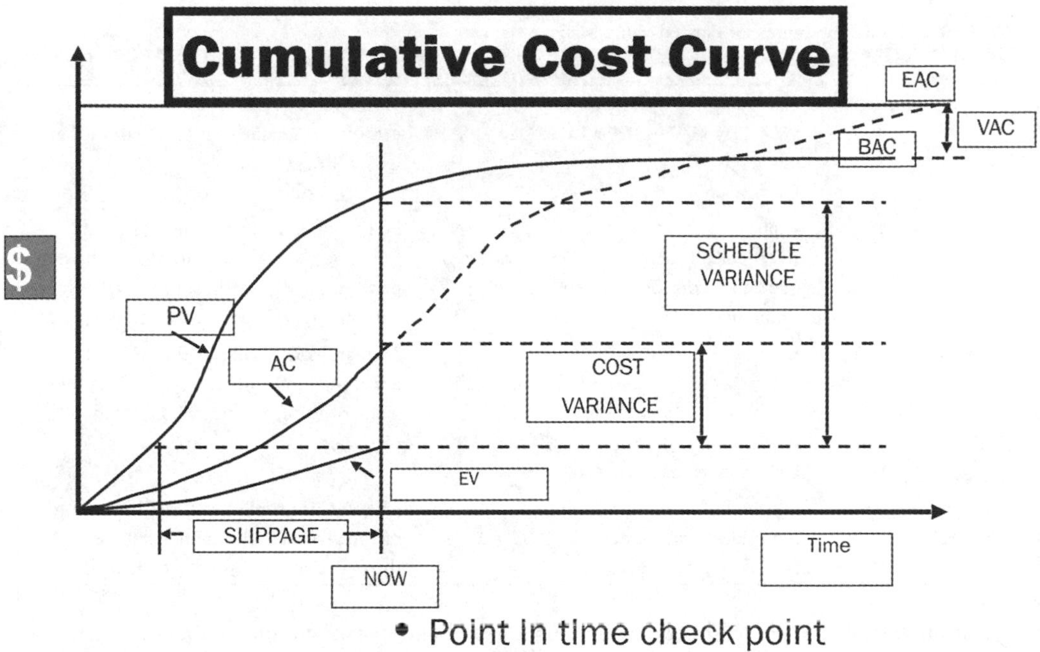

FIGURE 7.7 Sample Earned Value Chart

An important aspect of calculating earned value is that it is typically a point in time checkpoint, and to be effective it should be checked on a regular basis (early and often). Let's take the chart shown in Figure 7.7 and do the math.

Try This

EARNED VALUE EXAMPLE

You are the PM on a new project to build the sidewalls (protective barrier) for an ice hockey game. The assumptions used to calculate EV for this project are as follows:

- You have four days to build four walls for the ice arena.
- The duration estimate indicates it will take one day to build each side of the arena.
- The estimated cost (planned value) is $1,000 per wall.
- A checkpoint at day 3 shows you have only completed two and a half sides of the ice arena.

The information in the questions, tables, and answers that follow will guide you through the process of determining earned value on this project.

Question 1: What are the earned value management key-component values? (For the answer, see Table 7.7.)

TABLE 7.7 Key Components for Earned Value Management

EVM Component	Formula or Results	Comments
Planned value (PV)	$3,000 PV = Day 1 PV + Day 2 PV + Day 3 PV or PV = $1000 + $1000 + $1000	Checkpoint at Day 3 of a four-day project. Planned value cost at $1,000 per day is as follows: PV = 3 × $1,000 = $3,000
Actual cost (AC)	$2,900 AC = dollars spent at this time. For example: Labor ($1,500) + Materials ($800) + Equipment ($600)	You would only know this from the hours worked by the team times, the cost per hour, and of course the actual cost of equipment and building materials spent.
Earned value (EV)	$2,500 EV = Day 1 EV + Day 2 EV + Day 3 EV (EV = $1000 + $1000 + $500) or EV = 2.5 × $1,000 = $2,500	Two-and-a-half-sides of the ice arena are completed by Day 3. Therefore, the value of the work performed (completed) is $2,500.
Budget at completion (BAC)	$4,000 Four sides at $1,000 per side, BAC = 4 × $1,000 = $4,000	The BAC is usually set at the beginning of the project and can only change through approved change control.

Question 2: Is the project on schedule and on budget? (See Table 7.8 for the answers.)

Answer: In this case, the project is behind schedule and the budget is overspent.

TABLE 7.8 Schedule and Cost Variance Calculations

Earned Value Variances	Formula and Results	Interpretation
Schedule variance (SV)	SV = EV – PV $2,500 – $3,000 = –$500	Negative means that you are behind schedule (the project is delayed) or the schedule was not estimated accurately.
Cost variance (CV)	CV = EV – AC $2,500 – $2,900 = –$400	Negative means you have overspent the budget or underestimated the cost of the project.

Other key components of EVM are CPI and SPI; these indexes help you forecast the remaining cost to your project. Using the information provided in the preceding earned value case-study example, calculate the run rate (CPI and SPI) to see if you are getting your money's worth of performance for the money spent on setting up the walls at the ice arena.

Question 3: What are the CPI and SPI for the ice arena project, and are you receiving the work performance or cost performance you had planned for? (See Table 7.9 for the answer.)

Answer: Based on the results in the table (and the interpretation), the answer is "no" on both counts, which means you will miss both your target to complete and your budget.

TABLE 7.9 SPI and CPI Calculations

Earned Value Variances	Formula and Results	Interpretation
Schedule performance index (SPI)	SPI = EV / PV SPI = 2,500 / 3,000 = 0.83 (Note that 0.83 is rounded. If the calculation uses more decimal places, the results will vary.)	Less than 1.0 means you are getting less performance than planned against the schedule; in other words, you are performing at a rate that is 83 percent of your target schedule.
Cost performance index (CPI)	CPI = EV / AC CPI = 2,500 / 2,900 = 0.86 (Note that 0.86 is rounded. If the calculation uses more decimal places, the ETC results will vary.)	Less than 1.0 means you are getting less cost performance for each dollar spent (e.g., in this case, you're getting 86 cents for every dollar spent).

Now that you have key information about your project, you can use the results of the EVM calculations to apply the results of CPI and SPI toward the future. Here are the key questions that need to be answered before you forecast the future cost and schedule performance for the remainder of the project:

- Is the CPI (sometimes called "run rate" or "burn rate") representative of what the project will cost?
- Is the SPI a true representation of the performance you can expect as you go forward with the project?

The answers to these questions will help you decide whether you need to adjust the schedule or cost due to unforeseen problems or whether you need to take correction action to get the team and budget back on target.

The next tool and technique in the Control Costs process is forecasting. It is important to forecast the future cost and performance early and throughout the project life cycle. The components of earned value for forecasting are the following:

- **Estimate to complete (ETC)** answers the question of "what is the remaining cost from this point forward to finish the project?"
- **Estimate at completion (EAC)** answers the question of "what will be the total cost of the project be based on our new ETC?"
- **Variance at completion (VAC)** answers the question of "what is the amount over or under the original budget at completion (BAC) based on the latest cost information?"

See Table 7.10 for the forecast calculations for the ice hockey arena-wall project.

TABLE 7.10 Estimating Future Cost (ETC, EAC, and VAC)

EVM Component	Formula or Results	Comments
Estimate at completion (EAC)	EAC = BAC / CPI $4,000 / 0.86 = $4,651	The new estimated budget at the completion of the project based on EVM at this time. (Note: There are several ways to calculate EAC [see Table 7.5], and the decision should be based on the level of confidence in the actual cost [AC] and other factors.)
Estimate to complete (ETC)	ETC = EAC – AC $4,651 – $2,900 = $1,751	How much do you anticipate you need to spend to complete the project?
Variance at completion (VAC)	VAC = BAC – EAC $4,000 – $4,651 = – $651	Based on the information available, you expect to be $651 over budget at the end of the project. Again, minus is bad.

In the case of our ice hockey area setup project, with the estimated cost to complete (ETC) of $1,751 added to what we have already spent (AC) of $2,900, we can forecast the new estimate at completion (EAC) for the entire project to be $4,651. The overrun variance at completion (VAC) is $651.

The next step is to present the status and forecast amounts to the project sponsor along with your action plan to either get back on track or to justify additional funding. As you would expect, the project's forecast gets more and more accurate the closer to the end of the project. (Go figure. There we go with that *progressive elaboration* again.)

Tip

Accurate forecasting is essential to managing the costs on your project. Some companies go so far as to hold the PM accountable for an accurate project forecast (within ± 10%, e.g.). The reason is clear—the more accurate the forecast for each project, the more accurately the financial department can forecast across all their projects. You can see this at the corporate level each quarter when stock analysts predict (forecast) a company's earnings. It doesn't matter if the company made a profit and grew their revenue; if they missed the analysts' forecasts (expectations), especially if the number is lower than expected, then the company's stock will often go down.

To-Complete Performance Index (TCPI)

The next tool and technique in the Control Costs process is the to-complete performance index (TCPI). Basically, TCPI provides a way to calculate how much work it would take (future required cost efficiency) to achieve the original approved budget at completion. If the TCPI calculation is greater than 1.0 late in the project life cycle, this means the chances of being able to get back to the original baseline budget are not likely.

As shown in the previous Table 7.6, this can be calculated using the following formula:

$$TCPI = (BAC - EV) / (BAC - AC)$$

Or TCPI can be calculated by using the same formula above with EAC – AC (instead of BAC – AC) as the denominator to compare to your estimated at completion (EAC) cost.

Performance Reviews

Performance reviews compare cost performance over time as well as schedule activities or work packages that are either running over or under the budget. They also estimate the funds needed to complete the work in progress. The performance review is another tool in the Control Costs process. If used with EVM, it applies the following information:

- **Variance analysis.** Compares actual project performance to planned or expected performance. Cost and schedule variances are the most frequently analyzed.
- **Trend analysis.** Examines project performance over time to determine whether it is improving. Many graphical tools are available that can visually show trends on the project.
- **Earned value performance (EVP).** EVP compares the baseline plan to the actual schedule and cost performance and looks at the value of work performed to show the true status of the project.

Variance Analysis

The last of the tools and techniques in the Control Costs process focuses on cost performance measurement (CV, CPI) and is used to assess the extent of variation from the original cost baseline. The results of variance analysis provide the PM and team valuable information on cost performance and help them decide if correction or preventive action is required.

As always, PM software can be used to assist with the many tools and techniques to help you control costs on your projects.

Other Terms and Concepts in Cost Management

A few other terms and concepts are associated with cost management that you should be familiar with. I will only briefly touch on these topics because they are not used extensively in project management, unless, for example, you are on a project selection board that votes on which projects should be selected and funded.

Ask the Expert

Q: What are the real goals of cost management? And how do I know if the cost is the norm or an anomaly (one-off)?

A: The goals of cost management are simple:

- Focus on the end-cost results (deliverables, scope, schedule, products, etc.).
- Use the tools and resources available to determine what the project should cost.
- Work as a team to ensure that you are controlling cost to the best of your ability and are reporting it accurately.

I am not sure I have ever seen a project that is "normal." After all, that is what makes each project unique. Therefore, watch for the anomalies because there tend to be many; be sure to adjust accordingly. Note that these three goals should sound familiar (they align with the three take-away points from Chapter 2).

PRESENT VALUE

Present value (PV) is the value today of future cash flows and can be found by using the following formula:

$PV = FV / (1 + r) n$

Where:

- PV = Present value
- FV = Future value (see FV formulas, next)
- r = interest rate
- n = number of time periods

You can think about PV as "how much money do you need to put in the bank today (PV) at r percent interest if you want to reach a future cash flow of FV in n years?"

Tip

The good news is that present value is usually only mentioned once or twice on the PMI exam, and you will not likely have to remember the formula. You should know that present value is "less" than the amount of cash flow you receive in the future. In other words, if you see a question that asks for PV of $300,000, the answer would be a number less than $300,000.

NET PRESENT VALUE (NPV)

The first step is to review some of the terms associated with PPV.

The term *constant dollars* refers to the net present value relative to a fixed date. The term *current dollars* refers to the unadjusted value of the money. The term *discount rate* refers to a percentage used to calculate the NPV and reflects the time value of money.

For example, assuming a discount rate of 5%, the net present value of $2,000 ten years from now is $1,227.83. So if someone offered you $1,000 now or $2,000 ten years from now, you'd pick the latter because its net present value is higher.[5]

Net present value (NPV) is used in capital budgeting to analyze the profitability of an investment or project. FinAid.org offers the following definition of net present value (NPV):

> Net Present Value (NPV) is a way of comparing the value of money now with the value of money in the future. A dollar today is worth more than a dollar in the future, because inflation erodes the buying power of the future money, while money available today can be invested and grow. . . . Calculating NPV is difficult, in part, because it isn't clear what discount (interest) rate should be used, nor is it clear how to project future changes in the discount rate.[6]

Tip

For the PMP exam, you may have to calculate NPV. You need to know the formula and how to calculate it and that the project with the highest NPV provides the more favorable financial investment. In addition to the formula, net present value can often be calculated using tables and spreadsheets.

Generally, if NPV is positive, the investment choice is a good one. NPV in simple terms is the sum of PV for the period measured minus the investment costs for those same periods.

For example: To calculate NPV on a project (project A), use the sample data in Table 7.11. First, calculate the present value for income/revenue based on the interest rate as shown in the third column. Then, calculate the present value of cost over the number of periods as shown in the fifth column. Last, take the total present value of income/revenue minus the total costs and you get the net present value. In this example, NPV = 511 – 290 = 221.

TABLE 7.11 Sample NPV Calculation

Time Period	Income/Revenue	Present Value of Income/ Revenue at 10% Interest Rate	Costs	Present Value of Cost at 10% Interest Rate
0	0	0	200	200
1	100	90	100	90
2	200	166	0	0
3	300	255	0	0
Total		511		290

Here's how this helps in the project selection process. Take the example where the NPV of project A is 221 and compare this to another project (B) that has an NPV of 120. Which project has the most favorable NPV? Even though they are both positive NPV, you would recommend project A to your sponsor; it has the higher value, if all other things are equal.

FUTURE VALUE (FV)

Future value (FV) is the value of an asset or cash at a specified date in the future that is equivalent in value to a specified sum today. There are two ways to calculate FV:

- For an asset with simple annual interest:
  Original investment × (1 + (interest rate × number of years))
- For an asset with interest compounded annually:
  Original investment × ((1 + interest rate) ^ number of years)
- Consider the following examples from Investopedia.com: $1,000 invested for five years with simple annual interest of 10 percent would have a future value of $1,500.
- $1000 invested for five years at 10 percent, compounded annually, has a future value of $1,610.51.[7]

These calculations demonstrate that time literally is money—the value of the money you have now is not the same as it will be in the future and vice versa. Therefore, it is important to know how to calculate the time value of money so that you can distinguish among the different investments that offer you returns at different times.[8]

INTERNAL RATE OF RETURN (IRR)

The internal rate of return (IRR) is a capital-budgeting metric used by firms to decide whether they should make investments. It is also called "discounted cash flow rate of return" (DCFROR) or rate of return (ROR). IRR is an indicator of the "efficiency" or quality of an investment as opposed to net present value (NPV), which indicates value or magnitude.

Here's an easy way to relate this to project management. Say, for example, that you have to choose between projects A and B. Project A has an IRR of 20 percent, and project B has an IRR of 10 percent. Which do you choose?

Answer: You would choose project A because it has a higher efficiency (internal rate of return on the dollars invested).

PAYBACK PERIOD

Payback period is the number of time periods it takes to recover your investment in a project before you start making a profit. For example, project A has a payback period of ten months, and project B has a payback period of 24 months. Which would you choose to fund?

Answer: You would choose project A because it has a shorter payback period (sometimes known as the "break-even point").

OPPORTUNITY COST

Opportunity cost analysis is an important part of a company's decision-making process but is not treated as an actual cost in any financial statement.

Here's an example of opportunity cost: A person investing $10,000 in a particular stock is denied the chance, or opportunity, of gaining the interest that the $10,000 would have earned had it been left in a bank account instead. The opportunity cost of the decision to invest in the stock is the value of the interest that would have been made by leaving the money in the bank.

Note that opportunity cost is not the sum of the available alternatives when those alternatives are, in turn, mutually exclusive to each other. The opportunity cost of the city's decision to build a hospital on its vacant land is the loss of the land for other venues, such as an events center, or the money that could have been made from selling the land, because use for any one of those purposes would preclude the possibility to implement any of the other opportunities.

Here's another way to look at opportunity cost: it is the cost spent (given up) by selecting one project over another. The good news is, no calculations are needed. For example, project A has an NPV of $45,000, and project B has an NPV of $85,000. What is the opportunity cost of selecting project B?

Answer: $45,000 NPV of project A.

SUNK COSTS

Simply put, sunk costs are project costs that have been expended (spent). Be aware that according to general accounting standards (and it is usually true in project management as well), sunk costs should not be considered when deciding whether to continue or terminate a troubled project. This is a hard one because clearly you don't want to throw good money after bad.

For example, assume your company has approved $10,000 to fund a project to build a prototype medical product called Heart Beat II (HB2). Two months later, you see that a competitor has just announced the very same product for a lower per-unit price than at which you were estimating selling yours. No matter the outcome of the project, the money already spent is "sunk cost." The logical decision might be to terminate the project. However, your company sees a way to reduce production cost and anticipates very high demand for HB2. The decision to continue building the product should not be based on sunk cost but rather on the business need, the product's marketability, the potential benefits to your customer, the law of diminishing returns, and of course profit.

DEPRECIATION

Most people are familiar with the different types of depreciation, but just in case let's talk about a couple as a refresher.

In simple terms we can say that depreciation is the reduction in the value of an asset due to wear and tear, obsolescence, depletion, or other factors.

In accounting, *depreciation* is a term used to describe any method of spreading the purchase cost of an asset across its useful life, caused by normal wear and tear.

Straight-line depreciation is the simplest and most often used technique, in which the company estimates the salvage value of the asset at the end of the period during which it will be used to generate income (useful life) and expenses the original cost (less salvage value) in equal increments over that period. The *salvage value* is an estimate of the value of the asset at the time it will be sold or disposed of; it may be zero. Salvage value is also called "scrap value."

Another type of depreciation is *accelerated depreciation*. It has two forms, and both decline faster than using traditional straight-line depreciation:

- **Double declining balance.** The most common rate of accelerated depreciation used is double the straight-line rate. For this reason, this technique is referred to as the double declining balance method.

  To give you an example, say a business has an asset with $4,000 original cost, $100 salvage value, and five years of useful life. First, calculate the straight-line depreciation rate. Because the asset has five years of useful life, the straight-line depreciation rate is 20 percent per year (100% / 5 years). With the double declining balance method, as the name suggests, you would double that rate (40-percent depreciation rate) for the first two years and be left with 20 percent to be used the third year. You might use an accelerated depreciation on an asset that has a shorter life span.

  Book value at the beginning of the first year of depreciation is the original cost of the asset. Thereafter, book value equals original cost minus accumulated depreciation.

  Book Value = Original Cost – Accumulated Depreciation

  Book value at the end of one year becomes the book value at the beginning of the next year. The asset is depreciated until the book value equals the salvage value (or scrap value).

- **Sum of the years digits.** Sum of the years digits is a depreciation method that results in a more accelerated write-off than straight-line depreciation, but less than the double declining balance method. Under this method, annual depreciation is determined by multiplying the depreciable cost by a schedule of fractions.

Depreciable Cost = Original Cost – Salvage Value

Book Value = Original Cost – Accumulated Depreciation

For example, if an asset has an original cost of $1000, a useful life of five years, and a salvage value of $100, how do you compute its depreciation schedule? First, determine the years' digits. Because the asset has a useful life of five years, the years' digits are 5, 4, 3, 2, and 1. Next, calculate the sum of the digits (5 + 4 + 3 + 2 + 1 = 15).

Depreciation rates are as follows: 5/15 for the first year, 4/15 for the second year, 3/15 for the third year, 2/15 for the fourth year, and 1/15 for the fifth year.[9] Depreciation for year one would be $300, calculated as ($1,000 – $100) * 5 / 15, where $1,000 is original cost, $100 is the salvage value, and 5/15 is the rate of depreciation for year 1.

Summary of Project Cost Management

As mentioned at the beginning of this chapter, cost management is one of the primary constraints on projects, and costs should be managed as if your own money was being used.

Multiple studies show that a significant share of projects overrun their original timelines or are never completed. A study by PricewaterhouseCoopers, which reviewed 10,640 projects from 200 companies in 30 countries and across various industries, found that only 2.5 percent of the companies successfully completed 100 percent of their projects. A study published in the *Harvard Business Review*, which analyzed 1,471 IT projects, found that the average overrun was 27 percent, but one in six projects had a cost overrun of 200 percent on average and a schedule overrun of almost 70 percent. And we all have heard about large construction projects—the Channel Tunnel, Euro Disney, and Boston's "Big Dig"—that ended up costing almost double their original estimate.[10] Some of the likely reasons are poor initial cost estimates, unrealistic budgets, poor financial management, and changes in scope, any of which will likely yield a lower than expected return on investment (ROI). However, at the end of the day, most project failures can be tied back to poor project management discipline. The PM is ultimately responsible for successfully bringing your project in on time and on budget.

The good news is that a lot of good tools and techniques are available to help you manage cost. The best ways to manage cost on your project:

1. Stay alert and focused on project objectives and the associated costs.
2. Use the tools and resources available to effectively estimate, monitor, report, and manage costs.

Category Name	Daily Rate	Baseline Days	Actual Days	Baseline Cost *** Budget	Actual Cost To Date	Remaining Cost	Total Cost	Cost Variance
Summary of Staff				179,200	168,320	13,600	181,920	2,720
Project Team	400	138	180	55,200	72,000	4,000	76,000	20,800
Pilot End Users	400	62	34	24,800	13,600	500	14,100	-10,700
InterNet Support	560	70	67	39,200	37,520	3,500	41,020	1,820
Project Board	400	15	8	6,000	3,200	800	4,000	-2,000
Consulting	1,200	20	20	24,000	24,000	0	24,000	0
Extended Proj. Teams	400	75	45	30,000	18,000	4,800	22,800	-7,200
	Unit Cost	Units						
Hardware & Network				28,700	20,200	1,850	22,050	-6,650
Software	7,500	10		75,000	75,000		75,000	0
Project Training	1,500	4	4	6,000	6,000		6,000	0
Installation Training	1,500	10	8	15,000	13,300	785	14,085	-915
Miscellaneous				2,000	600	280	880	-1,120
Total Costs				305,900	283,420	30,115	299,935	-5,965

*** All Baseline Costs are derived from the approved Project Initiation Document Estimates

FIGURE 7.8 Case Study Sample Cost Estimating Spreadsheet

3. Work with the project team to ensure that everyone is doing their part to provide accurate cost estimates, develop and monitor budgets, and help manage cash flow.

Hopefully these three steps sound familiar by now as they are the three takeaway points for this book.

Also, you want to use earned value management (EVM), when possible and as appropriate, to ensure that the project's return on investment (ROI) is achieved.

One thing that is painfully clear is that if you and the project team are not diligent in managing cost and reporting status in a timely manner, you are at risk when it comes to cost management. Another thing to remember is that as a PM you need to look beyond identifying potential cost problems in order to make sound recommendations to keep the gaps (misses) from showing up in the future. See Figure 7.8 for a sample cost estimating spreadsheet.

References

1. "Project Margin," Inc.com, http://www.inc.com/encyclopedia/profit-margin.html, accessed March 12, 2017.

2. Rita Mulcahy, *PMP Exam Prep, Sixth Edition* (Minnetonka, MN: RMC Publications, Inc., April 2009), page 232.

3. US Department of Energy, "Performance Baseline Guide," DOE G 413.3-5A (September 23, 2011), https://www.google.com/search?q=Development+of+the+PB+begins+with+the+planning+cost%2C+schedule+estimate%2C+and+the+preliminary+scope+included+in+the+mission+need+statement%2C+and+is+further+defined+in+conceptual+design+documents.&ie=utf-8&o e=utf–8&aq=t&rls=org.mozilla:en-US:official&client=firefox-a.

4. Rita Mulcahy, *PMP Exam Prep, Eighth Edition* (Minnetonka, MN: RMC Publishing, Inc., 2013), page 266.

5. "Net Present Value," *FinAid*, http://www.finaid.org/loans/npv.phtml, accessed March 12, 2017.

6. Ibid.

7. "Future Value," *Investopedia*, http://www.investopedia.com/terms/f/futurevalue.asp, accessed March 12, 2017.

8. "Understanding the Time Value of Money," *Investopedia*, http://www.investopedia.com/articles/03/082703.asp, accessed March 12, 2017.

9. "Depreciation," *Wikipedia*, http://en.wikipedia.org/wiki/Depreciation, accessed March 12, 2017.

10. Benoit Hardy-Vallee, "The Cost of Bad Project Management," *Business Journal* (February 7, 2012), http://www.gallup.com/businessjournal/152429/cost-bad-project-management.aspx, accessed May 29, 2017.

8 Project Quality Management

Key Skills & Concepts

- Definition of quality
- Importance of managing project quality
- Quality is in the eyes of the customer
- How to achieve customer satisfaction
- How to measure quality
- Quality gurus (theorists)
- Key quality terms
- Continuous improvement
- Introduction to Six Sigma, Lean, and Kaizen
- Quality management processes
- Cost of quality conformance and nonconformance
- Types of reports and charts

The Definition of Quality (and How It Has Changed)

The definition of quality has changed through the years, depending on whom you talk to. PMI's definition in the first edition of the *PMBOK* was "the totality of characteristics of an entity that bear on its ability to satisfy stated or implied needs." My wife almost fell out of her chair when I read that to her in 1998 as I was preparing for the PMP exam. The good news is that in the latest edition of the *PMBOK*, the definition is much easier to remember and more applicable and simply states that "quality as a delivered performance or result is the degree to which a set of inherent characteristics fulfills requirements" (ISO9000-[20]).

According to BusinessDictionary.com, quality is a "measure of excellence or state of being free from defects, deficiencies, and significant variations." Quality in manufacturing is defined as a "measure of excellence or a state of being free of defects, deficiencies, and significant variations brought about by the strict and consistent adherence to measurable and verifiable standards to achieve uniformity of output that satisfies specific customer or user requirements."[1]

Importance of Managing Project Quality

How important is quality? Most people would say it is extremely important. In fact, the word is often used in advertising slogans. Here are some examples of classic slogans that begin with *quality*:

- Quality at your feet (Brown Shoe)
- Quality first . . . from America's first pen maker (Esterbrook Pen)
- The quality goes in before the name goes on (Zenith)
- The quality name in refrigeration and air conditioning (York)
- Quality runs deep (Rustoleum)
- Quality toys with a purpose (Tinkertoy)
- Quality you can trust (Crown Central Petroleum)

Quality Is in the Eyes of the Customer

How do you really know what a quality product or service is? As a project manager (PM), how do you know you have delivered a quality project?

The answer is simple: Quality is in the eyes of the customer. After all, the customer is paying for the product, service, or result of the project. The customer needs to feel the project is delivered to the agreed-upon specifications and that the project does what it was intended to do.

The tough part of measuring quality at the project level is that it tends to be elusive and in many cases is a moving target. Some things are extremely difficult to measure because the qualities are intangible. If you ask 100 project customers what their idea of quality is, you will likely get well over 100 different answers because their current views or expectations vary depending on when and how you ask the question (face-to-face interview, survey, email, by phone, etc.).

Early in the project life cycle, customers might simply say they want a "full-function" website to promote their products or services. In the middle of the life cycle, when customers see which functions and features are being developed, they may change their minds regarding the look and feel of their websites. They may end up wanting something totally different at the end of the project.

As you work the project, you and the team will gather more details from the customer and reach a higher degree of understanding as to what the customer wants the website (the product of the project) to look like. This should be accomplished through close communications and documented acceptance criteria.

Once you have an approved acceptance criteria based on what the customer wants, the team can begin to develop or prototype the website. This prototype will give the customer an opportunity to test the site to see how it responds and where the links point. The closer you get to the end of the project, the more the product should align with the customer's needs and expectations.

As a PM, the ideal solution is always to get a clear understanding of what the customer wants as early in the life cycle as possible. This is easier said than done, especially when the customer is not completely sure what they want or what they expect at the end of the project.

I am sure you have experienced an unclear scope definition on one or more of your projects. The situation usually goes something like this: your boss or the customer simply says, "Build a new website so shoppers can buy our products online quicker and easier." Or maybe they say, "We have had too many problems on our database servers lately. Put a team together to fix the problems."

Occasionally you get more precise project direction, such as "We need to reach a 15 percent increase in systems availability of our database servers." Or, "To reach our revenue goals we need to increase ticket sales by 10 percent." As clear as the expected results may be, the actual detailed requirements are usually as clear as mud. The reason in most cases is that the customer doesn't know how to articulate their own needs and expectations when it comes down to identifying the actual requirements. That is why they are paying you as the PM to "just fix it."

At the end of the project, the only way you will meet the expected results is if the requirements are clear, verified, documented, and, most important, approved. And, of course, that is just the starting point (the price of admission, so to speak). The next important step is to get a qualified team together and keep them focused on the approved scope. All of these steps are essential to achieving project quality.

How to Achieve Customer Satisfaction

"Poor quality blurs the lines between our responsibility as a company and the customer's."

—DAVE DEN OTTER, VP OPERATIONS AT COMPUTRONIX

The only way to achieve customer satisfaction is to interview the customer and gain an understanding of their needs and expectations. When you think you are crystal clear on what the customer wants, document it. Take the documented requirements back to the customer for verification. Customer verification can be conducted by simply asking, "Is this what you had in mind?" Once verified, you now have "formal acceptance" from the customer on what the project should deliver.

Once you have formal acceptance (agreement) of the requirements from the customer, you take these requirements to the project team to be evaluated for "do-ability." That is, can the project deliver what the customer wants, according to the specifications?

If the customer's expectations are realistic, and if the project team is capable of meeting those expectations, and if the project is officially accepted (chartered), then the work of managing the project can begin. When I say "managing the project," this includes managing customer expectations so that their requirements will be met. This necessitates a combination of conformance to requirements so the project produces what it is intended to produce, and fitness for use so the product or service satisfies the customer's needs.

Because quality is in the eyes of the customer, the best thing to do as the PM to help deliver quality on your project is follow these five steps:

1. You must have a clear understanding of what the customer wants.
2. You must ensure that the deliverables of the project are reasonable (doable), documented, and approved by the customer.
3. You must clearly communicate the customer's expectations and deliverables to the project stakeholders, specifically to the project team, which will complete the work of the project.
4. You must have realistic measurements that will be used for tracking and reporting the progress of the project.
5. You must effectively manage changes on your project.

Note

Following the five steps above will help you achieve customer satisfaction on your project.

How Do You Measure Quality?

For an accountant, the measure of quality is pretty clear—the ledger books must be balanced. What does it mean to say the books are balanced? It means all book entries (debits and credits) are in order and properly coded in accordance with approved accounting practices. All receipts are filed properly and are available in case of an audit. The bank statements match the tracking reports (spreadsheets, financial statements, etc.). The client receives reports in a timely manner, which clearly defines the account balances and potential financial exposures.

For our P&G case study, a measure of quality for the product was the help desk consolidation met all service level agreements for hold time (e.g., 90 percent of all calls to the help desk are answered within 30 seconds, hold times not to exceed 90 seconds on average, and first-time fix rate of 75 percent without having to transfer the caller to level-2 support person). And the project comprising help desk consolidation and transfer was to be successfully completed by the approved go-live date and the cost fell within ±5 percent of the approved budget with no disruption in daily operations.

Ask the Expert

Q: What is a good measure of quality when managing projects?

A: If the product of the project meets the specified (approved) requirements and if the product does what the project definition says it should do (fitness of use), and the project was delivered on-time and on-budget then you have met the quality standards for the project. Remember you can meet the product quality requirements and miss the project quality requirements or the other way around. Ideally you should meet both quality requirements for project and the product(s) being delivered.

When you're managing projects, what you measure and when you measure it are not always as clear as they are in accounting. So, what is a good measure of quality in project management? Any time you measure quality, you must have a baseline or reference point against which to measure.

A simple approach I like to use is what I call the "Texas Three-Step." After you have a baseline, you ask yourself and your team these three questions:

- **Where are we today compared to where we planned to be today?** As explained in earned value management (EVM) from Chapter 7, this is a good way to confirm current status, but you also need to review in real terms, not just dollars and cents.
- **How did we get here?** Take a look at "the road just taken." Was it the road or path you had planned to take? Or did you have obstacles that impacted the project and required you to take a different path? Lessons learned are a great tool for helping you understand what worked and what didn't work the way it should have (we must learn from our actions and our mistakes).
- **Where do we go from here?** Looking forward, what course corrections do you need to take to keep the project on track (or to get it back on track)?

When it comes to measuring quality, the approach is and always will be, "What is important to the customer?"

Sample Quality Measurements

For another real-world example of quality measurements, let's take a look at an example for setting up an ice-skating event (such as ice hockey and performance show on ice). The ice has to be set up to meet very rigid specifications to be considered safe for the skaters. If the ice is too warm, it becomes spongy and slow and the skaters have a difficult time making turns and stops. If the ice is too cold, it becomes brittle and is susceptible to cracking, and sprawls or holes form.

- The paint is to be applied as close to the concrete as possible without drips, drifting lines, or "pearling" of the white base coat.
- Ice "slab" temperature must be maintained at 18 to 19 degrees Fahrenheit (F).
- Surface temperature at a depth of one inch must be maintained at 21 degrees F.
- The ice has to be at a depth that's thick enough so the skaters can't dig down to the concrete (e.g., 2 inches for ice hockey).
- Edges are to be conditioned to eliminate any rough surfaces.

Quality Assurance and Control

- Dry and wet cuts must be used to keep the ice conditioned and smooth after practice.
- Depth checks are performed and recorded daily after each Zamboni conditioning to track and control the quality of the ice.
- Protective glass surround (barrier around the ice) is to be walked prior to every game to ensure it is secure, thus reducing the chance that glass will pop out during a game.

Sometimes talk is cheap. The main question is, does the company really know what we, as customers, want when it comes to quality? Do they know what is broken and what to do to fix it?

What Is Broken and How Do We Fix It?

Throughout the years, many of us woke up to news headlines about massive recalls on everything from faulty ignition switches to airbag recalls that affected millions of cars. In response to quality issues in the 1980s, Ford Motor Co., adopted the slogan "Quality is Job 1." Ford went on to drop this slogan after seventeen years because of the perception that in today's marketplace, high quality is a given and is no longer an important marketing variable. Quality is expected; it is not an option.

As always, other influencing factors are at work when it comes to ensuring quality. Could it be that even though quality is important (a given), the real focus on cost overrides quality? In the interest of being competitive, companies seem to be more concerned with the cost of quality than they are with providing quality in their products or services.

No one goes to work in the morning wanting to do a bad job. However, how many people do you know who go to work each day and just do enough to get by? I have seen entire departments of people who "jumped ship" from one company to another for a few bucks more per hour or for a signing bonus. It seems that the loyalty of the workforce has diminished during the last few years. Most unhappy employees feel it is the shift of work to other countries or companies that outsource work to the lowest bidder that has caused this drop in employee loyalty and moral. Companies that outsource or "off-shore" work outside of the country may benefit by defining their quality policies on a global perspective because, in reality, the quality of work or materials used outside of the United States may be defined differently in other countries.

With the shift of work or work reduction, there tends to be an increased level of uncertainty among the employees. Uncertainty causes distractions on the job and will affect the quality of work being performed. This can be seen in many industries, even in professional sports where athletes are traded from one team to another, causing a drop or change in performance. If you don't know where you will be working (or playing, in the case of an athlete) next month or next year, it is much harder to establish a sound attitude toward quality. People want to do a good job; however, the priorities seem to have shifted, and doing quality work is not as high a priority in today's workforce (in many cases).

Even in Japan, where the "job for life" concept went out the window several years ago, the quality of work is still there. Quality is an attitude.

How Do We Fix the Quality Problems?

Everything we say and do affects our reputation. There is an old saying that it takes a lifetime to build a reputation and just one second to destroy it. Perfection may not be fully attainable; however, we can perform our jobs with excellence. To do so it just takes a little more focus, a few extra minutes. For example, try reviewing a note one more time before you send it out, or try verifying the spreadsheet totals before distributing a report. How many times have you spent hours doing "damage control," or having to explain what you meant to say, or why your email said the meeting was at 2:00 a.m. instead of 2:00 p.m.?

You may save a lot of time and have a much better chance of maintaining a good reputation for quality if you plan ahead and don't rush. Always double-check your work. At the end of the day, quality is a matter of time and attitude.

Tip

It is no surprise that we are not at our best after working long hours "burning the midnight oil." It has been my experience that if I send an email after midnight, the quality is not as good as when I am rested. Therefore, my recommendation is do not send an email after midnight. Wait until the next morning and read it one last time before you send it (especially if the note is to your customer or your boss). You should always double-check for errors before you send important documents—maybe have a friend, coworker, or even your spouse (if willing) read over the email to check for errors. This could save the day and your reputation.

TABLE 8.1 Juran's Quality Trilogy

Quality Categories	Steps
Quality planning	Identify the customers. Determine the needs of those customers. Translate those needs into our language. Develop a product that can respond to those needs. Optimize the product features so as to meet our needs and customer needs.
Quality improvement	Develop a process that is able to produce the product. Optimize the process.
Quality control	Prove that the process can produce the product under operating conditions with minimal inspection. Transfer the process to Operations.

Gurus (Theorists) of Quality

There are many quality theorists (or gurus, as they are often called) in the world of project management. The gurus you need to be familiar with who have made significant contributions to quality in project management (and may appear on PMI exams) are the following:

- **Dr. Joseph M. Juran** defined quality as "fitness for use," applied Pareto's 80/20 principle to quality, and advocated top management involvement. He made many contributions to the field of quality management in his 70+ active working years. He was the first to incorporate the human aspect of quality management, which is referred to as Total Quality Management (TQM). His classic book, *Quality Control Handbook*, first released in 1951, is still the standard reference work for quality managers. Table 8.1 outlines the major points of Dr. Juran's quality management ideas.[2]
- **Dr. W. Edwards Deming** advocated quality improvement using the Plan-Do-Check-Act (PDCA) cycle and developed the 14 Steps to Total Quality Management. He "taught that by adopting appropriate principles of management, organizations can increase quality and simultaneously reduce costs (by reducing waste, rework, staff attrition, and litigation while increasing customer loyalty). The key is to practice continual improvement and think of manufacturing as a system, not as bits and pieces."[3]
- **Philip Crosby** popularized the concept of "do it right the first time." He believed management should take primary responsibility for quality, and workers should follow their managers' example. He defined the Four Absolutes of Quality Management:

1. Quality is conformance to requirements.
2. Quality prevention is preferable to quality inspection.
3. "Zero defects" is the quality performance standard.
4. Quality is measured in monetary terms—the price of nonconformance.[4]

Key Quality Terms

Before we get into a lot of details surrounding the quality processes, there are some terms and distinctions that are important for you to know (especially if you are planning to take the PMI exam).

Quality versus Grade

Quality and grade are not the same:

- **Quality** is the degree to which the characteristics of the product meet its specified requirements. Take meat, for example. Several factors go into determining the quality of the meat, including maturity, firmness, texture, color, and the amount and distribution of marbling.
- **Grade** is a category assigned to products or services having the same functional uses but with different technical characteristics. Looking at meat again (can you tell it is getting close to mealtime?), there are different applications (uses) and different grades (e.g., Prime, Choice, Select, and Standard). See Table 8.2 for a description of beef quality grades according to Meat Science, USDA Beef Quality and Yield Grade, Texas A&M AgriLife Extension Services.[5]

TABLE 8.2 Examples of Beef Quality Grades

Grade	Characteristics	Suggested Use
Prime	Has abundant marbling and is generally sold in restaurants and hotels.	Prime roasts and steaks are excellent for roasting, broiling, and grilling (dry heat methods).
Choice	Has less marbling than Prime grades, but is still high quality.	Choice grade may be cooked with dry heat. Be careful not to overcook roasts from rump, round, and blade chuck. A meat thermometer can be helpful in cooking to a safe temperature
Select	Leaner than the higher grades. Fairly tender but may lack some juiciness and flavor of higher grades.	Only the loin, ribs, and sirloin should be cooked with dry heat. Other cuts should be marinated before cooking or cooked with moisture.
Standard	Has no marbling. Will lack juiciness and flavor of higher grades.	Standard may be sold as ungraded or "store brand" meat.

Here is another example of quality and grade that will be easy for dog lovers to remember. Let's say we have a manufacturing plant that builds two different types of dog chew toys.

1. The first one is very simple and is built for small dogs who don't put much pressure on their toys. The requirement for each toy is that it can withstand a dachshund chewing on it for one hour at a time without cracking. It passes the quality check for this 100 percent of the time, and it has never been returned by a customer.
2. The second toy is top of the line. It plays music and glows in the dark. It is also designed to withstand a strong chewer and it is shown in the advertisement with a German shepherd. The requirement is that it can be chewed by a tiger for one hour and can be run over by a cement truck without cracking. It passes this test only 60 percent of the time, and customer returns of cracked toys run about 20 percent.

The first toy is low grade but high quality. The second is high grade but low quality.

Precision versus Accuracy

Precise means that the product is exact, as in performance. It is repeatable and gets the same measure every time. *Accuracy*, on the other hand, means the measured value is very close to the true value (hitting the bull's eye on a target), meaning a measurement is accurate if it correctly reflects the size of the thing being measured. Precision measurements are not necessarily accurate. A very accurate measurement is not necessarily precise. See the following examples (Figure 8.1):

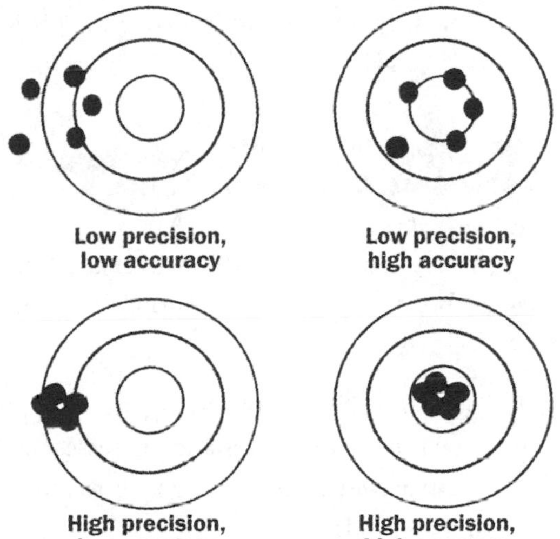

- In target shooting, a high score indicates the closeness to the bull's eye and is a measure of the shooter's accuracy.
- In target shooting, precision is the tightness of the pattern (cluster) when bullets hit the target close together. If the pattern is scattered (lots of space between the hits on the target), it is not precise. The smaller (or tighter) the pattern, the higher the precision. If the bullet hits are closely clustered but are not close to the bull's eye, the shooting is precise but not accurate.

Prevention over Inspection

Many quality experts feel that quality has to be "built in" (prevention) through planning and design, not "inspected in." There is usually a large cost (not just monetary) associated with inspection. If quality is built in, you are likely to save a lot of time and money (as well as saving your reputation and avoiding negative impacts to brand recognition) over the cost of inspection.

Inspecting quality means that you are not fixing the root cause of the problem. For example, if you are relying on inspection to ensure quality while spot-checking car parts on an assembly line, how many parts go through the line that are nonconforming? You can't inspect every part, so in this case you are letting bad parts get to the customer.

If you build quality in, you eliminate waste, scrap, and rework, which will save time, effort, and materials, and improve your reputation and brand recognition, as well as the profit margins.

You have probably heard the statement "do it right the first time" many times before. To ensure that you have long-term quality products, processes, or services, you need prevention. Prevention goes far beyond just "doing it right the first time." The PM and team need to look constantly for ways to improve the project over its life cycle by *monitoring* the product, process, or service.

Continuous Improvement

The Plan-Do-Check-Act (PDCA) cycle, mentioned earlier, is the basis for quality improvement, as defined by Walter Shewhart and later modified by W. Edwards Deming. The PDCA cycle is about creating a continuous, long-term improvement cycle. The details of the cycle are as follows:

1. **Plan.** From the top of the organization (or even across companies, as they do in Japan), establish the objectives and processes necessary to deliver results in accordance with the expected output. The goal is to ensure consistency in project management tools and methods.
2. **Do.** Implement the new processes. Everyone on the team is encouraged to look at innovative ways to improve the process flow, identify problems, and implement solutions (e.g., stop to fix the problem when it occurs).
3. **Check.** Measure the new processes by collecting actual process data and compare the outcome against the expected results to verify that the target is being met.

4. **Act.** Analyze the differences to determine their cause. Then make necessary adjustments to solutions and update action plans as needed. Also, identify future steps to make sure the problem doesn't resurface. Then you start the cycle again, thus continuing improvement.

International Organization for Standardization (ISO)

An organization you should be familiar with that helps ensure quality is the International Organization for Standardization (ISO). Founded in 1946, ISO is composed of national standards bodies from over 114 countries—for example, the American National Standards Institute (ANSI) is a member of ISO. ISO has defined a number of important computer standards, the most significant of which is perhaps OSI (Open Systems Interconnection), a standardized architecture for designing networks. Although ISO defines itself as a nongovernmental organization, it has the ability to set standards that often become law.

Here are some examples of ISO standards:

- ISO 9000 refers to a set of three standards (ISO 9000, ISO 9001, and ISO 9004). All three are referred to as "quality management system standards." For example, ISO 9004 provides a set of guidelines used to develop quality management systems. The ISO 9000 standards apply to all kinds of organizations across many industries, including manufacturing, processing, forestry, electronics, steel, computing, legal services, financial services, accounting, banking, recycling, aerospace, and construction.
- The ISO 14000 family of standards addresses various aspects of environmental management. The very first two standards (ISO 14001:2004 and ISO 14004:2004) deal with environmental management systems (EMS). The other standards and guidelines in the ISO 14000 group address specific environmental aspects, including labeling, performance evaluation, life-cycle analysis, communication, and auditing.

Introduction to Six Sigma, Lean, and Kaizen Initiatives

Six Sigma and Lean are two quality initiatives that have emerged at higher levels of interest in government and commercial organizations. These initiatives, combined with the previous focus on Kaizen (continuous improvement), tend to add confusion to people trying to improve project or product quality. A question that often comes up from clients and students alike is, "Which concept (or initiative) should we use to improve quality on our projects?"

Ask the Expert

Q: Is this a Six Sigma, Lean, or Kaizen project? Which concept should I use?

A: According to the article "Is This a Six Sigma, Lean, or Kaizen Project?" by Terence T. Burton, "This is a familiar question that is often [raised] by organizations. In fact, it's the wrong question. These concepts are nothing more than tools in your management toolbox. You don't fix a watch with a hammer, and you get the same results when you deploy Six Sigma, Lean, and Kaizen incorrectly. The fact is, a business problem is a business problem, and it needs to be fixed. Understanding the application of these tools to various improvement opportunities is the key to success."[6] With any tool, the application or use depends on the size and complexity of the project as well as the availability and affordability of the tool or model to use.

Before anyone can accurately answer the question about which initiative or tool to use on your specific project, you need a better understanding of the definition of each. Otherwise, you run the risk of seeing each quality issue as a nail, thus limiting yourself to using only one tool (a hammer).

What Is Six Sigma?

Six Sigma is a management-driven company-wide business initiative to generate breakthrough (innovative) results in business performance. Six Sigma is a focus on quality that strives for near perfection. It is a disciplined, data-driven approach and methodology for eliminating defects. A Six Sigma process is one in which 99.99966 percent of the products manufactured are statistically expected to be free of defects (3.4 defects per million). Six Sigma can be applied across businesses and industries, from manufacturing to services. Here are a couple of examples:

- Ford Motor Company began its Six Sigma push in 1999 when the director of quality for Ford's global truck business began looking for new ways to improve quality. Other companies were quick to jump on the bandwagon.
- General Electric, one of the most successful companies implementing Six Sigma, has estimated benefits on the order of $10 billion during the first five years of implementation. GE first began Six Sigma in 1995 after Motorola and Allied Signal blazed the Six Sigma trail. Since then, thousands of companies around the world have discovered the far reaching benefits of Six Sigma.[7]

The work processes tied to Six Sigma are Define, Measure, Analyze, Improve, and Control (DMAIC). It is important to note that Six Sigma is a business initiative, not a quality initiative. The theory is that if you improve business processes and work flow, then quality will follow.

What Is Lean?

Lean (the term) was first coined in the late 1980s (or 1990s, depending on which article/book you read). Lean is a system (or set of tools) that thrives on change and flexibility and focuses on reducing waste in the workplace. Lean can be used for organizing and managing projects, product development, ongoing operations, and supplier services. Many companies and organizations use Lean principles to reduce defects, streamline processes, reduce manufacturing space, and improve employee performance.

Specifically, Lean seeks to eliminate wait time between production stations, to avoid overprocessing (e.g., using too many steps in the process), and to reduce excess inventory. Lean also seeks out employee creativity to help solve problems and increase productivity.

According to the Lean Enterprise Institute website,

> Many of the key principles were pioneered by Henry Ford, who was the first person to integrate an entire production system, under what he termed "flow production." Following World War II, the Toyota Motor Company adapted Ford's principles as a means of compensating for its challenge of limited human, financial, and material resources. The Toyota Production System (or TPS), which evolved from this need, was one of the first managerial systems using Lean principles throughout the enterprise to produce a wide variety of products at lower volumes and many fewer defects than competitors.[8]

Try This

GO LEAN PROJECT

Your manager comes to you and says he wants his department to "Go Lean," and you have been selected to be the project manager to implement the quality initiative. The very next question from your manager is, "What is the expected completion date for this project?" What is your answer?

A. Six months from today

B. You need more information. For example, is this project part of an overall companywide initiative?

C. One year from today

D. On the Monday after Easter

Answer: B. You need more information because Lean must have top management sponsorship with companywide operational-level commitment, not just commitment from a single department. Lean implementation looks at quality problems throughout the operation. It requires system-wide focus and should be implemented across the entire organization.

Lean should be viewed as a culture change (developed over time). Lean is the set of "tools" that assist in the identification and steady elimination of wasted time, lost productivity, scrap, or rework. When waste is eliminated, quality improves and production time and cost are reduced. Examples of other "tools" are Value Stream Mapping, Five S, and Kanban (pull systems).

Note that Lean can only happen with planning, organization, and high-level management commitment to provide the resources needed to succeed.

What Is Kaizen?

Kaizen is a Japanese word meaning "continuous improvement." It comes from the words *kai*, which means "change," or "to correct," and *Zen*, which means "good." Kaizen is used in Lean manufacturing, the Toyota Production System (TPS), Just In Time (JIT) inventory, and other effective manufacturing strategies.

For Kaizen to work correctly it should involve every employee, from upper management to the cleaning crew. Everyone is encouraged to come up with improvement ideas (no matter how small) and make suggestions on a continuous basis. The ideas are based on making small changes along the way to improve productivity, safety, and efficiency to reduce extra steps and waste in the workplace.

Another quality program you may be aware of (so far not on the PMI exam) is the Five S program found predominantly in manufacturing and other types of businesses such as retail, warehouses, and even hospitals. The Five S program, usually part of Kaizen, is designed to establish a clean Visual Workplace. The Five S program focuses on having visual order and standardization. Here are the Five S's:

- **Sort.** First, make things clean and organized
- **Set in Order.** Organize, identify, and arrange everything in a work area
- **Shine.** Conduct regular cleaning and maintenance
- **Standardize.** Make it easy to maintain—simplify and standardize
- **Sustain.** Maintain what has been accomplished

The results you can expect are improved profitability, safety, and efficiency.

Project Quality Management Processes

Quality management must be planned into the project from the beginning. Quality must be ensured by the team. This means quality must be clearly defined and documented in both qualitative and quantitative terms, and it should be reviewed by all the stakeholders to make sure it will satisfy the needs for which it was developed. Once this is defined and agreed to by the project team, quality measurements must be implemented according to the approved guidelines. And last but not least, the team must continue to monitor quality to ensure that the project deliverables meet the planned quality performance requirements.

Monitoring quality to meet requirements is one thing; however, the PM and entire team should also continually seek ways to improve quality on the project. To help accomplish this continuous improvement, the PM and team need to be aware of and to exercise quality management processes. Quality management, according to PMI, includes the processes and activities to enable the PM and team to effectively manage the quality of the products (deliverables of the project) and of the overall project results by using proven project management processes, tools and techniques, and outputs. True quality is achieved when the PM and team demonstrate proven results through tracking, reporting, and managing quality over the entire project life cycle. Here are the three project quality management processes, according to PMI:

- **8.1: Plan Quality Management Process (Planning Process Group).** Includes identifying quality requirements and standards for the project and its deliverables and documenting how the project will demonstrate compliance with quality requirements.
- **8.2: Manage Quality (Executing Process Group).** The process of inspecting or auditing quality requirements and the results from quality control measurements to ensure appropriate quality standards and operational definitions are being used.
- **8.3: Control Quality (Monitoring and Controlling Process Group).** Involves monitoring and recording results of the execution of quality activities to assess performance and make necessary corrective actions through the change control process.

Tip

An easy way to remember the three processes for quality is to think of the first initials "PMC" (Plan, Manage, and Control). When you're preparing for the PMP exam, initials or acronyms often make the memorization a little easier.

Plan Quality Management Process (Planning Process Group)

The purpose of the Plan Quality Management process is to define requirements, industry practices, and the customer's quality standards for the product of the project and to provide information about and document how the project will comply with or achieve the defined quality requirements. An example of a customer's quality standards in an Agile project management environment may be the number of allowable software bugs (defects) per unit (module).

As with many of the PM processes, the Plan Quality Management process should be performed in parallel with other key project-planning processes, especially the risk and change control processes. Many tools and techniques are useful during the Plan Quality Management process. Figure 8.2 shows an overview of the inputs, tools and techniques, and the outputs for the Plan Quality Management process.

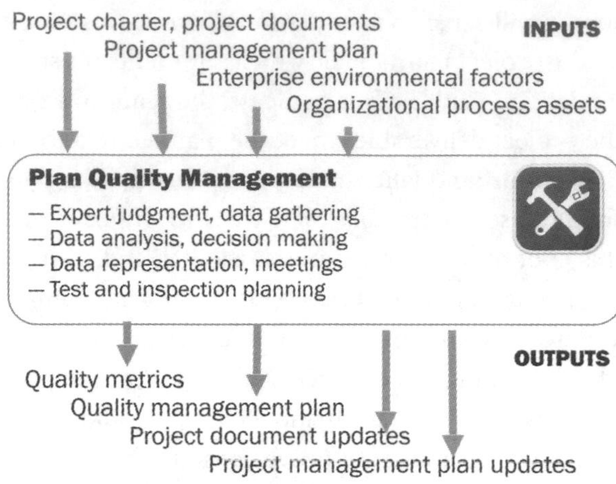

FIGURE 8.2 Plan Quality Management Process ITTOs

Tip

Keep in mind that part of the effort of creating standards and procedures for your project (based on your definition of quality) may also include any defined processes for how project management activities will be completed. In other words, when planning for how quality will be managed, it is also important to focus on how the work/activities will be monitored and measured to ensure the predictive results are being achieved.

A good way to track quality results is a technique PMI refers to as "data representation," which consists of using tools such as flowcharts (also referred to as process maps), logical data models, matrix diagrams, and mind maps to present project status.

A large part of data representation first requires data analysis, and there are many analytical tools available to assist in this effort.

Cost-Benefit Analysis

Most projects require a business case or cost case to help justify the need for them. Cost-benefit analysis is a relatively simple and widely used technique of weighing the benefits versus any costs of quality efforts and deciding whether to make a change (e.g., staying with an existing process or tool or going with one project vs. another).

As its name suggests, you simply list the benefits of a particular course of action as well as the savings or improvements realized and then subtract the costs associated with that action. Hopefully the benefits far outweigh the cost, thus making the project an easy sell. Cost-benefit analysis really helps decision makers choose the projects they want (or need) to sponsor.

Details of Cost of Quality (COQ)

Cost of quality (COQ) refers to the total cost of all efforts related to quality throughout the product life cycle. The decisions made during the project can impact the operational costs of quality as well. For example, the type of equipment or material used to build the product may not have a long life cycle or may require higher maintenance in the long run.

When calculating COQ, you also need to consider failure cost (cost of poor quality), potential cost of rework, cost of scrap, lost productivity (work stoppage), and so on. Costs can usually be broken into one of two categories: cost of conformance or cost of nonconformance. Using COQ means considering the appropriate amount of costs associated in achieving some specific level of quality.

COSTS OF CONFORMANCE

Here are some examples of the cost of conformance:

- Prevention costs (money spent during the project to avoid defects or failures)
  + Training
  + Document processes
  + Equipment
  + Time to "do it right the first time"
- Appraisal costs (to assess quality of the product)
  + Testing
  + Destructive testing loss (e.g., car safety testing)
  + Inspections

COSTS OF NONCONFORMANCE

Here are some examples of the cost of nonconformance:

- Internal failure costs (failures found by the project)
  + Rework
  + Scrap
- External failure costs (failures found by the customer)
  + Lost business
  + Warranty work
  + Liability

Control Charts

Control charts (PMI also refers to control charts as "data representation") are great tools for determining if a process or product is performing to expected levels. They can be used to track a variety of products, repetitive activities, cost and schedule variances, volume of

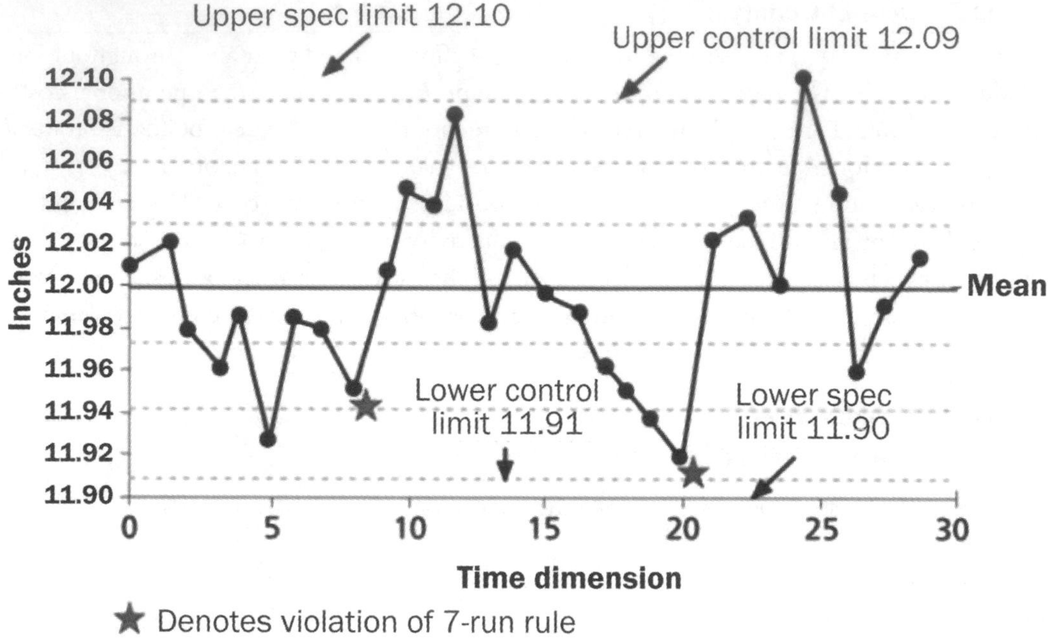

FIGURE 8.3 Sample Control Chart

output, and even the impact of changes to the project. Control charts or graphs can be used to show specific targets with upper and lower control limits tied to the acceptable requirements of the product.

If the product is not meeting the acceptable range (within approved control limits) in the specifications, there may be fallout (throwaway) parts or penalties associated with the out-of-limit parts or products. The control (specification) limits usually represent three standard deviations on either side of the centerline (or mean) of a normal distribution of data plotted in the control chart (see Figure 8.3).

When a process is within acceptable (control or warning) limits (generally ±3 sigma), it is said to be "in control" and doesn't need to be adjusted. When the process is outside the control limit, it should be monitored. If you see a "run" (seven consecutive points or events outside, above, or below the mean), that indicates the process is out of control and adjustments may be required.

Standard Deviation

When managing quality on a project, you may encounter the term *standard deviation*. People who have taken a statistics class in school are familiar with the term and might even under-

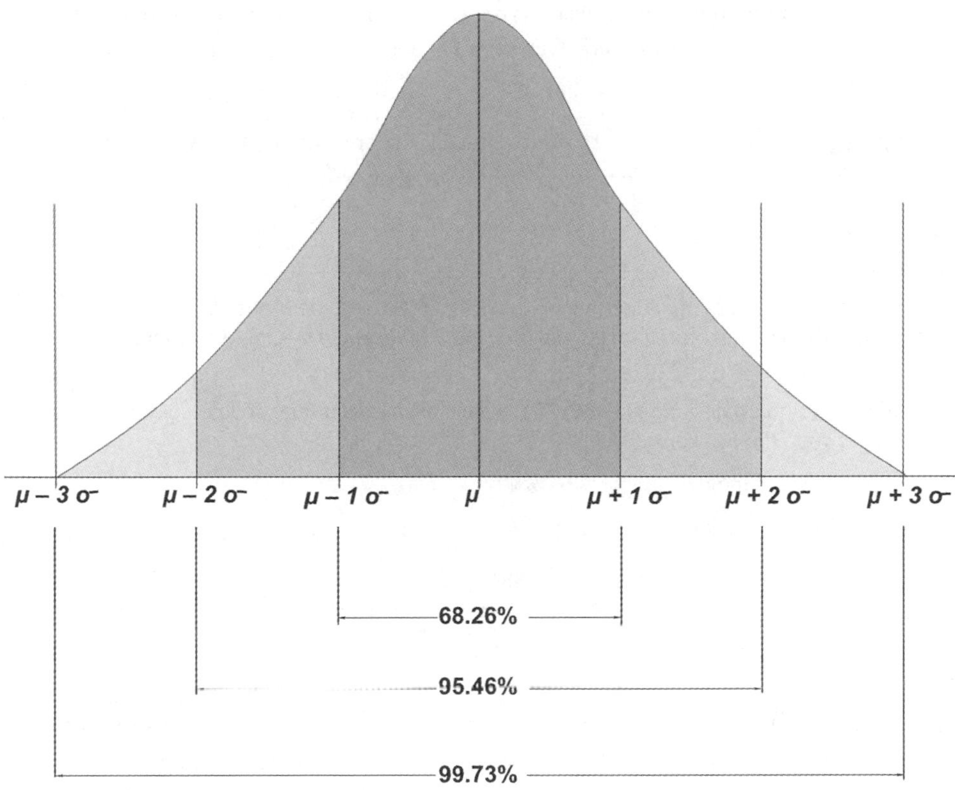

FIGURE 8.4 Sample Standard Deviation Chart

stand it. Standard deviation or sigma (σ is the Greek symbol for sigma) is a measure of the range or area of a normal distribution (bell curve) used to quantify the amount of variation from the mean (expected value) shown as a line in the middle of the chart. Sigma is taken from both sides of the mean and shows as a minus (–) on the left side and a plus (+) on the right side (see Figure 8.4).

> In statistics, standard deviation is a simple measure of the variability or dispersion of a data set. A low standard deviation indicates that the data points tend to be very close to the same value (the mean), while high standard deviation indicates that the data are "spread out" over a large range of values. For example, the average height for adult men in the United States is about 70 inches, with a standard deviation of around 3 inches. This means that most men (about 68%, assuming a normal distribution) have a height within 3 inches of the mean (between 67 and 73 inches), while almost all men (about 95%) have a height within 6 inches of the mean (between 64 and 76 inches). If the standard deviation

were zero, then all men would be exactly 70 inches high. If the standard deviation were 20 inches, then men would have much more variable heights, with a typical range of about 50 to 90 inches.[9]

A group of seven nonrandom data points shown on one side of the mean is referred to as the "rule of seven," indicating a process could be out of control.

Tip

Remember that half of a normal distribution curve is on the left side of the mean, and half is on the right side of the mean. If you are planning to take the PMP exam, you should memorize the following ranges:

±1 sigma (or standard deviations) = 68.26%, which is the percentage of data points (Occurrences) that fall between the two control limits

±2 sigma (or standard deviations) = 95.46%

±3 sigma (or standard deviations) = 99.73%

±6 sigma (or standard deviations) = 99.99966%

Benchmarking

Benchmarking is a process that uses standard measurements for comparing various things such as the cycle time, quality of a process or procedure, or method against an industry standard or best practice. Benchmarking provides a snapshot of how your business or organization's performance compares to these standards.

Certain groups conduct research and provide industry standards that can be used for benchmarking. These include the Gartner Group, Benchmarking Partners, and the Benchmarking Network, Inc., just to name a few.

Design of Experiments (DOE)

Design of experiments (DOE) is a statistical method or framework for identifying which factors may influence variables of a product or process. This is generally used during the quality planning process to determine the number and type of tests that may need to be run to ensure quality and the potential cost or outcome associated with the tests.

An example of DOE could be the study of rain, sun, and fertilizer on agricultural products for best growing conditions, or when a drug company conducts a series of tests on volunteers representing a sample group meeting certain criteria (e.g., age and level of fitness) using different doses, different frequencies, or even placebos to collect results and to determine which design of experiments yields the most favorable results for treating an illness.

Statistical Sampling

Statistical sampling is a way to obtain data without spending the time and money to observe or survey an entire population, because analyzing an entire population may take too long, cost too much, or be too destructive.

The best way to avoid a biased or unrepresentative sample is to select a random sample. A random sample is often defined as a sample where the probability that any individual member from the population selected as part of the sample is representative or the same as any other individual member of the population.

The sampling process frequently comprises several steps:

- Defining the population
- Selecting a sampling set of events possible to measure
- Determining a sampling method (e.g., interviews, surveys, etc.)
- Determining the sample size
- Implementing a sampling plan
- Collecting and analyzing data
- Reviewing the sampling results

Flowcharting

A flowchart is a graphical (data) representation of a process from beginning to end and shows relationships between steps, thus the term *flow*. It may be used to discover where quality problems exist on projects. Different design techniques and software tools are available to make this process easier. The flowchart can be used to show activities on the project, decision points (shown as a diamond-shaped image), and the order (or sequence) to follow. The use of arrows helps direct the viewer down the path based on decisions or answers to certain questions. Figure 8.5 shows a sample flowchart.

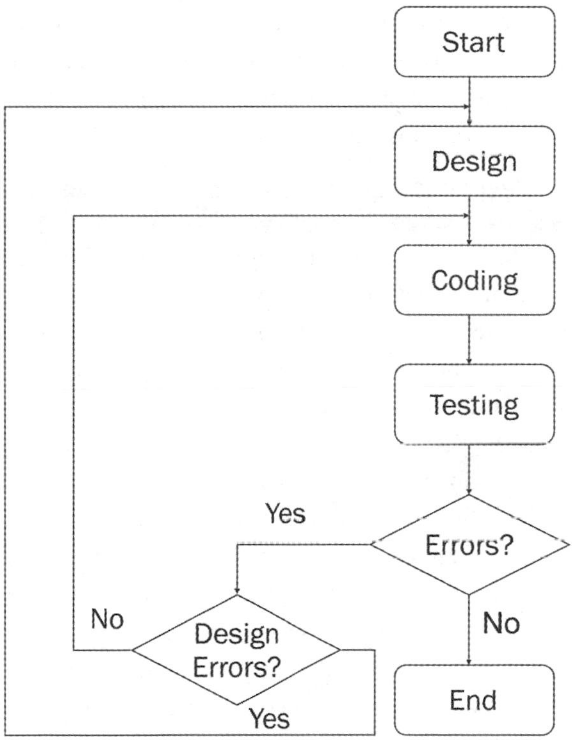

FIGURE 8.5 Sample Flowchart

Outputs of the Plan Quality Management Process

Here is a sample list of the primary outputs from the Plan Quality Management process:

- **Quality management plan (QMP).** Describes how the project team will implement the approved quality policies. The QMP is a key component of and provides inputs to the overall project management plan. The QMP can be formal or informal, and it can be very detailed or a high-level summary, depending on the needs of the project.
- **Quality metrics.** Describes operational details in very specific terms as to the product of the project as well as its features, functions (sometimes called "product attributes"), and any allowable tolerances. Quality metrics should be developed in advance so the project manager can effectively determine how the project is going. The quality metrics are used as inputs to the Manage Quality and Control Quality processes. Examples of quality metrics are failure rates (mean time between failures) of parts, budget or schedule control, on-time performance, defect frequency, and response time to fix problems.
- **Project documents updates.** As always, you want to use progressive elaboration to ensure the project plan and output documents are updated along the way when new information is learned or as changes occur. Examples of documents that might need to be updated are the responsibility assignment matrix (RAM) and the risk registry.

Manage Quality Process (Executing Process Group)

The Manage Quality process is in the Executing Process Group and uses data created during the Plan Quality process to identify whether processes and procedures are being followed and whether improvements can be made. The Manage Quality process involves the work of everyone (including the customer) involved with the project. The level of involvement in the quality management effort may differ among organizations, agencies, industries, and even the PM's style. In Agile projects, quality management is performed by the entire team throughout the project, where on traditional projects quality management is usually the responsibility of a specific team member or quality assurance representative. This process also includes auditing the quality requirements and the results from the quality control measurement to ensure that all appropriate quality standards are being met.

Some companies and organizations have a quality assurance (QA) representative or department as part of their management structure. The benefit of this person or department is that they help ensure that quality measures are accurate and communicated to the project stakeholders.

Quality assurance processes should be clearly documented and included in the quality plan as well as in the overall project management plan. Figure 8.6 shows an overview of the inputs, tools and techniques, and outputs for the Manage Quality process.

Quality Control Measures

Quality control measures—along with quality metrics, the process improvement plan, and performance information—are all things that need to be considered during the quality assurance process.

Quality control measures are the results of quality management activities. They are used to analyze and evaluate quality standards as established and approved at the project management office (PMO) and at the organizational level.

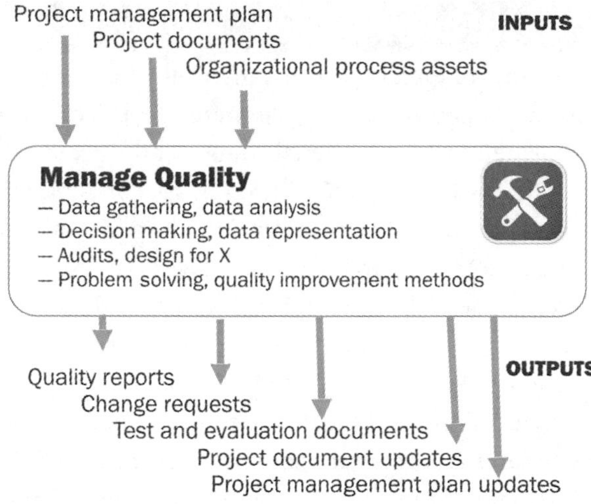

FIGURE 8.6 Manage Quality Process ITTOs

Quality Audits

One of the tools and techniques used in the Manage Quality process is quality audits. Audits typically are structured, independent reviews to determine whether project activities comply with organizational and project policics, processes, and procedures. Here are the reasons for quality audits:

- To identify best practices that can be shared across the organization
- To identify gaps or shortfalls for follow-up action
- To assist proactively in improving the implementation of approved processes
- To strive for continual improvement by identifying ways for the team to increase efficiency and performance

Other tools or techniques often used to help manage quality are:

- Data gathering (through benchmarking, brainstorming, interviews, and so on)
- Data analysis (using cost benefit analysis, cost of conformance, and other tools)
- Data representation (flowcharts, logical data models, diagrams, and mind maps)
- Problem solving
- Quality improvement methods

Some examples of the outputs of the Manage Quality process are quality reports, change requests, test and evaluation documents, and, as always, updates to project documents, as needed, to ensure the project is up to date.

Control Quality Process (Monitoring and Controlling Process Group)

The Control Quality process involves monitoring and recording the results of project execution via any measures that were identified during planning. Control Quality should be performed early and often throughout the project life cycle. This process is often performed by a quality control (QC) representative or department within an organization. The goal of the quality control team is to help ensure that quality is being performed to the approved tolerances, according to the specifications. This team is in place to prevent errors from reaching the customer. They perform this function through oversight and sampling, inspections, and other techniques to help ensure that quality is controlled.

The project team is responsible for complying with all quality standards, processes, and procedures. Control Quality is accomplished through the implementation of regular testing procedures according to the approved project definitions of quality and, more specifically, the refinement of these procedures by the project/quality control team using the following steps:

- Planning structured tests
- Following approved and documented specifications/requirements
- Conducting formal controlled testing according to standards
- Acting on the results of the tests (lessons learned)
- Updating documentation, processes, and procedures
- Using Quality Circle or similar review/implementation forums
- Following up to ensure continuous improvement (Plan-Do-Check-Act)

Successful companies and project managers place great emphasis on quality control. In "Quality Management Principles," Krister Forsberg states the following:

> With growing global competition, Quality Management is becoming increasingly important to the leadership and management of all organizations. Quality Management Principles provide understanding of and guidance on the application of Quality Management. By applying the following eight Quality Management Principles, organizations will produce benefits for customers, owners, people, suppliers and society at large.[10]

Here is a summary of Forsberg's quality management principles:

- **Principle 1. Customer-focused organization.** Organizations depend on their customers and therefore should understand current and future customer needs, meet customer requirements, and strive to exceed customer expectations.
- **Principle 2. Leadership.** Leaders establish unity of purpose, direction, and the internal environment of an organization. They create an environment in which people can become fully involved in achieving the organization's objectives.

- **Principle 3. Involvement of people.** People at all levels are the essence of an organization, and their full involvement enables their abilities to be used for the organization's benefit.
- **Principle 4. Process approach.** A desired result is achieved more efficiently when related resources and activities are managed as a process.
- **Principle 5. System approach to management.** Identifying, understanding, and managing a system of interrelated processes for a given objective all contribute to the effectiveness and efficiency of the organization.
- **Principle 6. Continual improvement.** Continual improvement is a permanent objective of the organization.
- **Principle 7. Factual approach to decision making.** Effective decisions and actions are based on the logical and intuitive analysis of data and information.
- **Principle 8. Mutually beneficial supplier relationships.** Mutually beneficial relationships between the organization and its supplier enhance the ability of both organizations to create value. Act promptly to resolve customer concerns. Enclose a brief survey form with the final invoice requesting information on the customer's opinions and expectations. Listen with great care to every one of your customer's ideas and suggestions, and thank them for their input.

For these principles to be effective, all business executives and managers first have to understand and then have to agree that quality management is essential to the success of the business. Once that agreement has been reached and you have full sponsorship at the highest level in the organization, the commitment must be communicated and enforced all the way down to each and every employee. All employees and managers must be involved in the process. All too often, employees are reluctant to report quality problems, feeling that they would be "rocking the boat" or seen as criticizing their coworkers to management. All employees must understand that the job of each employee and the prosperity of the company all depend on quality products and services and that teamwork and cooperation are essential to ensure quality.

Tools and Techniques for Control Quality Process

Many tools and techniques are used for Control Quality. Some of them are listed in this section. Check sheets are sometimes referred to as a tool used to control quality as well; they are simple sheets used for collecting data in real time. Figure 8.7 shows an overview of the inputs, tools and techniques, and the outputs for the Control Quality process.

The following is a list of what are often referred to as the Basic Seven Quality Tools, also known as Ishikawa's seven basic tools of quality control used for data representation:

- **Cause-and-effect diagrams.** These are also known as Fishbone or Ishikawa diagrams.
- **Control charts.** Walter Shewhart began using control charts in 1924.
- **Flowcharts.** These are used to identify failing process steps and used in risk analysis.
- **Histograms.** These are vertical bar charts, where the total area of a histogram always equals 1.
- **Pareto charts.** These charts use the 80/20 principle and show the number of defects by type or category (typically shown in a bar or histogram format).
- **Run charts.** These are line graphs similar to control charts, only without control limits.
- **Scatter diagrams.** These show the relationship between two variables.

INPUTS
Project management plan, project documents
Approved change requests, deliverables
Work performance data
Enterprise environmental factors
Organizational process assets

Control Quality
– Data gathering, data analysis
– Inspections, testing/product evaluations
– Data representation
– Meetings

OUTPUTS
Quality control measurements
Work performance information
Verified deliverables, change requests
Project document updates
Project management plan updates

FIGURE 8.7 Control Quality Process ITTOs

Here's a list of some quality control techniques:

- Statistical sampling
- Inspection
- Approved change-requests review

Pareto Diagram (Pareto's Law)

Named after Vilfredo Pareto, this diagram is used in quality assurance and is a special type of bar chart where the values being plotted are arranged in descending order (most frequent to least frequent). The graph is accompanied by a line on the graph that shows the cumulative totals of each category from left to right. Pareto diagrams are conceptually related to Pareto's Law (you may have heard of this as the 80/20 Rule or Principle), which states that a relatively small number of causes (20 percent) will typically produce the majority (80 percent) of the problems or defects. The Pareto diagram is a form of histogram (see Figure 8.8).

Lessons Learned

With every project, we learn more about what worked and what didn't. A good PM will document those lessons and use the information gained to improve on the next project and the next, which is why lessons learned are such a vital component in quality control. Collect and

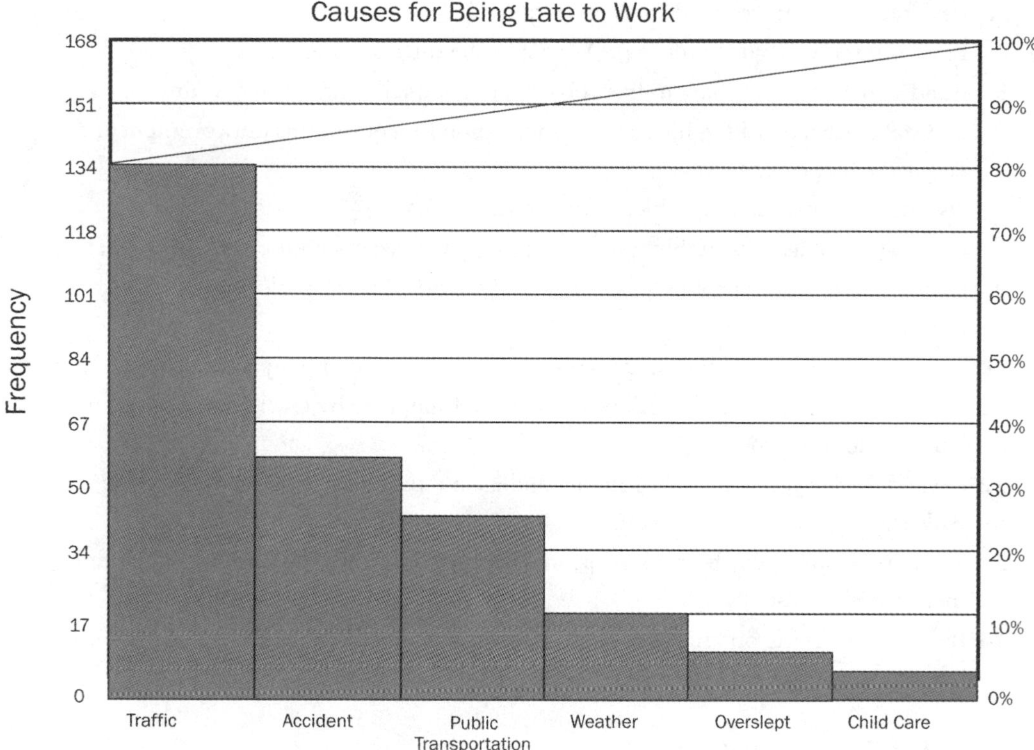

FIGURE 8.8 Sample Pareto Diagram (not to scale)

store documented lessons learned as an Organizational Process Asset in your information management system for future reference and use by others.

14 Principles of the Toyota Way

We have learned a great deal from the pioneers of quality, from the theorists and gurus mentioned in this chapter and from the many quality references shown as well. Another great reference for lessons learned is *The Toyota Way: 14 Management Principles from the World's Greatest Manufacturer*, by Jeffrey K. Liker (McGraw-Hill, 2004). These principles exemplify quality and have propelled the Toyota Motor Corporation into the "world's largest automobile manufacturer," as reported January 22, 2009 by Bloomberg News Service:

1. Base your management decision on the long-term philosophy, even at the expense of short-term financial goals.
2. Create continuous process flow to bring problems to the surface.

3. Use "pull" systems to avoid overproduction.
4. Level out the workload (*hijunka*). (Work like the tortoise, not the hare.)
5. Build a culture of stopping to fix problems, to get quality right the first time.
6. Use standardized tasks, which are the foundation for continuous improvement and employee empowerment.
7. Use visual control so no problems are hidden.
8. Use only reliable, thoroughly tested technology that serves your people and processes.
9. Grow leaders who thoroughly understand the work, live the philosophy, and teach it to others.
10. Develop exceptional people and teams who follow your company's philosophy.
11. Respect your extended network of partners and suppliers by challenging them and helping them improve.
12. Go and see for yourself to thoroughly understand the situation (known as *genchi genbutsu*).
13. Make decisions slowly by consensus, thoroughly considering all options; then implement decisions rapidly.
14. Become a learning organization through relentless reflection (*hansei*) and continuous improvement (*kaizen*).[11]

Managing Change Requests

You have heard me say this several times before, but when it comes to quality control, it is worth repeating: "Change is inevitable, except from a vending machine." In quality management, change, if managed properly, can be your friend. However, if it's not controlled, it can be your number one enemy. Therefore, plan for change, monitor it, and manage it to the best of your ability.

Summary of Project Quality Management

As mentioned, quality is an attitude; it is not optional if you and your company intend to be successful. When you truly listen to customers and understand what's important to them, you have a much better idea of what to measure. When you measure the right things and match the product of the project to a customer's needs and expectations, you are demonstrating that you and the team are focused on quality. When you are focused on quality results and using all the tools and resources available to produce quality products and services on your project, it will be clear that you have the right priorities and the right attitude to complete your project, reach your quality targets, and satisfy the demands of your customer.

References

1. "Quality," *BusinessDictionary.com*, http://tinyurl.com/quality-define, accessed May 30, 2017.

2. "Joseph M. Juran," *SkyMark*, 2015, http://www.skymark.com/resources/leaders/juran.asp, accessed May 30, 2017.

3. "Dr. Deming's Management Training," *Dharma Haven*, April 27, 1998, http://www.dharma-haven.org/five-havens/deming.htm, accessed March 12, 2017.

4. "Philip Crosby: The Fun Uncle of the Quality Revolution," *SkyMark*, http://www.skymark.com/resources/leaders/crosby.asp, accessed March 13, 2017.

5. Dan S. Hale, Kyle Goodson, and Jeffery W. Savel, "USDA Beef Quality and Yield Grades," *Meat Science, Texas A&M University*, http://meat.tamu.edu/beefgrading/, accessed March 8, 2013.

6. Terence T. Burton, "Is This a Six Sigma, Lean, or Kaizen Project?" *i Six Sigma*, http://www.isixsigma.com/new-to-six-sigma/how-is-six-sigma-different/six-sigma-lean-or-kaizen-project/, accessed March, 13, 2017.

7. Jack Welch, "What Is Six Sigma?" *i Six Sigma*, https://www.isixsigma.com/new-to-six-sigma/getting-started/what-six-sigma/, accessed March 13, 2017.

8. Lean Enterprise Institute, "A Brief History of Lean," *Lean.org*, http://www.lean.org/WhatsLean/History.cfm, accessed March 13, 2017.

9. "Standard Deviation," *Wikipedia*, http://en.wikipedia.org/wiki/Standard_deviation, accessed March 13, 2017.

10. Krister Forsberg, "The Quality Management Principles," *Quality Management Principles*, http://www.kristerforsberg.com/qmp/about.html, accessed March 13, 2017.

11. Jeffrey K. Liker, *The Toyota Way: 14 Management Principles from the World's Greatest Manufacturer* (New York: McGraw-Hill, 2004), http://www.goodreads.com/book/show/161789.The_Toyota_Way, accessed March 13, 2017.

9 Project Resource Management

Key Skills & Concepts

- Definition of project resource management
- The role of the PM in resource management
- Project resource management processes
- Resource staffing plan
- Ways to develop project teams
- Stages of team development (Tuckman Model)
- Types of project teams (including virtual)
- Skills needed to manage project teams
- Problem solving
- Types of power (leadership)
- Management and leadership styles
- Motivating the project team
- Managing conflict
- Motivational theories
- Managing customer expectations

Until now, we have spent most of our time in the Planning Process Group (refer to Table 3.1 in Chapter 3). We are now shifting gears, and this chapter is where the execution work of the project really begins. Most of the resource management processes are in the Executing Process Group.

Before we jump too deep into the Executing Process Group, allow me to set the stage a bit. You may recall the first process in the Executing Process Group from reading Chapter 4. As a reminder, Project Integration Management is the only Knowledge Area in the *PMBOK* that crosses all five Process Groups. The specific process I am referring to is "4.3: Direct and manage project work." The purpose of this process is to carry out the project plan. This is when you begin project execution (working the plan), and the only way to do that is with people (often referred to as *resources*). It is safe to say that people are the heartbeat of the project. They perform the activities, and they interact to come up with ideas and solutions. As a project manager, you will need to direct and manage these extremely important resources in order to succeed.

A good place to start is with a brief definition of what project resource management is. So let's roll up our shirt sleeves and get started.

Definition of Project Resource Management

Resource management includes the processes that organize, estimate, manage, and lead the project team, as well as other important resources such as equipment (hardware), materials, tools, software, and so on.

Resource management is slightly different from *personnel or human resource management* and is considered the planned strategic approach to managing an organization's most valued assets—the people working on projects to meet the objectives of the business as well as other resources such as software, equipment, and materials, to name a few. Resource management by definition includes the processes involved in managing people and other resources to meet business and organizational needs.

Tip

Most of the questions on the PMP exam regarding resource management come from everyday PM experiences. It is worth noting that PMI views resource management as falling into two general groups:

- **Administrative.** People who help organize the communications and documents of the project.
- **Behavioral management.** Management of team members. This group is covered in more detail later in this chapter.

Role of the Project Manager in Resource Management

When you have a team of any kind, you are likely to have conflict or at least differences of opinion. This can be healthy if handled properly; for example, it can facilitate constructive alternatives, the sharing of ideas, and open-mindedness. But it can also be disruptive, distracting, and counterproductive.

The success of the project is directly tied to the project manager's ability to lead and bring individuals together to form a cohesive, productive team. The project manager (PM) lives and dies by the team; this means you, as the PM, need to demonstrate strong organizational and communication skills. You need to be supportive (a cheerleader, a den mother, a coach, and an advocate) for the team.

Keeping the team focused on the deliverables of the project and working together to ensure against distractions and confusion is an extremely important role of the PM. As the PM you need to do the following:

- Be keenly aware of the importance of the team.
- Identify the team members and other key stakeholders on the project.
- Develop the resource and staffing plan (including skills and scheduling).
- Negotiate for skilled resources on the team as needed.
- Obtain funding, adequate workspace, and tools for the team.
- Get to know each team member's strengths and weaknesses.
- Establish trust and confidence with team members.
- Evaluate team member performance and provide feedback.
- Recognize and reward good performers.
- Help develop the team through strong leadership and guidance, including mentoring, education, and on-the-job (OJT) training.

As the PM, it is your role and responsibility to obtain, develop, and manage the team effectively. To do this well, you need to understand the processes that will assist you in this effort.

Project Resource Management Processes

Six processes are used most often to manage resources on a project. Even though these processes seem independent, they in fact overlap. Developing the team is an ongoing process, and, of course, there is always turnover in staff. On average, depending on the project, you should plan for at least 10 percent turnover in project team members. This means the cycle begins again and again as new team members rotate on and off your project. It is up to you to get the new members up to speed quickly so they can become productive contributors to the team.

The Resource Management processes according to PMI are as follows:

- **9.1 Plan Resource Management (Planning Process Group).** Identifying and documenting project roles and responsibilities, required skills, organizational relationships, and creating a staffing plan.
- **9.2 Estimate Activity Resources (Planning Process Group).** Estimating the number of project team member resources (people), types and quantities of supplies, materials, equipment, and so on to perform the work of the project.

- **9.3 Acquire Resources (Executing Process Group).** Confirming resource availability and obtaining the people, equipment, materials, and so on necessary to complete project activities.
- **9.4 Develop Team (Executing Process Group).** Improving competencies, team member interaction, and overall team environment to enhance project performance.
- **9.5 Manage Team (Executing Process Group).** Tracking individual team member performance, providing feedback, managing and resolving issues, and managing changes to optimize the team's performance.[1]
- **9.6 Control Resources (Monitoring and Controlling Process Group).** Ensuring that the physical Resources (people) assigned and allocated to the project are available when planned. This process involves monitoring all resources, including equipment, materials, subcontractors, vendors/suppliers, and certainly the team members needed to complete the project activities on schedule. The bottom line is controlling resources means having the right people, tools, materials, and equipment at the right time so as not to negatively impact the schedule.

Plan Resource Management Process (Planning Process Group)

The Plan Resource Management process is very important because if you don't plan properly for the right skills (or other resources), in the right place and at the right time, you will end up missing the boat. You'll experience schedule slips, people will be overworked, or the quality of the work will suffer due to lack of proper materials, equipment, skills, or fatigue.

Planning includes determining the five Ws (who, what, when, where, and why). The five Ws are especially important because you will need to justify why you need 15 people instead of 10, or you may have to prove why you need one person over another, especially if one is in a higher pay grade or is working on another project.

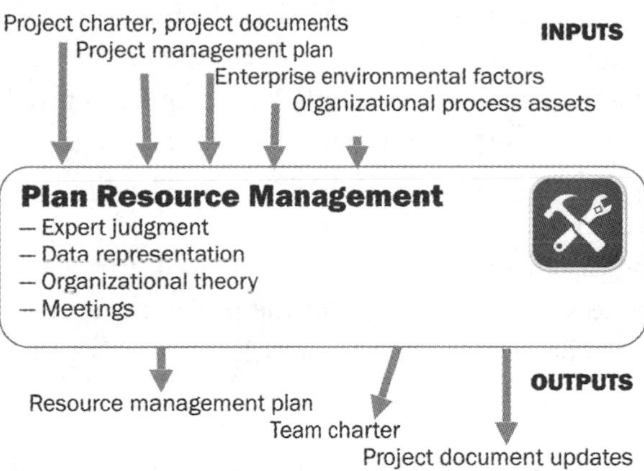

FIGURE 9.1 Plan Resource Management Process ITTOs

An overview of the inputs, tools and techniques, and outputs of this process are shown in Figure 9.1.

Ask the Expert

Q: I am the PM on an existing project and have a transition manager (Jack) on my project team who constantly disagrees with my ideas and work direction and makes negative comments in meetings. Jack was the project manager on this project and stepped down for personal reasons. He is highly respected by the team and the customer; however, he doesn't seem to respect me as the new PM. What do I do to get Jack on board and working together with me on this project?

A: I suggest you approach Jack, one-on-one and ask him to help you understand what is upsetting him. Let him know how important he is to the project, to the team, and to the customer. Show him respect and politely ask for the same courtesy. Try it. It never hurts to ask–it has worked for me.

Nothing is more frustrating than having a team member who is not willing to row in the same direction as the rest of the team. As part of the resource management plan, you need to ensure you have all the right people who are willing to work as a team and the right tools to get the job done properly. This is where the resource management and staffing plan fits in.

Resource Staffing Plan

The best way to determine the staffing needs and ultimately the cost of the resources is first to develop a responsibility (or resource) assignment matrix (RAM). The RAM will help identify the skills needed and help with work assignments. You can start with the job roles or skills needed to develop the RAM and then add the names of the people performing or filling the roles as they are assigned. In the real world of project management, you will likely hear team members referred to in a number of different ways—resources, staff, heartbeats, head-count, person months, or full-time equivalents (FTEs). What matters the most is that whatever you call the project team members, you must treat them with respect and as individuals.

When calculating labor hours per month of the work needed or performed on the project, most PMs use a monthly productive estimate of somewhere around 140 to 160 hours per month per person. The hours will vary depending on the productivity rate (expected time worked) assumed for the project, country labor laws, overtime expectations, and so on. The best way to sort out who is doing what on your project is to create a responsibility assignment matrix.

Developing a Responsibility Assignment Matrix (RAM)

The responsibility assignment matrix (RAM) is one of the many tools used for resource management as well as in risk and communications management planning. The good news is that there is no fixed rule on how to create a RAM. You can use a spreadsheet or create a table using many of the available software tools, or you can even use a notepad, just as long as the tool and format work for you and the team.

The RAM shown in Table 9.1 is for the P&G case study. It's for the call center based on an estimated call volume of 5,000 calls per month and level-1 and level-2 support for 12,500 people.

Note

A responsibility assignment matrix can be turned into a resource assignment matrix to include the names of people next to their assignments.

TABLE 9.1 Sample RAM

Responsibility	Primary	Secondary/Backup	Number of Staff Needed	Comments
Manager	1	3 shift team leads	4	Management
Level-1 call center agents	6	6	12	Use contractors for 30% of call center agents
Level-2 technical support	1 Team lead and 3 techs	3	7	Estimate 20 percent contractor staff and 10 percent can be remote

Another table similar to the RAM table that is often used is the RACI format (Responsible, Accountable, Consulted, and Informed). A sample of a RACI chart is shown in Table 9.2.

TABLE 9.2 RACI Chart

WBS Activity	George	Pam	Candy	Dawn	Ali
Collect requirements	A	R	C	I	I
Define code	R	A	I	I	C
Design code	I	A	R	C	I
Develop code	C	I	I	R	A
Code testing	I	I	A	I	R
Promote to production	R	A	C	I	I

To clarify the difference between *responsible* and *accountable*—you may have one person doing the work who is responsible for the activity; however, another person may be held accountable for the results of the work (for example, the PM is accountable in that if the work fails, the project will fail).

Clearly the RAM/RACI chart approach works best if the project team is identified and already assigned to the project. If the project team is not already assigned, you will need to acquire the project team and other resources.

Planning resources should include virtual team members, subcontractors, consultants, and volunteers as appropriate for staffing your project. Once you come up with a resource management plan, you will need to estimate activity resources.

Equally important to the five Ws is the age-old question, "How much is the project expected to cost?" Typically labor accounts for the highest cost on the project (an average of 80%). This is where resource management overlaps with scope, schedule, and especially cost management.

That brings us to the next process, which used to be in the Time Management Knowledge Area and moved over from the Time Management Knowledge Area with the changes in the *PMBOK Guide Sixth Edition*.

Estimate Activity Resources Process (Planning Process Group)

Now that you have a resource management plan in place, it is time to estimate activity resources needed to perform the work of the project. The best place to start is to map the resources to the WBS activities and, of course, to the scheduled milestones on your project.

Remember that resources include not only the people (labor) but also materials (supplies) and equipment (tools) needed to complete the work.

The Estimate Activity Resources process involves estimating the types and quantities of resources needed to perform each activity. This process should be closely coordinated with the Estimate Costs process in the Project Cost Management Knowledge Area (Chapter 7).

This is the time when you as the PM start getting very much involved with determining the types of skills and experience needed to complete the work of the project. There may be unique skills, knowledge, and capabilities needed, and you must begin to look at the time and cost to acquire, train (if needed), and organize the resources to address the activities you and the team have identified. As you add more people to the team, your job as the PM gets more complicated, especially in the execution phase. On construction projects, you need journeyman-level skills, people familiar with the building codes, and a realistic view of the time it takes to move from one activity (or process) to the next. Figure 9.2 shows an overview of the inputs, tools and techniques, and the outputs for the Estimate Activity Resources process.

Resource Calendars and Resource Leveling

In project management the team is the number-1 asset. The only way to manage the team, the individuals on the team, and other key resources is with organized scheduling. Knowing who needs to be where and when is like being an air traffic controller. Without the scheduling tools of resource calendars and resource leveling, you will have conflicts.

RESOURCE CALENDARS

As a PM, you live and die by the calendar. You need to know who is available on your team at all times. A resource calendar is a great way to do this, especially if you manage a large, geographically dispersed and/or virtual team. In Chapter 6 ("Project Schedule Management")

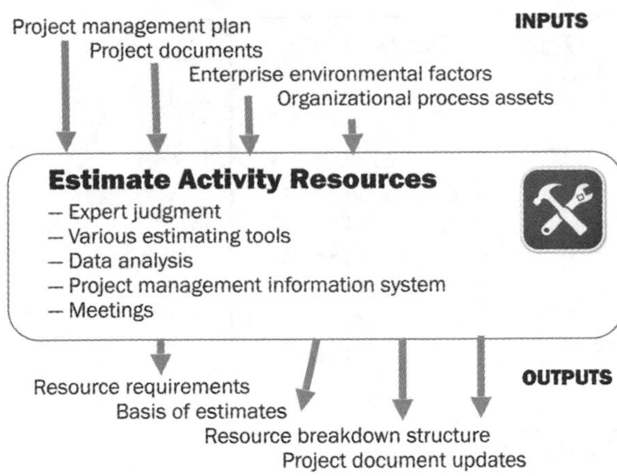

FIGURE 9.2 Estimate Activity Resources Process ITTOs

we introduced the resource calendar and showed an example (see Figure 6.12 for more details).

In a tight economy there may be overtime restrictions, or team members on your project might also be working other projects. This can be especially true in matrix management and functional organization structures. The problem occurs when you need work done on your project and the team members are not available. There can be many distractions from and constraints against getting and keeping highly skilled people focused on your project. The type of information that would go into a resource calendar includes, but is not limited to, name, skill set, availability (time period available to the project), planned vacation schedule, backup person, and manager name.

Try This

WHO'S ON FIRST? (KNOWING THE SCHEDULE)

You are the PM on a global project that requires "all hands on deck" availability during a critical test of a new call center scheduled to go live after the Labor Day weekend (a holiday in the United States on the first Monday of September). The majority of the project preparation work effort is to occur during the month of August. One of your team members in Asia casually mentions that most of the Asian team members will be out honoring religious holidays most of the month of August. What do you do? Take a few minutes to jot down possible solutions before reading the following answer.

Answer: If the schedule is set and the deliverable is firm, use team members from other countries that don't recognize the same holidays, or pay higher rates to the people who are available and willing to work over the holiday period to keep the project on schedule.

To manage resources effectively, you need to do your research ahead of time. You need to know that many countries in both Asia and Europe have major holidays and vacations during the month of August. Therefore, you should plan accordingly. Useful tools include a resource/responsibility assignment matrix (RAM) (see Figure 9.3) and, of course, a resource calendar for quick reference to see who is assigned to critical activities and whether they are available when needed.

The resource calendar can be used to identify risks, schedule duration, and needed backup skills. It also serves as a negotiation tool when critical path activities are at risk. This is where

Activity	Mary	Joey	Bob	Sue
Plan party	P			
Purchase food		P		S
Decorate office	S		P	
Serve the food		P	S	

Legend: P = Primary, S = Secondary

FIGURE 9.3 Sample Resource Assignment Matrix (RAM)

the PM needs to be focused and use all the resources available to the fullest extent possible. The PM must keep people informed, assigned, focused, engaged, and challenged, and must continue to reinforce the value of each person to the team and their role on the project.

RESOURCE LEVELING

Resource leveling does not mean knocking people over (like on the football or rugby field), even though the large workload many of us face tends to knock us over at times. Resource leveling is when you balance the work across the workers and not overload our friend the overachiever.

From a PM's perspective, resource leveling is a process used to examine a project for an unbalanced use of resources (usually people) over time and for resolving conflicts in worker availability or over allocation of work to help prevent "burnout."

Resource leveling is used to produce a resource-limited schedule. Leveling lengthens the schedule and increases cost in order to deal with a limited amount of resources, resource availability, and other resource constraints. A little-used function in project management software, this technique allows you to level the peaks and valleys of the schedule from one month to another, resulting in a more stable number of resources used on your project.

During project planning the PM and the team need to look closely at resource leveling to resolve potential conflicts early in the project life cycle. Note that this process is one that should be used over the course of the project; otherwise, you will likely impact one of the key constraints (time, cost, or scope).

When you use project scheduling software, resource leveling is a feature that can help you to calculate delays. However, don't let the scheduling software run amuck by making assumptions for you. Real resource leveling might require delaying tasks until resources are truly available.

In any case, leveling could result in a later project finish date, especially if the activities affected are on the critical path.

Try This

THE OVERACHIEVER ("PICK ME, COACH!")

During the project kickoff meeting, one of your team members who is known to be an overachiever (Greg) keeps volunteering for more work. Greg has always been quick to sign up for extra work. You think to yourself, "What a team player!" As you quietly wish you had a whole team of Gregs, you enter the assignments in the software scheduling tool and click the "Resource Leveling" button to verify that the work is balanced across the team. Your heart stops when you see that Greg has signed up for two years' worth of work on a one-year project. What do you do now? Take a few minutes to jot down a possible solution before looking at the following answer.

Answer: You pull the overachiever (OA) aside (one-on-one) and thank him for his willingness to take on the extra work. Then you explain that there are not enough days in a year for him to complete all the work he signed up for. Finally, you go through the work packages together to focus on the best use of the OA's time and reassign the extra work to other team members as equitably as possible.

The cost of the people assigned to the project is determined by several things, such as when the team members come onboard and at what salary rate, and when will they need to cycle off the project. Labor planning usually is measured in hours of effort at first and will vary depending on the type and size of the project. For example, on a small project you will have fewer people amongst whom to spread the work, and they end up being cross-functional. They become less specialized and have to perform work in many different areas (maybe even outside their areas of expertise). Later, the PM often has to translate the hours into dollars and will fall back to cost management (discussed in Chapter 7) to determine the overall cost of project labor and other costs to ensure adequate funding for the project budget.

You should note that three of the six resource management processes are in the Executing Process Group. This means that over half the work occurs during the execution phase, and therefore the lion's share of the budget will typically be spent during this phase. The reason for the higher cost is because the full project team is onboard and performing the activities of the project (full speed ahead). The cost of labor (number of people and types of skills) typically comes with an added cost for the tools and equipment needed to allow the team members to perform their duties on the project (workspace, computers, software licenses, phones, etc.). These costs are at full flow during this phase to keep the team productive.

Tip

You will likely see a question on the PMP exam similar to the following: "During which phase of the project is the majority of the budget spent?" The best answer should be "During the execution phase of the project."

Acquire Resources Process (Planning Process Group)

If you had to narrow the project down to a single most important asset, what would it be? Consider the following statement:

> Projects are performed by people, and most projects have more than one person working on the project. If you have more than one person working on your project, you have a team. In any team, you have people with a wide range of personalities, needs, experiences, and skills.

The project manager (no matter how good they are) cannot successfully complete the project without the project team. This means the number-1 asset on a project is the team. Figure 9.4 shows an overview of the inputs, tools and techniques, and the outputs for the Acquire Resources process.

Types of Project Teams

Teams come in all sizes and types. For purposes of project management, we will focus on two types of teams: the project management team and the project team (either of which may have members who work off-site [or virtual]).

The *project management team* is composed of a subset of the overall project team and includes the people who directly perform the management activities on the project. It is sometimes referred to as the core team, the executive team, or the leadership team. Team members are responsible for the overall management of the project, including the five Process Groups' various phases of the project. The project manage-

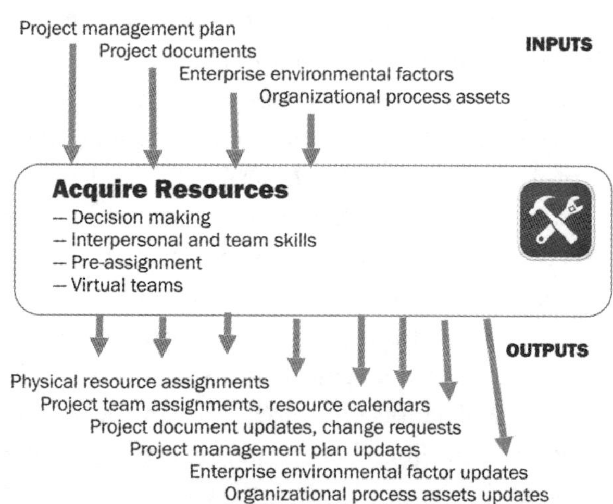

FIGURE 9.4 Acquire Resources Process ITTOs

ment team is everyone specifically responsible and accountable for the outcome (deliverables) of the project.

The *project team*, on the other hand, extends beyond the project management team and includes all stakeholders. You may recall from Chapter 2 that the definition of a stakeholder is anyone or any organization that is positively or negatively impacted by the project. The project team can be extensive, even on a small project, when you consider the end users, suppliers, support managers, executives, community, government, and even other companies. If you add team members working from other site locations or even different countries, you have virtual team members, which bring additional challenges.

The number and mix of stakeholders depend on the specific needs of the project. Because projects (and PMs) are unique, many factors should be considered when building your project team. The PM's leadership style is one of the many factors, as well as existing or new relationships, that play an important role in the success rate of the project.

Before we talk about leadership styles, let's take a look at the typical role of the PM when it comes to managing resources.

Where Do Project Teams Come From?

A key role of the PM is to establish the project team. On newer projects the PM may have full ownership and responsibility to build or acquire the team. When forming a team, strong negotiation skills are a plus to ensure that the best skills necessary for a productive team are acquired. In the case of existing projects, the project team (or at least the core project management team) may already be staffed or assigned.

Many companies have a centralized Human Resource (HR) department or project management office (or even virtual project management offices) to handle staffing and project assignments. In a centralized environment the PM may have little control over who is assigned to the project.

For purposes of this chapter, we will focus mostly on the project management team. As a PM, it is your responsibility to identify the project management team (even if some members are pre-assigned), and with assistance from the core leadership team you can further identify the overall project team—vendors, suppliers, and other key contacts, as necessary—to get a clear picture of the people involved (directly and indirectly) in the support of your project.

Emerging trends and project management styles are shifting away from traditional command and control organizational structures. This is driven by companies wanting to optimize resource utilization and in many cases minimize layers of management oversite.

This trend has resulted in new resource management methods. Some of these methods were introduced in Chapter 8, on quality management, such as Lean, Kaizen, Just-In-Time scheduling, and other management methods.

Other forms of teams that have emerged in recent years are the Agile (self-organized) project management team and virtual or distributed team.

What Are Agile Teams?

Agile teams or self-organized teams typically have little to no management oversite (decentralized control) and are focused on short-term goals and objectives. Agile works well in projects with high variability and requires strong collaboration among team members for success.

The Agile Manifesto was written in February 2001 by seventeen independent-minded software practitioners. The Agile Manifesto is based on twelve principles; a summary of the principles is shown below, but for more details go to Agile Alliance at https://www.agilealliance.org/agile101/the-agile-manifesto/.[2]

1. Customers satisfied by early and continuous delivery of valuable software.
2. Team welcomes changing requirements, even in late development.
3. Working software is delivered frequently (weeks rather than months).
4. Business people and developers have close, daily cooperation.
5. Projects are built around motivated individuals, who should be trusted.
6. Face-to-face conversation is the best form of communication (colocation).
7. Working software is the principal measure of progress.
8. Development is sustainable and can be maintained at a constant pace.
9. Continuous attention is paid to technical excellence and good design.
10. Simplicity—the art of maximizing the amount of work not done—is essential.
11. Best architectures, requirements, and designs emerge from self-organizing teams.
12. The team regularly reflects on how to become more effective, and adjusts accordingly.

What Are Virtual Teams?

The answer to this question is fast becoming the norm for projects all over the world. Virtual teams are groups of people who are geographically dispersed and who work across time, space, and organizational boundaries.

With the advent of the Internet, emerging software, and networking technology, the ability to work from anywhere in the world is not only possible but often preferred by companies and employees alike: "These technologies build the environment for virtual work in teams, with members who may never meet each other in person. Communicating by telephone and email, with work products shared electronically, virtual teams produce results without being co-located."[3]

Working at home can save money and increase productivity. For example, in 1988 I was working in downtown Chicago and living in Hoffman Estates, Illinois, a mere three-hour (round-trip) commute each day. I was working on a project that required a lot of computer time, and even though I had a PC at home, I was expected to be in the office every day. When I found out I needed surgery that required five weeks of recovery time, my boss was less than excited.

As it turns out, a couple of technical gurus in our office had started playing around with software that would allow remote access to our office computer and internal mail system. I asked if I could be their test subject, because this would enable me to work from home during my recovery period. We tested it, and it worked. Therefore, I was one of the first employees in our office to work from home on what we later called "The Home Office" program. My boss liked the idea a lot, and I was able to keep up with my project and work from the comfort of my home, saving hours of travel time.

Most companies now embrace partial or full-time home office employees. This practice saves office space and allows people to collaborate on projects at anytime from anywhere in the world. Even though these new channels of communications make virtual teams possible, they are often more difficult to manage than an onsite (colocated) team because of time zone differences, language barriers, and lack of oversight management.

Negotiation Skills

When acquiring a project team, you often need to put your negotiation skills to use.

Tip

> You are likely to see negotiations referred to frequently on the PMP exam related to obtaining resources, reducing cost, improving quality, improving schedule, collecting input/requirements from the team, determining project scope with the customer, and so on.

When it comes to negotiation skills, the PM should be aware of the following items:

- The purpose and priority of the project
- The needs of the organization, the team, and the customer
- Using the tools and resources available to analyze and prove needs before the negotiations (including picking a suitable location at an acceptable time)
- The relationship between parties and how to approach and negotiate accordingly
- The importance of working with decision makers
- Not asking for the best resources if they're not needed
- Understanding the influencing factors in negotiations
- Understanding the needs of the individual or group with whom you will negotiate

Once you have acquired the team members, you need to develop their skills to help bring them together into a productive, full-functioning team.

Develop Team Process (Executing Process Group)

This is the process where you don't want to spin your wheels. By this I mean you don't want turnover in personnel on your project. A high turnover rate is an indicator that something is wrong on your project. There may be extenuating circumstances why people move between projects—reorganizations, retirements, or resource actions (RAs) where people are released from their jobs. However, turnover can be directly related to a bad project or bad PM. Either it sucks the life out of a project (with lost time, lost money used to train the new team members, and lost productivity) or it revitalizes the project team with new skills, new experience, new ideas, and a newfound energy. Hopefully, you experience the latter on all your projects.

Here are the true benefits of solid team development:

- Less turnover
- Happy "campers" (happy project team members)
- Team spirit (good communications, collaboration, and camaraderie)
- Efficient results

Ways to Develop Your Team

Teamwork is a critical success factor on projects. It all starts with good communications (more on this topic in Chapter 10). It is up to the PM to communicate effectively to minimize confusion and maximize results. The PM is responsible for building a sense of teamwork (team spirit) and for motivating the team members so they want to work together for the greater good of the project. Here are some things you can do that will help build and develop your team members:

- Get to know your team members (including their strengths and weaknesses), and be there for them if they have questions or need support or assistance.
- Use a kickoff meeting to set the tone, communicate expectations, and get everyone on the same page.
- Schedule and manage regular team meetings to keep the team informed. (Don't just schedule meetings for the sake of meetings; they must be meaningful and informative.)
- Set up and communicate your recognition, award, or reward program (where the incentives may include on-time delivery of activities under the person's control).

- Allow time for one-on-one discussions and for team brainstorming for new ideas.
- Set the tone for open discussions and listen to your team (verbal and nonverbal cues).
- Consider a team charter (to set the ground rules or rules of engagement for team members). This can include how team meetings will be conducted, voting (if appropriate), and escalations (if there are disagreements or disputes).
- Provide timely team and individual evaluations and feedback so there are no surprises.
- Praise good performance through your established awards and recognition program.
- Be willing to change if things are not working as planned. For example, don't hold on to an employee just because he has been there forever and is a "good guy." Such a decision can't be personal; it has to be based on project performance.

Ask the Expert

Q: There is a guy named Jack on my project who has been a manager for many years and has decided to step down in rank while remaining on the project team. He is not used to actually doing the work, let alone taking directions from someone who is much younger in age. He is very resistant to change. What can I do to get him onboard?

A: First, you need to sit down in a quiet place and think through how best to approach Jack. It is important to have a one-on-one meeting to sort this out; make sure you conduct the meeting in a suitable (undisturbed) place. Picking the proper time, place, and approach is essential to a better outcome. Don't try to rush a meeting while Jack is driving you to a customer location (like a fellow PM friend of mine did), as you could be let out of the car to walk back to the office if the meeting doesn't go well. During the meeting, take the time to get to know Jack and better understand his concerns or his situation and then ask for his assistance on the project by appealing to his knowledge and experience. If that doesn't work, you may have to take more aggressive measures.

Develop Team Inputs, Tools and Techniques, and Outputs

The inputs, tools and techniques, and outputs that need to be considered as part of the project team development process are pretty straightforward yet very important. Figure 9.5 shows an overview of the inputs, tools and techniques, and the outputs for the Develop Team process.

Personally, I feel the outputs should include high team morale, effective collaboration, and team spirit, which lead to improved project results.

One way to ensure that the team members have the proper focus and the tools needed to perform their jobs well is to provide the right training and education to the team.

FIGURE 9.5 Develop Team Process ITTOs

Importance of Training and Education

Projects tend to be dynamic; they move quickly. (I once had a PM say he could feel the earth move beneath his feet because his project was experiencing change almost daily.) The only way to keep up with change is through training and education. With all the new technology, updated software tools, and new processes and techniques, change is constant. In fact, I like to say that the only constant is "change." One reason PMI requires professional development units (PDUs) as part of their continuing certification requirements (CCRs) is to ensure that we are keeping up with the changes in the profession. Other organizations also have similar types of credentials and require continuing education units (CEUs). Staying current and connected with the latest tools, techniques, and methods is essential to your ability to manage your project team effectively.

Consider training and education an investment in the future. Your team members will appreciate being viewed as important enough that their company is willing to spend the money (and allow them time off from the project) to stay current on new technology, tools and techniques, and process improvements. Unfortunately, education is sometimes the first thing that is cut when times are tough financially.

Team Building and the Five Stages of Team Development

Team building not only involves forming the team but also motivating the team members into a cohesive functioning group with the tools and talent needed to deliver the project successfully. Several of the tools and processes already discussed are, in essence, team-building activities—for example, the WBS, scope definition and management, time management, cost management, and especially risk management (more details on risk management can be found in Chapter 11). We talked earlier about the role of the PM in resource management. The PM's role in team building and skills development is also extremely important. The PM should start with obtaining top management support, gaining team-member commitment by creating a team identity, promoting trust and confidence, and fostering frequent and open communications. The single-most-important step above communications is to establish strong leadership skills.

Tip

> The true measure of success on a project is when team members come to you (the PM) at the end of the project and say they enjoyed working with you and offer to work with you on future projects. When they have trust and confidence in you as a project leader, you have a good, solid team relationship.

One of the most important skills in developing a team is how to handle project team problems. Problems, issues, and conflicts are a reality and need to be handled in different ways, depending on when they occur and the stakeholders involved. Problems tend to surface at different times and to varying degrees of impact on the team. In some cases conflicts are normal when building teams, so it is important for the PM to be aware of the five stages of team development.

Team Development

A number of theorists have conducted extensive research on the topic of team development and dynamics. However, one that tends to stand out is Dr. Bruce Tuckman and his five stages of team development:

> Dr. Bruce Tuckman published his Forming Storming Norming Performing team-development model in 1965. He added a fifth stage, adjourning, in the 1970s . . . Tuckman's model explains that as the team develops maturity and ability, relationships establish, and the leader changes leadership style. Beginning with a directing style, moving through coaching, then participating, finishing, delegating, and almost detached . . . This progression of team behavior and leadership style can be seen clearly in the Tannenbaum and Schmidt Continuum—the authority and freedom extended by the leader to the team increases while the control of the leader reduces.[4]

Let's take a closer look at Dr. Tuckman's five stages of team development.

Stage 1: Forming. There is high dependence on the project leader for guidance and direction; individual roles and responsibilities are unclear. The project leader must be prepared to answer lots of questions about the team's purpose, objectives, and external relationships. Processes are often ignored. Members test tolerance of the system and the team leader.

Stage 2: Storming. Decisions don't come easily within groups. Team members vie for position as they attempt to establish themselves in relation to other team members and the leader. There may be power struggles. The team needs to be focused on its goals to avoid becoming distracted by relationships and emotional issues. Compromises may be required to enable progress. Conflict among the team members is not uncommon in this stage.

Stage 3: Norming. Roles and responsibilities are clear and accepted. Big decisions are made by group agreement. Smaller decisions may be delegated to individuals or small teams within the group. Commitment and unity are strong. The team may engage in fun and social activities. The team discusses and develops its processes and working style. There is general respect for the leader, and some leadership is shared by the team. The project leader facilitates and enables the team.

Stage 4: Performing. The team is more strategically aware; the team knows clearly what it is doing and why. The team members have a shared vision and are able to stand on their own feet with no interference or participation from the leader. Disagreements occur, but now they are resolved within the team positively. Necessary changes to processes and structure are made by the team. The team is able to work toward achieving the goal of the project, and the members look after each other.

Stage 5: Adjourning. Adjourning, also referred to as the Deforming and Mourning stage, is very relevant to the people in the group and their well-being. Adjourning is the break-up of the group (hopefully when the project is completed successfully). Team members prepare to move on to new projects and may feel a sense of insecurity or threat from this change.

Skills Needed to Manage Project Teams (Including Virtual Teams)

Because the number-1 asset on a project is the team and because the team is made up of people, it is worth investing in understanding and developing people management skills. The following is from the article "Key People Skills for Virtual Project Managers," written by Dr. Ginger Levin and Dr. Parviz Rad:

> Effective and successful project managers and leaders must be extremely people oriented. They need to create an environment that is conducive to innovation, productivity, and high performance by using their human skills, along with their technical skills in areas such as scheduling, procurement, cost estimating and budgeting, monitoring and controlling, and risk management. Accordingly, they must maintain their technical and functional skills at the highest possible level, while enhancing their softer skills to meet the challenges of today and tomorrow.[5]

Social skills take on greater importance with virtual teams, and PMs need to facilitate and encourage successful interaction. It represents a dramatic change in how we work on projects and creates new challenges for the project team. When managing project teams, especially virtual teams, the PM needs the following important skills:

- **Networking.** The ability to assess and build the quality of working relationships.
- **Building trust and rapport.** Developing a positive attitude.
- **Motivation skills.** Ensuring that everyone is motivated on the team.
- **Communications (especially listening).** One of the most important skills to have.
- **Organizational skills.** Shows order and allows for higher productivity.
- **Counseling skills.** Used to overcome personal issues.
- **Appropriate use of power.** Power needs to be used accordingly.
- **Delegation.** A basic management skill and vital in project management.
- **Conflict management and problem solving.** Conflict can be a good thing when managed properly.
- **Negotiation.** It takes negotiation skills to make necessary changes.

All of us have had situations in which we let our emotions run wild, only to find we didn't have all the facts. That is why it is important to be sensitive, stay open-minded, and listen to your team. The signs may not be clear, so don't be too quick to judge.

The best way I have found to get people's attention and to help inspire creativity and improved performance is by providing recognition and rewards.

Recognize and Reward the Project Team and Individuals

Even if it is just a pair of new socks (you read that right), you need to find a way to recognize and reward good performance. You are probably thinking, "What a cheapskate!" Well, it worked in one situation on one of my more difficult projects.

The story goes like this: Once upon a time, there was a computer programmer (named Mark) working for me on a large project in Portland, Oregon. Mark was staying at a hotel for the duration of the nine-month project and had put in so many hours one week he didn't have time to drop his laundry off at the front desk for cleaning. One day he was getting dressed and had no clean socks, so Mark came to work wearing no socks. We all kidded him a bit, and at the end of the project I presented him with a new pair of socks for his dedication to the project and included a nice check as well. He was a great sport, and the team got a huge, endearing laugh out the socks.

Ask the Expert

Q: What should I do as the PM when a team member is distracted, sometimes falls asleep in meetings, is not taking the work seriously, and is talking back?

A: Pull the individual aside (one-on-one) and calmly and professionally ask the person to please explain the reason for their behavior. If there is no logical or acceptable response, you will need to be firm and explain this behavior is not acceptable. Give specific examples of how it is disrupting team meetings and is distracting the team. Have an action plan documented and in hand with acceptable options in mind to present to the individual. Here are some sample options for the distracted team member:

- An open apology to you and the team in the next meeting
- Additional work, because this person appears to have spare time available
- Possible performance rating reduction
- Moving off from the project or being fired

Be aware that there are times when the person may have a good reason for their actions, or at least they think they do. Therefore, be patient and listen. You may find they have a medical condition, are going through a personal situation, or have a work-related reason that may require your compassion or assistance.

Tip

Don't be too quick to judge. I once had a student who dozed off in class and would snore, which I found distracting and rude. I was getting upset and was considering how to reprimand him in class. Then I decided instead to give the class a 15-minute break so I could approach this student one-on-one. He explained to me that he was on heavy medication to prepare for a liver transplant. He was on the top of the recipients' list and was expecting a call at any time to go to the hospital. Imagine how embarrassed I would have felt if I called him out in class and then learned the news. I am glad I didn't make a fool of myself by jumping to the wrong conclusion.

Rewards and recognition can come in many forms or flavors. I know an outstanding PM who received a large award (of several thousand dollars) for successfully completing a challenging project ahead of schedule and under budget. His manager asked him to set up an awards dinner for the whole team. At the dinner his manager gave out awards to everyone on the team but failed to announce the PM's award, the largest of them all. The PM didn't get the team recognition, only a check. Even though the award was sizable, it was anticlimactic when it came without an announcement to the team. Some would say, "Don't give me applause—just send money." But at the end of the day we all like the open team recognition, even if it's just a pair of socks (given in the right situation).

Another example is of a team member (Jim) who was in a project meeting where I handed out commemorative, uncirculated coin sets to several of the team members. After the second one was handed out, Jim counted the face value of the coins and boldly announced the set was worth only a few dollars. His tune changed when he received a coin set, announcing that the coin set was truly priceless and would be worth a lot of money someday!

The moral to the story is that you can get great results by handing out recognition and awards even if the dollar value is low, as long as the recognition is meaningful and can be appreciated by the recipient and the team. Also remember that the high-dollar awards can seem meaningless if not presented in a favorable manner.

Manage Team Process (Executing Process Group)

The Manage Team process includes being involved with the team activities, having open communications, and making sure the team members are focused and productive.

Management and Leadership Styles

Managing people and being a leader are two different things. They have slightly different motivations and require slightly different approaches.

For example, managers tend to look at the daily operations and are focused on the following:

- The short-term perspective.
- Did everyone show up for work today?
- What have you done today?
- How are we going to accomplish this?

Leaders, on the other hand, look for ways to develop the team members and focus on the following:

- The long-term perspective.
- Is there a better way to do things?
- Coaching and mentoring the team.
- Working with the team for best results.

MANAGEMENT STYLES

Even though these are not in the *PMBOK*, you should be familiar with the different types of management styles:

- **Autocratic.** The manager makes all the decisions.
- **Democratic.** The team is involved in the decision-making process.
- **Laissez-faire.** The team is self-led (as in Agile project management).

- **Exceptional.** Looking at only the top and bottom 10 percent of performers (i.e., who is doing well and who is not).

Much like project management skills, the general management skills needed to effectively manage people are as follows:

- Strong communications skills
- Organizational skills
- Negotiating skills
- Problem-solving skills
- Leading and influencing people

Being a good manager doesn't mean the manager is a good leader. Strong leaders demonstrate slightly different styles.

LEADERSHIP STYLES

There are many different leadership styles, and several are described in the *PMBOK*. As a PM you need to be familiar with the different types of leadership styles. Your style will likely be slightly different from other PMs (or totally unique). Be aware that different situations and different team members will call for different leadership styles. It is best to be flexible and "mix it up" to meet your needs and the needs of the team. Here are a few leadership styles you may already be familiar with (the first seven in the list) and a few that PMI tends to focus on (the last six in the list below):

- **Directing.** Telling others what to do ("my way or the highway").
- **Autocratic.** Making decisions without outside information.
- **Facilitating.** Coordinating input from others to help solve problems or make decisions.
- **Coaching.** Instructing or inspiring others.
- **Supportive.** Being an advocate and providing assistance to the team and individuals.
- **Consultative.** Inviting ideas from others and assisting in the decision-making process.
- **Consensus.** Making decisions based on a process of group agreement.
- **Laissez-faire.** Allowing team to make its own decisions (like in Agile project management).
- **Transactional.** Focusing on goals, management by exception, and feedback.
- **Servant leadership.** Focusing on people, community, and commitment to others.
- **Transformational.** Empowering others; encouraging creativity and innovation.
- **Charismatic.** Inspiring others with high energy and self-confidence.
- **Interactional.** Combining transactional, transformational, and charismatic.

As PM, you will likely use different styles at different times. You will probably exhibit more management style on the front end of the project and more coaching style further into the project life cycle. A lot will also depend on the relationship and history you have with your team members.

Know the Capabilities of the Team Members

Know your team members' skills, experience, capabilities, and any limitations they may have. It can be embarrassing to assign someone to perform certain activities and then find they don't have the knowledge, skills, or education to perform these duties.

Problem Solving

When you effectively use strong project management skills, you may be able to avoid many problems. However, problems will occur. There are various ways to solve problems, and the first step is always to take the time to identify and understand the problem. Make sure you are focused on the problem and not a downstream result of the problem. Here is the recommended process to help solve problems:

1. Identify the root cause of the problem (focus on the cause and not the symptom).
2. Understand and analyze the problem (use available tools and resources to help).
3. Work out an agreeable solution (it may be a temporary workaround at first).
4. Solve the problem to the best of your ability using the resources available.
5. Monitor the situation after the problem has been resolved to ensure it doesn't reoccur.

Tip

For those of you planning to take the PMP exam, you can expect approximately 100 questions that require you to look at a situation (cost, schedule, resource, etc.) and make the best decision to help solve the problem.

Manage Project Team Inputs, Tools and Techniques, and Outputs

There are a number of inputs to consider during the managing of the project team process. Keep in mind that the main focus is on the team. When you have the staff assigned according to the project management plan, it's time to manage the team through use of the various tools and techniques available (see the list that follows). As mentioned earlier, when you have a team, you tend to have conflicts. Sources of conflict include resource constraints, interpersonal relationships, and competing demands. Figure 9.6 shows an overview of the inputs, tools and techniques, and the outputs for the Manage Project Team process.

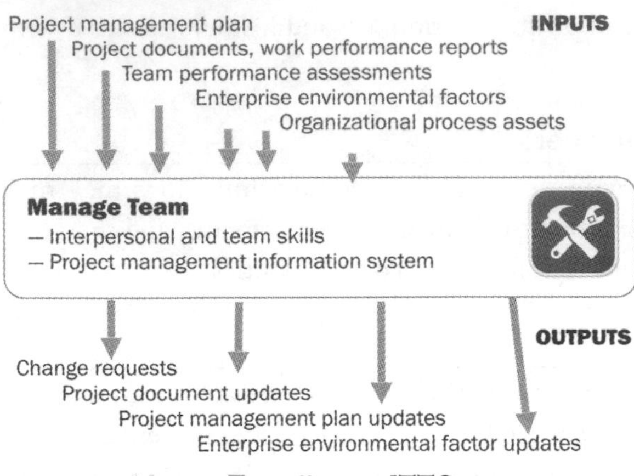

FIGURE 9.6 Manage Team Process ITTOs

How to Motivate the Team

To help you solve problems and conflicts on your project, it is always helpful to know how to motivate your team. This is a good place to look to professional sport coaches and people who have proven success in team motivation. They can provide great examples of ways to get the team to focus on the end results, to work together, and to use all the tools and resources available. (Sound familiar? It should, because this goes back to my three takeaway points in Chapter 2. By the time you get to the end of this book, you should be able to recite these in your sleep!)

Ask the Expert

Q: Pam writes, "I am a new PM, and my boss, coworkers, and team are constantly stopping by my office at all hours of the day just to introduce themselves and talk. I enjoyed this attention at first, but now it is becoming distracting and taking time away from my project. I don't want to be rude, but what can I do to minimize the distractions?"

A: The first question I ask myself in such a situation (and it has happened often) is, "Do I have a candy dish or other snacks on my desk?" The answer in most cases has been "yes." I hate to say this, but people can see candy as an open invitation to come by your desk. If this is the case with you, I recommend one of two things: take away the candy dish or have some work folders handy with tasks that need to be done and when someone stops by, give them the work. After a short period of time, people won't stop by as often. Try it—you'll be surprised how well it works. You may also want to consider the location of your guest chairs. Too close to the door invites people to come in and sit. Further away requires them to ask permission, at which point you can say, "Would you mind coming back in 15 minutes? I will finish what I'm working on and then I will be able to concentrate on your question."

Being a PM is like being a coach, teacher, or mentor. Here are some quotes I pulled from the Internet to help you coach and motivate your team:

- "The achievements of an organization are the results of the combined effort of each individual." —VINCE LOMBARDI
- "Practice the Golden-Rule of Management in everything you do: Manage others the way you would like to be managed." —BRIAN TRACY

- "Coaches have to watch for what they don't want to see and listen to what they don't want to hear." —JOHN MADDEN
- "Probably my best quality as a coach is that I ask a lot of challenging questions and let the person come up with the answer." —PHIL DIXON
- "People will exceed targets they set themselves." —GORDON DRYDEN
- "Coaching is 90 percent attitude and 10 percent technique." —AUTHOR UNKNOWN
- "A good coach passes on information quickly. They do not hold back information that affects my job." —BYRON AND CATHERINE PULSIFER, FROM "PEOPLE'S EXPECTATIONS OF A COACH"
- "You get the best effort from others not by lighting a fire beneath them, but by building a fire within." —BOB NELSON[6]

From personal experience I will add a couple of tips on coaching as well.

- Take time to listen. (This one is very difficult, as we tend to be busy formulating our thoughts for the answer and we don't fully hear the question.)
- Look at the situation from the other person's point of view. (This gives you a new perspective.)
- Think positively and be open-minded to new ideas and suggestions.
- Trust your team—give them room to grow. (People tend to rise to your level of expectation.)
- Recognize even the little things, and offer praise early and often. (Rewards are good.)

Try This

TAKE ME OUT TO THE BALL GAME: NETWORKING THE PROJECT TEAM

You are the PM for a large Information Technology (IT) systems support team. The team is so large and physically dispersed across several states and countries that you are experiencing difficulty getting the team members focused on the project activities and schedule. A critical date has been missed, and the customer is very upset. What do you do?

Answer: Take the team (including the customer) to a baseball game. That is exactly what a good friend of mine (and fellow project executive) did. He invited as many of the project team members, including the customer, that were within a short traveling distance to the local baseball stadium. He reserved a club room that enabled the project team to not only enjoy the game but intermingle, talk, relax, and get to know one another. The results were amazing.

Granted, getting the team together, even on the phone, is not easy if they are spread out in different locations and different time zones, especially if you don't have the budget to allow everyone to travel to a baseball game. However, maybe you can coordinate a similar get-together for the other locations concurrently so everyone can participate at some level. It is also good to give out T-shirts or baseball hats with a team slogan or logo. I have seen this approach work time after time, and it goes a long way toward helping build the team spirit.

Types of Power

As leader of a team, the PM needs to be aware of different types of power. Getting team members and stakeholders to cooperate is sometimes difficult, especially when managing virtual teams. Here are the different types of power you as the PM can use (or be aware of in case others are using these powers on you):

- **Positional (sometimes called formal, authoritative, or legitimate).** Based on a person's position in the company, e.g., formal position granted in the organization or team.
- **Informational.** Based on control of gathering or distribution of information.
- **Referent.** Based on creditability and the ability of a leader to influence others that respect or admire the individual. Referent power is often gained through strong interpersonal skills.
- **Situational.** Gained due to a unique situation such as a crisis that was handled well.

There is always more than one way to get things done. And the level of power and how you as the PM exercise the power and authority is related to your personality type.

Many of us have different personalities, and depending on the situation we may exercise power in different ways. Some personality types to consider are authentic, courteous, creative, and cultural. Before we exercise our power as a PM, it is good to use a personality style that works best for you given the situation and also to be aware of the different motivational theories.

Motivational Theories

One way to get the team motivated is to understand what drives them. Many behavioral science tools and techniques are available to assist you in better understanding what motivates individuals or teams. Here are a few that are not in the *PMBOK* but that you should be aware of if you are planning to take a PMI exam.

Maslow's Hierarchy of Needs

According to the article "Abraham Maslow's Hierarchy of Needs Motivational Model" at BusinessBalls.com, "Abraham Maslow developed the Hierarchy of Needs model in 1940–50 USA, and [his] theory remains valid today for understanding human motivation, management training, and personal development."[7] The article goes on to explain his theory:

> Each of us is motivated by needs. Our most basic needs are inborn, having evolved over tens of thousands of years. Abraham Maslow's Hierarchy of Needs helps to explain how these needs motivate us all.

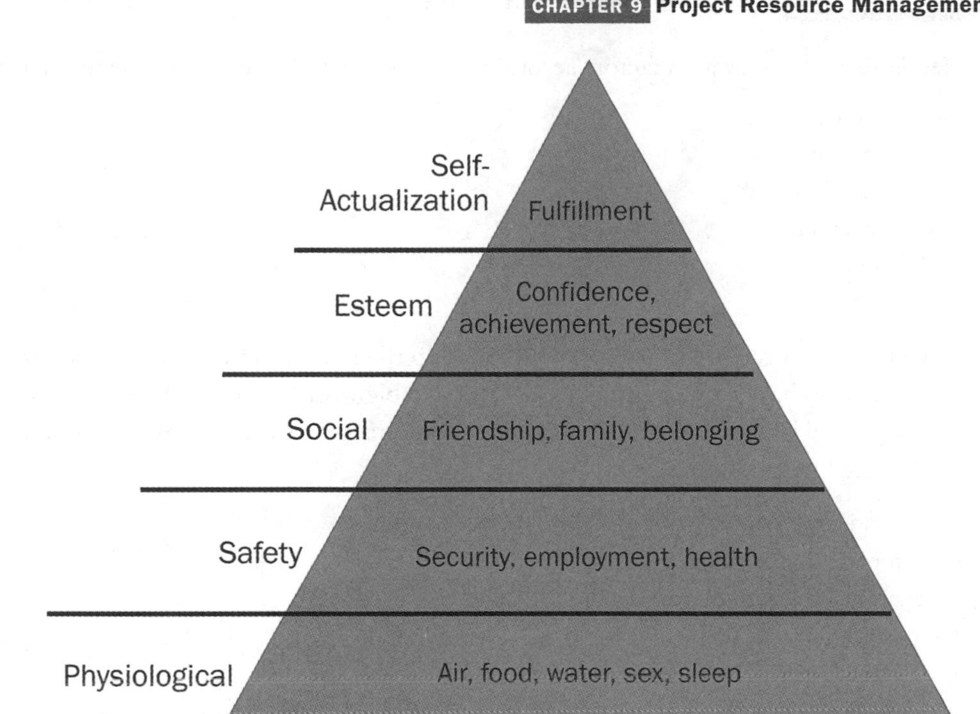

FIGURE 9.7 Maslow's Hierarchy of Needs

> Maslow's Hierarchy of Needs states that we must satisfy each need in turn, starting with the first, which deals with the most obvious needs for survival itself.
>
> Only when the lower order needs of physical and emotional well-being are satisfied are we concerned with the higher order needs of influence and personal development.
>
> Conversely, if the things that satisfy our lower order needs are swept away, we are no longer concerned about the maintenance of our higher order needs.

For example, if a person has reached the top (that is, has accomplished/self-actualized) and then is stranded on a desert isle, they immediately go to the bottom of the needs hierarchy pyramid to seek food, water, and shelter. Figure 9.7 shows Maslow's Hierarchy of Needs.

Herzberg's Motivator-Hygiene Theory

Frederick Irving Herzberg (1923–2000) was a psychologist who was also influential in business management. He is most famous for introducing the Motivator-Hygiene theory, which is also known as the Two-Factor Theory of Job Satisfaction. According to this theory, people are influenced by two factors: motivation factors and hygiene factors.[8]

Here's a list of motivation factors according to Herzberg's Motivator-Hygiene Theory:

- Achievement
- Recognition
- Work itself
- Responsibility
- Promotion
- Growth

Hygiene factors relate to how people respond to their environment. Because workers in certain countries have come to expect a safe and suitable working environment, we are more often dissatisfied by a bad environment and seldom satisfied by a good environment. Here's a list of some hygiene factors:

- Pay and benefits
- Company policy and administration
- Relationships with coworkers
- Physical environment
- Supervision
- Status
- Job security
- Salary

Wikipedia states the following about motivation and hygiene factors:

> Hygiene factors operate independently of motivation factors. An individual can be highly motivated in his work and be dissatisfied with his work environment. All hygiene factors are equally important, although their frequency of occurrence differs considerably. Hygiene improvements typically have short-term effects. Any improvements result in a short-term removal of, or prevention of, dissatisfaction. Hygiene needs are cyclical in nature and come back to a starting point. This leads to the "What have you done for me lately?" syndrome.[9]

McGregor Theory X and Theory Y

In his book *The Human Side of Enterprise* (published in 1960), Douglas McGregor examined theories on the behavior of individuals at work and formulated two models, known as Theory X and Theory Y.[10] Theory X is based on managers who believe that people need to be watched every minute, that they are incapable, and that they avoid work whenever possible. This is contrasted with Theory Y, in which managers believe people are self-motivated and work without supervision. Here's a list of assumptions for these theories:

THEORY X ASSUMPTIONS

- The average human being has an inherent dislike of work and will avoid it if possible.
- Most people must be controlled and threatened before they will work hard.
- The average person prefers to be directed and dislikes responsibility.

THEORY Y ASSUMPTIONS

- People are self-motivated, and work is as natural as play or rest.
- If a job is satisfying, the result will be commitment to the organization.
- The average person not only accepts but seeks responsibility.
- Workers use imagination, creativity, and ingenuity to solve work problems.

McClelland's Theory of Needs (or Acquired Needs Theory)

David McClelland's Theory of Needs states that people are often motivated by one of three needs. It is important for you as a PM to be aware of the different needs. The category of primary needs that a person falls into (see Table 9.3) would indicate how that person tends to be managed.

TABLE 9.3 McClelland's Theory of Needs

Primary Need	Behavioral Style
Achievement	Likes challenges and recognition
Affiliation	Tends to work well with others and seeks approval rather than recognition
Power (authority)	Seeks power, is usually socially oriented, and strives for leadership positions managing others. Likes to organize and influence others

Expectancy Theory

Another theory to be aware of is Expectancy Theory. This motivation theory was first proposed by Victor Vroom of the Yale School of Management and is based on the expectation by employees that their work efforts will lead to results and that they will be rewarded for their effort. Expectancy Theory is about choice. It explains the processes that an individual undergoes to make choices.

Expectancy Theory predicts that employees in an organization will be motivated when they believe the following:

- Putting in more effort will yield better job performance.
- Better job performance will lead to organizational rewards, such as an increase in salary or benefits.

Theories like the Expectancy Theory help us better understand what motivates people; however, the only way to know how your team is performing is to assess their results.

Team Performance Assessments

Team performance assessments can be informal or formal. The goal is to evaluate the team's performance to make the members aware of what is working and what is not.

Overall results of the project are influenced by each and every individual on the team and should be looked at from both the team perspective and the team member perspective.

The performance of a successful team is measured in a number of different ways, depending on the nature of the project. For example, if the project is time constrained (schedule dependent), then clearly a measure of team success is whether the project is being delivered on time.

Team assessment is used to determine team effectiveness, and the results can be detailed and specific or general. In either case the assessment should show how the team is measuring up to the agreed scope, cost, and schedule of the project. Here are some examples of team evaluation points:

- Is the team working together in a productive and cohesive manner?
- Are the improvements a result of a joint team effort or individual effort?
- What is the overall project team turnover rate? (Remember, this is a risk indicator as to whether or not things are going well on the project. If people are not happy, they will want to move on.)
- Is the team showing respect for the PM, project team leads, and other team members?
- What is the quality of the products being delivered by the project team?

The results of the team performance assessment should be used to analyze the situation and make improvements, as needed, to help ensure quality work. Any action taken should be documented with cause-and-effect details, including action plans for improvements. Examples of action items include suggesting specific education or training, mentoring, and the assistance of other team members.

Extra care should be given in assessing a virtual team because you can't see the team members face-to-face. You may also have contract performance clauses, country privacy issues, or other laws that must be considered when managing virtual project teams.

Understanding how your team is performing will also help in managing your customer's expectations.

Managing Customer Expectations

The customer is a key stakeholder and should have a representative as part of the project management team. Customers should provide review and approval for changes that affect the project triple constraints. They should also be involved in risk management and communications management. They should provide requirements of what they expect from the project, the target completion date, and what specific results they want to see at the end. As part of the team, they are privy to information that can cause concerns or conflicts. So, how do you manage customer expectations and conflict?

Note that conflict is not always bad; it can sometimes raise opportunities to improve the way you do things. You can enhance the relationship with your customer and your team by looking at conflict as a healthy way to learn new things. The main thing to remember is to be open-minded. Ask the customer questions. Make sure you understand what is important to the customer and what the customer's expectations are at the end of the project. You may be surprised, but it is better to find out sooner than later and lose valuable resources, time, and cost by going down the wrong path.

Ask the Expert

Q: I am the PM on a small project. My customer called recently with a request to mail a survey and invoices to their clients. The additional mailing requests are out of scope of the project. Therefore, I set up a meeting for 8:00 the next morning to discuss their requests. During the meeting, the customer demanded that the survey go out immediately. I calmly explained that the request was not in scope and that if the team was pulled off the project to perform the extra work, it would delay the overall project by one week. The customer was very upset and threatened to cancel the entire project. A shouting match ensued. How could I have handled this situation better?

A: When things heat up, I suggest you try taking a short break and have some coffee and rolls or donuts to calm the situation. It might make all the difference in the world. The customer could become more agreeable once you both take a minute to relax and get something to eat. (Perhaps the customer is a single parent with a sick child, was running late for the 8:00 a.m. meeting, and had skipped breakfast.) After you have your break, you can then pursue settling your differences in a more professional manner.

Signs of a Conflict

How do you know when conflict is looming? Some characteristics or triggers are listed here:

- Team members are working excessive hours (for example, more than 15 hours per week of overtime for long periods of time).
- The customer or team members are defensive during meetings or discussions.
- Relations are strained (the customer or team members are avoiding you).
- Tempers flare (outbreaks of emotions in meetings or one-on-ones).
- The customer is micromanaging the team (loss of confidence).
- High turnover of team members occurs (as mentioned earlier).

- Lots of extra meetings take place (meeting to prepare for meetings).
- Significant number of changes happen (dissatisfaction or disorganization).

Conflict Resolution

Now that you know some of the signs or triggers of conflict, the question is, How can you resolve conflict? The best way to resolve conflict is to understand it—what it is and how it will impact the project. Conflict, like change, is inevitable in the project environment. Conflict is a state of disharmony or opposition between people or forces when they, with perceived incompatible goals, seek to undermine each other's capability or objectives.

There are many sources of conflict, including lack of skilled resources, scheduling conflicts, cost constraints, different management and leadership styles, communications problems, change, and risk events.

When conflict is managed properly, the results are improved productivity, higher team morale, and higher-quality product and project deliverables.

Here are a few things to remember when it comes to managing conflict:

- Don't take yourself too seriously.
- Don't take the conflict personally.
- You need to know conflict is normal and helps you look at the options.
- It is a team issue and needs to be resolved early.
- Keep the conflict focused on problems and issues, not personalities.
- Be aware of the relative importance and impact of the conflict on the project.
- Be aware of the downstream results (ripple effects).
- Focus on the root cause of the conflict and not the symptoms.
- Help the team stay focused and motivate team members to help resolve conflict.

Techniques to Help Resolve Conflicts

One way of analyzing and understanding a problem is by interviewing the customer or parties involved. There are a number of techniques you can use to help resolve conflicts, as listed here:

- **Withdrawing/avoiding.** Retreating from the actual or potential conflict situation.
- **Smoothing/accommodating.** Emphasizing areas of agreement rather than areas of difference.
- **Compromising.** Searching for solutions that bring some degree of satisfaction to all parties. This is often viewed as a lose/lose situation as everyone gives up something.
- **Forcing.** Pushing one's view on others (someone wins and someone loses).

- **Collaborating.** Looking at multiple views from different perspectives (leads to consensus).
- **Confronting/problem solving.** This is a win/win situation because it treats the conflict as a problem to be solved by looking at alternatives (requires give-and-take approach by all parties).

Tip

PMI views confronting/problem solving as the best approach to resolve conflicts. You may even see a question or two concerning this technique on the PMP exam.

No matter what resolution approach you take, the end results depend on your ability to apply sound judgment and good interpersonal skills, including leadership and the ability to influence others to help solve conflicts. Conflict resolution is a team sport; the PM can't succeed without the team, and the team must be productive and fully functional to provide results. However, it is up to the PM to set the stage and to lead by example.

It is important to note that conflict resolution begins at home in your project team first. This is what resource management is all about. Here are the other key steps:

1. Make sure you have sponsorship for the project (turnover in executive sponsors can change the focus, funding, and fun on the project).
2. Make sure you have a clear and confirmed understanding of scope, target dates, and expectations from all key stakeholders (especially the customer).
3. Ensure clear communications, including listening at all times (no news is not always good news, and it leaves room for speculation and uncertainty in the ranks).
4. Treat all the people on your project with respect.
5. Be flexible and open-minded. Be firm when needed, but be compassionate as appropriate.

Managing the project team and the vast number of stakeholders on a project can be a huge job in itself. The key is to maintain a high degree of control over your resources which brings us to the final process in this Knowledge Area which is the Control Resources process.

Control Resources Process (Monitoring and Controlling Process Group)

Controlling resources (including the team) involves using the tools and techniques mentioned throughout this chapter to ensure the physical resources assigned and allocated to the project are available when needed. When you think about control, think about measurements, such as planned versus actual utilization against approved productivity (workload)

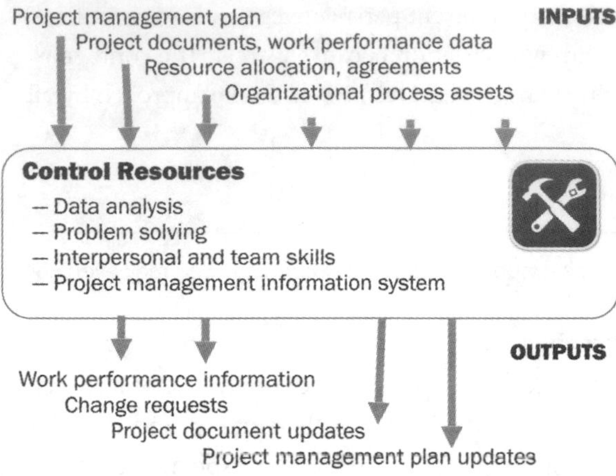

FIGURE 9.8 Control Resources Process ITTOs

rates. Control also includes knowing when to take corrective action in the event key resources are not available when needed.

Also remember that resources include supplies, materials, equipment, tools, software, and so on needed by the physical team members. The physical team often includes internal team and external (or extended) team members such as consultants, subject matter experts, volunteers, and so forth.

It is important to know that a big part of the PM's job is to ensure you have all the right resources at the right time and at the right place to get the job done according to the approved scope and schedule. Figure 9.8 shows the inputs, tools and techniques, and the outputs for the Control Resources process.

I realize there are many variables when it comes to resource management. Any time you deal with people, you have feelings and emotions to consider. The good news is you can find lots of help and collaboration via courses, mentors, coworkers, family, and friends. The thing to remember is you want to invest in this skill to help you and your team grow.

Summary of Project Resource Management

Resource management is truly the lifeblood of the project. Many organizations have found teaming to be an extremely effective way to accomplish project goals and objectives. As a project manager, having the knowledge and skills to acquire, develop, and manage teams effectively is a necessity. With the uniqueness of projects and team members, there is clearly a challenge for the PM to keep everyone focused on the end results. Deal with problems head on, quickly, yet with compassion and respect for all parties involved. Remember, the problem won't go away on its own and will likely grow the longer you allow it to remain unresolved.

When asked what I like most about project management, I have to say it's the people. Working with project teams from all over the world has opened my eyes to the benefits and barriers of managing diverse projects. The true measure of success is the size and breadth of your network, and your network is what makes the world of project management go round.

References

1. Kim Heldman, Claudia Baca, and Patti Jensen, *PMP Project Management Professional Exam Study Guide*, Second Edition (Indianapolis: Wiley Publishing Inc., 2007), pages 336 and 353.

2. *Agile Alliance,* "12 Principles behind the Agile Manifesto," June, 6, 2010, Kent Beck, James Grenning, Robert C. Martin, Mike Beedle, Jim Highsmith, Steve Mellor, Arie van Bennekum Andrew Hunt, Ken Schwaber, Alistair Cockburn, Ron Jeffries, Jeff Sutherland, Ward Cunningham, Jon Kern, Dave Thomas, Marin Fowler, Brian Marick, https://www.agilealliance.org/agile101/12-principles-behind-the-agile-manifesto/, accessed March 14, 2017.

3. "Virtual Team," *Wikipedia*, https://en.wikipedia.org/wiki/Virtual_team, accessed March 14, 2017.

4. "Bruce Tuckman's 1965 Forming Storming Norming Performing Team-Development Model," *Businessballs.com*, http://www.businessballs.com/tuckmanformingstormingnormingperforming.htm, accessed March 14, 2017.

5. Ginger Levin and Parviz Rad, "Achieving Project Management Success Using Virtual Teams," *Jimdo.com*, https://doimaqa.jimdo.com/2013/05/25/achieving-project-management-success-using-virtual-teams-online/, accessed March, 14, 2017.

6. "Coaching Quotes," *wow4u.com*, http://www.wow4u.com/coaching/, accessed March 14, 2017.

7. "Abraham Maslow's Hierarchy of Needs Motivational Model," *Businessballs.com*, http://www.businessballs.com/maslow.htm, accessed March 14, 2017.

8. "Frederick Herzberg's Motivation and Hygiene Factors," *Businessballs.com*, http://www.businessballs.com/herzberg.htm, accessed March 14, 2017.

9. "Frederick Herzberg," *Wikipedia*, http://en.wikipedia.org/wiki/Frederick_Herzberg, accessed March 14, 2017.

10. "Douglas McGregor's XY Theory, Managing an X Theory Boss, and William Ouchi's Theory Z," *Businessballs.com*, http://www.businessballs.com/mcgregor.htm, accessed March 14, 2017.

10 Project Communications Management

Key Skills & Concepts

- Importance of clear communications
- PM's role in communications
- Communications model
- The medium
- Virtual communications
- Communications methods
- Conducting effective meetings
- Communications management processes
- Agile project communications
- Communication channels (including formula)
- Communication blockers (barriers)
- Project management reports

There's communication, and then there's (or should be) *effective* two-way communications. Communication is the simple exchange of information between two or more parties. Edgar Dale's Cone of Experience is a model that incorporates several theories related to instructional design and learning processes. During the 1960s Dale theorized that learners retain more information by what they "do" as opposed to what is "heard," "read," or "observed." His research led to the development of the Cone of Experience (see the cone diagram in Figure 10.1). Today, this "learning by doing" has become known as "experiential learning" or "action learning."[1]

Basically there are two types of communication models.

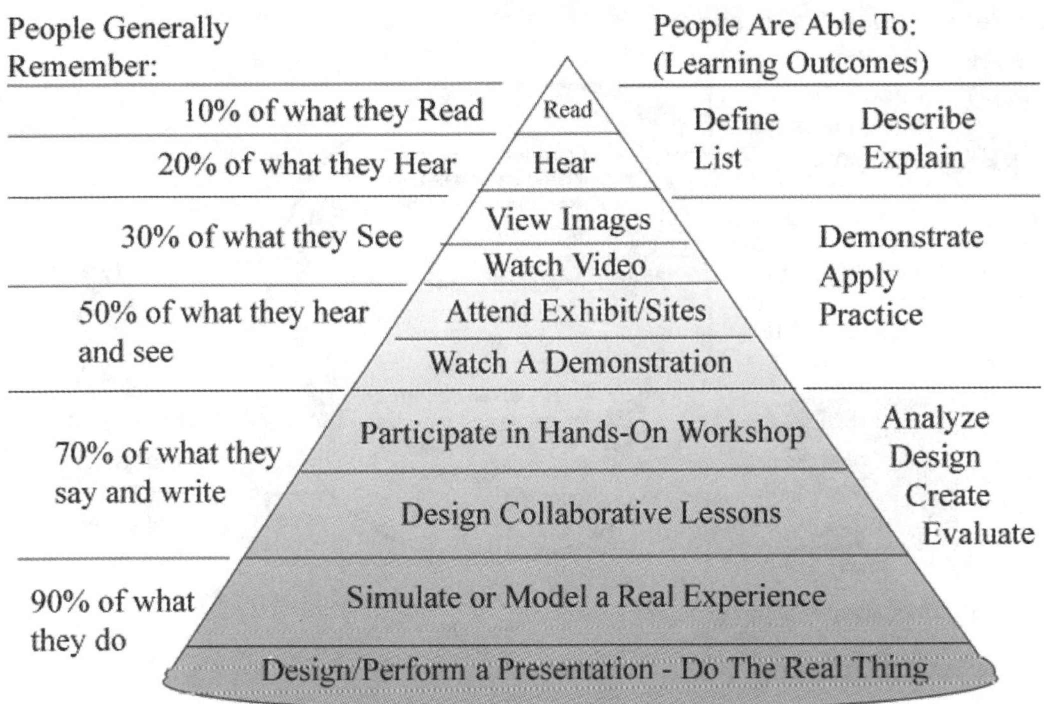

FIGURE 10.1 Dale's Cone of Experience Model

There is the basic *sender/receiver communications model*, which includes the two parties (sender and receiver) and also includes the message, yet this model focuses on the delivery of the message and not ensuring the message is understood. The three primary components of this model are listed here:

- Encode the message (into sound or text).
- Transmit the message (using a multimedia medium and avoiding noise or barriers).
- Decode the message (translating into a form useful to the receiver).

For the communication model to be effective, we must be aware of the three elements. For example, the information needs to be *encoded* (translated into thoughts or ideas that can be understood by others) by the sender. The sender then needs to select the appropriate method (or vehicle) to send (convey) the message—for example, a *medium* such as email, letter, text message, face-to-face encounter, or phone call. Then the receiver needs to *decode* the message (translating it back into understandable meaningful thoughts and ideas).

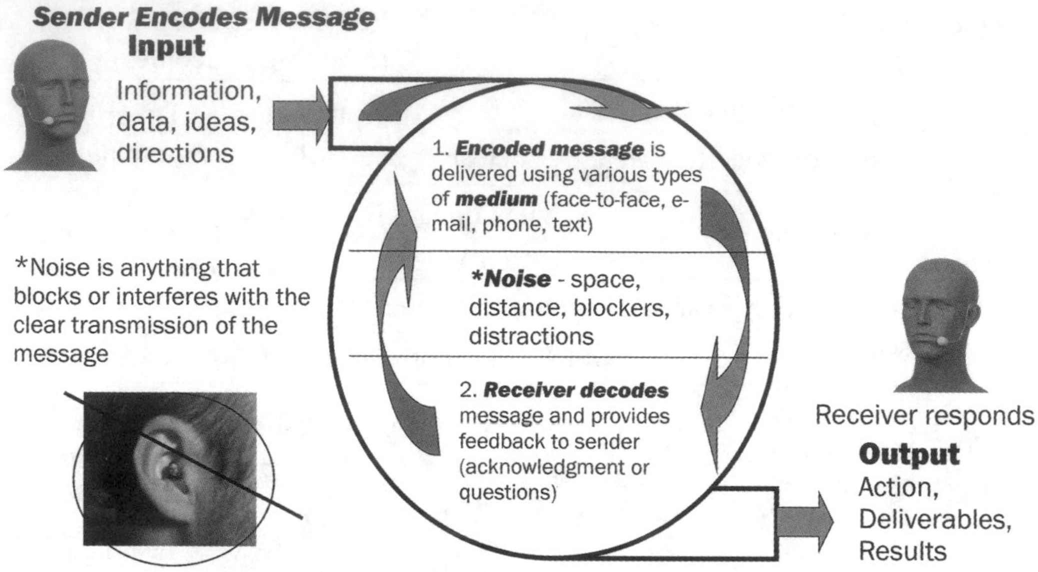

Sender Encodes Message
Input
Information, data, ideas, directions

1. ***Encoded message*** is delivered using various types of ***medium*** (face-to-face, e-mail, phone, text)

****Noise*** - space, distance, blockers, distractions

2. ***Receiver decodes*** message and provides feedback to sender (acknowledgment or questions)

*Noise is anything that blocks or interferes with the clear transmission of the message

Receiver responds
Output
Action, Deliverables, Results

FIGURE 10.2 Interactive Communication Model

Then there is the *interactive communications model*, which is also concerned with the message and medium for delivery of the message. The primary components that make up this communication model include making sure the message is understood.

- Acknowledgment by the receiver
- Feedback/response to the sender

Ideally the receiver provides *feedback* to the sender in the form of either an acknowledgment or additional questions to clarify the message. The intent is to have a communication circle of a clearly understood and actionable exchange of information, ideas, or directions that produce the desired results (see Figure 10.2).

The project manager (PM) needs to focus on effective communications. A coworker once told me many years ago that "effective communications is a connection between people that allows for the exchange of thoughts, feelings, and ideas, which leads to understanding."

For the communication to be successful, it also helps if all parties have a common language and similar knowledge of the topic. For the message to be clear and understood, there should be minimal *noise* (or interference) with the transmission of the message. Examples of noise include unfamiliar terms, lack of background information, distance (temporal or physical), and environmental factors (phones ringing, crowded room, etc.).

Tip

Because communication is so important in managing projects, you are likely to see several questions on the Project Management Professional (PMP) exam concerning communication in areas such as risk management, scope management, status reporting, and stakeholder management.

To recap, here are the components of the communication model:

- Sender
- Encoding
- Message
- Medium (with minimal noise)
- Decoding
- Receiver (including feedback/acknowledgment)

The Importance of Clear Communication

I saw a cute Hallmark birthday card recently that really says it all about communication. The card shows three elderly men walking along the beach. The first man says, "It's a windy day." The second man says, "No, I think its Thursday." And the third man says, "I'm thirsty, too. Let's go have a beer." This kind of conversation happens far too often where we hear only half of what is said, and we retain even less, especially with all the distractions we are faced with throughout the day. A big part of managing any project is communications, so as a PM, what is your role and how do you effectively manage the vast number and different types of communications on a project?

The PM's Role in Communications

Since good, clear communications is hugely important on all projects, the PM must have (or quickly develop) strong, effective communication skills to help you communicate with the team and other stakeholders about all aspects of the project. The PM must develop and refine this skill to plan and execute the work of the project as part of the Project Communications Management Knowledge Area.

The good news is that the communications model is simple to use; in fact, we use it from the time we learn to talk. The bad news is that if the model is not used effectively, you will send or receive the wrong message. Thus, the team is off building the wrong widget at the wrong time, or team members are so confused they don't know what you want and may just choose to ignore you.

As simple as the communication model is, communicating is one of the more difficult activities in managing a project. Talking is easy; communicating is a challenge! Being able to communicate effectively is a skill that is developed and honed your entire life. Communicating is not just about the *sender*. It is an interactive, two-way session in which both sender and receiver continuously influence each other as messages are cycled back and forth on sometimes nonverbal, barely perceptible levels.

Tip

To be prepared for your PMP exam, you need to know that PMs spend an average of 90 percent of their time communicating; any questions on communications management will likely be intermingled with other topics. For example, the WBS is a communications tool, and the scope and risk response strategy have to be clearly communicated to the team. As a PM, you communicate to yourself internally—even in your sleep. During light sleep is when some of the best ideas come to mind, so keep a pad and pencil next to your bed to capture those great ideas or reminders. This helps clear your mind so hopefully you can sleep and then deal with the reminders in the morning when you are fresh.

There are a multitude of reasons for good, clear, two-way communications. Here are some examples:

- To improve our working relationships
- To be able to adapt to change and to enable prompt action
- To understand different communication styles and to take advantage of the right style to eliminate confusion and influence positive results
- To increase the overall quality of the project team and the deliverables

As you probably already know, there are two primary types of communication: verbal and nonverbal. *Verbal* (or *auditory*) *communication* includes talking, singing, tone, and the pitch of your voice. *Paralanguage* (sometimes called *vocalic*) is the nonverbal cues of the voice such as pitch, volume, and intonation. Paralanguage may change the meaning of words.[2] Nonverbal communication includes body language, sign language, touch, and eye contact.

The Medium: How We Deliver the Message

Have you ever heard a person telling a joke mess up the punch line or put the emphasis on the wrong syllable? Or nail the punch line but hesitate at the wrong time or use the wrong word? When this happens, the receiver will likely say, "I don't get it," or they may get the joke but will think it wasn't funny. The only way to improve the delivery of a joke or any other communication is through practice.

Some of the more common communication delivery methods are face-to-face, written, and virtual (i.e., video messaging or teleconferences). Virtual is a whole new ballgame, as we adapt to a new generation of highly interactive, fast-paced, multitasking project managers.

The delivery method can be formal or informal, both of which will have different results. An important thing to remember is that your message is likely to be received incorrectly or the meaning lost depending on your delivery method, the timing, or the mood in which you deliver the message. This is especially noticeable in the face-to-face delivery method and almost impossible to discern (at least immediately) with the other delivery methods.

To ensure effective communication, the sender needs to select the appropriate delivery method depending on the situation. There is no "one-size-fits-all" delivery method. With the rapid growth of communication technology, sometimes there can be an overdependence on one type of communication. I cannot tell you how many times I have had fellow PMs complain to me that they were not getting a timely or proper response from a team member. When I asked how they had been communicating, they typically respond, "I sent them *three* emails!" I ask, "Did you go to their desk to talk to them face-to-face or try calling them?" "No" is the usual response. The younger generation has grown up in a digital age, and it is often difficult to get a face-to-face engagement, and when you do, it may be difficult to establish eye contact.

For a summary of delivery methods, see Table 10.1.

TABLE 10.1 Communication Delivery Methods

Delivery Method	When Used	Advantages	Comments
Spoken (face-to-face or remote as in virtual teams)	For important meetings or conferences (virtual conference calls for distant and geographically dispersed team members)	Shows importance of the meeting or event and is great for networking and building trust and confidence, as well as improving relationships	Can be challenging to schedule and can be distracting, especially with language or other barriers; be aware of expressions, acronyms, and technical jargon (special words or expressions used by a particular profession)
Written (physical or electronic)	For formal or informal, depending on the type of medium used	Works well in many ways to communicate to a broad, diverse audience	Generally, two categories: formal (letters, contracts, etc.) and informal (emails and texting, which is a whole new language in itself)
Haptic (nonverbal touching such as a handshake, hug, or pat on the back)	When in close proximity, as appropriate	Can show sincerity and friendship	Not always accepted and can be offensive in some cultures
Tactile gestures	In face-to-face or video meetings (in person or remote)	To express emotions or to accentuate or help visually explain an item or topic; gesturing helps conveys enthusiasm and energy to your audience	Be aware of gestures that can be distracting or even insulting; generally 55% of a message is conveyed by body language and only 7% in what is said; the remaining 38% is in tone, pitch, and volume

Virtual Communications

A mechanism that has grown in popularity is virtual communications. Some examples include the virtual classroom or videoconferencing, FaceTime, and Skype. This virtual face-to-face connection allows each participant to see the nonverbal communication that is occurring and allows for participants to develop a stronger sense of familiarity with individuals they may never meet in the same place. Some videoconferencing technology allows for the team to share files and their desktop screens so that everyone is looking at the same thing.

For entertainment purposes, there are also virtual "worlds" such as *Second Life* or *My Second Life*. In these virtual worlds a person can choose an avatar (a virtual alter ego) and walk, talk, or even fly around in virtual settings. According to the SecondLife.com website, "*Second Life* is a free online virtual world imagined and created by its users."[3] Some companies have even considered using this application for education and demonstration purposes.

Project Communications Management Processes

According to PMI, there are currently three processes associated with the Communications Management Knowledge Area:

- **10.1. Plan Communications Management (Planning Process Group).** Developing an appropriate approach and plan for project communications based on stakeholders' information needs and requirements, and available organizational assets.
- **10.2. Manage Communications (Executing Process Group).** The process of creating, collecting, distributing, storing, and retrieving, and the ultimate disposition of project information in accordance with the communications management plan.
- **10.3. Monitor Communications (Monitoring and Controlling Process Group).** Monitoring and controlling communications throughout the entire project life cycle to ensure information needs of the project stakeholders are met.

Plan Communications Management Process (Planning Process Group)

The PM and team need to work together when planning communications for the project. A good place to start is with the stakeholder register created during Identify Stakeholder process in the Initiation Process Group. This list will help you determine the level of communications needed, the frequency, the format, and reports needed, and after stakeholder analysis you will be able to further determine style and preference of communications that will best meet the needs of the many stakeholders on your project.

Try This

You just spent 12 hours (in a single day) putting together a detailed status report including schedule progress, risks and issues (a couple of staffing problems), several change requests, and financial reports to present to your project sponsor (Lynn) in two days. You know Lynn is a busy executive, so you want to start the meeting on time and bring her up to speed quickly.

You are a very experienced PM and know that sending her the information ahead of time will give her advance notice and hopefully allow the meeting (scheduled for 9:00 a.m.) to move smoothly.

At 8:55 a.m. the day of the meeting, Lynn storms into your office and asks for the report. You remind her that you sent the report in an email two days ago, and she replies: "I don't read email. Give me the darn report. We need to reschedule the meeting because I have not had time to prepare." Then she storms out. What do you do?

Answer: You hand her the report and ask if the 9:00 a.m. meeting is still on to go over the status reports, and she replies, "NO, I have not had time to review the reports!"

What should you have done?

Answer: You should have performed stakeholder analysis during the Plan Communications Management process to understand Lynn's preferred communications style and preferences to know that you should have hand-delivered the report instead of sending it in an email. Also, because she is a busy executive, you should have only provided a summary level report (i.e., milestone report) instead of all the details . . . better luck next time!

Sample Project Communications Plans

A well-planned project has a well-planned communication plan and strategy. A big part of project communications management is based on a number of factors, including the organizational structure, individual style and preference for communicating, culture, egos, relationships between the parties, and even politics within the organization.

The following tables provide examples of two project management communication plans.

The detailed sample communications plan shown in Table 10.2 is a modification of the Princeton Project Communication Plan.[4]

TABLE 10.2 Sample Communications Plan

What	Who/Target	Purpose	When/Frequency	Type/Method(s)
Initiation meeting	All lead project management team members.	Gather information for initiation plan.	First. Before project start date.	Meeting (colocated if possible).
Distribution of project plan	All key stakeholders.*	Distribute plan to alert stakeholders of project scope and to gain buy-in.	Before kickoff meeting. Before project start date.	Document distributed via hardcopy or electronically. May be posted on project team room or website. PM templates: Project scope "lite" and initiation plan.

continued on next page

TABLE 10.2—*continued*

What	Who/Target	Purpose	When/Frequency	Type/Method(s)
Project kickoff	All key stakeholders.*	Communicate plans and stakeholder roles/responsibilities. Encourage communication among stakeholders.	At or near project start date.	Meeting.
Status reports	All stakeholders and project office.	Update stakeholders on progress of the project.	Regularly scheduled. Monthly is recommended for large/midsize projects.	Distribute electronically and post in team room or via Web. PM template: status report.
Team meetings	Entire project team. Individual meetings for subteams, technical teams, and functional teams, as appropriate.	To review detailed plans (activities, resource assignments, and action items).	Regularly scheduled. Weekly is recommended for the entire team. Weekly or biweekly for subteams, as appropriate.	Meeting PM template: Detailed project plan and key project documents, as appropriate.
Project advisory group meetings (may apply only to larger projects)	Project advisory group and project manager.	Update project advisory group on status and discuss critical issues. Work through issues and change requests here before escalating to the sponsor(s).	Regularly scheduled. Monthly is recommended.	Meeting.
Sponsor meetings	Sponsor(s) and project manager.	Update sponsor(s) on status and discuss critical issues. Seek approval for changes to the project plan.	Regularly scheduled. Recommended biweekly or monthly, or as needed when issues cannot be resolved or changes need to be made to the project plan.	Meeting.
Executive sponsor meetings (may apply only to larger projects)	Executive sponsor(s) and project manager.	Update sponsor(s) on status and discuss critical issues. Seek approval for changes to the project plan.	Scheduled as needed when issues cannot be resolved or when changes need to be made to the project plan.	Meeting.

continued on next page

TABLE 10.2—*continued*

What	Who/Target	Purpose	When/Frequency	Type/Method(s)
PO audit/ reviews	Project office, project manager, select stakeholders, and possibly sponsors, if necessary.	Review status reports, issues, and risks. Identify and communicate potential risks and issues that may affect the schedule, budget, or deliverables.	Monthly. Scheduled by the project office.	Meeting/report. The project office will produce the report using their (auditors') template.
Post-project review	Project office, PM, and key stakeholders (including sponsors).	Identify improvement plans, lessons learned, what worked, and what could have gone better. Review accomplishments.	End of project or end of major phase.	Meeting/report. The PM or project office will produce the report.
Quarterly project review	Project office, project manager, and key stakeholders.	Review the overall health of the project and highlight areas that need action.	Quarterly, depending on size and criticality of the project. Scheduled by the project office.	Meeting/report. The project office will produce the report using an internal template.
Other	To be determined by the project manager and team.	General communications.	As needed.	Group meetings, Lunch-'n'-Learns, emails, webinars, webcasts, postings in project team room or website, etc.

* A *key stakeholder* is defined as a person whose support is critical to the project—if the support of a key stakeholder is withdrawn, the project may fail.

Case Study: Event Center Sample Communications Plan

For projects that are similar in nature and can be repeated, it is good to streamline the communications plan. Take our events center case study for example. Weekly meetings are conducted to streamline the flow and frequency of communications from the director of events to the operations managers. In these meetings the director uses an event data sheet (EDS) showing all the key information needed—dates, times, expected seating capacity, security and lighting for the event, and so on.

Based on the scope statement, here is a brief overview of the communications strategy, followed by a table showing when each communication should occur, who the assigned owner is, and a brief description of the communication activity.

- The event team will have weekly update/status meetings to review completed tasks and determine current work priorities. Minutes will be produced from all meetings.

- The event director will lead weekly meetings to review the previous event's lessons learned and the upcoming events for team awareness. A customized EDS will be used and distributed to the project team to show all pertinent information about the events with timelines, department assignments, key contacts, and other requirements for each event.

A streamlined communications plan is shown in Table 10.3.

TABLE 10.3 Sample Communications Plan

Frequency of Meeting	Owner/Tool Used	Description
As needed for project initiation (varies by event)	Event director and artist's agent or sponsor/contract	This is the initial meeting to finalize the event contract and requirements.
Three weeks prior to event	Event manager/event data sheet (EDS)	Meeting with all building staff to provide advanced information from the band and building requirements for the event.
Two weeks prior to event	Event manager / EDS	Distribution of the EDS to start the planning.
One week prior to event	Operations manager / EDS	Review requirements and begin staffing and facility changeover staging for event week.
Week of event	Project or changeover manager / EDS	Use the EDS as a guide for setup of the venue.
One week after event review	Full team / EDS	Review lessons learned.
Close the event communications	Sign-off by the project team and event manager	Document the results of the event, tickets sold, issues, and so on.

Plan Communications Management Tools and Techniques

Some tools and techniques associated with the Plan Communications process are expert judgment, communications requirements analysis, communications technology, models and methods, data representation, and interpersonal and team skills. These and other tools and techniques are discussed in detail in the *PMBOK Guide*.

FIGURE 10.3 Plan Communications Management Process ITTOs

Figure 10.3 shows an overview of the inputs, tools and techniques, and the outputs for the Plan Communications Management process.

COMMUNICATION-REQUIREMENTS ANALYSIS

To establish a communications plan, the PM and team often need to perform a communications-requirements analysis. The analysis varies depending on the project and will be more detailed for new or first-time projects.

One thing we tend to overlook as PMs is the complexity of the communications required. Even on a small project you can have dozens or even hundreds of stakeholders to consider during communications analysis. The number of lines of communication grows exponentially as the size of the project team grows.

Say, for example, you have four team members on your project. Here is the formula:

$$(n * (n - 1))/2$$

where n represents the number of stakeholders. For the sample project, the formula would look like this:

$$(4 * (4 - 1))/2, \text{ which equates to } (4 * 3)/2, \text{ and finally } 12/2 = 6$$

Therefore, you have six communication channels on your project. The number of lines of communication between the four team members is shown in Figure 10.4.

Now suppose you have ten people on your team. The calculation now is:

$$(10 * (10 - 1))/2, \text{ which equates to } (10 * 9)/2, \text{ and finally } 90/2 = 45$$

This means you have 45 different communication channels (or paths) among the ten team members. That's a lot of lines of communication. The more lines you have, the more room there is for a breakdown in communication, where someone is not clear and does the wrong thing. This could be devastating to the project. Now just imagine if you have 50 or 100 people on the project team!

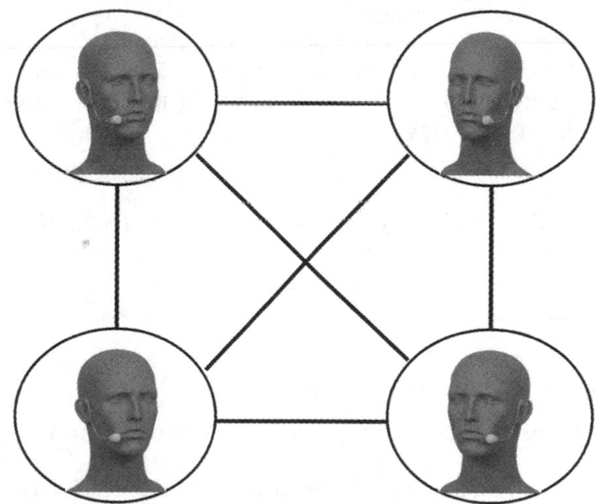

FIGURE 10.4 Communication Channels

COMMUNICATION TECHNOLOGY

Various methods are used to transfer information among project stakeholders. You also have a number of factors to consider when selecting the technologies or tools for this process:

- The urgency of the needed information

- The availability of the technology (both physically and from an affordability perspective)
- Telephony needs (e.g., phones, systems, and technology compatibility)
- The duration of the project and project environment (e.g., short- or long-term, and virtual or colocated team) and, of course, the size of the team

COMMUNICATION MODELS

We covered a communication model earlier in this chapter. Do you remember the seven components of the communications model? If not, go back now and review.

The one point I want to emphasize here is the noise factor. Don't let noise get in the way of clear communications. This includes physical noise, temporal distance, language barriers, poor phone connections, and distractions.

On one of my projects on the West Coast, the project office team room was a storage closet of just over 50 square feet. At times there were six to eight people in the room, and for meetings we often had to gather in the cafeteria, with all the traffic and distractions. Talk about lots of noise (interference) in trying to communicate with the team in this environment! It was difficult at best.

Ask the Expert

Q: Can you provide an example of the type of question the PMP exam asks regarding calculating the number of communication channels?

A: The PMP exam will likely ask a question similar to the following:

"There are four new team members added to your existing team of five. How many additional communication channels have been added?"

When answering a question like this, you will need to remember the formula used to calculate the number of communication channels, which is $(n * (n - 1))/2$, and you will need to read the question closely. To arrive at the answer, first calculate the current number of existing communication channels: $(5 \times 4)/2 = 10$. Then calculate the new total number of team members if four more are added: $5 + 4 = 9$. Plugging this number into the formula gives you the following:

$$(9 \times 8)/2, \text{ or } 72/2 = 36$$

Then you simply need to subtract your starting number of channels (10) from 36, and you get $36 - 10 = 26$. Therefore, 26 additional communication channels are created by adding four new team members to this project.

COMMUNICATION METHODS

You need to be aware of several communication methods. Here are just a few:

- **Interactive communications.** Communication occurs between two or more parties (one-on-one or in meetings).

- **Push communications.** Information is sent to specific recipients or in broadcast messages.
- **Pull communications.** Used for very large volumes of information or large audiences. The information is downloaded by the recipient from a central repository when needed.

How to Conduct Effective Meetings

Most projects that fail are doomed before 20 percent of the work has been completed. One reason, among the many possible, is poor communications. One way to communicate to a group of people is through meetings. As a PM, how will you run meetings (both internally and externally)? See the following sample list of things to consider when conducting meetings. Remember, PMs spend an average of 90 percent of their time communicating, and meetings are a big part of project communications.

- **Preplan the meeting.** What is the purpose/objective? Who will prepare the presentation materials? Who should attend? Who will facilitate? Who will lead the meeting? Where will the meeting be held? (Is the meeting room scheduled? Is the room large enough? Do you have the room properly set up for the type of meeting you are going to run?) Are distractions minimized? Who will document the minutes of the meeting? And who will follow up on "to-dos" or action items from the meeting?
- **Always set an agenda.** Clearly document who will present, what they will present, and when. Make sure the presenters are clear on the timing, and provide prompts or cues if they are about to run over their allotted time.
- **Always send the agenda to the attendees ahead of time** (usually at least a day or two ahead of the meeting). This can be used as a meeting reminder to attendees and to the presenters.
- **Preview the presentations if time allows** (depending on sensitivity of material and audience) just so there are no (or fewer) surprises.
- **Allow time for networking.** Keep this between five and eight minutes at the beginning or end of the meeting.
- **Maintain meeting integrity.** The meeting should start on time and end on time.
- **Manage the meeting.** If there are disruptions, such as someone spending too much time on a topic or getting carried away in the discussions, flag the topic for follow-up. Be sure to capture the discussion item and be sure to follow up; otherwise, you lose credibility.
- **Take control of the meeting.** Keep things on track and reschedule it if necessary.
- **Publish the minutes.** Post the minutes in the project team room in a timely manner (usually within one or two days after the meeting) and communicate the posting.

- **Consider putting caveats (qualifiers) in the minutes.** It is a good idea to put a statement in the minutes such as, "If anything has been omitted or misstated in the meeting minutes, please let me (host of the meeting) know within five business days. Note: no response to this note implies acceptance of the minutes as written."

Manage Communications Process (Executing Process Group)

All of us at one time or another have received a message or email that was not meant for us. Oh well, you simply delete it and move on. How about receiving an email that is to a cast of thousands and is about a meeting that has already taken place? Again you mumble to yourself and delete the message. But, what about the real slip-ups? You know the ones . . .

- **Clicking the "Reply to All" button.** The Reply to All button is a powerful tool. Talk about instant gratification. It's a quick-and-easy way to tell a lot of people that a meeting has been rescheduled or the new contract has been signed. But be very careful with your reply. It can get you into an embarrassing situation.
- **Responding with a message that doesn't match the question.** This is a result of not reading the whole email. I am guilty of this one myself. I have answered emails too quickly, only to find I missed the real question and had to send follow-up messages to clear things up.
- **Sending streaming (cascading) email.** These are emails containing notes from several people that are forwarded to person after person. Half the time the message gets so convoluted that by the time it comes to you, it makes no sense at all. This happens far too often and can be quite counterproductive. Often the email is ignored altogether.

Agile Project Communications

A growing form of project management is Agile Project Management methods. Agile project management is a response-driven iterative method of managing design and construction for engineering and software development type projects. Its intent is to provide new product or service development in a highly flexible and interactive manner. Because of the increased flexibility and results focus, this method of project management requires a slightly different approach to project communications.

Note

Agile places an emphasis on verbal and interactive communications rather than documentation, which can be time consuming and distracting. It is extremely important that everyone on the team understand the project objectives and protocols.

The general principle is based on the open concept (no surprises) of each individual speaking out when something needs to be said regarding an issue or potential risk, without reprisal. A sample list of some of the communications protocols are as follows:

- Feedback to help improve competency and interaction
- Stand-ups typically during development and short, concise daily meetings designed to keep the team informed of current and intended activities and to keep everyone focused
- Showcases or demonstrations, usually at the end of an iteration or sprint, for a broader audience (outside the project team) to see how the project is progressing
- Retrospectives (lessons learned) as the team's version of interactive (feedback) to see what went well, what needs work, and where improvements may be needed

The Manage Communications process in general involves making relevant information available to project stakeholders. This process occurs throughout the project life cycle and can come in many forms, such as formal requests for information from an auditor or sponsor or informal requests from anyone at any time.

So how do you effectively distribute information? The main thing is to do your homework. You should also make sure you have a good idea of who the stakeholders are and their level of interest in the project. Finally, have a clear communications plan. Always remember the communications model. Make sure you are clear on who the specific senders and receivers are, the message that needs to be received (actions to take, response needed, etc.), and how to ensure open communication channels for the feedback loop to ensure that the message is in fact getting through as intended.

Now you need to think about how you are going to distribute the information—what format to use, what delivery method to use, and the frequency of the distribution. Here are some tips to keep in mind:

- Tell the recipient up-front the purpose of the communication (FYI only, project status, decision required, input needed, etc.).
- Write the message as a news reporter would. Start with the most important information first, followed by deeper levels of detail or background.
- Have a clear communications plan and stick to it.
- Keep the message simple and concise. Use active voice instead of passive voice, and pay attention to your writing style. For example, using all capital letters seems like you are yelling; using all lowercase letters seems like you are either uneducated or don't care.

- Send the information only to the person who needs to take action, and copy only those people who have a need to know.
- Avoid streaming (or stacking) emails that have been forwarded and replied to several times already. To keep your response clean and to the point, delete the previous unnecessary messages when you reply.
- Use an action word or phrase in the subject line of the email: Action Required, FYI Only, At Your Convenience, Response Due By, and so on.
- Avoid using the "Reply to All" button unless you are certain everyone should know.
- Avoid sending and responding to emails after midnight or when you are tired or frustrated. They will likely miss the point, be confusing, or not be written in an appropriate "tone."
- Use effective meeting management techniques by sending out agendas, staying on time, and capturing and posting the minutes to the meeting (this is very important).
- Work on your presentation skills and facilitation techniques to be effective when running meetings.
- Remember that anything you send becomes public record instantly—even if you've sent it confidentially to one person.

Be sure you set some ground rules, communicate them to the team, and then make sure you follow these rules to set a good example. You should be familiar with the many dimensions of the communication activity, which include the following:

- Internal (within the project) and external (clients, other project team members, the public)
- Formal (reports, memos, briefings) and informal (emails, open discussions, phone calls)
- Vertical (up and down the organization) and horizontal (to peers, vendors)
- Official (newsletter, annual report) and unofficial (off-the-record communications)
- Written and oral (including sending text messages)
- Verbal and nonverbal (voice inflections, body language)

I talked earlier about building your skills to help you improve communication. Here are some communication skills you may want to develop or refine:

- Active listening (effective two-way communications)
- Questioning by probing ideas and situations so they are better understood and more effective. Keep asking "Why?" until you have a clear understanding.
- Education, training, and mentoring to increase knowledge and awareness
- Fact-finding to identify or confirm information
- Setting and managing expectations

- Resolving conflict to prevent any disruptive impact on the project
- Summarizing, recapping, and identifying the next steps

Manage Communications Tools and Techniques

Figure 10.5 shows an overview of the inputs, tools and techniques, and the outputs for the Manage Communications process. The *PMBOK* lists a sample of tools and techniques in this process.

FIGURE 10.5 Manage Communications Process ITTOs

- **Communications technology.** The choice of technology is an important consideration in the Manage Communications process. For example, say you have a younger project team and they are used to texting for real-time communications and with that comes a whole new language, including acronyms such as "LOL." Because of this you may need to adjust your communications technology; in other words, get on the bandwagon and learn more about texting and the language associated with this technology.
- **Communications models.** There are several communications models out there to choose from. For example, a *linear* model assumes that there is a clear-cut beginning and end to communication. It also displays no feedback from the receiver. A *transmission* model (or standard view of communication model), is sent in some form (as spoken language) from a sender to a receiver. This model allows for ongoing feedback between the sender and receiver. Barnlund (1970) proposed a *transactional* model of communication. The basic premise of the transactional model is that individuals are simultaneously engaging in the sending and receiving of messages (such as email or text messages).[5] And there are many others as well.
- **Communications methods.** For example, individual and group meetings, conferences, computer chats, texting, IM'ing, and other remote methods.
- **Information management systems.** For example, hard copy, soft copy (electronic), reverse 911 calls, and websites.

- **Performance reporting.** The act of collecting and distributing performance information, including status reports, progress measurements, and forecasts. Reports should be provided at the appropriate level for the intended audience. If a high-level manager simply wants to know if the project is on time and on budget, for example, a milestone report would be a much more fitting response than would a detailed specification report.

Manage Communications Outputs

Outputs from this process include project reports, presentations, records, feedback from stakeholders, and lessons learned documentation.

What Happens When We Don't Communicate Clearly?

Have you ever said something and didn't get the reaction you thought you would? Or have you said something that didn't come out clearly as planned? We have all experienced those embarrassing moments.

Here are a few tips to help you avoid classic communication blunders. The following are things you *don't* want to do:

- **Say too little.** The "I'm the leader, just trust me" line doesn't work these days. People usually do trust you, but they want to hear your thinking and reasoning.
- **Say too much.** You don't have to give every detail to every person. For most people, keep the discussion at a high level.
- **Talk to the wrong people.** You have to target your communication. For example, you don't want to tell the sponsor about the technical details if all the sponsor wants to hear is the current project status (is the project on schedule and on budget?). (Don't explain how to build a watch to someone who just wants to know the time.)
- **Lose sight of emotional impact.** Remember, when things are changing, emotions run high. Statements can be made that have lots of energy. Give people time to emotionally adjust to the change.
- **Rush the process.** Because you are the leader, you probably have processed the information before anyone else. Your grief, excitement, or passion is behind you. It's easy to rush others, expecting them to catch up. Give them time.
- **Look away or look uninterested.** Your nonverbal actions must be consistent with your spoken message. Ralph Waldo Emerson said it well: "What you do speaks so loudly that I cannot hear what you say."
- **Have bad timing.** Delivering the right solution at the wrong time can get you in trouble. It is like telling a joke: the punch line has to be in the right place at the right time for it to be funny. The same is true in when and how you communicate.

- **Use unconscious or distracting body language.** See the sidebar "Five Body Language Tips from the Presidential Debates."

Five Body Language Tips from the Presidential Debates

In general, we look for leaders who exhibit two sets of nonverbal signals: status and warmth. When we see status cues (broad arm movements, physical height, bold stride, decisive gestures, etc.), we feel the leader has confidence and authority. When we see warm body language (smiles, raised eyebrows, head tilts, smooth gestures, etc.) we believe the leader is empathetic and caring.

Both Hillary Clinton and Donald Trump display nonverbal behaviors that are considered "good" for a presidential candidate, both have body language challenges, and both have areas where their nonverbal strengths become liabilities. But these generalized strengths and weaknesses pale in comparison to the power of the beliefs and expectations of their respective supporters.[6]

Communication Blockers/Barriers

According to a fellow instructor, "People are free to interpret things according to their own frames of reference (everyone has different filters)."

The vague words in Table 10.4 can create huge misunderstandings and conflict. How do you avoid using vague words, terms, or phrases? Practice thinking about what you say and how you say it; then work on ways to say it without the use of vague terms. Another thing to keep in mind is the use of adverbs. Adverbs, when used as modifiers of verbs, are ambiguous. For example, if he quickly ran, then just how fast did he run? Adverbs do not answer the question of "to what degree or extent?" It is also important to remember that adjectives used as descriptors are relative to a reader's experiences. For example, by describing a person as tall without specifying a height allows the reader to draw on their own imagination, which may be different from that of the next person.

TABLE 10.4 Vague Words

soon	often	a lot	many	better
worse	bad	good	like	similar
later	difficult	easy	more	less
faster	efficient	timely	always	never
nice	stuff	things	everyone	guys

When possible, replace vague generalizations with more specific and concise wording, such as using measure of performance (MOPs). For example: The key deliverables of the project are to (1) reduce cost of services by 10 percent, (2) increase reliability by 12 percent, (3) increase market share by 10 percent, (4) deliver 90 percent of the test script by Friday noon to the tester for use in the acceptance test this weekend, and so on. Any time you can add specific measurements, it will take the guesswork out of the equation and help ensure best results.

Monitor Communications Process (Monitoring and Controlling Process Group)

Monitoring Communications is the process of ensuring that the information needs of the project and its stakeholders are met. One of the best ways to communicate is through project status or performance reports.

Reporting project performance involves collecting and distributing performance information, including status reports, measurements, and forecasts.

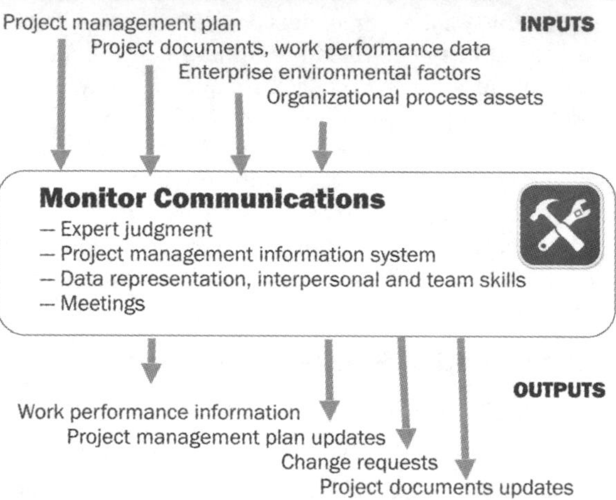

FIGURE 10.6 Monitor Communications Process ITTOs

Performance reports need to provide the stakeholders with an appropriate level of information according to their level of involvement in the project. One size doesn't always fit all when it comes to project reports.

Figure 10.6 shows an overview of the inputs, tools and techniques, and the outputs for the Monitor Communications process.

Ask the Expert

Q: My client continues to ask for more and more reports, more details, and in various formats. This has required me to assign a full-time person to generate all the reports for my project. What can I do to get this under control?

A: I recommend meeting with the key stakeholders and determining which reports are essential and which are just nice to have. If there are mixed results, take a vote or, worst case, stop sending what you and the team view as nonessential reports and see who complains. Another option is to determine the impact to the project (e.g., extra time and cost) and write a proposal to charge more for the additional reports. That should get someone's attention. If the stakeholders are not willing to pay extra, then reduce the number of reports and the problem is solved.

Tip

Performance reports are essential to the success of the project. Their importance is evident in the number of times performance reports show up in the *PMBOK* (over 50 times). Performance reports are referenced as inputs and outputs to many processes in many Knowledge Areas, such as integration management, risk management, HR, and communications. Therefore, you can expect a number of questions on these reports in the PMP (Project Management Professional) and CAPM (Certified Associate in Project Management) exams.

Monitor Communications Outputs

The primary output from the Monitor Communications process is work performance information in the form of actual performance reports. Reports are created and distributed at different intervals and to different stakeholder audiences. (See the list of report types shown below for details.)

The reports you create and distribute on your project will more than likely be customized to meet your needs and the needs of the stakeholders.

There is an old saying that goes something like this: "A job is never done until the paperwork is complete." The paperwork makes the finding or results real and auditable; it is the glue that keeps the project together.

Types of Performance Reports

The types of reports that go to the various stakeholders depend on a number of factors, including the size of the project, level of criticality, and impact to the community. Reports come in many types, and the following list shows only a few areas of focus for performance reports (according to PMI):

- Current status for project progress (usually reported on a weekly basis)
- Previous project performance analysis (trends, lessons learned, etc.)
- Risk and issue logs to know where the threats and opportunities might be
- Work completed during the period (earned value reports, percentage complete, etc.)
- Summary of changes reviewed, approved, and implemented during the period
- Specific approved measurements or metrics (e.g., schedule and budget results)
- Plan versus actual charts with variance analysis against the approved baseline
- Forecast reports, such as ETC (estimate to complete) and EAC (estimate at completion)
- Other relevant information, as needed, for review and discussion

Forecasting Methods

Forecasting involves dusting off your crystal ball to look at the future and determine if the current status is going to affect the future outcome of the project.

Several methods can be used to forecast your project:

- **Time series methods.** These methods involve the use of historical data as the basis for estimating the future (e.g., earned value, moving average, extrapolation, trend estimating, and various growth curves).
- **Causal/econometric methods.** These methods make the assumption that it is possible to identify the underlying (root cause) events that may affect the outcome. For example, the sales of ski passes are affected by the amount of snowfall at any given time. Some examples include linear and nonlinear regression, autoregressive moving average (ARMA), and econometrics.
- **Expert judgment methods.** These methods use the intuitive judgments of subject matter experts for cost estimates, probability and impact estimates, time estimates, and so on. Some tools and techniques used in this type of forecasting are the Delphi method, technology forecasting, and analogy forecasting (top-down from similar previous projects).

Other methods include simulation modeling, probabilistic forecasting, and ensemble forecasting.

Summary of Project Communications Management

Remember the importance of good two-way communications and that project managers spend about 90 percent of their time communicating. In the world of real estate, the famous motto is "location, location, location." In the world of project management, the motto should be "communication, communication, communication."

And don't forget the importance of listening. To be better communicators, we have to learn to listen. After all, you were given two ears and only one mouth, so you should listen twice as much as you talk.

When I first became a PM, I felt that I was not contributing to the work of the project. Sure, I was busy scheduling meetings, talking to stakeholders, preparing reports, running the numbers, and keeping track of the budget and schedule, but this didn't feel like real work. Then one day a team member said, "This project would fall apart without the work you do to organize, coordinate, and communicate what needs to be done." It was then I realized my worth on the project and accepted the fact that true project management involves managing the flow of communications, like a conductor of an orchestra.

So raise your baton and direct your team to success through effective communications management.

References

1. Raymond S. Pastore, "Principles of Teaching," *Teacherworld.com* (Spring 2003), http://teacherworld.com/potdale.html, accessed March 14, 2017.

2. "Nonverbal Communication," *Wikipedia*, http://en.wikipedia.org/wiki/Nonverbal_communication, accessed March 14, 2017.

3. "Explore Second Life," *Second Life*, http://secondlife.com/, accessed March 14, 2017.

4. "Project Communication Plan," *Princeton Project Methodology* (rev. October 3, 2003), *www.jrm4.com/FSU_Courses/LIS4910/communicationplan.odt*, accessed March 14, 2017.

5. "Models of Communication," *IACACT*, http://www.iacact.com/?q=models, accessed March 14, 2017.

6. Carol Kinsey Goman, "Body Language in the Presidential Debate Reveals More about Us Than about the Candidates," *Forbes* (September 27, 2016), https://www.forbes.com/sites/carolkinseygoman/2016/09/27/body-language-in-the-presidential-debate-said-more-about-us-than-about-the-candidates/#4bc84d531341, accessed March 14, 2017.

11 Project Risk Management

Key Skills & Concepts

- Definition of risk (uncertainty)
- Risk factors
- Threats and opportunities
- Risk tolerances and thresholds
- Risk management processes
- Risk identification
- Risk types and categories
- Probability and impact analysis
- Expected monetary value
- Monte Carlo analysis
- Decision tree analysis
- Contingency plans

Risk is often defined as "uncertainty" (a lack of knowledge about a potential event that can cause a positive or negative impact to the project). As mentioned previously, risk management must be done early and often. Risk is always considered to be in the future. It can have one or many causes and often has a cascading effect on other elements of the project. Risk management should be conducted as a team. It should be planned thoroughly because risk comes in many different flavors and most of the time can leave a very bad taste in your mouth (by costing you the project). The upside is you can minimize risks by following a few simple processes.

When is the last time your project team sat down and talked about risk? We are so focused on specific events and activities on the project that we rarely just talk about risk in general.

The bad news is risk is all around us; it is lurking in every corner and can happen at any time. Yet, for some reason, proactive risk management is often not formally practiced in projects; it is only discussed after a risk event has occurred.

Tip

Risk management is viewed as one of the toughest areas of the PMP exam. This is true for a couple reasons. The first reason is that PMI assumes that you and the team are managing risk (it is a given). However, the reality is that only a small percentage of projects in the real world actually have a risk management plan. The second reason is lack of experience. We hope we never encounter serious risks, so we tend to ignore or avoid them. Therefore, there are not a lot of experts in this field. Paying close attention to the material in this chapter will help you manage risk more effectively and score higher on the PMP exam.

When you get up in the morning and start down the stairs for that first cup of coffee, you probably aren't thinking about whether the kids forgot to put away their toys or whether the dog is still fast asleep on the top step, perhaps causing you to stumble and fall. Threats are everywhere. The really good news is that our brains and senses are constantly scanning (like radar) and will pick up potential danger without our even realizing we are doing it. A large number of accidents are avoided due to this internal radar and our quick reactions during times of danger.

The same is true on projects. In managing risk, a good project manager (PM) is constantly on the lookout for risk events, probability, impact, timing, gaps, or potential threats and opportunities.

Risk Factors

To be better risk managers, we need to better understand risk factors. Here are the primary factors to risk that always need to be considered on your project:

- The risk event itself (R)
- The probability (P) of occurrence
- The range of possible outcomes (impact [I] or amount at stake)

Other key considerations are *timing* and anticipated *frequency* of occurrence. Timing is an important consideration because the probability and impact change dramatically, depending on time of year (e.g., weather is a bigger risk for outdoor events such as picnics and weddings).

Threats, Opportunities, and Triggers

It is important to know that PMI views risk as not just a *threat* (negative event) but an *opportunity* (positive event). With proper planning, risk can be managed effectively with substantially reduced impact to the project. This means we have to think and talk about risk. We must plan for, train for, and be proactive about managing risk.

Most people have a pretty good idea about threats. A threat is a risk that has a negative impact on the project if it occurs. But how can a risk be an opportunity? Opportunities are risks that have a positive impact on the project should they occur. Here's a list of opportunities that can arise from risk:

- A supplier is out of stock for the building materials you ordered, and they upgrade the order to a higher-quality product.
- A team member retires and is replaced by someone with more experience, at less cost.
- A meeting is postponed and moved to a new location at a local branch office instead of at an expensive hotel.
- An ice hockey event is canceled because the team doesn't make the playoffs, and a professional rodeo agent calls to schedule the events center for the same dates that had been reserved. The rodeo event draws a large crowd in what would otherwise have been an empty arena.

Note

It is said that up to 90 percent of threats that are identified and analyzed by the project team during the risk management processes can be eliminated.

How can you predict when a risk is about to happen? The best way is to look for risk triggers. A trigger is a symptom or an early warning sign that indicates that a risk has a high probability of occurring. A trigger can simply be noise around the water cooler (that is, people talking and then stopping when the PM or a customer walks by), which may be a sign that there are staffing or other problems. Other triggers include market trends, foreclosures on housing (which have a ripple effect on the banking industry), or a series of budget cuts or resource actions that might signal that a company is thinking about a merger or reorganization. Any of these triggers should raise suspicions about the budget, staffing, or support on a project.

Identifying risk triggers is a critical team activity that creates team understanding of when risk events are about to occur. It can help the project team know when to implement a planned risk response strategy, under the Monitor Risk process.

In 1984 I was assigned to participate on the project team to set up and maintain a number of computer systems to score the Olympic Summer Games at 26 venues in the greater Los Angeles area. One of the first things we did was to sit down as a team (remember, risk is a team sport) and start identifying risks, such as traffic jams, communications and power blackouts, equipment failure, weather, and so on. The list was long, but we went through the risk management processes to make sure we had a plan for if (or when) the risk events occurred.

The project team felt that we did a pretty good job of identifying the risks, who would own the response strategy, the action items, and how we were going to ensure back-up plans so the Olympic scoring could go on. But we missed acting on a simple trigger—a damp, musty smell in a storage room (see the Try This element below for more details).

Watching for triggers (such as the damp smell in the storage room) and having a good mitigation plan would have helped reduce the risk probability or negative impact to the project. A good proactive mitigation plan would be to cover the equipment in the storage room with plastic in the event of rain or other potential contamination.

The project team in 1984 missed the trigger and didn't identify or mitigate this risk event. The team used hair dryers to blow-dry the equipment in the storage room. We learned our lesson.

Try This

DON'T RAIN ON MY PROJECT

You are a PM working at the Olympics. You come in one morning after a long steady rain the night before to find that the storage building where your computers, tools, and other equipment are stored is soaked. The roof leaked, and water is all over everything. What do you do?

A. Look at your project risk plan to see who was assigned to this risk event and then work with the risk owner to respond to the risk based on their documented response plan.

B. Look for someone to blame.

C. Gather the team to discuss a recovery plan.

D. Order new equipment, fast.

Answer: A. If you have planned properly, the risk event will have been identified, the owner assigned, and a response strategy will have been documented and approved.

Be Proactive: Plan for Risk and Mitigate Wherever Possible

Talk about being proactive—let's look at a risk event that could have cost 155 lives. It is hard to believe a few birds could take down an 85-ton airplane, but they did. I am sure you remember the 2009 incident dubbed the "Miracle on the Hudson," when a jetliner lost both engines in collisions with birds shortly after takeoff and made an emergency landing on the surface of the Hudson River in New York City: "When US Airways Flight 1549 was forced to make a splash landing in the Hudson River on Thursday, January 15, cool heads [Captain Chesley Sullenberger III] prevailed and what could have been an immense tragedy turned into 10 minutes of teamwork that has awed the nation."[1]

Even though airline pilots train for emergency situations in simulators, when you lose both engines in a real airplane just minutes after takeoff, the odds are against you. On Flight 1549, the pilot's training and experience really paid off. That is risk response at its finest.

Ask the Expert

Q: I am the PM on a project to mitigate the risk of bird strikes to airplanes at my local airport. What do I do first?

A: You start by doing your homework by first identifying the problem. You would find that bird strikes occur mostly around airports. Bird and other wildlife strikes to aircraft annually cause well over $700 million in damage to US civil and military aviation. Furthermore, these strikes put the lives of aircraft crew members and their passengers at risk: over 250 people have been killed worldwide as a result of wildlife strikes since 1988.[2] You also find that reports estimate that only 20 percent of all wildlife strikes are reported to the FAA. Therefore, the problem is bigger than the reports show.

Next, as a short-term solution you recommend that the airport use an integrated approach, with habitat modification, such as maintaining a consistent low grass height, as well as using noisemakers and other scare devices to drive birds away. Additionally, you would want to verify that pilots have a minimum number of hours spent in a simulator to practice how to deal with bird strike situations. Last, you might want to get a team of engineers together to determine ways to design deflectors of sorts to minimize the probability and impact to the airplane. Risk management is the key.

Risk Averse or Risk Prone (Which Are You?)

The sample project about mitigating bird strikes at an airport is a project that needs a project manager who is "risk averse." You want a perfectionist when it comes to people's lives. A person who is risk averse is someone who doesn't want to take risks.

On the other side of the coin are the people or companies that are willing to take risks. Thrill seekers who perform extreme sports (skydivers, race car drivers, etc.) or PMs who don't take the time to plan for risk are risk prone.

Appetite, Tolerance, and Threshold

If you have an appetite for risk, then you are willing to accept greater risks for greater rewards. Some years ago a friend of mine was involved with a research project exploring the use of open-source software modules to reduce development time. Open-source code can be problematic, but the potential savings in time and cost were deemed worthwhile by the customer. By assuming greater risk, the customer received a product without any licensing restrictions in a shorter amount of time and for less cost.

Risk tolerances are the areas of risk that are either acceptable or unacceptable. For example, a risk in health or safety for a company in the food-processing or drug-manufacturing business is totally unacceptable. There are some risks we are not willing to tolerate.

Risk thresholds, on the other hand, refer to the degree of risk a person or company is or is not willing to accept. In some cases a company's secret to success is tied to its willingness to take risks. This is especially true in the technology sector, where the name of the game is to push the envelope on new-product development to be the first to market whenever possible to gain market share. In this case risk thresholds must be high to achieve higher success and innovation. In the article "On The Edge: Setting the Thresholds," Carl Pritchard states the following:

> In establishing project plans (and more specifically, risk plans), project managers need to recognize the importance of elements that go beyond basic risk identification and assessment. One critical issue we often miss out on is the notion of the risk threshold. How much can we stand? How much of a schedule delay is too much? How much of a cost overrun can the organization tolerate? The formal, pat answer is often "no overruns are acceptable." But that's not realistic. Most projects can withstand some small overruns in terms of schedule or cost, or some small shortcomings in terms of requirements. Those represent our thresholds.[3]

Another way to show thresholds for identified risks is to determine their risk scores. You simply multiply probability by impact and then compare the risk score to the approved thresholds.

Approved thresholds for risk should be set depending on the size, type, and criticality of the project. There are many risk tools that assist in determining the risk score based on certain criteria. Often the scores are set in risk priority categories such as high/medium/low, red/yellow/green, or a numerical range from 1 to 10 or even 1 to 100 for more complex scoring. No matter what scoring system you or your company uses, the key is to have clearly defined thresholds and response strategies to align with the score.

Project Risk Management Processes

Project Risk Management includes seven processes, according to *PMBOK Guide Sixth Edition*, and includes conducting risk planning, identification, analysis (qualitative and quantitative), response strategy, implementing risk responses, and monitoring the project risks.

The majority of the processes (five of seven) are in the Planning Process Group, as you would imagine. A new process has been added in the sixth edition of *PMBOK Guide* and it is Implement Risk Response, which is in the Executing Process Group. The last process is the Monitor Risks process, which is in the Monitoring and Controlling Process Group.

Be careful to not let this preponderance of emphasis during the planning phase dull you to the critical importance of managing risks throughout the life of your project. You should plan to have at least weekly meetings to review your risk log. Otherwise, you will suffer a predictable fate we know as out of sight, out of mind, which equals missed risks and a higher probability of project failure!

The risk management processes are as follows:

- **11.1. Plan Risk Management (Planning Process Group).** Define how the team will perform risk management.
- **11.2. Identify Risks (Planning Process Group).** Determine which risks could occur and may affect the project.
- **11.3. Perform Qualitative Risk Analysis (Planning Process Group).** Analyze the risks identified and prioritize them to see which risks need further review or action based on probability and impact.
- **11.4. Perform Quantitative Risk Analysis (Planning Process Group).** Analyze the risks in numerical terms to see which ones potentially have the highest impact on project objectives.
- **11.5. Plan Risk Responses (Planning Process Group).** Create and document options and actions to enhance opportunities and reduce threats to the project's objectives.
- **11.6. Implement Risk Responses (Executing Process Group).** Implement (and execute) agreed-upon risk responses according to the plan should the risk event occur.
- **11.7. Monitor Risks (Monitoring and Controlling Process Group).** Make sure you have a risk strategy plan for how you and the team will monitor risks and that you also have a response strategy in place that can be effectively measured and tracked to ensure there are no surprises (as always, it is important to be on the lookout for new risks or the ripple effects from existing risks should they occur).

These processes are interactive with other processes in other Knowledge Areas. Risk management crosses all boundaries and can affect scope, schedule, cost, quality, and so on.

By now I am sure you get the importance of risk management, and with something this important you can expect many questions on the PMP exam. The best way to lock in on the processes is to memorize the order and how they tie to the Process Groups. You should remember the inputs, tools and techniques, and outputs to the processes, the risk factors, and response strategies (all of which are covered later in this chapter).

Plan Risk Management Process (Planning Process Group)

The first process in the Project Risk Management Knowledge Area is Risk Management Planning. The Plan Risk Management process involves deciding how to approach, define, plan, and execute the risk management activities for the project. As with many other processes, this one is definitely a team sport. With this process, the more stakeholders you have involved and the earlier in the life cycle the better. Key players such as the PM, sponsor, team, customer, and subject matter experts (SMEs) should take part in the planning process.

The amount of time spent and the number of resources involved in this process will vary based on a number of variables, such as the priority of the project, the overall size and complexity of the project, and the potential impact to the company, team, or community.

Tip

You might see a question on an exam that goes something like this: "The highest level of risk is encountered during which Process Group (or which phase of the project)?" Answer is the Initiating group. The earlier you are in the project life cycle, the higher the degree of uncertainty and the higher the risk. Another reason risk is higher at the beginning of a project is that there are many unknowns and that a decision made early in the project life cycle can take you down the wrong path, which often leads to higher cost, delayed schedule, and misuse of resources.

Plan Risk Management Data Flow

When planning for risk and how to manage it on your project, it is best to start by developing a risk management plan. The plan should include the interaction and dependencies across the various Knowledge Areas, people, departments, and organizations to ensure a clear picture of how you plan to identify, analyze, and manage risk on your project.

Plan Risk Management Inputs, Tools and Techniques, and Outputs

There are a number of inputs to consider during the Plan Risk Management process with several tools and techniques; however, there is but a single output. You may recall that inputs to a process are sometimes the output or outputs from the previous process, so a common thread exists between processes. This should help you when it comes time to study for the exam. Figure 11.1 shows an overview of the inputs, tools and techniques, and the outputs for the Plan Risk Management process.

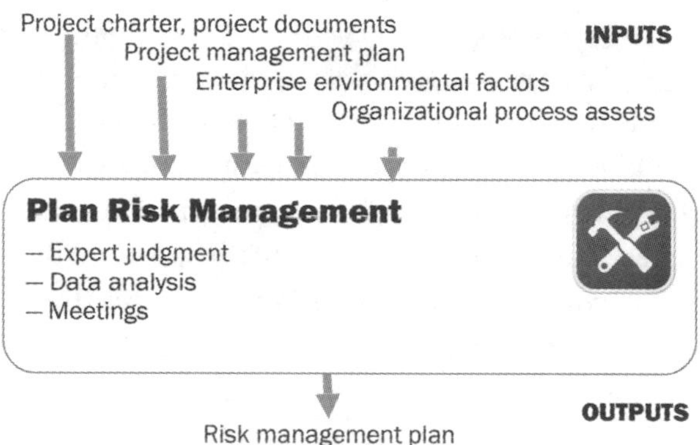

FIGURE 11.1 Plan Risk Management Process ITTOs

INPUTS

As important as inputs are for any process to be successful, inputs to risk management are essential. Note that in the case of risk management, there are inputs to the overall process as well as to each internal process. For example, historical information and lessons learned from previous projects may be relevant and are inputs to the overall risk management process. They should be reviewed prior to beginning the specific project planning process.

Remember that inputs should answer the following question: "What information, data, and resources do I need before I can begin this project (or process)?" All current and previous plans for the project should be considered when planning for risk management. In addition to the list of inputs shown in Figure 11.1, the following list breaks out the inputs for enterprise environmental factors and organizational process assets as they pertain to risk management:

- Enterprise environmental factors include attitude toward risk, tolerances, and the degree of risk (thresholds) the team or organization can accept.
- Organizational process assets include risk categories specific to the project, common definitions, templates, standards, concepts, and terms (potential penalties) of the contract.

RISK CATEGORIES (OR SOURCES OF RISK)

There are several categories of risk (sometimes referred to as *sources* of risk):

- **Internal.** Risks inside the project or organization (staffing/resource availability, other constraints, changes to the project, lack of proper planning, etc.).

- **External.** Risks outside the project team or organization (environmental factors, regulatory agencies, weather, shift in consumer demand, etc.). These risks can be predictable or unpredictable (see Table 11.1).
- **Technical.** Risks due to changes in technology, system upgrades, configuration, infrastructure, and support.
- **Unforeseeable.** Even though most risks can be identified, there is always a small percentage (approximately 10–15%) of risks that cannot be predicted.

TABLE 11.1 External Risk Examples

External Predictable	External Unpredictable
Market risks	Government or regulatory compliance
Operational risks	Unusual natural disasters
Environment impacts	Vandalism and sabotage
Inflation or currency exchange rates	Political unrest and labor strikes
Taxes	Supplier availability (bankruptcy, mergers, etc.)

Another way to help identify or categorize risk is by source. Looking at risk from its source (from the customer, supplier dependencies, and poor working conditions) might help you align the risk specifically with the potential impact to your project (cost, schedule, scope). A risk may also cross categories; for example, a lack of skilled resources can affect cost, quality, and schedule.

During the planning process you must understand that risks are either known or unknown. Risks that are known are those you can identify from previous projects or from common sense. Bird strikes, for example, are a known risk for the airlines. They do happen, and frequently. Therefore, airlines plan for this risk and train how to recover when it occurs.

In the United States, the "Great Flood of 1993" caused a number of levees to fail in Louisiana. This was a known risk. Agencies had performed Monte Carlo computer simulations (explained in more detail later in this chapter) and hundreds of "what-if" scenarios, but the planners determined that it would take a "perfect storm" (multiple events with high intensity) for such an event to happen. Well, it happened. The following is from "The Great USA Flood of 1993" by Lee W. Larson:

> The magnitude and severity of this flood event was simply overwhelming, and it ranks as one of the greatest natural disasters ever to hit the United States. Approximately 600 river forecast points in the Midwestern United States were above flood stage at the same time. Nearly 150 major rivers and tributaries were affected . . . Tens of thousands of people were evacuated, some never to return to their homes. At least 10,000 homes were totally destroyed.[4]

There will always be risks that catch us by surprise. They are considered to be unknown risks and are usually events that haven't happened before or were not even considered during the planning process. Because risk happens, we should plan for both the known and unknown risks. This involves going into the planning process (brainstorming session) open-minded and thinking of things that can go wrong both inside and outside the box.

Unknown risks cannot be managed proactively, which means the project team should create a contingency plan—an estimated budget amount (often referred to as *management reserves*) that is usually held outside the project budget at the management or government level. An example is the Federal Emergency Management Agency (FEMA) emergency funds.

TOOLS AND TECHNIQUES

The tools and techniques used in the Plan Risk Management process include the use of various analytical techniques for data analysis, expert judgment, and meetings. Analytical techniques may include performing a stakeholder risk profile analysis or creating strategic risk scoring sheets. For meetings, you should consider determining the frequency of meetings, an optimal format, and when they should occur. The team comes together to share ideas about what could go wrong on the project, the probability that risk will happen, and the potential impact if or when the risk occurs (analysis).

OUTPUTS

Outputs are the deliverables (finished products or results) of the process. Outputs in all cases should answer the question, "What should we have when the process is complete?" The only output for this Plan Risk Management process is the risk management plan itself, which includes a number of components. Here is a sample list of components:

- **Methodology.** Defines the approach your team plans to take in managing risk, including risk scoring, tracking tools, and other data sources used in performing risk management on your project.
- **Roles and responsibilities.** Defines who the key team members are for risk identification and analysis as well as risk owners for each identified risk in the plan.
- **Budget.** The approved cost management plan and baseline, risk contingency reserves, and so on.
- **Timing.** A description of when and how often risk review meetings should occur.
- **Risk categories.** A simple or detailed list of risks by category that you and your team select to document and track risks. A great way to do this is by using a Risk Breakdown Structure (RBS) to show risks by category or source. A sample RBS is shown in Figure 11.2.

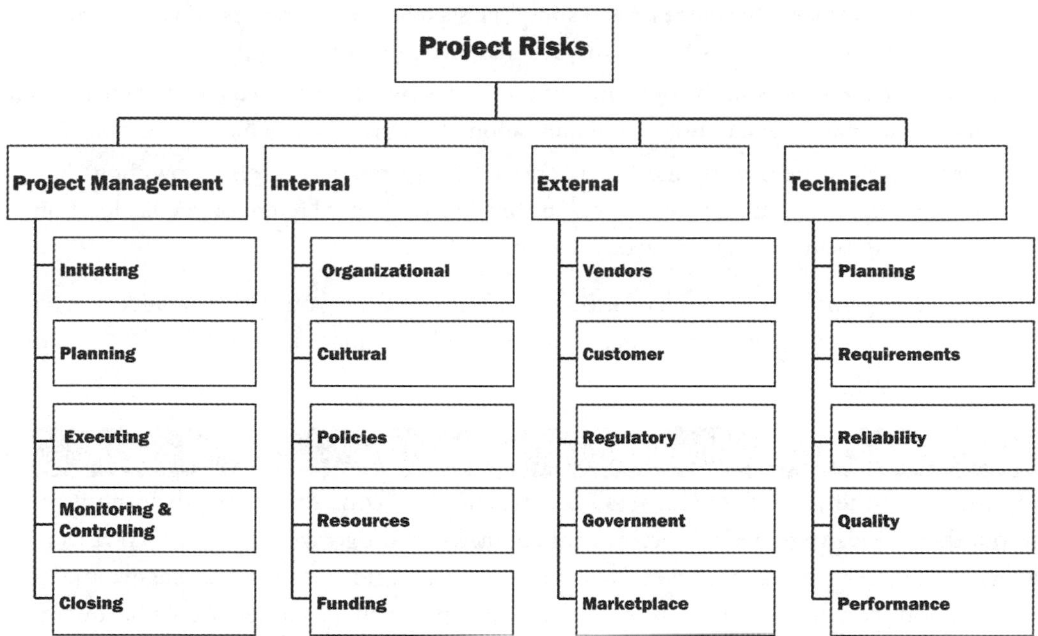

FIGURE 11.2 Sample Risk Breakdown Structure Categories

- **Definitions of risk probability and impact.** Different levels of probability and impact should be defined. Figure 11.3 shows a very simple matrix with associated definitions. These can be elaborated to five or more levels, depending on the complexity of the project and depth of information required by your company or sponsor.
- **Probability and Impact Matrix.** This can be by category and high level at first, or it can be detailed by work package; in either case it's designed to show the risk, probability, and impact. A matrix usually works best, and you can use a numbering system (1–10) or rating system (high, medium, and low) to show the level of risk in a particular area in the matrix. (A sample matrix is shown in Figure 11.3.)

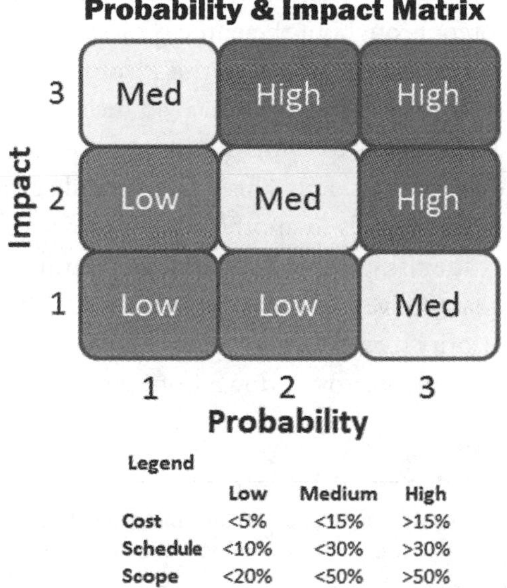

	Low	Medium	High
Cost	<5%	<15%	>15%
Schedule	<10%	<30%	>30%
Scope	<20%	<50%	>50%

FIGURE 11.3 Probability and Impact Matrix

- **Revised stakeholder tolerances.** More about the stakeholder tolerances, learned as you work through the process. So you may need to revise the plan accordingly.
- **Reporting formats.** How the outcomes of the process will be captured and documented for use in the analysis and ultimate communication of the risk management plan.
- **Tracking.** How the risk activities will be tracked and recorded. This also shows how the results will be used for future projects (lessons learned, record retention media, location, duration to store data, and how data are retrieved).

Some great templates are available to assist you in creating your risk management plan. See Figure 11.11 at the end of this chapter for a sample template from CVR/IT Consulting LLC.

Identify Risks Process (Planning Process Group)

In this process the work of the team (all key stakeholders) comes together; they should plan to put their heads together and brainstorm about what can go wrong and which risks may affect the project. This should be a collaborative session, not a traditional passive meeting run by a dominant leader. The session should be planned well, facilitated if possible by someone who can help capture the many potential risks that are identified. You should allow an adequate amount of time; sometimes these sessions go for hours. Also, as mentioned before, this process should begin early (at the onset of the project life cycle) and should be monitored throughout the entire project.

The reason I say the risk identification process session should be facilitated is because ground rules must be clear (no such thing as a bad idea or input, everyone has a voice, etc.). The intent is to think outside the box to collect all possible risks but to not evaluate any of them at this point. This process should be iterative, meaning there should be synergy where one idea leads to another. Don't worry about the prioritization or overall chance or impact of the risks; this will all come out during the analysis process. Analysis (both qualitative and quantitative) will separate out those risks that are high priority, medium priority, and low priority (based on probability and impact). Therefore, you should collect a long list to begin with and narrow it down from there.

Tip

If you see a question on the PMP exam that asks who should be involved in the Identify Risks process, the answer should be all stakeholders, including the customer, sponsor, project team, and so on.

How Do We Identify Risk?

The operative word is *we* in this question. And the answer is to use whatever tools and techniques you and the team can come up with that help to identify risks on your project.

The best way I have found to identify risk is through the facilitated brainstorming session mentioned previously, but I like the interview process as well. There are times when people are not open and candid in a workgroup session; therefore, one-on-one interviews tend to work really well in this situation. If possible, conduct the interview in a quiet location and take time to put the person at ease. Don't allow interruptions, be focused, and be present. When people feel comfortable in a "no-penalty" environment and they know they have your attention, they are more likely to open up with existing issues, concerns, and problems that you need to be aware of during the risk identification process. I have found that a quiet lunch or off-site meeting at a neutral location will help the person feel more at ease and willing to share any perceived and potential risks.

Another way to identify risk is to do your homework by reviewing all project-related documentation. The first thing you should do when assigned to a new or existing project is to review all the documentation available (including the documentation for similar previous projects). Keep in mind that PMI is big on lessons learned.

Consideration for Agile/Adaptive Environments

Some projects, such as software development and other similar projects, have many variables. As such, these projects have a higher degree of uncertainty than more traditional projects. In this case, Agile PMs may use an adaptive approach to manage the work products and cross-functional teams. The goal is to accelerate team and project knowledge by sharing and fully understanding risk in each phase or iteration of the project. Risks often change during each iteration and need to be identified, analyzed, and managed as appropriate during these iterative cycles. Remember that risks change depending on where you are in the life cycle, and as risks are identified it is necessary to update the risk register.

Two Levels of Risks

According to PMI, risks fall into one of two primary classifications:

- **Individual risks.** An uncertain event or condition that, if it occurs, has a positive or negative effect on one or more project objectives.
- **Overall project risks.** The effect of uncertainty on the project as a whole arising from various sources of risk that can impact the outcome of the project positively or negatively.

Ripple Effect

There are times when risks have a ripple effect; they ricochet around and have a residual impact on the project. The project team should be aware of these types of risks and plan accordingly. A ripple effect is an event that can happen both inside and outside the project. The ripple effect can be felt both upstream and downstream from the project and can impact the team, customer satisfaction, milestones, delivery dates, and so on.

Here are some examples:

- **Residual risks.** Risks that remain even after the original risk has been responded to (e.g., water damage that causes mildew or rust).
- **Secondary risks.** Risks that have side effects or cause other risks to occur (e.g., the risk of electrical shock due to a leaky roof).
- **Risk interaction.** Risks that don't play well together. For example, the interaction of two chemicals to clean a storage tank can cause toxic fumes, even resulting in death. Now there is a risk event you don't want to have to address!

Identify Risks Inputs, Tools and Techniques, and Outputs

Like the previous risk management process, this one has many inputs according to PMI. Also, there are many tools and techniques that can be used to help you and the project team identify risk, and the outputs are the risk register, risk report and updates to project documents as appropriate. See Figure 11.4 for an overview of the Identify Risks process inputs, tools and techniques, and outputs for this process.

INPUTS

Remember, when it comes to risk identification, you should look all around for anything that may jump up and impact (hurt or help) the project. Be sure to examine your other project management subplans and supporting project documents to help identify potential risks and sources of risks. Here's a sample list of inputs that should be considered, at a minimum:

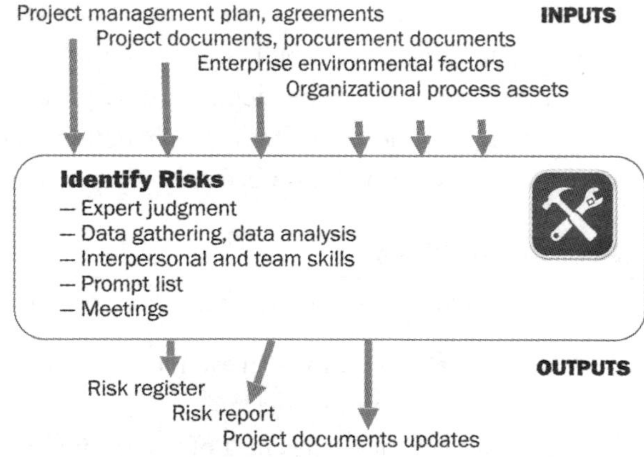

FIGURE 11.4 Identify Risks Process ITTOs

- **Project management plan.** This includes all the key areas of the project plan, such as how the project will be managed, executed, controlled, and ultimately closed.

Other project documents to consider as inputs are shown below:

- **Cost management plan.** Understanding the overall budget and level of priority the project has at the upper-management level will help you identify risks in this area. Look for indicators such as delays in order processing and delayed accounts payable, which can mean that no management approval or financial issues may exist in the company or department.
- **Schedule management plan.** Another great place to look for potential risks. Remember that the schedule is a key component of the project constraints and is often the highest source of conflict on the project.
- **Quality management plan.** Quality requirements pose threats. Therefore, this is a great place to look for potential risks on your project. Remember, quality is defined by the customer as to what is acceptable.
- **Resource management plan.** Yes, people and other resources such as hardware, software, equipment failures, and so on can pose risks to projects, either by not being available or not having the skills mix needed for the project. The resource management plan should fully describe the skills team members must have, a staffing plan, and a transition plan as the project comes to a close and team members are released to other projects.
- **Scope baseline.** The assumptions found in the scope statement that are approved as the baseline (including the WBS and WBS dictionary) are great sources of input to help identify risks.

For more details of inputs for this process see the *PMBOK Guide*.

Tip

High-level risks should have been defined early in the project charter. The best time for the PM to start the detailed risk identification process is during the creation of the work breakdown structure (WBS) (see Chapter 5). By doing these activities together, you may be able to combine two processes into one at the very start of the project.

TOOLS AND TECHNIQUES

Here are some of the tools and techniques used in the Identify Risks process:

- **Expert judgment.** Individuals with expert knowledge of project activities or subject matter experts should help with the risk identification process.
- **Documentation reviews.** This should be a disciplined and thorough review of existing project documentation with a view toward identifying potential risks.
- **Data gathering and analysis techniques.** You have a multitude of ways to gather data and key information about your project. Some of these have already been discussed, but for clarification I list a few of them here:

+ **Brainstorming.** One idea prompts another (synergy).
+ **Interviewing.** Also may be called "expert interviewing" on the exam.
+ **Delphi technique.** This technique provides a way to reach a consensus of experts. Experts participate anonymously through the use of a questionnaire or survey. A facilitator conducts an iterative process to narrow the field of possibilities until a consensus is drawn based on the results from the participating experts.

Tip

You should remember the Delphi technique if you are planning to take the PMP exam.

- **Diagramming techniques.** Various diagrams can be used for risk identification: cause-and-effect diagrams (also known as Ishikawa or fishbone diagrams), system or process-flow charts (show interrelationships), influence diagrams (graphical representations of situations or time-ordered events on the project), and mind mapping.[5]
- **Strengths, weaknesses, opportunities, and threats (SWOT) analysis.** Looks at the overall project to determine where the strengths and the possible weaknesses may exist as well as the opportunities and threats. SWOT analysis examines the project itself as well as the project management processes, various plans, resources, and organizational structures to help identify future risks.
- **Meetings.** This is a good way to get the team engaged and on the same page as far as needs and expectations. The information gathered during meetings with team members and other stakeholders can be used to create a risk register.

Ask the Expert

Q: What are the advantages of creating a risk register?

A: The advantages provided by creating a risk register start with the ability to organize the identified risks in a fashion that will assist in the analysis of those risks. The risk register should document the identified risks, the category (scope, quality, schedule, staffing, etc.), risk triggers (if known), and response strategies, as well as the assigned owner (who will monitor and respond to the risk). The risk register is also a great way to demonstrate your project management control to stakeholders.

OUTPUTS

A sample list of outputs to the Identify Risks process are risk reports, project document updates, and of course the risk register, which is a list of the identified risks and specific information about the risks. It is usually created in list or table format and often contains the following sample list of information (but is not limited to these things):

- **Risk register.** The risks should be described in as much detail as needed and should include the event, probability, impact, expected cause, and priority (to be determined during the analysis processes), including a list of potential responses. The responses should be determined by the assigned owner of the risk event, and responses should be focused on the high-priority risks found during the risk identification and risk analysis processes.
- **Risk report.** It is important to stay on top of risks and to report risks in a timely and accurate manner. The best way to do so is by setting up a risk report that should be reviewed frequently, usually as a team, and discussed in your weekly team meetings.

For details of tools and techniques, and outputs, see the *PMBOK Guide*.

Tip

Consider using a standard sentence structure for describing risk. I suggest something like this:

If **<cause>**, then **<risk>**, resulting in **<effect>**.

Using this simple approach allows you to be very specific in identifying your risks. Then it's much easier to determine mitigation and contingency strategies.

Whether you use this method or another, it's important that when describing a risk, do not use a single noun. I have frequently seen *weather* as a risk. It's hard to identify risk triggers or mitigation and contingency strategies when the description of the risk is so vague.

Better than a one-word descriptor, I feel a better approach is to write out a statement.

"If it rains on the day of the event, participants may not show up, causing a loss of revenue."

To this risk we can attach a seven-day weather report to identify the trigger: storm clouds are predicted. Also, with this description, you can develop mitigation and contingency strategies that could include setting up tents, providing umbrellas from a nearby hotel, moving the event inside, or sliding the event one day or one week.

If we are not specific enough, then we will miss critical triggers and not develop sufficient strategies to resolve.

Perform Qualitative Risk Analysis Process (Planning Process Group)

Qualitative risk analysis is used to assign priorities to the risks your team has identified in the risk register. Risks are prioritized by assessing the probability that each risk will occur and its impact if it does. Remember, always use the work performed in previous processes to help develop each downstream process. (You should recall that PMI calls this *progressive elaboration*. Remember this term.)

Tip

Remember that qualitative analysis is subjective analysis, which depends on judgment to determine or qualify the probability and impact to your project. You should also know that PMI (as does the real world) refers to the terms *probability* and *impact* in a number of different ways (refer to Table 11.2).

Be aware that risk probability and impact can be referred to using different terms (see Table 11.2), especially if you are planning to take a PMI exam.

TABLE 11.2 Other Terms Used for Probability and Impact

Probability	Impact
Likelihood	Consequence
Chance	Effort
Possibility	Outcome
Odds	Results

The Perform Qualitative Risk Analysis process involves an understanding of the stakeholder tolerance and thresholds discussed earlier. As with all risk management processes, this analysis should be performed early and often throughout the project life cycle.

Probability and impact can be determined in many different ways:

- Expert judgment (using people who are SMEs and who are experienced with the risk)
- Cost and time estimates as well as tools such as Monte Carlo analysis (computer simulation)
- Use of previous similar project risks (historical information or lessons learned)
- Delphi technique (mentioned earlier in the discussion of the Identify Risks process)

Probability and Impact Matrix

To determine the probability and impact to the project of the various risks, it is helpful to use a matrix (see Table 11.3). The matrix provides a good way to rate, sort, and rank (in order of priority) the risks that have been identified. The goal is to determine which risks will have the biggest impact on the project. Later, during the Response Planning process, you will assign a risk owner who will develop mitigation and response strategies. Table 11.3 is an example of a risk probability and impact matrix.

TABLE 11.3 Risk Probability and Impact Matrix

Risk	Probability	Impact	Priority	Owner
Staff availability	High	High	1	PM
Scheduling issues	High	High	2	PM and team
Budget acquisition	Med	High	3	Financial analyst
Equipment procurement	Med	Med	4	Asset manager
Creation of training materials	Low	Low	5	Course developer

Perform Qualitative Risk Analysis Inputs, Tools and Techniques, and Outputs

See Figure 11.5 for an overview of the inputs, tools and techniques, and outputs of the Perform Qualitative Risk Analysis process.

INPUTS

Here's a description of some inputs and tools and techniques to be considered when performing qualitative risk analysis:

- **Project management plan.** Including other plan documents such as the risk management plan and the communications plan
- **Project documents.** For example, scope baseline, schedule baseline, issues tracking log and procurement documents from a risk perspective (e.g., new technology, contract services, and the risk register)
- **Enterprise environmental factors.** Industry studies and risk databases
- **Organizational process assets.** Standard templates, common terms, and so on

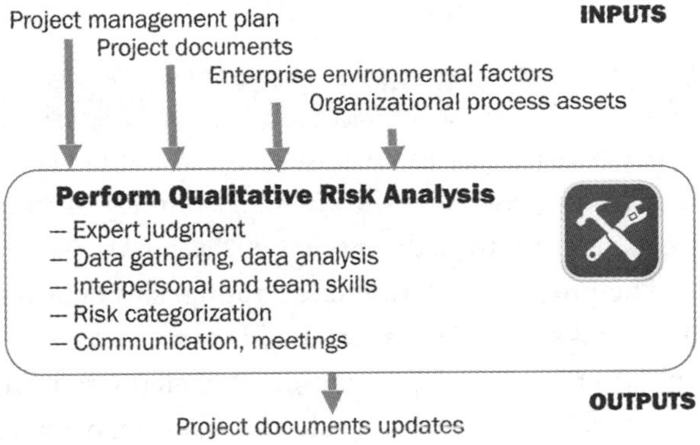

INPUTS
Project management plan
Project documents
Enterprise environmental factors
Organizational process assets

Perform Qualitative Risk Analysis
– Expert judgment
– Data gathering, data analysis
– Interpersonal and team skills
– Risk categorization
– Communication, meetings

OUTPUTS
Project documents updates

FIGURE 11.5 Perform Qualitative Risk Analysis Process ITTOs

TOOLS AND TECHNIQUES

Here are a few of the tools and techniques that can be used in this process:

- **Data gathering and analysis.** Data need to be accurate and unbiased for best results.
- **Risk probability and impact assessment.** This assessment looks into how likely a risk will occur and the magnitude of its impact (positive or negative). Please note that risks may be multifaceted, affecting cost, schedule, scope, quality, and so on.
- **Probability and impact matrix.** Discussed earlier in the "Probability and Impact Matrix" section.
- **Risk categorization.** Categorized by source of risk (use the RBS) or other categories.
- **Communications.** Communicate near-term response strategy for higher-impact risks.
- **Expert judgment.** Not only your knowledge and experience, but the knowledge and experience of others. However, always beware of expert bias. Experts will often have very strong opinions that might not fully reflect the current situation and that might not factor into technology and process improvements.

OUTPUTS

The primary outputs for this process are updates to project documents such as the risk register, cost and schedule plans, and updates to an assumption log, based on any new information acquired. Possible updates within the risk register could include causes of risk, near-term risk response activities, trend information that may be an indicator or trigger for potential risks, and any "watch lists" of lower-priority risks. Risks on the watch list may not require a response plan but are "watched" to see if either the probability or the impact increases, requiring a response.

Perform Quantitative Risk Analysis Process (Planning Process Group)

The Perform Quantitative Risk Analysis process is the numerical view of the effect of the (prioritized) risk events. You assign a numerical rating to only the highest-impact risks (sometimes referred to as the *amount-at-stake risks*).

The purpose of a numerical rating is to determine which risks warrant a response. The list of risks should get shorter and shorter after each wave of analysis. Clearly, you don't have enough time or money to respond to all the risks identified. The qualitative and quantitative analyses help narrow the field to a manageable number based on priority.

This process presents a quantitative (less subjective) approach to making decisions in the presence of uncertainty.

Quantitative Risk Analysis

Depending on the nature or lack of complexity of the project, you might not focus on this process as a separate activity. It might be consolidated with the qualitative analysis (at least during the first wave of the process).

Quantitative analysis includes the following:

- Additional investigation of risks that are rated high for probability or impact
- Further definition of the type, source, or category of risk
- Determining the type of quantitative analysis to be used—the type of probability distribution (normal, triangular, beta, etc.), statistical data, how the data are collected, how the data are tested, and so on
- Sensitivity analysis—determining which risks have the biggest impact (amount at stake)
- Expected monetary value (EMV) or the results of Monte Carlo simulations (discussed later in this chapter) or other computer simulations to determine the possible cost or impact to the project

Perform Quantitative Risk Analysis Inputs, Tools and Techniques, and Outputs

Figure 11.6 shows an overview of the inputs, tools and techniques, and the outputs for the Perform Quantitative Risk Analysis process.

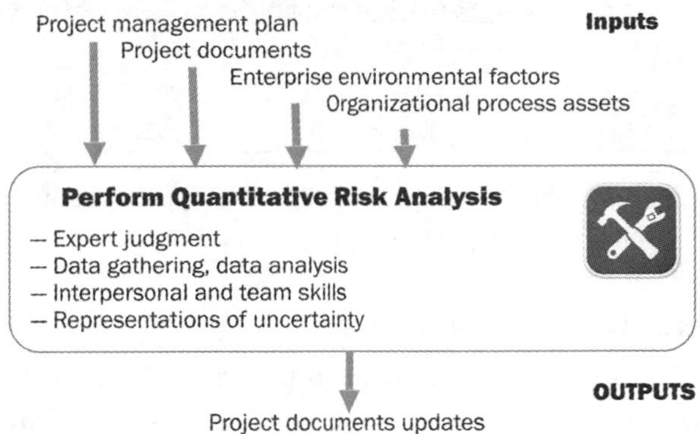

FIGURE 11.6 Perform Quantitative Risk Analysis Process ITTOs

INPUTS

Inputs that apply to this process are the same as for the Perform Qualitative Risk Analysis. For more details of inputs for this process, see the *PMBOK Guide*.

TOOLS AND TECHNIQUES

Here are descriptions of some of the tools and techniques that should be considered in this process:

- **Data gathering and representation techniques.** These include interviewing, data mining, and probability distributions.
- **Interpersonal and team skills.** Since this process involves a lot of data, which often comes from different stakeholders and sources, it is important to work with your team and key stakeholders to obtain, process, and understand the data.
- **Quantitative risk analysis and modeling techniques.** These include sensitivity analysis (also known as *tornado analysis* because of the structure of the chart data), EMV, and *Monte Carlo analysis*, and also strategies for threats and opportunities, contingent response strategies, and decision making based on the information available.
- **Representation of uncertainty.** This is creating the documents, charts, and so on to be able to clearly show the risks in a quantitative manner.
- **Expert Judgment.** This uses SMEs who specialize in quantitative analysis.

Some of the specific tools and techniques (or methods) used in quantitative analysis are shown below.

EXPECTED MONETARY VALUE (EMV)

One of the big questions that always comes up when attempting to manage risk is, "What's it going to cost?" One estimate that can be used to determine this is *expected monetary value* (EMV; see Table 11.4).

TABLE 11.4 EMV Calculations

Work Package	Probability	Impact	Expected Monetary Value (EMV)
1.11.2 Prevent network failure	20%	$10,000	$2,000
1.12.4 Perform system test	30%	$28,000	$8,400
2.5.8 Call Center server failure	50%	$12,000	$6,000

The formula is simple: EMV = P × I (probability times impact). EMV should be estimated for each work package on the WBS.

MONTE CARLO ANALYSIS

Monte Carlo analysis is a computerized mathematical technique used to determine possible outcomes by using random numbers. The simulations allow us to account for risk in quantitative analysis and are often used by professionals in many industries such as project management, finance, energy, engineering, research, and manufacturing in the decision-making process.

Many insurance and financial institutions use this computer software to run actuarial tables and "what-if" scenarios for the cost of premiums, retirement, and investment forecasts.

The Boeing 777 was tested extensively using Monte Carlo simulation software for everything from wing strength to flight capability after a bird strike to the engines.

For information only (as these steps are built into the software application), here are the basic steps involved in a Monte Carlo simulation:

1. Assess the range for the variables and determine the probability distribution.
2. Select a random value for each variable.
3. Run a deterministic analysis.
4. Repeat steps 2 and 3 many times to obtain probability distribution.

Tip

You should know the following regarding Monte Carlo analysis for PMI exams:

- Computer-based software used to quantify the overall risk to the project
- Evaluates the overall risk for the project shown in a probability distribution
- Can provide probability estimates for the project to complete on time or on budget
- Provides the probability of any activity being on the critical path
- Takes into account path convergence
- Translates uncertainties into impact probability on the total project

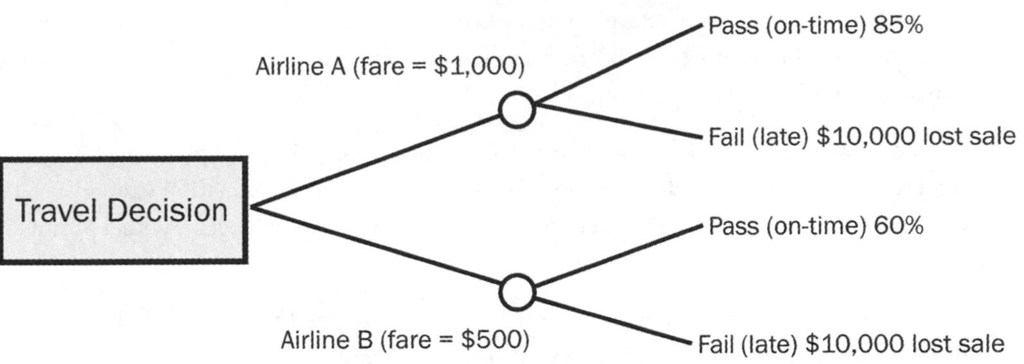

Airline A	(.15 x $10,000 = $1,500) + (.85 x $0.0 = $0.0) + $1,000 = $2,500
Airline B	(.40 x $10,000 = $4,000) + (.60 x $0.0 = $0.0) + $500 = $4,500

FIGURE 11.7 Decision Tree Diagram

DECISION TREE ANALYSIS

Decision trees are primarily used to assist the PM and team in making informed decisions about the risks and the alternatives being considered on the project. See example in Figure 11.7 in which the factors to consider are airline rates of on-time arrival and the risk of losing a sale in the event of a late arrival. Airline B has a lower fare but rates lower in on-time arrival.

A decision tree typically has the following attributes:

- Models a real situation
- Takes into account future events to help you make a decision today
- Can be used to help calculate the expected monctary value (probability times impact)
- Involves mutual exclusivity (where two events are independent of each other)

OUTPUTS

The only output to the Perform Quantitative Risk Analysis process is the updates to the project documents based on any new information acquired. These should include updates to the risk register describing statistical trends, updates to the prioritization list, and probabilistic analysis supported with facts and figures (e.g., the schedule contingency shows the project is in the 78th percentile and is expected to complete on time).

Plan Risk Responses Process (Planning Process Group)

Planning risk responses involves developing options and actions to reduce or eliminate the impact and probability of threats and to enhance opportunities. This process answers (or should answer) the following questions:

- What are we going to do if a particular risk event occurs (contingency planning)?
- Is there something we can do proactively before the risk occurs (mitigation strategy)?
- What can we do to increase the likelihood that an opportunity will occur, with a positive impact?

This process is also where the risk owner (the person assigned the risk) will document a response strategy and action for the risk event should it occur.

Risk Response Strategies

Risk response strategies are sometimes called *risk mitigation strategies*. Regardless of the name, the goal is clear: keep things from breaking and fix them quickly so they don't break again in the future. If something breaks the question becomes, "How can we make it better?"

Risk response strategies are different for threats and opportunities (see Table 11.5). Considering different strategies for responding to a risk can be a real benefit to the project. A Caltrans PM was once facing a potential delay to a new freeway project. The acquisition of property for a frontage road along the side of the freeway was running behind schedule. The project team could not think of a way to mitigate the risk. There were not any agencies or partners to whom they could realistically transfer the risk. Ideally, the PM wanted to just avoid the risk all together. By working with the sponsor, the PM was able to avoid the risk by funding the frontage road as a separate project with a later delivery date. The freeway was delivered on time, and the sponsor was happy because they were able to defer funding the frontage road to a time when funds were more available.

TABLE 11.5 Risk Response Strategies

Response Strategies for Threats	Response Strategies for Opportunities
Avoidance (do what you can to eliminate the threat)	Exploit (reverse of avoidance—seeks to eliminate the uncertainty of the risk, ensuring the opportunity is realized)
Mitigation (reduce probability or impact)	Enhance (reverse of mitigation—increase probability or impact)
Transfer (deflect or allocate; for example, by purchasing insurance)	Share (reverse of mitigation by writing joint responsibility in the contract or agreement)
Accept the risk (do nothing)	Accept the risk (do nothing)

Note

Transferring risk doesn't mean transferring all the ownership and accountability. For example, outsourcing work to a vendor or third-party supplier doesn't let you off the hook for schedule delays or poor workmanship. You are still responsible for the quality of the work. Also, remember that accepting risk may be appropriate for either threats or opportunities.

Risk response strategies vary from case to case and should be adapted to the project situation to the best of your ability. Knowing the cause of a potential risk will assist in formulating a proper response. Say, for example, you have two team members who are not showing up on time to meetings and are not meeting your expectations for performance on the project. In one case (Joan), it appears her performance is affected by a lack of experience and training. In the other case (Joey), it appears he is not interested in working on the project. Because the cause is different for each person, the response strategy you choose will likely be different for each. You may decide to provide additional training and mentoring for Joan but to release Joey from the project. For more examples of risk response strategies, see Table 11.6.

TABLE 11.6 Sample Risk Response Strategies

Description of Risk Response	Response Strategy
Remove a poor performer from the project team.	Avoid
Train team members to improve their performance.	Mitigate
Seek additional funding to cover increased cost of materials.	Accept
Adjust the schedule to allow the use of a more experienced person.	Exploit
Hire a vendor/subcontractor to perform some of the work.	Transfer
Order equipment early to take advantage of better pricing.	Enhance
Work with the customer to ensure requirements are clear and dependencies are met.	Share

Plan Risk Responses Inputs, Tools and Techniques, and Outputs

Figure 11.8 shows examples of inputs, tools and techniques, and outputs for the Plan Risk Responses process. For more details on the ITTOs for this process, see the *PMBOK Guide*.

INPUTS

To expand on the standard inputs such as the project management plan, project documents, enterprise environmental factors, and organizational process assets, here's a list of the more specific inputs that should be considered for this process:

- Risk management plan (including other project plans)
- Risk register
- Strategies for opportunities and/or threats

TOOLS AND TECHNIQUES

Here is a description of some of the tools and techniques that can be used in this process:

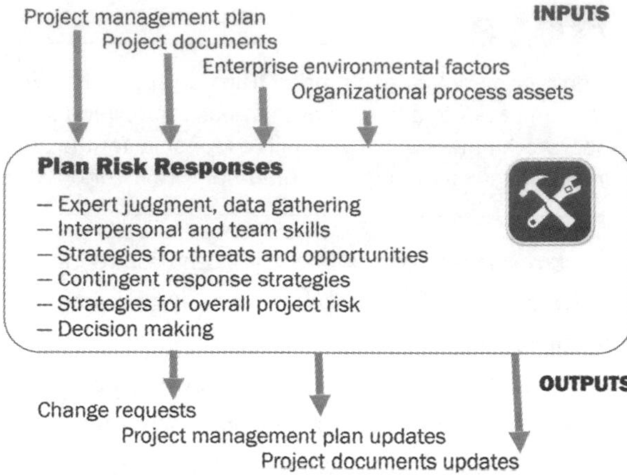

FIGURE 11.8 Plan Risk Responses Process ITTOs

- Strategy for dealing with negative risks and threats (avoid, transfer, mitigate, or accept).
- Strategy for dealing with positive risks and opportunities (exploit, enhance, share, or accept).
- Contingent response strategies (designed for certain events that will be triggered only if a specific event occurs). For example, the loss of a highly skilled expert may require a unique response to obtain a specific-skilled resource replacement.
- Expert judgment.

OUTPUTS

The outputs for this process include updates to the project management plan and other project documents. An important component of those updates may include risk-related contract decisions.

- **Change requests.** New information gathered during this process may lead to changes.
- **Updates to the project management plan and other project documents.**

The information collected from the Plan Risk Responses process will often influence the type of contract selected, the extent of shared risk, amount of insurance needed, or other key decisions.

Regardless of whether you are responding to threats or opportunities, there are some guidelines that should always be followed:

- Responses should be timely and well communicated.
- Responses must be appropriate to the significance of the risk.
- Responses should be cost effective (if possible).
- Responses must be realistic in nature.

- Responses can address multiple risks with a single root cause.
- Responses should involve the team and other stakeholders.

Now the planning is well in hand, the next (and newest) process is the implement risk responses process.

Implement Risk Responses Process (Executing Process Group)

This is the process of contacting the assigned risk owner when an identified risk event occurs and implementing the planned and approved risk response strategy to resolve the risk.

The goal of the implement risk responses process is to minimize individual project threats and to maximize individual project opportunities. One important aspect of this process is to plan ahead and identify a single or primary risk event owner to help identify, estimate, and implement the approved response action when the risk is realized. A good way to keep track of the risks and their status is through the use of a risk register or tracking log to include issues or problems that surface after the risk occurs. The inputs for this process are the project management plan, other project documents, and organizational process assets such as standard forms, tools, or templates. The outputs of this process are change requests and updates to project documents as appropriate.

Figure 11.9 shows an overview of the inputs, tools and techniques, and the outputs for the Implement Risk Responses process.

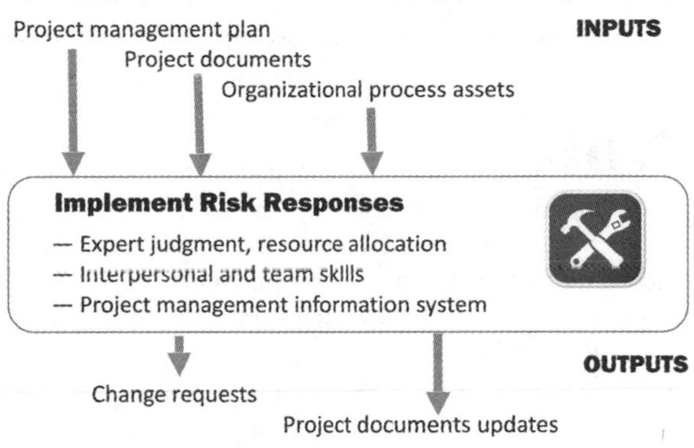

FIGURE 11.9 Implement Risk Responses Process ITTOs

Monitor Risks Process (Monitoring and Controlling Process Group)

After the risks have been identified and analyzed, the owners assigned, and the response strategies documented and communicated, it's time to monitor the risks. This is an ongoing process and needs to be reviewed and updated frequently. I recommend a weekly review, but what you choose depends on your project's length, complexity, and condition (troubled, stable, critical, etc.).

The Monitor Risks process involves monitoring when a risk trigger has occurred, implementing the approved risk response plan, tracking those risks that have been deemed high priority, watching out for all risks (even lower-probability threats in some cases), monitoring residual and secondary risks (ripple effect), and watching for new risks that may surface. To monitor risks effectively, you must be diligent in monitoring all risks, even though the majority of the focus is on those risks identified as most likely to occur or with high impact to the project.

Several tools and techniques are available for monitoring and controlling risks, such as risk assessments, risk audits, variance and trend analysis to look into the future for changes in risk probability and impact, technical performance measurements, reserve analysis, and meetings. Here are some of the questions that need to be asked, answered, and reviewed often during this process:

- Are the assumptions for a particular risk event still valid?
- Has anything changed on the project, such as scope, schedule, cost, staffing, expectations, type of materials, and requirements?
- Are the risk policies and procedures documented and up to date?
- Is the risk management plan being followed and reviewed regularly?
- Are contingency reserves still appropriate and sufficient if needed?

Note

The Monitor Risks process requires all team members to keep a close eye on their areas of the project. It is important to use good management skills to weigh the situation and make decisions about all risk events in a timely manner. The alternatives and options (risk response strategies) have to be clear and must be implemented as needed to meet the challenge of risk management on your project.

Risk Assessment (Reassessment) and Audits

There is a saying that has floated around in the world of project management that goes like this: It is not a matter of *if* your project will be audited, but *when*. This means that at some time in your PM career, you *will* likely be audited. Risk audits are specifically directed toward how you and the team are managing (or have managed) risk. The auditors will want to see your risk register; they will want to see how you identified and analyzed risks. Did you assign owners to the top risks? Did you collect documented risk response strategies for the top risks from the assigned owners?

Ask the Expert

Q: How do the PM and team ensure that they are prepared for an audit?

A: Through risk assessment, reassessment, and audit preparedness. It is important to stay focused on risk by keeping your risk register log up to date and making sure you are effectively tracking and managing project risk (both internal and external to the project as appropriate).

This preparedness also requires that you and the team get (and stay) up to date on all regulatory compliance requirements that may apply to your project. The key is to do your homework, research those areas that apply to your project or industry, and find someone to assist in this process. You do not want to fail an audit.

Regulatory Authority and Agencies

Regulatory authority is a government or public authority responsible for exercising autonomous power over some area of human activity in a supervisory or governing capacity. An independent regulatory agency is usually separate from other branches of the government.

Regulatory agencies deal in administrative rule-making, regulation, and enforcement (such as code enforcement over building codes), and in audit and regulatory compliance supervision. They provide oversight or governance for the benefit of the public at large.

The following is a short list of regulatory agencies that are sometimes involved with auditing projects in their areas of responsibility. For more details go to the Code of Federal Regulations (CFR) website,[6] or perform an Internet search on "regulatory agencies."

The Code of Federal Regulations (CFR) is a compilation of regulations issued by federal departments and includes the following:

- The Federal Communications Commission (FCC) is the US government agency that regulates and enforces the use of radio transmission frequencies (Title 47 CFR).
- Title 21 is the Department of Health and Human Services (DHHS) regulations.
- Title 29 is the Department of Labor regulations.
- The Security and Exchange Commission (SEC) oversees stock transactions and protects investors; maintains fair, orderly, and efficient markets; and facilitates capital formation.
- The Office of the Comptroller of the Currency (OCC) provides advice to help prevent borrowers from becoming victims of foreclosure-rescue scams.
- The US Food and Drug Administration (FDA) protects and promotes health and safety.
- The Sarbanes-Oxley (SOX) Act of 2002 affects how any accounting firm does business. Auditors and accountants pay close attention to the SOX Act when advising any business, large or small, on internal controls over financial reporting.

- The Interstate Commerce Commission (ICC) facilitates the transportation of products and services from one state to geographic points in other states.
- The Occupational Safety and Health Administration (OSHA) of the US Department of Labor facilitates workplace safety and health by issuing and enforcing standards to prevent work-related injuries, illnesses, and deaths.

Tip

The code of regulations and list of regulatory agencies are for reference only and will not likely be on the PMI exam.

Reserve Analysis

Part of risk management is analyzing the reserves needed to respond to or mitigate risk. We talked about reserves in cost management (Chapter 7). As a reminder, there are two types of reserves:

- **Contingency reserves.** Used for known unknowns (possible) risks. Estimated funds are typically held inside the project budget baseline. The response strategy and estimated cost should be clearly documented, monitored, and controlled.
- **Management reserves.** For unknown unknowns (totally unplanned) risks. Estimated funds are typically held outside the project budget baseline and can normally only be accessed with management approval.

Case Study Example

Matt and Jake are seasoned project managers and have many years of experience working on setting up and consolidating help desks (call centers). Even though the approved scope and schedule clearly direct the work of the project, there are times when the PMs are forced to make decisions "on the fly" in order to get the job completed in the most efficient way possible.

For example, during the setup of the new call center in Boulder, Colorado, they experienced a breakdown in communications with one of the subcontractors. The breakdown was on the type of cabling that needed to be run for the network connections to each desk for the call center agents. This mistake caused a major delay in the "go live" (launch) date because the project team had to reorder the correct cables, causing the schedule to slip by two weeks. Every day the crew is standing around waiting on the new cables is costing time and money.

This is one of those times when it is important to have a contingency (fall-back) plan with alternative (backup) options available. In this instance, although the options seem limited, the PMs have planned well; they have established a couple of response strategy options to ensure that the project got completed on time. The options were as follows:

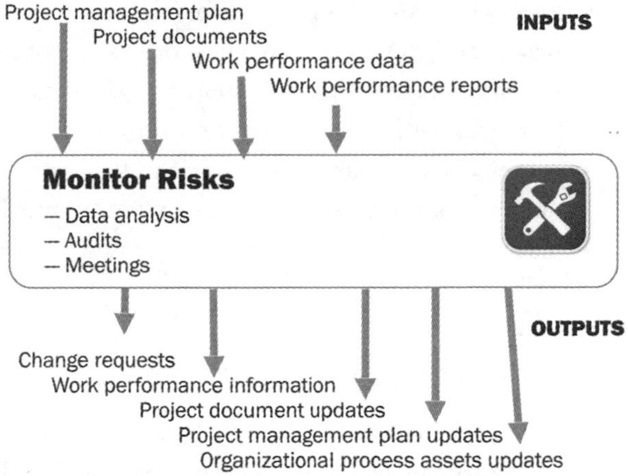

Project management plan
Project documents
Work performance data
Work performance reports
INPUTS

Monitor Risks
— Data analysis
— Audits
— Meetings

OUTPUTS
Change requests
Work performance information
Project document updates
Project management plan updates
Organizational process assets updates

FIGURE 11.10 Monitor Risks Process ITTOs

- **Option A.** Line up a second source supplier for materials that can provide the needed cabling on short notice and make sure the estimated cost of expediting the materials is held in the contingency-reserve fund.
- **Option B.** Use temporary labor to provide late-night assistance to help complete the cabling in time to meet the deadline (again, using contingency reserve funds).

Matt and Jake decided to use Option A and B to complete the correct cabling on time. Their risk management, solid project management, and contingency planning saved the day.

Monitor Risks Inputs, Tools and Techniques, and Outputs

Figure 11.10 shows an overview of the inputs, tools and techniques, and the outputs for the Monitor Risks process.

INPUTS

Some of the inputs for the Monitor Risks process are the same as previous processes (risk register and project management plan) and the outputs from the Plan Risk Responses process. The inputs for this process that should be considered:

- **Project management plan.**
- **Project documents such as the risk register.**
- **Work performance data.** Deliverable status, schedule progress, and costs.
- **Work performance reports.** Look for trends, forecasting data accuracy, and so on.

TOOLS AND TECHNIQUES

The tools and techniques often used in this process are unique and are as follows:

- **Risk reassessment.** Involves looking for secondary or new risks.
- **Risk audits.** Review effectiveness of risk responses, action taken, and so on.
- **Variance and trend analysis.** Statistical data that help answer the questions: Were the expected results achieved? Where do we go from here?
- **Technical performance measurement.** Requires objective, quantifiable measurements.
- **Reserve analysis.** Compare the plan to the actual use of reserves and future needs.
- **Meetings.** Regular status reviews are used to ensure proper focus and action.

OUTPUTS

The outputs to this process are as follows:

- **Work performance information.** Data transformed into reportable information.
- **Change requests.** Change is inevitable. As a result, change requests may need to be initiated to put the project back on track (this includes recommended correction and preventive actions).
- **Project management plan updates.** Progressive elaboration yields new information, new situations, and new risks, which all tend to drive updates to your project plan.
- **Project document updates.** The ripple effect requires updates to various project documents as the project progresses.
- **Organizational process assets updates.** Information from the risk management processes will produce information that can be used for current and future projects.

Reporting Status: Early and Often

Nothing is more embarrassing than discovering that the customer or project sponsor knows something before you do when it comes to your project. You need to be the air-traffic controller, the conductor of your project. You need to be the person reporting the status of a risk event, the expected impact to your project, and the action plans (fallback or back-out plans) you are taking to ensure that everything is under control.

Tip

Timely and accurate reporting is essential to risk management. Information is power when it comes to managing a project. Making sure you collect meaningful, accurate, and timely information can mean the difference between whether or not you meet your project objectives on time and on budget. There isn't a PM alive who hasn't wished to have known more about a difficult situation sooner rather than later. Our actions and reactions depend totally on timely and accurate reports (verbal or written) so we can make prompt, informed decisions.

Updates to Project Documents

For peace of mind and for audit purposes, you need to keep the project plan documents up to date and accurate. I recommend a Wiki, Dropbox, or SharePoint (electronic, easy-access team room) or a similar central repository to hold the master project control book (PCB). No matter what tools or techniques you choose, they must be managed effectively; otherwise, they will get outdated and may cause misinformation or confusion, which of course is counterproductive to the project.

Summary of Project Risk Management

Risk happens, so plan for it (remember that the majority of the processes in Project Risk Management Knowledge Area are planning processes).

Make sure you have identified and analyzed the risks. You also need to have assigned risk owners and a documented action (response) plan for the top risks. Report status promptly and with conviction. Be diligent in looking for future risks.

Wouldn't it be great if all the risks that occurred on your project were identified, analyzed, assigned, and addressed as planned? When a risk event happens, nothing is more satisfying than being able to report, "The risk was identified in our plan, the owner assigned to the risk has implemented the approved response according to the plan, and everything is under control." The best motto for risk management is, "Be prepared for anything." No one likes to be unpleasantly surprised on projects.

Remember the definition of risk is "uncertainty," so even if the risk is a known one, we don't always know if or when it will occur. The following list represents some common pitfalls and errors made in the area of risk management:

- Not conducting a thorough risk identification process with all stakeholders
- Not assigning owners to high profile risks (and having a back-up plan)
- Not documenting the risk response strategy clearly
- Not communicating the probability or impact to the project in a timely manner
- Not having adequate reserves to cover risks when they occur
- Not doing risk assessment early or often enough (and completely)
- Missing categories of risks (such as market impact, cultural risks, and customer risks)
- Conducting risk management with an unclear objective, scope, or target schedule
- Not obtaining project sponsor commitment to the project and the risk plan
- Not involving the team and all stakeholders in the risk management process
- Not monitoring your risk register regularly

Although an anticipated potential negative risk is still in the future, use mitigation strategies to minimize or eliminate its likelihood and magnitude. For opportunities, use proactive strategies to increase their likelihood and magnitude. Once a negative risk event occurs, it is elevated to the issue log, and its contingency plan must be executed by the risk owner. When unplanned risk events occur, enter them into the issue log and develop workaround plans.

When it comes to managing risk on your project, the best approach involves the same three takeaway points mentioned in other chapters:

1. Stay focused on the end results (especially on risk management).
2. Use the tools and resources available on your project to ensure effective risk management, such as the summary level sample shown in Figure 11.11 at the end of this chapter. (For the latest and complete risk management template, go to Dr. Gary Evans at CVR/IT Consulting LLC.[7])
3. Work as a team. This is especially true when managing risks. To aid in your understanding, a full Project Management Plan with Risk has been included as an example in Figure 11.11.

FIGURE 11.11 Sample Risk Management Plan Template, reprinted with permission from CVR/IT Consulting LLC

Sample Risk Management Plan Template	
Project Name:	
Prepared by:	
Date (MM/DD/YYYY):	

Risk Management Strategy

1. Define the risk management methodology to be used. Section 1 of this table defines your risk management process. The process is scalable to ensure that the level, type, and visibility of risk management are commensurate with both the risk and the importance of the project. Modify the text in this section to fit your process.

- **Risk Identification** – Identify risks through discussion with all major stakeholders. Also use the *Risk Assessment Questionnaire* and *Project Planning Risk Assessment Checklist*, augmented to include other project specific risks, as appropriate.
- **Risk Categorization** – Group the risks into categories by using the *Risk Assessment Questionnaire*. The project manager can create additional categories, as required.
- **Risk Probability and Impact Assessment** – Enter all risks into the *Risk Response Plan* document. For each risk identified, assess the risk event in terms of likelihood of occurrence (Risk Probability) and its effect on project objectives if the risk event occurs (Risk Severity = Impact Score). This information will be used to prioritize the risk using established threshold criteria.
- **Risk Prioritization** – Risks that meet the threshold criteria will be so noted in the *Risk Register*. These risks will be prioritized.
- **Risk Response Planning** – For each risk in the *Risk Register* that is above the Risk Threshold:
    - Determine options and actions to reduce the likelihood or consequences of impact to project objectives.
    - Determine the response based on a cost/benefit analysis (cost vs. expected effectiveness).
    - Describe the actions to be taken to mitigate the risk.
    - Describe the signs and symptoms (triggers) that may be indicators of risk event occurrence.
    - Describe the actions to be taken when the risk event occurs (contingency plan).
    - Assign responsibilities for each agreed-upon response.
    - Assign a "due date" where risk responses are time-sensitive.
    - Determine impact on project budget and schedule and make appropriate changes to the project plan.
    - Incorporate this information into the *Risk Register*.

continued on next page

FIGURE 11.11—*continued*

Risk Management Strategy

• **Risk Response Tracking:**
  • Dates and the actions taken to mitigate the risk.
  • Actions taken when the risk event occurred (contingency plan).
  • Incorporate this information into the *Risk Register*.

• **Risk Monitoring** – Establish systematic reviews and schedule them, ensuring the following reviews:
  • Ensure that all requirements of the *Risk Management Plan* are being implemented.
  • Assess currently defined risks as defined in the *Risk Register*.
  • Identify status of actions taken and evaluate effectiveness of actions taken.
  • Validate previous risk assessment (likelihood and impact).
  • Validate previous assumptions and state new assumptions.
  • Identify new risks and track risk response.
  • Establish communications.

• **Risk Control**
  • Validate mitigation strategies and alternatives.
  • Take corrective action when actual events occur.
  • Assess impact on the project of actions taken (cost, time, and resources).
  • Identify new risks resulting from risk mitigation actions.
  • Ensure the Project Plan (including the *Risk Management Plan*) is maintained.
  • Ensure change control addresses risks associated with the proposed change.
  • Revise the *Risk Assessment Questionnaire*, *Project Planning Risk Assessment Checklist*, and other risk management documents to capture results of mitigation actions.
  • Revise *Risk Register* and establish communications.

2. Define assumptions that have a significant impact on project risk:

continued on next page

FIGURE 11.11—*continued*

3. Define the roles and responsibilities unique to the risk management function:	
Risk Management Team:	<Team Members>
Risk Response Tracking Coordinator:	<Name>

4. Define risk management milestones (insert rows as needed):	
Milestone	Date (MM/DD/YYYY)
Risk Management Plan approved	
Risk Assessment Questionnaire tailored to project	
Risk Assessment and *Project Planning Risk Evaluation Checklist* complete	
Risk Management Reviews scheduled	

5. Define risk rating/scoring techniques. (The project will rate each identified risk [e.g., Impact Score = High, Medium, Low] based on the likelihood that the risk event will occur and the effect on the project's objectives if the risk event occurs. This will be a subjective evaluation based on the experience of those assigned to the project's risk management team.):

Default rating/scoring system is as follows:

- *Impact Score* can be rated as 1, 3, 5, 7, or 9 (1 = Very Low, 9 = Very High).
- *Probability* can be rated as 0.1, 0.3, 0.5, 0.7 or 0.9 (0.1 = Very Low, 0.9 = Very High).

6. Establish risk thresholds. (Modify the text below to show how the project team will plan for risk events, e.g., "The project will establish risk responses for risk events that have been determined to have a rating of 'High'.")

Risk priority is determined by calculating a Risk Score (= Impact × Probability) and then comparing that Risk Score to Priority thresholds.

Based on a sample scoring system, the lowest possible Risk Score is 1 × 0.1 = .01, and the highest possible Risk Score is 9 × 0.9 = 8.1

See Figure 11.1 for details and sample risk threshold scores.

7. Define risk communications:

continued on next page

FIGURE 11.11—*continued*

8. Define risk tracking process:

Project Risk Management Plan Approval/Signatures
Project Name:
Project Manager:

I have reviewed the information contained in this Project Risk Management Plan and agree:

Name	Title	Signature	Date
	Project Manager		
	Project Executive		
	Project Sponsor		

The signatures above indicate an understanding of the purpose and content of this document by those signing it. By signing this document, they agree to this as the formal Project Risk Management Plan *document.*

FIGURE 11.12 Sample Risk Management Plan (as part of a Project Management Plan)

	**Team 1** **Designated Drivers**	**PROJECT RISK MANAGEMENT PLAN TEMPLATE** *Rev. 2.1, 2/20/2017*

Project Risk Management Plan

Note: Any work not explicitly included in the Project Risk Plan Statement is implicitly excluded from the project.

Project Name:	Pour More (PM) Brewery Expansion
Prepared by:	Marty, Katie, Bryan, and Josh
Date (MM/DD/YYYY):	08/31/2017

Version History (insert rows as needed):

Version	Date (MM/DD/YYYY)	Comments
1.0	08/31/2017	Initial draft by the project manager
1.1	09/05/2017	Updates based on input from the project team
1.2	09/15/2017	Final draft submitted for review and approval

1. Executive/Project Summary

PM Brewery has announced the construction of a new facility near Boulder Canyon—a $5 million investment to develop a mixed-use facility that is to include a small brewery plant, a tasting room, office space, riverfront pub/eatery, and a riverfront beer garden. As a subset of the expansion, this project will provide the human resources necessary to launch and operate the facility. The people put in place by this project will provide excellence in operations and customer service, resulting in a high-quality customer experience.

"This expansion is an important and exciting milestone, not only for the company, but for the greater Boulder area and near-by communities," says President and Founder, Guz Slocher. "PM Brewery is reinvesting in our operation and locating a new production and pub facility in downtown Boulder that will bring dozens of quality jobs and vitality to a strategically important section of the city." This expansion is important to the PM Brewery future growth and to Boulder's economy.

1.1 Business or Project Objectives, product description, planned solution, e.g., problem to be solved, or product to be delivered:

The high level goal of this project is to manage and deliver the staffing and onboarding aspects of the larger Pour More Brewery Expansion project. This project will align its timing with the larger project to ensure support through the full life cycle of the expansion project.

continued on next page

FIGURE 11.12—*continued*

	**Team 1** **Designated Drivers**	**PROJECT RISK MANAGEMENT PLAN TEMPLATE** *Rev. 2.1, 2/20/2017*

1. Executive/Project Summary
1.2 Business Objectives (goals and benefits of the project to the organization):
The specific project goal will be to provide an excellent customer experience to our customers by hiring experienced, knowledgeable and customer-centric staff to meet the needs of the PM Brewery expansion. The project will help the business with strategic growth by increasing customer base and loyalty. Project Start Date: August 25, 2017 Target Completion Date: December 30, 2017

2. Project Scope
The project scope shall include Staffing and On-boarding to operate the new production and pub facilities.
2.1 Project Scope Details
Primary Deliverables: • **Staffing Plan** – Roadmap outlining the process for hiring and staffing • **On-Boarding** – Summary of hiring results including items that a new associate should complete before starting work • **Project Schedule** – Timeline of phases, gates, and milestones. Includes projected and actual • **Risk Management Plan** – Assessment of risks with mitigating action, contingencies, and tracking of progress • **Communications Plan** – Guide for communication practices within the core project team, with the external project team, with other stakeholders, and the sponsor • **Budget** – Summary of the projected costs (capital expenses, equipment expense, people)
Does Not Include (out of scope exclusions): • Construction • Setting up tasting room • Marketing, Promotion, and related PR activities
2.2 Project Completion Criteria (what has to be provided to meet project successful completion):
The primary criterion for this project is the completion of all staffing and on-boarding processes.

continued on next page

FIGURE 11.12—*continued*

	**Team 1** **Designated Drivers**	**PROJECT RISK MANAGEMENT PLAN TEMPLATE** *Rev. 2.1, 2/20/2017*

2.3 External Dependencies (such as client requirements, vendor/supplier deliverables):
• Hiring of a restaurant-staffing consultant firm that specializes in the following: staffing levels, recruiting and hiring process, and development of the position descriptions. • Leverage the staffing plan from the existing brewery to staff the new production facility.

2.4 Assumptions (e.g., customer to provide ongoing support when the project is complete, materials will be provided in English only, subcontractor provides their own tools, etc.):
• Appropriate consultants and recruiting agencies are available and able to meet our schedule requirements. • The required number of qualified candidates are available and want to work for PM Brewery.

2.5 Constraints (limitations such as schedule, budget, resources, or quality measures, etc.):

• Opening date is contingent upon a number of factors external to this project, including:
  • Successful completion of building construction, all interior finishing and decorating.
  • Appropriate certifications for: occupancy, food handling, safety, liquor, and music.
  • Potential budget impact with hiring external staffing agency.

3. Project Milestones Estimated Schedules – List key project milestones relative to project start.	
Project Milestones	Target Date (MM/DD/YYY)
• Project Start	08/25/2017
• Complete Project Plan Documents	08/30/2017
• Complete Staffing Plan	09/01/2017
• Source Job Candidates	09/15/2017
• Complete Hiring	09/30/2017
• Communication Project Status	10/01/2017
• Complete Training	10/30/2017
• Conduct Soft Opening (pilot)	11/25/2017
• Final Adjustments Made	11/30/2017
• Launch Grand Opening	12/25/2017
• Final Project Reports and Close the Project (Project Complete)	12/30/2017

FIGURE 11.12—*continued*

	**Team 1** **Designated Drivers**	**PROJECT RISK MANAGEMENT PLAN TEMPLATE** *Rev. 2.1, 2/20/2017*

4. Project Approach (how the project will be managed)

4.1 Primary Plans – Will the project have formal written plans – i.e., formal change control, shared project schedule, budget, quality measures, risk plan and issues tracking, etc.? Describe briefly in the space below:

The opening phase of this project requires the development of the Staffing Plan. The contents of this plan will drive the remainder of project through closing.

The Staffing Plan will outline the specifics of:

- Number and types of positions to be filled, including wage ranges, base rates, and expected average rates.
- Staffing schedule – when each of the positions are to be filled and on-boarded.
- Job descriptions for each type of position, including key skills, abilities and knowledge requirements, personality traits, etc.
- Hiring sequence and which positions will have influence on hiring of subordinates.
- Organizational chart outlining areas of responsibility.
- Training requirements and training providers.
- Outside resources to be utilized throughout the project.
- Performance standards for each position type.
- Performance management plan.
- On-boarding plan, including:
  - selection criteria;
  - paperwork requirements;
  - background checks, bonding, drug screening.
- The budget for this project is estimated to be $150,000, to include PM salary, outside consultants, and recruiters. The direct labor costs for new personnel hired to staff the facility while in training is included in this budget up to the point of grand opening.
- The staffing plan, and any revisions to that plan, must be approved in writing by the Project Sponsor and the Project Manager before any subsequent stages of the project may proceed.

FIGURE 11.12—*continued*

	**Team 1** **Designated Drivers**	**PROJECT RISK MANAGEMENT PLAN TEMPLATE** *Rev. 2.1, 2/20/2017*

4.2 Risk/Issue Management:

Risks are to be reported to the PM as they are identified. The PM will manage identified risks through the following process:

Log all identified risks.

Assess Probability of Occurrence: collaborate with the project team to assess each risk's probability of occurrence on the following scale:

Probability Range	*Description*	*Probability Value Used for Calculations*	*Numeric Score*
91–100%	Very likely to occur	95%	5
61–90%	Probably will occur	76%	4
41–60%	May occur about half the time	51%	3
11–40%	Unlikely to occur	26%	2
1–10%	Very unlikely to occur	5%	1

Assess Risk Impact and assign to one of the following risk impact categories:

Impact Description *An event that, if it occurs:*	*Example*	*Rating*	*Impact value used for calculations*	*Numeric Score*
Will cause project failure.	Schedule adjustment >2mo Cost impact >40%	Critical	Cost of variance	10
Will cause major cost/schedule increases. Secondary requirements may not be achieved.	Schedule adjustment > 1mo Cost impact >20%	Serious	Cost of variance	8
Will cause moderate cost/schedule increases, but important requirements will still be met.	Schedule adjustment >2wks Cost impact >10%	Moderate	Cost of variance	5
Will cause only a small cost/schedule increase. Requirements will still be achieved.	Schedule adjustment > 1 wk. Cost impact >5%	Minor	Cost of Variance	3
Will have no effect on the project.	Schedule adjustment <2d Cost impact <5%	Negligible	Cost of variance	1

FIGURE 11.12—*continued*

	**Team 1** **Designated Drivers**	**PROJECT RISK MANAGEMENT PLAN TEMPLATE** *Rev. 2.1, 2/20/2017*

Score the risk exposure or risk score as the product of the probability of occurrence and the impact scores. The PM will use the risk matrix table to compare risks as part of the prioritization process. Risk scores range from 1 (very low exposure) to 50 (very high exposure). There are no specific breakpoints in the exposure ranking, but those risks scored 20 or lower are generally considered low risk, 20–39 as moderate risk, and 40–50 as high risk.

	Impact				
Probability	*Negligible (1)*	*Minor (3)*	*Moderate (5)*	*Serious (8)*	*Critical (10)*
Very likely (5)	5	15	25	40	50
Probably (4)	4	12	20	32	40
~50% Chance (3)	3	9	15	24	30
Unlikely (2)	2	6	10	16	20
Very unlikely (1)	1	3	5	8	10

Take appropriate action (ranging from watch/no action to assign to a team member for immediate action), and communicate the change in risk environment in accordance with the communication management portion of this plan.

4.3 Change Management:

This plan, and all revisions to this plan, must be approved in writing by the Project Sponsor and the Project Manager. Each revision will be maintained as a separate electronic document in the project Google Docs folder, and signed hard copies of all versions are to be kept in a project binder in the PM's office.

FIGURE 11.12—*continued*

	**Team 1** **Designated Drivers**	**PROJECT RISK MANAGEMENT PLAN TEMPLATE** *Rev. 2.1, 2/20/2017*

4.4 Communication Management:
The PM will manage project communication to ensure successful completion of the project and to keep key stakeholders informed of status during the execution of the project. Communications are to include: • Core Project Team meetings – Weekly meetings to review action item register & status and update with new action items. • Project Management Plan Changes – all approved changes to this project management plan are to be recorded in the project folder in Google Docs, with copies (electronic or paper) to the Sponsor and members of the project team. • Staffing Plan Approval &/or Changes – all approved changes to this project management plan are to be recorded in the project folder in Google Docs, with copies (electronic or paper) to the Sponsor and members of the project team. • Risk Status – all changes in project risk and actions are to be recorded in the risk log (a shared Google Doc), with copies (electronic or paper) to the Sponsor and members of the project team. • Risk Mitigation/Contingency – where an identified risk is assigned to a member of the project team, the PM will meet personally with the assigned team member to devise strategies for mitigation/contingency, and agreed-upon actions will be added to the risk log. • Risk Review – all risks having a rating of >20 shall be reviewed/reassessed at least weekly by the PM, and progress on mitigating those risks shall be communicated to the Sponsor and project team via email. • Project Status Reporting – the PM will monitor project progress and will report status, exceptions, and issues on a biweekly schedule. Reports will be communicated to the Sponsor and the project team. • Project Status Review – the PM will also conduct status-review meetings on a monthly schedule commencing at the start of the 2nd month of the project. These review meetings are to include all key stakeholders (Sponsor, project team members, corporate marketing, etc.) and are to report and discuss project status. Minutes of these reviews are to be recorded in the project Docs folder and shared with all participants.

FIGURE 11.12—*continued*

	**Team 1** **Designated Drivers**	**PROJECT RISK MANAGEMENT PLAN TEMPLATE** *Rev. 2.1, 2/20/2017*

4.5 Resource Management:

The four-member Designated Drivers project management team will be responsible for managing the outcome of this project. The team includes Katie, Josh, Bryan, and Marty, and all are very experienced project managers.

The team members will each take the lead for different portions of the project, with the rest of the team supporting that phase, as follows:

	Project Section	*Lead*
1.	Overall Project Mgt. Plan	Marty
2.	Staffing Plan Execution	Katie
3.	Candidate Sourcing	Josh
4.	Onboarding & Training	Bryan

5. Authorizations (Modify lists as needed)

This section identifies the approvers/decision makers on the project who should review key documents, such as the Scope Statement, WBS, Project Schedule, Risk Management Plan, Staffing Plan, Communications Plan, and Project Budget for buy-in/sign-off:

- **Project Sponsor:** Guz Slocher, President & Founder
- **Project Manager:** Designated Drivers Team

Project deliverables will be approved/accepted by the:

- **Project Sponsor**
- **Key Stakeholders/Customer**

Specific task responsibilities of project resources will be defined in the Responsibility Assignment Matrix (RAM) or RACI table.

6. Project Management Plan Approval/Signatures/Date

I have reviewed the information contained in this Project Management Plan and agree:

Name	Role	Signature	Date (MM/DD/YYYY)
Guz Slocher	Project Sponsor	_GS_	08/31/2017
Designated Drivers Team	Project Manager	_DDT_	08/31/2017

References

1. "US Airways Flight 1549," *Wikipedia*, https://en.wikipedia.org/wiki/US_Airways_Flight_1549, accessed March 22, 2017.

2. *Bird Strike Committee USA*, www.birdstrike.org, accessed March 22, 2017.

3. Carl Pritchard, "On the Edge: Setting the Thresholds," *Project Connections*, http://www.projectconnections.com/articles/063000-pritchard.html, accessed March 22, 2017.

4. Lee W. Larson, "The Great USA Flood of 1993," http://www.nwrfc.noaa.gov/floods/papers/oh_2/great.htm, accessed March 22, 2017.

5. "Mind Map," *Wikipedia*, http://en.wikipedia.org/wiki/Mind_map, accessed March 22, 2017.

6. "Code of Federal Regulations," US Government Publishing Office, https://www.gpo.gov/fdsys/browse/collectionCfr.action?collectionCode=CFR, accessed March 22, 2017.

7. CVR/IT Consulting LLC, "Project Risk Management Plan Template" (Rev. 2.2, April 2, 2006), http://www.cvr-it.com/Samples/XRisk_Management_Plan_Template.pdf, accessed March 22, 2017.

12 Project Procurement Management

Key Skills & Concepts

- Procurement management process
- Definition of a contract
- Terms and conditions
- Elements of a legally binding contract
- Role of the project manager (buyer or seller)
- Types of contracts and who bears the burden of risk
- Make-or-buy analysis
- Project procurement documents: RFPs, RFQs, and RFBs
- Source selection process
- Bidder's conference and vendor selection process
- Statement of work (SOW)
- Buyer and seller relationship
- Contract change control
- Privity of contract and contract waiver
- Administrative closure
- *Force majeure*

Project Procurement Management includes the process to purchase or acquire goods and services from outside the project team. This chapter focuses on Project Procurement Management and the PMI recognized processes associated with managing project procurements. One of the primary tools or instruments used during procurement is a contract, agreement, statement of work, work order, or service level agreement (SLA). In this chapter we cover both topics as they usually go hand-in-hand when it comes to managing these important elements of a project.

Many project managers (PMs) are familiar with contracts, and most PMs are involved with procurement of goods and services, so the information in this chapter may simply serve as a refresher. However, you'll encounter tips and terms along the way that you will need to be familiar with, especially if you are planning to take the Project Management Institute (PMI) exam.

Also be aware that with any agreement or contract, there can be legal penalties or ramifications if not written or executed properly. With this in mind, it is important to realize that this area of project management can carry significant impact to the project, and as a PM you may want to call on the experts within your organization to assist as needed; that is, don't try and be a hero by writing contracts on your own.

Tip

Knowledge of how to manage contracts as well as key terms and conditions is important to PMs in the real world. However, you should note that PMI tends to focus mostly on procurement management. You'll encounter a few exam questions regarding the types of contracts, who bears the burden of risk between the buyer and seller on the different contracts, and even some calculations. Therefore, you should be familiar with these key aspects of contract management and how it fits into Project Procurement Management as a whole.

Definition of a Contract

A *contract* is a legal, mutually binding document, agreement, or exchange of promises between two or more parties to provide goods or services in exchange for something of value. Contracts usually have terms and conditions and can be used for a wide range of purposes—sale of property, terms of employment, settlement of disputes, ownership protection (when it comes to licensing, intellectual property, or copyright protection), and even tickets to a sporting event. That's right. A ticket to a baseball game, for example, has terms and conditions ("Holder is admitted on the condition of . . .").

In the entertainment world a contract may be referred to by various names: technical contract, appearance agreement, booking agreement, contract rider, and even engagement contract. Whatever you decide to call this piece of paper, it is essential. It provides protection to both the performer and the venue / events center. The goal of the agreement is that everything is laid out on the table and that both parties remain in total agreement. Once the contract or agreement is signed and dated, it becomes a legally binding document.

Contract Terms and Conditions

Terms and conditions (T&Cs) set the rights and obligations of the contracting parties. These include "general conditions," which are common to all types of contracts, as well as "special conditions," which are peculiar to a specific contract (e.g., contract change conditions, payment conditions, price variation clauses, and penalties).

T&Cs also define the business relationship between the buyer and seller, the roles and responsibilities of each party, and how the activities will be carried out throughout the established period of contract performance.

- **Terms.** Necessary statements that make the contract legally valid (e.g., "The total term duration of the project, including all approved deliverables, shall not exceed 12 months").

  Another contract term is for payment. In the entertainment world, for example, a contract term may state the following: "All payments (including performance amount plus 5 percent of ticket sales) will be in cash and are to be provided within 30 days following the concert."

  Other terms should include what happens if the event is canceled due to low ticket sales, weather, flight delays, and so on. These terms need to be spelled out.
- **Conditions.** Defined events that must happen in order for contingent terms in a contract to become fixed (e.g., "Late payment penalty of 10 percent of the total invoice will be added to the statement for payments not received by the 10th business day of the month following the date of the invoice").

Conditions should include any specific restrictions or expectations for the performer that the venue or hosting party has set. This can include the performer's expected attire, language, and music selection. This condition varies from place to place. The conditions can include the performer's own personal restrictions and expectations, such as guest lists, guest passes, dressing rooms, backstage refreshments (for example, brown M&Ms), and other hospitalities. The conditions depend on the individual performer and the venue's willingness and ability to meet the conditions of the contract.

The following list represents some items you might see in the terms and conditions (T&Cs) of a contract:

- **Acceptance.** Clearly defined project milestones and deliverables as well as what will be measured, reported, and deemed formally acceptable at completion.
- **Agent.** A person (or persons) specifically representing the buyer and/or seller.
- **Arbitration.** A method that describes how disputes, escalations, or issues will be handled as well as how this process will be assigned and billed (and who does it).
- **Assignment.** Describes the circumstances in which one party or the other can assign their rights and obligations to another party (such as an agent or manager).
- **Authority.** Who holds the power in a contract and under what conditions?
- **Bonds.** If bonding (performance assurance) is required by one party or the other.

- **Breach/default.** Failure of the seller to perform or deliver as promised in the contract.
- **Contract change process.** Defines the process, who will serve on the CCB (change control board), and the tool used to track and manage changes.
- **Incentives (if appropriate).** To reward achievement of objectives on the contract.
- **Indemnification (liability).** Who is liable under what conditions and how this is handled.
- **Personnel.** Key personnel involved or who have been requested to remain for a specified period of time to provide services on a contract.
- **Reporting.** Format, frequency, distribution list, tool, and so on.
- **Termination.** Stopping the work before it is complete.
- **Waivers.** How or if rights can be waived. As a PM, you need to understand how you may waive certain rights intentionally or unintentionally (e.g., allowing changes to occur without going through the change process).
- **Warranties.** Measure of quality and duration of coverage.

No wonder people develop headaches while reading contracts! They can be quite complex. What's more, legal jargon and even the placement of a comma can change the meaning of a contract.

Unless you speak "legalese," the best thing you can do is get a lawyer, procurement representative, or other subject matter expert (SME) involved to help ensure that you and the other parties understand the language of the contract. The good news is many great forms, templates, and software applications are available to make this easier. The bad news is there are way too many forms and templates to use, so it can be overwhelming.

Ask the Expert

Q: What's a real-world example of a contract misinterpretation that provides a good lesson learned?

A: Try this one on for size: On a contract long, long ago, the PM was reviewing the service level agreements (SLAs) for computer support (e.g., hours of support, system availability, and the financial penalties associated with missed SLAs). The contract language was not clear, and when the PM asked the contract manager to explain it, he simply said, "Don't worry. There will never be penalties against the SLAs because of the way the contract is worded." Well, the first time a critical server went out of operation due to a failure, the client came to the PM and said, "You owe several thousand dollars in penalties for the outage!" The customer had interpreted the contract language in one way, whereas the PM and team interpreted it differently. After heated discussions, the legal team was called back to rewrite the language around SLAs and penalties. A penalty was paid, and the contract was rewritten to ensure that there would be no confusion in the future. The moral to this story is that unclear language is not good: when left to interpretation, it can create a lot of confusion, expense, and ill feelings.

Elements of a Legally Binding Contract

Under normal circumstances, a contract must contain certain key elements to be legally binding and enforceable:

- **Offer and acceptance.** The contract must include an *offer* to provide goods or services and *acceptance* of the offer.

> **Note**
>
> A counteroffer is not an acceptance and will normally be treated as a rejection of the current offer.

- **Mutual consideration.** The mutual exchange of something of value. In order for the contract to be valid, the parties to a contract must exchange money or something of value. (In the case of the sale of an event ticket, e.g., the buyer receives something of value in the form of attendance to the game, and the seller receives money.)
- **Legal purpose.** A contract cannot violate legal, government, or public policy. For example, if a contract is for the sale of illegal drugs, the contract is not enforceable.
- **Legal capacity.** Buyer and seller must have legal capacity to enter into contract for exchange of products or services. For example, someone trying to sell something they don't own does not have legal capacity.

Other elements of a legally binding contract:

- **Good faith.** It is implicit in all contracts that the parties are acting in good faith. For example, if the seller of a "bike" knows the buyer thinks the purchase is of a motorcycle instead of a bicycle, the seller is not acting in good faith and the contract will not be enforceable.
- **Performance or delivery.** In order to be enforceable, the agreed-to action of the contract must be completed (e.g., the tickets have to be delivered as promised and payment received to complete the transaction).
- **Mutual consent.** There must be mutual consent between the buyer and seller (a "meeting of the minds") over products, services, or results to be provided and received.
- **Mutual understanding.** There must be a clear understanding by all parties to the contract of what is being provided and received. For example, in a contract for the sale of land, the buyer may think they are buying a lot to build a house on when the seller is actually contracting to sell a pad of land for commercial use (zoned for commercial use only). There is no meeting of the minds, and the contract will likely be held unenforceable.

Is an Oral Agreement Legally Binding?

There is an old saying, "an oral contract isn't worth the paper it's written on," which is so true. It can be very difficult to prove an oral contract exists without documented proof of the agreement. With an oral or "handshake" agreement, one party may be unable to enforce the agreement or may be forced to settle for less than the original bargain. The solution is to draft a contract (or agreement). It is always good practice to make some sort of written document, signed by both parties, to clarify the key terms of an agreement.

Definition of Procurement

Procurement is the acquisition of goods and services, usually from outside the project team. Generally, procurements are acquired via a contract or agreement. A simple procurement however, may not require contracts, formal agreements, or purchase orders. Complex procurements should involve finding vendors or suppliers who are willing to establish a long-term buyer/seller relationship.

Almost all purchasing decisions include factors such as price, shipping, delivery, quality of goods and services, benefits, and payment processing. Procurements may also involve making buying decisions that make use of economic-analysis methods such as cost-benefit analysis, cost-utility analysis, and risk analysis:

- **Cost-benefit analysis** involves looking at the total costs and all the benefits of a decision, then weighing the pros and cons to determine before the decision is made if the planned action is beneficial.

Centralized or Decentralized Procurement Structure

Contracts and procurement processes can be performed by the PM or a centralized department or organization, or they may be divided or spread over a number of different resources in the project organization. Contracts and procurement can be managed through either a centralized structure or a decentralized structure. In the case of a centralized structure, the processes are managed within a specific department or group within the organization that specializes in the processes needed to carry out this role. In a decentralized structure, the work is often performed by the PM. Clearly, there are advantages and disadvantages to both structures. Table 12.1 lists some of the differences.

TABLE 12.1 Differences in the Procurement Organizational Structures

Centralized Contracts/Procurement		Decentralized Contracts/Procurement	
Advantages	Disadvantages	Advantages	Disadvantages
Standard processes	Less flexibility	More PM flexibility	Unclear processes
Volume discounts	Rigid bid process	Quicker acquisitions	Higher prices
Consistency	Bureaucracy	Less bureaucracy	Inconsistency
Support experts, including legal	Administrative cost	Less overhead cost	Limited support, increased liability

Role of the Project Manager (Buyer or Seller?)

The PM can perform the role of either (or both) the buyer or the seller in a procurement transaction. For example, the PM may be the seller of project management services to a project sponsor (customer) and in turn contract for outside services from another group or company (in which case the PM is also a buyer of vendor/supplier services). Regardless of which side of the fence you are on, it's always a good idea to understand the other side's perspective and responsibilities from a PM standpoint.

Tip

PMI tends to view the PM as the buyer in the buyer/seller relationship. Also, note that on the PMP exam the Project Procurement Management Knowledge Area can be difficult for people who have little experience in dealing with contracts or procurement. It is good to have real-world experience; however, you need to look at this Knowledge Area from PMI's perspective as covered throughout this chapter.

As a PM, you will need to determine which products, goods, or services will be needed from outside the project team. As always, the procurements needed are totally dependent on the size, type of project, and staffing requirements (skills and people available) of the project.

The best approach for determining what you will need to administer the project deliverables successfully is to pull the project management team together and conduct a brainstorming session. Start with the work breakdown structure (WBS) and make a list of products, equipment, and services needed. Then initiate the make-or-buy analysis (discussed later in this chapter) to see whether or not your team can provide cost-effective products or services.

A PM needs to understand labor requirements and related costs clearly. Labor includes not only the people and their availability but the skills, education, and experience they bring to the table to deliver the project (e.g., programmer, construction manager, financial analyst, team leader, or contract manager). Then you must determine if your project team can perform these functions or if you will need to obtain (or procure) them from outside the project team. As for related cost, labor rates are often "loaded" or "burdened," which means that the rate includes overhead, benefits, profit, and other costs of doing business. These loaded rates are often highly protected by companies due to competition. Direct labor is generally the employee's salary or pay rate, whereas the bill rate is normally the loaded rate the buyer pays the seller. Make sure you know the difference.

Tip

I suggest you use the "80/20 principle," discussed in Chapter 8, to focus on the areas that are going to cost the most, especially labor. Also, don't shortchange yourself on the cost of managing the project's contracts and procurements, which can be independent of project costs. These activities take time, especially if they are unfamiliar, are not clear, or are misinterpreted.

Whenever possible, you will want to be involved in the contract and procurement process from the beginning of your project. If you are working in a centralized procurement organization, you will need to work closely with that department or group to initiate the proper requests, using the proper forms and procedures. If you attempt to work outside the process, the consequences can be disastrous—for example, not getting the best price from sellers, missing key information in the SOW, or even losing your job. (That's correct! If you don't utilize the right people or processes for procurement, it is often considered a "bypass" and can cost you your job.)

Project Procurement Management Processes

Project Procurement Management includes the processes to purchase or acquire the products, services, or results needed from *outside* the project team. Here's an overview of the project procurement processes:

- **12.1. Plan Procurement Management (Planning Process Group).** Involves documenting procurement decisions on how you will manage procurements and setting the seller-selection criteria on the project.
- **12.2. Conduct Procurements (Executing Process Group).** Involves initiating the bidder selection process, obtaining seller responses, choosing a seller, conducting final negotiations, and awarding the contract.
- **12.3. Control Procurements (Monitoring and Controlling Process Group).** Involves maintaining the procurement relationship with the vendor selected as well as monitoring contract performance and managing the changes and corrections needed to ensure compliance.

Plan Procurement Management Process (Planning Process Group)

The Plan Procurement Management process is all about understanding what needs to be obtained in the way of products, services, or results on the project, and then documenting the purchasing decisions and the approach you plan to take to identify the resources needed, such as marketing, advertising, vendors, subcontractors, and so on.

Tip

It is important to remember that the seller is often referred to as a vendor, supplier, subcontractor, provider, or even customer, and any of these terms tend to show up on PMI exams.

When planning procurements on a project, you have many things to consider, starting with the scope (and scope baseline), requirements document, schedule, budget, and contract type. This process should be closely tied to the cost and time available to deliver the project.

Plan Procurement Management Inputs, Tools and Techniques, and Outputs

A high-level overview of the inputs, tools and techniques, and outputs for the Plan Procurement Management process is described in the following sections (see Figure 12.1).

INPUTS

Because procurement is an important aspect of obtaining resources outside the project team, the list of inputs for this process is long. See the sample list below:

- **Project charter.** Provides the authorization to begin the project and for the PM to assign resources.
- **Business documents.** Includes documents such as mission and vision statements, business plans, and business strategy; that is, the ABC Company will implement the following strategies to achieve its goals of becoming the leading branded Internet Sports Network: (1) Create a compelling value proposition for sponsors

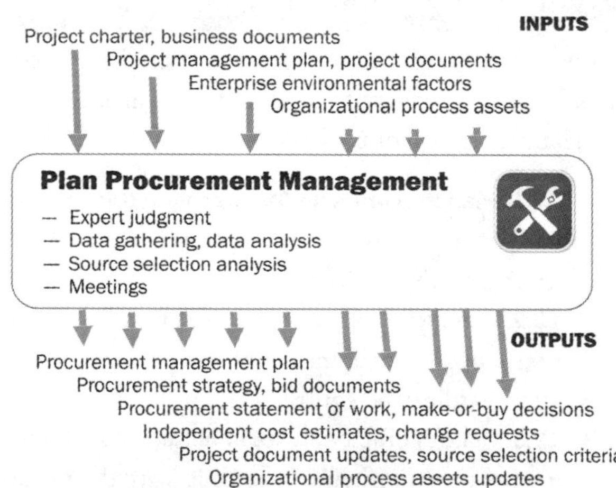

FIGURE 12.1 Plan Procurement Management Process ITTOs

and consumers, (2) build strong brand recognition, and (3) develop key industry relationships to promote our products and partnerships.

- **Project management plan.** Includes the scope baseline (scope statement, WBS, and the WBS dictionary).
- **Other project documents such as**
  - **Requirements documentation.** Includes contractual and legal implications around health, safety, security, performance, environmental considerations, insurance, and so on.
  - **Risk register.** Includes risk-related information, such as identified risks, owners, and response strategy, as it pertains to contracts and procurement.
  - **Risk related contract decisions.** Is insurance needed? Bonding of providers?
  - **Activity resource requirements.** Number of people and type of skills needed.
  - **Project schedule.** Constraints, timelines, specific deliverables, and target dates.
  - **Activity cost estimates.** From procurement activity, bid process, and cost of deliverables.
  - **Stakeholder register.** List of project participants and their specific interest in the successful completion of the project.
- **Enterprise environmental factors.** Type of structure, market conditions, supplier performance, relationship and credibility, and terms and conditions of the contract.
- **Organizational process assets.** Formal procurement policies, management systems used, and contract type (it is important to know who bears the burden of risk).

Hundreds of contracts and agreements are available to you as a project manager, so to keep this discussion simple, we cover only the ones mentioned in the *PMBOK Guide*.

Another important factor when choosing the contract type to use on your project is who will bear the burden of risk between the buyer and seller. Each contract type carries advantages and disadvantages, depending on which side of the table you are on.

The two primary types or categories of contracts recognized by PMI are detailed next.

FIXED-PRICE CONTRACTS

Fixed-price contracts involve setting a fixed (or lump sum) price for delivery of a product or service. This price is fixed at the time the contract is awarded. There may also be incentives incorporated into the contract—no down payment, delayed payments, factory rebates—but the price is usually the price. Of course, we try hard to negotiate the price down, but whatever price the seller and buyer agree upon becomes the fixed-price contract.

Here are the three types of fixed-price contracts mentioned in the *PMBOK*:

- **Firm Fixed Price (FFP).** This is the most common and is favored by most buyers because the price is set and the risk goes mostly to the seller. If the cost of services or materials goes up, the seller bears the burden of risk in this type of contract.

Note

A purchase order (PO) is the simplest form of a fixed-price contract. This type of contract is considered to be unilateral (signed by the buyer) as opposed to bilateral (signed by both parties).

- **Fixed-Price Incentive Fee (FPIF).** This contract gives the buyer and seller some flexibility in that it allows for variations in performance, with financial incentives tied to any agreed-upon results. For example, if the house is completed in time to move in before school starts, the seller gets an incentive fee based on a pre-negotiated amount. Here's an example:
  - **Contract** = $100,000 + $5,000 for each month the project is completed ahead of schedule. (Two months early = $10,000 + $100,000 = $110,000 total contract value.)
- **Fixed Price with Economic Price Adjustment (FP-EPA).** Used when the seller's performance period spans a considerable number of years, allowing for changes in labor and material costs. It is a fixed-price contract, but with a special provision allowing for predefined annual or final adjustments to the total price of the contract. Here's an example:
  - **Two-year contract** = $100,000 ($50,000/year) + $5,000-per-year cost of living adjustment (COLA) starting year 2 for the added cost of labor. (Year 1 = $50,000, year 2 = $55,000. Total contract value = $105,000.)

COST-REIMBURSABLE CONTRACTS

This contract category is advantageous to the seller and is commonly referred to as a *cost plus* (CP) contract. It involves payments (cost reimbursements) for all legitimate actual costs incurred for the work performed and includes some type of incentive (or fee representing seller profit) if the seller exceeds predefined objectives (such as schedule, cost, or performance targets). Cost-reimbursable contracts tend to pass the risk to the buyer. They also allow flexibility in the contract if the scope is not clear or if there are a high number of expected changes. This contract type is commonly used with research and development (R&D) projects.

Here are three of the common cost-reimbursable contracts:

- **Cost plus fixed fee (CPFF).** The seller is reimbursed for all allowable costs for performing the agreed-to work of the contract plus a fixed fee usually identified as a percentage. Here's an example:
  - Actual cost (e.g., labor and materials) = $100,000 + $5,000 (5%) fixed fee = $105,000.
- **Cost plus incentive fee (CPIF).** The seller is reimbursed for allowable costs for performing the contract work and receives a predetermined incentive fee based on achieving certain

performance objectives, such as completing the project on time (similar to FPIF). Here's an example:

+ Actual cost = $100,000 + $10,000 incentive at completion = $110,000 total contract value.

- **Cost plus award fee (CPAF).** The seller is reimbursed for all legitimate costs, but the majority of the fee is earned based on the satisfaction criteria preapproved by the seller and the buyer (e.g., the software application performs to requirements). Here's an example:
  + Actual cost = $90,000 + $20,000 award fee (if preapproved deliverables are met) = $110,000 total contract value.

Note

Cost-reimbursable contracts often include direct and indirect costs (see Chapter 7 for details on cost management). A contract of this type is beneficial when the scope of the project is not clearly or easily defined, or when there are a high number of changes expected.

TIME AND MATERIALS CONTRACTS

Time and materials (T&M) contracts (sometimes called *unit-price* or *time and means contracts*) are considered to be a "hybrid" type of contractual arrangement in that they have certain aspects of both fixed-fee and cost-reimbursable contracts. They are often viewed as "risk neutral," meaning the burden of risk is shared by both parties.

Sometimes the T&M contract is left open-ended to allow flexibility in the terms and conditions (T&Cs) of contract delivery. T&M contracts can resemble fixed-price contracts when specific parameters are set in the contract's T&Cs. Here's an example:

Time = 1,000 labor hours × the approved hourly rate ($50 per hour) = $50,000 + costs of materials (actual = $58,255) = $108,255 total contract value.

Tip

As a PM, you may not always be directly involved with, or be the decision maker in, the selection of which contract type will be used on your project (especially if you operate in a centralized procurement organization). However, for the purposes of the PMP exam, you need to be able to put yourself in the procurement manager's shoes and answer questions on the exam as if you are making these decisions as the PM from the buyer's perspective.

Things to Consider in Contract Selection

A number of factors need to be considered when it comes to the type of contract you (or your organization) select for your project, for instance:

- Contract type (sometimes predetermined by your company or organization).
- Relationship with the seller/vendor/supplier.
- Vendor's reputation and past performance. For example, do they deliver on time, with skilled, responsible people? Do they invoice in a timely manner? Are the invoices accurate? Do they stand behind their work? Do they comply with industry standards?
- Vendor's willingness to adjust schedule, skills, cost, and so on to meet project needs.
- Competition. (How does the seller compare to their competition?)
- Degree of risk on both parties (ideal is shared risk).
- Contract terms and conditions. (Are they rigid or flexible?)
- Other specific considerations unique to your project.

Advantages and Disadvantages by Contract Type

Table 12.2 provides a comparison of the contract types in the three primary categories and the advantages and disadvantages of each.

Tip

There will be a few questions on the PMP exam regarding contract types, so I recommend that you become familiar with the types, who bears the burden of risk between them, and the advantages and disadvantages of each contract type.

TABLE 12.2 Advantages and Disadvantages of the Contract Types

Fixed-Price (Lump Sum) Contracts	
Advantages	Disadvantages
Very common and easy to understand. Buyer knows the total price at the start of the project.	Can be more expensive than cost-reimbursable contract to help cover added risk to the seller.
Buyer has less risk and less work to manage (or audit) the invoices. FP contracts work well when the scope is clearly defined.	Seller may underprice the bid and overprice add-on services, features, or upgrades for higher profit.
Seller is responsible for controlling the costs.	Quality of work may suffer or the seller may cut corners if costs run higher than estimated. Also, there's little flexibility for change.
Cost-Reimbursable (CP) Contracts	
Advantages	Disadvantages
Typically less work to write the contract/SOW. CP contracts work well when additional or critical skills are needed to augment your staff.	Buyer has higher involvement to audit seller invoices closely. Additional procurement and administrative uplift (burden).
Seller has less contract risk.	Seller is not motivated to control costs.
Generally lower cost than FP contracts because of cost reimbursement instead of having to add in for unknown contingency.	Total price is unknown.

continued on next page

TABLE 12.2—*continued*

Time and Materials (T&M) Contracts	
Advantages	Disadvantages
Easy to create/manage. T&M contracts are effective when work needs to begin right away.	Profit margins are built into the hours billed.
Add flexible workforce (supplementing staff).	Seller has no incentive to control costs.
Usually for very specific products or services over a shorter, more manageable period of time.	Usually only appropriate for smaller projects.

Keep in mind that contracts can be complex, even if the project is not. This can be exacerbated when you are managing multiple projects or subcontracts at the same time. Each project life cycle can end at different times. With this in mind, it is important to keep a keen eye on the way one project may affect another when it comes to procurements. You may require certain skills, equipment, or other resources across many projects, and keeping everything organized by project may be a challenge. This is where strong organizational skills are essential (e.g., don't fall into a trap by signing a one-year lease for equipment on a six-month project).

Risk-Related Contract Decisions

Contract decisions should be based on the related risk. The main purpose of a contract is to protect you and the other party. From a PMI perspective, contracts are arranged according to the level of risk to the PM (buyer). The sliding scale in Figure 12.2 shows how risk shifts between the buyer and seller. You should be able to recognize who bears the burden of risk for each of the contract types typically used and recognized in the world of project management.

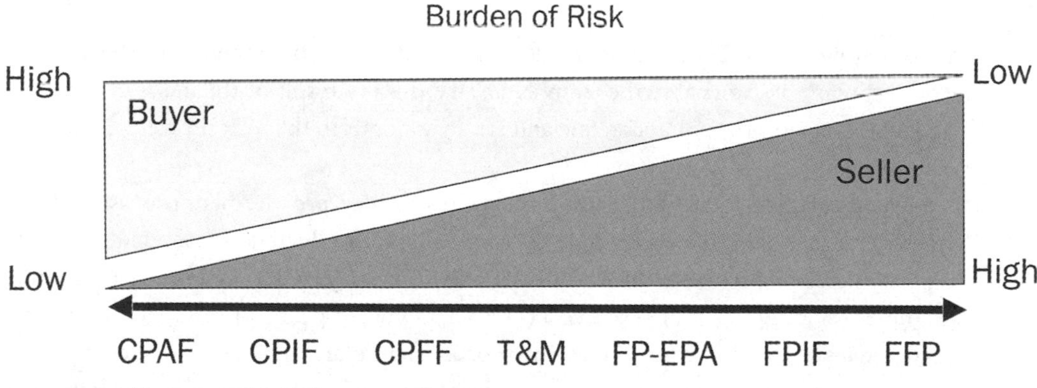

FIGURE 12.2 Contract Risk Scale

TOOLS AND TECHNIQUES

The sample list below shows some tools and techniques that can be used in the Plan Procurement Management process (for more details refer to the *PMBOK Guide*):

- **Make-or-buy analysis.** A technique used to determine if specific work can be performed with the skills and resources available on the project team or if this needs to be acquired outside the team. Again, the schedule will often influence this decision.
- **Expert judgment.** In the case of procurement planning, the experts sought out may be financial analysts, business analysts, contract or procurement specialists, and so on.
- **Market research.** What commercial products and services are available on the market? What is your independent estimate? Do your homework so you know what to expect.
- **Meetings.** They complement market research by serving as opportunities to work with companies and industry specialists to find appropriate solutions.

OUTPUTS

A sample list of potential outputs of the Plan Procurement Management process are as follows:

- **Procurement management plan.** A plan that includes the types of contract to be used, risk issues, and evaluation criteria for vendor selection.
- **Procurement strategy.** Tying together the procurement plan with business objectives.
- **Bid documents.** The documents used to solicit proposals from potential sellers, vendors, or suppliers.
- **Procurement statement of work (SOW).** Based on the project scope, a narrative description of the procurement work to be performed on the project.
- **Source selection criteria.** The key skills, deliverables, cost, and so on that will be considered as part of the vendor selection process (to be used during the conduct procurements process).
- **Make-or-buy decisions.** Conclusions and decisions made to perform the work internal to the project team or external to the team. Note that this is a result of the make-or-buy analysis performed as a tool/technique and is also an input to the next process (Conduct Procurements).
- **Independent cost estimates (ICE).** An output of the planning procurement process that helps generate a project life cycle estimate that is usually conducted independently of the Program Management Office (PMO) or department/agency by an outside organization. It examines the full project life-cycle cost (or Total Ownership Costs [TOC]) for a project.
- **Change requests.** Items that surface during procurement planning that require changes to the selection process or to the criteria when choosing a vendor.

- **Project documents updates.** Consideration of which project documents may need to be updated and updating as necessary. This could include updates to your requirements documents and traceability matrix. If a contract is put in place, how will that affect your risk register and risk owner?
- **Organizational process assets updates.** Updates to common tools and templates or other standard forms or assets used in the procurement processes within your organization, department, or agency.

Procurement Management Plan

To be successful in managing procurements, you should always have a plan. The procurement management plan should describe how the procurement processes will be managed. It should define the key characteristics of the project (such as concerns or issues that need to be considered during the process) and the policies used to select suppliers—for example, single source, preferred (preapproved) vendors, performance measurements, billing requirements (such as electronic, net 30-day, payment by auto-deposit, and so on).

Key components of the procurement plan may include the following:

- The type of contract to be used, terms and conditions, and who the signers will be
- Assumptions and constraints
- The risk plan and contingencies
- The bidder selection process and who will manage it
- The schedule, with date and time requirements or estimates
- The billing and reconciliation process
- The escalation or exception process (to handle grievances or disputes)
- Contract termination language (for example, 30-day written notice, nonperformance penalties, and early termination clause)
- The communications plan (e.g., frequency of meetings, format of documentation, where the documentation is kept, who takes minutes of the meetings, and level of participation from suppliers in the project processes)
- Performance measurements and evaluation criteria
- The overall schedule, documented deliverables, and major milestones

Note

The procurement management plan can be very detailed or high level. It can be formal or informal, depending on the needs of the project and the relationship (history) between the buyer and seller, as well as the level of confidence the seller will deliver as agreed to in the contract.

Make-or-Buy Analysis

The make-or-buy analysis helps the PM decide whether it is more cost efficient to produce the products/services inside the project team or to buy them outside the team from a supplier or vendor. There are times when it is more efficient to farm out (outsource) the work or lease equipment than to do the work internally to the team or purchase the equipment. Many factors need to be considered, such as frequency of use, overall cost of the alternative, proprietary property, schedule, resource availability, and so on.

Procurement Documents

As an output to the Plan Procurements process, you develop documents that will be used to solicit proposals from sellers/suppliers. These documents represent a detailed view of the work to be performed, products, or results expected as part of the vendor performance.

The term *proposal* is used generally to describe any one of the following documents to solicit proposals (bids) from prospective sellers or suppliers:

- **Request for proposal (RFP).** Sometimes called a *request for tender*. An RFP calls for a price from the seller and usually includes a detailed proposal for how the seller will perform the work, handle billing, receive payments, and so on.
- **Request for information (RFI).** Requests detailed description of how the seller can and will perform the work.
- **Request for bid (RFB) or invitation for bid (IFB).** Requests a price for the work to be performed (typically, the bid received has a time limit; e.g., 30 or 60 days).
- **Request for quote (RFQ).** Requests a price quote per item-hour or per unit of work.

Note

As the buyer, you (the PM) structure the request or invitation to meet your specific project needs. The documents should have sufficient details to address the specific products, services, or results you need to accomplish from the procurement.

Here are the steps to follow when the final decision is made on the type of documents you plan to use for soliciting proposals:

1. Identify the potential sellers. This is normally accomplished either by a current or past relationship with sellers (some companies have a preferred vendor/seller list) or by referrals from others. You can also simply use a phone directory or an Internet search.
2. When you have a list of sellers, you need to assess their ability to provide the needed products, services, or results in the timeframe they are needed.
3. Send out the invitation to bid to prospective sellers.

Note

The invitation should be clear on the requirements, return date, and bidder's conference information (described in the next section). This could include location, time, format, time allocated to each seller to present, and question-and-answer period.

Source (Seller) Selection Criteria

This process begins with distributing requests for products or services using the documents created in the preceding section. The documents describe the work to be performed and the initiation of the source selection process.

Assessment of potential sellers may include the following:

- **Overall life-cycle cost.** What is the total cost of ownership in the work to be performed (purchase cost plus operating cost—e.g., office equipment, office space, and disposal fees)? Are there licenses or royalties that will need to be paid?
- **Capability of meeting the needs of the contract.** Staffing technical skills, management or specialty skills (such as CAPM or PMP), and track record on past projects. Also, is training required and available if needed?
- **Risk rating.** Level of risk to the seller, past performance, and mitigation strategy.
- **Management approach.** Will the seller provide supervision, HR management (including payroll), and standard processes, methods, and procedures for the services to be performed?
- **Technical approach.** Does the seller have proven methods, measured results, and positive trends in quality performance? Do their services meet the procurement document requirements?
- **Warranty requirements.** Does the seller warrant the finished product, and for what time period? Are there property rights (licenses) for products or services the seller provides?
- **Financial status.** Are they financially sound to take on your project? Do they invoice in a timely manner and pay their bills on time? Can they handle wire transfers between banks?
- **References.** Are they willing and able to provide good references from previous clients?

The information and sample selection scoring (weighting) criteria in Table 12.3 represents a bid for call center (help desk) services.

Note

Keep in mind that the scoring criteria and weight numbering are subjective and must be meaningful and applicable to your specific project.

TABLE 12.3 Sample Scoring Criteria

Category	Weight
I. Functional Characteristics (This section evaluates the system and technologies.)	**40**
A. Redundancy/reliability/life cycle of technology proposed	10
B. Flexibility for interconnection with peripheral systems installed at other locations	1
C. System management tools and report capabilities	5
D. System expandability (scalability): ease of adds, deletes, moves, and changes	1
E. Integration of voice, data, video, and Internet	7
F. Flexibility for network and VRU (voice response unit) interface	7
G. User operational characteristics	1
H. Flexibility for multisite virtual network	8
II. Vendor Qualifications *(This section evaluates the vendor's capabilities to get the job done.)*	**25**
A. Strategy for long-range product development	5
B. Training and backup support	2
C. Installation capabilities	3
D. Maintenance capabilities	7
E. Installed base of comparable systems	6
F. Call center management strategy expertise	2
III. System Cost/Revenue Opportunities *(This section evaluates the costs over the useful life of the system or services, and any revenue opportunity enhancements available.)*	**35**
A. Discounted cash flow over system life cycle	5
B. Capability to minimize network costs	5
C. Capability of minimizing staffing costs	15
D. Capability of maximizing revenue production	10
Total:	**100**

KEY PERFORMANCE INDICATORS (KPIS)

The best approach is to start with identifying which criteria are required ("must have") and which are simply desired (on your "want" list from the seller). The must-have criteria might include a set of key performance indicators (KPIs) or service-level agreements (SLAs) that are tracked, measured, and reported on a regular basis. If the KPI or SLA is missed, penalties may be assessed on the seller (in this case, the call center service provider). Remember that special or critical support requirements may result in higher risk to the seller and possibly higher cost to the buyer. Here's a sample set of must-have criteria for a call center:

- Ninety percent of all calls to the center will be answered within 30 seconds.
- Once the call is answered, no more than 45 seconds of "hold time" will elapse.
- Seventy-five percent of caller problems will be resolved at the Level 1 call center without transferring the caller to a Level 2 support group. Note: Being able to resolve the caller's problems on the first call is sometimes known as the "first-time fix rate" or "first call resolution" (FCR).

Each "want" criterion must be given a relative weight to display its importance compared to all the other "want" items. The total of all "want" criteria should be 100 points, or 100 percent of the decision (in our example). For technology acquisitions, it is common to divide the "want" criteria into three major categories:

- Functional characteristics (such as the system and technology to be used)
- Vendor qualifications and capabilities of meeting the requirements of the contract
- System cost and revenue opportunity (see the sample criteria in Table 12.3)

Conduct Procurements Process (Executing Process Group)

The Conduct Procurements process involves obtaining seller responses and comparing the responses to the scoring (or weight) table. At this time ßyou have a clear set of selection criteria, procurement documents (such as RFP or RFQ), and a distribution list of the sellers you feel would be able to provide the goods or services you want to acquire. The request is sent to the sellers, and you begin collecting the responses.

Bidders' Conference

In some cases you may conduct a bidder's conference (sometimes called a contractor's conference, vendor's conference, or prebid conference). This is usually held at the (requesting) customer's site or a central location for more complex or larger contracts.

The bidder's conference is a way to get the request presented in an organized fashion to multiple vendor/suppliers by getting them together at the same time in the same place (colocated). This is a great opportunity to present the goods or services needed and the criteria that will be used in the selection process to ensure that all participants hear the same information in an unbiased manner. It is customary to allow a question-and-answer (Q&A) session during the conference in case the suppliers want clarification on any specifics of the project. Normally, the minutes and Q&As are posted online or distributed to all prospective bidders in a timely manner. Choosing among competitive bids can be a challenging process. It often involves having a committee representing a variety of disciplines and agendas. A fair and impartial analysis that results in a consensus decision is the goal, but competing priorities and hidden biases or agendas often slow down the process. This is where the work in the previous processes pays off—for example, you have an approved procurement plan and associated documents (including scoring criteria).

Source Selection: Selecting a Seller and Awarding a Contract

Once the bids are received from the sellers, your committee begins reviewing and analyzing the bids for compliance with your must-have criteria. Here are some insights into the selection process.

The vendor selection process can be a very complicated and emotional undertaking if you don't know how to approach it from the very start. Here are five steps to help you select the right vendor for your business and provide you with insight on contract negotiations and avoiding negotiation mistakes.

1. Analyze business requirements. This is the toughest part of the vendor selection process. Success here will put you on the right track in selecting the right vendor at the right price. Lack of effort, poor planning, or taking shortcuts will seriously jeopardize the success of the vendor selection process.
2. Define the product, material, or service. Writing a definition of the product, material, or service that you are selecting a vendor for will be the easiest task that you have to accomplish and the most important.
3. Define the technical and business requirements. If it is a service or software, then specific business requirements must be defined. The bigger the scope of the project, the more requirements you should have.
4. Define the vendor requirements. The vendor selection process would not be complete without listing the criteria that the vendor itself must meet in order to be considered and evaluated for the job.
5. Publish a requirements document for approval. Once all of the above steps are complete, aggregate your findings and requirements into a comprehensive document. The team members will share this document with the key employees in their areas and seek feedback. After the team members accomplish this, and the document is updated with appropriate feedback, the leader of the vendor selection team will present the updated requirements document to upper management to seek their feedback and approval. This document will be the basis for generating a request for proposal (RFP) or request for quote (RFQ)."[1]

Ask the Expert

Q: Do you have an example of a seller selection that can serve as a learning experience?

A: Yes, in response to an RFP from a seller to a bid for 24/7 (three 8-hour shifts per day) call center support, the seller stated they would provide support in two 12-hour shifts per day. When the seller was asked why they proposed different shift coverage, they said that it would be more efficient and save money to provide two-shift 12-hour coverage instead of three 8-hour shifts. When the truth came out, it was revealed that the company didn't have enough trained staff to perform coverage for three shifts. Needless to say, they were not awarded the contract.

Conduct Procurements Inputs, Tools and Techniques, and Outputs

An overview of the inputs, tools and techniques, and outputs for the Conduct Procurements process is described in the following sections (see Figure 12.3).

INPUTS

There are many inputs to be considered in the Conduct Procurements process, and a sample list of the inputs are seller proposals, project and procurement documentation, and, as usual, any enterprise environmental factors or organization process assets. Each of the inputs shown in Figure 12.3 is critical to the overall success of this process. As you work your way through this process, always make sure you consider the organizational process assets that already exist. Ignoring them could result in repeating mistakes your organization has already experienced.

TOOLS AND TECHNIQUES

When it comes time to work the Conduct Procurements process, there are a number of tools and techniques available. Each has its purpose and may be predetermined by your project management office (PMO), procurement department, or organization. The PM should be involved in this process even if it is being handled or managed by a centralized procurement department or group. Here is a brief description of some of the possible tools and techniques:

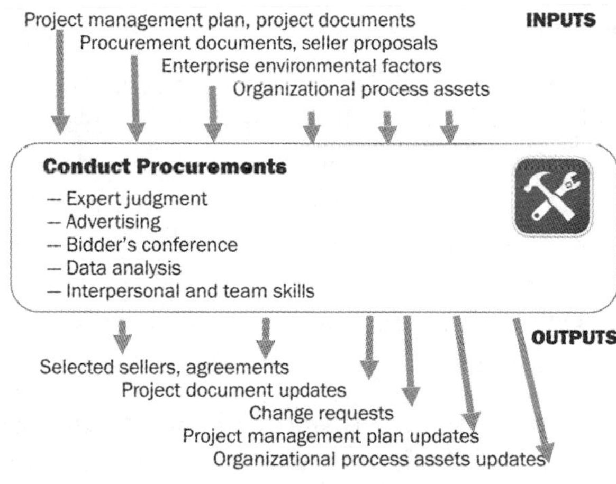

FIGURE 12.3 Conduct Procurements Process ITTOs

- **Bidder's conferences.** Includes contractor or vendor/supplier conferences, which are very useful, especially for complex projects.
- **Proposal evaluation techniques.** Using selection criteria based on procurement policies helps you evaluate proposals consistently.
- **Independent estimates.** Help evaluate the accuracy of bids. When you notice a large gap between bids, it may be an indication of poorly stated requirements—or, it could differentiate between experienced and inexperienced bidders.
- **Expert judgment.** Leverage the knowledge and experience of others whenever possible.
- **Advertising.** Advertising is a great way to solicit new vendors, suppliers, and customers to participate in the procurement process, ensuring best competitive prices, products, supplies, or services.
- **Analytical techniques.** There are many different techniques to analyze potential vendors, suppliers, or subcontractors. These techniques (or methods) are procedures used to analyze project problems and are usually time limited or task limited. Some basic and commonly used analytical techniques or methods may include the following:
    + Brainstorming
    + Benchmarking
    + Gap analysis
    + Mind maps
    + Pareto principle, Pareto principle 80-20 rule
- **Procurement negotiations.** An important tool or technique for conducting procurements is to use proven negotiation skills.

OUTPUTS

The outputs of the Conduct Procurements process include the following:

- **Selected sellers.** Based on selection criteria.
- **Agreements.** Awarded contracts, letters of agreement, SOW, etc.
- **Change requests.** Based on any new information.
- **Project management plan updates.** As appropriate.
- **Project document updates.** Such as resource calendars (work schedule, work periods, resource availability, and so on).
- **Organizational process assets updates.** As they pertain to conducting procurements process.

As a last step in this process, always remember to look back over your project management plan and other project and procurement documents to determine which may require updates.

Note

You should remember that the outputs from a given process typically become the inputs to the next process. Watch for the links–this will help when studying for PMI exams.

Control Procurements Process (Monitoring and Controlling Process Group)

The Control Procurements process involves managing procurement relationships and monitoring contract performance to ensure that the work (or product) is meeting quality requirements. Although proper planning is critical to get to this point, without a doubt this is one of the most important areas for the PM's management of the process to successful completion. The legal nature of the contractual relationship makes it extremely important for the project team to be fully aware of the implications of their actions when administering procurement. This is what is often referred to in the business world as a "bet your job" situation.

Most companies have established procurement policies and follow strict business-conduct guidelines pertaining to how contracts should be managed.

Tip

The best way to "do good and avoid evil" is to stay current on all your business conduct guidelines. Ensure that you follow all regulatory requirements and your company's code of ethics. The PMI Code of Ethics and Professional Conduct describing social responsibilities and ethics is available on the www.pmi.org website. I highly recommend that you print it out two to three weeks prior to taking the exam to get very familiar with this section and the two key categories ("Mandatory" and "Aspirational").

Managing the Relationship

The key to success when it comes to procurement is the relationship between the buyer and the seller. Honesty and integrity are critical. As the PM (assumed buyer), it is extremely important that you manage this relationship. The best way to manage the relationship during the administration of procurements is with a formal document of agreement) or statement of work (SOW) to establish the ground rules and the roles and responsibilities between the buyer and seller. Managing this relationship is critical to reducing risk to the project. By having very clear written and agreed-to expectations, you lay the framework for success. By ensuring that billing and payments occur according to the agreements made, you build trust. When problems or issues arise and you use the methods agreed to for resolution, you protect the relationship. So many of us fail in this area. We become frustrated by a lack of achieving an expectation without first analyzing (and including the other party in the process) what caused the problem. Be sure to treat others as *valued partners*.

Statement of Work (SOW)

Most PMs use SOWs or a similar type of document. For performance-based contracts, the SOW is often referred to as the "Performance Work Statement" (PWS) if it is a performance-based acquisition. A SOW is a narrative description of the services (or products/results) to be delivered on the project. Other titles include work order, request for service, service request, service order, and document of understanding (DOU). It doesn't matter what you call it in your world; you need to be familiar with the SOW from PMI's perspective, especially if you plan to take and pass the PMI exam.

The SOW should be developed from the approved scope baseline. It defines the specific work that will be performed from outside the project team. It can be viewed as a legally binding document and should sufficiently describe the work, quality deliverables, features, functions, metrics, due dates, specifications, estimated hours, duration, and so on. It should also include details of the location where work will be performed, hours of service, billing requirements, and key contacts (see the upcoming sample list of topics in a SOW). Some great SOW templates are available on the Internet. One example can be found at the CVR/IT Consulting LLC website (http://cvr-it.com/PM_Templates/).

Sample List of Topics in a Statement of Work (SOW)

Here are some key components you might see in an SOW:

- Introduction to the project (business need or justification)
- Problem statement or background (what the project will fix or address)
- Scope statement/baseline (including requirements for both products and the project)
- Seller and buyer requirements, deliverables, and milestones (including roles and responsibilities for all parties)
- Schedule duration (period of performance, target completion date, etc.)
- Change management plan, system, processes, and procedures
- Specific type of services and deliverables
- Rate structure (by skill type, expected hours, constraints, and costs)
- Hours of support or coverage
- Communications plan and expectations for meetings and status reporting
- Roles and responsibilities, special needs, training, mentoring, and so on
- Payment schedule and type (e.g., invoices must be paid within 30 days of receipt)
- Nondisclosure agreements (e.g., handling of confidential or proprietary information)

- Physical and logical security (e.g., user IDs, access codes, and passwords)
- Travel and discretionary expense reimbursement guidelines
- Approval signatures

Control Procurements Inputs, Tools and Techniques, and Outputs

The inputs, tools and techniques, and outputs for this process are further described in this section. Figure 12.4 shows the inputs, tools and techniques, and the outputs for the Control Procurements process.

INPUTS

The Control Procurements process has numerous inputs to consider and primarily include the contract and other specific performance and procurement agreements: agreements, selected sellers list, quality reports, and so on.

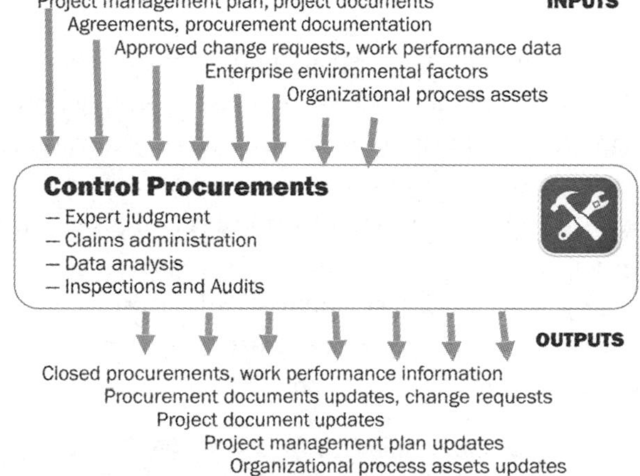

FIGURE 12.4 Control Procurements Process ITTOs

TOOLS AND TECHNIQUES

The tools and techniques for the Control Procurements process focus on results reporting, tight change control, and accountability in the process. Some of the tools and techniques include, but are not limited to, contract change control system, procurement performance reviews, and inspections and audits, as well as payment systems.

Contract Change Control

As mentioned previously, change control is essential, especially when you are managing procurements and contracts. When it comes to legal documents and liabilities, this is not a topic you want to take lightly. Changes to a project can have a direct effect on the contract, such as a modification to the scope of work or deliverables. Also, there may be a change in overall cost (price increases for products, materials, or services). It is important to ensure that all contract changes are reviewed, documented, and approved by both parties prior to implementation. I highly recommend that you seek support from your contracts and procurement experts when drafting and managing contracts and procurements.

Tip

You should be aware of the doctrine of *privity of contract*, which refers to the contractual relationship between the buyer and seller. You may see a question on the PMP or CAPM exam around this term. Simply stated, by the legal principle of privity of contract, a contract cannot confer rights or impose obligations except to the parties to the contract. For example, if Seller A enters into a contract to build a house for Buyer B, and Buyer B contracts Seller C (electrician) to install additional features in the house (such as wiring for a home theater system), and the house burns down because of faulty wiring by Seller C, Seller A will not be liable for the damages caused by Seller C.

Outputs

As with all outputs, keep in mind the ripple effect (*progressive elaboration*). When controlling the procurement process, you need to keep all procurement and project documents up to date. It is important to note that many organizations treat contract and procurement administration separately from operational or functional support. Although a PM may be involved with the administration of contracts and procurement, this process might be administered by supervisory or administrative support.

One of the primary outputs of the Control Procurements process is closing all procurements, reporting work performance information, and updating any procurement and project documentation based on the latest information.

Close Procurements

Close Procurements is no longer an independent PMI process; rather, it has been combined into the Close Project or Phase process in the Closing Process Group and falls in the Project Integration Management Knowledge Area of the sixth edition *PMBOK Guide*.

Close procurements involves completing each procurement activity and verifying that all work and deliverables were performed according to the terms and conditions of the contract.

The closure of procurements may be for the entire project or one or more phases. Closing procurements also includes administrative activities such as finalizing any open claims, updating records, and archiving all pertinent documents for future use.

The best place to start when it comes to closing procurements is the contract terms and conditions to make sure all contractual obligations have been fulfilled. Once you are sure you and the team have successfully completed all deliverables of the contract/procurements, you need to obtain formal acceptance from the sponsor (or sponsors) of the project. In some cases a formal audit may be performed prior to final payment.

A couple of things to think about when closing out the procurements are to ensure that you obtain formal acceptance of all deliverables on the contract, verifying that the work is satisfactory, complete, and warranted as appropriate and that all invoices are paid—and to make sure you have complete administrative closure. *Administrative closure* simply refers to those activities associated with claims processing, tracking changes to completion, record retention management, final payments, and so on.

A few tools and techniques for the closing procurements focus on ensuring proper control, handling any unsettled procurements, and making sure your records are complete and accurate on your project. Attend to the following:

- Procurement audits are structured reviews of the procurement processes.
- Procurement negotiations may include reaching satisfactory settlement of contract deliverables, which may be achieved through direct negotiation, or some form of alternative dispute resolution (ADR) may need to be explored.
- Records management systems usually consists of a specific set of process-related control functions and tools that are part of the overall project management information system.

The last thing you need when managing procurements on your project is loose ends. You must ensure that all procurements are closed properly, including the following:

- Closed procurement documents should include formal written notice from the buyer to the seller showing satisfactory acceptance of the project deliverables.
- Organizational process assets updates or other project document updates should be performed, which includes procurement document updates, deliverables acceptance, and lessons learned documentation reflecting the final status of the procurement.

Try This

FIXING ISSUES BEFORE TURNING OUT THE LIGHTS

You are the PM on a large project and are closing the procurements by conducting a lessons learned meeting. The customer makes a comment that some of the work was not completed properly and that they will not sign a formal acceptance statement for satisfactory project completion until the work is complete. Take a few moments to decide what you would do first and what you would do second. Then consult the following answer.

Answer:

1. Interview the customer to understand what work the customer feels was not completed. (As it turns out in this case, the work the customer is referring to was not in the original scope baseline, and the work was begun by the project team later in the life cycle.)
2. Interview the team to collect status and estimated completion. Find out why the work was started even though it was not in scope. Then work with the customer to document the work as follow-on activities given that it is not in the scope baseline. Explain that you will be happy to complete the work as a follow-on phase to the project once it is approved; however, you need to officially close the original project.

Contract Termination

Sherrie Bennett states the following in her article "Contract Termination" at Lawyers.com:

> There are many ways to terminate the obligations of a contract. Most often, parties conclude their contract obligations by performing them. However, sometimes problems arise and parties cannot or will not complete their obligations under the contract. Therefore, contracts may be terminated by reasons of *rescission*, *breach*, or *impossibility of performance*.[2]

Here are definitions of these three reasons for termination:

- **Rescission.** This may terminate the obligations of a contract in a variety of circumstances. One party may have the legal right to rescind the contract, or the parties together agree to terminate the contract. For example, event ticket sales are extremely low and the events center has another client to fill the spot (date), so both parties agree to a rescission of the contract.
- **Breach of contract (also called default).** Either or both parties have failed to perform an obligation as agreed to and expected under the contract. A breach may occur when one party
  - Refuses to perform the deliverables of the contract.
  - Does something that will prohibit the contract from being delivered.
  - Prevents the other party from performing its obligations.

  There are two types of breaches: material and immaterial.
  - **Material breach of contract.** This goes to the heart of the contract. The injured party can seek damages such as monetary payment to cover losses resulting from the breach of contract. For example, a rock star who shows up at a concert but doesn't bring his guitar has materially breached the contract to perform if he cannot play.
  - **Immaterial breach of contract.** This is more trivial and does not kill the contract. For example, let's say you have a service contract to maintain the air-conditioning system at the events center. The system is to be checked weekly on Fridays to ensure that the temperature in the arena is a constant 60 degrees (±2 degrees). Contrary to the contract, the service person misses a Friday inspection and comes in on Saturday instead. This act is a technical breach of the contract, but it is immaterial, unless for some reason the inspections needed to be done on Fridays rather than any other day.
- **Impossibility of performance.** The contract can be terminated if an unforeseen event prevents the performance of the contract (e.g., you contract with a famous singer to perform a concert and the performer gets laryngitis and is unable to sing). The contract is terminated by impossibility of performance. As always, there may be exceptions.

Additional Contract and Procurement Terms

Here are some additional terms you should be familiar with (especially for the PMP exam).

FORCE MAJEURE

Force majeure (French for "superior force") "is a common clause in contracts which essentially frees both parties from liability or obligation when an extraordinary event or circumstance beyond the control of the parties, such as a war, strike, riot, crime, or . . . an 'act of God' (for example, flooding, earthquake, volcano) prevents one or both parties from fulfilling their obligations under the contract. However, *force majeure* is not intended to excuse negligence or other malfeasance of a party, [if the] non-performance is caused by the usual and natural consequences of external forces (for example, predicted rain stops an outdoor event), or where the intervening circumstances are specifically contemplated."[3]

Letter of Intent or Letter of Agreement

Letter of intent (LOI) and *letter of agreement* (LOA) are terms that refer to the buyer's express interest in the seller. Even though these letters from the buyer are not normally considered to be contracts, they may be used during the engagement or proposal phase of negotiations to commit to a closer (best and final) review of the seller's proposal. There may be financial compensation written into the LOI or LOA that allows for a period of due diligence for the seller to verify the size and complexity of the project prior to entering into the final contract. LOIs and LOAs are often used when there are many unknowns associated with the project, such as new technology, unique conditions, uncertainty in the overall size or complexity of the project, and so on.

DUE DILIGENCE

Due diligence refers to the performance of an investigation of a business or person. A common example of due diligence in various industries is the process through which a potential buyer evaluates a target company's assets to ensure that the company has accurately stated inventory, revenues, and so on, prior to the acquisition (the goal is full disclosure of the seller's status in order to avoid surprises to the buyer after the contract is signed).

SINGLE AND SOLE SOURCE

You should be familiar with these terms of noncompetitive procurements:

- **Single source.** A single-source contract is made directly with a preferred seller, often without going through the full procurement process. This is normally used when you have a prior long-term relationship with the seller. It is based on trust and confidence.

- **Sole source.** With a sole-source contract, there is only one seller, due to special conditions, patents, or special skills that may exist with that seller.

Note

Single and sole source are both commonly referred to as *sole source*. These contracts carry a higher risk of nonperformance due to putting all your eggs in one basket.

Performing Contract Closure

Contract closure involves making sure all the unfinished work (loose ends) are tied up and formally completed. Often this may be difficult for the PM as many staff may have moved on to support other projects. Many steps are involved with procurement closure, depending upon the contract type (such as fixed price or cost reimbursable). These steps include product verification, administrative closure, financial closure (payments made/received), final reports, lessons learned, and updating all project documentation.

Tip

You will likely see situational questions on the PMI exam asking whether the project is closed. Also, you may see questions asking the difference between contract closure and administrative closure. The difference is that contract closure should occur first, followed by administrative closure.

All contract documents—such as the procurement plan, scope statement, WBS, and so on—need to be reviewed to ensure satisfactory completion. Reviewing all the project documentation (not just the contract) will assist with contract and procurement closure. Documents and areas of consideration include the following:

- Scope baseline
- Approved schedule, deliverables, and milestones
- Budget reports and other financial documents (such as invoices, payments)
- Inspections and audit results (as appropriate)
- Substantial completion (the stage in the progress of the Work when the Work, or a designated portion thereof, is sufficiently complete in accordance with the Contract Documents so that the Owner can occupy or use the Work, or a portion thereof, for its intended use)[4]
- Final completion (formal acceptance)
- Inventory closeout
- Release of liens/claims (formal)

Once the deliverables have been accepted by the customer and the contract has been closed, it's time to collect all the contract, procurement, and project information (conduct a lessons learned meeting), and to finalize the project control book for record retention. Remember, lessons learned should have been collected throughout the project, making the final lessons learned meeting even more effective. Make sure that more than one person knows where the contract files/documents are stored and that you have more than one key. Normally, following closure, the official contract file resides with the contracting official at the corporate office. This sounds simple enough, but entire warehouses are full of old project documents needed for audit or customer review but whose PM has since retired or moved on to another company. When the client comes back for Phase II or III of the project, unless you have key documents you will have to start all over; otherwise, you could fail an audit if the documents cannot be produced when needed.

Ask the Expert

Q: Can you provide an example of project documents needed on an old project?

A: Yes, a young PM called me a few years ago and asked if I had the scope statement, SOW, or WBS for a project I had worked on "some time ago." I finally found the documents in my archives. They were from over seven years ago, and the customer's recollection of the deliverables of the project was much grander than what was captured in these project documents. Needless to say, these documents saved the day and allowed the new PM to get and give a clear picture of the original project. This enabled the new PM to manage the customer expectations more effectively as they initiated Phase II of the project.

Summary of Project Procurement Management

Here are the things you need to remember about contract and procurement management:

- Know the different types of contracts and who bears the burden of risk between the buyer and seller for each.
- Know the procurement management processes (and be familiar with inputs, tools and techniques, and outputs of each).
- For the PMI exam, think of the PM as the buyer in the buyer/seller relationship.
- Be familiar with the elements of a legally binding contract.
- Understand the SOW and contract/agreement details on your project.
- Understand the evaluation criteria. Make them as objective as possible.
- Know the importance of good negotiation skills and the need to maintain a good buyer/seller relationship.

- Ensure that contract performance reporting/documentation is complete and accurate.
- Know the importance of obtaining formal acceptance and effectively closing procurements.

Note

Additional information on project closure is provided in Chapter 14.

References

1. Business Operations and Technology, "The Successful Vendor Selection Process," http://operationstech.about.com/od/vendorselection/a/VendorSelectBusinessReq.htm, accessed March 22, 2017.

2. "Reasons to End or Terminate Contracts," *Lawyers.com*, http://contracts.lawyers.com/contracts-basics/reasons-to-end-or-terminate-contracts.html, accessed March 23, 2017.

3. "Force Majeure," *Wikipedia*, http://en.wikipedia.org/wiki/Force_majeure, accessed March 23, 2017.

4. "'Substantial Completion' on the Construction Project: How Is It Defined?" *Construction Law in North Carolina* (AIA general conditions, A.9.8.1, 2010-07), http://constructionlawnc.com/2010/07/08/substantial-completion/, accessed March 23, 2017.

13 Project Stakeholder Management

Key Skills & Concepts

- Identifying stakeholders
- Stakeholder communications
- Stakeholder management processes
- Importance of planning and managing stakeholder engagement
- Developing a stakeholder strategy
- Interpersonal skills
- Transforming data into information

The first step in managing stakeholders is to identify who they are. You should remember from Chapter 2 that stakeholders are anyone or any organization that is positively or negatively affected by the project. Even on a small project, you could have hundreds of stakeholders that will be somehow involved or affected by the project. Once the stakeholders are identified, you will need to manage them. This step is so important that PMI added a whole new Knowledge Area in the *PMBOK Fifth Edition* addressing this topic. As you may have guessed, the Knowledge Area is called Project Stakeholder Management.

Why is stakeholder management so important? Your project's success or failure will be determined by the project's stakeholders. You may meet cost and schedule requirements but still fail to meet the needs of a particular stakeholder or a group of stakeholders. As project manager (PM), you must lead your team in identifying these stakeholders. By creating a strategy for identifying and managing stakeholders, the project team will not only know and understand "who's who" in the environment, but they will also understand when and how to include and communicate with them.

Agile/Adaptive Environment Considerations

Projects often experience a lot of change, especially early in the project lifecycle and especially in an Agile or Adaptive project environment. Because of the propensity for change in Agile projects and due to the fast and flexible nature of these projects, the PM and team need to be fully engaged with stakeholders. Being actively engaged with stakeholders helps builds trust and confidence between the PM and key stakeholders and goes a long way toward building strong, long-term relationships.

Stakeholder management should begin very early in project creation—during the initiation phase—and be reviewed and updated periodically throughout the life of the project. When you deal with entities outside your immediate project team, it is essential to capture stakeholder information about those who may impact your project, and you will need to adapt your strategy to any personnel changes that will occur over time. Projects can become stalled (delayed) because of an incomplete pass-down (transition or handoff) during personnel changes.

Tip

You may see a question on the PMP exam asking when a stakeholder has the most influence on a project. Remember that stakeholder influence is highest in the beginning and tends to become less as the project progresses.

A Key to Success

It was just after a regularly scheduled quarterly project review meeting with the executives, and Fred, a PM, sat out in the hotel hallway after his briefing. He was stooped over and holding his head. Across the hallway, John noticed Fred was shaken up a bit and went over to encourage him. The conversation went like this:

Fred: "I don't know how you do it John! How are you able to brief the executives and always come out unscathed? When I presented my project status, they said things like, 'We don't understand.' How could they not understand? I explained everything to them in detail. The CFO asked, 'Why are we just now hearing about this?' I sent him an email. Arghhh, this is so frustrating! What don't they get? Now they want to delay my project until they have time to review it in greater detail. There isn't enough time for that!"

John: "The CEO never reacts well to problems without solutions, especially when it's news to him and he first hears about it in these meetings. I learned years ago to include him in communications about significant problems early and solicit his input, sort of as a mentor. He doesn't seem to mind and enjoys the technical interaction. Then, when I brief the executives, he's already on board and takes care of any resistance. As for the CFO, he gets hundreds of emails a day. When it's something that's going to affect my budget, I send him an email with 'FLASH' at the front of the subject. Then I wait five minutes and call him. When I brief the board, they already know all the critical issues and are in agreement with the proposed solutions."

Herding Cats and Managing Stakeholders

A friend of mine was involved with the contract for the Navy/Marine Corps Intranet (NMCI). The navy was consolidating all of its many independent networks being run by various departments and agencies into just one network. It also standardized the many personal computer systems and software in use to a standard build and load. He was involved preaward in gathering requirements from various technical communities and then later for the deployment. When the contract was finally awarded to the EDS Company, they commissioned a popular commercial for the Super Bowl: Herding Cats. The one-minute commercial turns out to be a great example of what it's like managing a project.

- There's a difference between herding cats and cows.
- Herding cats is a team sport.
- It ain't easy.
- Being a cat herder is hard work—go figure!
- You can get ripped to shreds.
- It feels good when you bring in the herd!

All humor aside, taking on a project can be a nearly impossible task without preparation and planning. Part of this is knowing who your stakeholders are and identifying what their level of interest is. This includes knowing whether they are advocates, indifferent observers, or opponents of your project. Once this is understood, develop a plan to manage them by. For you to be successful, your stakeholders need to be engaged. How are you going to accomplish that? PMI states that stakeholder management strategy is about creation and maintenance of relationships between the project team and stakeholders, with the aim of satisfying their respective needs and requirements within project boundaries.

Project Stakeholder Management Processes

According to PMI, there are four processes associated with stakeholder management:

- **13.1. Identify Stakeholders (Initiating Process Group).** The process of identifying the people, groups, or organizations that could impact or be impacted by a decision, activity, or outcome of the project; and analyzing and documenting relevant information regarding their interests, involvement, interdependencies, influence, and potential impact on project success.
- **13.2. Plan Stakeholder Engagement (Planning Process Group).** The process of developing appropriate management strategies to engage stakeholders effectively throughout the

project life cycle, based on an analysis of their needs, interests, and potential impact on project success.

- **13.3. Manage Stakeholder Engagement (Executing Process Group).** The processes of communicating and working with stakeholders to meet their needs/expectations, addressing issues as they occur, and of fostering appropriate stakeholder engagement in project activities throughout the project life cycle.
- **13.4. Monitor Stakeholder Engagement (Monitoring and Controlling Process Group).** The process of monitoring overall stakeholder relationships and adjusting strategies, and maintaining plans for engaging stakeholders.

Identify Stakeholders Process (Initiating Process Group)

This process is extremely important to managing projects in the real world. It is critical to identify who the stakeholders are early in the project life cycle (see Figure 13.1). You need to know who the stakeholders are and their level of interest or influence on the project (e.g., funding sponsor, end users, or managers). If you need a refresher on who the project stakeholders are, see Chapter 2.

The Identify Stakeholders process is a great opportunity to bring your team together and brainstorm who will affect or be affected by the project. Schedule a meeting and

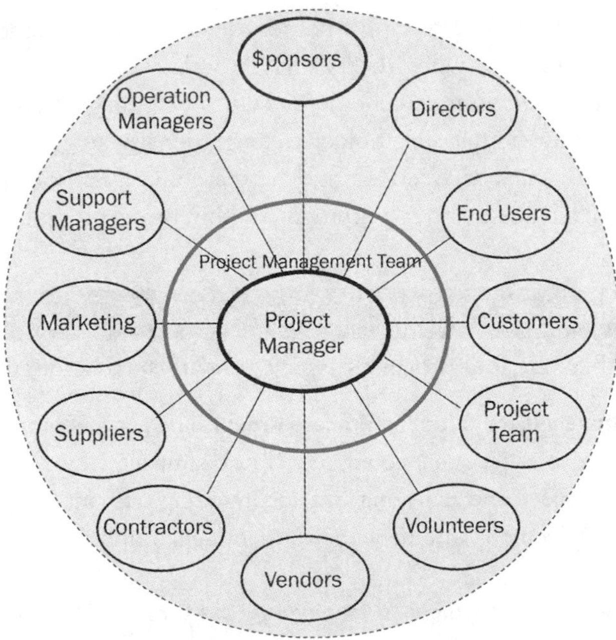

FIGURE 13.1 Who Are Project Stakeholders?

run some exercises, using the team to begin identifying stakeholders and understanding their roles. Maybe you will find groups of stakeholders who require unique communications. Build that into your strategy while planning. Figure 13.2 shows an overview of the inputs, tools and techniques, and outputs for the Identify Stakeholders process (see *PMBOK* for more details).

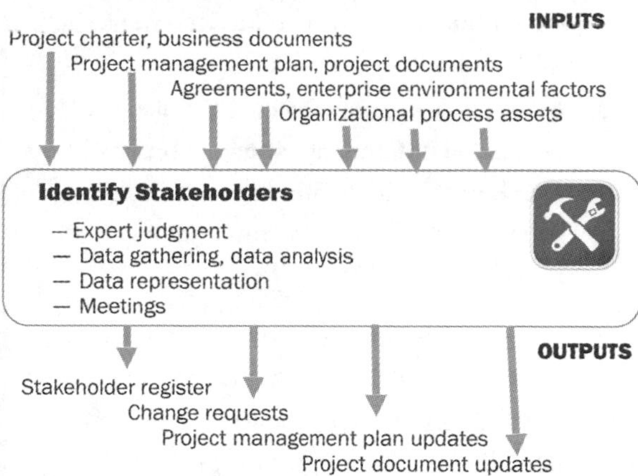

FIGURE 13.2 Identify Stakeholders Process ITTOs

Identify Stakeholders Inputs

Some of the inputs for the Identifying Stakeholders process are project charter, business and project documents including the project management plan, other project agreements, and of course the enterprise environmental factors and organizational process assets that need to be considered during the Identify Stakeholder process.

Identify Stakeholders Tools and Techniques

One of the more important tools and techniques for identifying stakeholders is stakeholder analysis. Three primary steps are involved.

1. **Identify all potential project stakeholders**, including their roles, departments, level of knowledge, and influence on the project or information (or funding) needed on the project. Are they decision makers or subject matter experts (SMEs) who can help technically? A good way to do this is to interview the stakeholders and expand your list based on the new information gained.
2. **Identify the potential impact or support of each stakeholder** and prioritize the key stakeholders to ensure communications flow appropriately. An effective tool in this case is a power/interest grid (see Figure 13.3). This allows you to group the stakeholders based on their active involvement or level of influence (power). This is a simple grid with quadrants: on the Y-axis is *Power* (from low to high), and on the X-axis is *Interest* (from low to high). Then as a team, you determine where your stakeholders should be placed on the grid. For example, from left to right in the bottom quadrants, insert *Monitor (Minimal Effort)* and *Keep Informed*. In the top two corners, put from left to right *Keep Satisfied* and *Manage Closely*. Then, it is a matter of coming to some agreement as a team on an agreed placement of each stakeholder. Variations of this method can also be used, including

power/influence grid, influence/impact grid, and salience models.

3. **Assess how key stakeholders are likely to respond in different situations** in order to plan better how to influence stakeholder support and to mitigate potential negative impact to the project.

The other tools and techniques usually associated with the Identify Stakeholders process are expert judgment and meetings. Meetings are especially important with Agile projects, and it is good to have the customer (or other key stakeholders) in attendance or represented to ensure clear and timely flow of information.

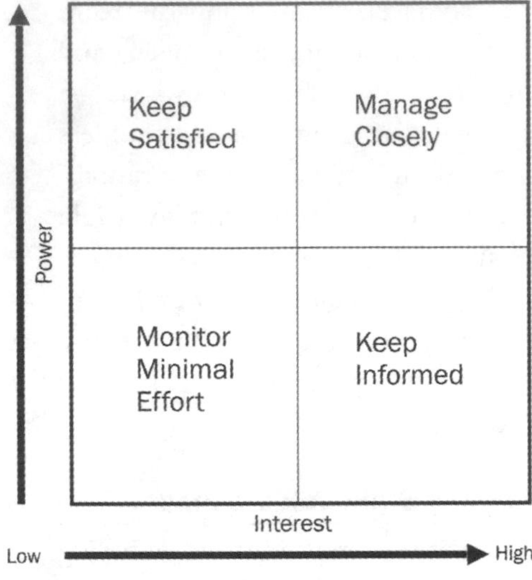

FIGURE 13.3 Sample Power and Interest Grid

Identify Stakeholders Outputs

Here are a few samples of outputs for the Identify Stakeholders process:

- **Stakeholder register.** This is a log that should include each stakeholder's name, organization, position (title), role on the project, contact information, and assessment information (such as expectations or level of influence), and stakeholder classification (such as supporter, neutral, or resister).
- **Change requests.** Changes are inevitable on any project, and keep in mind some changes can be positive, so don't just say no to change.
- **Project Management Plan Updates.** As more information is gained, there are times when it is appropriate to update the project management plan. Always keep track of changes to the PM Plan and other project documents as appropriate (version control).
- **Project Document Updates.** Updates are necessary to keep track of changes. When updating any project document, be aware of scope creep, and always document and communicate changes to the proper project stakeholders.

Now that the project stakeholders have been identified, it is time to start the planning process for stakeholder engagements.

Plan Stakeholder Engagement Process (Planning Process Group)

Here is where you develop strategies based on stakeholders identified in the register and factor in their needs, expectations, their level of interest in the project, and how their participation, or lack thereof, affects the success of the project. Figure 13.4 shows an overview of the inputs, tools and techniques, and outputs for the Plan Stakeholder Engagement process.

Try This

HOW TO PLAN COMMUNICATIONS FOR KEY STAKEHOLDERS

Say for a moment that you are the events center manager for an upcoming concert. How do you plan for the communications needs of the stakeholders (sponsors, team, etc.) for this event?

Answer: The best way to plan for communications is to brainstorm. Get the core project team together and make a list of who will be affected by this project. I like to use a spreadsheet or table for the project team—refer to sample RAM table (Table 9.1) and sample RACI Chart (Table 9.2) in Chapter 9. Then add to it for additional stakeholders, including their level of interest or power (i.e., decision maker, end user, support manager, or customer).

Stakeholder Engagement Management Strategy

Once you identify the stakeholders, you need to have a strategy to help guide the team and yourself in managing those stakeholders. The stakeholder register is an output of the Identify Stakeholders process, and it should provide direction on how you plan effective management of all the stakeholders affected by the project. Because projects are unique and stakeholders change, one thing is certain: you can't treat all stakeholders alike. For example, you would treat the sponsor of the project differently than you would a meddling manager (who, for some reason, wants extra deliverables added to the project even though the manager is not a decision maker and has no authority to make these kinds of demands or changes). To get an idea of the different stakeholder interests and the flow of communication to the various stakeholders, see Figure 13.5.

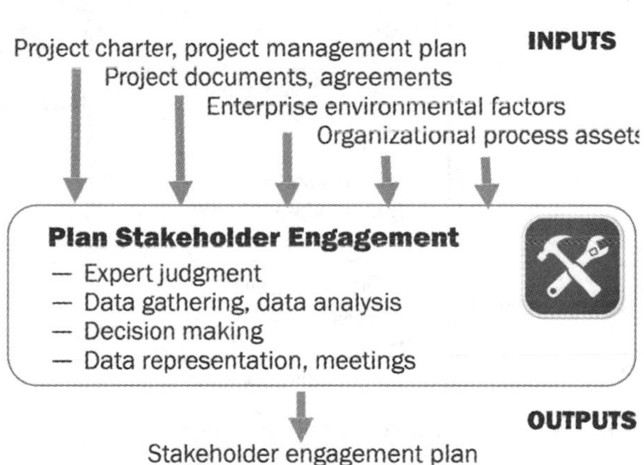

FIGURE 13.4 Plan Stakeholder Engagement Process ITTOs

Table 13.1 shows a stakeholder engagement assessment matrix that can be used to understand *current state* engagement and *desired-state* (future) engagement from individual stakeholders or groups of stakeholders.

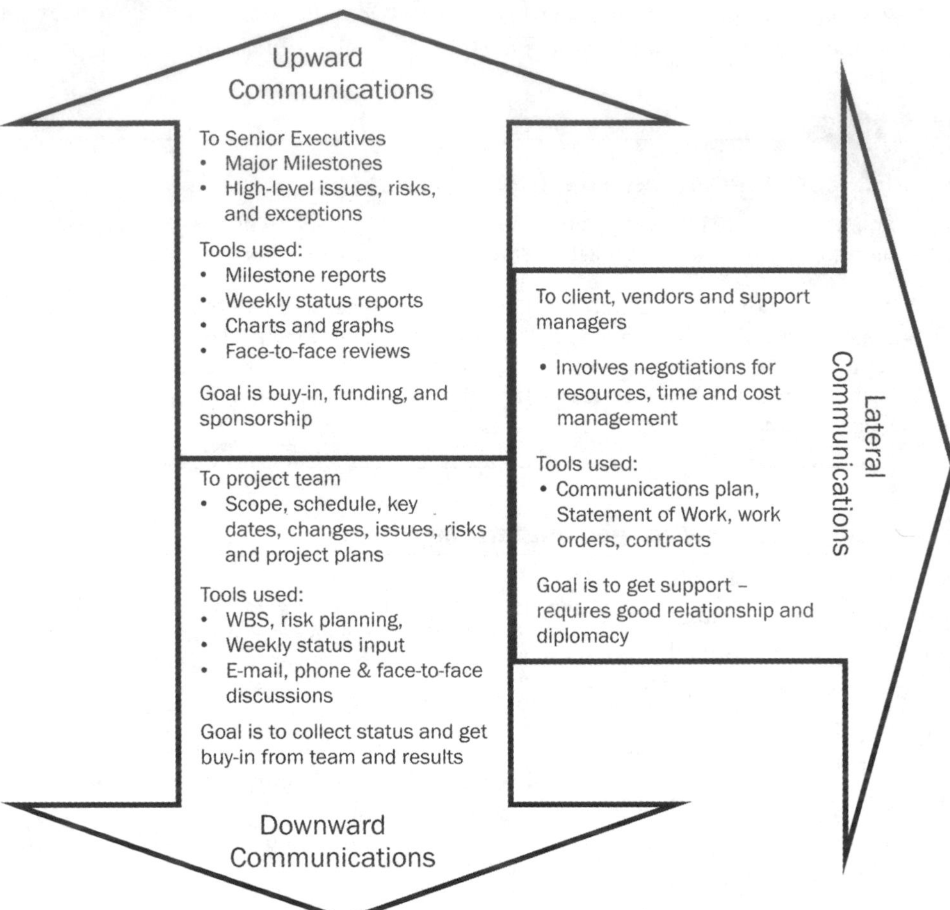

FIGURE 13.5 Communications Flow Diagram

TABLE 13.1 Stakeholder Engagement Matrix

Stakeholder	Unaware	Resistant	Neutral	Supportive	Leading
VP of Finance		C	==========>	D	
Sponsor			C	==========>	D
Engineering Director	C	===========	==========>	D	

Legend: C ==> Current state of engagement; D ==> Desired state of engagement

The arrows represent strategies and action plans needed to move stakeholders from where they are to where you need them to be. As progress is made, update the plan. Caution must be observed in developing, handling, and distributing this type of information.

Plan Stakeholder Engagement Process Outputs

The key output of the Plan Stakeholder Engagement process is the stakeholder engagement plan, which is a component of the project management plan. The stakeholder engagement plan should create effective strategies to increase stakeholder engagement.

Manage Stakeholder Engagement Process (Executing Process Group)

Here is where the active engagement with stakeholders occurs (during the Executing Process Group). Using the previously created stakeholder management plan and communications management plan tools, the PM uses interpersonal and management skills to relate information effectively to stakeholders. In these engagements issue logs are updated, change requests are processed, and updates to the project management plan are processed through the integrated change control process. Figure 13.6 provides an overview of the inputs, tools and techniques, and outputs of the Manage Stakeholder Engagement process.

This process, if not done properly, tends to come back to haunt you. After managing a lot of projects over 30 years, it has been my experience that managing (or attempting to manage) stakeholders takes the majority of time because of all the variables, including moods, egos, politics, and so on.

In today's world many people expect (or demand) instant gratification. Managing stakeholder expectations is not easy. The only way to help make managing stakeholder expectations easier is to establish a good working relationship with the key stakeholders (remember, the team is your number-1 asset on the project). You want to keep them happy. Also, don't forget the sponsors who are funding the project. They may need special care as well. Therefore, you need to learn how to play well with others, even when emotions run high and mood swings occur. Always keep your responses friendly and professional. Don't raise your voice, get cynical, or sarcastic. In Asia and other countries, raising your voice or showing emotion is a sign of weakness. You want to stay in control in all situations.

FIGURE 13.6 Manage Stakeholder Engagement Process ITTOs

Try This

MANAGING UNREALISTIC EXPECTATIONS (CASE STUDY)

Imagine for a moment that you are a project manager for a six-month transition of IT services from the customer's location (Cincinnati, Ohio) to Boulder, Colorado. The project is to mirror the computer system as is by simply setting up a clone of the current system's operating environment in Boulder, copying the system image over to the new system, and then running the tests. Sounds pretty simple, right?

Now throw in a little change in the customer expectations. For example, the client decides (after equipment has already been ordered based on an originally approved and priced configuration) to add new human resources and financial applications that require a significant increase in the system's processing power (double the usage). A larger computer system is needed and will cost another $500,000, and the software licenses will cost over $1 million beyond that. The impact to make these changes will extend the schedule by two to three months.

So the question is, How do you manage unrealistic expectations?

Answer: Meet with the customer to understand fully the reason for the customer's change. Then, armed with all the facts and figures, explain to the customer in a professional manner the impact to the project both in time and cost. Hopefully, the client will be reasonable and allow the extra time and additional pricing to match their new expectations. I have seen this go both ways, but in all cases the changed expectations strained the relationship. Therefore, always work on establishing a good relationship with stakeholders as early as possible. That is another key to success.

Managing stakeholder expectations involves frequent interaction, negotiations, regular meetings, and status reports to keep them in the loop. The old saying "no news is good news" doesn't hold true here. If you are not communicating with the stakeholders, they begin to wonder who is in charge and whether you are hiding something. Therefore, it is best to communicate early and often. Even if the news is bad, you need to keep the stakeholders informed. The key is to stay connected, communicate any problems, and most of all have an action plan. The key stakeholders have a right to know what is going on and how you are managing problems. The following stakeholder checklist is provided as a guide in managing the stakeholder processes:

1. Team brainstorming exercise to identify stakeholders (profile-analysis meetings).
2. Team affinity diagram exercise to sort people/groups into related groups.
3. Team grid model exercise to build consensus on stakeholder priority.
4. Team stakeholder engagement exercise. Create a mapping of stakeholders to their engagement levels (unaware, resistant, neutral, supportive, or leading) and the team's desired level for their engagement.
5. Plan strategies and actions to move stakeholders from current states to desired states.
6. Execute the plan, monitor, and update as necessary.

Manage Stakeholder Engagement Tools and Techniques

Here are some tools and techniques that can be used for this process:

- **Communication skills.** How you plan to communicate with the stakeholders.
- **Interpersonal and team skills.** Build trust, resolve conflict in a timely manner, and actively listen.
- **Management skills.** Work on negotiation, writing, and presentation skills, even public speaking techniques and style.

INTERPERSONAL SKILLS

Interpersonal skills are the life skills we use every day to communicate and interact with other people, both individually and in groups. People who have worked on developing strong interpersonal skills are usually more successful in both their professional and personal lives.[1]

Employers often seek to hire staff with *strong interpersonal skills*. They want people who will work well in a team and be able to communicate effectively with colleagues, customers, and clients.

Interpersonal skills are important not just in the workplace—our personal and social lives can also benefit from better interpersonal skills. People with good interpersonal skills are usually perceived as optimistic, calm, confident, and charismatic—qualities that are often endearing or appealing to others.

Through awareness of how you interact with others, and with practice, you can improve your interpersonal skills.

A list of interpersonal skills includes the following:

- **Verbal communication.** What we say and how we say it (refer to Chapter 10 for details).
- **Nonverbal communication.** What we communicate without words; body language.
- **Listening skills.** How we interpret both the verbal and nonverbal messages sent by others.
- **Negotiation skills.** Working with others to find a mutually agreeable outcome.
- **Problem solving.** Working with others to identify, define, and solve problems.
- **Decision making.** Exploring and analyzing options to make sound decisions.
- **Assertiveness.** Communicating our values, ideas, beliefs, opinions, needs, and wants.

YOU ALREADY HAVE INTERPERSONAL SKILLS

We've all been developing our interpersonal skills since childhood, usually subconsciously. Interpersonal skills become so natural that we may take them for granted, never thinking about how we communicate with other people. With a little time and effort you can develop these skills. Good interpersonal and team skills can improve many aspects of your life, professionally and socially. They lead to better understanding and relationships.

Interpersonal skills are also sometimes referred to as *social skills*, *people skills*, *soft skills*, *communication skills*, or *life skills*. Although these terms can include interpersonal skills, they tend to be broader and therefore may also refer to other types of skills.[2]

HOW TO DEVELOP YOUR INTERPERSONAL SKILLS

A variety of skills can help you to succeed in different areas of life, but the foundations for many other skills are strong interpersonal skills because these are relevant to personal relationships, social affairs, and professional lives. Without good interpersonal skills, it is often more difficult to develop other important life skills.[3]

- **Learn to listen.** Listening is not the same as hearing; take time to listen carefully to what others are saying through both their verbal and nonverbal (body language) communication.
- **Choose your words carefully.** Be very aware of the words you are using when talking to others. Take the time to formulate your thoughts before you speak—you want the words to be clear and understood. Also, learn to seek feedback to ensure that your message has been received and clearly understood.
- **Relax.** When we are nervous, we tend to talk more quickly and therefore less clearly. Being tense is also evident in our body language and other nonverbal communication. Instead, try to stay calm, make eye contact, and smile. Let your confidence shine.
- **Clarify.** Show an interest in the people you talk to. Ask questions and seek clarification on any points that could be easily misunderstood.
- **Be positive.** Try to remain positive and cheerful. People are much more likely to be drawn to you if you can maintain a positive attitude.
- **Empathize.** Understand that other people may have different points of view. Try to see things from their perspective. You may learn something whilst gaining the respect and trust of others.
- **Understand stress.** Learn to recognize, manage, and reduce stress in yourself and others. Although stress is not always bad, it can have a detrimental effect on your interpersonal communication. Learning how to recognize and manage stress, in yourself and others, is an important personal skill.
- **Learn to be assertive.** You should aim to be neither passive nor aggressive. Being assertive is about expressing your feelings and beliefs in a way that others can understand and respect. Assertiveness is fundamental to successful negotiation.
- **Reflect and improve.** Think about previous conversations and other interpersonal interactions; learn from your mistakes and successes. Always keep a positive attitude, but realize that you can always improve your communication skills.
- **Negotiate.** Learn how to negotiate effectively with others, paving the way to mutual respect, trust, and lasting interpersonal relations.

- **Learn to work well in groups.** We often find ourselves in group situations, professionally and socially—especially while working in project teams, which is when we need to be keenly aware of, and exercise, good interpersonal skills.

As you can see, interpersonal skills are closely tied to relationship building. Here are some additional tips to ensure success when managing stakeholders:

- Demonstrate integrity and honesty.
- Actively manage stakeholder expectations (interactively and proactively).
- Address concerns before they become larger issues or problems.
- Clarify and track issues using an issue-tracking log, and resolve them quickly.

Monitor Stakeholder Engagement Process (Monitoring and Controlling Process Group)

What does monitoring stakeholder engagement look like? Using this process, the PM monitors stakeholders and relationships identified and analyzed in the previous processes. The PM measures ongoing performance to the project stakeholder engagement management plan. As changes occur in the environment and project, the PM constantly updates the strategies and plans (*progressive elaboration*) for keeping stakeholders engaged. Figure 13.7 describes this process.

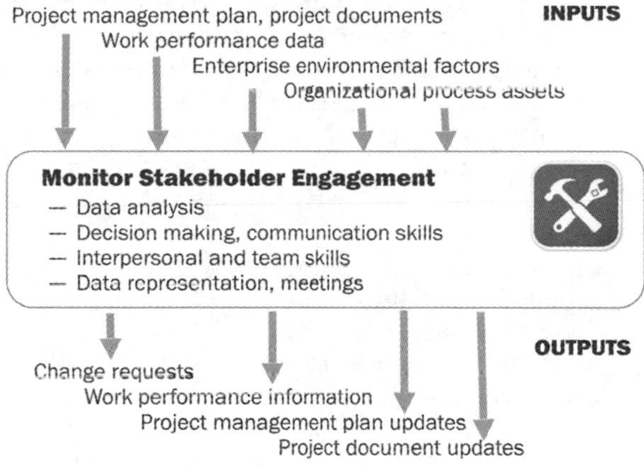

FIGURE 13.7 Monitor Stakeholder Engagement Process ITTOs

What Is an Issue Log Used For?

The issue log is an output to the Direct and Manage Project Work process and is a great tool for monitoring and managing stakeholder engagements. The issue log is not the same as the risk register, where known risks are captured. Risks have uncertainty; issues do not. The issue log is a result of managing and controlling stakeholder engagement. It is used to record a question, dispute, or matter under discussion when consensus is not reached within the group, and the log is then used to track progress on that matter.

An issue log isn't used just to record disagreements that arise during project execution. It is a useful tool to identify a problem, analyze it to explore alternate solutions, record a recommended solution, and then track the success of the solution to closure. Issues can easily arise from poorly defined requirements, and they can surface during the design or execution phases. For instance, in our case study, one of the contracts specified that a surface should be painted but failed to specify the color. Later, during the execution phase, this omission was noted during a team meeting when team members couldn't agree on the proper color. The issue was captured in the log and elevated to the sponsor for resolution. The team was able to present the issue to the sponsor with a color palette of available colors from which to choose. The customer chose the desired color and was satisfied with the team's process.

Another use of the issue log is for capturing and managing risk events that occur (no longer a risk, but now an issue). Once a risk event occurs, it is elevated to the issue log for further action.

A Tale of Two Competing Project Managers: Building Trust

A colleague of mine related a personal story from early in his career. While it wasn't something he was proud of, he said the lesson learned profoundly influenced how he managed professional relationships the rest of his career. It went something like this:

> I worked for a contractor on the West Coast supporting a program manager within an engineering division. My counterpart (working for the same company) on the East Coast supported a different program manager in the Program Management Office. We were constantly butting heads as we represented the competing interests of our direct customers. Over several months there were more than a few heated exchanges during customer status meetings. You can imagine how distressed our CEO was upon hearing stories of two of his managers' constantly locking horns (at odds, or not working together) on behalf of their customers' competing interests. One day, he pulled both of us aside and directly confronted us about our constant battling. The CEO told us his expectation was for both of us to work out our customers' concerns before any meetings and then brief the "agreed-to" plan. Confident that he had made his point, the CEO dropped the matter and continued on into the meeting.
>
> That meeting went okay. However, as time progressed, we eventually returned to our prior adversarial roles.
>
> Later in the year, at the company's annual retreat, there were a number of activities planned. One of them was whitewater rafting. The CEO arranged the crews so that both of us were in the same raft sitting opposite of each other. The river was only supposed to have a few Category 3 rapids, but after a healthy melt-off of winter snow, some were really Category 4 (a bit more dangerous). At first, neither of us wanted to acknowledge the presence of the other, but as we got farther down the river, we had to begin coordinating our efforts to safely navigate the rapids. After what seemed like several close calls, we actually began working together in unison. By the end of the trip, we were fast friends.
>
> What did that look like back in the office? We started seeking each other out early about conflicting issues, looking for ways to bring our customers together and make them successful. Eventually, our customers stopped competing with each other and started cooperating. Our products and services integrated more quickly, and our end users were more satisfied.

What was the lesson learned? Shared activities bring people together. Sharing a challenging experience together away from the office can solve a lot of problems in the office.

Tools and Techniques

The following section describes some of the tools and techniques that can be used during the Monitor Stakeholder Engagement process. Remember that tools and techniques transform inputs into outputs.

INFORMATION MANAGEMENT SYSTEMS

There are many information management systems commercially available today to aid in managing, monitoring, controlling, and publishing project information. Some provide controls over who can see what and also provide editing capabilities. When such systems are used, it is wise to have an agreed-upon standard for version control of the documents.

PROJECT STATUS REVIEW MEETINGS

Meetings, in general, are a fact of life for the project team, and as the PM you will be expected to lead many of them. Meetings are identified as a critical tool and technique in many of the Knowledge Areas in the *PMBOK Guide*. Meetings are important, including status review meetings, progress reporting, and change meetings, which are critical to the success of your project. Status review meetings should be defined in the communications plan with the following elements:

- Type of meeting (status review)
- Who should attend (expert judgment)
- Purpose (to exchange and analyze information about stakeholder engagement)
- When and where (location and time of day / week is important)
- Frequency

Presenters at status meetings should focus on the needs of the receivers of the status. The status also communicates what the team is doing and the progress being made, helping to identify new risks and issues. Status meetings are also an excellent forum to facilitate project integration across project areas. See Chapter 10 for more details on meetings.

Outputs

The following section describes examples of outputs from the Monitor Stakeholder Engagement process.

WORK PERFORMANCE INFORMATION

Work performance data are transformed into work performance information. Data alone don't tell the story or provide clear contexts for taking action. Data need to be interpreted and then applied within a framework leading to understanding. Work performance information organizes and summarizes performance data, which can then be communicated to stakeholders (reports). Table 13.2 provides some examples of each.

TABLE 13.2 Work Performance Data, Information, and Reports Examples

Work Performance Data	Work Performance Information	Work Performance Reports
Percent work complete	Status of deliverables	Status reports
Start/finish dates	Implementation status for change requests	Memos or emails
Number of defects	Forecasted estimates to complete	Justifications
Actual costs	Schedule variance	Electronic dashboards
Actual durations	Schedule performance index	Recommendations
Key performance indicators	Cost variance	Information notes
Number of change requests	Cost performance index	Updates

CHANGE REQUESTS

Change requests are an expected output of the Monitor Stakeholder Engagement process. As the project team interacts with the various stakeholders regarding progress of the project, team members will be able to more clearly communicate their needs. When those changes impact the baseline in any way, change requests should be completed and submitted to the change control board (CCB), following the approved process. Refer to Chapter 4 for more on integrated change control.

PROJECT DOCUMENT UPDATES

As with most other PMI processes, you should always be on the lookout for the need to update project documents (such as the PM Plan) based on any new information that comes up during the development of this and other processes.

Summary of Project Stakeholder Management

Identifying stakeholders on your project helps the PM build a picture of a project's stakeholder environment. Understanding your stakeholders and their needs will allow you to create a strategy for effectively managing them. Remember, one size does not fit all. A particular status report you create to satisfy the needs of one key stakeholder or group of stakeholders may not be appropriate for all stakeholders. Know which information should go where, when, and to whom, and make sure your team knows this too.

One of the fun aspects of project management is the people interaction. Be prepared to fine-tune your communication skills. As you deal with conflict, develop your interpersonal skills. This job will require negotiation, writing, presentation skills, and public speaking. So be prepared to be constantly improving your project management skills.

Monitoring and controlling stakeholders doesn't mean you manipulate them. Combining your communication, interpersonal, and management skills helps you build consensus with your stakeholders and plan effectively for overall project success.

References

1. "Interpersonal Skills," *Skills You Need: Helping You Develop Life Skills*, http://www.skillsyouneed.com/interpersonal-skills.html, accessed March 24, 2017.

2. Ibid.

3. Ibid.

14 Closing the Project: Are We There Yet?

Key Skills & Concepts

- Importance of properly closing the project
- Formal acceptance (getting the sign-off in writing)
- Closing Process Group
- Reverse engineering
- Exit criteria and common closure activities
- Lessons learned
- Conducting the lessons learned/closure meeting
- Rewards and recognition
- Finding team members a home
- Final project closure report
- Plan for record retention
- Reminder of the AIM strategy
- Next steps—where to go from here
- PMI Credentials
- PMI exams
- PMI exam objectives
- How to apply and prepare for a PMI exam
- Learning styles
- Study tips and what to expect on exam day
- Maintaining PMI credentials by earning Professional Development Units (PDUs)
- Objectives of this book
- Celebrate!

Congratulations, you are approaching the end of this project (and this book).

Closing a project is probably the least planned and potentially the most difficult part of managing projects. So how do you ensure that you bring your project to a successful close? The answer is by using good, sound project management discipline. You want to manage the project closure phase of the project life cycle just like any other phase—by using the five Process Groups, as appropriate. You should remember them by now; they are Initiating, Planning, Executing, Monitoring and Controlling, and Closing. You might think you can focus only on the Closing Process Group, but that is not the case. As mentioned before, all Process Groups work interactively and apply to all projects or phases of a project.

Importance of Project Closure

Closing the project or phase is as important as starting a new project. As the project manager, you need to manage project closure as a project in itself. That's right, you need to initiate project closure as well as validate the scope and deliverables of project closure. You need to make sure you have authorization to close out the project (potentially a separate project charter with focus on the closing phase). You need to plan for how to close the project or phase successfully and to ensure proper staffing, adequate time, sufficient budget, and so on to meet the approved closure dates and deliverables.

Formal Acceptance

One way to ensure proper project closure is to make it official by getting the final acceptance (sign-off) in writing. We covered risk management in Chapter 11 and how you must plan for and manage risk throughout the project life cycle. This is especially important during project closure. The project is not officially complete until the paperwork is done and signed by the approving sponsor(s).

Most PMs have a fear of surprises. Surprises are great for birthdays or other holidays but not when closing a project. One of the greatest surprises on any project is when you go to the project sponsor (or customer) to obtain formal acceptance of project completion and you discover they don't want the project to end. Either they really like the work performed and thus feel confident about adding more features or, on the other side of the coin, they feel they didn't get all they expected and want you to deliver more.

If you have planned well and properly documented the project scope and deliverables (what I call "lining up your ducks") by defining the acceptance criteria, communicating the plan and measurement objectives, and obtaining formal acceptance from the sponsor(s), then you should experience few or no surprises at the end of the project.

Tip

At the end of the project, the success or failure of a project depends entirely on measured results and perception. For example, a project may be on time and on budget but may not meet the customer's expectations. PMI feels issues and conflicts should be resolved in favor of the customer. Therefore, you need to manage customer (stakeholder) expectations effectively early and often, especially when closing the project.

Three Takeaway Points

A really good way to manage customer expectations, the project as a whole, and project closure is to remember the three key "takeaway points" from Chapter 2. In my opinion, they are essential to helping you successfully close out your projects. Hopefully, by now you remember them. If not, now is a good time to ask the expert for a refresher.

Ask the Expert

Q: What are the three takeaway points needed for success on any project or phase?

A: At this point, you should be able to recite these from memory. If you can't, learn them now:

- **Stay focused on the end goals and objectives.** You should be able to answer the following question confidently: Did you do what you said you would do on the project? For example, did you meet all project deliverables, effectively manage constraints, meet the approved budget and schedule, perform in a quality manner, and meet customer expectations?
- **Use the tools and resources available.** Did you effectively manage the resources, and did you effectively use tools such as standard processes, templates, checklists, this book, your organization's assets, and the *PMBOK Guide*?
- **Work as a team.** Did you manage the team effectively? Did you help grow the team and the individual team members through mentoring, partnering with the team, and other team-building activities? Always remember the project team is your number-1 asset.

Closing Project or Phase Process (Closing Process Group)

The Closing Project or Phase process is more important than ever based on the potential legal and customer satisfaction exposures. Keep in mind that many projects are created as a feasibility study, that is, business justification, product prototype, or other types of pilot programs or controlled releases to test the marketplace.

According to PMI, research shows that few project managers have the authority to officially (formally) and/or legally close a contract. PMs are responsible to determine when the work is complete and deliverables met (responsibilities transferred); however, the project sponsor (or customer) must sign off on (approve) the contract and deliverables to validate the project deliverables and contract completion.

Reverse Engineering

Reverse engineering (sometimes called "right-to-left planning") is a great way to close a project. You normally have a set (or fixed) target date for closure. So start by backing into the target date and allow enough time to shut down the project properly. The amount of time needed to close a project depends entirely on the size, type, and complexity of the project. In general, allow at least 60 to 90 days, due to the written notices that you need to send to suppliers to cancel services, to write leaser license-termination letters for hardware and software, and to give people sufficient notice to plan for their next assignment.

It doesn't matter if you are closing a long-term project that you have been working on for some time or if you are brought in on a fairly new short-term project that someone else has been managing—the approach should be the same. Manage the closing phase as a project (charter to close).

The Past Is a Crystal Ball into the Future

Wouldn't it be great if you knew how to reach success on your project before you even began? You can, and you don't even need a crystal ball to see into the future. The past has provided a lot of great historical information about why projects fail. We should be able to learn from past mistakes and move on to greater project success.

You may remember that in Chapter 2 we talked about why projects fail, and these reasons apply even when closing a project. To refresh your memory, here's a short summary:

- Lack of project management discipline (risk management, communications, change, time, cost and scope management, etc.). When closing a project, we tend to get in a hurry and think we just need to get to the "end of the game" and the project will be complete. However, you still need to exercise good project management practices for successful closure.
- Lack of user (key stakeholder) involvement. (Don't leave out the customer or users.)
- Lack of project sponsor commitment. (Sponsors tend to lose interest at the end of the project; remind them of what needs to be done and the need for their support.)
- Projects ending for the wrong reasons (assuming the problems are solved, or due to lack of sponsorship).
- Lack of properly trained or skilled people to work the project.
- Lack of cultural skills and ability to manage in a multicultural environment.

Exit Criteria

The exit criteria for a given project tends to be unique no matter how many times a similar project has been conducted. Even if the project has been done before, there are always certain factors that require a slightly different approach to the closing process for each project.

Exit criteria must align with the agreed-to measures for the project and may include quality, conformance to specific requirements, and successful completion of key deliverables such as products, services, and results.

Project Closure Activities

Here are some of the more common project closure activities:

- Provide final written reports (financial status, earned value reports, milestones, changes, successes, open issues, the location of updated documentation, etc.).
- Conduct contract closeout and overall administrative closure.
- Get formal acceptance of all deliverables. (This is extremely important.)
- Conduct a lessons learned session to capture what worked and what didn't work. Include the customer in this session.
- Update documentation for record retention. (Check with your asset manager or business controls coordinator for state and local, federal government [IRS, SEC], and company-specific requirements.)
- Conduct team and individual evaluations. Provide feedback to the employees and their managers.
- Provide rewards and recognition to the team and individuals for their contributions.
- Celebrate!

Sample Project Closure from the P&G Case Study

To carry on with our P&G case study, see Figure 14.1 for a real-world example of project closure. After each event/project, this checklist is used to determine the status of the facility, equipment, and preparedness for the next event. All identified follow-up activities will be initiated as appropriate.

FIGURE 14.1 Case Study Project Status Report

Project Status Report	
Project Name:	P&G IT Transition Project (help desk transition subproject only)
Prepared by:	George A.
Date (MM/DD/YYYY):	09/30/1995
Reporting Period:	03/01/1995 through 9/30/1995

FIGURE 14.1—*continued*

Either enter the status information in the sections below or create links to referenced documents (e.g., Link_To_…) by using Insert ➔ Hyperlink on your toolbar.

1. Executive Summary

Overall Status:

	Green[1] *(Controlled)*	Yellow[2] *(Caution)*	Red[3] *(Critical)*	Reason for Deviation
Budget:	[ ]	[X]	[ ]	Overran original approved budget due to changes in scope (added servers) and cable problems
Schedule:	[ ]	[X]	[ ]	Project was delayed due to P&G restrictions on access to their employees the first two months and approved changes in server configuration.
Scope:	[X]	[ ]	[ ]	Scope changes did occur which added risks to cost and schedule; however, the scope changes went through the review and approval process and were approved, allowing added time and cost to the project.
Quality:	[X]	[ ]	[ ]	All quality measures were met.
Risk:	[X]	[ ]	[ ]	Risk was high at first and was brought under control by strict use of the change control process.

[1] Project is within budget, scope and on schedule.
[2] Project has deviated slightly from the plan but should recover
[3] Project has fallen significantly behind schedule, is forecast to be significantly over budget, and/or has taken on tasks that are out of scope.

Comments:

- New information discovered during the initial project Kickoff meeting raised concerns about the schedule, budget, resources availability, and quality of the project.
- For best results, the overall IT project was broken into 5 major subproject components (per the PM Plan).
- In spite of the changes to the scope, schedule, and budget, the project was successfully managed to completion with formal acceptance by the customer.
- Lessons learned meetings were held and have been entered into the team-room electronic database for future reference.
- All exit criteria and quality measures was accomplished per final approved contract.
- A celebration party was hosted at the end of the project and rewards and recognition were presented to team members who demonstrated outstanding commitment, results, and customer satisfaction ratings.
- Formal project acceptance document was signed by the customer and project documents are stored in the electronic team-room (project control book).

FIGURE 14.1—*continued*

2. Controls
Issue Status (Issues requiring resolution by Project Team or Executive Committee): Link_To_Project_Issue_Log
• A big issue which created major delays at the beginning of the project was due to confusion on the part of middle management at the customer site. This was overcome with "waiver to contract" agreements to allow for control startup with minimal contact with the customer end-user representatives. Impact to the project was 60 day delay. • Another issue was a change in the server configuration and the additional hardware, software, and resources (for backup and test servers) required to expand the help desk problem and change request tickets. • There was also a cable issue (subcontractor installed the wrong cable type, and we had to rework with new cabling and labor to perform the rework in a timely manner (added cost and created two-week slip in the schedule).
Change Status (Changes raised for consideration that change the approved project baselines. Would require approval by the Project Sponsor and possibly the Executive Committee): Link_To_Project_Change_Request_Log
• Issues listed above were managed by using the approved change control system and all changes were reviewed, priced, and approved by the customer, which allowed the project team to reset the scope, schedule, and cost baselines. • All changes were managed in a prompt and professional manner, documented, communicated, and resolved to all key stakeholders' satisfaction during the entire project life cycle.
Risk Status (Report on any change in priority or status of major project risks and any risks discovered since earlier risk assessments, along with proposed risk response): Link_To_Risk_Response_Plan
• There were a number of risks (186 total) identified, evaluated, and prioritized to ensure prompt response when risk events occurred. There were several (8) unplanned risks that were managed to the customer's satisfaction. • The project risk management process was presented, enforced, and effectively managed throughout the project life cycle. The risk tracking log is located in the project control book (PCB) and will adhere to record retention requirements. • The biggest risks were limited resource availability, especially at the beginning of the project and several (8) changes that took place during crucial time periods throughout the project. All were managed to completion.

FIGURE 14.1—*continued*

3. Budget Report: Link_To_Cumulative_Cost_Curve

Expense	Budget to Date	Actual to Date	Variance	Estimate to Complete	Budget Total Cost	Estimate at Completion
Labor Total:	$358,000	$390,558	$32,558	$23,200	$358,000	$413,758
Project Team	$258,000	$285,000	$27,000	$22,000	$258,000	$307,000
External contractors	$100,000	$105,558	$5,558	$1,200	$100,000	$106,758
Hardware	$128,000	$228,285	$100,285	$12,000	$128,000	$240,285
Software	$185,000	$225,000	$40,000	$5,500	$185,000	$230,500
Other, e.g., travel, meals, etc.	$28,000	$34,668	$6,668	$1,000	$29,000	$35,668
Total (cost to production)	$699,000	$878,511	$179,511	$41,700	$700,000	$920,211

Comments:

4. Scheduled Milestones / Deliverables

List any Project Milestones that are late as well as Milestones due in the next 4 to 6 weeks.

Milestone	Approved Schedule	Actual	Issue #	Status
Project Start	02/01/1995	02/02/1995		Complete
Kick-off meeting	02/01/1995	02/05/1995		Complete
Collect requirements	02/05/1995	04/01/1995	001	Complete
Reset project start date	02/10/1995	05/01/1995	002	Complete
Setup new help desk in Boulder, CO	05/01/1995	09/30/1995	003	Complete
Complete physical inventory	03/30/1995	06/01/1995	004	Complete
Complete training	04/25/1995	07/30/1995	005	Complete
Project end (launch new Call Center)	06/01/1995	09/01/1995	006	Complete

FIGURE 14.1—*continued*

5. Accomplishments / Plans
Accomplishments during this Reporting Period (Should relate to milestones): • Final approved requirements (with approved changes). • All Requirements collected and approved after negotiated changes to the contract delivery date. • All approved deliverables were met based on approved new schedule. • Help desk fully operational and agents fully trained and ready to receive calls. Plans during the next Reporting Period (Should relate to milestones): • Final close-out of the project. • Lessons learned meeting. • Obtain final formal acceptance for the project.

6. Project Definition
This section is for reference. Provide the links indicated below.
Link_To_Project_Schedule
Link_To_Project_Budget
Link_To_Project_Scope_Statement

7. Project Status Report / Signatures			
Project Name:	P&G IT Transition		
Prepared by:	George A.		
I have reviewed the information contained in this Project Monthly Status Report *and agree:*			
Name	Title	Signature	Date (MM/DD/YYYY)
Lynn G.	P&G Project Executive	Lynn G.	09/30/1995
Bob X.	IBM Project Executive	Bob X.	09/30/1995
George A.	Project Manager	George A.	09/30/1995
Mark F.	IT Manager	Mark F.	09/30/1995

The signatures above indicate an understanding of the purpose and content of this document by those signing it. By signing this document, they agree to this as the formal Project Monthly Status Report *document.*

Conduct Lessons Learned Closure Meeting

History is our best teacher. It shows us how to do things better if we take the time to learn from our mistakes. If we don't apply the knowledge learned, we truly miss out on some valuable lessons that can be costly to our future projects. Too often we just dive in to the water before we realize we don't have on a life preserver. The words of Clarence Darrow are appropriate here: "History repeats itself. That's one of the things wrong with history."[1]

To help assess the results of your project, schedule a project team meeting and include the customer. Plan for at least two hours (more if the project is large or complex). Also, set the stage and expectations by sending an agenda ahead of time, and be sure to capture the minutes of this meeting. The lessons learned closure meeting works best if you provide questionnaires or surveys ahead of time so people can think about their answers prior to attending the meeting. Here are some key questions that need to be asked and answered:

- How did we do overall on the project? (Were the results achieved and anticipated?)
- Did we meet our documented objectives? (Did we deliver what we said we would?)
- Are the products, results, and services at the approved quality levels?
- Did we manage the customer and team expectations properly?
- Did we effectively manage changes by enforcing the change control process?
- What caused the most problems, and how can we keep them from coming back on our next project?
- Was the budget managed properly, or did we have to beg for more funding halfway through the project life cycle?
- Did we make the best use of our resources? (Did we use the right skills at the right time in the right place?)
- Did we exercise effective interpersonal skills?
- Did we use the lessons learned from previous similar projects, and did we capture lessons learned from the current project effectively?
- Does the customer agree that all deliverables were met as approved in the scope statement?

Some great lessons learned templates are available on the Internet. You can see a partial example in Figure 14.2.[2]

FIGURE 14.2 Sample Lessons Learned Template

Put your logo here	**Put your organization name here**	**PROJECT LESSONS LEARNED CHECKLIST TEMPLATE** *Rev. 1.2, 2/10/2017*

Project Lessons Learned Checklist	
Project Name:	
Prepared by:	
Date (MM/DD/YYYY):	

Use this Lessons Learned Checklist as an aid to understanding those factors that either helped or hindered your project.

- *Best used in group discussion among those who have a stake in the project*
- *May be used anytime as an aid to discussion, or may be used during Project Close as a part of the Lessons Learned exercise*

1. Project Lessons Learned Checklist

					Impact				
					Low			*High*	
No.	*Lesson Learned*	*Yes*	*No*	*N/A*	*1*	*2*	*3*	*4*	*5*
Place your cursor in the appropriate boxes and type an X. (Insert additional rows as needed.) **Yes** = *the project team agrees with the statement* **No** = *the project team does not agree with the statement* **N/A** = *this statement does not apply to the project* **Impact** = *the extent to which this factor had an impact on your project* Add a comment to any question where supporting detail would be helpful.									
Project Planning									
	Business objectives were specific, measurable, attainable, results-focused, and time-limited >								
	Product concept was appropriate to business objectives >								
	Project plan and schedule were well-documented, with appropriate structure and detail >								
	Project schedule encompassed all aspects of the project >								
	Tasks were defined adequately >								
	Stakeholders (e.g., sponsor, customer) had appropriate input into the project planning process >								
	Requirements were gathered to sufficient detail >								

FIGURE 14.2 Sample Lessons Learned Template—*continued*

Put your logo here	**Put your organization name here**	**PROJECT LESSONS LEARNED CHECKLIST TEMPLATE** *Rev. 1.2, 2/10/2017*

1. Project Lessons Learned Checklist									
					Impact				
					Low			*High*	
No.	*Lesson Learned*	*Yes*	*No*	*N/A*	*1*	*2*	*3*	*4*	*5*
Place your cursor in the appropriate boxes and type an X. (Insert additional rows as needed.) **Yes** = *the project team agrees with the statement* **No** = *the project team does not agree with the statement* **N/A** = *this statement does not apply to the project* **Impact** = *the extent to which this factor had an impact on your project* Add a comment to any question where supporting detail would be helpful.									
	Requirements were documented clearly >								
	Specifications were clear and well documented >								
	Test plan was adequate, understandable, and well documented >								
	External dependencies were identified, agreements signed >								
	Project budget was well defined >								
	End-of-phase criteria were clear for all project phases >								
	Project plan had buy-in from the stakeholders >								
	Stakeholders had easy access to project plan and schedule >								
Project Execution and Delivery									
	Project stuck to its original goals >								
	Changes in direction that did occur were of manageable frequency and magnitude >								
	Project baselines (scope, time, cost, quality) were well managed (e.g., changed through a formal change-control process) >								
	Design changes were well controlled >								
	Basic project management processes (e.g., risk management, issue management) were adequate >								
	Project tracked progress against baselines and reported accurate status >								

FIGURE 14.2 Sample Lessons Learned Template—*continued*

Put your logo here	**Put your organization name here**	**PROJECT LESSONS LEARNED CHECKLIST TEMPLATE** *Rev. 1.2, 2/10/2017*

1. Project Lessons Learned Checklist									
					Impact				
					Low			*High*	
No.	*Lesson Learned*	*Yes*	*No*	*N/A*	*1*	*2*	*3*	*4*	*5*
Place your cursor in the appropriate boxes and type an X. (Insert additional rows as needed.) **Yes** = *the project team agrees with the statement* **No** = *the project team does not agree with the statement* **N/A** = *this statement does not apply to the project* **Impact** = *the extent to which this factor had an impact on your project* Add a comment to any question where supporting detail would be helpful.									
	Procurement (e.g., RFP, contract with vendor) went smoothly >								
	Contracted vendor provided acceptable deliverables of appropriate quality, on time, and within budget >								
	Stakeholders were satisfied with the information they received >								
	The project had adequate quality control >								
	Requirements, specifications, and test plan were well managed (e.g., requirements management system was used) >								
	Risks were manageable >								
Human Factors									
	Project manager reported to the appropriate part of the organization >								
	Project manager was effective >								
	Project team was properly organized and staffed >								
	Project manager and staff received adequate training >								
	Project team's talent and experience were adequate >								
	Project team worked effectively on project goals >								
	Project team worked effectively with outside entities >								
	There was good communication within the project team >								
	Management gave this project adequate attention and time >								
	Resources were not overcommitted >								

FIGURE 14.2 Sample Lessons Learned Template—*continued*

Put your logo here	**Put your organization name here**	**PROJECT LESSONS LEARNED CHECKLIST TEMPLATE** *Rev. 1.2, 2/10/2017*

1. Project Lessons Learned Checklist									
					Impact				
					Low			*High*	
No.	*Lesson Learned*	*Yes*	*No*	*N/A*	*1*	*2*	*3*	*4*	*5*
Place your cursor in the appropriate boxes and type an X. (Insert additional rows as needed.) **Yes** = *the project team agrees with the statement* **No** = *the project team does not agree with the statement* **N/A** = *this statement does not apply to the project* **Impact** = *the extent to which this factor had an impact on your project* Add a comment to any question where supporting detail would be helpful.									
	Resources were consistently committed to project aims >								
	Functional areas cooperated well >								
	Conflicting departmental goals did not cause problems >								
	Authority and accountability were well defined and public >								
Overall									
	Initial cost and schedule estimates were accurate >								
	Product was delivered within amended schedule >								
	Product was delivered within amended budget >								
	Overall change control was effective >								
	External dependencies were understood and well managed >								
	Technology chosen was appropriate >								
	The project was a technological success >								
	Customer's needs/requirements were met >								
	Customer was satisfied with the product >								
	Project objectives were met >								
	Business objectives were met >								

FIGURE 14.2 Sample Lessons Learned Template—*continued*

Put your logo here	**Put your organization name here**	**PROJECT LESSONS LEARNED CHECKLIST TEMPLATE** *Rev. 1.2, 2/10/2017*

2. Project Lessons Learned Checklist – Agreement Form / Signatures			
Project Name			
Project Manager			
I have reviewed the information contained in this Project Lessons Learned Checklist *and agree.*			
Name	*Title*	*Signature*	*Date (MM/DD/YYYY)*

The signatures above indicate an understanding of the purpose and content of this document by those signing it. By signing this document, they agree to this as the formal Project Lessons Learned Checklist.

Documenting Results and Action Items

The project is not over until the paperwork is done. Documenting the results of the lessons learned and project closure meetings needs to be concise, with specifics of key findings, a clear short summary of events, feedback from the team, milestones, deliverables, any/all follow-up action items, warranty-period contacts, and so on. Here are the steps to take:

1. Completely and accurately document the project results. (This should match the scope baseline and milestones as well as address all approved changes.)
2. Document accomplishments and team member recognition.
3. Capture minutes of all meetings, especially lessons learned and closure meetings, including input from all stakeholders (customer, team, yourself as the PM, sponsors).
4. Plan for process improvement (remember Deming's "Plan-Do-Check-Act" cycle).

Most PMs like checklists or surveys to tell them how they did in managing the project. Table 14.1 is a sample post-project closure survey that includes questions about project definition, planning, defect and issues management, decision making, teamwork, leadership, and managing dependencies.[3]

TABLE 14.1 Sample Post-Project Closure Survey

Please evaluate each of the following statements using the scale: 1-Strongly disagree, 2-Disagree, 3-No opinion, 4-Agree, 5-Strongly agree						*Comments*
1	2	3	4	5	Project developed and used a project and risk plan.	
1	2	3	4	5	Problems were dealt with quickly and escalated properly when necessary.	
1	2	3	4	5	Schedule/budget problems were dealt with effectively.	
1	2	3	4	5	Resource problems were dealt with effectively.	
1	2	3	4	5	Specifications were modified only through approved change control/management.	
1	2	3	4	5	Project reviews were done at appropriate times.	
1	2	3	4	5	Communications were thorough, timely, and complete.	
1	2	3	4	5	Documentation was consistent and available when needed.	
1	2	3	4	5	Project status was reported honestly throughout the project.	
1	2	3	4	5	Reporting project difficulties resulted in solutions.	
1	2	3	4	5	Standard processes were used properly.	
1	2	3	4	5	The project had appropriate sponsorship and support.	

Rewards and Recognition

Most of us thrive on rewards and recognition. We like to know that we are appreciated and recognized for the extra effort we put forth on project activities (the long hours, hard work, and sacrifices we make). Therefore, as a PM you need to make sure that team members' efforts and good deeds are rewarded, even if it's only a pat on the back and a nice note or letter to the team member and that member's boss. Monetary rewards are great as well. Remember, your team is the number-1 asset on your project, and team members need to feel needed and appreciated.

Finding Homes for the Team and Assets

Breaking up the team is always the hard part. This is called the "adjourning" phase in the Bruce Tuckman model. When it comes time to close a project, emotions are mixed. Sometimes PMs feel sad that the project is coming to an end, the project team is moving on to the next project, and the fear of the unknown (the next project and starting all over again) tends to creep in. Sometimes PMs are happy both to see their hard work coming to successful closure and to recognize new project opportunities appearing just around the corner; that means they can apply all the lessons learned and their new experience to the next big project.

This is no time to shortchange the team. It is extremely important to work with each team member to find them a good project home to move to. If you look out for the team members, they will look out for you. We work in a small world, so don't be surprised when you go into a new project and find people you previously worked with are now your customer or boss (this has happened to me several times).

Tip

Another measure of success for you as the PM is when people are willing to work with you on the next project. I view this as the biggest compliment one can receive. The team (or at least key members of the team) is confident enough in your PM skills and ability to work with you again on future projects.

When it comes to finding a home for the assets, you need to be thorough and get transfer acceptance in writing. Find a home for all the equipment and then properly transfer the equipment. Cancel all appropriate software licenses or hardware leases, as needed. The last thing you want to happen is to have a supplier call you three to six months after the project has been closed down, looking for payment of an invoice. This has happened to many experienced PMs, and dealing with this situation is not fun, especially when the project budget is closed.

Final Project Report

The primary purpose of the final report is to acknowledge the accomplishments of the project and to communicate to everyone involved that the project is officially complete. A final project report should also thank all stakeholders and contributors as well as address whom to contact if questions arise or if records are required after the project is closed.

Regardless of the size of the project, here are some fundamental steps that, if used, will help ensure successful closure on your projects:

1. Use proven project management disciplines. This includes using organizational assets by diligently documenting and managing scope baseline, change, risk, scope, time, and cost.
2. Review and report status frequently and honestly (I recommend weekly).
3. Ensure clear two-way communications (use active listening).
4. Work with the stakeholders to ensure that they are focused on the closure activities.
5. Be an advocate for your project team (catch them doing something right!).

6. Verify the overall health of the project by asking yourself and the team the following questions:
   - Were deliverables produced on time, within the approved scope and budget?
   - Did the project satisfy the business requirements of the stakeholders? (E.g., was the problem solved or business result accomplished?)
   - Has the project met the business value goals? (Such goals might include cost savings, increased market share, and streamlined processes needed to improve quality.)
   - Most important, do the business owners (sponsors) believe the project was successful? Did you deliver a quality product and meet stakeholder expectations?
   - Last but not least, document, document, document, and communicate project results.

Plan for Record Retention

As part of formal acceptance, you should ensure that all final reports have been completed, reconciled, and approved. Make sure you have documented and planned for how to store the project documents. Record retention should include considerations of where to store the project documents, for how long, who will have access to the documents, and who the backup person is in case the primary contact is not readily available. Make sure these bases are covered in writing and are fully communicated to all the key stakeholders. PMs should be aware of their document retention policies or requirements (See Figure 14.1 and Figure 14.2 for details).

Celebrate!

Now it is time to celebrate. No matter how the atmosphere has been during the closing days of your project, bring it to a positive conclusion. Celebrate the success of the team, the individuals on the team, and the key support managers. A dinner or luncheon works best, but this might not be possible if the team is geographically dispersed or if some team members have already moved on to other projects. Still, you should strive to rally the team together to acknowledge team members' good work, even if the project was not a complete success.

Moving on to the next assignment or project is much easier for people when they have a chance to bring their last project to a friendly conclusion. For global or distributed teams, you might want to arrange a similar event for each location at roughly the same time and then conference in the different subgroups for a final thank you and send-off.

Next Steps: Where to Go from Here

The best way to reach success is to always have a plan and a strategy. I recommend the AIM strategy (discussed in Chapter 2). I feel strongly about this strategy for life in general and project management. Here it is again, as a reminder:

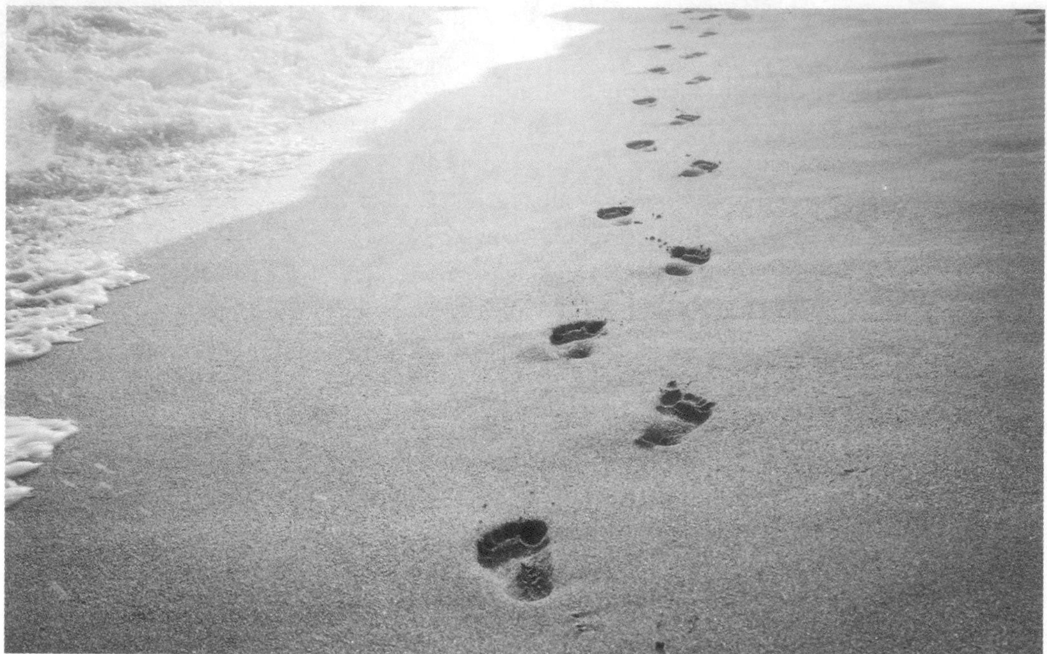

FIGURE 14.3 Next Steps—Footprints in the sand

1. Analyze the situation. (Develop the plan as a team and obtain formal acceptance for the project plan.)
2. Implement the approved plan. (Use available tools and resources.)
3. Manage the whole project, and nothing but the project.

For example, here are the steps you should follow if you are planning to take a PMI exam:

1. Apply for the exam online at www.pmi.org.
2. Study using the key resources (books, study groups, sample exams) available to you.
3. Consider creating index (flash) cards with questions on one side and answers on the back. Study them until you know all the answers, and then reverse the process by looking at the answers and being able to describe the questions.
4. Stay focused (make a project plan and stick to it).
5. Don't be too hard on yourself (allow for some downtime).
6. Don't cram for the exam the night before you take the test.
7. Celebrate your achievement upon successfully completing the exam.

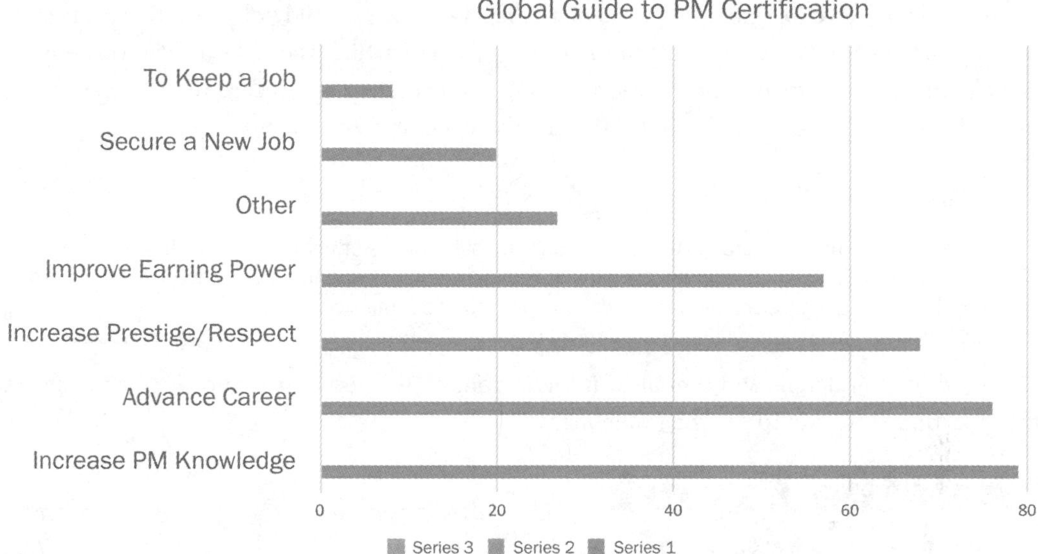

FIGURE 14.4 Reasons People Pursue PM Certification

Many great project managers are successful without being certified. You, too, can be a successful PM by following these simple rules (the three P's):

1. **Plan** well (preparation is the key).
2. **Perform** your role with clear direction and clear communications.
3. **Practice** (you need to keep developing your skills, apply lessons learned for continuous improvement, and stay current with the latest processes, tools, concepts, and methods).

Reasons People Pursue PMP Certification

PMP is the premier certification credential for project managers. When a PMI member audience was asked why they were pursuing this credential, the majority of the responses were to further their knowledge (79 percent), to advance in their career (76 percent), and to increase prestige/respect (68 percent), with the next highest being to increase earning power (57 percent) and a combined 28 percent to either secure a new job or hold on to an existing job. You can see all the responses in Figure 14.4.[4]

PMI Credentials

To begin the process of becoming certified in one of the PMI credentials, you first need to determine your level of experience and eligibility. Table 14.2 should help with this process. It refers to professional development units (PDUs), each of which is one hour of direct educational contact. For a further description of PDUs and current fees, please refer to the appropriate PMI certification handbook for the certification in which you are interested.

Note

To be eligible for the PMP credential, a candidate must meet the education and professional experience listed in Table 14.2, and all the project management experience must have been accrued within the last eight consecutive years prior to application submission.[6]

For additional details and the latest information, go to the www.pmi.org website (select the "Certification" tab to see the guidelines).

Ask the Expert

Q: Which credential is right for me?

A: It depends. The best way to determine the answer to this question is to look at your experience, your level of education, your current and future job roles, and your aspirations. Then, take a look at credential requirements listed in each PMI credential handbook. Each credential is designed to stand alone (no one credential serves as a prerequisite for another). However, you can pursue multiple credentials. Each credential complements the others. A partial list of PMI credentials is shown in Table 14.2. For the latest details, go to the PMI.org website and select "credentials" to view the various handbooks available.[5]

Examples of Credential Eligibility

To put this credential eligibility in perspective, let's look at three people with different levels of experience to see which credential is right for each of them:

- Joey has a minimum of 1,500 hours' experience working on project teams but has not led a project himself. He has a high school diploma and over 23 hours of project management education. Joey has a good foundational understanding of the *PMBOK* Process Groups, Knowledge Areas, and concepts. Joey should go for the CAPM-level credential (he is eligible with either 1,500 hours of experience or the 23 hours of PM education). The CAPM focuses on the *PMBOK*. With only 150 multiple-choice questions (compared to 200 in the PMP exam), it measures one's ability to understand the PM fundamentals according to the *PMBOK Guide*.

TABLE 14.2 PMI Credentials

	CAPM	PMP	PgMP	PMI-ACP	PMI-PBA
Full name	Certified Associate in Project Management	Project Management Professional	Program Management Professional	PMI Certified Agile Practitioner	PMI Professional in Business Analysis
Project role	Contributes to project team	Leads and directs project teams	Achieves the organizational objectives through defining and overseeing projects and resources	Demonstrates knowledge of Agile principles and tools and techniques across Agile methodologies	Perform duties under general supervision and are responsible for working with stakeholders to define an organization's business requirements in order to shape the output of projects and ensure they deliver the expected business benefit.
Eligibility requirements	High school diploma or global equivalent **AND** 1,500 hours' experience OR 23 hours' project management education	High school diploma or global equivalent + 5 years' project management experience + 35 hours' project management education **OR** bachelor's degree or global equivalent + 3 years' project management experience + 35 hours' project management education	High school diploma or global equivalent + 4 years' project management experience + 7 years' program management experience **OR** bachelor's degree / global equivalent + 4 years' project management experience + 4 years' program management experience	High school diploma or global equivalent + 2,000 hours over the last 5 years **OR** PMP or PgMP credential. **Note**: requires 21 hours of Agile practices education	High school diploma or global equivalent + 7,500 hours (5 years) working as a practitioner of business analysis + 35 education contact hours. This experience must have been earned in business analysis practices over the last 8 years. With bachelor's degree or higher + 2,000 hours working on project teams + 35 education contact hours in business analysis practices. Project experience can be inclusive of the 4,500 hours of business analysis experience listed. Includes any business analysis experience that occurred within the context of a project. This experience must have been earned in business analysis practices.

continued on next page

TABLE 14.2—*continued*

	CAPM	PMP	PgMP	PMI-ACP	PMI-PBA
Steps to obtaining credential	Application process + multiple-choice exam	Application process + multiple-choice exam	Three evaluations: application panel review + multiple-choice exam + multi rater assessment	Application process + multiple-choice exam	Application process+ multiple-choice exam
Exam information	3 hours; 150 questions	4 hours; 200 questions	4 hours; 170 questions	3 hours; 120 questions	4 hours; 200 questions
Fees for PMI members	US$225 €185	US$405, €340 (nonmember US$555)	US$1,500 €1250	US$435 €365	US$405, €340 (nonmember US$555)
Credential maintenance cycles and requirements	5 years; must retake the exam in the fifth year to recertify	3 years; 60 PDUs	3 years; 60 PDUs	3 years; 30 PDUs in Agile projects	3 years; 60 PDUs in business analysis topics.

- Suzy has over three years (36 non-overlapping months) of project management experience, leading and directing project teams over the past eight years. When she adds up her hours managing projects, she has more than 4,500 hours, and Suzy also has a bachelor's degree. She also has over 35 hours of formal project management education. Suzy has demonstrated her ability to "think on her feet" in real, live project situations and has a good grasp of project management principles, methods, and processes, according to the *PMBOK Guide*. Suzy should go for the PMP-level credential. She understands that the PMP exam focuses on the ability to apply sound judgment to project situations.
- Suzy's sister Mary currently has a high school diploma (no college degree). She does have a minimum of 7,500 hours of project management experience, leading and directing project teams over a five-year (60 nonoverlapping months) period in the last eight years. Mary also has over 35 hours of formal project management education, so she is also eligible to sit for the PMP exam.

Demystifying PMI Exams

Most people (myself included, before I took the test) are confused and intimidated by PMI exams. This is normal and expected because few people want or like to take tests, especially with the cost, the time to prepare, and the level of commitment required. The good news is that, depending on the type of exam you take, the exam is now only three to four hours long (prior to April 1998, the PMP exam was eight hours). Plus, the majority of the exams are computer-based testing (CBT), which means "touch screen" for less paper processing and quicker scoring (and to align with the electronic generation). You see the results of the test on the computer screen within minutes after completing the exam.

There is also a growing number of PMI Registered Education Providers (REPs). These are recognized companies, universities, and organizations that offer project management courses and certificate programs designed to help you prepare to pass the exam.

In order to further demystify the exams, let's start with a quick review of the different types of examinations PMI offers. The PMI exam types align with the credentials mentioned earlier, so only a brief summary of the types is provided here.

To begin, here are the two most common PMI exams:

- CAPM (Certified Associate in Project Management)
- PMP (Project Management Professional)

The other PMI exams are as follows:

- PgMP (Program Management Professional)
- PMI-ACP (PMI Agile Certified Practitioner)

- PMI-RMP (PM Risk Management Professional)
- PMI-SP (PM Scheduling Professional)
- PfMP (Portfolio Management Professional)
- PMI-PBA (PMI Professional in Business Analysis)

There are also two ways to take PMI exams:

- Computer-based testing (CBT)
- Paper-based testing (PBT)

Note

There are strict requirements to qualify to take the paper-based test. To be eligible, the candidate must live at least 186.5 miles (300 km) from a PMI-approved test site. Also, there is a reexamination fee should you need to retake the test. (See the PMI.org website for the latest fee amounts.) You are allowed to retake the exam up to three times during your 12-month approved period. The reexamination fee must be paid prior to each sitting for the exam.

Differences between the Exams

Because the PMP certification exam was introduced first, it has the highest number of credentialed project managers. It is by far the most sought-after exam of all the credentials. Because of its popularity, we will focus mostly on the details of the PMP exam.

According to PMI, the PMP exam is designed to determine your ability to demonstrate proficiency in each of the five Process Groups (also known as "domains"): Initiating, Planning, Executing, Monitoring and Controlling, and Closing.

The PMP exam is composed of 200 multiple-choice questions. Of the 200 questions, 25 are considered "pretest" questions. Pretest questions do not affect the score and are used in examinations as an effective and legitimate way to test the validity of future examination questions. All questions are randomly placed throughout the examination. Each question on the exam is developed and independently validated by global work groups (credential holders) and assigned a complexity rating.

Each exam is unique in that the system selects a random group of questions for each participant, and the number of correct answers needed to pass the exam depends on the complexity of the questions selected. For example, if many of the questions in your exam are higher in complexity, then you can pass with a slightly lower number of correct answers—say, 69 percent as opposed to 70 percent. (These percentages are examples only and are subject to change without notice.)

The allotted time to complete the PMP computer-based examination is four hours. The CAPM, on the other hand, has 150 multiple-choice questions, with three hours allotted to complete the test. These time limits are tightly controlled at the test center, and, in general, many people feel they have more than enough time to complete the exams. You can sign in and out to take short breaks, eat a snack, and so on—however, the clock is still ticking.

Candidates for the CAPM credential must be able to document their contribution to projects as subject matter experts (SMEs) and team members. They may also have served as project sponsors, facilitators, liaisons, or coordinators for the projects in which they participated, but they are not responsible for leading or directing the project team (which is the role of the project manager).

How to Save Money on the Cost of the Exam

The PMP exam cost US$555 in 2016 for the first sitting of a CBT. However, if you are a member of the PMI organization (which costs $125 to join), you receive a big discount on the exam. The discount is approximately US$150 (subject to change).

Membership also offers savings on chapter meetings, books, events, and so on. Therefore, it is recommended that you join the PMI chapter nearest you for at least one year (the year you plan to take the exam). Some employers will even pay for a year of membership dues because the savings (discount) on the exam fee alone is offset by the cost of a year of PMI membership dues.

The annual cost of membership in local PMI chapters varies depending on the chapter, and you can join additional special interest groups, now called Communities of Practice (CoPs), such as IT (Information Technology), IS (Information Systems), Agile, and SD (Software Development). Each CoP membership fee varies, so check out the www.pmi.org website for latest details.

PMP Exam Blueprint

The PMP examination is developed based on the PMP examination blueprint contained in the "Project Management Professional Examination Specification." The PMP exam blueprint details the percentage and number of questions contained in each project management Process Group. Table 14.3 shows the percentage and number of questions in each Process Group/domain included on the PMP exam, as of March 2017.

TABLE 14.3 PMP Exam Blueprint

Process Group/Domain	Percentage of Questions	Number of Questions
Initiating	13%	26
Planning	24%	48
Executing	31%	62
Monitoring and Controlling	25%	50
Closing	7%	14
Total	100%	200

Note

The percentages and the number of questions shown in Table 14.3 are subject to change. For the latest PMP exam or CAPM exam blueprint percentages, go to the PMI.org website.

PMI Exam Objectives (Skills Tested)

The PM must be able to make sound decisions and apply good judgment in order to move the project forward to achieve schedule and budget deadlines. As a PM, you must be able to address various real-world situations and work through them quickly to solve the many different problems faced by you and the project team.

The skills of the applicant that are tested (such as communications, risk management, cost and schedule management, team building, etc.) vary depending on the type of exam taken. For example, the PMP exam focuses on the ability of PMs to apply their knowledge, tools, techniques, and methods to manage projects effectively, whereas the CAPM exam focuses on the fundamental processes and a more academic view of project management (which tends to be more from the *PMBOK Guide*).

Tip

Keep in mind the latest focus, especially on the PMP exam, is on the role of the project manager, the tasks that they are expected to perform (such as strategic planning, business acumen, and so on), and their ability to "think on their feet" to solve project-related problems of any kind. The PM at this level must also have (or can articulate) project solutions in large project environments.

PMP Exam Objectives

The PMP Role Delineation Study conducted by PMI states that candidates for the PMP credential must do the following:

- Perform their duties under general supervision and be responsible for all aspects of the project for the life of the project
- Lead and direct cross-functional teams to deliver projects within the constraints of schedule, budget, and scope
- Demonstrate sufficient knowledge and experience to appropriately apply a methodology to projects that have reasonably well-defined project requirements and deliverables

Overall, the PMP exam is designed to determine your ability to demonstrate proficiency in leading and directing project teams in each of the five Process Groups listed next.

1. **Initiating the Project Process Group**
    - Conduct project selection methods
    - Define project scope
    - Document risks, assumptions, and constraints
    - Identify and perform stakeholder analysis
    - Develop project charter
    - Obtain project charter approval
2. **Planning the Project Process Group**
    - Define and record requirements, constraints, and assumptions
    - Develop the project management plan
    - Identify the project team and define roles and responsibilities
    - Create the work breakdown structure (WBS)
    - Define activities, estimate resources, and determine the budget
    - Develop the schedule and change management plan
    - Plan communications, quality, and procurement
    - Identify risks and define risk strategies
    - Conduct project kickoff meetings
3. **Executing the Project Process Group**
    - Execute activities defined in the project plan
    - Ensure common understanding and set expectations
    - Implement the procurement of project resources
    - Manage resource allocation
    - Implement quality management plan
    - Implement approved changes
    - Implement approved actions and workarounds
    - Improve team performance
4. **Monitoring and Controlling the Project Process Group**
    - Measure project performance
    - Verify and manage changes to the project
    - Ensure that project deliverables conform to quality standards
    - Monitor all risks and initiate a response strategy
5. **Closing the Project Process Group**
    - Obtain final acceptance for the project
    - Obtain financial, legal, and administrative closure

- Release project resources
- Identify, document, and communicate lessons learned
- Archive and retain project records
- Measure customer satisfaction

Note

Notice the use of verbs ("action" words) to define the various proficiency requirements among the Process Groups, for example, the Initiation and Planning Process Groups (e.g., *define*, *identify*, *develop*) and the Execution Process Group (e.g., *execute*, *ensure*, *implement*, and *manage*). Beginning each requirement with a verb emphasizes the change from the fourth edition to the fifth edition of the *PMBOK* to be more action-oriented responsibilities of a project manager. This may seem like a small change; however, it makes a big difference when it comes time to create the WBS or the schedule for your project.

The biggest change in the PMP exam (as of January 2016) is in the role of the project manager and the tasks and skills areas PMs are responsible to perform. The change in the PM's role is more strategic in nature, managing global projects and virtual teams. These changes were introduced in Chapter 2 of this book and are outlined in the PMP Exam Content Outline dated June 2015, http://www.pmi.org/~/media/PDF/Certifications/pmp-certification-exam-outline.ashx.

Even though the professional responsibilities (code of ethics) are not covered in the *PMBOK Guide*, a number of questions may appear on the PMP exam (and fewer on the CAPM exam) that relate to the ethical application of project management. Those questions are broken into four value categories in the Code of Ethics and Professional Conduct guidelines area of the PMP Handbook offered by PMI.[6] Here are the value categories:

- Responsibilities
- Respect
- Fairness
- Honesty

The focus areas for professional and social responsibilities are as follows:

- Ensure individual integrity.
- Contribute to the project management knowledge base.
- Enhance professional competence.
- Promote interaction among stakeholders.

CAPM Exam Objectives

Overall, the CAPM exam focuses on the PM's ability to work in a project team and understand the five Process Groups/domains, 10 Knowledge Areas, and 49 processes, according to the *PMBOK*. As previously mentioned, the CAPM is based more on the academic view of project management according to the *PMBOK* than on the applied practitioner view as tested in the PMP exam. The CAPM exam questions tend to be straightforward compared to the more situational ("What would you do if . . .") questions that you will find in the PMP exam.

Expected Results (First-Time Pass Rate)

The first-time pass rate is tightly controlled by PMI and changes occasionally and without notice; however, history indicates that the target is about 70 percent, compared to only 50 percent in 1998. This means seven out of ten people taking the PMP exam for the first time, on average, are smiling when they leave the test center. Unfortunately, three on average are not smiling and will have to try again later. PMI tends to be shy about publishing this information, which only rarely has been shown on the website.

How to Apply for a PMI Exam

Once you have selected the credential that is right for you, you need to submit an online application form to sit for the exam. Directions for the application, current pricing, and additional details are also available on the PMI website. Again, you have two ways to take a PMI exam: computer based or paper based (you must be physically located farther than 186.5 miles from a contracted PMI test facility to qualify for PBT).

Once your application has been reviewed, you will receive approval or denial within a matter of five to ten business days. Once approved, you have up to one year to schedule and sit for the exam.

Tip

Start the registration process as early as possible, and schedule a planned date to take the exam. This will make it real and help drive you to complete the process.

Ask the Expert

Q: Is the exam as hard as everyone says? And how much study time does it take?

A: It depends on your level of experience, your commitment to learn the language from PMI's perspective, and the amount of time you plan to prepare for the exam.

Note

The PMP exam can be tricky, with a high number (over 90%) of situational questions that require you to select the "best" answer from the PM's perspective and PMI's point of view. It is not a test of information from the *PMBOK*, as with the CAPM exam; you have to be able to determine which answer is the best among the answers available. There are also a high number of questions (approximately 100) that give a lengthy scenario to pose a problem to be solved and then ask you to provide an answer for what you would do first, or what you would do next. The goal is to see if you can "think on your feet" as a project manager and come up with the best solution given the information available. The PMP questions are very subjective.

The exam is difficult and ever changing. The biggest changes occurred in 1998 when PMI went to the computer-based exam and again in 2004 when PMI raised the bar on the requirements to pass the PMP exam (such as possessing project management experience actually leading and directing project teams). This change was made right after PMI launched the CAPM exam (for people who participate as a project team member). The most recent changes in these exams occurred January 2016, when PMI updated the role of the PM to be more global and strategic in nature to align projects with the overall needs of the business. Additional changes in the PMP and CAPM exams are expected to align to the latest *{MBOK Sixth Edition*, released third quarter January 2017. The exam typically changes every four years to align to the latest *PMBOK Guide*.

Tip

Many people feel you should allow at least two to four months to prepare for the exam, depending on how well you take tests and your level of project management experience. They also recommend taking as many sample questions as possible to get in the test-taking mode. Another good suggestion is to take a full (200-plus-question) sample exam in one sitting to get the feel for how long it will take you when you actually sit down to take the exam and to do this at least three times prior to taking the four-hour PMP exam or three-hour CAPM exam.

PMP Exam Application Checklist

It is best to apply for the exam online through the PMI.org website (select Certification; Overview; Find the Certification That Fits You Best offerings, select the appropriate button, and then click the Apply button). PMI also offers a "paper based exam"; however, you can only apply for this option if you live more than 186.5 miles from an approved testing center.

The following application checklist is a summary of the top three steps you need to take to apply for a PMI exam:

1. Complete the online application form, providing all the key information. Be sure to provide your name exactly as it appears on your government-issued identification card. You also need to fill out the experience verification section according to the credential exam for which you are applying, and provide documentation of the 35 hours (minimum) of education you've obtained.

   Tip

   Save a tree! You do not have to provide all the supporting documentation of your project experience unless you are audited. The backup documents are not sent to PMI unless requested.

   The time it takes to complete the application depends on the amount of detail and research necessary for credential eligibility (e.g., you will need contact information and details from previous projects).

2. Affirm that you have read and understand the policies and procedures outlined in the credential handbook, which is available on the PMI.org website.
3. Submit your payment according to the credential payment process (you will not be able to schedule your exam until full payment is received). PMI will review your application and provide an approval code. You will then need to contact a Prometric test center near you and call or go online to schedule an exam date.

Note

Prometric is an independent organization that provides comprehensive testing and assessment services to companies and organizations, such as PMI, across the globe. They offer an extensive, professional, and secure testing network from which tests are delivered in over 7,500 locations across 160 countries.

Manage the Exam Preparation like a Project

A good project manager is organized, gains satisfaction from checking off tasks, and can manage the exam as if it were a project (because it is). You can use the following steps as your project plan:

1. Review the courses and credentials available.
2. Review the requirements and eligibility.
3. Determine which exam is right for you and apply for it (see the "Timeline of the PMP Credential Process" section).
4. Build a project plan to guide you toward achieving your goals (and stick with it).
5. Set a realistic target date with key checkpoints to ensure you are on track.
6. Schedule the exam date, and mark it on your calendar. (Now it is real!)
7. Allow some "downtime" during the training and preparation process.
8. Tell your support group—your boss, coworkers, and family—that you are going into training.
9. Monitor your progress, and continue managing the process as a project.
10. Remember to stay focused on the exam using the tools and resources available (study materials and your study group) to achieve success on the exam.
11. Once you pass the exam, celebrate! You deserve it.

Timeline of the PMP Credential Process

As with other credentials, there is a timeline or flow for the PMP credential that must be followed to apply for a PMI exam. Remember that the time it takes to apply for the PMP credential will vary depending on how organized you are in compiling your project information, contacts, and so on that are required to complete the submission form. Also, remember that you will need to provide the detailed supporting documentation only if you are audited, so please don't plan to send mounds of paper to PMI.

The following bullets are from the "About PMP Credential" section of the PMP Credential Handbook at www.pmi.org. The handbook can be downloaded and used as a reference when the time comes to begin your application process.

- Once you start an online application, you cannot cancel it. You can save it unfinished, come back to it later, and edit any information you have already entered. The application will remain open for 90 days, during which time PMI will send you an email reminder to complete the application.
- The applicant completeness review (by PMI) takes five business days (when submitted online).
- The applicant payment process must be completed and confirmed before you can schedule your exam with Prometric.

- The audit process (if the application is selected by PMI for audit) takes five business days for notification, and you will have up to 90 days to respond if selected for audit.
- The examination eligibility period lasts one year from the date of application approval.
- The certification cycle is three years from the date the exam is passed; you must recertify by entering your PDUs online prior to your expiration date.

Note

To recertify once you attain a PMI credential, you must participate in the Continuing Certification Requirements (CCR) program to maintain active certification status. Additional details are provided in the "Maintaining Your PMI Credential" section later in this chapter.

Balancing Competing Demands

With the advent of portable, easy access to the Internet, it is far too easy to work extra hours even when you are on vacation. Many bosses have come to expect, or even demand, a higher level of accessibility to their employees. To be competitive, we often feel the need to "stay connected," so we keep pushing ourselves because we are afraid of falling out of favor with the boss, losing our job, or not getting that promotion we deserve. With the current times, there are scores of qualified workers who are more than willing to put in the extra time on the job and to get certified to increase their marketability.

When it comes to studying for the exam, you will find it far too easy to get distracted and lose focus. You will need to balance a variety of competing demands for your time, especially if you have a family with kids. Between your job, your family, and your friends, how will you ever find the time it takes to prepare for the exam? The answer is focus, commitment, and a support structure. If you can maintain focus and use your support group to help you meet your commitment to yourself, the satisfaction and rewards of passing the exam are immeasurable.

Start Training

It is never too early to start training—and by this I mean physical training. I actually set up an exercise bike in the bedroom with a rack on the handlebars to rest my study material on for easy reading. Then I set up a schedule (I chose three nights per week, one hour per night) to start with and gradually increased the duration and frequency as I got closer to the test date. After coming home from the office, I would spend at least 40 to 60 minutes going over exam preparation material while working out on an exercise bike. This allowed me to be in good shape both physically and mentally for the exam.

What to Expect on the PMP Exam

You should expect lots of situational-type questions. Remember, the PMP exam tests your ability to apply project management knowledge to a given situation and to be able to solve problems.

Here are some examples:

1. The project sponsor has indicated he will be making a lot of changes to the scope of the project during the Initiation and Planning phases. What is the *best* approach the project manager should take to manage the expected changes?

   A. Meet with the sponsor and tell him the changes will add cost to the project.

   B. Send a note to the sponsor's boss to figure out a way to assign him to another project.

   C. Include the sponsor early in the project to understand his/her needs and expectations. Work with him/her to ensure he is aware of and is in agreement with the change process.

   D. Just say no to changes—they are distracting to the project team.

Answer: C.

2. During a project team meeting, a software engineer indicates a need to provide a larger (newer technology) system to meet the long-term needs of the customer. The engineer admits this change will delay the project, but it needs to be done. As the PM, you remind the team for the need to focus on the approved plan. This is an example of what?

   A. Time management process

   B. Cost management process

   C. Scope management

   D. Work breakdown structure

Answer: C. Although it could be argued that this is a time/schedule management issue, or even a cost management issue, it really goes back to the original scope of the project. Managing scope effectively keeps other constraints (time and cost) under control.

Moving the Exam Date (Change Happens)

Once you are approved, you can contact Prometric to schedule your exam date within the 12-month approved PMI window to take the exam. Changing the exam date is not recommended. However, there may be certain circumstances that force you to move your exam date. Some reasons that would be accepted by PMI for moving the examination date include medical emergency, military deployment, or death or serious illness in the immediate family.

Rescheduling requires that you contact the test center directly no later than two business days prior to your scheduled exam date. You must provide your PMI Eligibility Identification number, group ID number, the location and type of exam you are scheduled to take, and the reason for rescheduling (there will be a fee). You may be able to avoid paying a reschedule fee if you reschedule over 30 days prior to your test date.

Tools to Use to Prepare for PMI Exams

Many books and classes are available to help you learn about project management, to build your knowledge, and to help prepare you for the PMI exam. The tools available to help you study for the exam (such as flash cards, sample exam question workbooks, and downloads) are plentiful; thus, it may be difficult to determine which ones are right for you. The best way to choose is to first look at your own learning style. You need to determine what makes you feel most comfortable and what style works best for you. Here are some examples:

- Dawn is a fast study and is usually not intimidated by tests (well, maybe a little). She is very organized and learns best by seeing the words and goes as far as rewriting her class notes in neat, color-coded script. She likes descriptive scenes, diagrams, and posters; always reads directions; and seeks out pictures to help visualize and understand the message. Dawn is using a "visual" learning style. Dawn used the *PMBOK*, a popular PMP exam preparation workbook, flash cards, and her own color-coded notes.
- George tends to sound out the words and uses a phonetic approach to learning. He is eager to talk. He tends to get distracted by sounds and noises (such as the television) and prefers verbal instructions rather than reading directions. George is using an "auditory" learning style. He studied for the PMP exam using recorded tapes he created with key study material. He listened to the tapes often while on the way to work, walking the dog, mowing the lawn—all to help "burn in" the material.

Study Tips

Depending on your learning style, you will need to decide which study tips work best for you. Many people find it helpful to obtain or record key materials, definitions, formulas, inputs, tools and techniques, and outputs for the various processes and then play back the tapes during their study periods. Sample exams, flash cards (some can be downloaded to your personal digital device), CDs, and more are available.

I chose to record key topics, and I replayed the recording while walking the dog, working in the yard, and so on. I covered one Knowledge Area per week over a planned study (training) period of 12 weeks. At the end of each week, I got up early on Saturday morning and took all the sample exam questions I could get my hands on for practice. At key intervals I would take the entire practice exam from my handy PMP exam preparation study guide to get used to a three–four-hour sit for the exam. I did this three times, until I felt comfortable in that test-taking mode. A good friend of mine only used sample exam questions from various sources and would spend hours taking and retaking the sample "exams" until he felt good about his answers. He passed the PMP on the first try.

Whatever methods and materials you use, make sure that the materials align with the version of the *PMBOK* that will be on the test.

Countless online and face-to-face exam preparation classes and workshops are available to help you prepare for the PMI exam. These usually cost anywhere from US$995 to US$3,395, depending on the provider, the duration of the class, the location, and the provider's success rate.

Note

Check with your local PMI chapter or other education providers in your area for available classes or study groups.

The Key Is to Stay Focused and Committed

Focus is the key; if you get distracted easily, as many of us do, you will need to work harder at staying focused on exam preparation. It is far too easy to put it off, even for a night, then two, and before you realize it, weeks or even months have passed.

There is a saying (quoted by an IBM system programmer in the book *The One Minute Manager*) that goes like this: "How do you get a year behind on a project?" Answer: "One day at a time."[7] This is where the commitment comes in to play. You will need the training discipline we mentioned earlier and the support of your family, friends, and coworkers to make this happen. Allow for some downtime to relax and get reenergized during the training cycle, and stay focused.

Tip

How can you stay focused? Answer: Make it real; go into training mode and ask your support group (friends, family, boss, and coworkers) to allow you the study time you need. You may have to remind them of your commitment and the date (put it on your calendar in bold print).

Exam Day Has Come

You must arrive at the testing center 30 minutes ahead of your scheduled start time. You must bring an original government-issued ID that has both a photo and a signature that matches your name exactly. The identification must include English characters (or a translation). It can be a valid driver's license, military ID, or passport. You must sign in and provide your unique PMI-approved identification code (you may be asked to provide your confirmation number from Prometric as well).

You will be provided with scratch paper and pencils. Some centers provide a simple calculator; others have the calculations available on the computer screen. Items that may not be allowed in the test area include cell phones, pagers, watches, food, drinks, books, notes, jackets or sweaters with pockets, and personal belongings. Also, visitors and children are not allowed in the testing facility.

Once you sign in, are seated at your computer, and begin the exam, it is best to do a quick brain dump of all the formulas you remember onto a page of scratch paper while they are fresh in your mind. This serves as a quick reference later on when you get to those questions in the exam.

The computer-based examination is preceded by a tutorial and followed by a survey, each of which is optional and can take up to 15 minutes to complete. The time used to complete the tutorial and survey is not included in the four hours allotted for the PMP exam or the three hours allotted for the CAPM exam. I suggest you take the tutorial to get settled in and to better understand the computer-based exam process.

Use the "Mark for Review" Option on the Exam

If you are not sure of the correct answer for any question, you can mark it for "review." At the end of the exam, you can select the option to review all marked questions. This will take you back through all the questions you marked for later review.

Note

You can also select the "Review All Questions" option, which I do *not* recommend, because the system takes you back to the beginning of the exam. Valuable time is taken going back over all the questions.

Once you are comfortable with your answers, press End (complete). The system will then ask if you are sure you want to end the exam. At this point you might think, "What do they know that I don't?" The tendency is to second-guess yourself. Instead, just press "Yes." You will be prompted to complete a survey. Shortly after the survey is submitted (which seems like several minutes), you will be presented with a screen that either states, "Congratulations, you passed," or reads, "Sorry, you did not pass the exam," in which case you need to try again later. Again, you can retake the test up to three times within the 12-month window from your approved date.

When you receive the "Congratulations, you passed" message and printout from the test facilitator, then go celebrate! You deserve it for all your hard work.

Maintaining Your PMI Credential (CCRs/PDUs)

Once you become certified, you will want to maintain your credentials. This is necessary to demonstrate your continued participation in the PM profession. PMI's program for maintaining your credentials is called continuing certification requirements (CCR). Your certification/CCR cycle begins the day you pass the PMI exam (except for CAPM) and ends on the same date three years later for all PMP and similar credential holders.

The way you meet the CCR requirements is you need to participate in professional development activities in which you earn professional development units (PDUs). PDUs are used to quantify approved professional activities. Typically, you earn one PDU for one hour spent in a planned, structured professional development activity. PMI changed the CCR Program in 2015 and now views PDUs in three talent areas, as shown below (See Figure 14.5).

PMI states that the ideal skill set—the Talent Triangle—is a combination of technical, leadership, and strategic and business management expertise. What this means to project and program talent is a focus on developing the additional skills you need to meet the evolving demands in your industry and in your profession. But in doing so, it also means new opportunities to elevate your value as a strategic partner in business success.[8] See the list below for an overview of the three "sides" of the talent triangle:

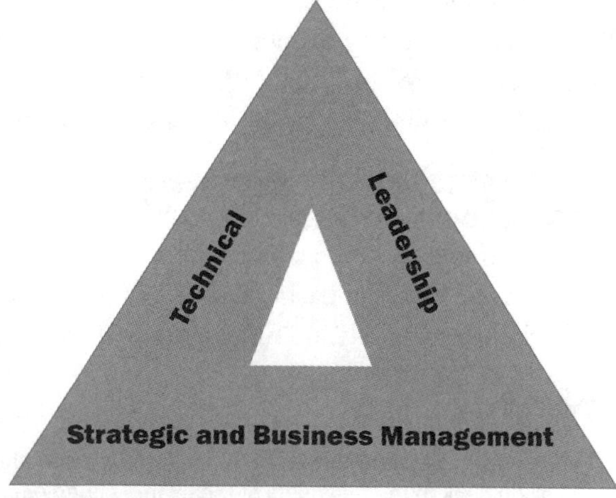

FIGURE 14.5 PMI Talent Triangle

- **Technical Project Management.** Advanced project management, techniques to improve your WBS, how to gather and document requirements, risk management for your portfolio, and so on
- **Leadership.** Negotiation, communication, motivation, problem solving, conflict resolution, and so on
- **Strategic and Business Management.** Product knowledge, industry knowledge, business acumen, innovation strategy alignment, market strategy alignment, differentiation strategy alignment, customer strategy alignment, finance, marketing, and so on.

Each PMI credential requires a certain number of PDUs per three-year credential cycle. Refer to the PMI.org website under the CCRP for the latest information because these numbers are subject to change. There are two categories of PDUs (Education and Give Back). You will be able to earn and claim PDUs for all of the activities listed below, including:

- Taking course from PMI R.E.P.s, universities, or your organization
- Attending educational activities and events offered by PMI chapters or other organizations
- Reading, attending a webinar, or participating in self-directed learning activities
- Creating new project management knowledge
- Volunteering
- Working as a project practitioner

A sample of the PMI credential requirements is shown in Table 14.4.

TABLE 14.4 PDU Requirements by Credential

Credential	Number of PDUs Needed in the Three-Year Cycle
CAPM (Certified Associate Project Manager)	No PDUs. Retaking the CAPM exam is required in the last year of your five-year cycle to recertify.
PMP (Project Management Professional)	60 PDUs over a three-year period (20 per year)
PgMP (Program Management Professional)	60 PDUs over a three-year period (20 per year)
PMI-ACP (Agile Certified Practitioner)	30 PDUs in Agile Project Management
PMI-RMP (Risk Management Professional)	30 PDUs over a three-year period in the specialized area of project risk management
PMI-SP (Scheduling Professional)	30 PDUs over a three-year period in the specialized area of project scheduling
PMI-PBA (Professional in Business Analysis)	60 PDUs over a three-year period (20 per year)

Note

For education PDUs, one hour of classroom contact usually equals one PDU.

Ask the Expert

Q: What is the best way to maintain my PMI credential?

A: The best way is to look first at the latest PMI Continuing Certification Requirements (CCR) Program and Talent Triangle (mentioned earlier in this chapter), and then follow these steps:

1. Start early by establishing a strategy for attaining your PDUs before your cycle begins. For example, set reminder dates on your calendar for any planned PMI events or education. Don't wait until year 3 of your cycle to start applying for PDUs.
2. Maintain a personal folder of all your PDU claim documents. The claim documents should be printed from the online registration process at the PMI.org website. This information will be valuable if your reporting form is randomly selected for audit.
3. Report activities soon after completion while dates and topics are fresh on your mind. This makes it easier to complete the Activity Reporting Form.
4. Take advantage of the opportunity to transfer PDUs from one cycle to the next. You can transfer up to 20 PDUs earned in the last year of your current cycle if you exceed the 60 total needed for the three-year cycle. For example, say you earn 20 PDUs the first year of your credential cycle, 30 PDUs the second year, and 30 PDUs in the third year. You have a total of 80 PDUs in your three-year cycle (you only need 60). In this scenario, you can carry over 20 PDUs from year 3 to your next recertification/CCR cycle. This is a great way to get a head start on the next cycle.
5. Make sure you have the registered program number for all REP classes you complete, which is required on the Activity Reporting Form.

Easy PDUs

You can even claim PDUs for reading project management material, magazines, and trade journals; collaborating with fellow PMs; and participating in free webinars and podcasts, which are often offered as demos and teasers for many PM education providers and for self-directed learning. You are limited to 15 such PDUs per three-year cycle (subject to change without notice).

Note

If you do not maintain an active certification status by meeting the CCR program requirements, your credential will expire and you will no longer be allowed to refer to yourself as a credential holder until you retake the exam and pass.

Your participation in continuing education activities indicates to your peers, employers, and clients that you are committed to ongoing professional development. Staying current on standard practices and policies, as well as keeping up with the latest processes and methods, is helpful in managing your projects in a professional and effective manner.

Ask the Expert

Q: How do I get the most out of my project management effort and experience?

A: I would like to offer these words (from an unknown author): "The best way to get where you want to go is to act like you are already there." This means you have a much greater chance of being successful if you perform with integrity, conviction, and commitment. Act like a leader.

To be successful, you must demonstrate your abilities, take charge, and then take action to move your projects forward with determination and direction.

Project Objectives for This Book

Here are the objectives I set for the "project" of writing this book:

- Provide useful information that readers can apply to their projects immediately.
- Provide readers with proven checklists to help guide them in managing their projects to a higher degree of success.
- Offer tips to help readers better understand what they need to do to apply for and prepare for the PMI exam.

I consider this book a success if I have accomplished one or more of these goals. However, the only way I will know is through feedback from you, the reader. Feel free to contact me through my website (www.eagle-business.com) to offer your feedback and suggestions and to let me know if I met my project goals.

Closing Statement: "Go Confidently in the Direction of Your Dreams"

I would like to leave you with a quote from Henry David Thoreau: "Go confidently in the direction of your dreams! Live the life you've imagined. As you simplify your life, the laws of the universe will be simpler."

To add to this quote, there is a saying I often use that seems to work well for managing projects or other important endeavors in your life and that is to "line up your ducks and feed them well." (See Figure 14.6).

I hope you enjoyed the book and may your ducks always be in a row!

FIGURE 14.6 Ducks in a Row

References

1. Clarence Darrow, *BrainyQuote*, https://www.brainyquote.com/quotes/quotes/c/clarenceda384906.html, accessed March 24, 2017.

2. "The Project Template Library," *CVR/IT Consulting LLC*, http://www.cvr-it.com/PM_Templates/, accessed March 24, 2017.

3. Tom Kendrick, *Identifying and Managing Project Risk: Essential Tools for Failure-Proofing Your Project*, 2nd ed. (New York: AMACOM, 2009), pages 296–298.

4. Scott R. Abraham and Gary D. Boetticher, "A Global Guide to Certification for Project Managers," http://sce.uhcl.edu/boetticher/Isa05.pdf, accessed March 24, 2017.

5. *PMP Credential Handbook*, http://www.pmi.org/~/media/PDF/Certifications/handbooks/project-management-professional-handbook-pmp.ashx, accessed March 24, 2017.

6. PMI's Code of Ethics and Professional Conduct, http://www.pmi.org/About-Us/Ethics/Code-of-Ethics.aspx, accessed March 24, 2017.

7. Kenneth Blanchard and Spencer Johnson, *The One Minute Manager* (New York: William Morrow and Company, 1982).

8. PMI CCR Talent Triangle, https://www.pmi.org/-/media/pmi/documents/public/pdf/certifications/talent-triangle-flyer.pdf, accessed March 24, 2017.

Abbreviations

AC	actual cost
ACP	Agile Certified Practitioner
ADR	alternative dispute resolution
AE	apportioned effort
AIM	Analyze, Implement, Manage
ANSI	American National Standards Institute
AOA	activity-on-arrow
AON	activity-on-node
ARMA	autoregressive moving average
BA	business analyst
BAC	budget at completion
BOEs	basis of estimates
BOM	bill of materials
CAPM	Certified Associate in Project Management
CBT	computer-based testing
CCB	change control board
CCRs	continuing certification requirements
CEO	chief executive officer
CEU	continuing education unit
CFO	chief financial officer
CFR	Code of Federal Regulations
CIPM	Certified International PM
CoPs	Communities of Practice
COQ	cost of quality
CP	critical path; cost plus
CPAF	cost plus award fee
CPFF	cost plus fixed fee
CPI	cost performance index
CPIF	cost plus incentive fee
CPM	critical path method
CSA	Canadian Standards Association
CSFs	critical success factors
CV	cost variance
DCFROR	discounted cash flow rate of return
DHHS	US Department of Health and Human Services
DMAIC	Define, Measure, Analyze, Improve, and Control
DOE	design of experiments
DOU	document of understanding
EAC	estimate at completion
EDS	event data sheet
EEFs	enterprise environmental factors
EF	early finish
EMS	environmental management systems
EMV	expected monetary value

ES	early start
ETC	estimate to complete
EV	earned value
EVA	earned value analysis or analyst
EVM	earned value management
EVP	earned value performance
FCC	Federal Communications Commission
FCR	first call resolution
FDA	US Food and Drug Administration
FEMA	Federal Emergency Management Agency
FF	finish-to-finish
FFP	firm fixed price
FNET	finish no earlier than
FNLT	finish no later than
FP-EPA	fixed price with economic price adjustment
FPIF	fixed-price incentive fee
FS	finish-to-start
FTE	full-time equivalent
FV	future value
HR	Human Resources
ICC	Interstate Commerce Commission
ICE	independent cost estimates
IFB	invitation for bid
IPMA	International Project Management Association
IRR	internal rate of return
IS	information system
ISO	International Organization for Standardization
IT	information technology
JAD	joint application development
JAR	joint application requirements
JIT	just-in-time
KPIs	key performance indicators
LF	late finish
LOA	letter of agreement
LOE	level of effort
LOI	letter of intent
LS	late start
MOPs	measures of performance
MRA	Multi-Rater Assessment
NPV	net present value
OA	overachiever
OBS	organizational breakdown structure
OCC	Office of the Comptroller of the Currency
OJT	on-the-job
OPC	order processing center
OPM	organizational project management
OSHA	Occupational Safety and Health Administration
OSI	Open Systems Interconnection
PB	performance baseline
PBT	paper-based testing
PCB	project control book
PCR	project change request
PDCA	Plan-Do-Check-Act
PDM	precedence diagramming method
PDU	professional development units
PERT	Program Evaluation Review Technique
PfMP	PMI Portfolio Management Professional
PgMP	Program Management Professional
PM	project manager
PMBOK	*A Guide to the Project Management Body of Knowledge*

PMI Project Management Institute
PMI-ACP PMI Agile Certified Practitioner
PMI-PBA PMI Professional in Business Analysis
PMI-RMP PMI Risk Management Professional
PMIS project management information system
PMI-SP PMI Scheduling Professional
PMO project management office
PMP Project Management Professional
PO purchase order
PtMP Portfolio Management Professional
PV planned value; present value
PWS Performance Work Statement
QC quality control
QFD quality function deployment
QMP quality management plan
R&D research and development
RACI Responsible, Accountable, Consulted, and Informed
RAM resource assignment matrix; responsibility assignment matrix
RBS risk breakdown structure; also resource breakdown structure
RCA root cause analysis
RDS Role Delineation Study
REP registered education provider
RFB request for bid
RFI request for information
RFP request for proposal
RFQ request for quote
RFS request for service
ROA return on assets
ROI return on investment
ROM rough order of magnitude (or order of magnitude)
ROR rate of return
ROS return on sales
SA service agreement
SD software development
SEC Security and Exchange Commission
SF start-to-finish
SLAs service-level agreements
SMART specific, measurable, attainable, relevant, and time bound
SMEs subject matter experts
SMS schedule management system
SNET start no earlier than
SNLT start no later than
SOP standard operating procedures
SOW statement of work
SOX Act Sarbanes-Oxley Act
SPI schedule performance index
SR service request
SS start-to-start
SV schedule variance
SWOT strengths, weaknesses, opportunities, and threats
T&Cs terms and conditions
T&M time and materials
TCPI to-complete performance index
TM time management
TOC total ownership costs
TPS Toyota Production System
TQM Total Quality Management
VAC variance at completion
WBS work breakdown structure
WP work package (used in the WBS)

Glossary

activity-on-arrow (AOA). A network diagramming technique used to identify activities, which are represented by arrows. Also called **arrow diagramming method (ADM)**.

activity-on-node (AON). A precedence diagramming method that uses boxes to denote schedule activities. These various boxes or "nodes" are connected from beginning to end with arrows to depict a logical progression of the dependencies between the schedule activities. *See also* **precedence diagramming method (PDM)**.

actual cost (AC). The total cost incurred and recorded for work performed. *See also* **earned value**.

administrative closure. Those activities associated with claims processing, tracking changes to completion, record retention management, final payments, and so on.

AIM. (1) *Analyze* the situation and get involved with the key stakeholders, develop the plan as a team, and obtain formal acceptance (approval) for the project plan. (2) *Implement* the approved plan. (3) *Manage* the whole project and nothing but the project.

AIM strategy. A strategy designed to break the solution down into a manageable flow and allow the PM and team to analyze the problem systematically, implement a solution, and manage the project effectively. *See also* **AIM**.

analogous estimating. A form of expert judgment, also called "top-down estimating," involving taking historical estimates from previous, similar projects (an analogy). This technique is used to determine the duration when the detailed information about the project is not available, usually during the early states of a project.

arrow diagramming method (ADM). Also called **activity-on-arrow (AOA)**. A network diagramming technique in which activities are represented by arrows.

audit ready. Being able to demonstrate that you are effectively managing all aspects of a project. *See also* **project control book**.

backward pass. A way of determining late finish or late start for an activity. *Contrast* **forward pass**.

basis of estimates (BOEs). Where you show the type of estimating tools and techniques used as well as other supporting details.

benchmarking. A process that uses standard measurements for comparing various things such as the cycle of time, quality of a process or procedure, or method against an industry standard or best practice. Benchmarking provides a snapshot of how your business or organization's performance compares to these standards.

bottom-up estimating. Using an estimate provided by a subject matter expert (SME), the aggregate cost estimate for a project is determined.

brainstorming. A good way for a group to generate and collect many ideas (uses synergy, where one idea helps build on another idea).

business risks. Risks that result in a gain or loss to the business. *Contrast* **pure (insurable) risk**; **residual risk**.

cause-and-effect diagram. Also called a Fishbone or Ishikawa diagram. Shows the causes of a specific event that affects the outcome of a product, service, or result. Useful in identifying the root cause of quality defects.

change control board (CCB). A formally chartered group responsible for reviewing, evaluating, approving, delaying, or rejecting changes to the project, and for recording and communicating such decisions. Should be a mixed panel of organizational and project representatives.

code of ethics. *See* **PMI Code of Ethics and Professional Conduct**.

colocated. Working in the same room or building.

contingency reserves. Used for known (possible) risks. Estimated funds are typically held inside the project budget. The response strategy and estimated cost should be clearly documented, monitored, and controlled.

continuing certification requirement (CCR). The program for maintaining PMI credentials. Certification begins the day the exam is passed and ends on the same date three years later for PMP credential holders.

contract. A legal, mutually binding document, agreement, or exchange of promises between two or more parties to provide goods or services in exchange for something of value. *See also* **terms and conditions (T&Cs)**.

control chart. A tool for determining if a process or product is performing to expected levels.

cost-benefit analysis. Involves looking at the total costs and all the benefits of a decision, then weighing the pros and cons to determine before the decision is made if the planned action is beneficial.

cost of quality (COQ). The total cost of all efforts related to quality throughout the product life cycle.

cost performance index (CPI). A measure of the relationship between the budgeted cost of work performed or earned value (EV) and the actual cost of work performed or actual cost (AC) as a ratio. The formula is CPI = EV / AC. A CPI greater than 1.0 indicates that actual cost is less than budgeted cost or that the project is under budget, while a CPI less than 1.0 indicates that the project is over budget.

cost-reimbursable contracts. Commonly used with research and development projects, this contract category involves payments for all legitimate actual costs incurred for the work performed and includes some type of incentive if the seller exceeds predefined objectives. These contracts are advantageous to the seller and pass the risk to the buyer. *Contrast* **fixed-price contracts**; **time and materials (T&M) contracts**.

cost variance (CV). A very important factor to measure project performance, **cost variance** indicates how much over or under budget the project is at a given point in time.

crashing. A way to compress scheduling that involves bringing in additional resources for the least incremental cost. *Contrast* **fast tracking**.

critical path (CP). The longest path through the network that represents the shortest amount of time to complete the project.

critical path method (CPM). A project modeling technique that helps determines the longest path of planned activities to logical end points or to the end of the project, and the earliest and latest that each activity can start and finish without making the project longer.

dangler. An unintended break in the network path or an activity in the network diagram that is missing a dependency from its predecessor or successor activity.

definitive estimate. A range of estimating accuracy used later in the life cycle or when confidence is high concerning the information available.

deliverable. A tangible or intangible object—for example, a report, document, server upgrade, building blueprints, or overall project plan—produced as a result of the project, intended to be delivered to a customer (either internal or external). *See also* **input**; **output**.

Delphi technique. Used to build a consensus of experts who participate anonymously. A request for information is sent to a select group of experts, their responses are compiled, and the results are sent back to the group for further review until consensus is reached.

depreciation. Any method of spreading the purchase cost of an asset across its useful life, caused by normal wear and tear. *See also* various depreciation methods.

design of experiments (DOE). A statistical method or framework for identifying which factors may influence variables of a product process, generally used during the quality planning process to determine the number and type of tests that may need to be run to ensure quality and the potential cost or outcome associated with the tests.

discretionary dependencies. Also called soft or preferred logic. The project team determines which dependencies are discretionary (those that can wait or those that should proceed) and the preferred logic sequence for best results.

double declining balance. This most common rate of accelerated depreciation used is double the straight-line rate. Thus, this technique is called the double declining balance. *Contrast* various other depreciation methods.

due diligence. The performance of an investigation of a business or person.

dummy activity. Dashed or dotted lines on an arrow diagram that indicates a dependency between two activities and carries zero time duration.

earned value (EV). The value of the work performed. *See also* **planned value**; **actual cost**.

earned value management (EVM). A project management technique for measuring progress and overall project performance. It can combine measurements of schedule, cost, and variances, including cost and schedule performance indexes, compared to the value of the work completed.

earned value performance (EVP). Compares the baseline plan to the actual schedule and cost performance and looks at the value of work performed to show the true status of the project.

enterprise environmental factors (EEFs). Refer to both internal and external environmental factors that surround or influence a project's success. EEFs are explicit or implied inputs to all PMI processes.

estimate at completion (EAC). What is the currently expected total cost of the total project (a forecast)?

estimate to complete (ETC). How much more is the expected cost to finish the project from this point on (a forecast)?

events data sheet (EDS). Serves as an all-in-one contract, scope statement, schedule of events, outline of special needs, and so on.

expected monetary value (EMV). A form of quantitative analysis that can be used to estimate the total cost of a decision or event on the project.

expert judgment. The use of SMEs who specialize in quantitative analysis. *See also* **subject matter expert (SME)**.

external dependencies. Whom outside the project team will you depend on for successful completion of the project.

fast tracking. A way to compress scheduling that involves doing things in parallel that are normally done in sequence. *Contrast* **crashing**.

feasibility study. A concept phase to determine whether the project is appropriate and if it will provide the correct solution to meet the need or solve the problem it is intended to resolve.

finish-to-finish (FF). A predecessor activity must finish before the successor can finish.

finish-to-start (FS). A predecessor activity must finish before the successor can start. This relationship is sequential in nature.

fixed-price contracts. Contracts that involve setting a fixed (or lump sum) price for delivery of a product or service, with the price fixed at the time the contract is awarded. *Contrast* **cost-reimbursable contracts**; **time and materials (T&M) contracts**.

float. Also called total float or slack. The amount of time an activity can be delayed from its early start without delaying the project finish date.

flowchart. A graphical representation of a process, usually showing relationships between steps.

force majeure. A common clause in contracts which essentially frees both parties from liability or obligation when an extraordinary event or circumstance beyond the control of the parties (such as a war, strike, or natural and unavoidable catastrophes) that prevents one or both parties from fulfilling their obligations under the contract.

formal acceptance. Final acceptance in writing, signed by the approving supervisor.

forward pass. A way of determining the early start or early finish for an activity. *Contrast* **backward pass**.

free float. Amount of time an activity can be delayed without delaying the early start of any immediately following (successor) activities.

functional. The basic organizational structure of a project team that is either hierarchical or by skill. *Contrast* **matrix**; **projectized**.

future value (FV). The value of an asset or cash at a specified date in the future that is equivalent in value to a specified sum today.

Gantt chart. A "time-scale network diagram" shown as a bar chart with no lines to indicate relationship between activities.

gold plating. Term in the world of project management for providing extras (giving away something that is not in the scope of the project).

governance. Controlled direction. As used in industry—especially in the IT (information technology) sector—describes the processes that need to exist for a successful project.

grade. A grade assigned to products or services having the same functional uses but with different technical characteristics.

group decision-making techniques. An assessment process with many alternatives to help prioritize requirements.

A Guide to the Project Management Body of Knowledge (PMBOK Guide). First published in 1996, this guide is recognized as a worldwide standard and provides common processes, principles, knowledge areas, tools and techniques, and a global project management discipline.

hammock activity. Also called summary activity. Represents a group or collection of related (or unrelated) activities aggregated at a summary level.

hard logic. *See* **mandatory**.

histogram. Vertical bar charts where the total area of the chart equals one.

input. Something that needs to be considered as part of the influencing factors to complete a process.

internal rate of return (IRR). Also called discounted cash flow rate of return. A capital-budgeting metric used by firms to decide whether they should make investments.

interpersonal skills. Also called social skills, people skills, soft skills, communication skills, or life skills. A set of personal skills closely tied to relationship building.

issue log. A result of managing and controlling stakeholder engagement, used to record a question, dispute, or matter under discussion when consensus is not reached within the group, and subsequently used to track progress on that matter.

iterative. A process for getting to a decision or desired result by initiating a series of repetitive cycles of analysis.

Kaizen. A Japanese word meaning continuous improvement.

key performance indicators (KPIs). Part of a set of must-have criteria that are tracked, measured, and reported on a regular basis.

Knowledge Areas. Fields of specialization. The ten PMI Knowledge Areas are Project Schedule Management, Scope Management, Time Management, Cost Management, Quality Management, Human Resource Management, Communications Management, Risk Management, Procurement Management, and Stakeholder Management.

lag time. Adds time to the start of an activity, allowing a delay in the successor activity.

lead time. Removes time from the start of an activity, allowing an acceleration of the successor activity.

Lean. A system (or set of tools) that thrives on change and flexibility and focuses on reducing waste in the workplace.

letter of agreement (LOA). Also called letter of intent (LOI). A letter from the buyer expressing interest in the seller, which can be used during the engagement or proposal phase of negotiations to commit a closer review of the seller's proposal.

letter of intent (LOI). *See* **letter of agreement (LOA)**.

level of effort (LOE). Work that must be done to support other work activities or the entire project effort. It is often used to define the amount of work performance within a time period and is measured in workdays or hours per day / week / month.

loops. Repeating sequences of activities contained within a process.

make-or-buy analysis. A technique used to determine if specific work can be performed with the skills and resources available on the project team or if this needs to be acquired outside the team.

make-or-buy decision. Conclusions and decisions made to perform the work internal to the project team or external to the team. Result of make-or-buy analysis.

management reserves. Money set aside outside the project cost baseline to cover cost of potential unknown or unplanned risk events.

mandatory. Also called hard logic. A mandatory dependency is one that *must be* carried out at a particular time. It is usually a requirement based on contracts, laws, company procedures, or regulatory compliance laws.

matrix. The basic organizational structure of a pool of people aligned similarly to the functional structure but used across multiple projects and organizations and with much more flexibility in cross-coverage between projects. *Contrast* **functional**; **projectized**.

methodology. A theoretical analysis of the methods applied to a particular field of study and/or of the principles associated with a branch of knowledge.

milestone. A major event in a project that allows project managers to more accurately determine whether or not the project is on schedule. Milestones have zero duration in time and require zero resources from the project team.

milestone chart. A type of chart excellent for reporting schedule status using milestones to a project sponsor or executive.

Monte Carlo analysis. A computer simulation used to determine possible outcomes that allows people to account for risk in quantitative analysis and decision making.

Multi-Rater Assessment (MRA). A team of raters assess one's history of demonstrated performance of tasks pertinent to program management.

near critical path. The path through the network with the lowest total float (if changes occur to the network, the near critical path may then become the critical path). *See also* **critical path**.

net present value (NPV). Used in capital budgeting to analyze the profitability of an investment or project. *See also* **present value (PV)**.

One Method. A way to calculate forward and backward pass in a network diagram that assumes the start day of one and advances one day from the early finish of an activity to the early start of the successor activity.

operation. The activity of operating something such as a machine or a business. Repeatable and ongoing, in production. *Contrast* **project**; **program**.

opportunity cost. The cost spent (given up) by selecting one project over another.

organizational breakdown structure (OBS). Shows the organization's departments, units, or teams aligned to the project activities or work packages that they are responsible for delivering. Also groups together similar project activities or "work packages" and relates them to the organization's structure. Used to define the responsibilities for project management, cost reporting, billing, budgeting, and project control.

organizational process assets. A company's processes, policies, and templates, and where lessons learned and historical information maintained by the company come into play.

organizational structure. The way a company or group is formed or aligned. For basic PMI structures, *see* **functional**; **matrix**; **projectized**.

output. The finished product or result of any process. *Contrast* **input**.

paralanguage (vocalic). Nonverbal cues of the voice such as pitch and tone. *Contrast* **verbal communication**.

parametric estimating. Estimating using a "cost per unit" (quantifiable/mathematical) model.

Pareto chart. Uses the 80/20 principle and shows the number of defects by type or category.

path convergence. Occurs when deliverables of two or more predecessor activities are required for the start of a single activity. *Contrast* **path divergence**.

path divergence. Occurs when deliverables of one predecessor activity are required for the start of two or more successor activities. *Contrast* **path convergence**.

payback period. Also called a break-even point. The number of time periods it takes to recover your investment in a project before you start making a profit.

PERT (Program Evaluation Review Technique) chart. A project management tool used to schedule, organize, and coordinate tasks within a project, using a bar chart with lines to indicate a relationship between activities in a time scale.

planned value (PV). *See also* **actual cost**; **earned value**.

PMI Code of Ethics and Professional Conduct. Acceptance of this code is required for PMP certification by PMI. It requires PM practitioners to demonstrate a commitment to ethical and professional conduct, including complying with laws, regulations, and organizational and professional politics.

PMI credentials. PMI's certification program for projects and program managers that establishes one's dedication and proficiency in project management.

PMI Registered Education Provider (REP). Recognized companies, universities, and organizations that offer project management courses and certificate programs.

portfolio. A collection of projects or programs and other work operations that are grouped together at a company level to achieve strategic business objectives.

portfolio management. The centralized management of one or more portfolios, which includes identifying, prioritizing, authorizing, managing, and controlling projects and programs, as well as the governance of the collective work to achieve specific strategic objectives.

precedence diagramming method (PDM). Also called activity-on-node (AON). Displays the activities in nodes (boxes) to visually show the relationships between activities.

predecessor. An activity that exists on a common logic path that occurs prior to a successor (or following) activity. *Contrast* **successor**.

present value (PV). The value today of future cash flows. *See also* **net present value (NPV)**.

privity of contract. The contractual relationship between the buyer and seller—a contract cannot confer rights or impose obligations except to the parties to the contract.

procedure. Working by using a series of steps to accomplish an end.

process. A series of actions or steps to bring about a planned result on a project.

Process Groups. A collection of one or more processes. Process groups are used in the initiation, planning, executing, controlling, and closing of a project.

procurement. The acquisition of goods and services.

product-oriented processes. Specify the products of the project (what the project will deliver). *Contrast* **project management processes**.

product scope. The feature or function identified, designed, and approved for the product that the project is to produce. *Contrast* **project scope**.

professional development unit (PDU). Used to quantify approved professional activities as part of PMI's continuing certification requirements (CCR) program. PDUs are obtained by following certain education programs, participating in professional development activities, and so on to maintain PMI credentials.

profit margin. An accounting measure designed to gauge the financial health of a business or industry, generally defined as the ratio of profits earned to total sales receipts (or costs) over some defined period. Profit margin is a measure of the amount of profit accruing to a firm from the sale of a product or service.

program. A collection (or group) of projects, longer in duration with no defined end date. *Contrast* **operation**; **project**.

Program Evaluation Review Technique chart. *See* **PERT (Program Evaluation Review Technique) chart**.

progressive elaboration. Involves continually looking for ways to improve on the work and results of a project.

project. A temporary endeavor undertaken to create a unique product, service, or result, with a definite start and end and clearly defined goals and objectives.

project charter. The authorization for a project or phase of a project to begin.

project control book (PCB). A binder or electronic folder holding documents or templates for a project.

project deliverable. *See* **deliverable**.

project float. *See* **float**.

project integration management. Includes the processes and activities needed to identify, define, combine, unify, and coordinate the various processes and activities with the project management process groups.

projectized. Aligned and managed by project, this type of organizational structure provides the project manager with the highest level of authority of all the structure types because the team usually reports directly to the PM. *See* **functional**; **matrix**.

project management. The application of knowledge, skills, tools, and techniques to project activities to meet approved requirements and deliverables of a project. Involves looking across the entire project, from requirements to what is being accomplished.

project management framework. Sets the stage for the overall structure of the project, including type of organization, products, services, deliverables, and results to be achieved from the project.

project management information system (PMIS). Where you should keep all your project plans and output documents. *See also* **project control book (PCB)**.

Project Management Institute (PMI). The world's leading not-for-profit professional membership association for the project, program, and portfolio management profession. Founded in 1969, PMI provides globally recognized standards, certifications, resources, tools, academic research, publications, professional development courses, and networking opportunities.

project management office (PMO). Emerging mostly in larger companies to set up a common approach to providing standards across many projects.

project management plan. A formal approved document that defines how the project is planned, executed, monitored and controlled, and closed. It may be a summary or a detailed document and may include baselines, subsidiary management plans, and other planning documents.

project management processes. Help ensure the effective flow of the project throughout its life cycle. *Contrast* **product-oriented processes**.

project management team. Also called the core team, executive team, or leadership team. A subset of the overall project team including the people who directly perform the management activities on the project. *Contrast* **project team**.

project phases. Steps of a beginning project before they become ongoing operations.

project scope. The work that needs to be accomplished to deliver a product, service, or result with approved specified features and functions. *Contrast* **product scope**.

project sponsor. An individual responsible for the strategic development and financial support of a project.

project team. Includes all stakeholders in a project. *Contrast* **project management team**.

pull communications. Used for very large volumes of information or large audiences. The information is downloaded from a central repository when needed. *Contrast* **push communications**.

pure (insurable) risks. Apply only to a loss (theft, fire, personal injury, etc.). *Contrast* **business risks**; **residual risks**.

push communications. Information is sent to specific recipients or in broadcast messages. *Contrast* **pull communications**.

quality. The degree to which characteristics of a product or service meet its specific requirements.

quality metrics. Describes operational details in very specific terms as to the product of the project as well as its features, functions, allowable tolerances, and so on.

Ready, Fire, Aim dilemma. A poor management habit that involves jumping ahead of plans on a project.

request for bid (RFB). Also called invitation for bid (IFB). A procurement document that requests a price for the work to be performed (typically, the bid received has a time limit).

request for information (RFI). A procurement document that requests detailed description of how the seller can and will perform the work.

request for proposal (RFP). Also called request for tender. A procurement document that requests price from the seller and usually involves a detailed proposal for how the seller will perform the work, handle billing, receive payments, and so on.

request for quote (RFQ). A procurement document that requests a price quote per item-hour or per unit of work.

requirements traceability matrix. Typically a spreadsheet or a table that shows requirements and the links to their source and traces them throughout the project life cycle.

residual risks. Risks that remain even after the original risk has been responded to. *Contrast* **business risks**; **pure (insurable) risks**.

resource breakdown structure (RBS). Breaks down the work by type of resource, such as programmers, plumbers, electricians, testers, trainers, and so on.

resource calendar. Used to identify risks, schedule duration, and needed backup skills.

resource leveling. A process used to examine a project for an unbalanced use of resources (usually people) over time and for resolving conflicts in worker availability or overallocation of work to prevent burnout.

responsibility assignment matrix (RAM). A tool used for HR management as well as in risk and communications management planning.

reverse engineering. Also called right-to-left planning. A way to close a project by backing into the target date and allowing enough time to shut down the project properly.

risk breakdown structure (RBS). A tool for project organization that shows how a risk should be managed—shows the risk events that have been identified, provides analysis of impact and probability, and identifies the risk event owner, should the risk occur.

risk response strategy. Also called risk mitigation strategy. An approach using various response techniques (e.g., transfer, accept, avoid, or mitigate) to decrease the probability of occurrence or impact of the risk to the project and to outline the steps necessary to address a risk.

risks. An uncertainty (a lack of knowledge about a potential event that can cause a positive or negative impact to the project). *See also* **secondary risks**.

rolling wave planning. An iterative, progressive detailing of the project management plan where one identifies the likely effects of new risks or changes to the project.

root cause analysis (RCA). The use of tools to find the cause of the problem.

rough order of magnitude (ROM). Also called order of magnitude (OM). A primary range of accuracy used to estimate the cost of a project early in the life cycle.

schedule performance index (SPI). Measures the success of project management to complete work on time, expressed as the ratio of the budgeted cost of work performed or earned value (EV) to the budgeted cost of work scheduled or planned value (PV). The formula is SPI = EV/PV. An SPI greater than 1.0 indicates that the project is ahead of schedule; an SPI less than 1.0 indicates that the project is behind schedule.

schedule variance. Indicates how much ahead or behind schedule a project is and can be calculated using the formula SV = EV – PV. This formula gives the variance in terms of cost, which will indicate how much cost of the work is yet to be completed per the schedule. Positive schedule variance indicates that a project is ahead of schedule; negative schedule variance indicates a project is behind schedule.

scope creep. Also called focus creep or requirement creep. Uncontrolled changes in a project's scope. *See also* **scope leap**.

scope leap. When project requirements change significantly from the start of the project to the end. *See also* **scope creep**.

scope statement. A narrative description of the purpose and objectives for the project as well as the specific business need or problem to be solved.

secondary risks. Risks that have side effects or cause other risks to occur.

self-directed learning. A category of PDU (professional development unit) as part of the recertification of PMI credentials by meeting continuing certification requirements (CCR).

Six Sigma. A management-driven companywide business initiative to generate innovative results in business performance through a disciplined, data-driven approach and methodology for eliminating defects. A Six Sigma process is one in which 99.99966 percent of the products manufactured are statistically expected to be free of defects.

slack. *See* **float**.

stakeholder register. Information about the stakeholders, their risk tolerances and thresholds, expectations, and level of support, and even their attitude toward the project.

standard deviation (or sigma). A measure of the range or area of a normal distribution from the mean.

start-to-finish (SF). A predecessor activity must start before the successor can finish (rarely used).

start-to-start (SS). A predecessor activity must start before the successor activity can start—this means two activities can run in tandem, but activity A must start before activity B.

statement of work (SOW). Also called a performance work statement (PWS), work order, request for service, service request, service order, and document of understanding (DOU). A narrative of the services, products, or results to be delivered on the project.

statistical sampling. A way to obtain data without spending the time and money to observe or to survey an entire a population.

straight-line depreciation. Simplest and most often used technique of spreading purchase cost, in which the company estimates the value of the asset at the end of the period during which it will be used to generate income (useful life). *Contrast* various other depreciation methods.

strengths, weaknesses, opportunities, and threats (SWOT) analysis. Looks at the overall project to determine whether the strengths and possible weaknesses may exist as well as the opportunities and threats, examining the project as well as project management processes, various plans, resources, and organization structure to help identify future risks.

subject matter expert (SME). Consulting experts who apply their knowledge and experience to a project.

successor. An activity on a common logic path that occurs after another activity.

sum of the years digits. A depreciation method that results in a more accelerated write-off than straight-line depreciation but less than double declining balance method. *Contrast* various other depreciation methods.

sunk cost. A project cost that has been expended (spent).

team room. A common thing you find in Agile projects is that the development team sits in a single open team room, or the project team may have an electronic project control book folder to store project documents and files.

terms and conditions (T&Cs). Sets the rights and obligations of the contracting parties, including general and special conditions and defining the business relationship between buyer and seller, the roles and responsibilities of each party, and how the activities will be carried out.

three-point estimating. A way of determining the range of estimating accuracy by estimating the probable date or cost using the weighted average of a three-point estimate.

tight matrix. To have the project team colocated (located in a single room or area).

time and materials (T&M) contracts. Also called unit-price contracts. A "hybrid" type of contractual arrangement employing certain aspects of both fixed-fee and cost-reimbursable contracts, viewed as "risk neutral," meaning the burden of risk is shared by both parties. *Contrast* **cost-reimbursable contracts**; **fixed-price contracts**.

time management system (TM system). A designed combination of processes, tools, and techniques that allow the PM and team to identify, analyze, sequence, and estimate the duration for all project activities.

to-complete performance index (TCPI). Provides a projection of the anticipated future performance required to achieve either the target budget at completion (BAC) or the estimate to complete (EAC).

tools and techniques. Methods in which the information (input) is applied to get the process to the intended result or product (output).

total float. *See* **float**.

trend analysis. Examines project performance over time to determine whether it is improving.

triple constraints. Restrictions of time, cost, and scope (or quality), often visually depicted as a triangle.

variance analysis. Compares actual project performance to planned or expected performance.

variance at completion (VAC). An earned value formula to tell how much variance is expected from the budget at the end of the project.

verbal (auditory) communication. Includes talking, singing, tone, and pitch of voice. *Contrast* **paralanguage**.

virtual team. A geographically dispersed group that works across time, space, and organizational boundaries.

work breakdown structure (WBS). A decomposition of the work to be performed on the project.

work package. A group of related tasks within a project. Work packages are the smallest unit of work that a project can be broken down to when creating a Work Breakdown Structure (WBS).

Zero Method. A way to calculate forward and backward pass in a network diagram that assumes the start day is zero and carries the same early finish value of an activity to the early start of its successor activity.

About the Author

GEORGE G. ANGEL, certified Project Management Professional (PMP), is founder and owner of Eagle Business Services, a project management education and consulting company since 1994. He has successfully managed multimillion dollar projects for over 30 years at IBM and was an innovative global education program manager for ten years.

As a leader in project management education, George has extensive experience in business, project and program management education, course development, teaching, and consulting. He provides high-quality training and consulting services to a broad range of clients, including universities, state and federal governments, international corporations, and private companies of all industries and sizes. He also delivers classes using a multitude of methods, including virtual classroom, online, and face-to-face to thousands of students from over 60 different countries.

George obtained his PMP certification in 1998 and IBM's Executive PM Certification in 2001. He served on IBM's Project Management Profession Review Board for over six years. He obtained a Stanford Advanced Project Management (SAPM) certificate in 2012 and is a Six Sigma Green Belt. He has also been a professional speaker at Project Management Institute (PMI) conferences and symposiums and has taught project management classes and workshops at Colorado State University since 2000, and at the University of Colorado since 2013, Front Range Community College, the State of Colorado, and IBM and other companies for over 20 years.

When not writing, teaching, or consulting, George can be found hiking, biking, skiing, scuba diving, or relaxing on the beach with his wife, two daughters, their husbands, and four grandchildren. You can contact him through the www.eagle-business.com website or send an email to gangel@gmail.com.

About the Technical Editor

JULIE M. CLARK, PMP AND CERTIFIED PUBLIC ACCOUNTANT. Julie began her professional career working for the public accounting firm now known as Deloitte. Each audit she managed was a project, and Julie found that she excelled at that aspect of the work. After leaving public accounting, Julie continued to work in accounting departments taking companies public, setting up new departments and running process improvement projects. After a stint as a Chief Financial Officer, she decided that running projects was what she most enjoyed. She ran a consulting company for seven years before accepting a position with a Denver-based energy company as a full-time project manager within the accounting department. After 28 years of managing projects, Julie decided to pursue her PMP certification and passed the exam in August 2015.

Julie holds a Bachelor of Science degree from Kansas State University in Accounting. When not at the office, you may find Julie hiking on the Colorado Trail, riding one of her motorcycles, gardening, or holding a dinner party.

Subject Matter Expert Reviewer

JOE KEIM, PMP. Joe is a certified Project Management Professional (PMP) and Lean Six Sigma Green Belt, and holds a Bachelor of Science degree from the University of La Verne in Organizational Management. He is cofounder of revivePM, a company focusing on recovering troubled projects by providing consulting and training to revive stakeholder relationships, revive project teams, and revive products and services. He has worked in the defense industry for over 30 years with direct project, program, and corporate management experience in aircraft programs, mission planning, decision-support systems, and software development. More recently, Joe joined the Continuing Education teaching staff at Colorado State University as an instructor in the Project Management Certification program.

Joe's extracurricular activities include hiking, biking, and photography. He is married to the lovely Lori D. Keim, and together they have five children and five wonderful grandchildren. You can contact him through the www.revivePM.com website or send an email to Joe.Keim@ revivePM.com or joskeim@gmail.com.

Index